*WONDER CONFRONTS CERTAINTY*

# WONDER
# CONFRONTS
# CERTAINTY

*Russian Writers on the Timeless Questions*
*and Why Their Answers Matter*

Gary Saul Morson

*The Belknap Press of Harvard University Press*
Cambridge, Massachusetts · London, England · 2023

*Library of Congress Cataloging-in-Publication Data*
Names: Morson, Gary Saul, 1948– author.
Title: Wonder confronts certainty : Russian writers on the timeless questions and
    why their answers matter / Gary Saul Morson.
Description: Cambridge, Massachusetts : The Belknap Press of Harvard
    University Press, 2023. | Includes bibliographical references and index.
Identifiers: LCCN 2022037065 | ISBN 9780674971806 (cloth)
Subjects: LCSH: Russian literature—19th century—History and criticism. |
    Russian literature—20th century—History and criticism. | Russian literature—
    Philosophy. | Intellectuals—Russia.
Classification: LCC PG2948 .M67 2023 | DDC 891.709—dc23/eng/20221013
LC record available at https://lccn.loc.gov/2022037065

*For Morton Schapiro*

Wonder Confronts Certainty.

—RUFUS MATTHEWSON

The capacity for astonishment is the poet's greatest virtue.

—OSIP MANDELSTAM

But do not the bewitching powers of all studies lie in that they continually open up to us new, unsuspected horizons, not yet understood, which entice us to proceed further and further ... ?

—PRINCE PETER KROPOTKIN

The shapes of divinity are many, and
The gods accomplish many things beyond hope;
The expected was not fulfilled
And god found a way for the unexpected.
That is how this affair turned out.

—EURIPIDES

Life by its very nature is dialogic. To live means to participate in dialogue.

—MIKHAIL BAKHTIN

# Contents

## Note to the Reader

I have tacitly modified translations. When no translator is indicated, the translation is my own. My elisions of a text are rendered as standard ellipses; when an ellipsis is in the original text it appears in brackets, to avoid confusion.

*WONDER CONFRONTS CERTAINTY*

# Introduction

## Great Conversations and Accursed Questions

WHEN MONTAIGNE arrives in the underworld, he tells Socrates that a lot has changed since his time. As Socrates expresses delight, Montaigne explains that change has been for the worse, and people have grown even more foolish. When the gods summon the great emperors to a boasting contest, Alexander, Caesar, and Octavius each claim to be the greatest leader, but the gods award the prize to Marcus Aurelius because he does not boast at all. Three satirists, Lucian, Erasmus, and Rabelais, discuss human folly and then go off to dine with Swift. Thoreau argues with Samuel Johnson about the human condition.

These conversations—by Fontenelle, Julian the Apostate, Voltaire, and Joseph Wood Krutch—exemplify a genre dating to antiquity. Usually called "The Dialogues of the Dead," a title used by the genre's first great master, Lucian, these works bring together thinkers who lived in different places and eras and therefore never met in life.[1] If one has ever wondered how Socrates would answer those who pointed out flaws in his arguments, this is the genre to consult. In the third book of *Gulliver's Travels*, a necromancer conjures up the shades of Homer and all his commentators. The great poet can make no sense of how he has been interpreted.

In the underworld and the Elysian Fields, in hell and heaven, everyone is everyone else's contemporary. The world's greatest minds and most powerful leaders confront each other and defend their beliefs from scrutiny more searching than they encountered in this world. What better way could there be to reveal fallacies, expose pretense, or progress closer to truth?

Participants in these dialogues may include sea nymphs, courtesans, and gods, but philosophers, and occasionally rulers, predominate. Today, popular intellectual historians have followed the spirit of this genre by reconstructing (and speculating about) encounters between real figures who knew each other. Matthew Stewart's *The Courtier and the Heretic* probes Leibniz's encounter with Spinoza; in *The Best of All Possible Worlds*, Steven Nadler explores Leibniz's arguments with Malebranche and Arnauld; Karl Popper and Ludwig Wittgenstein contend in David Edmonds's and John Edinow's *Wittgenstein's Poker*; and we trace the complex interactions of two friends, David Hume and Adam Smith, in Dennis C. Rasmussen's *The Infidel and The Professor*.[2] What makes these books especially interesting is that the questions the philosophers strive to answer remain, and will probably always remain, important.

Hume knew ancient dialogues of the dead well. Approaching his own death, he imagined begging Charon, the ferryman to the underworld, for a little more time to live: "Good Charon, I have been endeavoring to open the eyes of people; have a little patience only till I have the pleasure of seeing the churches shut up, and the Clergy sent upon their business; but Charon would reply, O you loitering rogue; that wont happen these 200 years; do you fancy I will give you a lease for so long a time? Get into the boat this instant."[3] Lucian and other authors use the genre to mock the foibles of philosophers who claim knowledge no one can have, and Hume, the master of skepticism and irony, does not hesitate to make fun of himself.

Interlocutors in these dialogues often address the ultimate questions of thought and life. In this respect, they extend the logic of Plato's *Symposium* and similar works, by choosing a setting beyond biographical time. Why limit oneself to conversations that really, or might really, have taken place? Would we not learn a great deal from overhearing Confucius, Zoroaster, Saint Paul, and Marcus Aurelius argue about life's meaning? Surely Shakespeare, the Marquis de Sade, Tolstoy, and Freud could add to the discussion of love in the *Symposium*?

Dialogues of the dead differ from symposia of the living not only because people of different eras and cultures converse, but also because, as shades living posthumously, they no longer consider the life circumstances in which they speak. What they say can no longer benefit or harm them. In Voltaire's dialogue, Erasmus regrets being unable to enjoy his greatest pleasure, undeceiving those who have gone astray, because "dead men ask the way from no one."[4] Everyday concerns do not shape the interlocutors' words, as they always do in life, because there are no everyday concerns. By the same token, culture and historical period do not matter because the otherworld transcends both.[5]

Thinkers can therefore express their ideas in a pure form, take them to their ultimate conclusions, or modify them in response to other, equally pure ideas. There is nothing to fear and nothing to gain. What really matters in these conversations is their freedom from context and immediate concerns.

Now consider that when Ivan speaks with Alyosha in the core chapters of *The Brothers Karamazov*, he imagines expressing his ultimate position as if he were outside life looking down on it. He claims that such conversations typify Russians:

> "And what have Russian boys [like us] been doing up till now, some of them, I mean? In this stinking tavern, for instance, here, they meet and sit down in a corner. They've never met in their lives before and, when they go out of the tavern, they won't meet again for forty years. And what do they talk about in that momentary halt in the tavern? Of the eternal questions, of the existence of God and immortality. And those who do not believe in God talk of socialism or anarchism, of the transformation of humanity on a new pattern, so that it all comes down to the same, they're the same questions turned inside out. And masses, masses of the most original Russian boys do nothing but talk of the eternal questions. Isn't it so?"
>
> "Yes, for real Russians the question of God's existence and of immortality, or, as you say, the same questions turned inside out, come first and foremost, of course, and so they should," said Alyosha, watching his brother with the same gentle and inquiring smile.
>
> "Well, Alyosha, it's sometimes very unwise to be Russian at all."[6]

One of the most profound conversations in world literature follows. The chapter "Rebellion" poses "the question of evil" more sharply and clearly than ever before, and "The Grand Inquisitor" examines the essential human characteristics that have shaped history and led to all our woes. These "Russian conversations" import the freedom of dialogues of the dead into everyday life. In some liminal space—a "stinking tavern," a train compartment, an inn at a crossroads—time seems suspended, and people talk from the depths of their souls as if they were already living outside time.

Dostoevsky loved this way of posing ultimate questions. The hero of Dostoevsky's story "The Dream of a Ridiculous Man" begins with the nihilistic conviction that "*nothing mattered* . . . I suddenly sensed that . . . *it wouldn't matter* whether the world existed or whether there was nothing anywhere." He proceeds to solipsism and feels "with all my being that nothing existed around me."[7] After resolving to kill himself, he encounters a little girl begging for help, ignores her, and—to his surprise—feels conscience-stricken at doing so. Perhaps something does matter? Imagining he has shot himself, he arrives in a world where sinless people live as in the golden age. Even though he loves them, he corrupts them with human selfishness, cruelty, and vice. Considering themselves enlightened, they develop the rationalist outlook of the nineteenth century.

When the hero awakes, he senses that meaning exists, finds the girl he rejected, and begins to preach his new truth to people who regard him as "ridiculous." In the journey to the other world, in his conversations with its inhabitants before and after their fall, and in the confrontation of his believing and nihilist convictions, he addresses timeless questions in their pure form.

No one addresses ultimate questions more wittily than the devil who insists on visiting Ivan Karamazov. Unlike earlier devils in world literature, this one knows the history of philosophy and theology. He refutes Descartes's "I think therefore I am." Since Christian theodicy justifies evil as part of a divine plan to achieve a higher good, he also argues, why do they blame me for supplying what the divine plan requires and what I was created to supply? "I love man genuinely, I've been greatly calumniated!" he repeats.[8]

Unlike Milton's Satan, Ivan's devil has read the literature about devils—the devil isn't illiterate after all!—and finds Goethe's Mephistopheles unappealing. In Bulgakov's novel *The Master and Margarita*, the devil who visits atheist Stalinist Russia reports his conversation with Kant about proving God's existence. It turns out that the book's hero, a novelist called "the Master," correctly imagines what Jesus and Pontius Pilate really said to each other, as the devil, who eavesdropped on their conversation, confirms.

What would Russian literature be without such passages? Dostoevsky manages to harmonize the fantastic with realism by having his otherworldly dialogues occur to dreamers, poets, and the insane. These transparent ways to save realism do not exhaust Dostoevsky's ingenuity. As Ivan's conversation with Alyosha illustrates, Dostoevsky creates conversations in this world that might as well be taking place in another. In *The Possessed*, Stavrogin discusses ultimate questions with Shatov in the dead of night, at a time felt to be outside of time. "We are two beings," Shatov remarks about their dialogue, "and have come together in infinity." Stavrogin answers: "You keep insisting we are outside the limits to time and space."[9] Later in the book, a monastery—a place outside "the world"—provides the setting for Stavrogin's conversation about life's significance with the wise monk Tikhon. In *Crime and Punishment* a murderer and a prostitute discuss the story of Lazarus rising from the dead. The antihero of *Notes from Underground* discusses free will, responsibility, and the nature of humanness with imagined antagonists in a locale ("underground") where he has retreated from living people. Prison provides the setting for such speculation in *The House of the Dead*, as it was to do for many Soviet writers.

Countless conversations of this sort take place in Russian literature. In work after work, dialogues of the dead—timeless considerations of ultimate questions—take place among the living. They include many of Russian literature's most memorable passages. In *War and Peace*, Pierre and Andrei converse several times about whether life has meaning. When one of them despairs, the other celebrates life, and so while their positions alternate, the same questions persist. In their most famous conversation, "the carriage and horses had long since been taken off and harnessed, the sun had sunk below the horizon, and an evening frost was starring the pools near the ferry, but to the amazement of the coachmen and ferryman, Pierre and Andrei continued to stand on the raft and talk." Oblivious of their immediate context, the heroes express their deepest thoughts and feelings. "I feel that beside myself, above me, there are spirits, and in the world there is truth," Pierre enthuses. "We must live, we must love, and we must believe not only that we live today on this scrap of earth, but that we have lived and shall live forever, there in the Whole." Andrei remains skeptical, but the conversation marks the beginning of a change in his sensibility. "Though outwardly he continued to live in the same way, inwardly a new life began for him."[10]

In Aleksey Pisemsky's novel *One Thousand Souls*, romanticism and practicality contend when Belavin and Kalinovich discuss whether analysis of life actually devours it.[11] When after many years apart Mikhalevich and Lavretsky meet for one night in Turgenev's *A Nest of Gentlefolk*, they stay up talking about "what life has taught" them. At first "irritated by the ever-ready enthusiasm of the Moscow student, perpetually at the boiling point," Lavretsky soon finds that "a heated argument had broken out between them, one of these endless arguments, of which only Russians are capable . . . they disputed about the most abstract subjects, and they disputed as though it were a matter of life and death for both."[12]

Several such conversations also occur in *Doctor Zhivago*, written a century later. Toward the novel's end, a stranger, who turns out to be Strelnikov, seeks out Zhivago and soon "they had been talking for hours. They talk as only Russians can talk, particularly as they talked then, desperate and frenzied."[13] In Grossman's *Life and Fate*, a Nazi death camp provides the setting for Bolshevik Mostovskoy's probing conversations with a Nazi officer and with the idealist Ikonnikov. Solzhenitsyn's Nerzhin, Rubin, and Sologdin engage in several such conversations as they work "in the first circle" of the sharashka (prison research institute). The "first circle" of Dante's hell, which provides the novel's title *In the First Circle*, is the ultimate boundary place ("limbo"). Example after example of living dialogues of the dead in Russian literature come to mind.

In this book I portray the Russian tradition as a dialogue of the dead (and a few still living) extending over centuries. Novelists and their characters, critics and ideologists, argue about ultimate questions that obsessed Russians and concern humanity everywhere and always. My interest is not primarily historical. I focus not so much on how the social circumstances of the day shaped each thinker's thought as on how the ideas of many profound thinkers confront each other in timeless debates about eternally relevant questions. After all, what makes great literature great—in fact, what makes a work literature in the first place rather than just a historical document—is its ability to transcend its immediate context. If all one sees in *Hamlet* is a document about its epoch, one has bypassed what is most important about it.[14]

It wasn't just "Russian boys" who loved to discuss "the eternal questions." As countless memoirists confirm, Russian "girls" also regarded a meaningful life as one devoted to some transcendent goal, such as establishing the Kingdom of God, conquering death, eliminating all injustice, or, if the goal of human life was still unknown, discovering just what it is. The Russian word *pravda*, it was commonly noted, means both Truth and Justice, and a worthy life was one devoted to *pravda*.

When Russian literature first began to be appreciated in the West, readers were struck by its forthright posing of ultimate questions, which polite French and English novels did not ask or, at best, left merely implicit. Russians could "feel ideas," as one Dostoevsky character explained. As psychologically acute as it was philosophically deep, Russian fiction not only depicted the human soul with unprecedented insight, it also engaged in lengthy discussions of psychological questions. *War and Peace* and *The Brothers Karamazov* contain little treatises on how the mind works, spoken by the author in the first case and by several characters in the second. Havelock Ellis attributed this readiness to set aside the polite evasion of fraught questions to a "deeply felt obligation to be sincere."[15] John Cowper Powys concurred: "There is so much that the other writers, even the realists among them, cannot, *will* not say. . . . But this Russian [Dostoevsky] has no mercy."[16]

The English wrote about manners, the Russians about the soul. "Indeed, it is the soul [itself] that is the chief character in Russian fiction," as Virginia Woolf noted in her essay "The Russian Point of View." Soul, in this sense of the deepest, quivering, personhood of a person—what Dostoevsky called "the person in the person"—is "alien" to the English, Woolf observed. "It is even antipathetic." But the novels of Dostoevsky "are composed purely and wholly of the stuff of the soul. Against our wills we are drawn in, whirled round, blinded, suffocated, and at the same time filled with a giddy rapture. Out[side] of Shakespeare, there is no more exciting reading." Ultimately, Russians realize, "we are souls, tortured, unhappy souls, whose only business is to talk, to reveal, to confess." Russian literature strikes some readers as one long confession.[17]

Russian authors, Woolf continues, offer English readers an entirely new experience. We no longer remain comfortably on shore but are immersed in the water, she explains. We read "feverishly, wildly, we rush on and on, now submerged, now in a moment of vision understanding more than we have ever understood before, and receiving such revelations as we are wont to get only from the press of life at its fullest . . . a new panorama of the human mind is open to us" as we see the naked human soul, "its passions, its tumult, its astonishing medley of beauty and vileness. . . . Out it tumbles at us, hot, scalding, mixed, marvelous, terrible, oppressive—the human soul."[18]

Woolf was far from alone in these reactions. In the first decades of the twentieth century, Russian fiction took Europe and America by storm. It was above all *serious*, in a way other fiction was not; it summoned people away from increasing wealth, technological progress, and rapidly growing scientific knowledge to heartfelt engagement with what life means. In Woolf's words, it made us ask: "But why live [at all]?"[19] For those who had lost religious faith, Russian literature became the place to contemplate essentially religious questions; and for those who retained it, Russian literature became a way to revitalize it. Critics and writers rushed to praise Russian fiction ever more extravagantly, and it was hardly surprising to find that Arnold Bennett claimed that "the twelve finest novels are all Russian."[20]

The reverential understanding of literature that had long been common-place among Russians deeply impressed Westerners on the lookout for moral guidance. You did not read Tolstoy, Dostoevsky, Turgenev, and Chekhov for pleasure. Often enough, they were not pleasant. Neither did you go to them to admire craft, as you might to Flaubert. To be sure, Chekhov's tales stood out as perfect formal gems virtually defining the short story genre, but other Russian masterpieces were—or appeared to be—what Henry James fa-mously called "large loose baggy monsters" that by some magic triumphed, by their unsurpassed psychological realism and moral urgency, over all aesthetic flaws.[21]

Russian literature shook awakened readers from moral torpor and shocked them into reexamining their lives. Like Tolstoy as Maxim Gorky described him, it fixed its relentless gaze on one and allowed no evasion.[22] Powys com-pared the experience of reading Dostoevsky to a physical assault. It was like a "hit in the face, at the end of a dark passage: a hit in the face followed by the fumbling of strange hands at one's throat."[23] The Russian novel did not let one alone. J. Middleton Murry, the author of the first serious study of Dostoevsky in English, experienced "a supersensual terror. For one awful moment I seem to see things with the eye of eternity." Evidently thinking of Ivan's meeting with Alyosha, Murry reports hearing "voices in certain unforgettable fragments of dialogue that have been spoken by one spirit to another in some ugly, mean tavern. . . . And I am afraid with a fear that chills me to remember . . . [a] time-less, metaphysical terror."[24]

In an age of materialism, utilitarianism, and smug confidence, critics re-peated, these Russians unabashedly revealed truths about life beyond any purported social science. Murry saw something prophetic in the appearance of Dostoevsky's works at the moment when the sheer "metaphysical obscenity" of a purportedly scientific approach toward all questions had established it-self. In the present crisis, his book begins, we must attend to his words "almost at the peril of our souls."[25]

The Russian novelists rendered moral questions palpable, urgent, and baf-flingly complex. The Soviet period—when the Gulag made the prison de-scribed in Dostoevsky's autobiographical novel *The House of the Dead* seem like a resort by comparison—sharpened the insights of the previous century.

## Literature Addressing Extreme Conditions

Russian writers and thinkers responded to their country's experience, which, in its very extremity, did not invite euphemisms. Evil was evil, as no one in the Gulag could doubt; if ever there was goodness, it was amidst immense suffering.

Before 1917, tsarist Russia exemplified repression, even after the serfs—who were effectively slaves and often called that—were freed in 1861. To many Western travelers and commentators, it seemed as if no country could be worse than Russia. Famously, the Marquis de Custine, an enemy of representative government who had lost his parents to the French terror, visited Russia in 1839 in the hope of proving the superiority of autocracy. Conditions so horrified him that he returned—as André Gide was to return from the USSR a century later—with his views entirely changed.[26] As Custine explained, by autocracy he had imagined the relatively benevolent monarchies of Austria and Prussia, where absolutism was tempered by civilized traditions. Russia demonstrated the horrors of arbitrary rule as no treatise ever could.

However tyrannical, tsarist Russia did not remotely compare with what replaced it. *Harvest of Sorrow*, Robert Conquest's 400-page classic study of the Soviet collectivization of agriculture from 1929 to 1933, begins by noting that "in the actions here recorded about twenty human lives were lost for, not every word, but every letter, in this book."[27] The deliberate creation of a famine claiming millions of lives was just one episode: millions of Soviet citizens had previously lost their lives under Lenin's War Communism and millions more would do so in the Great Terror of 1936–1938 and the forcible deportation to Siberia of whole nationalities in the 1940s. The Soviet Union paved the way for similar horrors committed in subsequent decades by other totalitarian regimes, most of them modeled on the USSR.

As Americans invent gadgets, Lenin invented an entirely new form of rule. Whether they celebrated or deplored it, Soviet Russian writers understood all too clearly that their totalitarian regime had no precedent. Lenin created the first state to be based on sheer terror, which, he insisted, was no temporary expedient but a permanent feature of the new society. This terror soon threatened not just ethnic minorities, class enemies, or other despised portions of the population, but literally everyone except the ruler. Under Stalin, thoughts, as well as actions, were criminalized. Punishable offenses included not just "treason" and "wrecking" but also *suspicion* of treason or wrecking—and, going a step further, association with someone guilty of being suspected of treason or wrecking. It was a crime in itself to be the wife of someone arrested, and there were special camps for wives of enemies of the people. For that matter, people were arrested arbitrarily by quota.

Particularly during the Great Terror, top party officials, generals, and admirals were especially likely to be arrested. So were the secret police themselves.

When NKVD (secret police) agents anticipated their own imminent arrest, they often committed suicide rather than face the tortures they themselves had inflicted. I know of no earlier society that made terror routine for everyone, celebrated "mercilessness" as a virtue, and taught schoolchildren that compassion is criminal. Nor have I heard of one, before the Soviet Union, that sentenced endless people, known to be innocent, to slave labor with insufficient calories, sometimes (as in the infamous Kolyma) at sixty degrees below zero; and having done so, forbade the use of felt boots or other warm clothing. In his memoirs of the camps, Dimitri Panin wondered why anyone faults ancient Egyptian slavery, since those forced laborers, unlike those in the Gulag, had families, received proper food, and, of course, did not lose digits to frostbite.[28]

In conditions like these, ultimate questions pressed all the more urgently. It is difficult to imagine anyone in Auschwitz or the Gulag regarding evil as a mere social convention. Neither did the distinction between truth and falsehood appear to be purely relative to one's point of view. As there are few atheists in foxholes, there were (if memoirists are to be believed) few radical skeptics at Kolyma.

People asked: How did an ideology promising human liberation produce such an outcome? Why did many guiltless people, sentenced to torture and concentration camps, never cease to doubt the ideology that condemned them? How did the regime recruit agents not only to torture people according to protocol but also to devise exquisite new ways of inflicting pain? And how did those recruits regard what they did for a living? What self-justifications do those who commit monstrous crimes invoke, what moral alibis do they seize upon, and what makes excuses persuasive to them? What do extreme suffering and unspeakable cruelty show about human psychology? When does death become preferable to life? Can we draw lessons about guilt, self-deception, political and philosophical convictions, social change, revolution, and how one should live?

"Anyone who has survived his first year in a camp," observed Panin, "knows ... [that] a doctrine that purports to define a man's relationship toward the world at large is truly tested only under extremely trying circumstances."[29] People in extreme conditions often faced the choice of saving their lives at the expense of someone else's, and memoirists, including atheists, observed that the ones most likely to refuse to survive on such terms were the believers—whether Baptist, Russian Orthodox, Muslim, or Jewish did not seem to matter. By contrast, educated nonbelievers, confident in their sense of right and wrong, succumbed the fastest when their lives or welfare were at stake. Prisoners with advanced degrees asked: Were believers strong from simplicity or wisdom? Did hell on earth strengthen faith and could it be the road to it? Was it sometimes a blessing in disguise? It was dangerous to take in the orphaned children of arrested parents; why was it, the educated reflected, that sophisticated members of the intelligentsia would not run the risk while uneducated old ladies did? Was Tolstoy right that sometimes sophistication leads one further from truth?

In light of Russian and Soviet experience, could one believe in a law of progress or, indeed, in any historical laws? Did devotion to justice sometimes produce the greatest injustice? Is utopia a worthy goal that, even if unreachable, offers guidance on what to strive for, or is it instead the devil's most insidious temptation?

What is the responsibility of those who witness or endure such evil? Having barely survived the camps, as some did, should they risk another sentence by recording what they had experienced? Could those who had not gone through what they had endured even understand them? Some returnees, realizing they could not, refused to rejoin their families, from whom they were forever alienated.

How should evil be memorialized? Some argued it shouldn't be and regarded forgetting as the way to health. Others considered deliberate forgetting a sin almost as great as the sins being forgotten and, indeed, as preparation for more to come. Does the devil prompt us to inaction as well as to action? Could the greatest of all evils be neglect?

Those who survived Nazi camps also confronted such questions and, some Russians grasped, were the people best able to understand their own experience. Vasily Grossman—the first person to report on the Holocaust as it unfolded on Soviet soil, and whose breathtaking article "The Hell of Treblinka" was entered as evidence at Nuremberg—pointedly included a Nazi camp in his pair of novels *Stalingrad* and *Life and Fate*, which allowed him to enunciate questions that, for those able to read between the lines, applied to Soviet camps as well.

Ultimate questions first posed in the nineteenth century, and made still more pointed by Soviet experience, fill the pages of Russian literature, criticism, and moral thought. They gave birth to distinctively Russian genres. Is it any wonder that it was a Russian writer, Eugene Zamyatin, whose novel *We* pioneered the literary form we now call the dystopia—works that, like Huxley's *Brave New World* and Orwell's *1984*, depict a hellish (or dystopian) world resulting from utopian aspirations? (Huxley and Orwell knew Zamyatin's book and in turn inspired many more dystopias.) Is it surprising that the first prison camp novel,

Dostoevsky's *House of the Dead*, should have been Russian? Or that Russians, who created modern terrorism, also specialized in a genre that might be called the terrorist novel? In addition to masterpieces examining terrorism, such as Dostoevsky's *The Possessed* and Andrey Bely's *Petersburg*, this genre also—amazingly enough—included riveting fiction written by prominent terrorists themselves.

Above all, Russians specialized in, though they did not invent, the novel of ideas. By the novel of ideas I mean realist fiction, focused on the complexities of human psychology and the social conditions peculiar to a specific time and place, that tests theories by examining the sources of their appeal and the consequences of accepting them. George Eliot, Henry James, Joseph Conrad, Honoré de Balzac, and others produced splendid examples of the form, and Russian writers knew European predecessors well. *Père Goriot* helped shape *Crime and Punishment* as *Middlemarch* influenced *Anna Karenina* before the predominant direction of influence reversed. Then Tolstoy and Dostoevsky achieved renown as the supreme masters of the form and set the standard for Western writers. Turgenev, Chekhov, Grossman, Pasternak, and Solzhenitsyn also produced significant fiction of ideas. The power of these works derives in part from the profundity of their insights and in part from the inventiveness of the literary means employed to express them. We will examine both.

## Hume's Backgammon

In George Eliot's *Middlemarch*, which is arguably the greatest non-Russian philosophical novel, the narrator, who is given to pointed aphorisms and sage philosophical digressions, comments on the role ideas play in English life. Abstractions fascinate several of the novel's characters, but, the narrator explains, "the great safeguard of society and domestic life was, that opinions were not acted on. Sane people did what their neighbors did, so that if any lunatics were at large, one might know and avoid them." Eliot's hero Lydgate may have held radical opinions, she comments, but "in warming himself at French social theories he had brought away no smell of scorching. We may handle even extreme opinions with impunity while our furniture, our dinner giving, and preference for armorial bearings in our own case, link us indissolubly with the established order."[30]

That judgment doubtless pertained well to nineteenth-century England, but no such "safeguard" linked the Russian intelligentsia with the established order. The signs of "scorching" were everywhere, and members of the Russian intelligentsia, in real life and in fiction, scorned reluctance to put radical ideas into practice.

Eliot's observations probably allude to David Hume's well-known meditation about the tenuous hold that bold philosophical systems like his have on the mind. After arriving at a form of skepticism so radical that it would seem impossible to live at all, Hume remarks:

> As long as our attention is bent upon the subject, the philosophical and study'd principle may prevail; but the moment we relax our thoughts nature will display herself, and draw us back to our former opinion. Nay, she has sometimes such an influence, that she may stop our progress, even in the midst of the most profound reflections and keep us from running on with all the consequences of any philosophical opinion.[31]

As book one of the *Treatise of Human Nature* draws to a close, Hume first evokes the paralyzing despair afflicting anyone taking his conclusions to heart and then reflects that no one could actually do so:

> Most fortunately it happens, that since reason is incapable of dispelling these clouds, nature herself suffices to that purpose, and cures me of this philosophical melancholy and delirium, either by relaxing this bent of mind, or by some avocation, and lively impression of my senses, which obliterate all these chimeras. I dine, I play a game of back-gammon, I converse, and am merry with my friends; and when after three or four hour's amusement, I wou'd return to these speculations, they appear so cold, and strain'd, and ridiculous, that I cannot find in my heart to enter them any farther.[32]

If "nature herself" had acted on the Russian intelligentsia as it did on Hume, Russian history would have turned out quite differently, and the Russian ideological novel would scarcely have been possible. Most likely, Russia would never have adopted Bolshevism or any other disastrous "philosophical and study'd principle." Doubtless, its people would have been better off, but then we could not have traced the real implications of extreme principles. We would also know less about the way doctrines (or chimeras) may take insidious hold of our minds, whether individual or collective.

Far from tempering philosophical enthusiasm, Russian "nature" intensified it. To be Russian was to be immoderate. Good sense was for Englishmen, and prudence for Germans. Several Russian thinkers prided themselves on this national characteristic. Unlike Europeans, Herzen boasted, Russians will never stop halfway, never stage a revolution to replace one ruler with another, and never content themselves with mere liberal reform. For them, freedom restrained by law is no freedom at all, and step-by-step social improvement entails immoral tolerance of injustice. Evil must somehow be eliminated at a stroke.

Russia produced the first translation of *The Origin of Species*, but Darwin's repeated maxim that "nature takes no leaps" aroused incredulity. Gradualism might appeal to the Westerners, Herzen explained, but Russians will never accept compromise, middle-class happiness, and restrained ideas: "Russia will never be *juste-milieu*. . . . Possibly we ask too much, and shall achieve nothing."[33]

Dostoevsky observed that when educated Russians borrowed Western ideas—as they did with abandon—they utterly transformed them by discovering (that is, inventing) "the Russian aspect of their teachings." "Please allow me this funny phrase, 'the Russian aspect of their teachings' because a Russian aspect of their teachings really does exist," Dostoevsky explained. "It consists of those conclusions drawn from their teachings that take on the form of an invincible axiom, conclusions that are drawn only in Russia; in Europe, as people say, the possibility of these conclusions is not even suspected."[34] Whether we are speaking of Darwin, Mill, Strauss, Buckle, or even hard scientists who did not venture beyond their own field, Russian thinkers passed their ideas through what Joseph Frank has aptly called "the Russian prism."[35]

First, the borrowed idea would be extended from one domain to all; next, it would be rendered as abstract as possible; then it would be taken to the most extreme conclusion imaginable; usually, it would be enlisted in the cause of some utopian ideology; and at last it would underwrite radical action, like terrorism. If two radical camps quarreled, each side would invoke these Russified European ideas to berate the other. "Poor Avernarius," Nikolai Berdyaev observed. "He never suspected that his name, innocent and remote from worldly strife, would figure in the quarrel of the Bolsheviks and Mensheviks. . . . Most European philosophers . . . do not suspect the role they play in our intelligentsia's quibbles and quarrels, and they would be astonished to learn how their ponderous thoughts are turned into flimsy pamphlets," and those pamphlets used to inspire revolutionary action.[36]

Extremes begat ever greater extremes. As in Dostoevsky's novels, where a scandal that seems to be the scene's climax catalyzes a greater scandal, which in turn sparks a still greater one, a more extreme step is always possible. Acting according to a theory justifying murder, Raskolnikov, the hero of Dostoevsky's *Crime and Punishment*, kills an old pawnbroker and her sister. He goes on to argue that "extraordinary people," like Solon and Napoleon, not only may but should commit crimes when doing so advances a great idea. That would seem horrifying enough. And yet, Porfiry Petrovich, the detective pursuing Raskolnikov, observes: "It's as well that you only killed the old woman. If you'd invented another theory you might perhaps have done something a thousand times more serious."[37]

What would be "a thousand times more serious" is revolutionary killing such as Dostoevsky was to predict in *The Possessed*. This book, alone among nineteenth-century works, foresaw what we have come to call totalitarianism, not only in scale but also in detail. Surveying the carnage of Lenin and his successors in the Soviet Union, China, Cambodia, and elsewhere, people have repeatedly asked: how did Dostoevsky know? The answer is that he appreciated how Russian revolutionaries thought—he was himself a former radical who had served time in Siberia—and asked what such people would do if, having gained power, they could actually use their extreme ideas as a blueprint for practice. Hume in power would not have governed like Lenin.

## When We Begin, and Why

Beginning with the reign of Alexander II (1855–1881), the Russian tendency to take ideas to extremes magnified otherwise indiscernible implications. The scrawl of manuscripts became the handwriting on the wall. Accursed questions writ large stand out all the more legibly. If, from our perspective, Russian debates seem exaggerated, then our assumptions, as Solzhenitsyn insisted, appear naïve in the light of Russian experience.[38] Russians still have a lot to learn from the West, but by the same token we would benefit from following Russian debates from 1855 until the present.[39]

Why begin with the reign of Alexander II? For one thing, it was during this period that the questions I examine first received clear formulation. The intelligentsia, in the special Russian sense of the word we shall examine, was born, while the great philosophical novels of Turgenev, Dostoevsky, and Tolstoy elucidated and contested intelligentsia beliefs.

In the early 1860s, Nikolai Chernyshevsky wrote his utopian narrative *What Is to Be Done?*, which was to become, in effect, a Bible (or as some said, a Koran) for Russian radicals, not only because of its ideas but also because of its models for behavior. "In my sixteen years at the [Odessa] university," wrote Professor P. P. Tsitovich, "I never did meet a student who had not read the famous novel while he was still in school."[40] According to one legend, scholars deduced the Russian literacy rate from the number of copies in circulation.

Chernyshevsky's articles, as well as those of Dobrolyubov, Pisarev, and other radical journalists, defined a distinct view of the world that was to dominate intelligentsia thought. Chernyshevsky himself achieved secular sainthood (parodied in Nabokov's novel *The Gift*). The Soviet regime claimed him as its most illustrious Russian predecessor. Lenin adored Chernyshevsky, would brook no criticism of *What Is to Be Done?*, and borrowed the title for one of his most famous works.

The 1870s witnessed the birth of Russian populism (*narodnichestvo*), a term Americans trace to the 1890s but which, in its distinctively Russian variant, named a movement born two decades earlier. Young *intelligents* (members of the intelligentsia) heeded Herzen's call to "go to the people," that is, to leave the city for the countryside in order to instruct uneducated peasants and, if possible, stir them to revolt. Pyotr Lavrov and Nikolai Mikhailovsky, the leading populist theoreticians, articulated an idea that was to obsess the intelligentsia and give birth to a type called "the repentant nobleman." What required "repentance" was not upper-class privilege or wealth but high culture itself, which, these penitent *intelligents* reasoned, depended on resources extracted from already impoverished peasants. "Mankind has paid dearly so that a few thinkers sitting up in their studies could discuss its progress," Lavrov famously observed.[41]

Some concluded that high culture, as morally tainted, should be entirely destroyed. Others rejected education which, they held, could only lead to a new class of oppressors. Still others denounced pure scientific research. We shall examine some splendid fiction, notably the stories of Vsevolod Garshin and the sketches of Gleb Uspensky, that captured the sense of guilt the authors themselves experienced.

The idea of "the justification of culture," to use Berdyaev's phrase, was, at first, distinctively Russian. Western Europeans often rejected one cultural movement in favor of another, but no one of any influence advocated abolishing high culture and education as such. Even the Soviets did not go so far, and it was not until the Chinese Cultural Revolution and the rule of the Khmer Rouge that such thinking was put into practice. Russian ideas travel.

For many Russians, populism entailed worshipping the supposed wisdom of the people (that is, peasants), an idea pioneered by the Slavophiles decades before and now adopted by the radical left. "Everyone, without distinction of viewpoint," Vladimir Korolenko recalled, "recognized that in those peasant masses there was ripening, or perhaps had already ripened, some Word that would resolve all doubts."[42] Could one anticipate what that Word would be? "The people lay on our horizon like a cloud into which men peered, trying to discern or guess the shapes swarming within it. In so doing, different men saw different things, but they all peered anxiously."[43] To their dismay, radicals who went to the countryside discovered that the "people" either did not understand or knowingly rejected *intelligents*, a disappointment Turgenev described in his last major novel, *Virgin Soil*.

Early populism fostered an argument used from then on. Instead of advancing reasons demonstrating the advisability of a given action, thinkers might simply argue that it is what "the people" demand. The people could not be wrong. Both left and right used this argument to justify Russian military intervention in the Balkans in 1876. Perhaps only Tolstoy, who delighted in opposing prevailing opinion, rejected both this war and the infallibility of "the people." In the eighth part of *Anna Karenina*, Tolstoy's hero Levin, along with his wise father-in-law, contend that the common people neither know nor care about the concerns attributed to them. What's more, they can err like anyone else. For that matter, there is no good reason to accept the idea of a unified people in the first place. "That word 'people' is so vague," Levin shockingly observes.[44]

The 1870s also witnessed the birth of Russian terrorism. The People's Will not only successfully murdered government officials, it also created a whole new way of life.[45] Russia became the first country where young men and women, when asked their intended career, might answer "terrorist," an honored, if dangerous, profession.[46] Like the priesthood, it was a profession that ran in families. Unlike the priesthood, it included women, who constituted about a third of the movement and held key leadership positions. Sofya Perovskaia, for instance, directed the operation that killed the tsar. Following family tradition, brothers and sisters joined the terrorist movement together, as the Lenin and Kropotkin siblings did. As some now associate terrorism with radical Islamists, nineteenth-century Europeans associated it with "Russian nihilism."

Terrorism obviously raised moral questions about the justification of maiming and killing not only targets but innocent bystanders as well. It also contradicted a view of history as governed by iron laws, since terror made sense only if the course of events could be altered and only if individuals—both terrorists and their victims—could affect its direction. As terrorists murdered, stood trial, suffered punishment, and, in many cases, escaped, they gave rise to a mythology and martyrology that conferred sanctity on killing.

Radical ideology did not go unchallenged. Tolstoy, Dostoevsky, Turgenev, and other writers examined its moral, cultural, epistemological, and psychological premises. Debates between the writers and the radical critics, as well as between characters within the great novels, defined the great "questions" of Russian thought.

## The Tsar-Liberator

The death of Nicholas I in 1855, along with Russia's defeat in the Crimean War (1853–1856), excited hopes for change. An old saying advised that every new tsar is a liberal until he begins to exercise power, but with Alexander II hopes for major reforms proved justified.[47] Overcoming the resistance of serf-owning nobles, he fulfilled the dreams of generations by liberating Russia's serfs, both those in private hands and those owned by the crown itself. At a stroke, some fifty-five million people, or 70 percent of the population, were freed from bondage and acquired civil rights. I do not know whether the imperial rescript of February 19, 1861, was, as some have called it, the most extensive legislative act in history, but it decisively changed more lives than had the reforms of all other tsars. And unlike the almost simultaneously emancipated American slaves, liberated Russian serfs received land, however inadequate the allotments often were.[48]

To be sure, even after gaining their liberty, peasants continued to be bound to their traditional communes, which remained responsible for collecting taxes and supplying army recruits. Nonetheless, former serfs gained the basis of human dignity. No longer could they be bought and sold or lost at cards. They could now marry without an owner's permission, possess property, engage in trade, enter into legally binding contracts, and sue or be sued in court.

February 19—the date became synonymous with emancipation—marked only the first of several "great reforms." The judiciary statutes (*sudebnye ustavy*) of 1864 transformed the legal system from top to bottom. The old system—archaic, corrupt, arbitrary, based on class status rather than equality before the law, and relying on secret procedure—prompted even the Slavophile Ivan Aksakov to remark: "The old court! At the mere recollection of it one's hair stands on end and one's flesh begins to creep!"[49] By contrast, the new, westernized court system presumed equality before the law, the right to be heard before an impartial tribunal, no punishment without a fair trial, uniformity and relative simplicity of legal procedure, preliminary investigation of crimes not by the police but by examining magistrates, and, perhaps most important, the independence of the judiciary. Judges could be removed only for malfeasance in office. The establishment of trial by jury and the right to defense in criminal cases virtually created the class of lawyers, who were to form the backbone of the Russian liberal movement.

Although no prominent figures advocated a return to the old system, the westernized new one provoked thoughtful objections, notably by Dostoevsky. Probably history's greatest court reporter, Dostoevsky probed the moral problems raised when a silver-tongued attorney sways a jury. One such attorney, based on the real Vladimir Spasovich, figures prominently in the twelfth book of *The Brothers Karamazov*.[50] Dostoevsky shrewdly detected some simplistic, if not false, assumptions about human psychology, especially the nature of intentions and their relation to action. Some of his essays on this topic rank among the most profound examinations of intention and choice ever written. He also recognized, as did Tolstoy, that institutions presuppose a specific cultural context and cannot readily be transported elsewhere. Russian juries, Dostoevsky explained, do not grasp the importance of upholding the law when doing so entails condemning someone whom, as Christians, they are inclined to pardon. Even the educated were easily seduced when crimes, including assassinations, were motivated by radical politics, especially if the accused was a woman.

In a series of measures culminating in the rescript of 1874, Alexander II also modernized the military along Western lines. In a country where elementary schools were all but nonexistent, the army now provided privates with basic instruction in reading and writing. The worst forms of corporal punishment were abolished. For the first time, people from all social groups had an obligation to serve. Most important, the term of military service was reduced from twenty-five years, effectively a life sentence, to six. A number of lesser reforms modernized government. A single state treasury was established, a state bank was created, and the annual budget was published. Any one of these would have been a major accomplishment under other tsars.

In 1864, local self-governmental bodies (*zemstva*) were established, and over the decades, they provided local nobility with hands-on experience in governing. The specialists they hired (including teachers, doctors, and veterinarians) were to populate both the liberal and radical movements. The *zemstvo* reform was extended to cities in 1870. With participation in public affairs a novelty, the basic habits necessary to make any such assembly work had to be painfully acquired. The comic scene in *Anna Karenina*, where Tolstoy's hero Levin can make no sense of voting or assembling coalitions in a legislative body, suggests that Russians might be temperamentally unsuited to parliamentary procedure. Reforms had been adopted so rapidly that the habits and knowledge they presumed had not yet developed.

## Why Was the Tsar-Liberator the Terrorists' Target?

After a series of assassination attempts, taking many innocent lives, the People's Will at last succeeded in killing Alexander II on March 1, 1881, which brought reform to an abrupt halt and led to the polarization that was to shape Russian thought and politics thereafter. Why was it during Alexander II's reign, rather than that of his reactionary predecessor Nicholas I or his repressive successor Alexander III, that the Russian terrorist movement began? Why was it the tsar-liberator who was assassinated?

Apologists for the radicals, and many struck by the romance of their dangerous lives, credulously accepted the claim that government obstinacy forced high-minded Russians into terrorism. The terrorist and novelist Sergei Kravchinsky, known in the West by his pseudonym Stepniak, insisted that killing was the only choice. "There was nothing to hope for in legal and pacific means," Stepniak explained with a straight face in his book *Underground Russia.* "After 1866 a man must have been either blind or a hypocrite to believe in the possibility of any improvement, except by violent means."[51] But as we have just seen, significant reforms were enacted in 1870 and 1874. The very day the tsar was killed he had approved a plan moving in the direction of a constitution, a reform his successor immediately canceled. Historian Adam Ulam remarked in reply to this justification for violence that it was not government refusal to reform but "their numerical weakness"—the radicals had virtually no support among the peasants they claimed to represent—that made terrorism the only option.[52] One thing the People's Will did not represent was the people's will.

Elsewhere in his book, Stepniak himself attributes the turn to terrorism not to government recalcitrance but to the ethos of the radicals themselves reflecting "the Russian mind": "It is a fact, highly characteristic of the Russian mind, this tendency to become excited, even to fanaticism, about certain things which would simply meet with approval or disapproval from a man of Western Europe."[53] Since no reforms can be perfect, this explanation suggests that nothing the tsar could have done would have prevented the rise of terrorism.

In any case, the demand for violence and the founding of revolutionary groups dates from before 1866. In 1862, the proclamation "Young Russia," written by P. G. Zaichnevsky and others, declared:

There is only one way out of this oppressive and terrible situation . . . and that is revolution—bloody and merciless revolution—a revolution that must radically change all the foundations of contemporary society without exception and destroy the supporters of the present regime.

We do not fear it, although we know that rivers of blood will flow and innocent victims too will perish; we foresee all this, but we still welcome its approach . . . [54]

The routine use of the word "merciless" as a term of praise was to become a staple of revolutionary rhetoric, as those who have read Lenin, Stalin, and other Bolsheviks will recognize. One never uses the least amount of force necessary or suppresses opposition, so far as possible, with mercy. Other rhetorical features of this proclamation also became part of revolutionary tradition, including uncompromising terminology and obligatory redundancy. It is not enough to say that change must be radical, it must transform "all" the foundations and do so "without exception." Zaichnevsky's readiness to slaughter innocent people, not just opponents, looked forward to later terrorists' dynamite in crowded public places and to Lenin's taking of random hostages and Stalin's arrests by quota. The "Russian mind," or at least the mind of the intelligentsia, favored maximalism in action as well as rhetoric.

Zaichnevsky's tract continues with the usual demands: abolition of marriage and the family, with children raised communally; prices of goods fixed at "their real cost"; and communes to which everyone would have to belong. After calling for "the party" to "seize dictatorial power," the proclamation inconsistently demands elections to a national assembly. The Bolsheviks—having seized dictatorial power while promising a constituent assembly—were to resolve this contradiction by dissolving the Constituent Assembly, where Bolsheviks held only a quarter of the seats, on its first day by armed force. "Young Russia" anticipates a more compliant assembly by insuring that "its membership does not include any supporters of the present regime (if there are any such left alive)."[55]

"Take up your axes!" the proclamation concludes. Kill opponents "without pity . . . kill them on the square if that foul scum dares to come out, kill them in their houses, kill them in the narrow alleys of the towns, kill them in the wide streets of the capital cities, kill them in the villages and hamlets!" Again looking forward to later revolutionaries, Zaichnevsky insists that to be neutral is as worthy of death as outright opposition: "when the time comes, he who is not with us is against us, and he who is against us is our enemy, and enemies must be destroyed by all possible means." Within a few years, this bloodthirsty proclamation came to seem tame, almost amateurish, in comparison with Sergei Nechaev's "Catechism of a Revolutionary."[56]

To explain the assassination of the tsar-liberator, some scholars have pointed to Alexis de Tocqueville's well-known observation that "the most dangerous moment for a bad government is generally that in which it sets about reform."[57] The more changes it offers, the more seem possible. Demands cascade, and all reforms, no matter how extensive, fall short and prove the regime's recalcitrance. Tocqueville's explanation applies well to Alexander II.

Others attribute Russian maximalism to the fact that noblemen and intellectuals, with no experience of actual governing, did not understand compromise, which seemed like a euphemism for unprincipled cowardice. The term "politics," in the sense of give and take, earned the same opprobrium, as Ulam observed. Real politics was not the art of the possible but the art of the miraculous.

It was also the art of the urgent. Maximal change was not only imperative, it had to be achieved right now, without delay, immediately. There was not a moment to be lost, so there could be no careful process of preparation. "The revolutionary does not *prepare* but *makes* the revolution," Peter Tkachov explained. "Then make it. Do it right away. It is criminal to be indecisive, to delay."[58] In his memoirs, Korolenko recalls the thrill he and other young people experienced at Tkachov's rejection of laborious preparation and contempt for strategic delay: "At the centre of his article was the image of the martyred people, put on a cross. And now—he wrote—we are urged to study chemistry in order to analyse the chemical composition of the cross, botany in order to determine the type of wood, anatomy in order to discover what tissues have been damaged by the nails."[59]

The revolutionary (and terrorist) of this sort lived in a special temporality—let us call it *terrorist time*—exactly opposite to the temporality of realist novels, where characters develop gradually and plot unfolds slowly. In this sense, the realist novel ran counter to the very pace of Russian radical thought. Describing why he rejected strains of Marxism that prescribed waiting until capitalism and the proletariat had matured, Nikolay Valentinov, whose friends called this sort of thinking "requiem Marxism," stressed that Lenin's appeal lay in his insistence that action could be taken right away. "We responded heart and soul to its calls to 'will'" and urgent action in the present moment.[60]

Whatever its causes, the habits of formulating issues in extreme terms, rejecting all compromise, and insisting that change be immediate, led to disastrous results. In addition to replacing the reforming tsar Alexander II with the reactionary Alexander III, the terrorist frame of mind led, and was almost bound to lead, to the sort of tyranny to which Russia succumbed. In *The Gulag Archipelago* Solzhenitsyn cites the 1862 proclamation and comments:

> "What is it we want? The good, the happiness of Russia. Achieving a new life, a better life, without casualties is impossible, because we cannot afford delay—we need speedy, immediate reform!"
>
> What a false path! They, the zealots, could not afford to wait, and so they sanctioned human sacrifice . . . to bring universal happiness nearer! They could not afford to wait, and so we, their great-grandsons, are not at the same point as they were (when the peasants were freed), but much farther behind.[61]

Terrorist time led to the time of terror.

The tendency to extremism, maximalism, and urgency had this one benefit: it allowed Russians, and incidentally us, to see the potential consequences of ideas and actions usually taken only part way.

## Literary Intensity

As the great Russian conversation took recognizable form, thinkers articulated its fundamental questions and outlined possible solutions. Alfred North Whitehead famously remarked, "The safest characterization of the European philosophical tradition is that it consists of a series of footnotes to Plato."[62] In much the same spirit, we may say that Russian thought is a series of footnotes to Tolstoy, Dostoevsky, and other thinkers of the 1860s and 1870s.

Alexander II's reign witnessed an amazing, perhaps even unsurpassed, concentration of literary genius. English literary creativity extends over centuries, but Russia's greatest works were produced in an astonishingly short time. The most influential nineteenth-century Russian literary critic Vissarion Belinsky dated the beginning of Russian literature—by which he meant literature as understood in the West—to the year 1739.[63] It would, of course, be impossible to single out a year for the beginning of Greek, Latin, French, or English literature.

The Russian eighteenth century was a time of apprenticeship and the development of an appropriate language for literary creation. If we set aside compositions of interest only to specialists in Russian literary history, the first truly great Russian works date to the early nineteenth century. A wag has remarked that the most significant event in eighteenth-century Russian literature was the birth of Pushkin in 1799. A mere century after Pushkin's first masterpieces, Russian literature had achieved the status of its much more venerable counterparts.

Pushkin published the first canto of his spectacular novel in verse, *Eugene Onegin*, in 1825. It stands as the first Russian work of worldwide significance. By comparison, *The Canterbury Tales*, which dates from the late fourteenth century, is old enough that its Middle English requires notes to decipher. The manuscript of *Beowulf*, which describes events that took place in the sixth century, dates from the eleventh century or earlier and is written in what to modern English readers is a foreign language. If the first English masterpiece were, let us suppose, Wordsworth's "Immortality Ode" (completed 1804) or Jane Austen's *Sense and Sensibility* (1811), the shape of English literary history would more closely resemble Russia's. To match the pace of Russian achievement, all its greatest authors—Chaucer, Shakespeare, and Milton, along with Pope, Samuel Johnson, Dickens, and George Eliot—would have to have been contemporaries or near contemporaries. Imagine French literature beginning with Balzac.

As a result, Russian literary history is "telescoped." Literary and philosophical movements occurring centuries apart came to Russian consciousness together and so seemed simultaneous, as they did not in their countries of origin. Cervantes rubbed shoulders with Richardson, and Bacon with Kant. Geniuses from different epochs came to life and argued with each other in a real-life "dialogue of the dead." Of course, telescoping characterizes not just Russian literature but Russian culture as a whole since Peter the Great's rapid westernization.

Even in the short span of Russian literary history, some periods proved much more creative than others. It is a commonplace that the overwhelming majority of Russia's greatest masterpieces were produced within the lifetime of one person, Leo Tolstoy (1828–1910). Pushkin completed *Eugene Onegin* in 1831 and composed his stories, "little tragedies," and some great lyric poems after 1828. This span of years also includes all the great works of Gogol, Lermontov, Goncharov, Leskov, Turgenev, Dostoevsky, Chekhov, and, of course, Tolstoy himself. When Belinsky published annual reviews of Russian literature in the 1840s, he seemed to be asking: did we catch up with the West this year? In fact, he was able to comment in each of these reviews on works that have become classics. The pulse of literary history throbbed.

It throbbed most strongly and rapidly while Alexander II reigned. With the possible exception of Shakespearean England or classical Greece, there has probably never been a period of greater literary creativity. And the Russian efflorescence was still more concentrated. The age of Alexander II lasted a mere quarter century, while a century and a half separates Aeschylus's *The Persians* (472 BCE) from the death of Aristotle (322 BCE). Three quarters of a century, as opposed to one quarter, elapsed between Shakespeare's first plays (early 1590s) and Milton's *Paradise Lost* (1667).

During those few years, Turgenev published *Rudin, A Nest of Gentlefolk, On the Eve, Fathers and Children, Smoke,* and *Virgin Soil,* as well as several exemplary stories. Dostoevsky's four great novels—*Crime and Punishment, The Idiot, The Possessed,* and *The Brothers Karamazov*—all appeared in the 1860s and 1870s, along with his novellas *Notes from Underground* and *The House of the Dead* and some spectacular stories. Tolstoy published *War and Peace* and *Anna Karenina.* Like fifty-story buildings in Manhattan, masterpieces like Saltykov-Shchedrin's *The Golovyovs,* Leskov's *The Enchanted Wanderer,* and Herzen's *My Past and Thoughts* are barely noticeable in the presence of such towering giants and usually have to be omitted from surveys of the period.

Alexander II's reign also witnessed the publication of thinkers whose ideas Russians have debated ever since. In addition to Chernyshevsky, Dobrolyubov, and other radical materialists, the anarchist Mikhail Bakunin published several key works while Mikhailovsky and Lavrov defined Russian populism. Sergei Nechaev's conspiracies and infamous "Catechism of a Revolutionary" (to which Bakunin may have contributed) inspired Dostoevsky's *Possessed,* in which the key revolutionary, Peter Stepanovich, is based on Nechaev. Both Nechaev and Peter Tkachov formulated ideas that led to Lenin's concept of a revolutionary party.

It doesn't stop there. Physiologist Ivan Sechenov's *Reflexes of the Brain* (1863) outlined a neurological reduction of mind to brain and drew conclusions that read as if they had appeared only recently.[64] (Sechenov's best-known disciple, Ivan Pavlov, who was also strongly influenced by Pisarev, began his studies in the 1870s.) Dmitri Mendeleev invented the periodic table of the elements (published 1869) and, like Sechenov, entered into debates on philosophical materialism.[65] The first translations of Darwin's *Origin of Species* and Marx's *Capital* were into Russian, and they exercised enormous influence right from the start. We can appreciate how widespread were the ideas of Darwin and Sechenov when that unintellectual sybarite, Stiva Oblonsky in *Anna Karenina,* invokes them to justify his behavior.

In art, what is often considered the first significant Russian school of painting, the Wanderers (*peredvizhniki*), began and produced its greatest masterpieces. Its best-known works included psychologically revealing portraits and scenes of everyday life (genre)—the same topics shaping the realist novel—as well as landscapes that recall those of Turgenev.[66] In music it was the era of Anton Rubinstein and the "Mighty Handful" of Mily Balakirev, César Cui, Nikolay Rimsky-Korsakov, Alexander Borodin, and Modest Musorgsky. Musorgsky, "a young military officer who had been devouring the works of Darwin and living in a typical student commune of the sixties," composed works shaped by the ideological debates of the time, including his operas, *Boris Godunov* and *Khovanshchina*, along with his piano suite, *Pictures at an Exhibition*.[67] Tchaikovsky produced his first significant compositions.

Painting, music, chemistry, physiology: none remained in its own domain, as all took part in the ideological debates of the novelists and critics. Sechenov originally submitted *Reflexes of the Brain* to the journal *The Contemporary*, aimed at a general intellectual readership and edited by the poet Nikolai Nekrasov.[68] Influential intelligentsia critics often deplored scientific work confined to its discipline or undertaken for its own sake. It had to be done for the good of "the people" or to advance "the cause." As Pisarev argued, it was much more important to popularize science, and with it a materialist worldview, than to make new discoveries. That idea only gained strength until, in the Soviet period, it led to the demand that science be "Party-minded." After World War II, any other view of science was denounced as "bourgeois" and "cosmopolitan" (a code word for "Jewish"), an official position with which the scientist hero of Grossman's *Life and Fate* has to contend.

It has often been suggested that one reason Russians have excelled for so long in mathematics is that it is the only field that, under tsars or Soviets, has never been interpreted ideologically and so has been safe from censorship. In fact, even Russia's great mathematician, Nikolai Lobachevsky, credited with inventing non-Euclidian geometry, was yoked into current philosophical arguments. In his conversation with Alyosha, Ivan Karamazov uses Lobachevsky's counterintuitive ideas to symbolize moral justifications beyond human reason.

## Reading a Thick Journal

To appreciate the intensity of intellectual life in these years, let us consider two issues of the influential "thick" journal *Russkii vestnik* (*The Russian Herald*), edited by Mikhail Katkov.[69] *The Russian Herald* called itself "A Literary and Political Journal," but, like other "thick" journals, it covered a lot more than literature and politics, including, especially, history and the sciences. It really was thick, with each monthly issue containing some four hundred closely printed pages. Its heart was the literary masterpieces it published, and I imagine that no editor in history was as fortunate in his regular contributors as Katkov. At one point he had to choose between Tolstoy's and Dostoevsky's latest novels. (He correctly picked *Anna Karenina*, since the novel Dostoevsky offered, *A Raw Youth*, turned out to be something of a failure.)

During the 1860s and 1970s, *The Russian Herald* featured three Turgenev novels (*On the Eve, Fathers and Children*, and *Smoke*); Dostoevsky's four major long novels; and Tolstoy's *War and Peace* and *Anna Karenina* (except for part 8, which Katkov declined to publish) along with Tolstoy's novellas "Family Happiness" and "The Cossacks." As if that were not enough, the journal also published satirist Mikhail Saltykov-Shchedrin, the classic playwright Alexander Ostrovsky, and storywriter Nikolai Leskov, while serializing translations of foreign fiction.

Glance at the table of contents for February 1866 and April 1866. *The Russian Herald* published the January and February issues together; the March and April issues appeared the same way, so an examination of February and April by themselves neglects half of each eight hundred page number subscribers received.

## February

In the four hundred pages for February 1866, readers discovered the latest installments of both Dostoevsky's *Crime and Punishment* and Tolstoy's *The Year 1805*, which Tolstoy renamed *War and Peace* when he decided to continue the story into 1806. And so Russia's two best-known masterpieces appeared together. It's as if *Hamlet* made its debut alongside *Paradise Lost*, or *The Iliad* next to *Oedipus the King*, with each author aware of the other.

The joint appearance of these novels made possible a dialogue of allusions. When Dostoevsky's detective Porfiry Petrovich taunts Raskolnikov with his unjustified faith in rational planning, he observes:

> You are still . . . so to say, in your first youth, so you put intellect above everything, like all young people. Playful wit and abstract argument fas-

cinate you for all the world like the old Austrian Hofkriegsrath, as far as
I can judge of military matters, that is: on paper they'd beaten Napoleon
and taken him prisoner, and there in their study they worked it all out in
the cleverest fashion, but look you, General Mack surrendered with his
whole army, he-he-he!"[70]

Porfiry Petrovich alludes to Tolstoy's rejection of a "science of war," a skepticism Porfiry extends to criminology. Tolstoy describes General Mack
showing up with bandaged head at General Kutuzov's headquarters right
after losing his army: "'You see before you the unfortunate Mack,' he said, his
voice breaking."[71] Is Raskolnikov headed for a similar defeat? Does Porfiry
Petrovich read *The Russian Herald*?

*War and Peace* is a lot longer than *Crime and Punishment*, and so Dostoevsky's next novel, *The Idiot*, could also be serialized alongside it in *The Russian
Herald*. It, too, alludes to Tolstoy and invites allusive answers. Critics routinely
point out that, like Tolstoy, the hero of *The Idiot* is named Lev Nikolaevich;
while the surname Myshkin, which means mouse, seems to invert the meaning
of "Tolstoy," which means stout. The connections between the two works extend much further.

The pages for February 1866 also include an installment of Wilkie Collins's
*Armadale* in Russian translation. A section entitled "Russian literature" re-
views a volume of Sergei Soloviev's *History of Russia*, a monument of Rus-
sian historical writing. Subscribers could also find an extract from poet
Sergey Glinka's notebooks and a new lyric by one of Russia's greatest poets,
Afanasy Fet.

There was a lot more. Ya. K. Grot's article on the eighteenth-century poet
Derzhavin defends his personal and poetic reputation against recent accusations, both literary and political. In N. A. Popov's "Duchy of Warsaw"
readers discovered an account of European politics centering on Poland from
1808 to 1812. General Rostovtsov, the subject of N. A. Semenov's article, was a
public official, a botanist, and, most important, a significant figure in the
1861 liberation of the serfs. The essay devoted to a book entitled *Moscow
Flora, or a Description of Higher Plants and a Botanical-Geographical Review of
Moscow Province* features arguments against the tendency of Russian bota-
nists to entertain imaginative scientific theories before completing basic de-
scriptive work. M. I. Subbotin, the author of the piece on the sectarian Old
Believers, served as a professor in the curiously named Department of the
History and Unmasking [of the Old Believer Movement] at the Moscow
Theological Academy.[72]

The April issue contains more of *Crime and Punishment*, *The Year 1805*, and *Armadale*, along with a novel by Bozhena Nemtsova, a writer in the Czech national revival movement. N. A. Veselovsky, the author of the article on the music of the Slavs, was to develop into one of Russia's foremost literary historians and theorists. Korb's diary, an Austrian diplomat's scathing attack on Russian character and customs, evidently was bound to strike a nerve. The article on American Protestantism and its relation to Eastern Orthodoxy reflects the Slavophile hope that Protestant leaders might convert. Also considered are a book on geology and "Aleko's" monthly impressions of European politics.

Has there ever been such an intensity of creative energy or so urgent a desire to absorb available knowledge in all fields?

## The Life of Realism

Let us eavesdrop on Russians debating the ultimate questions. Since we cannot survey an entire civilization of almost two centuries, we will limit our discussion to writers addressing them most directly and profoundly.

The greatness of Russian poetry is indisputable, but it is not the richest source for exploring the issues I wish to consider. As Woolf and her contemporaries recognized, Russian prose, on which the worldwide reputation of Russian literature rests, conducts a philosophical quest to be found nowhere else. Space does not permit discussion of nonverbal arts. With some exceptions, I regretfully omit discussing theology and academic philosophy.

In the Soviet period, the Party required writers, as "the engineers of human souls," to represent not the world people actually experience but the glorious communist paradise in the making. The horrors of totalitarianism, of course, remained unmentionable except for a brief and very partial relaxation during Nikita Khrushchev's de-Stalinization campaign. To call for "sincerity," as Vladimir Pomerantz did in his essay "On Sincerity in Literature" (1953), constituted a challenge to official writing.

In this context, realism (as opposed to unrealistic socialist realism), far from seeming passé as it did in the West, became something shocking. It readily expressed an urgent moral demand for those who would, in Solzhenitsyn's phrase, "live not by lies." Realism demanded courage, and the art of the past—the uncompromising fidelity to actual experience found in the Russian classics—became avant-garde. "Probably no great novel of the last sixty years," wrote Robert Chandler about Vasily Grossman's daring novel *Life and Fate*, "is so untouched by the influence of Modernism."[73] The same may be said of Varlam Shalamov's stories and Solzhenitsyn's novels.

In the shadow of the Gulag, work outside the realist tradition, unless it contrived to address moral issues with the seriousness of Tolstoy and Dostoevsky, seemed to many a betrayal of the essential spirit of Russian literature. Modernism—when understood as gratuitous formal experimentation, defiance of tradition for shock value, and empty revolutionary gestures—repelled Solzhenitsyn, who denounced "a falsely understood 'avant-gardism'—a raucous, impatient 'avant-gardism' at any cost." The early twentieth-century Russian modernists, in his view, paved the way for the Bolshevik destruction of art: "Before erupting on the streets of Petrograd, this cataclysmic revolution erupted on the pages of the artistic and literary journals of the capital's bohemian circles."[74]

Postmodernism, in Solzhenitsyn's view, was still worse. The early twentieth-century modernists could not have imagined where their revolutionism would lead, but postmodernists lived and wrote when totalitarian disasters were well known. Self-referential play in the shadow of Auschwitz and Kolyma seemed obscene, while moral relativism and the rejection of "truth" as entirely a matter of one's point of view were incomprehensible. Did Nazi gas chambers and the torture chambers of the Lubyanka exist, or did they not? These supposedly sophisticated doctrines, Solzhenitsyn objected, dismissed all that twentieth-century experience had taught at so enormous a price. "Yes, they say, Communist doctrines were a great lie; but then again, absolute truths do not exist anyhow, and trying to find them out is pointless. Nor is it worth the trouble to strive for some kind of higher meaning."[75] Postmodernism betrays everything the Russian classics represent: "And in one sweeping gesture of vexation, classical Russian literature—which never disdained reality and sought the truth—is dismissed as next to worthless. . . . And so it has once again become fashionable in Russia to ridicule, debunk, and toss overboard the great Russian literature, steeped as it is in love and compassion toward all human beings, and especially those who suffer."[76] Without at all endorsing Solzhenitsyn's view of Russian modernism and postmodernism, which have produced many important works, I shall largely confine myself to the realist tradition, broadly conceived.

Russian realism, like the Russian empire itself, continually appropriated new territory. Tolstoy and other novelists regarded the realism practiced in the West as not realistic enough, and so they invented new ways to strip away artifice still present in the most realistic prose. Tolstoy's greatness, many critics and writers argue, derives from his ability to lay bare human experience not as it has been captured in even the best art but as it is in unadorned life. When Matthew Arnold observed that "we are not to take *Anna Karénine* as a work of art; we are to take it as a piece of life," he grasped what Tolstoy had in mind.[77] The artifact must banish the artificial. Away with foreshadowing, symbols not present in the real world, and closure tying up all loose ends!

It is hardly surprising, then, that Russian writers cultivated genres that, while still fictional, bordered on the factual, like Tolstoy's *Childhood, Boyhood,* and *Youth* or Dostoevsky's *The House of the Dead*.[78] Recognizably autobiographical fiction plays an especially large role in the Russian tradition.

Going still further, Russian writers found ways to include nonfiction in traditionally fictional genres. Like *Middlemarch, War and Peace* contains wise commentary by the narrator on human vanity and self-deception, but it also includes, as no great English novel does, essays by the author himself that stand outside the fiction altogether and at one point were even published separately. Dostoevsky invented what he called a "new genre" by transforming a periodical into a work of art. Subscribers discovered stories and drafts for stories, sketches and parables, autobiographical anecdotes and literary criticism, political commentary and court reporting—all written by Dostoevsky himself and interacting to make each issue an integral, though composite, whole.[79] Entitled *A Writer's Diary: A Monthly Publication*, Dostoevsky's experiment was, if not entirely successful, something unique.

The Russian Formalists, who developed the idea of a "literature of fact," also produced works resisting ready classification. Boris Eichenbaum's *My Periodical* takes off where *A Writer's Diary* left off, and Yuri Tynyanov's *The Death of Vazir-Mukhtar*, a thoroughly documented biographical novel about the dramatist Alexander Griboyedov, lies somewhere between fiction and literary criticism. Formalist theory explored how the boundaries of "literariness" expand and contract, so that a conventional form—like the petition or the friendly letter—that usually served a purely pragmatic function might be transformed into a literary genre.[80] For that matter, even behavior could, in some periods, take on the character of literary performance, as the life of poets did in the romantic period. "The readers [of romantic poetry] cried: 'Author! author!'," observed Boris Tomashevsky, "but they were actually calling for the slender youth in a cloak, with a lyre in his hands and an enigmatic expression on his face."[81] As we shall see, Russians took this tendency to make behavior literary to an extreme. When someone living an already "literized" life wrote fiction, the process came full circle. Literature's imperialistic ambitions knew no limit.

His hostility to formal experimentation for its own sake notwithstanding, Solzhenitsyn was ready to try anything when it served his realist purposes. His series of novels—if that is what they are—on the Russian Revolution, *The Red Wheel*, includes documents, street scenes as they might be filmed, polemical digressions correcting historical falsifications, and essays longer than any of Tolstoy's, some set in small print so impatient readers can skip over them. Nothing could be further from fiction than his *Gulag Archipelago*, the whole point of which is its documentary accuracy, and yet it is subtitled, for reasons we will explore, "An Experiment in Literary Investigation."

In much the same spirit, the recent Nobel laureate Svetlana Alexievich developed another form of nonfictional literature, one in which, as she put it, she became an ear listening to and recording voices otherwise lost. Crafting literature from intimate interviews, she orchestrated the quiet confessions of sufferers and tyrants. In this way, Alexievich explained, she extended the central impulse of the Russian literary tradition.

To be sure, the canon of English literature also includes nonfictional works, like Gibbon's *Decline and Fall of the Roman Empire* and Boswell's *Life of Johnson*, but these books came to be regarded as literary after the fact, because they proved of interest beyond their original purpose. Today we read Gibbon not primarily for information about Rome and Byzantium—there are more reliable sources—but for its brilliant prose and sage observations about human nature. Russian nonfictional literature, by contrast, usually reflects a desire to arrive at truth unavailable by nonliterary means, or, at times, the need to dignify or immortalize harrowing experience through membership in the canon. Several memoirs of the Gulag or Stalinist terror—like Evgeniya Ginzburg's *Into the Whirlwind* and Nadezhda Mandelstam's *Hope Against Hope*—have become literary classics.

## "Journalists" and Thinkers

The novelists interacted with figures who proved at least as influential. These *zhurnalisty*—more closely resembling publicists, propagandists, or ideologues than journalists in the American sense—provoked key arguments. There is no telling the history of Russian thought without Vissarion Belinsky and his successors, some of whom also became prominent political actors. Bakunin, Herzen, Nechaev, Tkachov, Lavrov, Kropotkin, Struve, Lenin, Trotsky, and Stalin not only propounded controversial ideas but were also, of course, political actors.

Academic philosophy existed, of course, and some proved significant, but the most influential Russian philosophical thought developed outside philosophy departments. Beginning with Herzen and Belinsky in the 1830s and 1840s, it often took the form of literary criticism. Chernyshevsky's brilliant essay on Tolstoy's early works and his trenchant article on Turgenev's *Asya*, "The Russian at the Rendez-vous," probably initiated the philosophical debates of the 1860s. Almost as important were Dobrolyubov's "What Is Oblomovitis?" (on Goncharov's *Oblomov*) and "When Will the Real Day Come?" (on Turgenev's *On the Eve*) as well as several of Dmitri Pisarev's essays, including "Bazarov" (on Turgenev's *Fathers and Children*).

Even those Russian critics who disparaged "tendentious" analyses in favor of aesthetic or formal readings could at times not help expressing an overall philosophy of life. The Russian Formalists derided any human interest in art—"blood in art is not bloody," Victor Shklovsky quipped—but they nonetheless articulated their own moral worldview and the role of literature in it. For them, life warred with habit. "Habitualization devours works, clothes, furniture, one's wife, and the fear of war," Shklovsky proclaimed, and art exists to make us pay attention to experience. It does so by rendering the familiar strange, as if we were seeing it for the first time. Art exists so "that one may recover the sensation of life; it exists . . . to make the stone *stoney*."[82] In Russia, it would seem, even a formalist had to be a moralist.

Criticism of Dostoevsky's works constituted an important *philosophical* genre, to which many of Russia's greatest thinkers—Vladimir Soloviev, Vasily Rozanov, Vyacheslav Ivanov, Dmitri Merezhkovsky, Berdyaev, and of course Mikhail Bakhtin—contributed.[83] Bakhtin's book on Dostoevsky invites reading either as philosophically informed literary criticism or as philosophical speculation illustrated with examples from Dostoevsky's fiction. The same is true of his books on Goethe and Rabelais; and when Bakhtin analyzed literary genres, he depicted each as an implicit philosophy of human experience. One finds a quite different understanding of human personality in ancient biography, like Plutarch's *Lives*, on the one hand, and in the realist novel, on the other. Realist novels, in Bakhtin's view, convey humanity's deepest understanding of itself. So what was Bakhtin primarily: a literary theorist or a philosopher? In his interview with the scholar Victor Duvakin two years before his death, he directly addressed this question when he called himself "a philosopher more than a philologist. And that's who I am today. I am a philosopher. A thinker."[84]

One reason often adduced for writing philosophy as literary criticism was to circumvent the censorship, and that consideration certainly played a role. Even when authorities could not easily be fooled that way, the tradition had been established. But subterfuge was not the only reason. If, as Bakhtin argued, the greatest wisdom resides in literature, then philosophers might capture—or as Bakhtin wrote, "transcribe"—some of that wisdom in the form of philosophically oriented literary criticism. To understand the human mind, could one do better than probe Dostoevsky's insights? Literary criticism played such an important role in Russian thought because literature itself did.

Histories of Russian philosophy differ markedly from their English or American counterparts. They more closely resemble intellectual histories of influential "thinkers," as if the main line of Western philosophy ran through Samuel Johnson, Goethe, Kierkegaard, Coleridge, Nietzsche, Bergson, and Freud. Aesthetics, politics, and ethics weigh much more heavily than logic and epistemology. Analytic philosophy, in the Anglo-American tradition, barely exists. Consult the standard histories of Russian philosophy and you will discover chapters on Tolstoy and Dostoevsky. Would anyone write a history of American philosophy centering on Hawthorne and Melville and paying more attention to Henry James than to his brother William?

## The Disputants

To sharpen our focus, we will, at the cost of some simplification, begin by considering what I take to be the tradition's central conflict. Writing in 1909, the critic Mikhail Gershenzon observed that "In Russia an almost infallible gauge of the strength of an artist's genius is the extent of his hatred for the intelligentsia."[85] Gershenzon uses the word "intelligentsia" in a specifically Russian sense that we will explain in detail. For the moment, we can say that he means, roughly speaking, radical ideologues. To be sure, Gershenzon exaggerated for rhetorical effect. All the same, if we regard Russia's greatest writers as Tolstoy, Dostoevsky, and Chekhov, whom he cites, Gershenzon is largely correct.

How could the great writers *not* resist intelligentsia demands, which included enlisting literature for crudely propagandistic "tendencies"? As the Soviet period was to show, such strictures make outstanding art almost impossible. What's more, the great realists insisted above all on their independence and on fidelity to the truth as they saw it, even if that truth did not support progressive polemics. In a letter to A. N. Pleshcheev responding to criticisms that his story "The Name-Day Party" was not properly tendentious, Chekhov replied, "Does my last story really show no 'tendency'? You tell me that my stories lack a protesting element. . . . But don't I protest from the beginning of my story to the end against lies? Isn't that a tendency?"[86]

As Chekhov well knew, from the intelligentsia's point of view, it was not. The tsarist censorship was bad enough, but the intelligentsia added what was called "the second censorship." If these "toads and crocodiles" ever gained power, Chekhov complained, "they will rule in ways not known even at the time of the Inquisition in Spain," an apparent exaggeration that proved an understatement.[87]

With his characteristic aristocratic disdain, Tolstoy dismissed the increasingly radical intelligentsia as more pathetic than dangerous, and as too hopelessly out of touch with reality to cause much harm. In *Resurrection*, the hero, Nekhliudov—a name Tolstoy often used for a main character resembling himself—interviews an imprisoned revolutionary *intelligent*, who confides to him the secrets of the terrorist People's Will. "Her speech was intermingled with a great many long words, which she seemed to think everybody knew, but which Nekhliudov had never heard of." Neither, of course, had the workers and peasants she hoped to rouse: "Nekhliudov looked at her miserable little neck, her thin, unkempt hair, and wondered why she had been doing all these strange things. . . . He pitied her, but not as he pitied Menshoff, the peasant, kept for no fault of his own in the stinking prison. She was pitiable because of all the confusion that filled her mind."[88] Only Dostoevsky foresaw the unprecedented carnage that *intelligents* in power would cause.

After Lenin, Trotsky, Stalin, and other *intelligents* seized power, their way of thinking became official. From that point on, great writers found themselves at odds with a disputant much more dangerous than Bakunin, Lavrov, the People's Will, or the Socialist Revolutionary Combat Organization. The masterpieces produced under Soviet conditions testify to the courage of their authors as no nineteenth-century work ever did or could have. Tolstoy sought martyrdom by trying to provoke the tsar to imprison him; no Soviet writer had to go out of his way to get arrested.

Realism and fidelity to empirical reality constituted a special threat called "bourgeois objectivism." Chief Party ideologist Mikhail Suslov told Vasily Grossman that his novel *Life and Fate* would not be publishable for two centuries.[89] "Why," he asked, "should we add your book to the nuclear bombs that our enemies are getting ready for us?"[90] Grossman did not even submit his more explicitly critical novel, *Forever Flowing*.

Since the sixteenth century, when Prince Kurbsky escaped to Poland and sent defiant letters to Tsar Ivan the Terrible, Russian literature has included significant works written or published in emigration. Russian literary history, unlike that of any other major European country aside from Poland, cannot be narrated without including significant works written or published abroad. In the 1920s, the vast number of Russians who escaped Bolshevik rule included Nabokov and Ivan Bunin, Russia's first Nobel Prize winner. Beginning with Zamyatin's *We*, works smuggled abroad enriched the émigré tradition. Indeed, from the mid-1930s on, virtually all masterpieces—and there were many—were either circulated illegally in samizdat, written "for the drawer" (like Bulgakov's *Master and Margarita*), or published abroad (like *Doctor Zhivago, Life and Fate*, and *The Gulag Archipelago*).[91]

Reading such literature, as well as writing it, entailed significant risk, as was true in no Western country. To appreciate Soviet literary culture one must grasp that reading its greatest works was in itself a political act.[92] Is it any wonder, then, that Russian literature, already devoted to ultimate questions about life's significance, became even more serious? Or that Russian writers, once abroad, found it difficult to understand the West's high culture once they found themselves, in Solzhenitsyn's apt phrase, "between two millstones"?[93]

For Solzhenitsyn, the Soviet experience demonstrated the naiveté of Western intellectuals who congratulate themselves on their sophistication. American intellectuals, in turn, regarded Solzhenitsyn's way of speaking as out of date at best and repugnant at worst. Would any influential American writer insist, as Solzhenitsyn did, that "the greatness of a people is to be sought ... in the level of its inner development, in its breadth of soul"?[94] Solzhenitsyn knew quite well how such assertions sounded. From his perspective, comfortable westerners fail to grasp what human beings are capable of. What's more, they take for granted that life's goal is personal well-being.

Most nineteenth-century thinkers imagined that progress is "a shining and unswerving vector," Solzhenitsyn observed, but "it turned out to be a complex and twisted curve, which brought us back to the very same eternal questions which loomed in earlier years, except that facing those questions then was easier." Could anyone familiar with the Gulag deny what Solzhenitsyn called "the intrinsic evil in man?"[95]

The two chapters comprising Part I examine the main disputants, the writers and the intelligentsia. Because intense discussions of the Russian kind require and shape distinct personality types, Part II examines three important ones, which I call the Wanderer, the Idealist, and the Revolutionist. The six chapters of Part III each examine one of the accursed questions: the proper role of theory, the nature and basis of ethics, ethical responsibility and the ways people avoid it, whether time is open so that real alternatives exist, the relative importance of the prosaic and the dramatic, and, finally, whether life has any meaning and if so, what it might be. These questions overlap and we shall often find ourselves circling back and addressing the same issues, and sometimes the same passages, from a new angle. The conclusion addresses the question that makes discussion of all other questions possible, the nature and importance of dialogue and a dialogic understanding of truth.

Beginning with the great period of Russian literature, the time of Dostoevsky, Tolstoy, Herzen, Turgenev, and Chekhov, Russians argued about the ultimate questions. Once defined, those questions persisted, provoking responses again and again. The earlier statements retained the power to speak as if their authors were still present, and when later thinkers found earlier views mistaken, they contested them as they might have done in a face-to-face confrontation. The extreme conditions of the Soviet period shed new light on familiar questions and gave some of them, especially moral ones, unprecedented intensity. One does not have to be Russian to appreciate that the issues debated pertain to all of us and will never lose their vitality. So long as people wonder about what is most essentially human, about whether morality has any nonarbitrary basis, about the relation of abstract theory to lived experience, about life's meaning, and other such topics—so long will Russian literature command an enthusiastic audience.

# PART ONE

# THE DISPUTANTS

# 1 Russian Literature

> A book is a squarish chunk of hot, smoking conscience—and nothing else!
>
> —BORIS PASTERNAK

AS INSTALLMENTS OF TOLSTOY'S *Anna Karenina* were appearing in *The Russian Herald*, Dostoevsky reviewed it in his one-person periodical, *A Writer's Diary*. Although *The Russian Herald* had chosen to publish Tolstoy's novel in preference to Dostoevsky's *A Raw Youth*, Dostoevsky could not have expressed greater enthusiasm. In an article entitled "*Anna Karenina* as a Fact of Special Significance," he praised the book not only for its "perfection as a work of art," and not only as a masterpiece superior to any in Europe, but also for proving that Russians can make a real contribution to world culture. "If the Russian genius could give birth to this *fact*," he concluded, "then it is not doomed to impotence and ... can provide something *of its own*, it can create its *own* word."[1] For Dostoevsky, this novel vindicated the very existence of Russian culture and, indeed, the Russian people.

No country has ever valued literature more than Russia. Would any Englishman or Frenchman presume that his people's existence required vindication? To be sure, other countries (including America) have shared a cultural inferiority complex, but it is hard to imagine an American finding national vindication in a novel. Literature exists to represent life, we naturally think, but Russians often speak as if life existed to provide material for literature: Is that why God created the Russian people?

"The artist communes with God," Boris Pasternak explained to Leonard Bernstein, "and God puts on various performances so that he can have something to write about."[2]

The Russian tradition "proclaims the primacy of literature over life," short story writer Tatyana Tolstaya observed in her essay "Pushkin's Children."

> Life is nothing—a fog, a mirage, fata morgana. But the word . . . represents a power greater than that of the atom. This is an entirely Russian point of view, with no parallel in the West. And everyone in Russia, it seems, shares it: the tsars and their slaves, censors and dissidents, writers and critics, liberals and conservatives. He who has articulated a Word has accomplished a Deed.[3]

For Tolstaya, to be Russian is to be one of Pushkin's children—it is to be defined by Russian literature.

When Krymov, a dedicated Communist in Grossman's novel *Stalingrad*, finds himself under arrest, he thinks of lines from the *Odyssey*: "Tell me, why are you weeping? Why do you listen so sadly, / Hearing these stories of Trojans and Greeks, of long-ago battles? / All was decreed by the Gods—to make songs for far-off descendants."[4] At the end of book 8 of the *Odyssey*, Alcinous voices these lines to the stranger we know to be Odysseus, who weeps hearing songs of the Trojan War. Homer seems to suggest—or so Grossman's character supposes—that the Trojan war was fought so that epics, the foundations of Greek culture, could be composed to memorialize it. Russia, in Grossman's view, has preserved this sense of history as material for literature. The gods have inflicted countless tragedies on Russia so that novels about them could be written. Varlam Shalamov, arguably the best short story writer since Chekhov, told Pasternak, "our time will be justified because you lived in it."[5] Literature could justify an epoch as well as a nation.

The writer Vladimir Korolenko, who was part Ukrainian and part Russian, was once asked which country he considered his homeland. His reply is famous: "[My] homeland became, first and foremost, Russian literature."[6] Svetlana Alexievich echoed Korolenko's words when, at the end of her speech accepting the Nobel Prize for literature, she explained: "I have three homes: my Belarusian land, the homeland of my father, where I have lived my whole life; Ukraine, the homeland of my mother, where I was born; and Russia's great culture, without which I cannot imagine myself."[7] By Russia's great culture, she made clear, she meant Russian literature. The fact that both her parents came from other nations did not matter. As numerous Russian émigrés have felt, one lives in Russia through its books. Like Jews, Russians are people of the book—or, rather, books.[8]

It went without saying that one must be prepared to die for one's homeland. Russian literature has always been dangerous. The great poet Osip Mandelstam, author of a lyric mocking Stalin, knew, as his friends told him, that he had in effect written a suicide note. His wife Nadezhda observed in her memoirs, a Russian literary classic, that "In choosing the manner of his death, M. was counting on one remarkable feature of our leaders: their boundless, almost superstitious regard for poetry. 'Why do you complain?' M. used to say. 'Poetry is respected only in this country—people are killed for it. There's no place where more people are killed for it.'"[9] One can kill poets, but poetry itself, Nadezhda Mandelstam explained, "is a law unto itself: it is impossible to bury it alive and even a powerful propaganda machinery such as ours cannot prevent it from living on. 'I am easy in my mind,' [poet Anna] Akhmatova said to me in the sixties. 'We have seen how durable poetry is.'" The best-known line from Mikhail Bukgakov's novel *The Master and Margarita* expresses a similar thought. When the devil returns the manuscript the Master has burned to ashes, he remarks, "manuscripts don't burn."[10]

The Mandelstams's assessment of the regime's respect for literature did not exaggerate. Stalin in particular understood literature's importance. That is why he lured Maxim Gorky, the émigré writer who had criticized Lenin's war against free expression, back to Russia. Gorky's prestige, both literary and political, lent legitimacy to Soviet socialist realism's claim to be the proper heir to Russia's great literary tradition. In a similar spirit, Stalin enticed novelist Alexei Tolstoy to return from emigration so that a Tolstoy—no name carried so much literary charisma—would praise the Stalinist worldview. My teacher, Victor Erlich, would not pronounce this writer's name but referred instead to "the turncoat," that is, the betrayer of the Russian literary tradition. Another teacher, historian Firuz Kazemzadeh, who grew up in Stalinist Russia, recalled that at the height of the Great Terror of 1936–1938, someone who knocked on Alexei Tolstoy's door would be told by his valet from before the revolution: "The count is engaged [*graf zanyat*]." So valuable was the name Tolstoy that its bearer could use his prerevolutionary title.

It surprises many to learn that Stalin himself was a voracious reader. As Stephen Kotkin observed, "Stalin had a passion for books, which he marked up and filled with placeholders to find passages. (His personal library would ultimately grow to more than 20,000 volumes.)" "The Leader (*vozhd'*) would always ask what I was reading," recalled Artyom Sergeev, who lived for a while in the Stalin household. Recommending the Russian classics, Stalin observed that "during wartime there would be a lot of situations you had never encountered before in your life.... But if you read a lot, then in your memory you will already have the answers how to conduct yourself and what to do. Literature will tell you."[11] Novelist Konstantin Simonov, who spoke with Stalin several times, noted the leader's keen interest in and extensive knowledge of literature.[12] That knowledge impressed many writers.

Novelist Mikhail Sholokhov recalled that when he encountered trouble getting his novel *With Sweat and Blood* published, he appealed to Stalin, who read the manuscript over the next three nights. Summoned to a meeting, Sholokhov found, along with Stalin, the editor of *Pravda*, Lev Mekhlis; People's Commissar for Military and Naval Affairs, Kliment Voroshilov; and the person in charge of economic development, Sergo Ordzhonikidze. Could one imagine any Western president or prime minister worrying about whether a novel would be published—or making sure that his ministers in charge of the military and the economy would hear his verdict? Sholokhov was allowed to publish his novel with its title changed to *Virgin Soil Upturned*.[13]

In *The Readers of "Novy Mir"* Denis Kozlov includes a lengthy list of Politburo decrees concerning literary journals. An American might ask, hadn't they anything better to think about? The prestige of Russian literature made such concern routine. To use Kozlov's phrase, Russia is "literature-centered." It was especially so after World War II when, even more than usual, literature and literary journals interested not only highbrow intellectuals, but also "engineers, workers, teachers, doctors, students and soldiers." During the "Thaw" following Stalin's death, "readers lined up in libraries for months" and "gatherings of readers were sometimes monitored by mounted police."[14]

The "era of stagnation" under Brezhnev may have made life difficult for Russian citizens, recalled Tolstaya, but interest in literature grew even more intense. "Literature was valued above everything. Books became a common form of currency. In order to acquire certain rare books, people would spend huge sums or laboriously retype the books themselves on old typewriters.... People stole journals from their neighbors' mailboxes. Thieves broke into apartments in order to carry away books."[15]

"One text would be on everyone's mind at a given time," observed Kathleen Parthé. It might be a piece of *samizdat*, a neologism based on the Soviet acronym *gosizdat*—state publishing house—and meaning "self-publishing" house: people hand-copied books word by word. Or it might be an especially bold piece of official literature. "From late 1987 into 1989 [the period of *glas-*

*nost*] everyone on the metros and buses seemed to be reading the same thing at the same time," observed American journalist David Remnick. "One month it was *Doctor Zhivago*, the next it was *Life and Fate*." This "one-text" phenomenon, as Parthé calls it, was not new: the nineteenth-century critic Nikolai Strakhov recalled that "only *Crime and Punishment* was read during 1866, only it was spoken about."[16]

As numerous memoirists testify, literature played a special role in the Gulag. Evgeniya Ginzburg recalled how literate prisoners, reciting memorized verse, said to themselves, "But we, wise men and poets, keeper of the secrets and the faith, shall carry the lighted candles into the catacombs." Of course, she reflected, they were not at all wise. "Nevertheless, we did manage to carry our 'lighted candles' into solitary confinement, into the huts and punishment cells, and through the blizzard-lashed marches in Kolyma. These lamps of ours alone were what enabled us to emerge from the pitch-darkness."[17]

If one knew Russian poetry by heart, it appeared, one's humanness remained. Olga Adamova-Sliozberg recalled that in one prison she was allowed a single book a week:

> That was when I understood what a really good book was: a book that would make you feel human again when you'd read it! For so long now it had been drilled into our heads that we weren't human, that we were the dregs, garbage ... not just by the prison guards, whom we despised, but by the newspapers, which we still hadn't learned to disbelieve ...
>
> But here were Tolstoy and Dostoevsky speaking to me, and in my human essence I felt myself their equal.[18]

Released from camp, the narrator of Shalamov's story "The Train" visits a used book shop, not to buy books, since he has no place to keep them, but just to feel them in his hands. "To hold books, to stand next to the counter of a bookstore was ... like a glass of the water of life." Even more revealing is Fleming, a prisoner Shalamov (or his narrator) encounters in "The Used Book Dealer." A former NKVD officer, Fleming "told with reverence how he had touched the file of the executed poet Gumilyov.... It was just as if he had touched the Kaaba [sacred to Muslims], such was the bliss, the purification in every feature of his face. I couldn't help think that this too was a means of being introduced to poetry." To be sure, the narrator concedes, "the moral values of poetry are not transmitted in the process."[19]

## A Single Enterprise

Regarded as a sacred legacy, Russian literature is perhaps best compared not to French or English literature, but to the Hebrew Bible when the canon was open and books could still be added. "The artist communes with God." If literature is holy, not everyone is entitled to write it, much as, in the Orthodox tradition, not everyone was worthy to paint an icon. Those who were thought worthy achieved quasi-sacred status; those who were not did not truly belong to the tradition. When Solzhenitsyn condemned the postmodernists for insufficient reverence for the classics he was saying, in effect, that they may be authors writing in Russian, but, however talented, they do not truly belong to "Russian literature."[20]

"Among the Hebrew people," Gogol explained, many would prophesy, but "only one among them was chosen by God, he whose phrases were entered into the holy book of the Hebrew people; all the others probably spoke superfluously." For Gogol, the same is true of those Russian poets who "feel the hand of God."[21] Many compose verses, but few are poets; many write, but few belong to Russian literature. To be sure, lesser writers could still achieve a measure of immortality through association with the greats, the way the minor poet Kyukhelbeker is remembered because of his friendship with Pushkin.

As the acknowledged "father" of Russian literature, Pushkin stands above criticism. Negative comments about him or about Tatyana, the heroine of Pushkin's novel *Eugene Onegin*, may elicit charges of "blasphemy." People make pilgrimages to "Pushkin places"—as one might go through the stations of the cross—associated with events in his life. Wisdom is discovered in his most trivial comment or the most banal incident from his life, a practice the absurdist Daniil Kharms parodied in his "Anecdotes from Pushkin Life": "Once Petrushevsky broke his watch and sent for Pushkin. Pushkin came, looked at Petrushevsky's watch, and put it back on the chair. 'What do you say, Brother Pushkin?' Petrushevsky asked. 'The wheels stopped going round,' Pushkin said."[22]

"In the lyricism of our poets," Gogol claimed, "there is something which is not in the poets of other nations, namely a kind of biblicism."[23] It was common to read Pushkin's poem "The Prophet," based on Isaiah's account of his divine election (Isaiah 2:6–10), as a revelation of a similar status for Pushkin. That status could be transmitted to others. As Moses anointed Joshua and Elijah anointed Elisha, so Lermontov achieved recognition as Pushkin's successor, first with his poem "The Death of a Poet" and then, remarkably enough, by losing his life, as Pushkin did, in a duel.

In her article on the Russian writer's prophetic status, Pamela Davidson points to the importance of this sense of prophetic continuity.[24] Dostoevsky's famous speech about Pushkin described him as the prophet announcing Russia's "panhuman" word destined to save the world.[25] Because Pushkin died when his creative power was at its height, Dostoevsky concluded, "he unquestionably took some great secret with him to his grave. And so now we must puzzle out this secret without him."[26] As Davidson notes, Dostoevsky's enthusiastic speech amounted to a claim of prophetic status for Dostoevsky himself and, indeed, people often apply the epithet "prophet" to him.[27]

To be sure, the image of the poet as prophet was a commonplace in European romanticism. As visionaries, poets, in Shelley's well-known words, are "the unacknowledged legislators of the world."[28] In Russia, they are acknowledged. "Hasn't it always been understood," asks Innokenty Volodin in Solzhenitsyn's novel *In the First Circle*, "[that] a major writer in our country . . . is a sort of second government?"[29] Realist prose writers enjoyed the same status, which indeed came to pertain to the very concept of the Russian writer, regardless of movement or genre. It is hard to imagine Anthony Trollope, George Eliot, or Flaubert being viewed that way.

Russian literature, like the Bible, came to be perceived not as a series of separate books but as a single ongoing work composed over many generations. When I was a graduate student, I discovered that Russians do not read poetry the way I had been taught in my English classes. A Russian poem was typically not appreciated as a discrete artifact, a well-wrought urn requiring nothing outside it, but as a link in a tradition to which it constantly alluded. Each word was, potentially, such an allusion, and each poem a microcosm of the canon as a whole. To be sure, Russian novels are not necessarily read this way, unless they invite doing so; but they do so often. Call your novel *Petersburg*, or just set the action in that city, and a whole range of works—including Pushkin's "Bronze Horseman," Gogol's Petersburg tales, Dostoevsky's *Crime and Punishment*, and others—enter into dialogue with it.[30]

Classics cite classics frequently. Solzhenitsyn's arguments with Tolstoy in *The Red Wheel* recall similar discussions of Russian classics in *Life and Fate*, *Doctor Zhivago*, and other works. As English novels presume readers' familiarity with the King James Bible, so Russian fiction presumes readers' intimate knowledge of that quasi-Bible, the Russian classics.

"From Aksakov and Turgenev to Chekhov, and even to Gorky, Bunin, and other writers of their generation, the Russian realistic novel may and must be regarded as one literary growth," observed D. S. Mirsky in his classic *History of Russian Literature*.[31] Critic and translator Max Hayward concurred: "It is a

striking feature of Russian literature . . . that it is, as it were, a single enterprise in which no one writer can be separated from another. Each one of them
is best viewed through the many-sided prism constituted by all of them taken
together. A later generation consciously takes up the motifs of its predecessors . . . in the light of the intervening historical experience."[32] This sense of
the tradition as a "single enterprise," even a single sacred work, still continues.

## Everything Belongs

No topic remains unliterary: as the Bible addresses all of life, so does
Russian literature. It keeps examining new, apparently unpoetic, topics and
appropriating nonliterary forms to do so. Long before socialist realism celebrated collective farming, *Anna Karenina* described Levin's evolving ideas
about English seed oats, threshing machines, and similar topics.[33]

Whether pertaining to society, the psyche, history, philosophy, or everyday life, an idea became significant only when discussed in literature or, at
least, literary criticism. This encyclopedic quality of Russian literature was
noted decades before the 1860s and 1870s. In his "Review of Russian Literature for 1831," the Slavophile Ivan Kireevsky asserted that literature is more
important in Russia than elsewhere because a wise government frees people
from politics. As a result, he explained, it is literature that occupies all minds
and becomes the venue for discussion of all topics. "That is why in Russia not
only literary men but every citizen of his fatherland must follow the progress
of literature."[34]

Without praising tsarist restrictions on political discussion, Russian literature's most influential critic, Vissarion Belinsky, made a similar point. His
"Thoughts and Notes on Literature" (1846) begins: "Whatever our literature
may be, it has far greater significance for us than may appear; in it, and it
alone, is contained the whole of our intellectual life."[35] The radical critic Nikolai
Chernyshevsky concurred:

> In those countries where intellectual life has attained a high level of
> development, one can speak of a "division of labor" among the various
> branches of intellectual activity. Only one of those branches is known
> to us: literature. For that reason . . . literature has a greater role in
> our intellectual life than French, German, and English literature play in
> the intellectual life of their respective countries, and it bears greater re-
> sponsibilities than the literature of other nations. Russian literature . . .
> has the direct duty of taking an interest in the kind of subject matter

that has elsewhere passed into the special competence of other fields of intellectual activity.[36]

If Levin could discuss agriculture, why not the centrifugal casting of sewerage pipes (in Vladimir Dudintsev's 1956 novel *Not By Bread Alone*)? Victor Erlich referred to "Soviet variations on the boy meets tractor theme."[37]

## The Russian Conscience

"Prophet" was only one of the roles Russian writers could play. Readers readily regarded realists as the nation's "conscience" and the discoverers of otherwise unavailable truths. The Russian writer spoke for "*pravda*," a Russian word meaning both justice ("rightness" in a moral sense) and truth ("rightness" as factual correctness).

Dmitri Likhachev—usually considered the greatest scholar of Russian medieval literature—deplored the Soviet regime's treatment of literature. He diagnosed a Pushkin shortage. It was easy enough to buy insipid approved authors, but hard "to buy Leskov, Bunin, or even Pushkin, Gogol, Lermontov, which comprise our national pride"; and it was a major achievement to "push through" (get published) an edition of humorist Mikhail Zoshchenko. For Likhachev, this state of affairs assumes the greatest moral significance:

> Literature is the conscience of a society, its soul. The honor and merit of a writer consists in defending truth and the right to that truth under the most unfavorable circumstances.... As a specialist on ancient Russian literature, I can say with conviction that Russian literature has never kept silent. Can you really consider literature literature, or a writer a writer if they side-step the truth, if they silence it or try to falsify it? Literature which does not evoke a pang of conscience is already a lie. And to lie in literature, you will agree, is the worst form of lying.[38]

"You will agree": Likhachev can count on his readers sharing this view of literature. Works not evoking "a pang of conscience" do not qualify as literature at all. An author who declines to battle for independent thought can put words on paper but is not truly a writer. "I do not agree that writing is a profession," Likhachev comments. "To be a writer is fate. It is a life."[39] One does not choose to be a writer; the writer is chosen by life. For Likhachev, and the readers whom he has in mind, these ideas constitute not an academic "theory of literature" but something far more important. For what can be of greater significance to a society than its conscience, its soul?

This view of the writer as national conscience was already commonplace during Alexander II's reign. Chernyshevsky praised Tolstoy's early stories for their contribution to "high social morality" capable of cleansing us from "inherited sins." "The literature of our time," he continued, "is the noblest manifestation of the purest moral feeling, in each of its remarkable works without exception." This statement borders on tautology, since without "pure moral feeling" a work could not be "remarkable" in the first place.[40]

As anarchist Peter Kropotkin observed in his *Memoirs of a Revolutionist* (1899), Russian literature, as the nation's conscience, shapes morality and plays the most important role in a young person's education. "In Russia there is not a man or woman of mark . . . who does not owe the first impulse toward a higher development to his or her teacher of literature." Other teachers instruct in their own subject, Kropotkin explains, but it is the teacher of literature who unites all learning into a meaningful and ennobling whole: "Only the teacher of literature . . . can bind together the separate historical and humanitarian sciences, unify them by a broad philosophical and humane conception, and awaken higher ideas and inspirations in the brains and hearts of young people. In Russia, that necessary task falls quite naturally upon the teacher of Russian literature."[41]

Given this high moral calling, the writer must appreciate, and persuade readers to care about, the suffering of others. Alexievich, who discovered new ways to elucidate pain, observed that "suffering is our capital, our natural resource. Not oil or gas—but suffering. It is the only thing we are able to produce consistently." With her trademark irony, she remarked that Russian history provides endless material for the writer: "The two most important words in Russian are 'war' and 'prison.'"[42]

In *The Unwomanly Face of War*, Alexievich described pain, properly understood, as a key to "the mystery of life itself." Nothing else reveals that mystery so well:

> I listen to the pain [. . .] Pain as the proof of past life. There are no other proofs, I don't trust other proofs. Words have more than once led us away from truth. I think of suffering as the highest form of information, having a direct connection with mystery. With the mystery of life. All of Russian literature is about that. It has written more about suffering than about love.[43]

"All of Russian literature is about that": what isn't about suffering isn't Russian literature.

Just as one can be expelled from Russia, one can be exiled from Russian literature if one acts against conscience and refuses to sympathize with sufferers, especially other writers. At the Twenty-Third Party Congress in 1966, Sholokhov condemned dissident writers Andrei Sinyavsky and Yuli Daniel, recently tried for publishing their "slanderous" works abroad. Daniel had been sentenced to five years and Sinyavsky to seven in a strict regime labor camp. "If these delinquents with their black consciences pulled the same stunt back in the twenties when people were judged not in accordance with strictly delineated articles of the Criminal Code but instead operated with a 'revolutionary understanding of what is right,'" Sholokhov thundered, "oh how these turncoats would have received an altogether different form of punishment."[44]

Editor and author Alexander Tvardovsky wrote in his diary that "Sholokhov is now a former writer." In an open letter, the writer Lydia Chukovskaia also condemned Sholokhov in the name of Russian literature. Never before, she observed, had a Russian writer claimed that the punishment of a fellow writer was not harsh enough! "It was surprising to hear such rude, unnuanced declarations from the author of *The Quiet Don*, which extends empathy even to individuals who committed crimes against the revolution," she observed. Sholokhov had evidently forgotten what every true Russian writer and reader knows: that literature, as the highest ideal, stands above the criminal code. "Literature," she wrote, "cannot be judged by courts." Because Sholokhov had joined those who did judge it, Tvardovsky, Chukovskaia, and others expelled this author, whose best work they still admired, from Russian literature.[45]

Long before Likhachev, Alexievich, and Chukovskaia, at the time when this view of Russian literature was still fresh, a character in Turgenev's novel *Rudin* mocks it. The misanthropic Pigasov explains why he does not care "for our contemporary [Russian] literature":

> I crossed the Oka [river] lately in a ferry boat with a gentleman. The ferry got fixed in a narrow place; they had to drag the carriages ashore by hand. This gentleman had a very heavy coach. While the ferrymen were straining themselves to drag the coach to the bank, the gentleman groaned so, standing in the ferry, that one felt quite sorry for him [...] Well, I thought, here's a fresh illustration of the division of labor! That's just like our modern literature; other people work, and it does the groaning.[46]

## Revealing Truth

In addition to serving as a national conscience, the Russian writer, the tradition holds, enjoys special access to truth. In *The Master and Margarita*, the Master's novel about Jesus and Pontius Pilate turns out to coincide perfectly with what actually happened. Where it differs from the Gospel, it is the Gospel that is mistaken, and the Master's novel itself offers the correct explanation for the difference.

The Master intuits the truth because he is just that, a literary master. Predominant opinion since Belinsky has held that to know the full truth about historical events, one needs not only factual histories, but also historical novels.[47] The historians discover facts, the novelist reveals the deeper truth. What that "deeper truth" entails varies from writer to writer and epoch to epoch, but it always includes the meaning of events.

Stalin supposedly said that "a single death is a tragedy, a million is a statistic," and that, at least, is how academic historians usually narrate.[48] They argue about the total number but do not dwell on each death. How could they? Great writers, by contrast, restore the sense that every death is uniquely tragic. The millions murdered by Stalin each died as individuals, as we ourselves might have. When Solzhenitsyn subtitled *The Gulag Archipelago* "An Experiment in Literary Investigation," he signaled, among other things, his intention to create that feeling of vicarious suffering in his readers.

Reviewing a book on the history of Ukraine, Belinsky observed that "histories like these have their value and their merits as material for the historian-artist by a scholarly hand. [But] one can grasp the meaning and probe the vital core of facts only by poetical intuition. . . . Hence it is clear that history requires creativeness."[49] Historians must not go beyond the sources, Belinsky argued, but a literary work can teach us more about a bygone time than even direct experience ever could.

Dobrolyubov's celebrated essay "When Will the Real Day Come?" (a title answering that of Turgenev's novel *On the Eve*) argues that, whether the author knows it or not, a great literary work reveals the most profound truths about society. That is why an astute critic can derive significant insights inaccessible by other means:

> We have no other way of knowing . . . what is beginning to permeate and predominate in the moral life of society but literature. . . . That is why we think that as soon as it is recognized that an author-artist possesses talent,

that is, the ability to feel and depict the phenomena with lifelike truth, this very recognition creates legitimate ground for taking his productions as a basis for the discussion of the milieu, the epoch, which prompted the author to write this or that production.[50]

The demands of great literature shape what the author shows, sometimes even contrary to his intention. For this reason, Dobrolyubov argues, "if Mr. Turgenev touches upon any question in a story of his . . . it can be taken as a guarantee that this question is rising, or soon will rise, in the mind of the educated of society." It is important to explain all this, Dobrolyubov informed his readers, "in order to justify our method, namely, to interpret the phenomena of life on the basis of a literary production."[51]

This is an odd sort of sociology: rather than gather empirical facts about a society, read its fiction. So long as writers are talented enough, you will grasp what is most important. Russian social thinkers routinely discussed fictional characters—Onegin, Pechorin, Chatsky, Oblomov, Bazarov—as if they were real people; or, more precisely, as if they were realer than real people.[52] Katkov, Pisarev, and others supplied details about Bazarov's life as if they were dealing with a real person documented elsewhere.

Belinsky still invoked the romantic concept of intuition to explain the writer's insight, and Dobrolyubov resorted to the vague concept of "talent," but Tolstoy, with razor-sharp logic, offered a clearer explanation. Mikhailov, the painter Anna and Vronsky visit in the fifth part of *Anna Karenina*, winces when they ascribe his impressive work to "talent." By this word, he reflects, they mean "an inborn and almost physical aptitude apart from brain and heart, and in which they tried to find an expression for all the artist had gained from life." Mikhailov knows they err in attributing his success to "technique." It actually derives from his constant practice in noticing what others miss. Through a lifetime, he has taught himself to discern telling details and to retain them for future use. "If to a little child or to his cook were revealed what he saw, it or she" could paint as he did. Tolstoy thought the same about his own astonishing realism.[53]

Think of it this way: there is an obvious proof that Tolstoy, George Eliot, and some other novelists understood people better than the greatest psychologists. If psychologists knew people as well as these novelists did, they could present portraits of people as believable as Anna Karenina and Dorothea Brooke, but none has even come close. These writers must know something that psychologists still struggle to grasp. The same may be said of their portraits of society.

*War and Peace* frequently explains why historians err about facts as well as meaning. The events novels describe are usually fictional, of course, but the shape of those events—the depiction of *how* things happen—is true. When historians create narratives that are false to the *way* things happen, the novelist will detect their naïveté. In a number of passages in *War and Peace*, Tolstoy first paraphrases or quotes a historian's account of an incident which, he argues, simply could not be true because things do not happen that way. Much of *War and Peace* consists of what might be called "negative narration"—an analysis of what could not have happened. Tolstoy often presents his alternative account as, if not necessarily correct, at least more likely than received historical narratives.[54]

In his essay "Some Words About the Book *War and Peace*," Tolstoy offers reasons that his account differs from those of historians. For one thing, historians describe historical figures when they make significant decisions or perform notable actions. After all, that is what documentation mostly contains. The result is a falsification, "a necessary lie," because "Kutuzov did not always hold a telescope, point at the enemy, or ride a white horse." By making the most of sparse documentation and imagining the rest, the novelist can represent historical actors' "relation to all sides of life." The novelist depicts people as what people always are, complex individuals with a diversity of inconsistent emotions, concerns, interests, and flaws. If these accounts go beyond verifiable sources, they at least show how people actually behave.[55]

Still more important, "the historian has to deal with the results of an event, the artist with the fact of the event." Seeking causes, historians detect in events the seeds of what came later as if those later events were already there, just as foreshadowed incidents in novels may be found in subsequent pages. For the novelist, this sense of historical time is a fallacy—Tolstoy calls it "the fallacy of retrospection"—because each moment possesses its own integrity and the potential to lead in many directions. For the historian, events of the past are just that, past; for the novelist, they are previous presents.[56]

Historians, moreover, describe events as much more orderly than they could possibly have been. Tolstoy famously presented battle—for the first time!—not as described in narratives (the left flank moves here, the right one there) but as sheer chaos, a view that was still striking when John Keegan wrote his classic study, *The Face of Battle*.[57] Ask soldiers right after a battle what they experienced, Tolstoy suggested, "and you will form a majestic, complex, infinitely varied, depressing, and indistinct impression."[58] But then officers must write reports and, to do so, base their accounts on earlier ones and so make them appear much more orderly than the events actually were. Then higher-level officers combine several reports in the same way, and finally, an official account is drawn up. And then something especially curious happens: people begin to "remember" events according to the official story, to the point where soldiers miles apart report, quite sincerely, that they witnessed the same incidents. Both *War and Peace* and *Anna Karenina* explore the dynamics of memory, which makes the world more orderly than it is, a process that continues with each act of recollection. Historians, in Tolstoy's view, may recognize conscious distortion in official reports, but do not show sufficient awareness of unconscious misrepresentations introduced by the very act of narrating.[59]

Tolstoy's explanation of novelists' superior insight goes too far, of course. But whether warranted or not, his unconventional account of the Napoleonic wars has become the conventional one, a template for later historians. Fictional events, like fictional characters, came to define reality.

Alexievich also claims to have made discoveries that historians did not make, and perhaps could not have made. Like Tolstoy, she wants to get beyond the official reports—"the canon," as she calls it—to discover what the experience of war was really like, especially for women. All those stories "about how certain people heroically killed other people and won" focus on men. "Women's war has its own colors, its own smells, its own lighting, and its own range of feelings. Its own words. There are no heroes and incredible feats, there are only people who are busy doing inhumanly human things."[60]

Women's experience of war is not only overlooked, but also difficult to elicit, and so Alexievich, like Solzhenitsyn, had to conduct an experiment in literary investigation. She needed to get women to talk frankly and intimately about what they had never put into words. Expressing their memories sometimes surprised these women. Alexievich's role as interlocutor extended far beyond asking questions and recording answers; like a psychoanalyst, she had to participate in a difficult and painful process of self-discovery.

Having elicited these revelations, Alexievich had to present them. "It took me a long time to find a genre that corresponded to the way I viewed the world [. . .] to the way my eyes saw and ears heard," she recalls. What her ears heard especially acutely was the tones of the conversational "human voice." "It's important to catch words in flight, as they're born . . . not to miss the conversational part of life. . . . It seems surprising that this could be literature. But I want to make every bit of our life into literature."[61]

Like men, Alexievich soon learned, women do not want to say anything that might discredit the mythology of the war and so she had to spend a lot of time with them, "sometimes a whole day," drinking tea and looking at photos of grandchildren. "After a certain time, you never know when or why, suddenly comes this long-awaited moment, when the person departs from the canon . . . I must seize that moment!" "Texts, texts. Texts everywhere" if you know how to find them and how to listen in the right way. "I listen [. . .] I turn more and more into a big ear, listening all the time to another person. I 'read' voices." Becoming literature, these voices reveal unsuspected truth. This truth is "the truth about life and death in general." To grasp it, "I have to gain breadth. . . . To ask Dostoevsky's question: How much human being is in a human being, and how to protect this human being in oneself."[62] The tradition lives: Alexievich regards her literary experiment as a continuation of Dostoevsky's.

Historians have missed "the story told by an unnoticed witness and participant. Yes, that interests me, that I would like to make into literature." This sort of literature, realism extended beyond fiction, can help us "discern the eternally human" in specific people: "The tremor of eternity. That which is in human beings at all times."[63]

The voice of conscience and the discoverer of truths: these roles are closely linked because a moral imperative directs the writer to reveal hidden truths—and directs the reader to learn them, even when, as often happens, it is perilous to do so. That sense of the reader's obligation also forms an intrinsic part of the Russian literary tradition. In "The Hell of Treblinka," Grossman explained: "It is the writer's duty to tell the truth, and it is a reader's civic duty to learn this truth. To turn away, to close one's eyes and walk past is to insult the memory of those who have perished."[64] Russian literature, made by writers and readers together, not only reveals the truth but also, no less morally important, remembers it.

## The Two Traditions

In 1909 seven prominent thinkers joined to produce the anthology *Landmarks: A Collection of Essays on the Russian Intelligentsia*.[65] Here we may single out one of its key observations: it is possible to trace two traditions in Russian literature and thought. One consisted of writers whose greatness lay in the literary masterpieces they produced or the original ideas they developed. Among prose writers, Gogol, Turgenev, Goncharov, Tolstoy, and Chekhov belong to this tradition; among poets, Pushkin, Lermontov, Tyutchev, and Fet; among philosophers, Chaadaev and Vladimir Soloviev.

The other tradition, according to the *Landmarks* contributors, celebrated radical "journalists" (in the Russian sense of makers of public opinion), especially Belinsky, Dobrolyubov, Pisarev, Lavrov, Mikhailovsky, and, above all, Chernyshevsky. Among fiction writers, adherents of this tradition preferred those "burning with indignation," as the revolutionary Lev Tikhomirov explained, and especially those who "did not trouble themselves about art." Chernyshevsky's journalistic collaborator Nikolai Shelgunov recalled: "creative writers formed the rearguard of the movement; the avant-gardes of the advancing literary hordes consisted of publicists."[66]

The radical canon gave pride of place to Chernyshevsky's utopian fiction *What Is to Be Done?* If one judges this book from a literary point of view, it is hard to see why it was more celebrated and influential than any other work of nineteenth-century literature. Most critics have wondered how it could have been celebrated at all. Turgenev famously remarked that reading its appalling prose produced a sensation of physical repulsion, and the rumor circulated that the tsarist censorship had allowed the book to appear in the belief that it was so bad it would discredit the radical movement.[67]

For that matter, the book itself proclaims its lack of literary merit. "I possess not one bit of literary talent," the author tells readers. "I even lack full command of the language. But that doesn't mean a thing; read on, dearest public, it will be well worth your while. Truth is a good thing . . . now that I've warned you that I have no talent whatever, you know that any merit to be found in my tale is due to its truthfulness."[68]

In his memoirs, Nikolay Valentinov recalled a conversation with Lenin about Chernyshevsky's book. "One is amazed," Valentinov had remarked, "how people could take any interest or pleasure in such a thing. It would be difficult to imagine anything more untalented, crude, and at the same time pretentious. Most of the pages of this celebrated novel are written in unreadable language." Lenin could not believe his ears. "Do you realize what you are saying?" he had indignantly replied. "How could such a monstrous and absurd idea come into your mind. . . . I declare that it's impermissible to call *What is to Be Done?* crude and untalented. Hundreds of people became revolutionaries under its influence. . . . *He completely transformed my outlook.*"[69]

These opposing views of *What Is to Be Done?* capture in a nutshell the difference between tradition and radical counter-tradition. When you think of Russian literature, do you have in mind Tolstoy or Chernyshevsky, Dostoevsky or Gorky, Chekhov or Lenin? One can already discern the divergence of the two traditions in the first years of Alexander II's reign. As early as 1858, Tolstoy felt that the pressure to produce politically acceptable works was intolerable. Writing to V. P. Botkin in 1858, he asked:

> What would you say if now, when the filthy stream of politics is trying to swallow everything, and to soil if not do away with art—what would you say about the people who believe in art's independence and its immortality coming together and demonstrating this truth both by deed (the practice of art) and word (criticism), and trying to save what is eternal and independent from the accidental, one-sided, and all-pervasive political influence?[70]

Tolstoy then proposed that "Turgenev, you, Fet, myself, and everyone who shared and *will continue* to share our convictions" should found a journal that will "attract all that is artistic. . . . The journal won't try to prove anything or know anything. Its one criterion will be educated taste."[71]

Turgenev's novel *Fathers and Children* (1861) also defends the claims of art against propaganda.[72] Bazarov, the novel's hero, largely shares Chernyshevsky's views about art, but learns to his dismay that this aesthetic "nihilism" is not only mistaken but also leaves him vulnerable to manipulation.

In his article "Apropos of *Fathers and Children*," Turgenev observed that too many critics presume that a novelist starts with an idea he wants to prove and then selects a character suitable to prove it. That may be true of the sort of writer the radicals favor, but not about "what goes on in the mind" of a novelist like himself. The author of a major literary work, Turgenev insisted, concerns himself not primarily with advancing his philosophical beliefs but with loyalty to the complex truth, which, often enough, runs counter to those beliefs. The critics, in short, "refuse to believe that to reproduce truth and the reality of life correctly and powerfully is the greatest happiness for an author, even if this truth does not coincide with his own sympathies."[73]

To illustrate his point, Turgenev reminded readers that even though he is an incorrigible westernizer, the character Panshin in *A Nest of Gentlefolk* shows up the vulgarity of westernizers. "Why did I do so?" Turgenev asked. "*Because in the given case life . . . happened to be like that*, and what I wanted above all was to be sincere and truthful." Characters often surprise realist authors. By contrast, Chernyshevsky's characters, as mere mouthpieces, could not possibly say or do something unexpected.[74]

To allow for such surprises, Turgenev continued, writers require freedom from all pressure to enunciate approved ideas. "What one needs is freedom, absolute freedom of opinions and ideas" so that one can be guided not by preconceived beliefs or the most cherished feelings but by "a truthfulness that is inexorable in relation to one's own feelings." For the true writer, the creative process is one of discovery, not of mere expression, and it is that process that makes characters believable and plots plausible.[75] Chekhov also resented the unceasing pressure to make his work tendentious, or even to pass clear judgment on his characters. A writer's job, he maintained, is not to solve questions but to present them correctly.

The fundamental disagreement between the two traditions, then, concerned not only which writers to favor but also what literature was supposed to be. Radicals denounced calls for "artistic freedom" and defenses of works without an unambiguous political tendency as "art for art's sake" appealing only to aristocrats, bourgeois individualists, or supporters of existing injustice. In his 1905 essay "Party Organization and Party Literature," Lenin proclaimed:

> Down with non-partisan writers! Down with literary supermen! Literature must become *part* of the common cause of the proletariat, "a cog and a screw" of one single great Social-Democratic mechanism set in motion by the entire politically conscious vanguard of the entire working class. Literature must become a component of organized, planned and integrated Social Democratic Party work. . . . I daresay there will ever be hysterical intellectuals to raise a howl about such a comparison, which degrades, deadens, "bureaucratizes" the free battle of ideas, freedom of criticism, freedom of literary creation, etc., etc. Such outcries, in point of fact, would be nothing more than an expression of bourgeois intellectual individualism.[76]

The Soviets made this essay the basis of their literary policy.

One has to agree, I think, with Rufus Mathewson's revision of received American opinion about the Russian literary tradition:

> The conventional view, echoed by Edmund Wilson, for example . . . that writer and radical critic in Russia coexisted in some form of loose, untroubled alliance based on their shared opposition to the status quo, must yield to a new understanding of what bound them together and what finally separated them . . . the grounds for communion between them were undermined by deeper disagreements. . . . In 1860 there was a crucial separation which established a fundamental polarity in thinking about literature.[77]

This polarity, Mathewson argues, continued into the Soviet period.

Andrei Zhdanov (Stalin's point man in the 1946 attack on Anna Akhmatova, Mikhail Zoshchenko, and all insufficiently Party-minded writers) appealed to the radical tradition from which Soviet literature took its cue: "The finest aspect of Soviet literature is its carrying on of the best traditions of nineteenth-century Russian literature, traditions established by our great revolutionary democrats, Belinsky, Dobrolyubov, Chernyshevsky, and Saltykov-Shchedrin, continued by Plekhanov and scientifically elaborated by Lenin and Stalin."[78] Zhdanov's "best tradition" of Russian literature includes, except for Saltykov-Shchedrin, only "journalists" and revolutionaries. It omits Turgenev, Tolstoy, Dostoevsky, and Chekhov.

## What Is Truth?

The radicals did not, of course, describe themselves as opposed to truthfulness. Rather, they redefined "truth" to include not only the observable present reality but also the inevitable future in the making. Great writers discern "types"—in the sense of prototypes—of people who are rare at present but bound to predominate in the future. They have what Belinsky called "the clairvoyant gift of presaging the future by the signs of the present."[79]

In *What Is to Be Done?* the major heroes shaping the plot—Lopukhov, Kirsanov, and Vera Pavlovna—expect that in the near future most people will exhibit their own still unusual virtues. The heroes' advanced beliefs will also be commonplace. These heroes are "the new people" of the book's subtitle, "From Tales About New People." "This type appeared quite recently," the author explains, "but now it's propagating quite quickly." We can judge how quickly when we reflect that six years ago "these people couldn't even be found . . . three years ago they were despised" and in a few years "what this type says will be done by all." Soon enough, resembling these "decent people" will be "the only option."[80]

As soon as that imminent future arrives, the process will be repeated, and the new people will yield to still newer people, as superior to them as they are to unenlightened folk today. One such newer person has in fact already appeared, the author tells us—the almost superhuman Rakhmetov, who plays almost no role in the action because his hour has not yet come. All the same, we can be sure: If Lopukhov and Vera are the best people, then Rakhmetov is "the flower of the best people"; if they are the salt of the earth, then he is "the salt of the salt of the earth."[81] I know of no other work that presents this type of the second order.

The Soviets would label fidelity to present facts "bourgeois objectivism." It was the best that could be expected from the age of realism, but must give way to socialist realism, which shows the ideal world inevitably coming. The socialist realist author was expected to focus on the people of the future, "positive heroes" exhibiting complete "Party-mindedness." True positive heroes do not have to bring their thinking into accord with the Party, a process requiring effort; they exhibit Party-mindedness so thorough that no effort is required. Complexity, self-division, the agonies of choice so brilliantly depicted in nineteenth-century fiction now appear as so many signs of the accursed past. To depict people of the present that way is, in Soviet thinking, to slip into "psychologism."[82]

Chernyshevsky's characters who had overcome psychology complexity presaged Soviet positive heroes. Lopukhov never suffers a moment's doubt. The Soviet Union endeavored to create real people no less certain. When the two traditions confront each other, Matthewson observed, "wonder confronts certainty."[83]

## Two Truths

To be sure, Soviet theoreticians observed, it is too early to discover many positive heroes resembling those in socialist realist literature. But that is precisely why such literature is needed. As Comintern Secretary Karl Radek observed, "We do not photograph life. In the totality of phenomena we seek out the main phenomenon. Presenting everything without discrimination is not realism. Realism means that we make a selection from the point of view of what is essential, from the point of view of guiding principles."[84] If this use of the term "realism" seems odd, think of the philosophical distinction between realism (which affirms the reality of abstract universals) and nominalism (they are merely convenient names).

Here, then, is a key difference between the two traditions as they reappeared in the Soviet period. For official writers, who regarded themselves as the heirs of Chernyshevsky and the radical journalists, reality is essentially Platonic. What is most real is not the brute facts, but something higher. Truth is not empirical, as "bourgeois objectivists" suppose, but "typical": it is the truth of the world certain to come. By contrast, the writers who adhered to the traditions of Tolstoy, Dostoevsky, and Chekhov insisted on representing the world as we see it, depicting people as they are rather than as "positive heroes," and conveying the truth of actual experience.

Vasily Grossman encountered trouble publishing his first novel, set in a mining community, which contained passages an editor deemed "counter-revolutionary." Grossman appealed to Gorky, the most influential Soviet literary figure. "I described what I saw while living and working for three years at mine Smolyanka-11. I wrote the truth. It may be a harsh truth. But the truth can never be counterrevolutionary." Gorky replied: "It is not enough to say, 'I wrote the truth.' The author should ask himself two questions: 'First, which truth? And second, why?' We know that there are two truths and that in our world, it is the vile and dirty truth of the past that quantitatively predominates. But this truth is being replaced by another truth that has been born and continues to grow."[85]

Grossman never forgot this reply, which, in his view, amounted to calling lies a higher truth. He did everything possible to adhere to truth as the great realists had understood it. In Grossman's novel *Stalingrad*, Marusya dislikes Zhenya's painting, which she calls "strange daubs no one can understand," and advises her to produce propaganda posters instead. "But I know what you'll say next," Marusya continues, "You'll start going on about truth to life [...] How many times do I have to tell you that there are two truths? There's the truth of the reality forced on us by the accursed past. And there's the truth of the reality that will defeat the past. It's this second truth, the truth of the future, that *I* want to live by."

"You talk about people," Zhenya counters, "as if it isn't women who bring them into the world but newspaper editors." Their friend Sofya Osipovna replies as Grossman would: "No, Marusya," she insists. "You're wrong. I can tell you as a surgeon that there is one truth, not two. When I cut someone's leg off, I don't know two truths. If we start pretending there are two truths, we're in trouble."[86]

When Alexievich submitted the manuscript of *The Unwomanly Face of War*, the censor objected: "you show the filth of the war. The underwear. You make our Victory terrible [...] What is it you're after?" When she replied: "the truth," the censor countered: "You think the truth is what's there in life.... It's such a lowly thing for you. Earthly. No, the truth is what we dream about. It's how we want to be!"[87]

## Life as Performance

The radicals proved especially given to viewing life in exalted literary terms. The Decembrist revolutionaries of 1825 had already imagined themselves as the heroes of a great drama, in which even failure would be a tragic success.

According to tradition, the Decembrist poet Alexander Odoevsky enthused just before the uprising, "O, how gloriously we will die!"[88] The Decembrists—or rather the well-crafted legends about them—inspired many others to revolt. Those legends drew on the verse and life of the executed Decembrist poet Kondraty Ryleev. It is noteworthy that Herzen's first significant publication abroad, *Polar Star* (begun 1855), took its name from the publication edited by Ryleev and fellow Decembrist Alexander Bestuzhev. The cover of Herzen's periodical displayed an engraving of the five executed Decembrists. Legends about "the wives of the Decembrists," who chose to follow their condemned husbands to Siberia, provided a model for radical women.

As historian Aileen Kelly has observed, "in their tragic defeat, followed by death and exile, the rebels provided their countrymen with a collective ideal of the romantic hero *par excellence*."[89] The imitation of literary exemplars, though not limited to revolutionaries, became especially characteristic of them, and constituted an essential part of revolutionary tradition. Characters from their favorite works, especially the heroes of *What Is to Be Done?*, proved astonishingly influential among young people. As a result, these prophecies, as Chernyshevsky regarded the personality types he created, became more or less self-fulfilling.

In Western countries, of course, romanticism also inspired young people to imitate the life (and death) of Goethe's Werther (*The Sorrows of Young Werther*) and of Byron, both the man and the heroes of his poems. But in Russia this practice not only had deeper roots, it also persisted, indeed gained momentum, long after the romantic era.[90]

This persistence once again testifies to the enormous prestige of Russian literature. As Boris Gasparov has noted, Russians not only regarded their literature as "containing the solution to moral problems, . . . the answer to cardinal philosophical questions . . . [and] a political program for the transformation of society," but also as "an all-embracing 'guide to life' . . . a codex of individual behavior."[91]

Dobrolyubov concluded his essay about Turgenev's *On the Eve* with a call for, and prediction of, Russians resembling the novel's intrepid Bulgarian hero, Insarov. Turgenev, in Dobrolyubov's view, had provided a model worthy of imitation. "We need him [this Russian Insarov]; without him our lives seem to be wasted. . . . That day will come at last! . . . the eve is never far from the next day; only a matter of one night separates them."[92]

Although some radicals took the portrait of Bazarov in *Fathers and Children* as a slander on the younger generation, others imitated Turgenev's hero not only by adopting Bazarov's ideas but also by copying his manners.

In his article "Bazarov Once Again," Herzen, having described people who "endeavored to base their actions and words on Bazarovism," speculates on the process by which literature, having represented behavior, inspires it:

> This mutual interaction of people and books is a strange thing. A book takes its whole shape from the society that spawns it, then generalizes the material, renders it clearer and sharper, and as a consequence reality is transformed. The originals become caricatures of their own sharply drawn portraits and real people take on the character of their literary shadows. . . . Young Russians were almost all out of *What Is to Be Done?* after 1862, with the addition of a few of Bazarov's traits.[93]

In short, if romanticism led people to imitate literary characters, realism engendered a two-stage process. First, authors based novelistic characters on real people, sharpened their features, and presented their distilled essence as a type. Then readers copied these characters and so rendered reality itself literary.

Again, no work proved more influential than *What Is to Be Done?* As A. M. Skabichevsky recalled, it became common to set up producers' cooperatives and residential communes modeled on Vera Pavlovna's. "Fictitious marriages in order to liberate the daughters of generals and merchants from familial despotism in imitation of Lopukhov and Vera Pavlovna became normal phenomena" and women liberated this way usually reported "vatic dreams" resembling Vera Pavlovna's.[94] Sexual relations copied those in the novel.

Revolutionaries, including Nikolai Ishutin (a founder of a group of aspiring assassins calling itself "Hell") and Dmitri Karakazov (who attempted to assassinate Alexander II in 1866), took Chernyshevsky's hero Rakhmetov as a model. The last words of *What Is to Be Done?* are "4 April 1863"—presumably the date of its completion—and Karakazov chose the third anniversary of that date for his planned assassination!

Imitating Rakhmetov usually included eating as little as possible, performing gymnastics, and reading in a particular way. "I grew up on Chernyshevsky," the revolutionary M. P. Sazhin recalled, and "Rakhmetov was my ideal. Of course, I couldn't bring myself to sleep on a bed of nails [like Rakhmetov], but I did sleep on bare boards for a year." Rakhmetov's sole weakness, a fondness for cigars, also became a proper revolutionary failing.[95]

Not surprisingly, writers satirized the penchant for imitating literary characters, and none more so than Dostoevsky. At the beginning of *The Brothers*

*Karamazov*, the narrator explains the strange decision of Dmitri's mother Adelaida Ivanovna, a wealthy and beautiful woman, to marry the hideous Fyodor Pavlovich. She probably was imitating a literary type, the narrator explains, and, like many young people, wanted to enact the conventional radical actions of her day, a process that, the narrator suggests, still continues. Her clichéd action was "an echo of other people's ideas," ideas he enumerates using the approved clichéd language for describing them. She probably desired "to show her feminine independence, to override class distinctions and the despotism of her family." So blinded was she to reality that she took Fyodor Pavlovich for "one of the bold and ironical spirits of that progressive epoch" whereas he was in fact "an ill-natured buffoon and nothing more."[96] Almost everyone in *The Possessed* seems to be playing a literary role, and when Stavrogin's behavior puzzles his mother, Pyotr Stepanovich mendaciously explains it by comparing him to Shakespeare's Prince Hal (and is Pyotr Stepanovich therefore his Falstaff?).

The lives (or rather legends) of writers also functioned as "literary facts" and, as the century wore on, proliferated into different genres. As a former radical who survived a mock execution, Dostoevsky contributed to the legendary traditions of both the writer and the persecuted radical.

Model biographies for terrorists, drawn from a variety of literary sources, inspired numerous young men and women to adopt this dangerous but glamorous life. The terrorist Sergei Kravchinsky fled abroad after stalking and stabbing General Nikolai Mezentsev, the head of Russia's security police, with a stiletto and twisting it in the wound. Having escaped, he turned to literature, or rather, to mythology.

Under the name Stepniak, Kravchinsky published two books romanticizing terrorism and terrorists: a novel, *Career of a Nihilist*, written in English, and *Underground Russia*, written in Italian but rapidly translated into Russian and widely known. Presented as nonfiction, *Underground Russia* more closely resembles a Russian Orthodox paterikon, a collection of incidents from saints' lives. Stepniak ascribed almost superhuman qualities to terrorist men and women. The terrorist, he exclaimed,

> is noble, terrible, irresistibly fascinating, for he combines in himself the two sublimities of human grandeur: the martyr and the hero.... The force of mind, the indomitable energy, and the spirit of sacrifice which his [romantic] predecessor attained [only] in the beauty of his dreams, he attains in the grandeur of his mission, in the strong passions which this marvelous, intoxicating vertiginous struggle arouses in his

heart. . . . Proud as Satan rebelling against God . . . the Terrorist is immortal. . . . It is this . . . imposing mission, it is this certainty of approaching victory, which gives him that cool and calculating enthusiasm, that almost superhuman energy, which astounds the world.[97]

Model biographies evolved for terrorist women as well as men; for those from poor backgrounds as well as noblemen; and for Christians as well as Byronic heroes.

Terrorists eagerly imitated a whole series of dramatic actions. Leonid Andreyev's appallingly bad story "The Seven Who Were Hanged" celebrates the cool determination with which condemned terrorists face their last moments. Trials offered each worthy killer what terrorist Vera Figner called "the consoling consciousness that the moment of his test has come." The "test" included the delivery of an appropriate speech—which the authorities were foolish enough to allow—like the one that serves as the climax of Maxim Gorky's cloying novel *Mother*. Audiences at trials also played a prescribed role in what might be called reverse show trials, since the speeches of the accused indicted the authorities. In her article on the career of terrorist Mariya Spiridonova, Sally Boniece describes the mendacious creation of "facts" to fit the myth of what one publication called "a pure virginal being, a flower of spiritual beauty that only the highest culture of Russia could produce."[98]

In Solzhenitsyn's *August 1914*, Veronika's two aunts recite one revolutionary cliché after another in order to persuade their niece to follow family tradition and become a terrorist. They describe how the celebrated terrorist Vera Zasulich was inspired by Chernyshevsky's hero, "the great Rakhmetov." She even got to enact another revolutionary ritual, "the romantic experience of visiting an incarcerated hero as his supposed bride-to be." The life of Vera Figner, the aunts enthuse, deserves an epic. Such women, they say, are "the glory of Russia! The aging Turgenev was thrilled." Many real people died so that inspired killers could act out a quasi-fictional role.[99]

Remarkably enough, the most famous of all terrorists, Boris Savinkov, also wrote (under the pseudonym Ropshin) a series of novels about terrorists.[100] As Lynn Ellen Patyk has observed, Savinkov began both careers at the same time, in 1903, when he published his first story and joined the Socialist Realist Combat Organization. Under his leadership, that organized group of terrorists would successfully murder Minister of the Interior Vyacheslav von Plehve (1904) and the tsar's uncle, Grand Duke Sergei, governor-general of Moscow (1905).

In 1909, Savinkov published *Pale Horse*, the first of a series of novels devoted to terrorism. They contributed to what Patyk calls "Ropshin-Savinkov's self-mythologization" on the basis of "Russian modernism's neo-romantic cultural mythologies." Savinkov chose his life-genre carefully. "As a member of the gentry, a cosmopolitan aesthete, and a dandy, Savinkov embraced a model of authorship bequeathed to Russian literature by . . . Lord Byron and nativized by Alexander Pushkin and Mikhail Lermontov, all of whom remained among Savinkov's favorites."[101] He saved reviews of his books along with clippings about his terrorist exploits. The same project included both.

It is clear that Savinkov wrote novels and memoirs to glorify his terrorism. But I suspect the reverse is also true: he turned to terrorism in the first place in order to provide compelling material for fiction. It is well known that he was indifferent to ideology and would ply his trade under any banner. Terrorism and literature, revolution and reading: he brought Russia's two most prestigious occupations together.

## Two Canons

The revolutionaries and the writers each celebrated their own literary canon, and the two canons have competed ever since the early years of Alexander II's reign. The first, sometimes called "aesthetic," consists of the masterpieces that usually come to mind. In the second, radical "journalists" and revolutionaries played the dominant role and *What Is to Be Done?* towered over all other works of art. The terrorist Lev Tikhomirov discovered the greatest creative talent "in the revolutionary publications [such as] . . . *The People's Will*."[102]

With this alternative canon in mind, many Russian radicals participated in the Russian sanctification of literature and authors. "Never . . . did writers occupy such an honored place as here in Russia," Nikolai Shelgunov observed. This radical journalist described authors' public readings of their works in the way one might characterize a religious revival. "It wasn't just enthusiasm, but some kind of raving that accurately expressed the fervor that the writer called forth from the public."[103]

True, some radicals rejected literature altogether. According to Pisarev, Pushkin "reinforces the prejudices of society—those very prejudices which every thinking person is called upon to eradicate."[104] "You like Pushkin?" he asked. "If you please, just look at him!"—"our nice, pretty-pretty Pushkin," "the drowsy figure of a lounging lizard," "the mountebank addicted to petty juggling tricks," "the soul of Russian manorial wit."[105]

Calling his brand of materialism "realism," Pisarev insisted that "aesthetics and realism are irreconcilably hostile to each other, and realism must radically destroy aesthetics . . . aesthetics is the stubbornest element of intellectual stagnation and the surest enemy of rational progress."[106] Pisarev entitled his best-known article on this theme "The Destruction of Aesthetics."

To be sure, as historian Eugene Lampert observed, Pisarev "could not always make up his mind whether he was attacking the idealist notion of beauty, or all art, or merely the primacy of 'form' over 'matter' in a work of art."[107] And Pisarev himself was something of an aesthete. All the same, it was his most uncompromising formulations about literature that achieved the greatest notoriety. Art, he declared, is useless, while "a thoroughgoing realism absolutely despises everything that does not bring substantial utility."[108] The addiction to art, he sniffed, resembles "the sickly attachment of an aged spinster to cats, parrots, and pug-dogs."[109]

To talk of art and beauty "while every object of art was bought with money extracted from starving peasants or underpaid workers," Kropotkin explained, "inspired him [the nihilist] with disgust . . . [that] the nihilist expressed in the sweeping assertion, 'A pair of boots is more important than all your Madonnas and all your refined talk about Shakespeare.'"[110]

Since Russian literature was regarded as sacred, the delicious thrill of blasphemy accompanied such comments. If you wanted to shock, you would do far better to reject the Russian classics than to denounce religion. In their futurist manifesto, "A Slap in the Face of Public Taste," David Burlyuk, Alexander Kruchhenykh, Victor Khlebnikov, and Vladimir Mayakovsky famously declared: "The past is too tight. The Academy and Pushkin are less intelligible than hieroglyphics. Throw Pushkin, Dostoevsky, Tolstoy, etc., etc. overboard from the ship of Modernity." Of course, by this time the manifesto was itself a literary genre.[111]

The Bolshevik revolution led many to ask whether the high culture of the past, as the product of a hostile social class, should be rejected. In his poem "It's Too Early to Rejoice" (1918), Mayakovsky demanded that great artworks be lined up against the wall and summarily executed. Aleksei Gastev, a leading spokesman for the "Smithy" (*Kuznitsa*) group, called for a complete transformation of art as part of a movement to "mechanize not only . . . production" but also "everyday thinking . . . [to] render individual thinking impossible." Only collectivized art, completely different from the individualistic art of the past, should be possible.[112] At the first conference of the Proletkult (Proletarian Cultural and Educational Organization, founded in 1917), historian Richard Stites observed, a euphoric Proletkultist insisted "that all culture of the past might be called bourgeois, that within it—except for natural science and technical skills . . . there was nothing worthy of life, and that the Proletkult would begin the work of destroying the old culture." Stites also pointed to the statement of a founding member of the Proletkult, Pavel Bessalko, that writers no longer needed "their older brothers," the prerevolutionary classics; and to the plan of Tambov Proletkultists "to burn all the books in the belief that the shelves would be filled on the first of the new year with nothing but proletarian works!" If, as Marxist doctrine held, culture was merely a superstructure built on an economic base, then it seemed to follow that the superior base of socialism would inevitably generate culture superior to any existing before.[113]

Reasoning of this sort in fact eventually led to mass destruction of cultural artifacts by the Khmer Rouge and by Maoist Red Guards, but the prestige of Russian literature, and the belief in its unmatched power, inclined the Bolsheviks to a different solution. Socialist realism would become the governing Soviet aesthetic, but prerevolutionary realism would still be honored as a glorious Russian achievement. Instead of being destroyed or forgotten, the Russian classics would be reinterpreted in a Marxist-Leninist framework.

A few cultural historians have detected in this decision the germ of Communism's demise. By retaining the "aesthetic" tradition, the Bolsheviks preserved the values it conveyed, these historians reason, values directly counter to those of Bolshevism. Alexander Yakovlev, the Politburo member who has been called the intellectual force behind Gorbachev's *glasnost*, traced his own reformist views to his youthful reading of great literature. "Fortunately for us," he observed, "the 'Brave New World' was not fully realized in Russia. Although ideology, newspapers, and official documents were all pure 'newspeak,' alongside them existed the immortal treasure of Western and Russian literature. Reprinted, read, and admired, it helped to preserve sanity among those faced with the crazy Stalinist reality and to save the innermost, humanistic aspect of Russian culture."[114] By Western literature, Yakovlev means those works—for instance, the novels of Sterne, Balzac, and Dickens—that had been absorbed into the canon and that were read in the Russian manner. "Humanistic" works—the Russian classics and the foreign works that joined them—retained what Denis Kozlov called "an independent power, and the classics' authority could one day be turned against the language and objectives of indoctrination."[115]

Most recently, Yuri Slezkine's celebrated study of postrevolutionary Russian culture, *The House of Government*, concludes that "the Bolsheviks did not realize that by having their children read Tolstoy . . . they were digging the grave of their revolution." The children of millenarian Bolshevik leaders read "the treasures of world literature" at home—such as Dickens, Balzac, and Tolstoy—and largely neglected the canon of socialist realism. "What most of these books had in common," Slezkine observes, "was their antimillenarian humanism" that ran directly counter to Bolshevik ethics.[116]

Slezkine doubtless exaggerates the role of Russian literature in ending communism, but the very fact that a renowned historian of Russia could advance such a thesis is telling. Where but in Russia might it seem plausible that a regime and civilization firmly in power could have been overthrown by the reading of classic realist fiction?[117]

# 2  The Intelligentsia

> No class in Russian history has had a more momentous
> impact on the destinies of that nation or indeed of the modern
> world [than the intelligentsia].
>
> —MARTIN MALIA

"IN RUSSIA AN ALMOST INFALLIBLE GAUGE of the strength of an artist's genius is the extent of his hatred for the intelligentsia," declared critic Mikhail Gershenzon in the notorious anthology *Landmarks: A Collection of Essays on the Russian Intelligentsia* (1909).[1] If ever a book caused a scandal in prerevolutionary Russia, this was it. The volume, in which seven prominent thinkers sharply criticized the intelligentsia, became the period's most widely debated— or rather, vilified—publication. It went through five editions in about a year, the fifth with an appendix listing over two hundred books and articles written in response.[2] Individuals, journals, and even political parties published replies that not only excoriated the anthology but also betrayed the sense of an affront. We can appreciate how notorious this book on the intelligentsia became if we consider that one recent historian, assuming that every *intelligent* (member of the intelligentsia) had read it, took its circulation figures as a first step in calculating the size of the intelligentsia.[3]

To grasp why this anthology struck a nerve, one must first appreciate that its seven prominent contributors used the term intelligentsia in a sense very different from its meaning in English today. England had never had an intelligentsia in this sense, and, so far as the seven thinkers were concerned, this was a condition to which Russians should aspire.

The word intelligentsia originated in Russia, where it was coined about 1860.[4] It is notoriously difficult to define the Russian term for a variety of reasons.[5] For one thing, the group that the term originally designated grew and differentiated over subsequent decades. For another, the question "what is the intelligentsia?" soon indicated not a request for an empirical description but a program for Russia's future. Instead of asking how Russia should develop, one specified what the intelligentsia should become. Or as Solzhenitsyn explained, "The chief difficulty dogging all these searches [for the meaning of intelligentsia] has lain not in an inability . . . to characterize an actually existing social group, but in a disparity of *desires*: who *would we like* to see included in the name *intelligentsia?*"[6]

Still more confusing, the term could be used in various senses, some quite broad, and others much narrower. When the narrator of Turgenev's "Strange Story" (1869) visits a provincial town, an old acquaintance informs him that "there'll be a big ball in the Hall of the Nobility the day after tomorrow. I advise you to go; there are some pretty girls here. And you'll see all our intelligentsia, too"[7]—a "broad" usage of the term very different from the narrower one referring to people like Bazarov in Turgenev's *Fathers and Children*.[8] It became common to refer to the narrower usage as "the intelligentsia in the strict sense of the term" or "the intelligentsia proper."[9] This is the meaning the *Landmarks* contributors had in mind, as their outraged readers correctly assumed.[10]

Our concern here will be with the intelligentsia in this strict sense, which was often identified by the people it did *not* include. "We would never think of the clergy, for instance, as part of the intelligentsia, would we?" asks Varsonofiev in Solzhenitsyn's *August 1914*. "And nobody with what are called 'retrograde' views is considered an *intelligent,* even if he's the greatest philosopher of his time. But all students are automatically *intelligents,* even those who fail their exams."[11]

It was not enough to be educated. As historian Stuart Ramsey Tompkins paraphrases an observation common in studies of the intelligentsia, "Western writers are inclined to confuse the intelligentsia with the 'intelligent' in the sense of 'educated' people. Nothing could be further from the truth."[12] No matter how well (or ill) educated one was, one had to think in the right way. In *Landmarks*, the liberal (formerly Marxist) politician Peter Struve observed that "the word 'intelligentsia' can, of course be used in various senses. . . . Obviously, by 'intelligentsia' we do not mean . . . the 'educated class.' . . . The intelligentsia [in the strict sense] is a totally unique factor in Russian political development" and only includes those of a particular political persuasion.[13]

"The intelligentsia, in this political definition," Struve explained, "made its appearance only during the age of reforms," that is, the reign of Alexander II.[14] Struve specified that earlier thinkers like Radishchev, Novikov, and Chaadaev, who were clearly well educated and what we would today call intellectuals, do not qualify as *intelligents* "in our sense of the word"; neither do Pushkin, Gogol, and Lermontov.[15]

To be sure, the intelligentsia that took shape under Alexander II had antecedents, and it has long been common to describe the alienated thinkers of the previous generation—the "fathers" in Turgenev's formulation—as forming a sort of pre-intelligentsia or proto-intelligentsia. Herzen and Bakunin in particular lived to play an important role in the 1860s and, in Bakunin's case, in the 1870s.[16] And if anyone was universally celebrated as the intelligentsia's progenitor, it was Vissarion Belinsky. As we shall see, Belinsky's personality, at least as much as his ideas, appealed to many who agreed on little else. The populist guru Mikhailovsky cherished a bust of Belinsky, and it was to Belinsky that Turgenev dedicated *Fathers and Children*—perhaps because both fathers and children revered him.

In his classic *History of Russian Social Thought* (1907), the populist historian R. V. Ivanov-Razumnik observed that the term intelligentsia was coined precisely because a new social type had made its appearance. The intelligentsia "in the contemporary meaning of the term" was born when the *raznochintsy*— "people of various [non-noble] ranks"—began to populate the educated world.[17] As Turgenev dramatizes in *Fathers and Children*, the *raznochintsy* contributed their distinctive worldview, way of life, and sense of identity, thereby creating a new group called, from that time on, the intelligentsia.

Ivanov-Razumnik explained that this newborn intelligentsia largely coincided with the people described by the thinker Pyotr Lavrov as "critically thinking individuals." Lavrov, and Ivanov-Razumnik after him, distinguished this group from "the cultured part of society because culture, like education, is only an external formal sign, not a defining attribute" of this type. No profession, they agreed, gives one "a patent to the intelligentsia"; in particular, neither professors nor academics have "the slightest right to number themselves in the intelligentsia." Or as Ivanov-Razumnik put it, "Not everyone saying 'Lord! Lord!' will enter the kingdom of heaven, and not every 'cultured' person enters into the group of the intelligentsia."[18]

However counterintuitive it may seem, poets and artists, no matter how successful, may or may not have qualified as *intelligents*. Only a writer who "fights with evil" in the approved way belonged.[19] Literary quality was beside the point. Although it seems "preposterous" to say so, Solzhenitsyn remarked,

not only did the intelligentsia exclude many engineers and scholars in mathematical or technical fields, but also "the greatest Russian writers and
philosophers—Dostoevsky, Tolstoy, Vladimir Soloviev—did not belong to
the intelligentsia either!"[20] The *Landmarks* contributors presented themselves
as "*ex-intelligents.*"[21]

It might therefore seem that the intelligentsia in the strict sense constituted a subset of the educated, but—as Lavrov, Ivanov-Razumnik, and many
others repeated—that is not the case because many *intelligents* had very little
education.[22] If we were to use Venn diagrams, the oval representing the intelligentsia would overlap with, rather than be located entirely within, the more
numerous group of the educated.

In short, education was optional. In Turgenev's novel *Virgin Soil*, one *intelligent*, Markelov, "had read little—and chiefly books relating to the cause—
Herzen in especial. . . . His limited intellect went for one point only; what he
did not understand, for him did not exist."[23] Indeed, it was entirely possible,
Ivanov-Razumnik observed, that "some sort of semi-literate tradesman
would rank above" a great writer, so long as he met the group's defining criteria.[24] As the decades wore on, more and more workers and peasants from
the countryside became *intelligents*.

In his study of Russian society (1885), the revolutionary Lev Tikhomirov
deemed it essential to understand what the intelligentsia is *not*. In his view, it
excludes anyone but revolutionaries. Tikhomirov, too, regarded professors as
atypical and explained that they played almost no role. How could they, when
they were state employees? In fact, "the position of professor is scarcely compatible with the playing of any important part in the intelligentsia movement."[25]

For Tikhomirov, the intelligentsia's most typical members were "journalists," and among them, only radical publicists. A Westerner might presume
that Mikhail Katkov, the editor of *The Russian Herald*—the thick journal that
published *Crime and Punishment* and *War and Peace*—would necessarily be a
prominent *intelligent*, but from the Russian perspective that presumption
would have been absurd.[26] "Ask the first Russian you meet. He will burst out
laughing. 'Katkov of the intelligentsia.' What an idea! They are two things
wide as the poles asunder."[27] In an article responding to *Landmarks*, N. A.
Gredeskul explicitly excluded any but radicals from "our traditional form of
the intelligentsia."[28] As a political conservative, Katkov was automatically
disqualified.

How radical did one have to be, and how actively committed to a revolutionary cause? Historian Stuart Ramsay Tompkins applied the term in the
narrowest way when he defined "intelligentsia" as "a collective noun to include

persons sometimes called 'intelligenty' [*intelligents*] by the Russians. Although seeming to embrace a group of persons of superior intelligence, it actually designated only a small minority fanatically devoted to the cause of revolution."[29] In his study of *The Russian Tradition*, Tibor Szamuely concurred: "The history of the Russian revolutionary movement is the history of the Russian intelligentsia. The Russian Revolution was the product of the intelligentsia, and revolution was the intelligentsia's *raison d'être*. In no other European country did a social stratum exist that remained, through three or four generations, exclusively and specifically devoted to the idea of revolution."[30] Boris Elkin and others regarded this definition as too narrow.[31] For our purposes, it does not matter exactly where one draws the line, so long as one recognizes that the core group that Tompkins and Szamuely had in mind represented the ideal type, however small in number. The influence of that type extended far. That is why even "the comparative moderates ... though they might have disagreed with the extremists, could not but feel ashamed of their own moderacy, and tried to make up for it by defending the extremists." The moderates, too, did not doubt that compromise was "an unspeakable betrayal of all that was sacred and good." After all, as *intelligents*, they were "brought up ... within the same ideological framework" and so "inwardly agreed with this assessment of their behavior."[32]

The Russian intelligentsia, observers routinely insisted, was *sui generis*: nothing like it had ever existed in other countries. As D. N. Ovsyaniko-Kulikovsky remarked in another classic study, *The History of the Russian Intelligentsia*, the intelligentsia elsewhere "carries on its work" without constantly posing the questions, "'What is the intelligentsia and what is the meaning of its existence?,' 'who is to blame* that it does not find its real calling?'—[and] 'what is to be done?'"[33] An *intelligent* was always asking what exactly is a true *intelligent*?

## Three Criteria

### Criterion One: Identity

If learning, professional education, or artistic achievement do not make one an *intelligent*, what does? Roughly speaking, we may specify three criteria.

To begin with, *intelligents* identified primarily *as intelligents* rather than as members of their social class, ethnic group, religion, or profession. When a nobleman joined the intelligentsia, he left his status and former life behind, the way a monk does when joining a monastery—a comparison often made. Tikhomirov cited Count Rostopchin's comment: "I can understand the French bourgeois bringing about the revolution to get his rights, but how am I to understand the Russian noble making a revolution to lose them?"[34] Tikhomirov answered that once they become revolutionaries, Russian nobles identify not with the class into which they were born but with the order they had joined, the intelligentsia.[35]

The "people of various ranks"—the ones who established the intelligentsia—are better thought of as people of no rank. They defined themselves as lying outside the whole system of ranks, classes, or legal estates. Or as Ivanov-Razumnik explained, the intelligentsia is defined by its *"vnesoslovnost' i vneklassovnost'"* (roughly, their estatelessness and classlessness).[36] By using his title of count, thereby insisting on his social class, Tolstoy thumbed his nose at the intelligentsia.

It was as if in joining the intelligentsia one was purged of all social characteristics, a process resembling what anthropologists describe as a rite of passage. Casting off one's old identity, one entered the state that Victor Turner called liminality, "a cultural realm that has few or none of the attributes of the past." Only then could one assume the new identity with all its attributes. As we shall see later, for many Russian *intelligents*, these attributes included a form of liminality itself, as if the transitional stage of the process was the goal.[37]

Losing one's identity appealed strongly to those who experienced it as a burden. Jews ceased to be Jews—Trotsky denied being Jewish at all—and it was common for traditional Jewish parents to mourn children as dead (they sat *shiva*) when they joined a group of intelligentsia radicals.[38] Peasants, too, became deracinated (declassinated?), as those who idealized them often noted with regret. Nobles, or rather former nobles, no longer looked down upon them, a change perhaps unattainable otherwise. Like the Freemasons Tolstoy describes in *War and Peace*, intelligentsia circles allowed people from all origins to mix.

Taking one's profession seriously, unless it was that of "journalist" or "revolutionary," was as repugnant as identifying with one's social class. Proper *intelligents* regarded their work as a temporary expedient or necessary evil. In Dostoevsky's *The Possessed*, one character asks whether it is wise to hire an engineer who, as an *intelligent*, believes in universal destruction.[39]

As A. S. Izgoev observed in *Landmarks*, the average *intelligent* "does not know his job and does not like it. He is a poor teacher . . . an impractical technician, etc. He regards his profession as . . . a sideline that does not deserve respect. If he is enthusiastic about his profession and devotes himself to it whole-heartedly, he can expect the cruelest remarks from his friends."[40] One did

not graduate from university to embark on a career, but remained, like Tro-
fimov in Chekhov's play *The Cherry Orchard*, an "eternal student"—or better
still, an ex-student, since expulsion became what Ronald Hingley calls "a
Nihilist diploma."[41]

In Solzhenitsyn's *August 1914*, Sonya, a radical young woman, and her revolutionary friend Naum confront her engineer father Ilya Isakovich and his
friend, the engineer Obodovsky.[42] Contrary to intelligentsia protocol, Ilya
Isakovich takes his profession with the utmost seriousness and views "the split
between revolutionaries and engineers" as one separating wreckers from
builders. "You ought to be ashamed of yourself, Papa!" Sonya exclaims in
horror. "The whole intelligentsia is for revolution!"

In reply, her father challenges her definition of intelligentsia: "Don't we belong to the intelligentsia, then? We engineers who make and build everything
of importance—don't we count as intelligents?" The answer, from her perspective, is no, and so "an anguished wail [came] from Sonya." Throughout the
discussion, "Naum and Sonya were . . . so full of scorn that they had forgotten
to eat."

For the two engineers, the real issue is the intelligentsia's attitude toward
work. Ilya Isakovich asks, where does "your party gets its funds? All those
meeting places, safe houses, disguises, bombs, all the moving around, the
escapes, the literature—where does the money come from?" Much of it, as
everyone knew, came from "expropriations"—the euphemism for robberies—and
so Naum indignantly refuses to answer. "Well, there we have it," Ilya Isakovich
concludes. "There are thousands of you. It's a long time since any of you had a
job. And we aren't supposed to ask any questions. Yet you don't consider
yourselves exploiters." For Solzhenitsyn, the "engineers" represent the path not
taken, the Russian future sacrificed to totalitarianism.

## Criterion One (continued): Identity and the Personal

The ideal *intelligent* abandoned not just social class and profession but personal connections as well. As the editor Nicholas Kurochkin lectured his staff
at *The Book Herald*: "The man of journalism should separate himself from all
personal tastes and wishes . . . the knowledge that he is a useful and true servant of society is the only moral satisfaction of the man of journalism."[43] *Intelligents* took that "only" quite seriously. At the extreme, *intelligents* would even
renounce ties to family, or, as Tikhomirov puts it, "they became foes of their
brothers, their nearest relatives."[44] The terrorist group Hell (which included
the man who tried to assassinate the tsar in 1866) expected its members to
surrender not only family times but even their names. The executive committee

of the terrorist group the People's Will demanded total commitment: "Promise to dedicate all your spiritual strength to the revolution, give up for its sake all family ties and personal sympathies, all loves and friendships. . . . Do not keep any private property. . . . Give all of yourself to the secret society, give up your individual will."[45]

Terrorist Sergei Nechaev's formulation is the best known: as a revolutionary, the *intelligent* becomes

> a doomed man. He has no interests, no affairs, no feelings, no habits, no property, not even a name. . . . In the very depth of his being . . . he has severed every tie with the civil order, with the educated world, and with all laws, conventions, ethics, and generally accepted rules of this world. He is an implacable enemy of this world and if he continues to inhabit it, it is only to destroy it more effectively.[46]

In the demand to renounce property, one's name, and "this world," we again appreciate why the intelligentsia was often compared to a monastic order.[47] In Boris Savinkov's novel about terrorist *intelligents*, *What Never Happened*, the hero's sister realizes that he doesn't write to her because, as the Gospel according to Luke instructs, "If any man come to me, and hate not his father, and mother, and wife, and children, and brethren, and sisters, yea, and his own life, he cannot be my disciple" (Luke 14:26).

As countless commentators have observed, the classic background for an *intelligent* was priest's child or seminary student (often both), to the point where referring to someone as a seminarian could be equivalent, in our terms, to calling him a "red."[48] Ex-seminarians included Chernyshevsky and Stalin.[49]

To be sure, not every *intelligent* went so far, much as not every Christian became a monk. Most *intelligents* did not sever all ties with class and profession, let alone with family and friends, but even those who did not honored those who did. "Although only a few individuals can fulfill this dream that dwells in the intelligentsia's heart," observed Sergei Bulgakov, "it serves as the general standard of judgment."[50]

## Criterion One (continued): Identity and Tradition

In identifying as *intelligents*, people participated in a tradition. Indeed, "consciousness of a tradition," historian Philip Pomper noted, was often what marked one as an *intelligent*.[51] *Intelligents* looked to their own "calendar of intelligentsia saints," as Sergei Bulgakov called it.[52] In *November 1916*, Solzhenitsyn observes that:

the passion of the Social Democrats for anniversaries and red-letter days was as full-blooded as that of the royal family. There was a revolutionary calendar showing strike days of obligation: 22 January, 17 April (anniversary of the shootings on the Lena goldfields), 1 May, obviously . . . also [. . .] also [. . .] also . . . And each of these dates . . . meant an obligation to strike which only traitors to the working class could evade.[53]

Some days were limited to a particular group or party, others more generally shared. Such differences were trivial, the narrator of Solzhenitsyn's *August 1914* explains, because "the factional divisions of the Russian intelligentsia were of little real importance. The whole intelligentsia was ultimately a single tendency, a single party, one and indivisible in its hatred of the autocracy."[54] Despite their different revolutionary sympathies, Veronika's aunts Adalia and Agnessa repeatedly refer to one date after another the way Americans might mention July 4, as if each date's significance could be taken for granted. What's more, "Agnessa was superstitious about dates: 'Have any of you noticed what day the war began? The day the Sveaborg rising was put down. History is exacting retribution!'"[55]

Shocked by Veronika's interest in art, rather than revolutionary politics, Adalia laments: "Your aunt and I cannot understand how you can ignore the great, the sacred tradition that goes all the way back to the Decembrists."[56] The aunts share a special jargon marking their membership in intelligentsia tradition: "Stolypin neckties" (hangman's nooses), "action" (revolutionary deed, such as assassination), "history" as an entity with agency of its own, and many other expressions. People were always taking a "Hannibalic oath" to destroy autocracy. For initiates, there was a martyrology to be studied and rituals of initiation to be observed. "In our day," Adalia recalls with enthusiasm, "girls used to be blessed—you were, Nesa!—with [terrorist] Vera Figner's portrait, as though it were an icon. And that determined your whole future life, didn't it?"[57] The more rituals, dates, expressions, and traditions one learned, the more one's intelligentsia identity was affirmed.

## Criterion Two: Beliefs

*Intelligents* shared, or were supposed to share, a set of beliefs, especially political beliefs. Historians have remarked on the oddness of this form of identification. As Martin Malia has noted, "No recognized system of social analysis, either those known to the intelligentsia itself or those since elaborated by modern sociology, makes provision for a 'class' held together only by the bond of 'consciousness,' 'critical thought,' or moral passion."[58] This Russian development would prove attractive elsewhere. "One of the key concepts the rest of the world has imported from Russia," notes Laurie Manchester, "is that of an intelligentsia [in the Russian sense]."[59]

Menshevik leader Theodore Dan, in a tone suggesting he was stating an indisputable truism, defined the intelligentsia as "a special group united by a certain political solidarity." Although this group encompasses a gamut of world outlooks and parties, Dan explained, "what is common to all educated people included in it is their political and social radicalism."[60] For some commentators, including Dan, educated people who did not share these beliefs were by definition not *intelligents*. For others, like the intellectual historian D. N. Ovsyaniko-Kulikovsky, proper opinion did not define the intelligentsia but was an empirical fact about it.[61] If so, that fact could change, and by the last years of the tsarist regime, had begun to do so.

Either way, what united the intelligentsia, what made it a distinctive group, was ideology. That is presumably why Sonya (in *August 1914*) can be so sure that "the whole intelligentsia is for revolution!"[62]

So great was the prestige of the intelligentsia that right from the beginning its ideology became the "standard of judgment" for respectable society generally. As Dobrolyubov remarked in his article on Turgenev's *On the Eve* (1860), "today even those who dislike progressive ideas must pretend to like them to gain admission to decent society."[63] Tikhomirov agreed: "these purely revolutionary principles" of the intelligentsia "are admitted as the foundation of their general philosophy by people who do not look upon themselves . . . as belonging to the revolutionary camp."[64] One reason it is hard to define the intelligentsia is that so many dwelled in the penumbra cast by the core group.

Although prescribed intelligentsia beliefs varied from decade to decade and group to group, they always included some form of socialism or anarchism and almost always some form of materialism and atheism.[65] As historian Richard Pipes observed, "Materialism, utilitarianism, and positivism became the ideology of the Russian intelligentsia and the test which determined qualifications for membership. No one who believed in God and the immortality of the soul, no matter how otherwise 'enlightened' and 'progressive,' could lay claim to being an intelligent."[66] Tolstoy's belief in God also placed him outside the intelligentsia.

What "socialism" meant was almost always left vague, usually with the explanation Bazarov gives in *Fathers and Children*: our present business is destruction, those who come after will decide what to build.

Socialism so conceived was not so much an economic doctrine—like government ownership of the means of production and distribution—as a utopian or millenarian vision of a world that had banished evil once and for all. Terrorist Vera Figner explained that she "accepted the idea of socialism at first instinctively," understanding it to mean nothing more than "altruistic thought . . . equality, fraternity, and universal happiness."[67] The word had no precise definition inviting rational scrutiny. Rather, it functioned, in Solzhenitsyn's words, as "a vague, rosy notion of something noble and good, of equality, communal ownership, and justice: the advent of these things will bring instant euphoria and a social order beyond reproach."[68] "Establish tomorrow a socialist system of distribution," declares Matvei in *November 1916*, "and right away there'll be enough and to spare for everyone. Hunger will cease the day after the revolution. Everything will appear . . . an age of abundance will set in. . . . People will start producing all that is needed with such enthusiasm!"[69]

Like "revolution" and "the people," socialism so conceived is what the Left Socialist Revolutionary I. N. Steinberg called "a magic word . . . there was enchantment in the very sound" of such a word.[70] It was an article of faith that all problems—not just those we think of as social but also death and other unwelcome facts—had social causes and could be remedied by the revolutionary seizure of political power in the name of the right ideology.[71] As Gershenzon paraphrased the point, "Public opinion . . . maintained that all life's woes have political causes; with the collapse of the [tsarist] police state, health and courage, as well as freedom, would at once prevail. Everyone blindly believed this assertion, which removed all responsibility from the individual. This was one reason why the hopes for revolution assumed the character of religious chiliasm [i.e., millenarianism]."[72] No one was responsible for his or her actions because actions are completely determined by the social environment, which alone is responsible for crime. As in all utopian thinking, evil derives from a single cause, which the utopian thinker knows how to eliminate.

The *Landmarks* contributors, by contrast, proclaimed "the practical primacy of spiritual life over the external forms of community" and pointed to the appalling morals of *intelligents* in their daily lives.[73] Why should we believe that people who cannot properly arrange their own lives could arrange the lives of everyone else, or that those who now behave badly now would behave better as political dictators?

As the enlightened characters in *What Is to Be Done?* repeat, there is no "human nature" since people are infinitely malleable. All utopian thinkers share this view, for how else could human malfeasance be eliminated?[74] It was this line of thinking that led the Soviets for many years to ban genetics, which suggested that behavior does not derive entirely from social causes. In Russian utopianism, the new human being was expected to improve without limit and soon tower over all earlier generations and all people in capitalist countries. As Trotsky eloquently invoked this intelligentsia truism, "Man will become immeasurably stronger, wiser and subtler; his body will become more harmonized, his movements more rhythmic, his voice more musical. . . . The average human type will rise to the heights of an Aristotle, a Goethe, or a Marx. And above this ridge new peaks will rise."[75]

Although socialism does not logically entail atheism, the intelligentsia usually treated the two as virtually synonymous. As Sergei Bulgakov observed, "Atheism is the common faith, into which all who enter the bosom of the humanistic intelligentsia church are baptized." Far from being controversial, Bulgakov continued, atheism is entirely taken for granted, to the point where "it is considered a mark of bad taste even to talk about it." No arguments justify atheism; it is, ironically enough, "taken on faith, and preserves the characteristics of a naïve religious belief," doubtless reflecting the fact that so many important *intelligents* came from a clerical background.[76] As Dostoevsky liked to say, Russians do not accept atheism, they believe in it.

Taking every idea to the extreme, the intelligentsia typically divided the world into good and evil, with no middle ground. Recall that Pyotr Zaichnevsky had written in his bloodthirsty manifesto of 1862, "Remember that . . . anyone who is not with us is against us, and an enemy, and that every method is used to destroy an enemy."[77] To tolerate other opinions, or consider the views of those who disagree, was to show lack of commitment to the cause. Elena Shtakenshneider memorably referred to what was called the "second censorship": "I once worked up the courage to tell my friends that I don't like Nekrasov. That I don't like Herzen—I wouldn't have the courage. . . . We now have two censorships and, as it were, two governments, and it's hard to say which one is more severe."[78] When Herzen himself, toward the end of his life, began to favor gradual rather than revolutionary change, he recognized that "to say this in the circle in which we live demands, if not more, then certainly not less, courage than to take a most extreme side on all questions."[79]

Even Pyotr Lavrov—who believed that "apart from the individual there are no great principles"—envisaged using collective violence to compel each individual to assent:

Beyond the bounds of the inessential, the freedom of action of the party's members and its tolerance of those outside it ceases. If any member oversteps these bounds, he is no longer a member of the party, but its enemy. If anyone outside the party disagrees with it on essential issues, he, too, is an enemy. Against those enemies the party directs and must direct the whole force of its organization . . . with all its resources, concentrating its blows.[80]

Remarkably enough, many liberals, despite their professed belief in constitutional democracy, shared this ethos of intolerance. In an essay distinguishing two types of Russian liberals, represented by Vasily Maklakov and Pavel Miliukov, historian Michael Karpovich stressed that Miliukov, though the leader of the Constitutional Democratic (Kadet) Party, objected to Maklakov's "philosophy of compromise." One might imagine that the essence of democratic politics lies in just such a philosophy, but for Miliukov, as for the radicals, such a view reflects weak-kneed "relativism." Perhaps because of his experience as a lawyer, Miliukov opined, Maklakov had acquired the habit of "seeing a share of truth on the opposite side, and a share of error on his own." No politician, Miliukov asserted, can afford such an "objective" attitude. Miliukov went on to affirm the Kadet Party's "implacable opposition" to Manchester liberalism.[81] Was he a liberal at all?

If even the most influential liberals could think this way, the shadow of intelligentsia radicals evidently extended quite far. As we have seen, when applied to literature, such a view threatened to reduce it to crude propaganda. The "second censorship" often weighed more heavily than the tsarist one, which only forbade ("negative censorship") but did not prescribe ("positive censorship") what to say. Dismissing "the wood lice and mollusks we call the intelligentsia," Chekhov warned that "under the banner of science, art, and oppressed freethinking among us in Russia, such toads and crocodiles will rule in ways not known even at the time of the inquisition in Spain."[82] Dostoevsky referred to *intelligents* as people proudly wearing an ideological "uniform."[83]

In short, as historian Martha Bohachevsky-Chomiak suggested in her study *Sergei N. Trubetskoi: An Intellectual Among the Intelligentsia in Prerevolutionary Russia*, if by an "intellectual" we mean an independent thinker, then the Russian term *intelligent*—which translators often render as "intellectual"—is really closer to its opposite.[84] The *Landmarks* contributors implored educated Russians to cease being *intelligents* and become, instead, what we would call intellectuals.

## Criterion Three: Manners, Dress, and Way of Life

> If you give me your attention, I will tell you what I am:
> I'm a genuine philanthropist—all other kinds are sham.
> Each little fault of temper and each social defect
> In my erring fellow-creatures I endeavor to correct. . . .
> I love my fellow creatures—I do all the good I can—
> Yet everybody says I'm such a disagreeable man!
>     And I can't think why!
>
> —GILBERT AND SULLIVAN, PRINCESS IDA[85]

In some periods, especially during the intelligentsia's founding decades, *intelligents* wore not only a figurative "uniform" but also a literal one, or something close to it. The revolutionary Elizaveta Kovalskaia recalled meeting a young woman "with close-cropped hair . . . [who] wore an outfit that seemed almost to have become the uniform" for radical feminists.[86] For the nihilists of the 1860s, as Skabichevsky recalled, it was "obligatory" to eat and dress in the approved way. The dress code inverted received norms:

> The desire to look different from the despised philistines extended to the very external appearance of the new men, and thus appeared the notorious costumes in which the youth of the 1860s and the 1870s showed themselves off. Plaids and gnarled walking sticks, short-hair [for women] and hair to the shoulders [for men], dark glasses, Fra Diavolo hats and Polish caps—my God, all of that was bathed in such a poetic aureole then, and how it made the young hearts beat.[87]

Hingley mentioned blue-tinted spectacles, a heavy walking stick, untidy clothes, and dirty, chewed fingernails.[88] Irina Paperno cited "a perceptive (though disapproving) portrait of a female nihilist" published in 1864:

> Most nigilistki [female nihilists] are usually very plain and exceedingly ungracious . . . they dress with no taste, and in impossibly filthy fashion, rarely wash their hands, never clean their nails, often wear glasses, always cut their hair, and sometimes even shave it off. . . . They . . . light their cigarettes not from a candle, but from men who smoke, are uninhibited in their choice of expression, live either alone or in phalansteries, and talk most of all about the exploitation of labor, about the silliness of marriage and family, and about anatomy.[89]

To be sure, when *intelligents* became terrorists, it paid for them to be less conspicuous. Hingley mentioned one revolutionary, Mokrievich, watching another, Lermontov, being shadowed by the police: "what a sight! Every fold of his clothing practically screamed 'criminal' at you: the black felt hat on his head, the grey plaid on his shoulders, and the blue spectacles on his nose! ... and on my first day as a member of the political underground, I made a definite decision to comport myself quite differently."[90]

Slovenliness was next to partyness, an ethic that the intelligentsia maintained in the decade after the revolution. Checking into a sanatorium in 1926, radical author Alexander Serafimovich, who like many others worried about degenerating into orderliness, wrote to a friend that the facility "is so beautifully appointed that I am afraid I might turn into a bourgeois myself.... In order to resist such a transformation, I have been spitting into all the corners and onto the floor ... and lying in bed with my shoes on and hair uncombed. It seems to be helping."[91]

Bad manners became good manners. As in the Gilbert and Sullivan song cited above, rudeness became a sign of frankness and old-fashioned politeness a sham. For *intelligents*, as Peter Kropotkin explained, all conventional forms of "outward politeness" became so many signs of hypocrisy, while rudeness (of the right kind) indicated "absolute sincerity."[92] "The [intelligentsia] nihilist," Kropotkin enthused "carried his love of sincerity into the minutest details of everyday life. He discarded the conventional forms of society talk, and expressed his opinions in a blunt and terse way, even with a certain affectation of outward roughness."[93] But if the roughness was itself an affectation, was not the sincerity it signified insincere? And didn't rudeness become its own form of hypocritical manners?

Chernyshevsky's hero Rakhmetov served as a model. As the novel's narrator explains,

> Yes, however rude Rakhmetov's manners, everyone remained convinced that he acted as he did because it was the most sensible and simplest way to act. He would utter his harshest words and most horrible reproaches in such a way that no reasonable man could take offense. In spite of this phenomenal rudeness, he was basically a very tactful person.... He began each and every delicate explanation by saying, "You are aware that I speak without any personal emotion ... I consider it inappropriate to take offense at anything said in earnest ... I have the following rule: I always offer my opinion when I should but never impose it on anyone."[94]

Not just any bad manners would do. Chernyshevsky—whom Tolstoy referred to as "the gentleman who stinks of bedbugs"[95]—came by his unaristocratic manners honestly, but people of higher birth sometimes required lessons. In Savinkov's novel *What Never Happened*, Misha Bolotov at last locates Party headquarters and learns to "talk fluently about the Party, about 'progressive minimum,' 'labor republic,' the 'socialization of the land.'" But when he is at last about to meet the "mysterious committee" of terrorists, he worries about his first impression. After all, "they might not take him for a revolutionist but for 'a mother's son'" and so, after considering what to wear, and "examining himself in the mirror, he thought he looked both elegant and democratic."[96]

The intelligentsia also reversed codes governing the relation of the sexes. The new men did not rise to offer chairs to women entering the room. When George woos Tanya in Stepniak's novel *The Career of a Nihilist*, he "did not . . . pay her a single compliment. No self-respecting man of the generation which championed so hotly women's rights would permit himself such a vulgarity, nor would any girl of their set listen without offense."[97] Guided by an antirule, the new morals varied among inconsistencies, tending to extreme puritanism on some occasions and to promiscuity on others.

If a wife fell in love with another man, the husband was supposed to bless the new union (as Lopukhov does in *What Is to Be Done?*). In Chekhov's story "Enemies," Abogin's wife, pretending to be ill, sends him off to fetch a doctor so she can elope with her lover; when Abogin finds out, he is insulted not so much at her leaving as at her distrusting him to act the proper role! The alternative solution was the love triangle, like the one among Mayakovsky, Lily Brik, and Osip Brik. The threesome established it, Irina Paperno surmised, in accordance with intelligentsia code.[98]

If a husband did not provide a meaningful life dedicated to the cause, Paperno also explained, then his wife was entitled to leave him (and the children).[99] In *Crime and Punishment*, Lebeziatnikov, Dostoevsky's caricature of an *intelligent*, praises a woman who, after seven years of marriage, abandoned her husband and children. Her suitably "frank" letter to him explained her actions:

> "I can never forgive you that you deceived me by concealing from me that there is another organization of society by means of communes. I have only lately learned it from a great-hearted man to whom I have given myself and with whom I am establishing a commune. I speak plainly because I consider it dishonest to deceive you . . ." That's how letters like that ought to be written![100]

The whole complex of intelligentsia behavior, morals, dress, manners, and beliefs lent themselves to parody, which, like caricature, works by exaggerating or otherwise foregrounding something real. Lebeziatnikov, Dostoevsky's narrator observes, "was one of the numerous and varied legions of dullards, of half-animate abortions, conceited, half-educated coxcombs, who attach themselves to the idea most in fashion only to vulgarize it and who caricature every cause they serve, however sincerely."[101]

Lebeziatnikov lauds the skeptical Luzhin for (supposedly) "being ready to contribute to the establishment of the new commune, or to abstain from christening his future children, or to acquiesce if [his bride] Dunya were to take a lover a month after marriage."[102] Dispensing with conventional politeness, Lebeziatnikov aims to "assist the cause of enlightenment and propaganda . . . and the more harshly, perhaps, the better . . . there's no need of gentleness, on the contrary, what's wanted is protest."[103] He voices several progressive clichés: the social environment is everything "and man himself is nothing"; prostitutes are simply exercising the right to dispose of their capital; it is possible to cure the insane by logical argument; and there is no honor outside utility: "I understand only one word: *useful!*"[104]

Intelligentsia manners repelled Herzen, who never renounced the aristocratic habits characteristic of the previous generation. "Every one of them had some tic," he remarked in his article on the new *intelligents*, "The Superfluous and the Jaundiced," "and apart from that personal tic they all had one in common, a devouring, irritating, and distorted vanity. . . . All of them were hypochondriacs and physically ill, did not drink wine, and . . . reminded one of monks who from love of their neighbor came to hating all humanity. . . . One half of them were constantly repenting, the other half constantly chastising."[105] What especially annoyed Herzen was their self-righteousness and "knack of administering a reprimand in the style of a director, uttered contemptuously with eyes screwed up. . . . Tone is not a matter of no importance."

From *Fathers and Children* (1861) to *Virgin Soil* (1877), Turgenev, too, sketched both serious portraits and caricatures of *intelligents*, at times in the same work. In *Fathers and Children* they meet. When Sitnikov drags Arkady and Bazarov to Kukshina's, they discover her laboring to behave unconstrainedly as a true *intelligent* should. Looking at her, one felt like asking: "What's the matter? Are you . . . bored? Or shy? What are you fidgeting about?" Rolling cigarettes between fingers "brown with tobacco stain," she cites nihilist authorities to justify denouncing all authorities. She cannot drop enough approved names—Liebig, Macaulay, Proudhon—or flaunt sufficient progressive opinions. "'They tell me you've been singing the praises of George Sand again,'" she lectures Sitnikov. "'How can people compare her with Emerson? . . . I am sure she's never heard of embryology, and in these days—what can be done without that?' (Evodkya [Kukshina] even threw up her hands.)"[106]

Kukshina tells Bazarov she is planning a trip to Heidelberg, and when he asks, why Heidelberg? she replies: "How can you ask? Why [the chemist] Bunsen's there!" Over lunch Kukshina "chattered without pause; Sitnikov seconded her. They discussed at length the question whether marriage was a prejudice or a crime" and similar progressive drivel.[107] The discussion recalls the one seriously offered as a model in *What Is to Be Done?*: Lopukhov, Vera Pavlovna, and their guests joyfully elucidate "the chemical basis of agriculture according to Liebig's theory; the laws governing historical progress—an unavoidable subject of conversation in such circles at that time; [and] the great importance of distinguishing real desires . . . from phantasmic desires."[108]

## Liberators and Cannon Fodder

Although intelligentsia ideologies evolved, one tenet remained constant: a special role was always conferred on the intelligentsia itself. Numerically small, the intelligentsia would nevertheless, by virtue of its theoretical insights and total commitment, bring revolutionary change to establish justice in Russia and, perhaps, the world. From Lavrov's idea of "critically thinking individuals" to Lenin's concept of the Party as the "vanguard" of the working class, the intelligentsia—or an especially enlightened part of it—putatively constituted a group of superior people. Give me a place to stand and a lever long enough, Archimedes is supposed to have said, and I will move the world. For the intelligentsia, ideology provided both ground and lever to magnify their power.

From the start, Dostoevsky appreciated the significance of the intelligentsia's exalted view of itself. The hero of *Crime and Punishment* (1866), Raskolnikov, divides humanity into two groups, the numerous people "of the present" and the few "people of the future." The latter, a small group of "extraordinary" human beings, bring progress and a "new word," while the former, the vast majority of "ordinary" people who are always "conservative and law-abiding," defend the past. They exist as mere ethnographic "material that serves only to reproduce its kind . . . they live under control and love to be controlled."[109]

Precisely because they promote new ideas, the extraordinary people possess the right, indeed the obligation, to break old laws and commit what others regard as crimes. "If such a one is forced for the sake of his idea to step over a corpse or wade through blood, he can, I maintain, find within him-self . . . sanction for wading through blood," Raskolnikov explains. For ex-ample, "if the discoveries of Kepler and Newton could not have been made known except by sacrificing the lives of one, a dozen, a hundred, or more men, Newton would have had the right, would have been in duty bound [. . .] to *elim-inate* the dozen or the hundred men for the sake of making his discoveries known."[110] The revolutionaries in *The Possessed* raise the ante to "a hundred million heads."[111]

Critics who paraphrase Raskolnikov's argument often refer to it as his "Napoleonic" theory and cite his examples of heroic lawbreakers: "Lycurgus, Solon, Mahomet, Napoleon, and so on."[112] But the key point is that there are many "grades and subdivisions" of extraordinary people, not just exceedingly infrequent geniuses like Napoleon. Together, they form a group of the espe-cially enlightened.[113] Ever the social scientist, Raskolnikov presumes that the division of people into the two main categories and their various subdivisions "must follow with unfailing regularity some law of nature . . . there certainly is and must be a definite law, it cannot be a matter of chance."[114]

Raskolnikov oscillates between theories that, however incompatible with each other, all justify his right to kill. It as if theories did not lead to a conclu-sion, but the conclusion generated theories justifying it. Would the intelli-gentsia soon reason that way? Dostoevsky was apparently asking. Raskolnikov's friend Razumikhin voices the author's apprehension: "what is really *original* in all this . . . to my horror, is that you sanction bloodshed *in the name of con-science*, and, excuse my saying so, with such fanaticism."[115]

Some *intelligents* advocated rousing the people by "education," but the first significant attempt to do so failed utterly. As we shall discuss in Chapter 4, the "Going to the People" (*Khozhdenie v narod*) movement of 1874–1875 met with incomprehension, and often outright resistance, from the people (the peasants) themselves. Even if the people could be enlightened, it seemed, the process would evidently take a long time. A significant part of the intelli-gentsia felt too great a sense of urgency to wait. Little alternative remained to terrorism by a cell of trained killers or to a small, Jacobin-type political party seizing power by force.

Some *intelligents* disappointed with "going to the people" formed the terrorist People's Will. And, of course, a small group of disciplined revolutionaries— Lenin's Bolsheviks—eventually mounted a successful coup in October 1917. Lenin appreciated that a theorist of the 1860s, Peter Tkachev (now sometimes remembered as "the first Bolshevik"), had already formulated this strategy. "Don't you understand," asked Tkachev, "that a revolution . . . differs from peaceful progress in that a minority makes the first and a majority the second? Don't you understand that a revolutionist . . . differs from a philosophical Philistine precisely in the fact that he doesn't wait for the current of historical events to point out the minute but selects it himself?"[116] While other Marxists were content to wait until advanced capitalism's contradictions would necessarily lead to revolution, Lenin selected the precise time to mount his coup.[117]

Revolution would be made not by but in the name of "the people," or later "the working class." Almost always, peasants and workers were allowed no voice of their own. Mere "material," the people always remain, in Sergei Bulgakov's words, "a passive object of activity, the nation or humanity that is being saved."[118] In all likelihood, no one alive ever belongs to that saved "humanity"; it is people of the future who will benefit from the intelligentsia's activity. As Semyon Frank paraphrased this way of looking at things,

> the abstract idea of happiness in the remote future destroys the concrete moral relationship of one individual to another and the vital sensation of love for one's neighbor, one's contemporaries, and their current needs. The socialist is not an altruist. True, he too is striving for human happiness, but he does not love living people, only his *idea*. . . . Since he is sacrificing himself to this idea, he does not hesitate to sacrifice others as well.[119]

Terrorists, therefore, felt little or no compunction about killing dozens of innocent bystanders and they eventually engaged in random killing (throwing bombs into cafes).[120] Herzen, as well as Dostoevsky, foresaw such an outcome. For such revolutionaries, Herzen warned as early as 1862, living people serve only as "the cannon fodder of liberation." "The great idea of revolution," he explained, "quickly went too far toward the police, the inquisition, and terror . . . a desire for speed led to treating them [the people] like the material of well-being, like the human flesh of liberation, *la chair du bonheur public* [the flesh of social well-being], like Napoleonic cannon-fodder."[121]

Lenin made it quite clear that the desires and views of existing proletarians, whether individually or as a group, did not matter. "It is immaterial what this or that proletarian, or even the entire proletariat presently imagines its aims to be," he explained. "What is important is what it is and what according to its being it will be compelled by history to do." Trotsky concurred: "The Party expresses the basic interests of the working class . . . through the revolutionary vanguard which, when necessary, compels the laggard tail to catch up with the head."[122] This position was far from new; Tkachev had argued for it long before: "Since the people themselves do not understand their own good, what is truly good for them must be forced upon them."[123] This is Raskolnikovism with a vengeance.

Is it any wonder, then, that the Party crushed the Workers' Opposition in 1922, which would have given trade unions power independent of the Party? Or that it never allowed Soviet workers a voice of their own? Some anarchists foresaw just such a tyranny, enforced by self-appointed liberators aspiring to control everyone else according to some putative "science." "Monopolists of science," as Bakunin called them, cared only for their abstractions and not at all for living people. For Bakunin, the worst of these monopolists was Marx, and his followers would prove the most tyrannical "scientists." "According to Mr. Marx," he famously declared, "the people should not only not abolish [the state], but, on the contrary fortify and strengthen it, and in this form turn it over to their benefactors, guardians, and teachers, the chiefs of the Communist Party—in other words, to Mr. Marx and his friends . . . state engineers . . . will form the new privileged political-scientific class." Bakunin therefore preached "the revolt of life against science, or, rather, against the government of science."[124]

Jan Machajski (whose followers were known as Makhaevists) further developed these ideas, which later reached America in ex-Trotskyite James Burnham's sociological classic, *The Managerial Revolution* (1941). Still later, they formed the basis of Yugoslav dissident Milovan Djilas's *The New Class* (1957). The original Makhaevists voiced a full-throated anti-intellectualism, sometimes expressed, interestingly enough, in highly intellectual studies. In his article "So What Then *Is* the Intelligentsia?"—a title invoking the countless articles on the same subject—the Makhaevist Evgeny Lozinsky described higher education as a form of capital and the intelligentsia as a class of capitalists.[125] Although anarchists and Makhaevists advanced some implausible, even repellent, ideas, they accurately foresaw that Russian Marxists would tyrannize in the name of liberty.

## The Intelligentsia after the Revolution: Stage One

> Berdyaev is mistaken when he says that the intelligentsia was destroyed
> by the people for which it once made such sacrifices. The intelligentsia

destroyed itself, burning out of itself . . . everything that
conflicted with the cult of power.

—Nadezhda Mandelstam, *Hope Against Hope*[126]

What happened to the intelligentsia after a portion of it, the Bolsheviks,
seized power?[127] The answer again depends on what we mean by the intelligentsia, a question that becomes all the more ambiguous after 1917. Do we
have in mind a particular group of people, regardless of what that group might
be called? Or are we asking about the usage of a word, which, especially in
tumultuous times, may switch its referent?[128] Or, as Solzhenitsyn reminded
us, are we prescribing what the intelligentsia should be?

Let us follow Solzhenitsyn's and Nadezhda Mandelstam's discussion of the
postrevolutionary intelligentsia. Both identified three stages; they had been
prepared for when, in the decade preceding the revolution, a new stratum had
appeared. Initially small, but rapidly growing, this new stratum, if not for the
Bolshevik takeover, would soon have outnumbered the classic intelligentsia,
"in the wake of which the term [intelligentsia] itself would have splintered."[129]
Solzhenitsyn cited the *Landmarks* contributors as shapers of the new tendency. Unlike the classic intelligentsia, Nadezhda Mandelstam agreed, this
new group, this "intelligentsia in a different sense," consisted of "humanist
thinkers who value honor and decency," which they refused to equate with
ideology and or reduce to politics.[130] They emphasized each person's inner life.[131]
They represented "the Russia that might have been" had there been no Bolshevik coup.

In the Soviet intelligentsia's first stage, lasting through the 1920s, many *intelligents* (particularly those belonging to other radical parties) died at the hands
of the Bolsheviks, while others found themselves in exile. Life abroad was
hard, Solzhenitsyn acidly remarked, but it "did at least grant the remnants of
the Russian intelligentsia a few more decades for excuses."[132] He portrayed
those remaining in the Soviet Union still more savagely. "Titillated by a stream
of temptations," especially the desire to participate in supposedly inevitable
social progress, they rushed "to acknowledge the newly arrived iron Necessity
as the long awaited Freedom . . . to submerge their 'I' in the Natural Order, to
gulp down that hot draft of proletarian air in pursuit of the Progressive Class
as it marched away into the radiant future."[133]

Did they really believe the revolutionary enthusiasm they professed?
While some proclaimed the new truth hypocritically, Solzhenitsyn explains,
most engaged in "fervent self-persuasion" to save themselves "from spiritual

collapse, for they gave themselves up to the new faith in all sincerity and entirely of their own free will."[134]

Such self-persuasion, Solzhenitsyn opined, proved easy because, even before the revolution, numerous *intelligents* had already developed the habit of supporting violence contrary to their own principles.[135] "I confess I am rather in favor of a more humane policy," concedes a moderate among revolutionaries in *The Possessed*, "but as all are on the other side, I go along with all the rest."[136] Such support, which played a key role in the Bolshevik seizure of power, naturally continued under Bolshevik rule. Fascinated by the psychology behind political "self-persuasion," Solzhenitsyn examined it frequently in *November 1916*. "Paralyzed by the clamor to their left," he writes of those who should have known better, "people refused to take a stand: let whoever wants try to stop it, I won't. They would sign any sort of protest, whether or not they agreed with it."[137]

The intelligentsia, in short, fell into what Solzhenitsyn called "a hypnotic trance, having willingly let themselves be hypnotized." Self-hypnosis of this kind afflicts not only Russians, he continued. To the extent that a society's educated people begin to resemble the classic Russian intelligentsia, deliberate suspension of moral judgment becomes common. Indeed, Solzhenitsyn warned, "the process is repeating itself in the West today" (i.e., 1974).[138]

In her chapter "Capitulation," Mandelstam argued that by such thinking the old intelligentsia destroyed itself. "This was the period of mass surrender when they [*intelligents*] all took the path marked out by the pre-revolutionary extremists and their post-revolutionary successors."[139] Many even joined the Cheka—Lenin's new secret police. "The Chekists were the avant-garde of the 'new people,'" she noted, "and they had indeed basically revised, in the manner of the Superman, all ordinary human values." Soon enough, these cultured practitioners of official terror were replaced by people of a different type "who had no values at all."[140]

What exactly made these *intelligents* act contrary to their values? For one thing, Mandelstam explained, they could not bear to oppose anything called "revolutionary." For another, they came to accept an overpowering idea, "that there is an irrefutable scientific truth by means of which . . . people can foresee the future, change the course of history at will, and make it rational," thereby achieving "heaven on earth." Still more important "for them was the end of all doubt, and the possibility of absolute faith in the new, scientifically obtained truth."[141] As Dostoevsky's Grand Inquisitor explains, certain basic facts of human nature—the lure of certainty, the irresistible appeal of escaping from doubt, the comfort of joining in collective affirmation—predispose people to surrendering their consciences.

Even some humanists and Christians adopted the new "science," which dismissed the commandment "Thou shalt not kill" as bourgeois morality, rejected concepts like "honor" and "conscience" as relics, and denied that freedom had ever existed or could have existed. The same was true of art: instead of art, the new dispensation held, there was only "bourgeois art" and "proletarian art." In effect, these doctrines translated into Marxist language the traditional intelligentsia view—championed by Chernyshevsky and his followers—that so appalled Turgenev, Dostoevsky, Tolstoy, and Chekhov.

Even the Formalist critic Victor Shklovsky and the poet Osip Mandelstam, Nadezhda's husband, found it hard to resist the tide. They suffered from "the fear of being left out in the cold, of not moving with the times."[142] Finding himself "alone on every road," Osip briefly tried to conform.

Osip "really was in a state of confusion," Nadezhda explained. "It is not so simple to go against everybody and against the times. To some degree, as we stood at the crossroads, we all had the temptation to rush after everyone else, to join the crowd that knew where it was going. The power of the 'general will' is enormous—to resist it is much harder than people think."[143]

Looking back on the twenties, those still smitten with the idea of revolution, along with the few artists and thinkers who somehow survived the next decade's purges, tried to treat the terrible 1930s as an unforeseeable deviation. "They deny responsibility for what happened later. But how can they?" Nadezhda Mandelstam asked. Even in the twenties some artistic groups implored the Party to suppress other artistic groups. "It was, after all, these people of the twenties who demolished the old [humanistic] values and invented the formulas that even now come in so handy to justify the unprecedented experiment undertaken by our young State: you can't make an omelet without breaking eggs. Every new killing was excused on the grounds that we were building a remarkable 'new' world."[144] Did Stalin destroy the old intelligentsia, or had it already destroyed itself?[145]

## The Intelligentsia after the Revolution: Stages Two and Three

With the old intelligentsia discredited or gone, Solzhenitsyn explained, the label *intelligent* first became a term of abuse (usually accompanied by the adjective "spineless") and then indicated an entirely different group of people.[146] Used in this new way, the term "intelligentsia" referred to "the whole educated stratum, every person who has been to school above the seventh grade," or, as Andrei Amalrik observed, the entire middle class.[147] Even when applied more narrowly to professionals, technocrats, and bureaucrats, Nadezhda Mandelstam observed, the term designated people sharing nothing with those tracing their intellectual lineage to *Landmarks* and the nineteenth-century classics—nothing "except perhaps their spectacles and false teeth."[148]

Solzhenitsyn and Mandelstam agreed that a third stage of the Soviet intelligentsia had begun. Some dissidents, who were reviving the "new stratum" of prerevolutionary humanist thinkers, might constitute the nucleus of a new intelligentsia. "Is not that nucleus whose beginnings we think we already discern today," Solzhenitsyn asked, "a repetition of the one that the revolution cut short, is it not the essence of a 'latter-day *Vekhi* [*Landmarks*]'?"[149]

What unites these new humanists, according to Solzhenitsyn, is "the purity of their aspirations . . . spiritual selflessness in the name of truth. . . . This intelligentsia will have been brought up not so much in libraries as on spiritual sufferings."[150] Like the nineteenth-century intelligentsia, they are not all well-educated; "even 'illiterate [religious] sectarians' and some obscure milkmaid down on the collective farm are members of this nucleus of goodness." They do not share an ideology, as nineteenth-century *intelligents* did, but a spirituality—"a thirst for truth, a craving to cleanse their souls."[151]

If so, Solzhenitsyn concluded, then we may need a new word for such people. "It would be better if we declared the word 'intelligentsia' . . . dead for the time being. Of course, Russia will be unable to manage without a substitute for the intelligentsia, but the new word will be formed not from 'understand' or 'know' but from something *spiritual*."[152]

Nadezhda Mandelstam also detected the beginnings of a new intelligentsia accepting the humanistic values of the prerevolutionary "new stratum" and the Russian classics: You will not catch these people saying, "You can't swim against the tide" or "You can't make an omelet without breaking eggs." "In other words, the values we thought had been abolished forever are being restored. . . . This has come as a surprise both to those who never gave up these values and to those who tried to bury them once and for all. Somehow or other they lived on underground."[153] Authors continued to write "for the drawer" and humanists survived in some Soviet equivalent of the catacombs.

If the initiative in destroying humanistic values had "belonged to the intelligentsia of the twenties," Mandelstam argued, then "at the present day we are witnessing the reverse process." Unlike its nineteenth-century predecessor, but in accord with the great writers, the new intelligentsia adheres to no specific ideology. It values, instead, "the ability to think critically . . . freedom of thought, criticism, humanism."[154]

One feature of this new intelligentsia differentiates it from Western counterparts, even those with similar values. Osip Mandelstam once asked what makes someone a true member of the intelligentsia. To be sure, he did not use that word, Nadezhda explained, since it had already become a term of abuse, but he had in mind people like those who were to constitute the new intelligentsia. The key quality is, again, not higher education. It is, rather, a "feeling about poetry. Poetry does indeed have a very special place in this country." The birth of the new intelligentsia therefore accompanies "a craving for poetry never seen before—it is the golden treasury in which our values are preserved; it brings people back to life, awakens their conscience and stirs them to thought."[155]

"The golden treasury of our values," poetry or, Russian literature more broadly, remains the Russian Bible that "brings people back to life" and "awakens their conscience." It once seemed certain that the Bolshevik takeover represented the definitive triumph of the radical intelligentsia over the great writers, the victory of Gorky over Gogol and Chernyshevsky over Chekhov. Now we are witnessing the old values reborn under the name of their prerevolutionary antagonist, the intelligentsia.[156]

In *The Master and Margarita*, the Master, having discovered that his new acquaintance is the official poet Ivan Bezdomny, groans because all official poetry is terrible. "Tell me yourself," he demands, "are your poems any good?" "Horrible!" Bezdomny concedes. "Then don't write any more," the master implores; and when Bezdomny agrees, "they sealed the vow with a handshake."[157] If only others could be persuaded as easily, Bulgakov implies, the tradition of great literature, which the persecuted master carries on, would revive.

Discouraged at the reception of his work, and blamed for every old and new ideological error, the Master burns his manuscript. I take the scene where the devil restores it—"manuscripts don't burn"—as a promise of the great tradition's revival, which Solzhenitsyn and Mandelstam celebrated decades later.

Even then, of course, the new intelligentsia was small and its ability to influence society lay in the future. In the interim, its promise remained, in both senses of the word, fiction.

# PART TWO

# THREE TYPES OF THINKER

# 3  The Wanderer

## Pilgrim of Ideas

> These homeless Russian wanderers continue their wandering
> even now and, it seems, are unlikely to disappear for a long
> time yet.
>
> —FYODOR DOSTOEVSKY

"BY THE MERCY OF GOD I am a Christian, by my deeds a great sinner, by
calling a homeless wanderer of the lowest origins, roaming from place to
place. Here, see my belongings: a bag of dry crusts on my back and the Holy
Bible in my breast pocket; that's it." So begins a remarkable book published in
1884 as *Candid Tales of a Wanderer to His Spiritual Father* (*Otkrovennye rass-
kazy strannika dukhovnomu svoemu otsu*) and translated into English as *The
Way of a Pilgrim*.[1] It tells the story of a wanderer's search for the answer to a
deep theological mystery: what is the meaning of the command, which the
Liturgy takes from the Epistle to the Thessalonians, to "pray without ceasing"?
(1 Thessalonians 5:17). Since one must attend to everyday affairs if only to
survive, how can one do nothing but pray?

The pilgrim recognizes that a deep truth—both philosophical and
psychological—lies at the heart of this mystery. "A strong desire and curiosity
took hold of me and wouldn't leave me, day and night. And so I began to go
from church to church, listening to sermons on prayer," and from wise man to
wise man, asking each to answer his questions.[2] In his many adventures, the

wanderer discovers fundamental truths about the meaning of human exis-tence, the inner workings of the soul, and the ways of God.

Readers familiar with Russian literature have remarked on the important role pilgrims play in Russian life and consciousness.[3] In Western Europe, pil-grimages, so common in the Middle Ages, had long ceased to occupy the at-tention of the educated, but in Russia their significance only grew. In *War and Peace*, Princess Marya converses with pilgrims; story writer Nikolai Leskov knew them well and portrayed them in "The Sealed Angel" and "The En-chanted Wanderer"; the pilgrim Makar Dolgoruky offers spiritual wisdom in Dostoevsky's novel *The Raw Youth*; and the heroine of Turgenev's "Strange Story" runs off with a pilgrim to follow a pilgrim's life. Legends affirmed that Tsar Alexander I had not died as reported but had become the holy vagabond Fyodor Kuzmich. This legend inspired Tolstoy's story "Posthumous Notes of the Elder Fyodor Kuzmich," in which the former tsar describes the spiri-tual journey leading him to embrace a pilgrim's life. The image of the wan-derer in search of truth haunted the Russian imagination.

"It was my good fortune to come in personal contact with wandering Russia during approximately ten years of this [twentieth] century, with the Russia that is searching for God and divine truth," reported Nicholas Berdyaev in *The Russian Idea*. "I can speak about this phenomenon which is so character-istic of Russia, not from books but as the outcome of personal impressions." Berdyaev conversed with wanderers of many sects: "'immortalists' and Bap-tists and Tolstoyans of various kinds, and *khlysty* [roughly, flagellants] and . . . theosophists from among the [common] people." He had the hardest time con-versing with the Dobrolyubovtsi, he reported, since they had taken a vow of silence. All sects considered this world and this life evil and therefore were searching for "another world, another life."[4]

In Berdyaev's view, educated Russians shared the same frame of mind, adapted to secular philosophies borrowed from Western Europe. "Not only physical but spiritual pilgrimage exists," he explained. Instead of wandering from place to place, educated Russians often progress from ideology to ide-ology. Their sages are Hegel and Schelling and Marx, and in seeking ultimate truth they also pursue the millennium, the salvation of all humanity. In this sense, "the whole of the revolutionary intelligentsia were pilgrims."[5]

When Father Zosima tells Ivan Karamazov that, underneath his cloak of worldly indifference, he is seeking the answer to ultimate questions about life's meaning and about good and evil, Ivan asks whether his inquiry will ever be answered "in the affirmative"—that is, if he will ever discover true goodness and meaning. Zosima replies: "If it can't be decided in the affirmative, it will never be decided in the negative," by which he means that Ivan will either find the answer or keep seeking it; he will never rest content without an answer or with a philosophy that regards morals and meaning as mere social conventions. "You know that is the peculiarity of your heart, and all its suffering is due to it," Zosima continues. "But thank the Creator who has given you a lofty heart capable of such suffering ... God grant that your heart will attain the answer on earth, and may God bless your path."[6] Ivan's marvelous discourses— in "Rebellion," "The Grand Inquisitor," and his conversation with the devil— evidently represent stages of his pilgrimage to "attain the answer on earth."

In his famous Pushkin speech, Dostoevsky praised the great poet for having identified "the type of the Russian wanderer, who continues his wandering even in our days; having been the first to divine, through his brilliant instinct, that wanderer's historical fate and in his enormous significance in our future destiny."[7] In Dostoevsky's view, the educated Russian, separated by his country's rapid westernization from his native roots, desperately seeks meaning, repeatedly thinks he has found it, and faces repeated disappointment, like Aleko, the hero of Pushkin's early poem, "The Gypsies." In this hero Pushkin depicted, for the first time, "a type that has become a permanent feature in our Russian land. These homeless Russian wanderers continue their wandering even now and, it seems, are unlikely to disappear for a long time yet." They no longer "frequent the camps of the gypsies to look for universal ideals ... they go running off to socialism ... they take their new faith to a different field and work it zealously" in order to find happiness not just for themselves but for all humanity. "For what the Russian wanderer needs is the happiness of the whole world in order to find his own peace of mind." To be sure, only a "'chosen few,' merely a tenth of those who began to be troubled" become noticeable wanderers but "through them the remaining vast majority will be deprived of their peace of mind."[8]

In Dostoevsky's reading, it is not just "superfluous men" like Pushkin's Eugene Onegin or Lermontov's Pechorin who represent spiritual wanderers, so do all the ideological heroes, in literature or reality, who devote their lives to serving one ideal after another. These heroes (and heroines) will always fail, in Dostoevsky's view, so long as they remain uprooted from real life and look for the kingdom of God in social utopias rather than in their own souls.

The narrator of Chekhov's story "Uprooted" (1887), on a visit to the Svatagorsky monastery, discovers that thousands of people, including innumerable pilgrims, have flocked there for the festivals of St. John the Divine and St. Nikolay the Wonder-worker. He finds the sight of such crowds anything but uplifting: "Looking at the confusion, listening to the uproar, one fancied that in this living hotch-potch no one understood anyone, that everyone was looking for something and would not find it."[9]

Asked to share his hostel room, the narrator finds himself lodged with Aleksandr Ivanich, a twenty-two-year-old man of indeterminate background. "I was unwilling to believe that he was one of those vagabond imposters with whom every conventual establishment where they give food and lodging is flooded, and who give themselves out as divinity students, expelled for standing up for justice"—that is, who pretend to be persecuted *intelligents*.[10] Aleksandr Ivanich turns out to be a converted Jew, who grew up amid dirt and poverty in a small town where he could study nothing but Talmud. Having run away, he has tried occupation after occupation, been injured, and at last converted to Russian Orthodox Christianity. When the narrator asks why he abandoned something so fundamental as the faith into which he was born, Aleksandr Ivanich offers no satisfactory explanation. All he can say is that the New Testament is the completion of the Old, "a formula not his own, but acquired—which did not explain the question in the least. . . . There was nothing for it but to accept the idea that my companion had been impelled to change his religion by the same restless spirit which had flung him like a chip of wood from town to town, and which he, using the generally accepted formula, called the craving for enlightenment."[11] His enthusiasm gazing at the religious procession makes clear that he did not convert to improve his fortunes.

When the narrator gives him a pair of boots, Aleksandr Ivanich can only express his delight by saying, "I should thank you, but I know you consider thanks a convention"—as a nihilist would.[12] Has he adopted intelligentsia beliefs or just assumed that the narrator holds them?

The narrator reflects on how many such people there are in Russia:

> Among the pilgrims some hundreds of such homeless wanderers were waiting for the morning, and further away, if one could picture to oneself the whole of Russia, a vast multitude of such uprooted creatures were pacing at that moment along highroads and side-tracks. . . . As I fell asleep I imagined how amazed and perhaps overjoyed all these people would have been if reasoning and words could be found to prove to them that their life was as little in need of justification as any other.[13]

Perhaps well-read pilgrims of the spirit could have used the same reassurance.

## "An Uninterrupted Succession of Convictions"

Berdyaev was right: as spiritual wanderers journeyed from place to holy place, educated wanderers jolted from idea to enlightening idea. Grigory Petrovich Likharev, the hero of Chekhov's story "On the Road" ("Na Puti," 1886) typifies just such an educated Russian or, as the hero himself says, all Russians. No sooner does one infallible truth fail than he flings himself head-long into another. The experience of repeated disconfirmation never teaches him caution or skepticism. Always as certain of his present philosophy as he was of the ones preceding it, he retains an absolute intolerance of anyone who thinks differently.

We find Likharev on the road—or as I prefer to think of the title, en route—literally as well as figuratively. It is Christmas Eve and a terrible storm rages outside an inn where Likharev and his eight-year-old daughter doze in the "travelers' room." In spite of the fact that Likharev's features are coarse and heavy, taken together "they gave the effect of something harmonious and even beautiful. Such is the lucky star, as it is called, of the Russian face: the coarser and harsher its features the softer and more good-natured it looks."[14] We are evidently dealing with a Russian everyman.

The storm resembles now an angry chained dog, now a battle followed by "sobs, shrieks, howls of wrath." "Something rabid, malicious, and profoundly unhappy seemed to be flinging itself about the tavern with the ferocity of a wild beast trying to break in.... In all of this was heard now malicious yearning [zlobstvuyushchaya toska], now unsatisfied hatred, now abusive im-potence of someone who at some time became accustomed to triumph."[15] Words derived from zloba (malice, spite) occur three times in this brief para-graph. They define the atmosphere, symbolic and real, in which Likharev's journey takes place.

A young noblewoman, Mademoiselle Ilovayskaya, arrives. She expresses disappointment that she cannot make it to her destination that night even though it is only a few versts away. As the little girl watches her remove layer after layer of warm clothing, she sees at last a lady who "recalled the portraits of medieval English ladies." The little girl's complaints lead both her father and the new guest to comfort her. Likharev speaks to her "in the tone in which men who have been drinking excuse themselves to their stern spouses," and Chekhov refers several times to the way his voice, his motions, and his very body all seem to express guilt.[16]

Marya Mikhailovna Ilovayskaya, we learn, must manage her father's large estate since her father and brother are totally negligent. Now on her way to look after them on their small farm, she remarks that men in general are "an irresponsible lot."[17] She evidently takes pride in her ability to do for them what they cannot or will not do for themselves.

Ilovayskaya's remark that her brother and father do not believe in God prompts Likharev to reveal his own deepest beliefs. His greatest faith is in faith itself, which he regards as

> a faculty of the spirit. . . . So far as I can judge by myself, by the people I have seen in my time, and by all that is done around us, this faculty is present in Russians in the highest degree. Russian life presents us with an uninterrupted succession of convictions and aspirations, and, if you care to know, it has not yet the faintest notion of lack of faith or skepticism. If a Russian does not believe in God, it means he believes in something else.[18]

Not only are Russians ready to embrace faith of whatever kind, Likharev observes, but they also pride themselves on that characteristic. Skepticism and cautious assertion mark one as not truly Russian in spirit.

Even by Russian standards, Likharev continues, "nature has implanted in my breast an extraordinary capacity for belief. I was in the ranks of the Atheists and Nihilists, but there was not one hour in my life in which I ceased to believe."[19] It is possible to make absolute negation an object of worship and, as Likharev suggests, that was the spirit of Russian nihilism.

When as a boy Likharev heard his mother say that "soup is the great thing in life," he ate soup ten times a day until he "was disgusted and stupefied." When his nurse told him fairy tales, he left out poisoned cakes to tempt goblins and house spirits. And when he began to read, things got worse: "I . . . hired boys to torture me for being a Christian."[20] His enthusiasm proved infectious, and whatever he did, he was able to induce others to join him.

Science became mystical revelation. Learning that the earth revolves around the sun and that white light comprises seven colors, he "wandered about . . . like one possessed, preaching my truths, was horrified by ignorance" and "glowed with hatred for anyone who saw in white light nothing but white light."[21] Hatred accompanied certainty as inevitably as objects cast shadows in sunlight.

Likharev has leapt from science to science, regarding each as a key to life's meaning and the answer to all questions. The one thing science has never meant to him, or other Russian *intelligents* who worshipped science, was the feature that, from Francis Bacon on, has defined it: the skeptical weighing of evidence. "And I gave myself up to science, heart and soul, passionately, as to the woman one loves. I was its slave. . . . But my enthusiasm did not last long." Likharev soon discovered a trap: no matter which science he chose, he always found that it "has a beginning but not an end," and so he could never arrive at a final answer. Zoology has discovered 35,000 species and chemistry reckons sixty elements, but adding one, or a thousand, to these numbers brings us no closer to final answers. "I saw through this trick when I discovered the 35,001-st and felt no satisfaction." But however often faith proved groundless, "I had no time to suffer from disillusionment, as I was soon possessed by a new faith."[22]

After nihilism, Likharev embraced populism. When Russian youth "went to the people" in the early 1870s, he joined them. "I loved the Russian people with poignant intensity; I loved their God and believed in Him."[23] Likharev shared, and apparently still shares, the belief that somehow Russian peasants carry a deep wisdom. As the story's readers were aware, Russians who disagreed on everything else often shared a belief in "the people."

Time and again, new interests overwhelm Likharev. "My enthusiasm was endless," first in working for the abolition of private property, then, like Tolstoy, in preaching "non-resistance to evil."[24] Did he preach love while hating all who disagreed?

## The Costs of Enthusiasm

For Ilovayskaya, this life of enthusiasms contrasts vividly with her self-imposed, endless occupation of managing her family's practical affairs. "You have had a lively time," she remarks wistfully. "You have something to remember," as she does not.[25]

Likharev offers an unexpected reply. He now explains that the tone of self-irony we have sensed expresses his awareness of the costs such a life has imposed on himself and others. He has wasted not only his own fortune, but his wife's as well, not to mention the fortunes of others who have followed him. He has never known peace, suffered constant distress even from his hopes, and five times found himself in prison. Still worse, he has never paid attention to the ordinary "process of life itself. Would you believe it, I don't remember a single spring, I never noticed how my wife loved me, how my children were born."[26] In focusing entirely on the ideal, he has missed everything real.

Thinking of humanity in the abstract, he has behaved cruelly to particular people, and this cruelty now troubles his conscience: "How often I have hated and despised those whom I ought to have loved, and *vice versa*." He has never intentionally lied or done evil, but, he explains, "I cannot boast that I have no one's life upon my conscience, for my wife died before my eyes, worn out by my reckless activity." Her death prompted his latest enthusiasm, the idealization of women.[27]

## The Russian Woman

Enthusiasm for "the Russian woman" infected people across the political spectrum and continued for generations. Women's importance among the revolutionary intelligentsia grew especially strongly. The hagiography that developed around "the wives of the Decembrists," who followed their husbands into Siberian exile, radicalized young women for generations.

In the last years of Alexander II's reign, and again at the beginning of the twentieth century, women played a prominent role in the Russian terrorist movement. Anna Geifman estimates that they constituted a quarter of all terrorists, a far greater proportion than anywhere else.[28] Sophia Perovskaya, we have already seen, directed the assassination of Alexander II in 1881, and Vera Figner, whose memoirs we will consider later, assumed leadership of the terrorist People's Will after the other leaders had been arrested. These and other women, hailed for their idealism, self-sacrifice, and saintliness, served as revolutionary icons.

In his classic *Underground Russia*, Stepniak praised Vera Zasulich, whose attack on General Trepov catalyzed the terrorist movement, as "an angel of vengeance, not a terrorist." Her act illuminated what Stepniak called "the Terrorism" with "its divine aureola, and gave to it the sanction of sacrifice."[29] He described the "beautiful"[30] Perovskaya as "an inspired priestess; for under her cuirass of polished steel, a woman's heart was always beating. Women, it must be confessed, are much more richly endowed with this divine flame than men. This is why the almost religious fervor of the Russian Revolutionary movement must in general be attributed to them; and while they take part in it, it will be invincible."[31]

Enthusiasm for "the Russian woman" prevailed on the right as well. Women came to embody purity, Christian self-sacrifice, and saintly devotion far beyond the capacity of fickle men. In the May 1876 issue of *A Writer's Diary*, Dostoevsky proclaimed that while the Russian man over the past twenty years has succumbed to "the vices of acquisition, cynicism, and materialism," the Russian woman has experienced "an upsurge in her strivings [that] has been lofty, frank, and fearless." In such women we find "one of the pledges of our renewal."[32] In "Again About Women," an article in the *Diary*'s next issue, Dostoevsky described an eighteen-year-old seeking his approval to serve

Russian volunteers as a nurse. Unlike so many other proponents of a cause, she displayed "not the slightest element of vanity, conceit, or infatuation with one's own heroism."[33] In both articles, Dostoevsky advocated higher education for women in order to make the most of their superior moral qualities.

In his Pushkin speech, Dostoevsky contrasted this ideal type of woman with the Russian ideological wanderer. In Tatyana, the heroine of *Eugene Onegin*, Pushkin achieved "the apotheosis of Russian womanhood," as Turgenev did in his portrayal of Liza, the heroine of *A Nest of Gentlefolk*. Unlike male ideological wanderers, Dostoevsky explained, these heroines understand that one cannot establish human happiness on the bones of innocent victims.[34] Stepniak idolized women as holy killers; Dostoevsky celebrated them for rejecting even the smallest act of violence.

## What Does Not Happen

Already intrigued by Likharev, Ilovayskaya listens with special attention to his praise of woman's capacity for self-sacrifice and willingness to give her life for an idea or a man representing it. Women, he explains, have followed him more than once. "I have turned a nun into a Nihilist who, as I learned afterwards, shot a gendarme; my wife never left me for a minute in my wanderings, and like a weathercock changed her faith in step with my changing enthusiasm."[35] Like him, these women have believed most passionately not in some idea but in passionate belief itself.

Without being aware of it, Ilovayskaya, like the other women who have followed him, becomes infected with Likharev's enthusiasm, all the more so because this time he has placed his faith in women like herself. Women, she realizes, "were ... the object of his new enthusiasm or, as he said himself, his new faith! For the first time in her life she saw a man carried away, fervently believing." For all the frantic awkwardness of his gesticulations, "there was a feeling of such beauty in the fire of his eyes, in his words, in all the movements of his huge body, that without noticing what she was doing she stood facing him as though rooted to the spot, and gazed into his face with delight."[36]

To prove his point about Russian women, Likharev asks: And wouldn't you, too, follow a man you loved to the North Pole? When she says she would, we know she is ready to do so. For the first time, "God's world seemed to her fantastic, full of marvels and magical forces. All that she had heard was ringing in her ears, and human life presented itself to her as a beautiful poetic fairy-tale without end."[37]

When Likharev sets off into the snowstorm in the morning, it is clear that he could easily persuade her to join him. She stares "as though she wanted to say something to him" but "she only looked at him through her long eyelashes with little specks of snow on them." He senses that she would follow him "without question or reasonings." But he does not ask her, and as his sleigh disappears into the distance they watch each other, his eyes, as ever, "seeking something in the clouds of snow."[38] As so often in Chekhov, we sense the significance of what does *not* happen.

## *"Kill the Yid"*

Entranced by this romantic picture, readers often miss one jarring note just before the story ends. It is now Christmas, and a crowd gathers. As it shouts and sings, Ilovayskaya can make out only these lines:

> Hey, you, Russian lad,
> Take your thin knife,
> We will kill, we will kill the Yid,
> The son of misery [. . .]

Likharev listens with pleasure to these appalling verses, "looking feelingly at the singers and tapping his feet in time."[39] He smiles at Ilovayskaya, and she smiles back. They wish each other a happy Christmas.

They hear nothing but a traditional Christmas song, and he apparently approves of anything that comes from the people. But if we reflect on Russian events in the years shortly before the publication of Chekhov's story in 1886, we recognize that the murderous words had immediate contemporary relevance few readers could have missed.

Russia had just witnessed a series of bloody pogroms following the assassination of Alexander II, perhaps provoked by the fact that a Jewess played an important role among the terrorists. In contrast to earlier pogroms in Russia's southern provinces, these were directed not just against property but against people as well. *The People's Will*, the organ of the group that killed the tsar, reported that "in Elisabethgrad, where the pogroms began, one hundred houses were destroyed, twenty people killed, one hundred wounded."[40]

We usually think of Russian pogroms as inspired, or at least tacitly condoned, by the government. That was true in the early twentieth century, but not two decades earlier. The anti-Jewish riots of the early 1880s emerged spontaneously, and, far from encouraging them, the government detected in them a dangerous breakdown of public order. When the reactionary Dmitri Tolstoy became minister of the interior in 1882, he vowed to suppress "these scoundrels" and had more than five thousand arrested.[41]

It was not the government but the revolutionaries who cheered the pogroms as an upsurge of popular violence that might be turned against the authorities. On August 30, 1881, the executive committee of the People's Will issued a manifesto, written in Ukrainian and addressed to "good people and all honest folk in the Ukraine." It began: "It is from the Jews that the Ukrainian folk suffer most of all. Who has gobbled up all the lands and forests? Who runs every tavern? Jews! . . . Whatever you do, wherever you turn, you run into the Jew. It is he who bosses and cheats you, he who drinks the peasant's blood."[42]

As historian Adam Ulam observed, such statements have "been a source of deep embarrassment to many historians of the liberation movement. Some break off the narrative in 1881, largely, one suspects, to avoid dealing with this episode."[43] Historians sympathetic to the revolutionaries also fail to mention that the terrorist heroine Vera Figner took several copies of this anti-Jewish manifesto to circulate in Odessa.

Another member of the executive committee, the populist Vladimir Zhebunyev, reported on the spot for the *Bulletin of the People's Will* about an incipient pogrom: "Excitement grew before my eyes," he wrote. Instead of believing in the tsar as they used to, "now the people have begun to realize that there exist ordinary mortals who strive manfully for their welfare. This is a great achievement of which every revolutionary ought to be proud."[44]

"Personally, of course I had no animosity against the Jews," Zhebunyev explained, "but my thoughts and feelings have become one with the people, and I was counting hours and minutes till the pogroms started."[45] He expressed deep disappointment that imperial soldiers arrived to prevent riots. Tikhomirov, another member of the People's Will executive committee, struck a similar tone. To be sure, massacres of Jews are revolting, he conceded, but one must remember that

> in those countries where anti-Semitic disturbances are most common, the Jews make up the majority of the most implacable exploiters of men. Meanwhile, their treatment of the people is irritating beyond all conception, and of inconceivable brutality. . . . Of course not all the Jews are not exploiters. . . . But when the people see that seventy-five or even ninety per cent, of those that devour them are Jews, they soon look upon these as all in the same boat.[46]

The article in *The People's Will* reporting the events in Elisabethgrad posed a question:

> Concerning the Jewish pogroms, many have been curious about the attitude we socialist revolutionaries adopt toward such cases of popular *retribution*. . . . We do not have the right to condemn or even remain neutral toward such manifestations of the people's anger. We are bound to espouse the aspirations of all those *justly* enraged who enter upon an active struggle, and we must consciously seize *leadership of those forces* and endorse their point of view.[47]

The revolutionaries, the article continued, could use these outbursts for something much more widespread: "If the bombs again will not help . . . then we will prevail with the aid of a nationwide wave of terror. . . . Come the day of retribution and the people will be merciless."[48]

With his usual tact, Chekhov makes no direct comment on the popular verses that charm Likharev and Ilovayskaya. But the story suggests that the Russian need to believe, to commit oneself wholeheartedly to one cause or another, can inflict immense harm not only on one's family and followers, as Likharev has come to realize, but on many others as well. We may recall the nun who, inspired by him, became a murderer. Once indiscriminate violence becomes welcome, is there any limit to that harm?

Chekhov suggests: perhaps the greatest brutality comes from humane, well-educated idealists.

## The Type Embodied

Several Russian writers experienced a life-changing conversion. Tolstoy's *Confession*, Kropotkin's *Memoirs of a Revolutionist*, Solzhenitsyn's *Gulag Archipelago*, and Dostoevsky's sketch "The Peasant Marey" all tell the story of what Dostoevsky called the rebirth of convictions. Conversion shapes the plot of several of Tolstoy's novels and stories. In Chapter 8, we shall examine conversions occasioned by extreme Soviet conditions.

Wanderers like Likharev and his real-life counterparts differ from these writers and characters because they experience not one but many conversions. For them, each final truth proves to be a penultimate one. Berdyaev, for example, narrated his life story as a series of leaps from one worldview to another. Consider these chapters in his autobiography:

2.  Solitude. Anguish. Freedom. Revolt. Pity. Doubts and Wrestlings of the Spirit. Reflections on *Eros*.
3.  First Conversion. Search for the Meaning of Life.
5.  Conversion to Socialism. The Domain of Revolution, Marxism and Idealism.
7.  The Movement Toward Christianity. The Drama of Religion. New Encounters.[49]

What remained common throughout these changes was Berdyaev's demand for final answers and his rejection of all compromise. His attitude, he explained, "has always been accompanied by non-acceptance of the world as it was given me, by an inability to be merged with the world."[50] As a result, "I was imbued with an irresistible eschatological impulse, which could not be satisfied by any given world. My love for life was a love for the meaning of life. . . . My greatest sin has probably been my inability and refusal to bear the stuff of the commonplace, that which constitutes the very 'stuff of life,' or to see light through the unspeakable darkness of the commonplace."[51] Likharev, too, dismisses the commonplace.

## Belinsky

It is hard to overestimate the importance of Vissarion Belinsky for understanding the tone and content of Russian thought. Russia's prototypical ideological wanderer, he provided the model for countless others to follow.

Before he had been dead a decade, Belinsky had already achieved mythic status. When the Slavophile Ivan Aksakov, who disapproved of Belinsky's views, went on a pilgrimage to Russian provincial towns in 1856, he discovered constant reverence not for figures from the Slavic past, as he had hoped, but for the westernizer Belinsky. "The name of Belinsky," he wrote, "is known to every thinking young man, to everyone who is hungry for a breath of fresh air in the reeking bog of provincial life. There is not a country schoolmaster who does not know—and know by heart—Belinsky's letter to Gogol. . . . Slavophile influence is negligible . . . Belinsky's proselytes increase."[52] And they continued to increase.

As the historian Eugene Lampert observed, Belinsky was, and increasingly came to be regarded as, "typical of the whole Russian intelligentsia"—typical in the Russian sense of "quintessential" or "an extreme example of." He came to be adored as "the first . . . in the long gallery of Russian rebels to embody the image of the eternal revolutionary, to bear, like Cain, the indelible sign of man's unfinished wayfaring."[53]

Everyone claimed him. Reading his works rather selectively, the Soviets deified him as the forerunner of socialist realist criticism. Others took a very different view. In his celebrated memoirs, *The Extraordinary Decade*, the moderate liberal A. P. Annenkov insisted that Belinsky's fundamental beliefs "can be called *conservative*, in the broad sense of the word, rather than revolutionary, as they were later reputed to be by the combined forces of the enemies of the press and of reforms in the structure of Russian life."[54] In Annenkov's view, the radicals mistook Belinsky's passionate idealism for revolutionary commitment. In fact, one can find support in Belinsky's writings for almost any position on the political spectrum.

Turgenev regarded him as a friend and dedicated *Fathers and Children* to him. Elements of Belinsky, above all supreme intellectual integrity, go into the portrait of the novel's hero, Bazarov. Dostoevsky broke with Belinsky and found his acknowledged heirs, Chernyshevsky and Dorbolyubov, distasteful and dangerous, but he remained under the spell of Belinsky's personality. Several of Ivan Karamazov's most famous statements paraphrase Belinsky.[55]

So who was Belinsky? To begin with, he was undoubtedly the most important literary critic in Russian history. To an astonishing degree, it was Belinsky who made the Russian canon. He demonstrated an uncanny ability to recognize the seeds of genius from a writer's first, and still highly imperfect, efforts. For Belinsky's discerning eye, Turgenev's poem "Parasha," which no one would read today if it were not Turgenev's first work, promised masterpieces to come. When "The Song of the Merchant Kalashnikov" appeared anonymously, Belinsky appreciated that whoever the poet might be—it turned out to be Lermontov—was a talent of the first rank. Belinsky also recognized the poetic promise of the sixteen-year-old Nekrasov, and he made the reputations of Gogol and Goncharov. Although Pushkin was already quite well-known, it was Belinsky's articles on him that, as Isaiah Berlin observed, "established his importance, not merely as a poet of magnificent genius, but as being, in the literal sense, the creator of Russian literature, of its language, its direction, and its place in the national life."[56] Pushkin, whose aristocratic manners and cultivated irony distanced him from the plebian Belinsky, could only remark: "That strange fellow for some reason is very fond of me."[57]

Annenkov, whose book might have been called "Belinsky and His Contemporaries," recalled the time when Belinsky, unable to contain himself, hurriedly explained to him that an extraordinary new novel had come into his hands. The author was some "beginner, a new talent; what this gentleman looks like and what his mental capacity is I do not know as yet," but his novel "reveals such secrets of life and characters in Russia as no one has even dreamed of."[58] The unknown author was Dostoevsky, who was to recall his meeting with Belinsky as the happiest event of his life. He remembered Belinsky saying to him "ardently, with burning eyes: 'Do you yourself know what you have written?' . . . raising his voice to a shriek, as was his habit . . . 'have you yourself comprehended all the terrible truth that you have shown us?'" What struck Belinsky most was Dostoevsky's understanding of a humiliation so profound that the humiliated person "does not dare claim even the right to his own unhappiness."[59] The work in question—*Poor Folk*—does not remotely measure up to those that would make Dostoevsky world famous, but Belinsky could discern what even Dostoevsky, by his own account, did not suspect.

And yet, it was not Belinsky's critical acumen that made his reputation. It was, rather, his personality. Herzen recalled him as frail, unprepossessing, ill-dressed, shy, and consumptive, but also, when roused to moral indignation, as a man with

> the spirit of a gladiator! . . . when the muscles of his cheeks began to quiver and his voice to burst out, then he was worth seeing; he pounced upon his opponent like a panther, he tore him to pieces, made him a ridiculous, a piteous object, and incidentally developed his own thought, with unusual power and poetry. The dispute would often end in blood, which flowed from the sick man's throat; pale, gasping . . . he would lift his handkerchief to his mouth with shaking hand and stop, deeply mortified, crushed by his physical weakness. How I loved and how I pitied him at those moments![60]

Contemporaries fell under the spell of Belinsky's reckless commitment to truth and righteousness combined with his ascetic lifestyle and willingness to sacrifice himself for his ideas. With utter integrity and complete disregard of his own interests, he never temporized or compromised. "If you are a person susceptible of thinking and holding convictions," he told Annenkov, "may you not be swayed from your path either by the reckonings of self-interest, or by considerations of personal or social life . . . or by the seductions of people's perfidious friendship intent on depriving you, in exchange for their paltry offerings, of your most precious treasure—independence of mind and pure love of truth!"[61] He was always breaking with people. "I am a Jew by nature," he wrote to Herzen, "and cannot eat at the same table with Philistines."[62]

Abstract questions "gnawed at him incessantly," Turgenev recalled. "He did not allow himself a moment's peace and . . . day and night he kept worrying over the questions he put to himself." Every question was urgent. "As soon as I came to see him," Turgenev continued, "he would at once get up from the sofa, looking haggard and ill . . . and . . . coughing continuously and with a pulse of one hundred a minute, and a hectic flush on his cheeks, he would begin the conversation at the point we had left off the day before. Although his enthusiasm and sincerity carried me away, I would tire after two or three hours and want to break for food. 'We haven't decided the question of the existence of God,' he said to me once with bitter reproach, 'and you want to eat!'"[63]

His acquaintances called him "*neistovyi Vissarion*"—furious (or frenzied) Vissarion—and sometimes simply Orlando Furioso. According to Annenkov, he became "the living embodiment of the images devised by poetry to convey the anguished strivings . . . of a restless heart and seething mind."[64] He took ideas personally: "for me," he remarked, "to think, to feel, to understand and to suffer are one and the same thing."[65] Abstractions were palpable to him, and he sensed theories as more real than lived experience, as did some Russian thinkers to follow. "Everything that is particular, contingent, and irrational is an *illusion*, . . . *appearance* and not *essence*," he wrote in 1840. "Man eats, drinks, dresses himself: this is the world of illusions."[66] No wonder German philosophy, and especially Hegel, appealed to him. Herzen remarked that the two people who best understood Hegel, Proudhon and Belinsky, did not know a word of German.[67] Herzen meant that Belinsky, in the true Russian spirit, discerned logical consequences Hegel himself had not seen and drew conclusions more extreme than any Hegel would have countenanced.

In Dostoevsky's novel *The Possessed*, Shatov, reminding us of Belinsky, famously remarks that he can *feel* ideas. "There are thoughts that live in me for only half an hour," Belinsky wrote. "How do they live? In such a way that when they leave me they must tear away my blood and nerves."[68]

## How Many Stages?

A Don Juan of theories, Belinsky embraced and abandoned them one after another. Goncharov "thinks I am a weathercock," he once remarked. "I admit I change my views, but I change them as one changes kopeck for a ruble!"[69] Biographers dispute how often he switched philosophies and argue about how to periodize his thought. Some enumerate philosophers he came to love: Fichte, Feuerbach, Hegel (especially), and French socialists. Others begin with his youthful rebelliousness, followed by a period of extreme conservativism, and then an all-embracing radicalism. Shortly before his death, Belinsky himself described three stages: "God was my first thought, mankind—my second, man—my third and last one."[70] Apart from the obvious schematism of this account, which differs from the messy and jerky picture suggested by his writings, one may doubt that his "last" stage would not have proven a penultimate one.

Time and again Belinsky believed that, after much searching and many errors, he had at last discovered the ultimate truth. He often experienced severe doubt as one idea began to lose its appeal, but he would never accept it with qualifications, regard it as applicable to many but not all cases, or maintain that it was on the whole true if one does not push it too far. For Belinsky, the whole point of a philosophy was to be pushed "too far."

Each time he adopted a new belief, he came to hate those with whom he used to agree. For Belinsky as with Robespierre, Herzen observed, "men are nothing, convictions everything."[71] An "idealist even in his hatred," as Lampert calls him, he could turn against people for no personal reason whatsoever but only for their beliefs.[72] "What is most exasperating," he explained to Annenkov, "is that people here are still unable to view a man's thought apart from the man himself, to conceive of a man losing his time, ruining his health, and *making enemies* out of fidelity to a deeply felt opinion, out of love for an abstract idea."[73] He felt this idealistic hatred even for people long dead, and treated figures from the past as if he knew them personally. "He had hosts of foes and antipathies both in the contemporary world and in the realm of shades," Annenkov observed. "Belinsky became the contemporary, as it were, of the various epochs he encountered in his reading" not only in his hatreds but also in his loves, and he would defend the reputation of some hero from centuries past against all present critics "to the furthest possible extent."[74] Belinsky lived as if he were already a participant in Lucianic "Dialogues of the Dead."

## Belief and Intolerance

One might suppose that a person capable of changing his opinions so frequently might respect the right of others to differ. After all, if he was wrong once, might he not be wrong again? That was a conclusion Belinsky never drew and could not imagine drawing. For him, true belief necessarily entailed intolerance of all other beliefs. In his most famous composition, the letter of March 1, 1841, to his friend V. P. Botkin, Belinsky explained: "A year ago my views were diametrically opposite to what they are today.... Do you know that my present self painfully detests my past self, and if I had the power and authority it would go ill with those who are today what I was a year ago."[75]

Logically speaking, of course, there is no reason that one cannot be committed to one idea while extending the same right to others. After all, one can believe deeply in tolerance of diverse opinions, freedom of speech, and everything Americans sum up with the phrase "the First Amendment." But in Russian thought, both tolerance and moderation became signs of insincerity, a willingness to betray one's convictions, or sheer hypocrisy. In the mid-nineteenth century, such charges were routinely leveled against moderate liberals like Annenkov, Turgenev, and the liberal thinker Boris Chicherin. In the early twentieth century, the liberal Kadet (Constitutional Democratic) party liked to boast that it was the most *radical* liberal party in the world!

## Reconciliation with Reality

Of all Belinsky's turnabouts, the one that most shocked his contemporaries was what he called his "reconciliation with reality." Having fallen under Hegel's spell, he interpreted the German philosopher's famous dictum, "all that is real is rational," to mean that all facts are justified simply because they are facts. "Do you know that from your point of view," Herzen cajoled him, "you can prove that the monstrous tyranny under which we live is rational and ought to exist?" "There is not a doubt about it," Belinsky replied.[76] In a series of articles, Belinsky defended "the sacred quality" of tsarist autocracy,[77] and in a letter to his friend Stankevich he enthused:

> A new world opened up before us. "Might is right and right is might." No, I cannot describe to you with what emotion I heard those words. It was a liberation. I understood the meaning of the downfall of empires, the legitimacy of conquerors; I understood that there is no crude material force nor conquest by sword or bayonet, nothing arbitrary, nothing accidental. . . . The word Reality became for me the equivalent of the word God.[78]

Scholars sometimes overlook two conclusions from this reasoning that would prove especially influential in Russian thought. To begin with, Belinsky maintained that the enlightened person must overcome all contrary beliefs, eradicate individuality, and become a perfect tool of legitimate state power. In Belinsky's words, such a person "must acknowledge the intellectual whims of his own person to be a sham and a delusion, must subordinate himself to the rules and regulations of the state, which is the only criterion of truth on earth, must delve down to the Idea lying at its depths, must convert all its mighty content into his own personal convictions and by doing so, cease being a representative of fortuitous and private points of view."[79] Substitute "Party" for "state" and this becomes a fair paraphrase of the Soviet doctrine of *partiinost'* (partyness).

Second, Belinsky's "reconciliation" anticipated the thesis about extraordinary people we have called Raskolnikovism. As the agents of History, such people are not bound by the morality obligatory for others. For these superior beings, Annenkov recalled, Belinsky "established special rights and privileges. Even a special morality, for great artists, great lawmakers, for geniuses in general, who were empowered to devise special roads and to lead their contemporaries . . . along those roads without regard for their protests, perturbations, sympathies and antipathies. No more complete a withdrawal in favor of the privileged and elect of Fate could possibly be professed."[80]

Complete transformation of the human being into the embodiment of the absolutely true Idea and total subordination of others to the superior person who embodies it: though inspired by Hegel, these precepts would soon be applied to any idea held to be the infallible standard of justice. We may think of this as the Russian idea about ideas.

## Belinsky and Ivan Karamazov

Belinsky's most quoted comments concern his disillusionment with Hegel, with the reconciliation with reality, and, perhaps, with theory itself. These are the comments that Ivan Karamazov paraphrases and other thinkers echo throughout Russian literature and history.

"I have a special reason to harbor a grudge against Hegel," Belinsky wrote to V. P. Botkin in his letter of March 1, 1841, "for I feel that I have been loyal to him" and, under his spell, have justified human suffering. Hegel directs our attention to the absolute Idea, Belinsky explained, but he came to understand that it is not the Idea that matters, but each individual: "the fate of a subject, an individual, a personality, is more important than the fate of the world." Hegel bids us forget about individuals, endeavor instead to perfect ourselves, and "climb the top rung of the ladder of evolution." Belinsky replies to "Yegor Fydorovich"—an ironic transformation of Hegel's name "Georg Friedrich" into a Russian name and patronymic—

> that if I did succeed in reaching the top of the evolutionary ladder, I would demand even there an account from you of all the victims of accident,

superstition, the Inquisition, Philip II, etc., etc.; otherwise I will throw myself headlong from the top rung. I will not have happiness even if you gave it to me gratis unless I feel assured about every one of my blood brothers. . . . Disharmony is said to be a condition of harmony: that may be very profitable and pleasant for music lovers, but certainly not for those whose fates are destined to express the idea of disharmony.[81]

Ivan Karamazov echoes Belinsky's comment about the necessity of "disharmony" when, after recounting a horrific case of child abuse, he paraphrases the common answer that mankind could not have known good without also knowing evil. Ivan replies, in Belinsky's spirit: "Why should he know that diabolical good and evil when it costs so much? Why, the whole world of knowledge is not worth that [abused] child's prayer to 'dear, kind God!'"[82]

Most famously, Ivan paraphrases Belinsky's comment, that happiness is not worth a single person's unjust suffering, when he asks Alyosha:

"I challenge you—answer. Imagine that you are creating a fabric of human destiny with the object of making people happy in the end, giving them peace and rest at last, but that it was essential and inevitable to torture to death only one tiny creature . . . and to found that edifice on its unavenged tears, would you consent to be the architect on those conditions? . . ."

"No, I wouldn't consent," said Alyosha softly.[83]

Ivan's approach to such questions discredits not only one theoretical justification of evil after another, and not only all that have ever been formulated, but also all that ever *could* be. Rather than offer arguments against specific theories, he asks his listener to compare them with the images of suffering children he has presented. Would any decent person prefer the theory to the child? It is clear that this question could be asked of any theory, past, present, or to come.

Against theories, Ivan, in Belinsky's spirit, offers specific *cases*; against abstract argument he cites concrete facts about unjust suffering. "'I understand nothing,' Ivan went on, as though in delirium. 'I don't want to understand anything now. I want to stick to the fact. I made up my mind long ago not to understand. If I try to understand anything, I shall be false to the fact and I have determined to stick to the fact.'"[84] Ivan is the last in a series of Dostoevsky's heroes who, having placed their faith in a theory, learn the limitations not only of that theory but of Theory itself. In *Crime and Punishment*, Raskolnikov embraces a series of contradictory theories to justify murder: one allows it because morality is mere "prejudice," while another not only allows but demands it on inexorable, absolute moral grounds. Raskolnikov eventually learns that his mistake lay in the theoretical cast of mind itself.

Dostoevsky's heroes come to recognize that no theory could justify cruelty, but Belinsky transformed even that insight into a theoretical justification of cruelty! The answer to one theory is always another. If the philosophy of the Absolute leads to violence against individual persons, then a new philosophy rejecting violence must justify violence against the adherents of the old philosophy! Was that not what the French revolutionaries defending the rights of man had done? Belinsky once referred to the guillotine as the sign of the highest civilization.[85] It is as if Ivan Karamazov had decided that the proper response to gratuitous cruelty was indiscriminate massacre.

In another letter to Botkin (June 28, 1841), Belinsky reported that after reading Plutarch "I have developed a sort of wild, frenzied, fanatical love of freedom and independence of the human personality which are possible only in a society founded on truth and virtue."[86] Since these beloved goods are possible "only" in a society founded on truth and virtue, one is justified taking the most extreme actions to create it. Or as Belinsky explained: "Human personality has become my obsession which I fear may drive me mad. I am beginning to love mankind à la Marat: to make the least part of it happy I believe I could destroy the rest of it with fire and sword. . . . I feel that if I were king I would surely become a tyrant."[87]

## *The Harm That Good Men Do*[88]

Chekhov and Dostoevsky both understood that fanatical idealism, even in the name of alleviating the misery of each person, contains the potential for unspeakable cruelty. What creates this potential is the whole-hearted, unquestioned adherence to a purportedly infallible theory, outside of which no morality is possible.

One might suppose that it takes a cruel person to commit cruel acts, but both authors insisted that is not so. The call to kill Jews does not give the kindly, populist Likharev a moment's pause. In his article "One of Today's Falsehoods," Dostoevsky, himself a former member of the radical Petrashavsky circle, argued against the common idea that terrorists, like the recent Nechaevists, must be ignorant, disreputable people, "monsters" or "scoundrels." On the contrary, Dostoevsky explained, they are often well-educated idealists. I know that because "I myself am an old 'Nechaevist': I also stood on the scaffold condemned to death and I assure you that I stood in the company of educated people. . . . There was not a single 'monster' or 'scoundrel' among the Petrashevsky circle."[89]

Like the Nechaevists, Dostoevsky continued, the Petrashavtsy might also have gone to all lengths under the spell of "new ideas" that "seemed to be sacred and moral in the highest degree" because they promised to regenerate the world. "Even in 1846 Belinsky had initiated me into the whole *truth* of this coming 'regenerated world' and into the whole *sanctity* of the future communist society. . . . So then why do you think that even murder . . . would have stopped us?"[90]

Wanderers abandon one theory for another, but the greatest danger lies in theory itself. Dostoevsky concluded: It is not villains who commit the most villainous acts. On the contrary, it is idealist believers in some utopian theory. The greatest evil results from attempts to abolish it altogether. "And herein lies the real horror: that in Russia one can commit the foulest and most villainous act without being in the least a villain! And . . . this is more possible in Russia than anywhere else. . . . The possibility of considering oneself—sometimes even being, in fact—an honorable person while committing obvious and undeniable villainy—that is our whole affliction today!"[91]

Russian history would vindicate this insight. The greater wisdom, events demonstrated, belonged not to Likharev but to Chekhov, not to theoretical wanderers but to the great realist writers.

# 4 The Idealist

## *Incorrigible and Disappointed*

> He had a peculiar talent—a talent for *humanity*. He possessed
> an extraordinarily fine delicate scent for pain in general.
>
> —Anton Chekhov, "A Nervous Breakdown"

Don Quixote fascinated the Russians because quixotic people seemed to be everywhere. Even Russian peasants, Ivan Turgenev noted in his celebrated essay "Hamlet and Don Quixote," refer to Don Quixotes. As the essay's title suggests, Hamlet and Don Quixote represented for Turgenev "two fundamental, and fundamentally opposed, qualities of human nature," the idealist and the skeptic.[1] Although Turgenev's fiction offers examples of both, he focused primarily on idealists, whom he described with remarkable pathos and insight. His own generation, the "men of the forties," famously embraced both idealist (in the sense of nonmaterialist) philosophy and idealistic (in the sense of devotion to noble ideals) ways of living.

According to an early nineteenth-century witticism, the British ruled the seas, the French dominated the land, while the Germans lived in the air ("in the clouds"). If so, then the Russians, who took German philosophy to extremes the Germans themselves never imagined, dwelled in the upper stratosphere, where air thins to the nothingness of space.

With his trademark irony directed at his earlier self, Alexander Herzen described the young thinkers of the 1840s as people for whom abstractions, especially lofty ones suffusing life with meaning, seemed more real than immediate surroundings or familiar people. "People who loved each other avoided each other for weeks at a time because they disagreed about the definition of 'all-embracing spirit,' or had taken as a personal insult an opinion on 'the absolute personality and existence in itself' . . . I have the right to say this because, carried away by the current of the time, I wrote myself in exactly in the same way, and was actually surprised when Perevoshchikov, the well-known astronomer, described this language as 'the twittering of birds.'"[2] Dostoevsky's underground man (another "man of the forties") calls these idealists "Schillers" devoted unreservedly to "all that is sublime and beautiful," but, as P. V. Annenkov noted in his memoirs, "even Schiller himself . . . was declared to be an infantile genius who could never ascend to . . . the heights of dispassionate contemplation of ideas and laws governing human beings."[3]

Looking back, Herzen regretted that he had broken with his friend, history professor T. N. Granovsky, "over theoretical convictions; but to us they were not something extraneous but the real foundation of our lives."[4] The name Granovsky soon became synonymous with incorrigible idealism because of his luminous, high-minded personality and his inspired public lectures on medieval history. These lectures, memoirists testify, constituted an "event" that had no precedent. They attracted, in Annenkov's words, "not only the scholars, the literary parties, and his usual ecstatic auditors—the young people of the University—but also the whole *educated* class of the city, from old men straight from the card tables to young misses still breathless with their success on the dance floor."[5] As Granovsky's first course of lectures ended, Herzen recalled, "everyone leapt up in a kind of intoxication, ladies waved their handkerchiefs, others rushed to the platform, pressed his hands and asked for his portrait. . . . There was no possibility of getting out. . . . The . . . fury of approbation doubled." When an exhausted Granovsky made his way to his office, Herzen concluded, "I flung myself on his neck and we wept in silence."[6]

In one lecture, Granovsky praised the nobility and achievements of Charlemagne, "the restorer of civilization," who exemplified "what the real role of any power, any majesty on earth should be." Russians have all the benefit of that example, he told the audience, "without paying any price" since Europeans had paid it "through bloody toil and bitter sacrifice."[7] Russians' debt of gratitude to medieval European heroes must therefore be all the greater.

For Granovsky, ideals mattered more than practical results. Even ineffective good deeds, as the product of noble intentions, surpass everything else in importance. "The great actors in history and the small . . . are alike bound by the duty to labor by the sweat of their brow," he remarked in a lecture on

Louis IX. "But they bear responsibility only for the purity of their intentions. . . . Their actions enter history as mysteriously as a seed falls in the soil. The ripening of the harvest, the time of the harvesting, and the yield all belong to God."[8] Turgenev concluded "Hamlet and Don Quixote" with a paraphrase of the quixotic Granovsky's faith: "Everything will pass, everything will disappear—the most noble rank, the most supreme power, the most all-encompassing genius. . . . But good deeds do not float away like smoke; they are more enduring than the most striking beauty. 'Everything changes,' said the Apostle. 'Only love remains.'"[9]

It was just this way of thinking that repelled Chernyshevsky and his followers. When they called themselves "realists," they meant they did not resemble idealists like Granovsky.

## Idealist Type One (Incorrigible): Don Quixote and Granovsky

So who was Don Quixote, in Turgenev's estimation? He was the opposite of the type we have called the wanderer because he remained steadfast in his loyalty to a single ideal, as unshakably devoted to it as the Knight of the Doleful Countenance was to Dulcinea of El Toboso. "Like an ancient tree," Turgenev explained, "he has dug his roots deeply into the soil, and he is inherently incapable of betraying his convictions or of transferring them from one object to another."[10]

The Don Quixotes of this world value above all "faith in something eternal and immutable . . . in the truth that exists outside the individual . . . the truth that . . . is worthy of constant service and profound sacrifice." The idealist values his life "to the extent it can serve as a means for promulgating those ideals."[11] Before Hamlet would embark on a risky adventure, he "would weigh all the consequences, all the probabilities of success," but the Quixotes, for whom success is beside the point, scorn such an approach as missing the whole point of self-sacrifice.

And what happens when reality forces itself on the idealist? What if Dulcinea should turn out to be ill-smelling and ugly, something base mistaken for an ideal? The distinguishing mark of this type of idealist is the ability to explain away all counterevidence. If facts contradict the ideal, then the facts must yield. For Cervantes's Don Quixote, discrepancies, which are always illusory, result from enchantments wrought by evil magicians. "In our own time, in our travels," Turgenev observed, "we ourselves have seen people die for an equally nonexistent Dulcinea, or for something coarse and often dirty, in which they have caught sight of their ideal, the transformation of which they also attribute to the influence of evil—we almost said 'magicians'—evil incidents and evil individuals."[12] No matter what blows fate may inflict, these idealists cannot be disillusioned because for them only illusions are real.

In his article "A Lie Is Saved by A Lie," Dostoevsky described how Don Quixote begins to wonder about passages in those "most truthful books" of knight-errantry in which sorcerers send an army of a hundred thousand men against the hero who, invoking his fair lady, keeps swinging his sword until a few hours later he has annihilated them all. It suddenly strikes Don Quixote that killing each man would take a few seconds and that, mathematically speaking, the process would take much longer than the allotted time. Oddly enough, this absurd knight, willing to believe in one preposterous fantasy after another, "suddenly *began yearning for realism!*" His faith is shaken on this point; and if this is a lie, why could not everything else in these books be equally false? "And so, to save the truth, he invents another fantasy . . . twice, thrice as fantastic as the first one."[13] The explanation, he decides, is that these were not armies of real men, but only of slugs resembling real men, and so the hero could kill several at one blow.

In just this way, Dostoevsky explained, quixotic idealists save one lie by another. What's more, there is something quixotic in all of us. "Say you've come to cherish a certain dream, an idea, a theory, a conviction." If you have "exaggerated and distorted" things to validate your belief, "doubt weighs upon your mind and teases it. . . . Now . . . won't you admit even to yourself what it was that suddenly set your mind at rest? Didn't you invent a new dream, a new lie, even a terribly crude one, perhaps, but one that you were quick to embrace lovingly only because it resolved your initial doubt?"[14] The incorrigible idealist will always find a way to dismiss the strongest counterevidence. To the extent they resemble such idealists, other people do the same.

## Two Idealists

The eponymous hero of Turgenev's story "Yakov Pasinkov" speaks with "a peculiar sort of sweet huskiness . . . while his whole face faintly glowed. On his lips the words 'goodness,' 'truth,' 'life,' 'science, 'love' . . . never struck a false note. . . . Without strain, without effort, he stepped into the realm of the ideal; his pure soul was at any moment ready to stand before the 'holy shrine of beauty'. . . . Pasinkov was an idealist, one of the last idealists whom it has been my lot to come across." When he read poetry, "it positively seemed to me that we were slowly, gradually, getting away from earth, and soaring away to some radiant, glorious land of mystery."[15] Pasinkov never discovers that someone loved him. His eyes raised on high, the idealist misses what is most important in reality.

All the same, Pasinkov understands something that practical people never will. "Peace to your ashes, unpractical man, simple-hearted idealist!" the narrator thinks as the story ends. "God grant to all practical men—to whom you were always incomprehensible, and who, perhaps, will laugh even now over you in the grave—God grant to them to experience even a hundredth part of those pure delights in which, in spite of fate and men, your poor and unambitious life was so rich!"[16]

Having outlived the time when youthful idealism is attractive, the hero of Turgenev's *Rudin* has accomplished nothing and lives off those charmed by his idealistic rhetoric. "The very breath of inspiration . . . was felt in his impatient improvising. He did not seek out words; they came obediently and spontaneously to his lips, and each word seemed to flow straight from his soul, and was burning with all the fire of conviction." Somehow when Rudin struck "one chord of the heart [he] set all the others vaguely quivering and resounding." When he reads the heroine German poetry, which has sunk deep roots in his soul, "he drew her after him. . . . Unimagined splendors were revealed there to her earnest eyes . . . a stream of divine visions, of new, illuminating ideas, seemed to flow in rhythmic music into her soul, and in her heart, moved with the high delight of noble feeling, slowly was kindled and fanned into a flame the holy spark of enthusiasm."[17]

Years before, Rudin, as a member of one of the idealist circles of the time, could already make everything "disconnected . . . fall into a whole . . . before our very eyes. . . . Nothing remained meaningless . . . in everything there was design . . . everything took on a clear and yet mystic significance; every isolated event of life fell into harmony . . . we felt ourselves to be . . . the living vessels of eternal truth." As the novel draws to a close, Rudin, without irony, compares himself to Don Quixote: "What Don Quixote felt then, I feel now."[18]

## The Irony of Origins

Annenkov described Turgenev as intensely interested in how ideals shape, and are shaped by, a personality. Russians, he knew, give themselves to ideals with abandon, and in this quality he "discovered a special kind of creativity in Russia, a creativity in the realm of ideals . . . no matter how chimerical, immature, and sad those ideals might have appeared to be." As a result, Annenkov explained, "all Turgenev's literary activity can be defined as a long, detailed, and poetically annotated catalogue of ideas that circulated in the Russian land . . . over the course of thirty years."[19]

While the intelligentsia valued their ideas and ideals as absolute truths, they interested Turgenev primarily as expressions of character. In Annenkov's view, Turgenev cared less about people's opinions than about "the psychological bases of their opinions, the reasons determining this or that choice of doctrines and outlooks. Study of person always stood in the forefront for him; convictions were valued not so much for their content as for the light they shed on the inner life of a man. This was a feature he shared with the majority of artists," especially realist novelists.[20]

In this respect, Turgenev exemplified, and to a great extent developed, the key techniques of the fiction of ideas. If philosophers test ideas for their agreement with logic and evidence, writers of realist fiction examine why they seem persuasive to a particular person. A hero may imagine that he holds a belief because it is plainly true or indisputably just, but the novelist recognizes how cognitive biases, the strategic selection of evidence, and the egoistic pleasure of holding a superior opinion, all shape that belief and give it cogency. In this way the novelist casts what I like to call an "irony of origins" over the idea, a form of scrutiny decidedly unwelcome to the one who accepts the idea with unexamined and uncritical fervor.[21]

Turgenev's best portraits of idealists work in just this way. In *Fathers and Children*, the young Arkady imagines he has adopted the new ideal of "nihilism" as intellectually superior to his father's romantic idealism, but readers discern that it enables a youthful rebellion that might have fixed equally well on any idea shocking to his father. As Arkady exhibits his recently acquired opinions, "he was conscious of a little awkwardness, that awkwardness that usually overtakes a youth when he has just ceased to be a child and has come back to a place where they are accustomed to regard him and treat him like a child. He made his sentences quite unnecessarily long . . . [and] with an exaggerated carelessness he poured into his glass far more wine that he really wanted, and drank it all off."[22] When he discovers his father has a mistress and that she is embarrassed to show herself, Arkady seizes the chance to demonstrate his progressiveness:

> "She has no need to be ashamed . . . you are aware of my views" (it was very sweet of Arkady to utter that word). . . . Arkady's voice had been shaky at the beginning; he felt himself magnanimous, though at the same time he realized he was delivering something like a lecture

to his father; but the sound of one's own voice has a powerful effect on a man, and Arkady brought out his last words resolutely, even with emphasis.[23]

Arkady delights in his "views" while Turgenev focuses on the psychologically complex process of enunciating them.

Ironically enough, Arkady is as idealistic as his father, whom he resembles more than he knows. He seems to forget that nihilists, as Bazarov remarks to Arkady's uncle, have contempt for high-minded views of any sort. "Liberalism, progress, principles," Bazarov exclaims, "what a lot of foreign [...] and useless words."[24] When Akrady denounces all authorities, he looks for approval to his own authority, Bazarov, who repeatedly winces at the idealistic rhetoric employed to defend "realism." "We are bound to carry out these requirements," Arkady intones "with dignity." "We have no right to yield to the satisfaction of our personal egoism.' This last phrase apparently displeased Bazarov; there was a flavor of philosophy, that is to say, romanticism about it . . . but he did not think it necessary to correct his young disciple."[25]

Arkady has apparently forgotten that a nihilist is *supposed* to be egoistic, indeed, that, as Chernyshevsky argued, no one can be anything else. When he does defend egoism, Arkady attributes to it all the virtues of altruism.

By the same token, Arkady, like so many young Russians to come, accepts materialism for idealistic reasons. He worships matter—not the matter one can touch but the idea of matter, which is as rarefied as any spirit. It is no less a metaphysical entity than Truth or Beauty or the Idea. In the notebooks to *The Possessed*, Dostoevsky has a character ask: "Is [such] matter material?"[26]

## Idealism's Progeny

Turgenev shows us just how incorrigible Russian idealism must be if it could inform doctrines diametrically opposed to it. He treated idealism with condescending appreciation and described it with the same gentle irony employed in his descriptions of young love. Dostoevsky took idealists much more seriously. With remarkable foresight, he detected in them the seeds of the violent radical intelligentsia they would engender. What the two groups shared was a faith in abstractions as more real, and more important, than living people.

Dostoevsky's political novel *The Possessed* focuses on 1860s revolutionaries, but it begins and ends with a man of the forties, Stepan Trofimovich Verkhovensky, who was modeled on Granovsky and in the notebooks is called Granovsky. Like the historical Granovsky, Stepan Trofimovich once delivered brilliant history lectures at the university. After that, the novel's narrator explains, Stepan Trofimovich published, "in a progressive monthly review, which translated Dickens and advocated the views of George Sand, the beginning of a very profound investigation into the causes, I believe, of the extraordinary moral nobility of certain knights at a certain epoch, or something of that nature. Some lofty and exceptionally noble idea was maintained in it, anyway."[27]

No less cloudy, Stepan Trofimovich's narrative poem also conveyed an "exceptionally noble" idea in "some sort of allegory in lyrical-dramatic form." As the narrator describes this production, we learn it contains "a chorus of incorporeal powers of some sort, and at the end a chorus of spirits not yet living but very eager to come to life" who "sing about something very indefinite . . . even insects sing, a tortoise comes on the scene with certain sacramental Latin words . . . if they converse, it is simply to abuse one another vaguely, but with a tinge of higher meaning." Stepan Trofimovich professes political opinions that are, so far as one can make sense of them, vaguely and loftily oppositional. They exemplify what the narrator calls "the higher liberalism"—that is, liberalism "without any definite aim"—the sort of liberalism "only possible in Russia."[28] In the notebooks, Stepan Trofimovich's radical son calls him "a whining, civic-minded old woman" and he dies of diarrhea.[29]

Idealism of this sort resembles a theatrical pose, and Stepan Trofimovich constantly strikes poses. Turgenev's Rudin, too, loves the sound of his own rhetoric, but with Stepan Trofimovich self-dramatization becomes the defining feature of his character. In the novel's notebooks Dostoevsky explains: "Granovsky [that is, Stepan Trofimovich] was truly pure, and ardently wished to do good, yet . . . he couldn't help playing a role and inevitably became a phraseur." He loves to pretend he is persecuted, and "without being conscious of it he has placed himself on a pedestal, as a sort of holy relic to be worshipped by pilgrims. Loves it."[30]

If all these weaknesses seem rather harmless, the novel's plot shows they are anything but. The lachrymose idealism Stepan Trofimovich displays as Stavrogin's tutor distorts the boy's emotions and psychology, while his appalling neglect of his son Pyotr Stepanovich engenders his revolutionary cynicism. Pyotr Stepanovich resembles (and was loosely based on) the bloodthirsty Nechaev, as he is called in the notebooks. And so "Granovsky" literally gives birth to "Nechaev," the idealist to the terrorist.

Revolutionary killers, in other words, act out the implications of the idealists' utopian dreams. "Haven't you been telling us," "Nechaev" asks "Granovsky," "how various ... literary men ... were, together with Belinsky, discussing such-and-such or such-and-such detail of the society of the future? It all started with your age."[31] To his chagrin, Stepan Trofimovich recognizes the kinship of the nihilists' beliefs with his. They have vulgarized his idea, to be sure, but it is recognizably the same idea or, as he puts it, they have taken it and dragged it through the streets.

This process of successive vulgarizations shows no sign of stopping. In the notebooks, "Granovsky" exclaims to "Nechaev": "Monster! If it is true ... that yours is the product of my own uprooted generation, that it is we who in due course engendered the Utopists of 8 years ago [Chernyshevsky and his followers], and after them in *due progression* you, in that case, tell me, what will they be like who replace you?"[32]

Nechaev replies that they will make today's violent men look gentle by comparison. They did.

Contrary to some Western critics, Dostoevsky meant not that most radicals of the 1860s resembled Nechaev, but that the potential effects of their ideas could prove far worse than either their defenders or critics imagine. The fact that the novel's descriptions of what we have come to call totalitarianism proved astonishingly accurate—and that Dostoevsky was the only nineteenth-century thinker to describe the danger in detail—suggests that he was on to something.

From Dostoevsky's perspective, the key error making idealists so dangerous is their faith in "abstraction." In the novel's notebooks Dostoevsky reminds himself:

> #### About Granovsky
>
> N.B. *The most important:* Abstractness of thought, the abstractness of one's own life and of one's social position, may be, in some persons, the cause of extraordinary cruelty toward people.... This is sometimes the case with men engaged in abstract speculation, even though theirs may be an extremely refined intellect, and their reflections of the most profound.[33]

## Idealist Type Two (Disappointed): Garshin and Uspensky

With the rise of Russian populism in the 1870s, a different type of idealist came to prominence. Driven by guilt for unmerited privilege, these new idealists worshipped "the people" and other unfortunates, including workers and prostitutes. "I know all my own sins and those of others, and how papa made our fortune," declares Lisa in Turgenev's *A Nest of Gentlefolk.* "I know it all. For all that there must be expiation."[34]

Somehow the debt to the people had to be paid. But could it be? And what if the people did not at all resemble the oppressed noble souls of the educated imagination? Unlike the Don Quixotes of the 1840s, their populist heirs repeatedly recognized disappointing facts that they could neither wish nor rationalize away.[35]

The writers Vsevolod Garshin and Gleb Uspensky, friends who exemplify this type of idealist, described with impressive power their disappointment and their struggles to deal with it. Perhaps, they wondered, the problem lay not with the peasantry but with their perception of it? Could the people's virtue be hiding under a deceptive surface? "Not one great phenomenon in the realm of the soul is visible on the surface of Russian life," Uspensky wrote hopefully of "the people."[36] If the people's goodness could not be discerned, that was all the more proof it was concealed. This way of thinking transformed the absence of evidence into evidence and discovered in "apparent muteness" the record of "inaudible" spiritual voices.[37] The problem was that Uspensky spent considerable time with the peasants and encountered one proof after another that in the depths, no less than on the surface, peasant values were vile.

In that case—if the peasants really do adhere to values educated people regard as morally repellent—perhaps it is the educated who should change their way of thinking? Peasant evil, be thou my good! It was a hard position to maintain when peasants not only behaved with heartrending cruelty to each other but also especially admired worldly success produced by cheating.

Evil and suffering, it turned out, proved far more resistant to amelioration by high ideals than idealists had supposed. This realization only magnified the idealists' guilt, inasmuch as a debt that cannot be repaid grows ever larger. Garshin, Uspensky, and other populist idealists suffered doubly, from guilt over the condition of the people and despair that something had to be done but nothing could be. Both writers suffered mental breakdowns, and as one traces the lives of noted early populists, nervous breakdowns, severe alcoholism, and suicide recur, as they do in Garshin's poignant stories. Historian James Billington referred appropriately to "the agony of populist art."[38]

## A Talent for Humanity

A cult figure whose readings provoked ecstatic responses, the charismatic Garshin struck one young woman as "a perfect model for an icon of our Savior.

His large, dark, deep-set eyes looked at me . . . with such melancholy kindness, as though pleading with me, a mere teenager, to have pity on him and on the whole world."[39] Like so many others, the artist Ilya Repin (the greatest of the "Itinerants" and perhaps Russia's greatest realist painter) was struck by Garshin's distinctive personal beauty. In his famous painting of Tsar Ivan the Terrible just after he has murdered his son in a rage, Repin gave the dead tsarevich Garshin's face. Repin's portrait of Garshin, one of his most psychologically acute, shows a young man at his writing desk, afflicted with a deep, almost metaphysical sadness. Garshin, in turn, published art criticism praising the Itinerants, in particular Repin's riveting canvas "Barge Haulers on the Volga" (1870–1873), which became an icon for popular suffering. When Likharev, the hero of Chekhov's "On the Road," embraces populism, he briefly works as a barge hauler.

This "martyr of the spirit," another contemporary observed of Garshin, "suffered from an illness from which it is morally wrong to recover." Replying to those who doubted that saintly figures like Dostoevsky's Alyosha Karamazov actually existed, some readers cited Garshin as proof they did.[40]

The radical materialism of Chernyshevsky, Pisarev, and the nihilists repelled Garshin. Nihilist *intelligents*, imitating Turgenev's Bazarov, dissected frogs to prove their materialist conviction that people are just complex lower animals.[41] Pisarev famously declared that the salvation of the Russian people lies in the splayed—that is, cut open—frog (*rasplastannoi lyagushke*).[42] Legend has it that when Garshin tried to dissect a frog, he was overcome with pity and sewed it back up.[43]

After Garshin, in a fit of despair, committed suicide by throwing himself down a flight of stairs, literary Russia—including both Chekhov and Tolstoy, who greatly admired his stories—was shocked. Chekhov contributed one of his best stories, "A Nervous Breakdown," to a volume commemorating the dead writer. Chekhov depicts the peculiar illness from which it is perhaps immoral to recover as "a talent for *humanity*." Like Garshin, the story's hero, Vasilev

> possessed an extraordinarily fine delicate scent for pain. As a good actor reflects in himself the movements and voice of others, so Vasilev could reflect in his soul the sufferings of others. When he saw tears, he wept; besides a sick man, he felt sick himself and moaned; if he saw an act of violence, he felt as though he himself were the victim of it, he was frightened as a child, and in his fright ran to help. The pain of others worked on his nerves, excited him, roused him to a state of frenzy, and so on.[44]

No one valued empathy more than Chekhov, and the absence of it creates the tragedy of many of his stories and plays. And yet in "A Nervous Breakdown," the hero suffers from too much empathy, an inability not to let it overwhelm him. What's more, he is apt to "raise every trifle to the level of a [social] question."[45]

As the story begins, two of Vasilev's friends, a medical student and a pupil at a school of painting, persuade him to join them in an innocent (for that epoch) amusement, a sort of pub crawl through the city's bordellos. Having derived his knowledge of prostitutes from books, Vasilev pictures them as delicate beings constantly enduring insult and contemplating their own degradation. He recalls the story of one prostitute "with a guilty smile" who, out of shame, will only see men in the dark, and another about a self-sacrificing young man who loves and proposes to a prostitute, who considers herself "unworthy of such happiness [and] takes poison." He imagines that prostitutes "all acknowledge their sin and hope for salvation."[46]

Instead, Vasilev encounters a world utterly different from any he could have imagined. To begin with, the décor of the eight bordellos he visits all exhibit a special kind of bad taste that expresses the positive attraction of evil and vice. He recognizes a style "intentional in its ugliness, not accidental, but elaborated in the course of years . . . he saw that it all had to be like this and that if a single one of the women had been dressed like a human being, or even if there had been one decent engraving on the wall, the general tone of the whole street would have suffered."[47]

Still worse, the women "had nothing in common" with the ones he had expected. "It seemed to him that he was seeing not fallen women, but some different world, quite apart, alien to him and incomprehensible."[48] The more Vasilev sees, the more morally corrupt the women appear. "It was clear to him that the thing was far worse than he could have believed" because these women display not only the absence of human dignity but a sort of inverse dignity, a parody of humanness matching the bordello's aesthetics of ugliness. "There is vice," he thought, "but neither consciousness of sin nor hope of salvation. They are bought and sold, steeped in wine and abominations, while they, like sheep, are stupid, indifferent, and don't understand. . . . It was clear to him, too, that everything that is called human dignity, personal rights, the Divine image and semblance, were defiled to their very foundations."[49]

The disgust Vasilev experiences strikes him as criminal and so his guilt grows even stronger. "He was tormented by the thought that he, a decent and loving man . . . hated these women and felt nothing but repulsion towards them." He asks himself the same question that disappointed populists asked:

could the problem be that "I am not trying to understand them. . . . One must understand them and not judge."[50]

And perhaps the rest of us are as guilty as they are? "Not only the street and the stupid women were responsible," Vasilev reasons, so are all those who go about their lives indifferent to such horror, which is to say, almost everyone. His friends' manifest wickedness strikes him. If these women die prematurely after a given number of encounters, and men like his friends visit so many prostitutes in a lifetime, then, he reasons, one can calculate exactly how many deaths each man occasions. "One of two things," he thinks. "Either we only fancy prostitution is an evil . . . or if prostitution really is as great an evil as is generally assumed, these dear friends of mine are as much slave-owners, violators, and murderers" as are to be found. "What is the use of their humanity, their medicine, their painting?"[51]

As Vasilev returns home, "his soul was possessed by an unaccountable faint-hearted terror. . . . 'It's beginning,' he thought. 'I am going to have a breakdown.'"[52] At home, lying on his bed, he experiences the overwhelming need to solve the problem of prostitution right away. Readers could not have missed that the radical intelligentsia professed the same urgency, the same refusal to consider mere reform or gradual improvements, with respect to several other social problems. It was as if the intelligentsia as a group suffered from the same nervous derangement as Vasilev, with the difference that Vasilev recognized his state of mind as an illness.

Not only must Vasiliev solve this unsolvable problem totally and immediately, he must do so in a way that consumes every fiber of his being. His "extraordinarily fine delicate scent for pain" can be satisfied with nothing less and soon he senses his moral essence ebbing away. "If at that moment someone had performed a great deed of mercy or had committed a revolting outrage, he would have felt the same repulsion for both actions."[53] The thought of suicide competes with the knowledge that this agony, which he has experienced before, lasts only three days. At last, his friends take him to a psychiatrist who regards the malady as purely physiological and writes prescriptions.

## Garshin the Disillusioned

Garshin's fiction, perhaps the most underrated in Russian literature, displays the same "talent for humanity" and empathy for pain that Chekhov described. Idealism confronted with recalcitrant and unforgiving reality shapes the plots of several of his stories. In "Attalea Princeps," a Brazilian palm tree in a Russian greenhouse dreams of escaping imprisonment and breathing the air of freedom. Directing all her energy to growing taller, she plans to break the greenhouse glass and reach the world outside. Eventually she succeeds, but this is frigid Russia, not tropical Brazil, and so the tree realizes she must die. "Is this all?" she asks herself. "Is this all I languished and suffered for so much?"[54] Ideals fail not only when unattainable but, still worse, when attained, as most revolutions show.

When war broke out with Turkey, Garshin, though an opponent of all violence, enlisted as a private, a form of "going to the people." He went to war, he explained, not even thinking of killing but only of sharing the common soldiers' suffering. "Is it more moral," he asked those who objected to serving in the imperial army, "to stay behind, with one's arms folded, while that soldier is going to die for us?"[55]

Some remarkable stories came out of this experience. The hero of "Reminiscences of Private Ivanov," has enlisted, as Garshin did, to study the people. "Yes, it has become the latest fashion these days," remarks the officer Wenzel with irony. "Even literature elevates the peasant and makes a sort of pearl of creation of him." Ivanov deplores Wenzel's sternness, verging on brutality, to the soldiers under his command, but eventually discovers that Wenzel had once been an idealist like himself, had shared his view of the people, and even "closely followed Russian literature." But experience of actual peasant soldiers had shattered his naïve idealism. "All that remained of the so-called good books on contact with reality," he remarks, "proved to be sentimental nonsense."[56] Though he may cry about using his fists, he has learned, the hard way, that the soldiers respond to nothing else and that the discipline he instills may save their lives in battle. His soldiers perform the best. Is Wenzel Ivanov's—and all idealists'—future?

## *Garshin's Aesthetics of Ugliness*

When Chekhov made Vasilev experience "repulsion," he presumably had in mind Garshin's rare ability to depict disgust, and, indeed, to make readers share it. When ideals conflict with reality, disappointment is only the first result. The next is disgust, leading to a nauseating despair. Just as the bordello decorations achieve a positive ugliness, and the prostitutes exhibit an inverse humanity, so reality itself proves not just recalcitrant but aggressively nauseating. If only nature were nothing worse than morally neutral, as scientists assure us!

"Four Days," the story that made Garshin famous, describes another Russian soldier who has joined the army without considering that he might hurt someone. "I meant no harm to anyone when I went to fight," the hero explains.

"The idea that I too would kill people somehow escaped me. I only saw *myself* as exposing *my* breast to the bullets." In the confusion of battle, the hero bayonets a Turk and then, severely wounded, is left for dead beside the Turk's corpse. He spends four days witnessing and smelling the decomposition of the Turk's body, a process he describes in excruciating detail. "His skin . . . had gone pale and yellowish; his face had swollen, drawing the skin so tight it had burst behind the ear. Maggots were squirming around there. His feet, wedged into his boots, had swollen and enormous bubbles oozed out between the hooks." So nauseating is the smell that he tries to drag his inert, injured body away from it and, despite the intense pain, at last moves a few feet into fresher air. But then "the wind changes and wafts toward me a stink so strong that it makes me want to vomit. My empty stomach goes into sharp, painful spasms. . . . And the stinking, tainted air washes over me."[57]

Then it gets worse. "That day my neighbor became so hideous as to beggar description. . . . His face was gone. It had slid off the bones."[58] The narrator had prepared whole heads in anatomy class, but had never seen anything like this. Aristotle thought of soul as that which gives an organism's matter its form; if so, then disgust is our response to the half-completed process of losing form. Skeletons frighten, but they do not disgust as a still decomposing corpse does.[59] We vomit when seeing organic matter becoming soulless. Until his lucky rescue, the hero can only imagine he is looking at himself in a few days. Could this experience have shown him human life shorn of prettifying disguises?

What sort of art is this that evokes nausea?[60] Garshin explores this peculiar aesthetics in "Artists," a story in which the diaries of two artists alternate. Dedov, a landscape painter, believes in beauty and excels at rendering it. Real art, he explains, "attunes man's soul to a mood of gentle wistfulness, it softens the heart."[61] His friend Ryabinin, a populist loosely based on the Itinerants, chooses to paint a worker whose horrible job is to press his chest against a rivet on the inside of a boiler while another man hammers on it. These "human anvils" do not survive long.[62] They represent all the suffering that people inflict on each other.

For Dedov, such a subject defeats the very purpose of art. "Looking for the poetic in the mud! . . . all this peasant trend in art, in my opinion, is sheer ugliness. Who wants these notorious 'Volga Bargemen' of Repin's? . . . Where is the beauty, harmony, refinement?" Ryabinin, he correctly observes, aims at the very reverse of beauty, "the positively ugly."[63]

In Dostoevsky's novel *The Idiot*, Ippolit Terentyev reflects on Holbein's naturalistic painting of Christ in the Tomb, which shows the corpse of a man who endured great suffering just as it would really be. "It is simply nature," Ippolit thinks, and looking at it one cannot help asking: "if death is so awful and the laws of nature so mighty, can they be overcome . . . when even He did not conquer them? . . . And if the Teacher could have seen Himself on the eve of the Crucifixion, would He have gone up to the cross and have died as He did?" What Holbein has achieved is an art of ugliness, a form rendering formlessness. Ippolit asks: "Is it possible to perceive as an image that which has no image?" Evidently it is.[64]

Dedov hopes to soothe his audience by allowing it to appreciate beauty, while Ryabinin refuses to allow viewers to contemplate his painting as a mere work of art. On the contrary, he strives to obliterate aesthetic distance and draw them into the subject's world, where they become morally responsible for the suffering they witness. "Bound to canvas by the spell of my power," Ryabinin addresses the workman he has depicted, "come forth, gaze down upon these dress coats and trains, and shout to them: I am a festering sore! Smite their hearts, give them no sleep, rise as a ghost before their eyes! Kill their peace of mind, as thou hast killed mine."[65]

The process of painting this sort of picture consumes the artist, who dwells within the horrible world he depicts. Ryabinin tries covering up his picture when not working on it, but it haunts him anyway. He falls ill, experiences terrifying nightmares, and, when he at last recovers, gives up painting altogether.

When successful, art of this sort seizes us by the throat so we cannot ignore it and must respond to it as moral beings. Tolstoy also aimed at this effect in some of his stories, especially "Sevastopol in December" and "The Death of Ivan Ilych."[66] In the Soviet period, the danger of reading forbidden works literally made its readers accomplices in a crime. This is a characteristically Russian way of reading. I have already quoted Grossman's comment in "The Hell of Treblinka": "It is the writer's duty to tell the truth, and it is a reader's civic duty to learn this truth. To turn away, to close one's eyes and walk past is to insult the memory of those who have perished."[67]

## The Idealist's Double Vision

Drawing on his own sad experience in an asylum, Garshin's best-known story, "The Scarlet Flower," depicts an idealist who knows he is mad and yet believes his insane reasoning. If madness is understood metaphorically, this description fits many idealists of this type. "His condition was a peculiar mixture of sane reasoning and nonsense," the narrator explains. The hero knows that he lives among mental patients and yet also discerns in each of them "some incognito or secretly disguised person."[68] Some idealists, as Garshin knew by experience, also find a way to believe in what they simultaneously recognize as impossible.

The story's hero believes in his mission. He has been called upon "to fulfill a task which he vaguely envisaged as a gigantic enterprise aimed at destroying the evil of the world." All evil, he decides, proceeds from three red flowers growing in the asylum yard. Each flower is red because it has absorbed "all the innocently spilt blood" of humanity. . . . It was a mysterious, sinister creature, the opposite of God . . . in a modest innocent guise."[69] One by one, the hero contrives to pick the flowers, each time holding it to his breast all night to defeat its evil by absorbing it into himself. As in "Artists," taking responsibility entails self-destruction. Despite the ample diet ordered by the doctor, the hero loses weight rapidly. His mission consumes him. For an idealist of this type, it would not be a real mission otherwise.

"Soon now, soon," this utopian dreamer assures himself, "the iron bars would fall apart and all the people imprisoned here would be set free and rush to all corners of the earth, and the world, with a shudder, would throw off its shabby old covering and appear in all its glorious and shining new beauty." Having picked the third flower, he dies convinced that he has rid the world of evil. By morning "his face was calm and serene; the emaciated features . . . expressed a kind of proud elation . . . they tried to unclench his hand to take the crimson flower out, but his hand had stiffened in death, and he carried his trophy away to the grave." Garshin knew that his own utopianism was futile at best.[70]

The success of Garshin's stories derives from his ability to convey the pathos of the idealist's experience while also registering its appearance to others. Dedov's views about Ryabinin, especially concerning the futility of his choices, ring true; Wenzel turns out to be sadly wise; and the narrator of "The Scarlet Flower" makes us sympathize with the utopian madman without forgetting that, whatever sentimentalists might say, he is truly mad. As the madman's reasoning is both sane and nonsensical, Garshin creates a double perspective in which both the ideal and the real claim their due.

This double perspective was Garshin's own. Unlike many populists, he could not wholly commit himself. To the revolutionary poet Yakubovich, this quixotic figure was "a Hamlet of Our Time."[71] Somehow Turgenev's opposite personality types, Don Quixote and Hamlet, combined unstably within him. Could that be one reason that Garshin dedicated "The Scarlet Flower" to Turgenev's memory?

## Uspensky and the Psychology of Populism

In *The Crisis of Russian Populism*, historian Richard Wortman argued persuasively that the populists did not share an ideology, as Soviet historians contended, but rather an ethos—a set of "hopes, fears, longings, and hatreds that were merely given shape by one or another ideological formulation." Populism, he explained, was "not merely a rationale adopted to promote change, but an integral and essential part of the personality of those espousing it." Disappointment therefore threatened "not only the premises of radical action, but the individual's conception of himself as well."[72]

Writer Gleb Uspensky gave heartfelt expression to the populist ethos. For him, "the people" were not just a group of agricultural laborers but also a moral icon. The people, he maintained, are "patient, and powerful in misfortune, young in heart, manfully strong, yet gentle as a child, the people who bear everything on their shoulders, the people that we love, the people that we go to for the cure of our spiritual ills."[73]

But to share an ethos is not to possess knowledge. It is to ascribe features based not on empirical fact but on the need to alleviate "our spiritual ills." "The People are still a theory for us and stand before us as a riddle," Dostoevsky pointed out. "All of us who love the People look at them as if at a theory and, it seems, not one of us loves them as they really are but only as each of us imagines them to be."[74]

Populists above all shared a psychology. Having broken with their families, many experienced a sense of "fatherlessness" (a theme running through the period's writings) and a profound feeling of loneliness, often intensified by guilt over their families' relative privilege.[75] Such guilt plagued Uspensky's life from childhood on and became the reigning emotion of his personality. Feeling responsible for his cruel grandfather and complicit in his ancestors' sins, Uspensky saw everything in the world reproaching him. In church, he recalled, "I was guilty before the saints, the images, the chandeliers. In school I was guilty before everyone from the guard . . . to the hanger of my coat; on the street every dog (so it seemed to me!) awaited my appearance, if not to devour me then at least to take a bite."[76]

Like some Dostoevsky characters, Uspensky yearned for suffering. "I felt that I had to encounter something revolting, to come across something that would poison my existence. . . . My thought, beginning to torment me again, sought something distressing, some outrage, if only to relieve the unpleasant sensation of the awakening of pain by paining me in more or less the same way."[77]

When the young Uspensky arrived in the capital, he vowed to begin a new life, compose "a new spiritual genealogy," and entirely remake his very self. "When 'the year of '61' came it was absolutely impossible to take any of my personal past forward with me into the future," he recalled. "I could take nothing, not a drop; to live at all I had to forget the past down to the last drop and erase myself of all the traits it had instilled."[78] That, of course, is impossible, just as no revolution, however far-reaching, eliminates all traces of the past.

The intelligentsia did not measure up to Uspensky's moral standards, and so he, like so many others, sought his ideal in "the people." The populist leader Mark Natanson called on *intelligents* to be the humble servants of the people, whom he viewed as morally superior because they lived in communes and so had already rejected private property. The term *narodnik* (populist, from *narod*, people), originally a term of derision, became a badge of honor.[79]

Although peasants seemed culturally remote, Chernyshevsky's "anthropological principle" assured *intelligents* that all people are virtually identical (they all have the same spleen, as Turgenev's Bazarov puts the point). If so, Chernyshevsky reasoned, "you don't have to worry about studying [the people] in order to know what they need.... Assume that the same calculations and motivations act upon ordinary individuals among the people that act upon ordinary individuals in your sphere and that will be correct." The peasants, as Chernyshevsky imagined them, were intelligentsia doubles, sharing intelligentsia ideals and outlook.[80] Nothing could have been further from the truth.

Some concluded that *intelligents* should erase whatever differentiated them from the peasants by imitating them—or, as it was said, fusing with them. These *intelligents* learned a peasant trade and went to the countryside, only to discover that the peasants dismissed these fake shoemakers and locksmiths. What's more, peasants revered tsarist authority and accepted the grossest superstitions.

But perhaps appearances were deceiving? The young nobleman Peter Chervinsky argued, with more hope than evidence, that behind these "crude and coarse ... and sometimes scandalous" superstitions, there dwells "a great feeling ... in embryonic form—the urge to submit one's egoistic self to something broader and more elevated to which man has moral obligations and on occasion may wish to sacrifice his individuality."[81] This feeling, of course, was an intelligentsia ideal attributed gratuitously to the peasants, but the appeal of "embryonic form" as an explanatory metaphor is that it dispenses with any need for visible evidence.

Populist theoretician Mikhailovsky disagreed. In his view, peasant bru-tality, which derived from corruption of their original state, had proceeded so far that peasants no longer knew their own best interest. Far from imitating them, the intelligentsia must grasp that "the problem consists in sincerely and honorably recognizing the [true] interests of the people as one's goal, while preserving only what corresponds to those interests."[82] How the intelligentsia, which knew nothing about agriculture or peasant life, was to know peasant interests better than the peasants themselves was not explained.

## The Incurable

Seeking his ideal and relief from guilt, Uspensky moved to the countryside, where he wrote brilliant sketches and stories. They often take the form of an educated narrator, resembling Uspensky himself, encountering an interesting person and discovering his history. In the process, the narrator also acquires unexpected, usually unwelcome, knowledge about the countryside. Either the narrator or the one he comes to know struggles to understand rural evil.

In "The Incurable" (1875)—a title that might be applied to Uspensky himself—the narrator visits a rural friend, a village doctor, and accompanies him on his rounds "in the capacity of a simple observer."[83] In the end, this ob-server observes himself and questions his right to live as he does.

Poverty and ignorance predominate in this region, which is economically dying. When the narrator asks people how they live, the answer is "God knows how." When he asks, "But how precisely?" they reply: "Precisely in that way—somehow or other." Despair and fatalism reign. "Sadness, the premoni-tion that everything that happened to the inhabitants must end only in the grave, the consciousness that it is impossible for there to be anything better: such an unrelieved and heavy condition of the soul penetrated everything and everyone, even seemed to suffuse the very air the village breathed."[84]

In the second part of the story, a deacon, given to drink, visits the doctor. To the doctor's mounting irritation, he beats around the bush, speaks incom-prehensibly, and mutters something about the iron the doctor has prescribed for him while obviously having something else in mind. At last, the deacon asks the doctor to prescribe some iron for the soul. Is the soul somehow material, he wonders, and does soul material come in different sorts, the way other matter does? If I take powders for the body, he asks, what can I take for the soul? Perhaps books? "Powders for the body, books for the soul?"[85]

The deacon then asks to borrow a book—not some periodical but some-thing timeless and "fundamental," something from the very beginning of history.

When the doctor offers him a book about the ancient Greeks, the deacon asks if there is anything earlier, and at last accepts a book about ancient India. "The thought of that poor man, who thought to cure his spiritual illness with books and powders," the narrator recalls, "did not abandon me. What was his spiritual wound? And what illness was this? . . . I decided I would certainly find an occasion to speak with him and ask him about it."[86]

The narrator at last discovers that the deacon used to live selfishly and cynically—"my conscience proved to be a swine"—until he encountered a village schoolteacher instructing peasant children.[87] He learns to his amazement that she was a wealthy woman who, in contrast to what the deacon and everyone he knows have assumed, recognized that property could not provide a meaningful life.

"I was aroused to think about all the domestic filth" and his thoroughly swinish life, the deacon explains. Everything he used to take for granted troubled him. At last, the deacon talks with the schoolteacher about what makes a life meaningful, about not taking wealth earned by others' labor, about helping the poor, and, above all, about conscience (*sovest'*). From then on, the deacon no longer looks at things the same way. Now he knows that a person can live either "in the name of his belly" or "in the name of truth."[88]

"And that, gracious sir," the deacon continues, "is how evil, torment, and illness came upon me. Unexpectedly, something divine flew into my swinish soul." Reconsidering his life, he feels ever-increasing remorse, gives up working, drinks, and behaves disgracefully: a truly "swinish person awoke in me . . . a swinish person made itself known." That is how he came to wonder: "the body . . . can be helped by various medicines, but the soul . . . by reading?—What do you think, will it be possible by such means to renew oneself so one can live anew honestly and nobly?"[89]

After listening to the deacon's story, the narrator asks himself, "as a simple observer": What if what is happening to the deacon is happening to the people? What if their illness is really a sign of future health? What if the illness is in fact "thought," a step to spiritual renewal?

> With quiet, quiet, unnoticed steps it [thought] is penetrating into the deadest corners of the Russian land, inserting itself into souls completely unprepared for it. In the midst of this apparently dead quiet, in this seeming silence of sleep, grain by grain of sand and drop by drop of blood, slowly and audibly, the frightened, downtrodden, and forgotten Russian soul is reconstituting itself, and—most important—reconstituting itself in the name of the strictest truth.[90]

By the magic of a metaphor—illness implies the possibility of recovery—everything that tells against idealization of the peasant becomes so much evidence for it. And yet, the title of the story remains "The Incurable." Which is it?

## Admiring Evil

The more Uspensky came to know the countryside, the greater grew the gap between ideal and reality. The peasants he encountered were not just ignorant, superstitious, and violent to outsiders, they also behaved inhumanely to each other. Still worse, they admired those whose success depended primarily on cruelty and corruption.

Uspensky recounts the story of one peasant who accumulates capital by prostituting his wife and cheating a retired army officer. Dazzled by his success, the other peasants elect him elder, and when he embezzles commune funds from them, they admire him all the more. "The whole village knew that his wife was consorting with the devil," Uspensky explains, "but the very ability, the knowledge of how to go about it, how to turn things to one's advantage—this conquered everyone." By contrast, an honest peasant, who failed at everything because of this very honesty, earned only contempt.[91]

Stories of this kind accumulate. The more power peasants had over their own lives, the worse they behaved to each other. They valued a person less than a horse. Far from serving as an insurance policy for its members in times of misfortune, the commune functioned as another tool of oppression. Uspensky records how one commune leaves a family deprived of its breadwinner to starve, and when a nearby landowner offers to sell the commune land on advantageous terms, the peasants so distrust each other—with good reason—that they cannot act together. When the peasants are to award a tavern concession, the would-be merchant gets them drunk to secure favorable terms. In court, peasants testify to anything, even to their own personal harm, for vodka.

Faced with such evidence, Uspensky could no longer attribute peasant evil to poverty. After all, when they had plentiful resources, they drank more or devised new forms of cruelty. Their problem, he concluded, was not economic, but moral. The radical populist press regarded such indictments as blasphemous. Georgi Plekhanov, a populist who would soon become "the first Russian Marxist," insisted that communal principles still governed peasant thinking: "the commune pities everyone." Peasants' "direct feeling" (*neposredstvennoe chuvstvo*), Plekhanov argued, endowed them with natural morality. In response, Uspensky mocked his critics' "sickly sweet" and "slobbering" attitude toward the people.[92]

## Sheep without Fold

Several Uspensky stories picture idealists like himself struggling with the terrible truth about the peasantry. In "Sheep without Fold" (*Ovtsa bez stada*), the narrator, bored by the usual dachas (vacation cottages), chooses to go "somewhere remote, to the quiet of the genuine countryside."[93] He suffers from loneliness until asked to officiate at a christening, where he meets people. Gradually "I began to unravel the essential secret . . . of this incomprehensible everyday laboring life."[94]

He meets Luksan Luksanych, a nobleman "trying to do what in journalistic language is called 'fusing'" with the people. When the narrator explains he has come for the summer, the nobleman asks ironically: "Only for the summer? Not to 'fuse'?" Evidently, this nobleman once idealized the people, who now disgust him. He tells one horrifying story after another about how peasants mistreat each other. They especially respect one successful peasant who enjoys watching animals die and "loved to look at suffering," which he is all too capable of inflicting.[95] Nothing matters more to them than vodka. "One can't fuse with you, only booze with you!"[96]

"What a stupid word—fusing," Luksan Luksanych tells the narrator before relating his history. Suffering from a spiritual malaise—literally, "bitter taste" (*oskomina*)—and a feeling that his life has been pointless, he traveled abroad where he overheard a conversation about peasant virtues. One interlocutor explained that civilized people suffer from the division of labor, which distorts the personality.[97] Peasants, by contrast, do a bit of everything. Because of this multifaceted life, he continued, "no one on earth is more fortunate than the peasant [with his] . . . incorruptible gaiety, pure as a child's soul. . . . Who is healthy, strong, magnanimous? . . . again, the peasant."[98] Listening to this eulogy, Luksan Luksanych felt order returning to his soul and resolved to go to the countryside and "fuse."

I lived "in the most conscious-stricken epoch of Russian life," Luksan Luksanych explains. "It was time for society to remember that there is something called conscience" and that one had to act "right away, at this very minute" (*seichas zhe, siyu minutu*), "serve in this huge infirmary, and by every means help cure the sick, the cripples." But when he acted on this plan, even opening a school for the peasants, it all seemed fake. His malaise returned, and within half a year he decided that his calling lay not with the peasants but with the intelligentsia "in the scene of Russian progress."[99] But despair pursued him. Once more he escaped abroad, where he at last began to understand his life.

Having been raised by a peasant nurse, and having grown up playing with peasant children, this nobleman was at heart a peasant living a gentleman's life and yet could never actually be a peasant. He was at home nowhere, which is why he kept going from place to place, literally as well as figuratively. "I arrived at a fatal question: what was I after all? . . . I am simply a sheep without a fold."[100]

Luksan Luksanych tells the narrator that, in spite of all he knows about the peasants, he plans to stay in the countryside, but when the narrator returns some months later, he finds that Luksan Luksanych has left. As the story ends, the narrator senses something "unspoken and unexplained," both about "this ailing and broken figure" and the peasant world he has seen.[101]

## Evil Justified

Uspensky could not rest content with his awful discoveries. In his stories about the peasant Ivan Ermolaevich, he arrived at a new way to reconcile ideals with reality. Ivan Ermolaevich at first repels the narrator with his cruelty and egoism, his despotic rule of his family, and his contempt for "friendship, comradeliness, or the mutual consciousness of the benefits of communal labor."[102] With no ideals at all, he looks at people in crudely economic terms. Then it dawned on Uspensky: what if Ivan Ermolaevich embodied the "natural truth"? Could he in fact be a master of "the poetry" of the countryside, a sort of artist of life as he found it? Perhaps the cruelest actions in the countryside happened naturally and spontaneously so that "one devours another [but] without base motivation"?[103] "In the thoughts, acts, and words of Ivan Ermolaevich," he decides, "there was not one petty detail that did not have the most real basis that was not completely intelligible to Ivan, while my life is continually burdened by thoughts and acts which have no link between them."[104]

Ivan Ermolaveich, Uspensky concludes, is the true idealist. If things looked different, the problem lay not with Ivan Ermolaevich but with Uspensky and those like him. "No, he is not guilty, I, the educated Russian, I am mostly decisively guilty."[105]

"Unable to reconcile the real world with the ideal," Wortman rightly concludes, "he idealized reality and renounced all claims to judgment."[106] It is a solution that has led many Russian thinkers to justify terrible injustice simply because it exists. We may recall Belinsky's "reconciliation with reality," based on Hegel's dictum that everything real is rational, which led him to justify tsarist (and any other) tyranny. If Uspensky praised Ivan Ermolaevich's despotism as "natural," Hegelians and Marxists applauded the "historical." Whatever the favored word, this way of thinking could, and in the twentieth century did, justify policies costing millions of lives.

## How Love Becomes Hatred and Benevolence Motivates Cruelty

In their writings and by their life stories, Uspensky and Garshin offer important lessons about the dangers of idealism and the psychology giving rise to it. They also exemplify the troubling consequences of basing politics on guilt, which may lead people to adopt whatever solution promises psychological relief even if it does not help—or even positively harms—the victims on whose behalf guilt is felt.

Pondering the injustice of inheriting wealth when poor peasants have nothing, Levin, the hero of *Anna Karenina*, says that "the important thing for me is to feel that I'm not guilty."[107] That way of thinking, which he later amends, makes him, rather than the poor peasants, the issue. Tolstoy knows that all too often, we support policies without even examining if they work because they relieve our guilt.

Dostoevsky asserted that something still worse can happen to lovers of humanity or other idealists. By a psychological process he called "the law of reflection of ideas," love can be transformed into its opposite. "In a family dying of starvation," for instance,

> the father or mother, toward the end when the sufferings of the children become unbearable, will begin to hate those same children whom they had previously loved so much, precisely because their suffering has become *unbearable*. Moreover, I maintain that the awareness of one's own utter inability to assist or bring any aid or relief at all to suffering humanity, coupled with one's complete conviction of the existence of that suffering, can even *transform the love of humanity in your heart to hatred of humanity*.[108]

Those interested in motivating people to help others do not usually appreciate the danger of inducing guilt. As Dostoevsky repeatedly shows, that strategy can backfire in many ways.

Contrary to what we usually assume, guilt for having injured people can make us even crueler to them. When Fyodor Pavlovich Karamazov is asked why he hates someone so much, he replies: "I'll tell you. He had done me no harm, but I once played a nasty trick on him and ever since I have hated him."[109] That reaction makes no logical sense, but it does make psychological sense. We hate our victim precisely because he has been the occasion of our suffering pangs of conscience and, in that sense, causing them. We must learn to forgive not only those who have wronged us but also those we have wronged. The danger of idealistic guilt, and of politics based on repentance, is another lesson of Russian literature.

Danger also lurks in rebellion directed not against this or that wrong but against the very nature of things, when the goal is to tear up all evil, like that scarlet flower, by the roots. "One cannot live in rebellion" (*buntom zhit' nel'zya*) against the universe, as Ivan Karamazov says, and if one tries one may wind up a murderer or a madman—or in Ivan's case, both.[110] If some evil persists despite our efforts—as it always does—one may resort to unlimited violence against anyone seen as sustaining it. Alternatively, one might, like Belinsky, Uspensky, and others, wind up promoting that evil as true goodness.

## Behaving "Swinishly"

Like Luksan Luksanych, Uspensky found himself continually escaping from wherever he was only to find despair pursuing him everywhere. He traveled more and more, taking thirty-seven trips in 1885. As Wortman points out, on one occasion Uspensky arrived in the capital at 11 p.m. only to leave the next day at 2 p.m. "without seeing anyone, doing anything, or even knowing his original reason for coming." His guilt and sense of unworthiness kept increasing and he began to imagine cruel punishment in the other world, "inexpiable sin . . . hellish torment, hooks driven into the ribs, the fire, the flame, and the stench."[111] Hallucinations haunted him.

Uspensky lost his grip on reality. "The 'eternal life' of the countryside has . . . aggravated and undone my nerves," he wrote, and he spent his last years in an asylum. The metaphor of "swinishness," a quality he had always despised and sensed in himself, now became literal for him. Seeing his face as a snout, he came to believe he was a pig and behaved accordingly.[112]

Idealistic personalities of both types, the incorrigible and the disappointed, outlived the populist era. The first has lent to Russian thought especially intense resistance to disconfirmation, the second a tone of guilty urgency. Russian history, no less than Russian literature, has shown why, despite its appeal, extreme idealistic thinking can be so dangerous.

# 5 The Revolutionist

## Pure Violence

The will to destroy is also a creative will.

—MIKHAIL BAKUNIN

VIOLENCE FASCINATES. Apart from any professed goals, revolution may appeal as an ecstatic release of energy. As cultural theorist Slavoj Žižek has memorably observed, "In every authentic revolutionary explosion there is an element of 'pure' violence, i.e. an authentic political revolution cannot be measured by the standard . . . to what extent life got better for the majority afterward—it is a goal in itself . . . one should directly admit revolutionary violence as a liberating end in itself."[1] The same may be said of terrorism. "[Terror is] justified violence against the practical inert," Jean-Paul Sartre explained. "The permanent feature of every freedom should be the violent negation of necessity."[2]

## Magic Words

When the émigré anarchist Jan Machajski learned in 1917 of the revolution in Russia, he decided to return, even though he opposed everything the new government stood for. "It's not yet my revolution," he explained, "but it is a revolution, so I'm going to it."[3] Apart from any goals, the idea of revolution itself proved irresistible to many.

"Russia at the dawn of the twentieth century knew no more magic word than 'revolution,'" explained the Left Socialist Revolutionary I. N. Steinberg, who joined the early Bolshevik government. "There was enchantment in the very sound of the word ... even as they pronounced the sacred words, 'Long Live the Revolution,' the Russians felt obscurely that they were already halfway to liberation."[4]

"The people," "socialism," "revolution": these magic words disarmed rational thought. The people, as everyone knew, could be superstitious and brutal; some versions of socialism might easily prove tyrannical; and revolution, which could be made by anyone with any goal, might lead to disaster far worse than the order it destroyed. So the philosopher Mikhail Bakhtin reasoned. "I did not welcome the February Revolution," he explained. "I thought, or I should say in my circle we believed that it'll all certainly end very badly. . . . We were right in our predictions."[5]

Unlike Bakhtin, most educated people succumbed to the revolutionary spell. In *Hope Against Hope*, Nadezhda Mandelstam eloquently described its charm. "My brother Yevgenii Yakovlevich used to say that the decisive part in the subjugation of the intelligentsia was played not by terror or bribery (though God knows there was enough of both), but by the word 'Revolution,' which none of them could bear to give up. It is a word to which whole nations have succumbed, and its force was such that one wonders why our rulers still needed prisons and capital punishment." Even Nadezhda's husband, the sensitive poet Osip Mandelstam, who would die at Bolshevik hands, succumbed. "At such moments he would say that he wanted to be with everybody else, and he feared that the Revolution might pass him by."[6]

"The mystique of revolution," as historian Leonard Schapiro called it, shaped cultural and political life in the decades immediately preceding 1917.[7] "Revolution was becoming the fashion," observed Socialist Revolutionary leader Victor Chernov.[8] Terrorism, applauded even by many of its designated victims, practically defined this epoch. As we have noted, Russia was the first country where "terrorist" became an honorable, if dangerous, profession, commanding especially great prestige among the young and continuing in families for generations. The extent of terrorism was breathtaking, a "mass phenomenon," as historian Anna Geifman outlined in her authoritative study *Thou Shalt Kill: Revolutionary Terrorism in Russia, 1894–1917*:

> During a one-year period beginning in October 1905, a total of 3,611 government officials of all ranks were killed and wounded throughout the empire. . . . By the end of 1907 the total number of state officials who

had been killed or injured came to nearly 4,500. The picture becomes a particularly terrifying one in consideration of the fact that an additional 2,180 private individuals were killed and 2,350 wounded in terrorist attacks between 1905 and 1907.... From the beginning of January 1908 through mid-May of 1910, the authorities recorded 19,957 terrorist attacks and revolutionary robberies, as a result of which 732 government officials and 3,051 private persons were killed, while 1,072 officials and 2,829 private persons were wounded.... In the month of October 1906 [alone], 362 politically motivated robberies took place, and on a single day, 30 October, the Police Department received some 15 reports of expropriations at various state institutions.[9]

These figures do not include many local murders and robberies, which went unrecorded. Killing and maiming (throwing sulfuric acid into the face) evolved into a sport where victims were just "moving targets. In 1906–1907, these 'woodchoppers' (*drovokoly*), as one revolutionary labeled them ... competed against each other to see who had committed the greatest number of robberies and murders, and often exhibited jealousy over others' successes." One anecdote told of an editor, asked if the biography of the new governor should be run, replying: "No, don't bother. We'll send it directly to the obituary department."[10]

After 1905, terror became so commonplace that newspapers ceased publishing descriptions of each attack. "Instead," Geifman explained, "they introduced new sections dedicated exclusively to chronicling violent acts, in which they printed daily lists of political assassinations and expropriations [robberies] throughout the empire." In Belostok, one combat organization consisted entirely of school children.[11] At the beginning of the twentieth century, approximately one quarter of the terrorists were women, who were especially valued in the practice of "sadistic cruelty" to victims.[12] "Robbery, extortion and murder became more common than traffic accidents."[13]

## Revolution for the Sake of Revolution

For many terrorists, goals, programs, and ideology were irrelevant. What they loved was revolutionary activity itself. Let us call this type of revolutionary a *revolutionist*.

Many revolutionaries were not revolutionists, and Lenin expressed contempt for the type, which he regarded as less than serious. In his view, revolutionism was a form of romanticism, and he called it "petty-bourgeois revolutionism," "dilletante-anarchist revolutionism," and, most famously, an "infantile disorder" (*detskaya bolezn'*).[14] "The greatest danger . . . that confronts a genuine revolution," he wrote, "is exaggeration of revolutionariness . . . when they begin to write 'revolution' with a capital R, to elevate 'revolution' to something almost divine," he observed.[15] And yet even Lenin "believed in terror as a good in itself," as Robert Conquest pointed out. "In 1908 he had written of 'real, nation-wide terror, which reinvigorates the country and through which the Great French Revolution achieved glory.' Many similar pronouncements could be cited."[16] Terror motivated by hatred and revenge especially attracted Lenin.

Time and again, the means for achieving a goal became the goal itself. If at first the end was a particular kind of society and revolution the means, revolution soon became the end. By the same logic, if at first revolution was the end and terrorism the means, terrorism soon became the end in itself. As for Pushkin "the goal of poetry is poetry," for the revolutionist the goal of terrorism was terrorism.

## Pure Violence: Bakunin

No one symbolized the cult of revolution for its own sake more than Mikhail Bakunin, celebrated as the founder of modern anarchism.[17] But Bakunin called for revolution long before he was an anarchist, and at times he supported the antithesis of anarchism, dictatorship, when that seemed more revolutionary.[18] He rushed to Paris to participate in the 1848 uprising, an experience that was probably his most blissful. "I was on my feet the whole day, took part in absolutely every meeting, gathering, club, procession, walk, demonstration," he recalled. "In a word, I inhaled with all my senses, with all my pores, the intoxicating atmosphere of revolution. It was a banquet without beginning or end."[19]

As Bakunin's biographer Aileen Kelly observed, "rather than revolt being the means to anarchist ends, anarchy was [for him] no more than an extension of the liberating spirit of revolt."[20] In his best-known work, *God and the State*, Bakunin described the essence of humanness—the highest faculty of the soul—as rebellion. In persuading Adam and Eve to defy God, he explained, Satan made them truly human, so in a sense, it is Satan who is man's creator. By the same token, people who give in to obedience or endeavor to live a peaceful life all but revert to a prehuman state. According to this logic, the goal of rebellion does not really matter. Aristotle deemed philosophy as the highest form of human flourishing; Bakunin made the same claim for revolution.

The title *God and the State* belongs not to Bakunin but to two disciples, Carlo Cafiero and Elisée Reclus, who discovered the manuscript among his posthumous papers. It breaks off in mid-sentence, they explain, because Bakunin, always seething with energy, never took the time to finish one work before "others were already under way.'My life itself is a fragment,' he said to those who criticized his writings."[21] The prose of an anarchist, it wanders, digresses, loses the thread, repeats, and contradicts itself. One footnote, begun in the original manuscript with its continuation discovered elsewhere, runs to sixty pages, almost as many as the pamphlet itself.[22] Bakunin seems to be running off in all directions at once.

According to his friend Herzen, Bakunin lectured about, encouraged, and organized revolution all day and every day. "In the brief minutes he had free he rushed to his writing-table, cleared a little space from cigarette ash, and set to work to write five, ten, fifteen letters to Semipalatinsk and Arad, to Belgrade, Moldavia and Belokrinitsa. In the middle of a letter he would fling aside his pen and bring up to date the views of some old-fashioned Dalmatian, then, without finishing his exhortation, snatch up the pen and go on writing." No wonder he never finished anything or bothered to reconcile inconsistent ideas born on the spur of the moment. "He was fretted by prolonged study, by the weighing of pros and cons," Herzen explained. Everything about him, including his appetite, his "gigantic stature and the everlasting sweat he was in, everything, in fact, was on a superhuman scale."[23]

In November 1861, Herzen received a letter from Bakunin breathlessly explaining that he had escaped from Siberia and had made his way to San Francisco. The letter then switched abruptly to plans for fomenting new revolutions: "The destruction, the complete destruction of the Austrian empire will be my last word."[24] Always in a hurry, Herzen observed, he longed for any action if only it were in the midst of danger and promised destruction. "I wait my . . . fiancée, revolution," Bakunin proclaimed. "We will be really happy— that is, we will become ourselves, only when the whole world is engulfed in fire."[25] One fellow radical remarked that "On the first day of the revolution he is simply a treasure, but on the day after he ought to be shot!"[26]

As a result of Bakunin's haste and carelessness, some of his followers were arrested. In contrast to Lenin, who waited for the "revolutionary moment," Bakunin, to the frustration of other radicals, instigated rebellions even when they were bound to fail. His friend and fellow revolutionary, the poet Nikolai

Ogarev, grew frustrated with Bakunin's counterproductive insistence that it was always the right time for an uprising. "You want everything to happen now, as quickly as possible, and you cause a disturbance, but this does not advance matters," Ogarev wrote to him. "It is time to recognize that it is we who live for the cause, not the cause that exists for us."[27]

## Terrorism for the Sake of Terrorism: Savinkov

As noted earlier, the best known of all terrorists operating in Russia, Boris Savinkov, also published novels, and it remains unclear whether he wrote novels to dramatize his terrorist achievements or practiced terrorism to obtain material for his novels. In either case, Savinkov did not care about ideology and would practice his craft for anyone. "Why, I live for murder, only for murder," proclaims Bolotov, the hero of Savinkov's novel *What Never Happened*. "His whole existence lay in the 'work,' in terror," Bolotov observes of a comrade. "He had fallen in love, yes, yes, fallen in love with terror."[28] The hero of another Savinkov novel, *Pale Horse*, muses that "my entire life is a struggle. I can't refrain from it. But I don't know in whose name I am struggling. That's how I want it. I drink my wine undiluted."[29] Struggle wants to be pure.

Savinkov's terrorist achievements working for the Socialist Revolutionary Combat Organization were astonishing. Under his direction, the Combat Organization assassinated minister of the interior Vyacheslav von Plehve in 1904 and Grand Duke Sergei in 1905. The accounts of these missions in his *Memoirs of a Terrorist* convey the thrill of his exploits. After the revolution of February 1917, Savinkov served as acting minister of war under Alexander Kerensky and then, after the Bolshevik coup, worked for both the Whites and the anarchist Greens to overthrow the new government. In 1924 he returned from exile to head a new anti-Bolshevik terrorist organization, but it proved to be a Bolshevik fabrication invented to lure him back to Russia. Arrested and condemned, he again switched sides and joined the Bolsheviks. Like the hero of *Pale Horse*, Savinkov could not live without practicing terror.[30]

For revolutionists, aiding workers and peasants was at best secondary. One of the first female terrorists, Vera Zasulich, recalled that "sympathy for the sufferings of the people did not move me. . . . I had never heard of the horrors of serfdom at Biakolovo [where she grew up]—and I don't think there were any."[31] In his memoirs, Savinkov observed that the famous terrorist Dora Brilliant "lived only by one thing—her faith in terror. . . . Questions of program did not interest her."[32] Helping to organize assassinations was not enough for terrorist Pokotilov, Savinkov recalled. He wanted to do the actual killing: "I believe in terror. For me the whole revolution is in terror."[33]

"It is surprising how quickly the urge to take blood manifested itself in radical literature, and how soon afterwards words led to deeds," noted historian Daniel Brower.[34] Although Stepniak, Kropotkin, and others were to maintain in works intended for European progressive society that they turned to terror only as a last resort—as the only response left when the regime had renounced all reforms—this excuse (as we have noted) does not pass the smell test.[35] Remarkably, Kropotkin argued that no one could have believed in reform after 1862—that is, one year after the liberation of the serfs and two years before the judicial reform, undoubtedly the two most far-reaching changes between 1725 and 1917.[36] As we have seen, Peter Zaichnevsky called for "rivers of blood" in "Young Russia" (1862);[37] the conspiratorial organization "Hell" was formed in 1864; Karakozov attempted to assassinate the tsar in 1866. It seems clear that terrorism exercised its appeal in spite of the reforms, not because they had ceased. Its beginnings pretty much coincide with the birth of the intelligentsia itself in the early 1860s.

In *Pale Horse*, a group of terrorists discusses the morality of terrorism. It is noteworthy that the question they dispute is not whether terrorism is justified—that is a foregone conclusion—but which justification to pick. In much the same way, Dostoevsky's Raskolnikov, whom the narrator of *Pale Horse* mentions in this passage, switches between incompatible justifications for murdering the old pawnbroker woman. In neither novel is any justification the actual reason for deciding on murder; rather, it is the decision to murder that leads to the search for a justification. In that case, one might inquire, why not dispense with justifications? Or as George asks in *Pale Horse*, does the very need for justification "perhaps hide some cowardice?"[38]

## Risk

If relieving human suffering is beside the point, why would someone kill, rob, and risk her life? What motivates the revolutionist to engage in terror?

This problem concerned both the terrorists themselves and the novelists who wrote about them. Turgenev composed stories tracing the terrorist impulse to purely psychological causes that may also operate apart from any political purpose. In "A Desperate Character," dated the year of Alexander II's assassination (1881), the narrator recalls eight people discussing "contemporary affairs and men." "I don't understand these [contemporary] men!" interlocutor A. observes. "They're such desperate fellows [. . .] Really, desperate

[...] There has never been anything like it before." To the contrary, interlocutor P. (Poltyev) replies: this type has a history. Just as the poet Yazykov was said to "have enthusiasm without an object," so other people, then and now, display "desperateness . . . without an object."[39] No one, he declares could illustrate this type better than his nephew Misha Poltyev, whose story he proceeds to narrate.

Having grown up in a conservative and pious household, Misha sells his family estate for a song the moment his parents die. Always smelling of spirits, he engages in one madcap adventure after another, as if risk was a goal in itself. "I have seen something of riotous living in my day," P. observes, "but in this there was a sort of violence, a sort of frenzy of self-destruction, a desperation!"[40] The riskier the wager, the greater its appeal.

On a bet Misha descends into a steep ravine likely to kill anyone who enters it. Since he can no longer pay his losses, no one will play cards with him, so on one occasion he offers to shoot himself in the hand if he loses. Even though he wins, he shoots himself in the hand anyway, just to show he would have kept his word had he lost! He himself does not know why he behaves this way. It's a given that he will court risk but begs his uncle for reasons to do so:

> "Come, you tell me what I ought to do, what to risk my life for? This instant . . .
> "But you simply must live [. . .] Why risk your life?"
> "I can't! [. . .] You say I act thoughtlessly . . . If one starts thinking—good God, all that comes into one's head! It's only Germans who can think!"[41]

Whatever a German is, a true Russian is the opposite: that seems to be a constant of Russian thought.[42] But Misha is hardly staking his life on a card out of patriotism. Or as his uncle asks: "Why ever do you drag Russia in?"[43]

Encountering Misha reduced to beggary, his uncle offers to feed, clothe, and house him, on the condition that he stop drinking. Overjoyed, Misha consents, but soon regrets foregoing not only drink but also risk. "'I can't live like this!' he shrieked at the top of his voice. 'I can't live in your respectable, thrice-accused house! It makes me sick, and ashamed to live so quietly." Years later, when Poltyev learns of his nephew's death, he reflects that, despite all the obvious differences between him and the desperate characters (presumably the terrorists) of the present, "still, a philosopher, you must admit, would find a family likeness between him and them.... And what it all comes from, I leave the philosopher to decide."[44]

## Roulette and Revolution

According to Savinkov, a fundamental feature of the terrorist Karpovich's character "was his daring.... The more dangerous the enterprise, the more eager he was to undertake it."[45] In *August 1914*, Solzhenitsyn depicts Dmitri Bogrov, the assassin of prerevolutionary Russia's last great prime minister, as a compulsive gambler.[46] At Monte Carlo he frequented the high-stakes room. "There was no thrill like it! In half an hour you could live through a whole lifetime."[47] Terrorism represented just another kind of roulette, and in *Landmarks* Peter Struve observed that the psychology of gambling had conditioned the intelligentsia to believe that progress does not require patient work but is instead "a jackpot to be won at the gambling table of history."[48]

As a compulsive gambler as well as a former revolutionary, Dostoevsky appreciated their psychological connection. In two works he was writing simultaneously, *Crime and Punishment* and *The Gambler*, he explored the intoxicating appeal of risk and the thrill of danger. Raskolnikov, the hero of *Crime and Punishment*, is by nature a risk taker, the opposite of his prudent friend Razumikhin, who works tirelessly to improve his condition step by step. When the servant Nastasya asks Raskolnikov why he has given up earning money, he dismisses small gains. Like a revolutionary, he will settle for nothing less than a complete transformation, or, as he tells Nastasya, he wants "a whole fortune all at once." Razumikhin criticizes the radical intelligentsia for just this way of thinking.[49]

Raskolnikov returns to the scene of his crime in order to reexperience the intense thrill of the moment when he was trapped in his victims' apartment and about to be discovered by two men in the corridor. At that perilous moment, he had slipped into "in a sort of delirium," had heard with frenzied alarm the men ringing the doorbell and had watched in helpless horror the latch being pulled so hard it almost detached from the wall. He had wondered what those men would do when they realized that if the door was latched from inside, someone up to no good must be there! Having returned to the apartment as it was being repainted, Raskolnikov "went into the passage and pulled the bell. The same bell, the same cracked note. He rang it a second and a third time; he listened and remembered. The hideous and agonizingly fearful sensation he had felt then began to come back more and more vividly. He shuddered at every ring and it gave him more and more satisfaction."[50]

For much the same reason, Raskolnikov cannot resist almost confessing to Zametov. He builds suspense, leads up to the moment of maximal intensity when he is bound to confess—and then pretends it was all a joke planned in advance, when in fact he himself did not know until the last possible moment what he would do. Does he refrain from confessing to make it possible to experience the same thrill again? By now danger has become irresistible.

Just as for revolutionists the future society became almost irrelevant, so for the hero of *The Gambler* the ostensible goal of gambling, winning vast sums, ceases to matter.[51] Roulette enthralls Arkady Ivanovich because, as he observes, "I was possessed by an intense craving for risk." When he does win a fortune, he squanders it so as to start the process all over again. He was "risking more than life, and I dared to risk it," he enthuses. He loves the thought of instantaneous transformation from something worse than beggary to colossal wealth. "The point is that—one turn of the wheel and all will be changed. . . . What am I now? Zero. What may I be tomorrow? Tomorrow I may rise from the dead." After each such resurrection, he seeks new entombment.[52]

"It was not the money that I wanted," he explains, but the sheer intensity of feeling. "With what a tremor, with what a thrill at my heart, I hear the croupier's cry. . . . Even on my way to the gambling hall, as soon as I hear, two rooms away, the clink of the scattered money I almost go into convulsions." The more horrible it will be if he loses, the more he wants to play: "there really is something peculiar in the feeling when, alone in a strange land . . . and not knowing whether you will have anything to eat that day—you stake your last gulden, your very last!"[53]

As terrorists could not bear to give up their trade even when their party called for a strategic respite, so Arkady Ivanovich becomes addicted to play. "I even dream of playing," he tells the practical Englishman Mr. Astley, and as the novel closes, Astley tells him that "you have not only given up life, all your interests, private and public, the duties of a man and a citizen, your friends . . . you have even given up your memories . . . I am sure you have forgotten all the best feelings you had. . . . You will be here [gambling] still in ten years' time."[54]

Mr. Astley and Arkady Ivanovich agree that "roulette is a game preeminently for Russians," who regard work, prudence, and moderation as unbearable—as something for Germans—and define themselves as people of extremes. "To my mind all Russians are like that, or disposed to be like that," Astley asserts. "If it is not roulette it is something similar."[55]

Peace is bourgeois. "What would I be doing if I were not involved in terror?" asks the hero of *Pale Horse*. "I don't know. . . . But I know one thing for certain: I don't want to live a peaceful life. . . . What's my life without struggle, without the joyful awareness that worldly laws are not for me?" He cannot do without that "joyful awareness," and, from this perspective, the lives of victims, including mere bystanders, do not matter. "I felt bored as I always do," he remarks of his state of mind when not engaged in his "work."[56] Geifman quoted one terrorist: "I cannot live peacefully. I like danger, so as to feel the thrill."[57]

## Listen to the Music

In his essay "The Intelligentsia and the Revolution" (1918), poet Alexander Blok discovered in violence an antidote to "the *boredom*, the *triviality*" of ordinary life.[58] It will "make everything over . . . change our false, boring, hideous life . . . *this* is called *revolution*." The goal matters less than "the roar" which is "always about something *grand*—always." Russian artists, Blok insisted, must embrace everything opposed to "practical sense, moderation, tidiness; 'all that threatens ruin' [has] held for them 'ineffable delights' (Pushkin)." They must reject constitutional democracy, the rule of law, and parliamentary procedure as "such a dull and dreadful somnolence, such a thunderous yawn . . . such nameless horror."[59]

In the intensity of Blok's revolutionary fervor, Schapiro observed, "there is something of that pathos of destruction for its own sake which was so dominant [for Blok] both in Bakunin and Wagner."[60] In Blok's view, the artistic spirit even demands the destruction of art itself. "Do not be alarmed when citadels, palaces, pictures, books are destroyed" because in their place—can't you hear it?—there is "the music." Which is "more frightening," Blok asks, "the arson and lynchings in one camp, or this oppressive lack of musicality in the other?" The bourgeoisie "never dreamt of any music except the piano," and many limited souls "are going insane from the lynchings," but the intelligentsia must embrace the violent music of revolution. "With your whole body, your whole heart, your whole consciousness," Blok concluded, "listen to the Revolution."[61]

## Living in Liminality

Terrorists may sense themselves living in a special sort of timeless time and enjoying what anthropologist Victor Turner called "a permanent condition of sacred 'outsiderhood' . . . a statusless status." This, Turner explains, is a status of "liminality": "Liminal entities are neither here nor there; they are betwixt and between the positions assigned and arrayed by law, custom, convention and ceremonial. . . . The great human temptation, found most prominently among utopians, is to resist giving up the good and pleasurable qualities of that one phase [liminality] to make way for what may be the necessary hardships and dangers of the next."[62]

On his way to assassinate the tsar, Andrei, the hero of Stepniak's novel *The Career of a Nihilist*, senses his total outsiderhood from all living people. "Whilst still a living man in full command of his mental and physical energy," Stepniak explains, "he had the strange, but perfectly tangible sensation of being already dead, looking upon himself, all those connected with him, and the whole world, with the unruffled, somewhat pitying serenity of a stranger." This feeling of living posthumously frees him from ordinary concerns and places him beyond good and evil. He becomes a superman, or, in the novel's last words, one of "the chosen few."[63]

Consequences, for oneself and others, no longer matter. The present moment is all there is. Sheer liminality—betweenness, transitionality, contradiction, and freedom from all definition—becomes addictive. It confers the sense—so long as the transitional moment lasts—that anything is possible. Enthusiasm for such a moment at first bewitches Pasternak's Doctor Zhivago, who experiences revolution as "this thing that had never been before, this miracle of history, this revelation" suddenly disrupting the old world. The miracle has arrived as a pure "suddenly," which "begins not from the beginning but from the middle. . . . That's real genius. Only real greatness can be so out of place and untimely." It is "untimely" in both senses, completely unexpected and outside of time.[64]

Zhivago comes to regret this enthusiasm for liminality and people at home in it. "Something definite should have been achieved," he tells Lara. "But it turns out that those who inspired the revolution aren't at home in anything except change and turmoil. . . . For them transitional periods, worlds in the making, are an end in themselves. They aren't trained for anything else, they don't know anything except that." Trapped in liminality, in "never-ending preparations," they cannot create anything, let alone an earthly utopia. "Man is born to live, not to prepare for life," Zhivago concludes. "Life itself, the phenomenon of life, the gift of life, is so breath-takingly serious!"[65]

## Metaphysical Hatred

Blok's excitement at blowing up cathedrals and destroying books exemplifies the pleasure afforded by sheer destruction. One might suppose that those engaged in killing, stealing, and bombing would have a specific set of changes they wanted to implement, but it was often considered pointless, even bad form, to insist on a program. In Turgenev's *Fathers and Children*, dated 1861, this attitude is already commonplace among the young radicals, as we recognize when the thoroughly unoriginal Arkady voices it. When his father remarks, "you destroy everything [. . .] But one must construct too, you know," Arkady is ready with the prescribed answer: "That's not our business now." "But how destroy without even knowing why?" Arkady's uncle asks. Arkady is again prepared: "We shall destroy, because we are a force."[66]

Bakunin symbolized destructiveness for its own sake. His famous aphorism—"the will to destroy is also a creative will"—was constantly quoted, and, as J. Frank Goodwin observed, "appeared in the flyers of several groups, including the 'Anti-Authoritarians,' the 'international' group of Anarcho-Communists in Georgia, and groups in Belostok, Kiev, and Odessa."[67] One group of Anarcho-Communists called upon workers and peasants to "remember the testament of the great Bakunin."[68]

Such revolutionaries, as historian Richard Stites observes of a group of Anarcho-Futurists, envisioned "a clarifying and purifying destruction, the creation of a charred landscape of ruined churches and museums and of paintings and books reduced to ashes. For these people, and many like them, the Revolution was to be a long black light of devastation—their black banner signified nothingness, the void, annihilation."[69]

Bakunin tried to foment spontaneous destruction, a contradiction he seems not to have appreciated. In his view, revolutionaries should join with brigands and other violent criminals, who must be regarded as elemental revolutionaries. "The Catechism of a Revolutionary," which Bakunin apparently coauthored with Nechaev, recommended an alliance "with the evil world of brigands, who in Russia comprise the true and only revolutionaries."[70] As Geifman notes, one reason it is so hard to count the number of terrorist crimes is that so many criminals operated under the banner of terrorism, while terrorists, having expropriated property for their party, sometimes went into business for themselves. Plekhanov observed: "It is impossible to guess where a comrade anarchist ends and where a bandit begins."[71] When the goal is pure violence, why not also profit by it?

Such "revolutionism," Semyon Frank observed in *Landmarks*, "reflects the metaphysical absolutization of the value of destruction."[72] It is fed, in his view, by a sort of metaphysical hatred. If anxiety is fear always looking for an object, then this sort of hatred, for much the same reason, can never be satisfied. It feeds on itself.

The longing for what Schiller called "total revolution," historian Bernard Yack observed, entails "the discovery of [ever] new objects of hatred."[73] Frank explained that "*hatred* is always the psychological incentive and accompaniment of destruction, and to the degree that destruction overshadows other forms of activity, hatred displaces other impulses in the psychic life of the Russian *intelligent*." This displacement takes place even in the gentlest person because it is not "in any way a personal or selfish hatred. His faith *obliges* him to hate; hatred serves as the most profound and passionate *ethical* impulse of his life."[74]

Memoirists who knew Lenin personally stressed the role of sheer hatred in shaping his choice of violence not whenever necessary but whenever possible. Lenin may have loved people "in general" and in the abstract, Gorky wrote in 1924 from self-imposed exile. But "his love looked far ahead, through the mists of hatred."[75] Lenin lived by hatred, leapt to hatred, and relied on hatred as a source of energy. Whenever some other revolutionary disagreed with him, recalled his associate Nikolai Valentinov, "Lenin became 'rabid' during his attacks, as he himself admitted. . . . He violently hated all of them, wanted to 'smash their faces in, to stick the convict's badge on them, to insult them, to trample them underfoot, to spit on them."[76] Defeating, even killing, them was not enough, as it would have been if the security of the new regime were the sole purpose of violence.

While serving in the Bolshevik government, Steinberg noted how Lenin's face "brightened" at the very thought of mass "extermination." He quoted Lenin's demand for "the cruelest revolutionary terror": "*Thousands of enemies must pay*. . . . From now on the hymn of the working class will be a hymn of hatred and revenge, more terrible than the hymn which the Germans sing against Britain."[77]

It was in this frame of mind, Steinberg recalled, that Lenin demanded "mass terror" and the deporting or shooting of "hundreds of prostitutes"; the immediate arrest of Socialist Revolutionaries and the taking of hostages; the killing of "entire families"; and the introduction by the Cheka (secret police) of "physical torture." At such moments, Lenin's sober tactics yielded to, or perhaps were eagerly implemented by, rage and rabid hatred. He called for maximum cruelty not only against opponents but also against workers and peasants who did not identify their own interest with his, and he suspected "criminal" weakness whenever a Bolshevik favored less cruel tactics as more effective.[78]

That was true of Stalin as well. According to a well-known anecdote, which exists in many variants, Bolshevik leader Lev Kamenev described a group picnic of Bolshevik leaders in the early 1920s. When someone asked, what is the best thing in the world? Kamenev answered "books," Radek "a woman, your woman." For Stalin it was revenge against one's enemies. He ostensibly added: "My greatest pleasure is to choose one's victim, prepare one's plan minutely, slake an implacable vengeance, and then go to bed. There's nothing sweeter in the world."[79] Many have doubted the story and assumed Kamenev told it for self-interested reasons. Perhaps most remarkable is the motive Stephen Kotkin suggests: far from denigrating Stalin, Kamenev "was ingratiating himself with Stalin"![80] For a true Leninist, nothing could be sweeter than hate-filled revenge.

When hatred motivated terrorists, the "people" did not matter. Far from professing concern for the suffering masses, Savinkov observed, the terrorist Fyodor Nazarov held them in "contempt. . . . His words and actions glowed with hatred for the well fed and oppressors rather than with love for the hungry and injured."[81] In *Pale Horse*, Vanya compares the hero George to a cabman who, having lost all his wealth in a fire, now takes out his spite by "lashing his horse across the eyes. . . . That is just what you are doing, George. You want to lash everyone across the eyes." Indeed, Vanya explains, that is true of all of us. "What do we live by, my friend? We live by bare hatred. We don't know how to love."[82]

## Art and Martyrdom

Terrorism for its own sake could become a form of art. "Infatuated with the terrorist 'art for art's sake,'" its practitioners would take pride in their artistic excellence.[83] Savinkov observed this motive. The legendary Kaliayev, he explained, loved revolutionary terror the way he loved revolutionary poets like Bryusov, Bal'mont, and Blok, who were "at that time still strangers to the revolutionists": "A born poet, he loved art" of both kinds.[84] Is this what novelist-terrorist Savinkov would have said about himself?

Among female terrorists, especially those with a religious background, the goal was often martyrdom. "Self-sacrifice . . . for many revolutionary women [became] a goal in itself," observed Donna Oliver. "Helping others was in some ways secondary to the true goal of satisfying the thirst for martyrdom"—a thirst that Oliver traces to the Russian Orthodox tradition of kenoticism.[85] Princes Boris and Gleb became the first Russian saints not for anything they had done but for allowing themselves to be killed without resistance, like Jesus. In this way of thinking, goals pollute the sacrifice by making it utilitarian and therefore impure.

Vera Zasulich, we recall, explicitly denied that sympathy for the sufferings of the oppressed had anything to do with her becoming a terrorist. Martyrdom did. Fascinated in girlhood by Jesus's death, a sacrifice made when everyone had abandoned him, she never prayed to him because "I didn't want his intercession," didn't want him to save her; on the contrary, "I wanted to . . . save Him." When she lost her faith in God, Zasulich retained her desire for "a crown of thorns" and so was drawn to Nechaev and his doctrine that "a revolutionary is a doomed man."[86] For those who thought this way, the danger of violence and killing became their very point. In *Crime and Punishment*, Dostoevsky suggests that a similar motive, among others, guided Raskolnikov to his double murder: crime *for* punishment.

As a girl, Vera, the heroine of Sofya Kovalevskaya's novel *The Nihilist Girl* (*Nigilistka*), reads her nanny stories from *The Lives of Forty Martyred Men and Thirty Martyred Women*, with which she becomes obsessed. "'Why wasn't I born then?' Vera often thought with regret." She reads the account of "three English missionaries in China who had been burned at the stake by savage heathens." A neighbor, Vasiliev, at last tells her "'there are martyrs now as well.' Vera stared at him in amazement for some time. 'Ah, yes, in China,' she finally declared. Vasiliev laughed again. 'No need to look so far away. . . . Haven't you heard that here in Russia they arrest people, exile them to Siberia, and sometimes even hang them? How can you ask if there are martyrs?'"[87] The time of the saints had returned, and with it the opportunity for martyrdom (for whatever cause).

Even those who did not seek a martyr's death found self-sacrifice appealing. When she joined the executive committee of the People's Will, Vera Figner recalled, she was required to "forget . . . all ties of kinship, and all personal sympathies, love, and friendships . . . taking no thought of anything else, and sparing no one and nothing . . . to have no personal property . . . to renounce one's individual desires" and more. Far from discouraging her and others, these prescribed sacrifices proved appealing. Indeed, "if these demands had been less exigent," she observed, "they would not have satisfied us."[88]

## Self-Assertion

The fact that such motives for violence are entirely selfish did not disturb Savinkov in the least; nor was he concerned that some other revolutionaries regarded the hero of *Pale Horse* as little more than a Nietzschean cynic. George, the hero of the novel, laughs at Vanya's concern for other people:

"Why are you laughing, George?"

"You sound just like a parish priest."

"Well, so be it. But you tell me—can one live without love?"

"Of course one can."

"How? Tell me?"

"You spit at the whole world."

"Are you joking, George?"

"No, I'm not joking."[89]

Sheer self-assertion motivates George as it evidently motivated Savinkov himself. George—he has an English name presumably because in one assassination Savinkov had assumed the identity of an Englishman—expresses utter contempt for all moral justifications of killing. They say, respect one's fellow man, but what if "there's no respect [in me?]," asks George in the passage that gives *Pale Horse* its title. "I'm on the border of life and death. What do I care for words about sin? I can say about myself: 'And I looked, and beheld a pale horse: and his name that sat on him was Death.'"[90] In the presence of that horse "there is no life, and therefore no law. For death knows no law." All is permitted.

Such a terrorist kills for himself, and George eventually murders, for personal reasons, a romantic rival. In the past he could justify his killing as necessary for the revolution, he reflects. But now "I [have] killed for myself. I wanted to kill and I did. Who's the judge? Who condemns me? Who justifies me?.... Why is it all right to kill for the terror ... but for oneself—impossible? Who will answer me?"[91] Justifications are as pointless as condemnations because morality does not figure in George's thinking at all. The only difference between this killing and his earlier ones is that he has at last discarded the pretense of killing in the name of justice. He has embraced pure self-assertion.

For George, there is no moral difference between killing for a cause and just because one wants to. A pure cynic, he compares life to a puppet show (*balagan*). "The curtain has gone up and, we are on the stage. Pale Pierrot has fallen in love with Pierette. He swears his eternal love. Pierette has a fiancé. A toy pistol fires and blood flows—red cranberry juice. A street organ squeaks offstage. Curtain." As others worry about right and wrong, "the tedious merry-go-round turns. People fly into the flame like moths.... And does it really matter?" To someone who sees things as they are, it's all a "farce ... open to the public."[92]

George remembers an autumn day on the seashore when a fog obscured all outlines. That is what life is like. "There's no outline, no end or beginning. Is it vaudeville or drama? Cranberry juice or blood? A farce or real life? I don't know. Who does?"[93] The obvious answer—the person whose blood is spilled—does not impress him.

Like the Byronic heroes of Pushkin's *Eugene Onegin* and Lermontov's *Hero of Our Time*, on whom George is evidently modeled, George imagines himself as one of those "extraordinary people" whom Raskolnikov also has in mind.[94] "On the square below my window people are rushing around like black ants. Each one is busy with his . . . petty cares of the day. I despise them. Wasn't Fyodor right in essence when he said, '[I] Wish they all could be finished off with a bomb, with no exception'?" Self-assertion here verges on self-deification. "Since I have no God," George thinks, "I shall be my own god."[95]

In Savinkov's *What Never Happened*, Olga instructs Volodya about superior people:

> If a man has resolved on everything, if he has borne everything, understood everything . . . if he has looked down into the deepest of the deep . . . into the horrifying darkness, and if he has felt no terror . . . tell me, do you think he is like all the rest? . . . Or has he, perhaps, a power over people? . . . To a man like that all is permissible. You hear: all. For him there is no sin, no forbidden thing, no crime.[96]

As danger provided the conditions of martyrdom for some, it allowed others to feel their superiority to the timid adherents of ordinary morality.

Bakunin's self-assertion, like everything about him, exceeded all measure. As Aileen Kelly has shown, the reason that he could simultaneously embrace contradictory positions, such as absolute anarchism and revolutionary dictatorship, is that both satisfied his psychological needs. Those needs, indeed, explain why he turned to revolution in the first place. In Kelly's reading, what remained constant in Bakunin's tumultuous life was his quest to overcome alienation and achieve "personal wholeness," a goal he first pursued with German philosophy and later by revolutionary activity. "A mystically conceived personal wholeness remained for him the ultimate 'reality,'" Kelly explains. "Generalizing from his own needs," he came to see his personal goal "as the goal of all humanity." What differentiates his later revolutionism from his early idealism is that he sought "to realize his fantasy through the transformation of the external world. His urge for self-assertion would find expression in the idealization of the act of revolution and the will of the revolutionary leader." For Bakunin, "the attraction of all messianic socialism was that it invested the inner dialectic of the personality with apocalyptic significance." In effect, he advanced "a mystical theory of self-realization through revolutionary action."[97] Revolution for the sake of revolution was practiced by Bakunin for the sake of Bakunin.

## Suicide Substitute

Terrorism also appealed to those already intent on suicide. "Many times in my youth I had the desire to end my life," explained Boris Vnorovsky, "but each time I banished the thought, knowing what sorrow" it would cause his parents. Attending a meeting of revolutionary students, he continued, he found a better way to die. "The purpose of my life was clearly determined. What remained to be done was to find a definite program."[98] In Andrey Bely's novel *Petersburg*, Nikolay Appolonovich also discovers in terrorism a substitute for suicide.

Suicide was the purpose; some program or other an afterthought. It was just this sort of reasoning that shaped the greatest Soviet comedy, Nikolai Erdman's *The Suicide*. When word gets around that Semyon Podsekalnikov plans to kill himself, various people plead with him to leave a note saying he did it for their cause! Why waste a good suicide? If he is to adhere to the best traditions of the intelligentsia, after all, he must end his life not for selfish reasons, blaming no one else, but as a protest against some injustice. The *intelligent* Aristarkh Dominikovich Goloschapov explains:

> *Aristarkh:* You cannot do that, Citizen Podsekalnikov [. . .] Who needs this, just tell me, "no one is to blame"? On the contrary, you ought to blame and accuse, Citizen Podsekalnikov. You are shooting yourself. Splendid. An excellent idea. Go right ahead. . . . But when you shoot, shoot yourself as a member of society. Don't forget you are not alone, Citizen Podsekalnikov. Just look around you, look at our intelligentsia . . . I'm afraid you don't quite understand why you're shooting yourself. Let me explain it for you.
>
> *Semyon:* By all means, please do.
>
> *Aristarkh:* You want to perish for the sake of truth.
>
> *Semyon:* Say, that's an idea!. . . .
>
> *Aristarkh:* The whole Russian intelligentsia will gather around your coffin, Citizen Podsekalnikov. The elite of the nation will carry

you from here onto the street. You will be buried with wreaths, Citizen Podsekalnikov. Your catafalque will sink in flowers, and beautiful horses with white pompoms will bear you to the cemetery, Citizen Podeskalnikov.

*Semyon:* Wow, what a life![99]

As suggested reasons, each with the appropriate suicide note, proliferate, it becomes unclear which one, if any, Podsekalnikov will choose:

*Alexander:* Tell me, comrades, what do you pay for when you buy a lottery ticket? For fate. For participating in a risk, comrades. That's the present situation with Podsekalnikov. The unforgettable deceased is still alive, but there is a large number of suicide notes. . . . For example, there are such notes as these: "I am dying as a victim of nationalism—crushed by the Jews." "Life is unbearable due to insufficient living space." "In my death, do not blame anyone except our beloved Soviet government," and so on, and so on. All of these notes will be offered to him, and which one he'll choose, comrades, I have no way of knowing.

*Aristarkh:* By the way, comrades, he has already chosen one. He is shooting himself for the sake of the intelligentsia. . . . What concerns the Russian intelligentsia cannot wait any longer.

*Pugachev:* How about trade, comrades, do you think it can wait?

*Victor:* How about sacred art? . . .

*Aristarkh:* Try to recall how it used to be. In earlier days, people who had ideas were willing to die for them. But now those who have ideas want to live. . . . It is now more than ever that we need ideologically dead bodies. . . .

*Raisa:* One dead man is not enough to go around.[100]

## Liberal Support

The mystique of the revolutionist enchanted many peaceful folk. Without their encouragement, as historians have pointed out, the revolutionaries could not have succeeded. The terrorists could count on support of all kinds, and the killers occupied the moral high ground.

In *The Career of a Nihilist*, Stepniak characterizes Repin, the liberal father of a daughter married to a terrorist, as "one of that huge and diversified circle of friendly people which in Russia surrounds each and all the conspirators." Repin loves his son-in-law and, despite his own old-fashioned skepticism, still finds his "singleness of purpose" attractive. "So—[with] the peculiar feeling of the best among the Liberals toward the revolutionists helping him," Repin does what he can to aid the conspirators.[101]

In her memoirs, terrorist Vera Figner explained that "society" could not resist the "magnetic" charm of "the cult of dynamite and the revolver." So common was terror that "society saw no escape from the existing [dangerous] condition; one group sympathized with the violence practiced by the party, while others regarded it only as a necessary evil—but even they applauded the valor and skill of the champion." Besides, "the repetition of such events made them a normal part of society's life" and respectable people regarded it as bad taste to be shocked by it. What ultimately brought society to the terrorists' side, Figner stressed, was the mystique of danger that made them shine as "examples of self-sacrifice and heroism, persons of rare civic virtues."[102]

The Russian liberal party, the Kadets (Constitutional Democrats), and its predecessor, the Union of Liberation, cheered and encouraged the terrorists.[103] Although they did not themselves practice violence, they collected funds for terrorists. Historians often explain this support as a tactic. If the government could be pressured to yield significant political power, the Kadets must have reasoned, then they would be the beneficiaries. True enough, but the charm of revolutionism also played a significant role. Neither the Kadet Party nor its newspaper *Rech'* ever denounced terrorism, as Geifman points out, even when revolutionaries tossed explosives into Riga streetcars or threw bombs, made more lethal by the addition of nails and bullets, into a large family café with two hundred customers present in order "to see how the foul bourgeois would squirm in death agony." When a confused terrorist murdered an elderly man she mistook for the minister of the interior, *Rech'* opined: "In these difficult times, it does not matter if there is one person more or less in the world." Kadet leader N. N. Shchepkin declared that the party "no longer considers the so-called political criminals to be criminals." On the contrary, they were saints: in an article in *Rech'* praising terrorist "Marusia" (an affectionate version of Maria) Spiridonova following her murder of Tambov official Gavrila Luzhenovsky, V. Azov enthused: "her life [*zhizn'*] ended. And then her saint's life [*zhitie*] began."[104]

Amazingly enough, the Kadets condemned all government attempts to defend itself. Seizing killers on the street was treacherous while arresting women assassins offended feminine modesty. Terrorists "undertook their acts relatively confident that if caught and tried they would in all likelihood be rescued from the most severe measures by the interference of their liberal lawyers, and by pressure from the sympathetic public opinion of society at large." One police department official described the paralyzing effect of leniency on the regime's defenders: "The latest verdicts in political trials are truly horrifying," he explained. "For after several months, all those convicted, having [already] spent their terms in confinement, return to the path of revolutionary activity with redoubled energy."[105]

Despite propaganda circulated at home and abroad, punishment was anything but brutal. Spiridonova, who spent ten years in penal servitude for murdering a tsarist official, observed that in her prison "there was complete freedom. The prisoners ... were allowed to take walks deep into the forests for the whole day.... Fathers and husbands ... lived with their [families] and showed up at the prison just to make themselves seen." In Kiev an imprisoned group of revolutionaries directed a local strike and issued proclamations. Escape was astonishingly easy, to the point where, the police official discouraged by short sentences observed, "the only people who did not run away ... were those who did not want to do so."[106]

## Liberal Self-Destruction

Shortly after Pyotr Stolypin became chair of the Council of Ministers in 1906, terrorists tossed bombs into his residence during an open house he was holding for petitioners. Twenty-seven people were killed and thirty-two wounded, including Stolypin's two children. In fact, assassinations were a daily event; the commander of the Black Sea fleet and the governors of Saratov and Warsaw died at the hands of terrorists. Monarchists responded with counterterrorism. As historian Richard Pipes pointed out, "no government in the world could have remained passive in the face of such violence."[107] Stolypin then introduced field courts to try and punish those whose guilt was obvious; the accused were allowed witnesses but not lawyers. This law remained in effect for eight months and some one thousand death sentences were handed down. Outraged liberals condemned Stolypin and treated the terrorists as victims rather than as perpetrators of violence. One Kadet leader, Fyodor Rodichev, referred to the new gallows as "Stolypin's neckties," a term that was constantly repeated.

Although Nicholas II granted a political amnesty in April 1906, the Kadets insisted on "total" amnesty, including terrorists pledged to continue their killing.[108]

Solzhenitsyn also cites the famous statement by Kadet leader I. Petrunkevich: "Condemn terror? Never! That would mean the moral death of the party."[109]

Didn't the liberals see that they were playing with fire? Before 1917 was over, the Bolsheviks proclaimed the Kadets "enemies of the people" who were "outside the law," which meant anyone could do anything to them. Almost immediately two Kadet ex-ministers in the provisional government, patients in a Petersburg hospital, were lynched.[110] And that was just the beginning.

The Bolsheviks sentenced not only the Kadets, but also the various openly revolutionary parties, to annihilation. In June 1918 they condemned Mensheviks and Socialist Revolutionaries as counterrevolutionaries, and by late summer, Lenin was practicing terror against them.[111] The show trial of the Socialist Revolutionaries took place in 1922.[112] From the very start, the Bolsheviks arrested the families, including children, of renowned non-Bolshevik revolutionaries. The eleven-year-old daughter of Socialist Revolutionary leader Victor Chernov "spent weeks of semi-starvation in an icy cell in the infamous Lubyanka prison."[113]

Many Socialist Revolutionaries and Mensheviks were shocked that the Bolsheviks would treat fellow revolutionaries much worse than the tsars had ever done and that the terror they had directed at others was now directed at them. Since Lenin never concealed his preference for violence, and had amply demonstrated his absolute intolerance of any disagreement, their naïveté was all the more remarkable.[114]

Could the reason for their surprise, and for Kadet applause for terrorism, lie in the mystique of the revolutionist and the magical appeal of political violence itself?

## The Slide

Numerous critics have noticed what might be called "the slide," the tendency to adopt more and more extreme violence. This process, of course, has occurred in many countries, as Russian radicals, who obsessively studied the French Revolution, recognized. "A typical struggle between Jacobins and anti-Jacobins, terrorists and anti-terrorists, led to the decisive victory of the Jacobins and terrorists," historian Philip Pomper observed of the French and Russian examples.[115] The process of radicalization, once started, repeats and the terrorists grow ever more terrible.

Geifman stresses the emergence in this way of "terrorists of the new type" who eagerly embraced the seamy side of revolutionism.[116] From killing specific people only when necessary, they rapidly advanced to killing random people whenever possible. Soon enough, sheer sadism became common. "The need to inflict pain was transformed from an abnormal compulsion experienced only by unbalanced personalities into a formally verbalized obligation for all committed revolutionaries," Geifman explains. Some people were thrown into vats of boiling water; others were mutilated both before and after death.[117] When Stalin introduced torture as the normal investigatory procedure halfway through the Great Terror, he was drawing on revolutionary tradition.

What explains this dynamic, which, as Pomper observed, has been "repeated in the history of other revolutionary organizations, both populist and Marxist"?[118]

To answer this question, Pomper pointed to yet another motive for terrorism practiced as an end in itself: the craving of lonely and alienated young people for an especially tightly knit community, a family bound together by the imminence of death. That craving proved especially intense with adolescents (some 22 percent of Socialist Revolutionary terrorists were between the ages of fifteen and nineteen) and children.[119] Once committed to the life of a professional revolutionary, a young person formed "close ties . . . in the process of apprenticeship, commitment, shared sacrifices, and satisfying organizational work—in short, socialization in a kind of 'radical fraternity.'" It was this socialization that, in Pomper's view, "created the emotional basis for acceptance of escalation to increasingly radical tactics."[120]

The terrorist novels of Savinkov and Stepniak evoke the deliciously tragic aura of love facing imminent death when, as Stepniak phrases it, "the sword of Damocles hung constantly" over lovers' heads. When Andrei and Tania marry in *The Career of a Nihilist*, Stepniak explains that this union differed from ordinary ones because "they had not even any illusion as to its longevity. . . . Any day and hour might be their last. . . . But they did not complain of this. The dangers which surrounded their path were the torch-bearers of their love" and made it burn all the more intensely.[121]

The proximity of death intensifies and transforms friendship as well. True comradeship subsists only among revolutionary comrades. It exists only in the fraternity of the Party.

When Stalin accused old Bolsheviks of preposterous crimes they could not possibly have committed, they confessed—or so this explanation goes—because they could not imagine life outside the Party. Arthur Koestler's novel *Darkness at Noon* explores the psychology of such an emotional tie with great subtlety. When the novel's hero—based on Bolshevik leader Nikolai Bukharin, whom Stalin had executed—reviews his life, he finds that it does not exist outside the Party. "His past was the movement, the Party; present and future, too, belonged to the Party, were inseparably bound up with its fate; but his past was identical with it."[122]

## Terror without End

The dynamic of ever-increasing violence also derives from another cause. For those addicted to the thrill of danger and the intensity of the moment, familiar violence soon becomes routine and ceases to have the desired effect. As with addictive drugs, larger and larger doses are needed. The war on boredom grows boring; repeated violence soon seems almost peaceful; and the struggle against everydayness turns into an everyday affair that one must struggle against.

When the Bolsheviks seized power, they hastened to employ terror. A decree on "Red Terror" (the Bolsheviks adopted the term proudly), issued on December 20, 1917, created the infamous Cheka (later called OGPU, NKVD, MVD, and KGB). In 1918 the Politburo began organizing "concentration camps" (again, their term). Lenin made absolutely clear that Bolsheviks were to regard terror not as a last resort but as the default option.

To staff the rapidly growing Cheka, Lenin recruited former agents of the Okhrana (tsarist secret police), who wound up operating alongside their former prisoners, the revolutionary terrorists.[123] These terrorists were numerous and eager for suitable employment, and many who had worked for parties opposed to Bolsheviks "joined and often led such organs of state-sponsored terrorism as the provincial and district sections of the infamous Cheka.... Former terrorists also worked in the revolutionary tribunals [with summary power to condemn the accused to death]" and in other "repressive organs."[124] This readiness to work for one's erstwhile opponents reflects the spirit of pure revolutionism where ideology matters less than the practice of terrorism itself.

## Terrorists as Rulers

> There is no greater joy, there is no better music
> Then a crushing sound of smashed bones and lives.
> —POEM IN THE ANTHOLOGY *CHEKA SMILE*[125]

What would those addicted to terror do now that the only restraint on them, the tsarist police, no longer existed? The answer was, in Geifman's words, "unrestricted violence" against "real and alleged counterrevolutionaries, as well as the peaceful population of remote areas. Mass murder, robbery, rape, beatings, and torture were common ... startling sadism was rampant within the Cheka, the tribunals, the people's militia ... and local Soviet government appointees."[126]

We usually think of mass terror as Stalin's idea, but, as numerous historians have pointed out, that is a mistake. The mass terror that characterized Soviet rule in the 1930s resumed Leninist practice, which in turn grew directly out of the Russian terrorist tradition.[127] Stalin was himself a former terrorist bandit.

The glee with which Bolshevik leaders encouraged, indeed demanded, violence still shocks those who read about it. Trotsky insisted that Bolsheviks must "put an end once and for all of the papist-Quaker babble about the sanctity of human life" and in a telegram to comrades in Astrakhan instructed: "Execute mercilessly." Right from the start, the Cheka arrested and executed people randomly. "We must execute not only the guilty," explained Commissar of Justice Nikolai Krylenko. "Execution of the innocent will impress the masses even more." Lenin recommended public hanging as especially impressive.[128]

During the Red Terror the government decreed that "class enemies *and their relatives*" be dispatched to concentration camps.[129] Stalin's policy of arresting families, relatives, and even ex-spouses of "enemies of the people" drew on previous Bolshevik practice.

In the ninety-two years between the Decembrist revolt of 1825 and the revolution of 1917, the tsarist regime, regarded everywhere as Europe's most oppressive, issued 6,321 death sentences, not all of which were carried out. In two months of terror, the new Bolshevik regime executed between 10,000 and 15,000.[130] Continuing the practice of some prerevolutionary terrorists, the Cheka made torture commonplace, with local Cheka units developing expertise in particular ways of inflicting pain. One specialized in scalping, another in burning alive, still another in crucifixion. The Kiev Cheka liked to put prisoners in a coffin with a decaying body. "Throughout the country," S. P. Mel'gunov wrote in his study *"Krasnyi terror" v Rossii* [*Red Terror in Russia*], "without investigation or trial, the Chekists . . . tortured old men and raped schoolgirls and killed parents before the eyes of their children. They impaled people . . . [and] locked them in cells where the floor was covered in corpses."[131] Lenin, believe it or not, regarded his agents as too soft. "If we are guilty of anything," he maintained, "it is of having been too humane, too benevolent."[132]

"As early as 26 October (8 November [in the new calendar])," Dmitri Volkogonov wrote in his biography of Lenin, the Bolshevik leader "personally penned a draft on workers' control in which 'negligence, the concealment of supplies, accounts, and so on will be punished by confiscation of property and up to five years' imprisonment.'"[133] October 26 / November 8 was the day after the Bolsheviks seized power. The decree's telling phrase "and so on" (or etc.)

recurred in Lenin's orders, for example in the August 1918 directive "to apply mass terror immediately, to execute and exterminate hundreds of prostitutes, drunken soldiers, former officers, etc." When the Petrograd Soviet restrained elements who wanted to practice random terror, Lenin reversed them: "This is unheard of!" he wrote. "The energy and mass nature of the terror must be encouraged."[134]

Something beyond Machiavellian ruthlessness was involved. The Red Terror was also revolutionism without limit.

## Terror as Law

"When we are reproached with cruelty," Lenin declared, "we wonder how people can forget the most elementary Marxism."[135] He had a point: why would anyone who had read Bolshevik pronouncements, including Lenin's many calls for terror and civil war, have expected anything else?

Lenin made it clear that terror was no temporary expedient until power was secure. In his famous article "A Contribution to the History of the Question of the Dictatorship," he wrote: "The scientific term 'dictatorship' means nothing more nor less than authority untrammeled by any laws, absolutely unrestricted by any rules whatever, and based directly on force. The term 'dictatorship' *has no other meaning but this*—mark this well, Kadet gentlemen."[136] He insisted that this power to do absolutely anything to anyone at any time must become a permanent feature of the new society. When D. I. Kursky, People's commissar of justice, was formulating the new Russian (RSFSR) legal code, Lenin instructed: "The law should not abolish terror ... it should be substantiated and legalized in principle, without evasion or embellishment."[137] The thrill of terror would never have to end.

## The Revolutionist's Suicide

The tumult did subside, if only temporarily. Eventually, the mass famine created by the attempt to abolish money, criminalize speculation (that is, any buying, selling, or trading outside of official control), and rely solely on force to make peasants surrender their grain, compelled the regime to adopt the New Economic Policy (NEP) restoring a measure of market activity. This respite was to be as brief as possible. "It is the biggest mistake to think that the NEP will put an end to the terror," Lenin wrote to Bolshevik leader Lev Kamenev in 1922. "We shall return to the terror, and to economic terror."[138]

All the same, the NEP struck many as a betrayal of revolutionary hopes. Especially distressing to revolutionists was the return to everyday life. Blok, who had heard the music of revolution, despaired "when bureaucracy, dishonesty, and corruption inevitably began to replace the élan of 1917." "The louse has conquered the world," he wrote.[139] Mayakovsky's image for the triumph of everydayness was "the bedbug" (the title of his most famous play).

Sooner or later, liminality must end and everyday life return. The disappointed belief that the liminal condition might continue forever, and revolutionary thrill never end, occasioned a special revolutionist's suicide. In the poem attached to his suicide note, Mayakovsky famously lamented: "Love's boat has smashed against everydayness [*byt*]."[140]

Historians and memoirists have often wondered how Stalin could persuade millions of people to turn on each other. Why did so many young idealists flock to the countryside to enforce a famine engineered to take the lives of millions of peasants—to take bits of food from emaciated families starving before their eyes and prevent them from fishing or gathering tiny amounts of grain left in the fields? How did the regime recruit so many agents willing to torture innocent people during interrogation?

One answer may be that Stalin offered a return to revolutionary élan, a new liminality, when anything is possible. The already fantastic five-year plan would be finished in four years; Alexei Stakhanov could mine 102 tons of coal, fourteen times his quota, in six hours; human nature would be entirely remade. At one point Stalin had to caution against the widespread belief that Bolsheviks can literally "achieve anything" and do so "in a trice" in defiance of the laws of nature binding on non-Leninists.[141] The Great Terror of 1936–1938 waged war on everydayness as it promised to create what historian Stephen Kotkin has called "permanent emergency rule."[142]

Far from a betrayal of revolutionary hopes, as anti-Stalinist Marxists later claimed, Stalinist terror may have revived them. It is worth noting that Western intellectual sympathy for the Soviet regime, once so far-reaching, virtually disappeared when it later became much less repressive.

Terror appealed to the revolutionism in so many of us.

## Herzen's Courage

Late in his life, Alexander Herzen recognized the dangers of revolutionism, exemplified by his old friend Bakunin. In his letters "To an Old Comrade," Herzen rebuked Bakunin for promoting revolution always and everywhere, regardless of circumstances. He called to mind cases where young people rushed into hopeless insurrections, lost their lives, and wound up strengthening their opponents. In addition to prudence in the choice and timing of methods, Herzen continued, one also needs a firm idea what will replace the old order, or one may wind up creating conditions as bad as or worse than before. "Too impatient people" may thoughtlessly destroy what should be preserved. "In dealing a blow to the old world," Herzen cautioned, the new order "not only must save all that is worth saving but leave intact that which does not interfere, which is different and original." "Every impatient attempt to evade or skip a stage" risks establishing a "world of moral slavery and subjection to authority" instead of "the world of *freedom of thought*."[143]

In the most famous passage of these open letters, Herzen rejected the revolutionist contempt for moderation. "The term 'gradual progress' holds no terrors for me. . . . Mathematics is transmitted gradually; why then assume that man can be inoculated with final deductions . . . like a vaccination against smallpox?" The alternative to thoughtful, steady improvement is "civilization by means of the knout and liberation by means of the guillotine." "Or should we rush into battle and . . . proceed to establish the new order, the new form of emancipation, by resorting to a massacre?"[144]

In short, Herzen confessed, "I do not believe in the former revolutionary paths." With an eye on intelligentsia intolerance, Herzen concluded his second letter with a comment we have already cited: "To say this in the circle in which we live demands, if not more, then certainly not less courage and independence than to take a most extreme side in all questions."[145] For Herzen, such courage to speak truth to intelligentsia power is needed because, in spite of all that experience might demonstrate, revolutionary élan maintains its appeal, and perhaps always will. Good intentions pave the road to hell even when earlier roads leading there are clearly visible.

Some thinkers have sadly concluded that the enchantment Nadezhda Mandelstam recognized in the word revolution, "to which whole nations have succumbed," continues to bewitch intellectuals. In his argument with dissident scientist Andrei Sakharov, Solzhenitsyn accused him of having "contracted the squint characteristic of the age—viewing all revolutions with general approval." This failing is not "personal," Solzhenitsyn opined, but "is the result . . . of the general hypnosis of a whole generation, which cannot wake up abruptly" and learn the danger of revolutionism in its many forms. "No," Solzhenitsyn admonished, "let us not wish either 'revolution' or 'counter-revolution' on our worst enemies."[146]

## Grossman's Question

Vasily Grossman's *Life and Fate* poses a question: Why did so many people not only accept unprecedented cruelty to others but even rush to their own annihilation? Secret police chief Yezhov was not the only one to proclaim on his way to execution that he would die with Stalin's name on his lips. In her memoirs *Into the Whirlwind*, Evgeniya Ginzburg wondered at innocent people sent to the Gulag who remain loyal Stalinists.[147]

It is all the more remarkable, then, that Ginzburg, though critical of Stalin, remained a Leninist and continued to approve of the collectivization of agriculture that took millions of lives! "I felt obscurely," she explained, "that Stalin was the inspiration behind the nightmare events in our party, but I could not say that I disagreed with the party line, it would have been a lie. I had honestly and with all my heart supported the policies of industrializing the country and collectivizing the land, and these were the basic points of the party line."[148] She did not understand editor Alexander Tvardovsky's shock that she objected only to Stalin's persecution of innocent Communists: "She thought it quite natural when they were exterminating the Russian peasantry."[149]

Evidently, her emotional tie to revolution mattered more to her than its disastrous results:

> And yet even now, after everything that has happened to us, would we have voted for any régime other than the soviet, the one that had grown as close to us as our hearts and as natural to us as breathing? All I had—the thousands of books I had read, the memories of my youth, even the endurance that kept me going—I owed to the revolution, which had become my world when I was still a child. What interesting lives we had led, and how wonderfully everything had begun![150]

Mystified by reactions like these, which he also describes in his novel *Forever Flowing*, Grossman ponders "cases of huge queues being formed by people awaiting execution—and it was the victims themselves who regulated the movement of those queues. . . . Millions of people lived in vast camps that had not only been built by prisoners but even guarded by them."[151]

For Grossman, the twentieth century demonstrates that revolutionism, almost irrespective of ideology, can lead people to do anything. The magic of "the Revolution" renders destruction and murder sacred. "The violence of a totalitarian State is so great as to be no longer a means to an end; it becomes an object of mystical worship," the narrator of *Life and Fate* observes:

> How else can one explain the way certain intelligent, thinking Jews declared the slaughter of the Jews to be necessary for the happiness of mankind? That in view of this they were willing to take their own children to be executed—ready to carry out the sacrifice once demanded of Abraham? How else can one explain the case of a gifted, intelligent poet, himself a peasant by birth, who with sincere conviction wrote a long poem celebrating the terrible years of suffering undergone by the peasantry, years that had swallowed up his own father, an honest and simple laborer?[152]

## Understanding the Preposterous

Westerners have often expressed surprise at Stalin's doctrine of the intensification of the class struggle (that is, of violence) *after* the revolution when no more enemies were visible—the doctrine that justified "liquidating" millions.[153] Why go to the expense of employing vast number of interrogators to torture people into confessing obviously imaginary crimes? Many regimes destroy their enemies, but why murder the unshakably loyal? "Hitler went after the Jews ... Communists, and Social Democrats, but in the USSR Stalin savaged his own loyal elites," Kotkin observed. He did things that neither Hitler nor any other tyrannical leader had ever done or could have done.

> Could Hitler—had he been so inclined—have compelled the imprisonment and execution of ... the personnel of Nazi central ministries, thousands of his Wehrmacht high command—as well as the Reich's diplomatic corps and its espionage agents. ... Could Hitler also have decimated the Gestapo even *while* it was carrying out a mass bloodletting. ... And could the German people have been told, and would the German people have found plausible, that almost everyone who had come to power with the Nazi revolution turned out to be a foreign agent and saboteur?[154]

As Kotkin concluded, "even among ideological dictatorships, [Soviet] Communism stands out." What sense did it make to execute almost all top army and navy officers on the eve of war, and why would secret police agents willingly torture their own—that is, themselves in the near future? "There is in Stalin's terror," historian Adam Ulam observed, "an element of sheer preposterousness which defies explanation."[155]

If one is looking for the usual sort of rational explanation, it may be true that Stalin's actions make no sense. But if one bears in mind the logic of revolutionism—which demands constant intensification, shock, and the deliberate defiance of everyday thinking—they fit the prerevolutionary pattern, now with unlimited power at the revolutionists' disposal.

## Zhivago's Regret

When Yuri Zhivago sees the horrors revolution has brought, he regrets his early days of revolutionary fervor: "Only once in his life had this uncompromising language and single-mindedness filled him with enthusiasm. Was it possible that he must pay for that rash enthusiasm all his life, by never hearing, year by year, anything but these unchanging, shrill, crazy exclamations and demands. . . . Was it possible that because of one moment of overgenerous response he had been enslaved forever?"[156]

Zhivago understands that no experience can ever extinguish revolutionism's appeal. In *Revolutionary Dreams*, Richard Stites cited Lev Kopelev's evocation of "rosy memories of the twenties" as "a 'golden age'. . . . Today we know that the romantic revolutionary passions which we recalled so many times with such sweet sorrow degenerated in some men into a fervent desire to serve as executioners." All the same, and despite all the consequences, Kopelev continued, the fervor of those "revolutionary passions" should be cherished. "I still think that the time was alive and bursting with youth. Not only with my tender youth and that of people of my own age, but with the youth of the century."[157]

Stites shared this sentiment. The Stalinist outcome, in his view, must not diminish utopian hopes and revolutionary passions. To be sure, he conceded, "it may be natural in the second half of the twentieth century—the most self-consciously brutal in the history of mankind—to scorn utopian ideals." And of course, he added, "utopianism is often naïve, innocent, and childlike."

> But what virtue is more admired in the whole catalogue of human art and sensibility than childlike enthusiasm . . . ? What is more lamented than our loss of youth, romance, openness to change, thirst for adventure, and the absence of refined callousness and cold sense of "reality"? These characteristics of the utopian imagination appeal to every gen-

eration that discovers it.... The warming springtime of human hope does not give in to the wintry smiles of the cynic and the realist; it blossoms and it perishes in the sad autumnal winds. And then it is born again—forever and ever.[158]

This perpetual vitality is precisely what Doctor Zhivago fears. It ensures that experience, if it is remembered at all, will never matter. "'What an enviable blindness!' thought the doctor.... Don't they remember their own plans and measures, which long since turned life upside down? What kind of people are they, to go on raving with this never-cooling, feverish ardor, year in, year out ... to know nothing, to see nothing ... ?'"[159]

One lesson of the Russian experience is that no consequences will extinguish the youthful appeal of the thrilling, dangerous, and addictive violence of the devoted revolutionist.

Another is that the danger of revolutionism is not confined to the destruction it immediately causes. It may lead to ever more horror exceeding anything presently imaginable.

# PART THREE

# TIMELESS QUESTIONS

# 6  What Can't Theory Account For?

## Theoretism and Its Discontents

> Abstraction is dear to me:
> From it I create my life [ . . . ]
> I love everything secluded and recondite.
>
> —ZINAIDA GIPPIUS

"IT HAS BEEN SAID that 'green is the tree of life and grey the theory thereof,'" wrote Nicholas Berdyaev in his autobiography, but for Berdyaev himself, and for Russian thinkers as he views them, 'the reverse is true: 'grey is the tree of life and green the theory thereof.' . . . What is known as 'life' . . . is, as often as not, an embodiment of the commonplace. . . . 'Theory,' on the other hand may be understood as creative vision . . . which raises us above the habits of daily life."[1]

"We made friends, quarreled, made up, quarreled again and made up again, were at loggerheads, loved one another madly, lived and fell in love by theory, by the book, spontaneously and consciously," Belinsky wrote to his friend V. P. Botkin.[2] "Spontaneously," because living by abstractions was natural to such thinkers; "consciously," because they chose to pursue this natural inclination as far as possible.

Belinsky, we have seen, experienced abstractions as more vital than the people and conditions around him. He, and those who resembled him, regarded everything empirical, individual, and contingent as so many phantoms. As in Plato's allegory of the cave, those who treat the empirical as the real are deluded by mere shadows.

"Everything that is particular, contingent, and irrational is *illusion . . . appearance* and not *essence*," Belinsky wrote. "Man eats, drinks, dresses himself: that is the world of illusions because his spirit plays no part in it. [On the other hand,] Man feels, thinks, knows himself to be an organ and a vessel of spirit, a finite particularization of the general and infinite: that is the world of *reality*."[3] For Belinsky, as for so many of his contemporaries, it was Hegel who offered a new revelation, but over subsequent decades other systematizers played this role. In a self-critical moment, Belinsky referred to "the terrific spell which is cast on common sense by the spirit of system and the charm of a cut and dried idea accepted as gospel . . . the spirit of system and doctrine has an astonishing power to befuddle the clearest of minds."[4]

Herzen became one of Russia's great debunkers of systems, but in the 1840s their charm seduced him, too. He later offered a much-quoted description of the mind wholly devoted to theory:

> One must live philosophy through, not assimilate it formally. To suffer through the phenomenology of spirit [of Hegel], to bleed with the heart's hot blood . . . and surrender everything to truth—such is the lyrical poem of education in science. Science becomes a terrible vampire, a spirit, which cannot be banished by any invocation because man himself has called it forth out of his own breast. . . . One must abandon the pleasant thought of engaging at a certain time of day in conversation with philosophers.[5]

For Herzen, the feeling of wholly surrendering to philosophical ideas resembles the sensations of gamblers staking their last thaler. For those willing to risk everything, everything changes: "he who loses his soul *will win it*." Then philosophy reveals truths like those "written in fiery letters by the prophet Daniel."[6]

For the rest of his life, Herzen would describe philosophical propositions in religious terms. Given his skepticism of religious dogma, that comparison cut two ways. To use Isaiah Berlin's famous terms, he became in turns hedgehog and fox; not only Hegel's systematizing but also Voltaire's skepticism entranced him.[7] "There is no universally valid idea from which man has not woven a rope to bind his own feet, and if possible, the feet of others," Herzen warned. "Love, friendship, tribal loyalty, and finally even *love of freedom* have served as inexhaustible sources of moral oppression and servitude."[8]

Bakhtin coined the term "theoretism" to designate the belief that abstractions are more real than experience.[9] For the theoretist, the concrete facts of reality can illustrate his system but can never overturn it, any more than a badly drawn triangle could refute trigonometry. As Bakhtin defined his neologism, not every theory qualifies as theoretism. Theories may be tentative, open to revision, and capable of being disconfirmed in light of new facts. That is how Francis Bacon described the scientific enterprise.

Here then is the first great accursed question we shall examine: what is the proper role of social theory? How certain could it be? How should specific individual people and events be understood and evaluated? Is there contingency or a residue that theory cannot account for? Should a good theory be open or closed to disconfirmation, and should we accept it as more or less real than the reality it explains? Newton, after all, did not keep examining how individual apples fall; he formulated a universal law of gravity. Would it not be possible to do the same for people, and should we try? What are the ethical and political implications of each view of theory? What behavior does each invite?

## Argument by Dynamite: Vera Figner

Dostoevsky's Grand Inquisitor divides people into two groups, the vanishingly few willing to live in a world of uncertainty and the overwhelming majority who require indubitable answers. The former value freedom while the latter—let us call them certaintists—willingly surrender it to authorities claiming perfect knowledge. The certaintist's ideal world tolerates no disagreement, which seems as demented as disputing the Pythagorean theorem. In short, as the Inquisitor explains, "the universal and everlasting craving of humanity" is "to find some one to worship . . . man seeks to worship what is established beyond dispute, so that all men would agree at once to worship it . . . what is essential is that all may be *together* in it."[10]

The specific doctrine accepted by such worshippers matters less than its capacity to banish doubt. In the Soviet period, skepticism constituted "spineless liberalism," the philosophy of weaklings professing a pusillanimous "agnosticism" instead of forthright atheism. How could anything short of total commitment constitute a virtue?

The Bolsheviks were not the only ones to reject skepticism. "My thinking does not proceed by way of some inner dialogue, in which I meet and resolve doubts and objections raised by my own mind," Berdyaev explained. "On the contrary, I always tended to project the objections to my thought outward into the opponents of my ideas and convictions, with whom I then proceeded to wage war. . . . Have I ever doubted at all?"[11]

It should come as no surprise that terrorists despised doubt. How could hesitant souls, constantly reexamining their own premises, ever resolve to kill? In her memoir, terrorist Vera Figner addressed readers who, she evidently assumed, agree with her, as if anyone worth addressing would have to. She therefore wrote matter-of-factly about how, in the failed attempt to assassinate the tsar by dynamiting the winter palace, "fifty soldiers were mutilated and killed. The amount of dynamite proved insufficient however, to destroy the dining room on the upper floor" and kill the tsar. All the same, "society, at any rate its more intelligent element, greeted our activity with great enthusiasm, and offered us sympathetic aid and ardent approval."[12]

Explaining how she became a terrorist, Figner identified not a gradual process but a series of sudden revelations. Once a truth had been revealed to her, she boasted, doubting was impossible and action became mandatory. Since no truth was qualified, the action taken always had to be the most extreme possible.

"From Uncle I heard for the first time the theory of utilitarianism," she recalled. "'The greatest good for the greatest number of men,' said Uncle, 'should be the aim of every person,' and I was impressed by this thought. My mind was not encumbered with notions and doubts. . . . On the contrary, the doctrine of utilitarianism at once appeared to me a manifest truth."

It was also the whole truth: there was never any competing principle to consider. "It was inconceivable for me not to act upon that which I had acknowledged as true . . . every truth once recognized as such thereby became compulsory for my will."[13]

Why did utilitarianism entail liberalism in England while in Russia it became synonymous with revolutionary terrorism? The answer may be that in England it figured as one of many truths. When it led to unappealing results, John Stuart Mill was willing to question it; indeed, he insisted on questioning his own beliefs and giving a fair hearing to opposing views. "He who knows only his own side of the case knows little of that," he famously argued.[14] That was not the part of Mill that appealed to Russians.

Figner lost respect for her father when he replied to a serious question, "I do not know." This answer filled her with "burning shame."[15] Admirable people *know*, they do not merely opine. Reasonable people do not differ.

According to Aristotle, practical judgment, based on experience rather than logical deduction, can at best be true "on the whole and for the most part" (one of Aristotle's favorite phrases). "Our discussion will be adequate if it has as much clearness as the subject-matter admits of, for precision is not to be sought for alike in all discussions," Aristotle explained in the *Nichomachean Ethics*. "We must be content, then, in speaking of such subjects . . . to indicate the truth roughly and in outline, and in speaking about things which are only for the most part true and with premises of the same kind to reach conclusions that are no better. For it is the mark of an educated man to look for precision in each class of things just so far as the nature of the subject admits; it is evidently foolish to accept probable reasoning from a mathematician and to demand from a rhetorician [a practitioner of practical reason] scientific proofs."[16]

For thinkers like Figner, and for the Russian intelligentsia generally, however, only theoretical reasoning capable of reaching infallible conclusions constituted true knowledge. One reason liberal democracy never thrived in Russia is that it depends on a strong sense of *opinion*, the awareness that events may prove one mistaken and vindicate the opinions of others. If the truth lies all on one side, why allow for open discussion or more than one party? When a Russian liberal movement developed in the 1890s, it had to contend with the feeling, which even liberals shared, that openness to different points of view testified not to a commitment to truth but to intellectual flabbiness.

In Figner's view, only someone obstinate, selfish, and "deaf to the lamentations of the people, and . . . the serious investigations of the scholar" could disagree with her. "And if all means of convincing him have been tried and alike found fruitless, then there remains, for the revolutionist only physical violence: the dagger, the revolver, and dynamite."[17]

## *The Perspicuity of Facts: Chernyshevsky and Lenin*

As religious fundamentalists insist on the perfect "perspicuity" (lucidity) of the Bible, Chernyshevsky and his followers maintained the utter reliability of our senses. The world is exactly the way we perceive it. If it were not, how could our knowledge of it be certain?

In Chernyshevsky's view, the sort of skeptical arguments advanced by Hume and Kant constituted "metaphysical nonsense." As critics pointed out, he dismissed them without understanding them. For example, he frequently confused the contention that we do not experience things in themselves with denial of an external world. As surely as "we know of ourselves that we are human beings," he declared with assurance, "we have knowledge of an infinite variety of objects—a direct, immediate knowledge of objects in themselves."[18]

"We know objects. We know them exactly as they are in reality," Chernyshevsky repeated. If those who claim that "knowledge gained by this means [vision] is untrustworthy or does not correspond to the real qualities of objects" would only look at a tree and then peer at the reflection of that tree in the pupils of another person's eyes, they would see that the two images match perfectly. "What follows? The eye neither adds nor takes away anything whatever. . . . There is no difference. . . . But does not 'the interior sensation' . . . or 'the activity of our consciousness' alter something in the picture? We know it does not."[19]

Of course, comparing how I see an object with how I see its reflection (in pupils or anywhere else) is comparing my own two perceptions, not my perception with that of another person. Besides, even if two people's perception of a given object coincide, they might both be conditioned by the dispositions of the human mind.[20] With a wave of the hand, Chernyshevsky dismissed such skepticism as obviously false.

A fervent admirer of Chernyshevsky, Lenin advanced essentially the same arguments about the perfect reliability of our sensations. In his treatise *Materialism and Empirio-Criticism* (1909), which was to exercise enormous influence on Soviet science, he rejected utterly (as he always rejected anything) Henri Poincaré's assertion that modern physics has entered a "period of doubt." For Lenin, doubt was itself reactionary—a form of "agnosticism" leading to "fideism" and "mysticism."[21]

When doubters refer to belief in a simple and absolutely reliable "copy" theory of knowledge as "naïve realism," Lenin maintained, they engage in "*sophistry* of the cheapest kind. The 'naïve realism' of any healthy person who has not been an inmate of a lunatic asylum or a pupil of the idealist philosophers consists in the view that things . . . exist *independently* of our sensation . . . and of man in general."[22] Here Lenin, no less than Chernyshevsky, equates skepticism about the reliability of our perceptions with denial of a world outside them. The same confusion continued in official Soviet philosophy.

## "Agnosticism"

Lenin referred to his opponents' self-characterization as "seekers" of truth with derision. Dialectical materialists do not seek truth; they already possess it. "As for myself," he sarcastically concluded his preface, "I too am a 'seeker' in philosophy." But what Lenin is seeking, he explained, is the reason his opponents, instead of avowing already disclosed Marxist truth, "are offering something incredibly muddled, confused, and reactionary."[23] The last adjective is especially important, because, for Lenin, mistakes in any field necessarily reflect class interests.

It is hard to overestimate the influence Lenin's derision of "agnosticism" exerted on Soviet science. Treating his assertions as infallible, the Soviets rejected theories in the hard sciences whenever they seemed to suggest that human knowledge had limits. To take just one example, at an "All-Union Conference on the Theory of the Chemical Structure of Organic Bonds" held in 1951, the Soviets denounced the chemical theory of resonance (originally proposed by Heisenberg and Pauling).[24] Quantum theory had led to the conclusion that it may be impossible to draw a single structural diagram of a molecule; the real structure may be seen as the "superposition of all the possible individual structures, or by their 'resonance.'" For the Soviets, the refusal to specify a single structural formula constituted "agnosticism," which meant that "resonance" contradicted dialectical materialism. The several paradoxes suggested by quantum theory, in fact, led to its rejection during the Stalin era on a variety of grounds. Relativity theory was also convicted of agnosticism because it denied any absolute frame of reference and the objective singularity of lengths, time intervals, and simultaneity.[25]

For Lenin and his Soviet followers, Marxism-Leninism was not just one science alongside others. Physics, chemistry, and biology were still changing while Marxism-Leninism had reached the truth once and for all. In his memoirs of Lenin, Valentinov—who supplied Lenin with material to write *Materialism and Empirio-Criticism*—recorded his shock at Lenin's certainty not only that Marx and Engels were absolutely correct, but that no fundamental principle they enunciated, about anything, could ever be changed. "Nothing in Marxism is subject to revision," Lenin told him. "There is only one answer to revisionism: smash its face in!"[26]

It is therefore more than curious to call Marxism-Leninism "scientific." After all, science, as distinguished from religious or philosophical dogma, is subject to revision in light of evidence. For that matter, the very way science establishes theories is by subjecting them to tests that might prove them false. One cannot prove a scientific theory by citing some infallible text or by aggressively asserting it. But that is exactly what Lenin did and thought one should do. As V. V. Zenkovsky observed in his classic *History of Russian Philosophy*, "everything that 'corresponds' to the position of dialectical materialism and strengthens it, is accepted without reservations; everything that fails to correspond to it is rejected *for this reason alone*."[27] Whatever this form of thinking was, it was not scientific.

Valentinov (and others) professed amazement that Lenin had not kept up with research in the fields he wrote about. Taking over an economy to be run entirely by government fiat, he had no conception of the "marginal revolution" (dating to about the time of Lenin's birth in 1870), usually considered the key concept making modern economic thought possible. When Valentinov pointed out mistakes or contradictions in Marx's *Capital*, Lenin soon relegated him "to the camp of 'the enemy.'"[28]

## Lenin's Infallible Method

Soviet thinkers praised Lenin's essay on empirio-criticism for revealing an entirely new way to assess any discipline's ideas. This new method depends on a theoretist worldview and, indeed, may be its logical consequence.

Using older methods, Marxist theoretician Georgi Plekhanov had already refuted empirio-criticism by an internal theoretical critique, much as a physicist might disprove a theory by standard disciplinary criteria. Lenin demonstrated an entirely different and infallible procedure: look at the question through the eyes of "party-mindedness" (*partiinost'*), arguably the key concept in Soviet philosophy. One need not know physics or chemistry to recognize a false physical or chemical proposition. Instead, one could examine its consequences for the Party program, as Lenin had done by pointing out empirio-criticism's reactionary implications. If the proposition in question ran counter to the Party program, it was wrong. That is why the Politburo could rule on problems in the hard sciences. This method worked infallibly not because of some mysterious ability of Politburo members to discern reality, but because *partiinost' defined* correctness; to imagine Party doctrine might itself be tested by some criteria external to it was itself reactionary and therefore false. Empirio-criticism and "resonance" were necessarily mistaken because they served the wrong class interests.

Official Soviet philosophy argued: bourgeois thinkers imagine that truth depends on empirical facts. But as Marx explained in *Theses on Feuerbach*, "contemplative" philosophy (even if materialist) falls short because it "does not understand sensuousness as a practical activity. . . . The philosophers have only *interpreted* the world, in various ways; the point, however, is to *change* it."[29] An idea is true not because it corresponds to "objective" facts, but because it produces the right results; and for the Soviets, the right results are those desired by the proletariat, which is to say, by the Communist Party of the Soviet Union (CPSU). As for Catholics the pope is the vicar of God, so for dialectical materialists the CPSU is the vicar of History. And while the popes claimed infallibility only when speaking *ex cathedra* and only on doctrinal matters, the CPSU is infallible about everything because, as the embodiment of History, it cannot be wrong.

In his speech "The Tasks of the Youth Leagues," Lenin explained that Bolsheviks must accept as ethical and scientific only what aids "the struggle of all working people against the exploiters," that is, only what advances the Party's interests.[30] What serves the Party is true. When one psychologist whose theories had been rejected as contrary to the Party program replied that they were based on experimental findings, he was told: "This theory (even though it may be 'experimentally' established! . . .) is methodologically perverted and leads to harmful practices."[31] Following facts without the guidance of theory constituted what Lenin had called "tailism" (*khvostizm*)—that is, being dragged behind rather than leading. Thus, the best-known Soviet figure studying intellectually disabled children found himself accused of "arithmetical tailism, with a terrible panic in the face of 'objective facts,' without a precise Leninist Party acuity and vigilance in his approach, without any attempt to work out the system of study on a dialectical basis."[32]

What happened when an approved theory failed to yield expected results? What if an economic program did not raise production as expected or Lysenko's theory of plant breeding did not improve agriculture? Since the theory could not be wrong, the explanation had to be sabotage, treason, or espionage. Sabotage was not just a legal and political crime, but also an epistemological category essential to the Bolshevik theory of knowledge: it explained failed predictions. Westerners often wonder at the outlandish charges against technical specialists: could anyone really believe that the mistakes of weather forecasters were sabotage meant to spoil the crop or that astronomers were terrorists because they had advanced non-Marxist views of sunspots?[33] But if one looks at matters from a Party-minded, Marxist-Leninist perspective, then such conclusions are almost unavoidable.

When in Erdman's play *The Suicide*, Serafima catches Egor spying at a woman through a keyhole, he explains:

> *Egor:* I looked at her, Serafima Ilyinichna, from a Marxist viewpoint, and in this point there cannot be . . . pornography.

> *Serafima:* Are you suggesting that from that point you see differently . . . ?

*Egor:* Not only differently, but completely the opposite. I experi-
mented on myself several times. You see, you're walking down a
boulevard and you suddenly notice some dame coming right at
you. . . . her beauty is so astounding that all you can do is close
your eyes and start panting. But immediately you check yourself
and think, "Let me look at her . . . from the Marxist viewpoint."
And [. . .] you look [. . .] and what do you think . . . everything
disappears like magic. Such repulsiveness is formed out of the
woman that I can't even describe it. . . . I can look at everything
from this viewpoint. Do you want me, Serafima Ilyinichna, to
look at you right now from this viewpoint?

*Serafima:* God forbid!

*Egor:* I'll do it just the same.[34]

## Science as Superstition

What authorizes a claim of infallibility? In an age of unquestioned faith, divine revelation precludes error. What God says is not just his personal
opinion. "The Holy Spirit is no skeptic," Luther wrote to the ever-skeptical
Erasmus, "and what He has written into our hearts are not doubts or opinions, but assertions, more certain and more firm than all human experience
and life itself."[35]

In a secular world, it is often "science" that underwrites claims of infallibility. Ever since Newton demonstrated that the amazingly complex movements of the planets could be explained by four simple laws, countless "moral
Newtonians," as historian Élie Halévy famously called them, have claimed to
have done the same for the social world.[36] Helvétius, Bentham, Comte,
Spencer, Marx, Freud, Pavlov, Skinner, Diamond: these are only a few of the
best-known claimants.[37] Whether authorized by God or science, assertions
are certainties.

Beginning with Chernyshevsky, the Russian intelligentsia tended to treat
science as a body of unchangeable dogma. To explain this essentially religious
conception of science, critics pointed to the clerical origin of so many influential *intelligents*. Having lost faith, former seminarians usually did not replace it
with careful examination of evidence. Rather, they traded a spiritual dogmatism for a materialist one. For these thinkers, science did not produce what
Max Weber called the "disenchantment [Entzauberung] of the world" but its
reenchantment.

As Herzen observed, the "men of the 'sixties" embraced not science but "the religion of science."[38] The three most famous Western authors advocating a thoroughgoing materialism—Büchner, Vogt, and Moleschott—figured as prophets of the new dispensation. In *Fathers and Children*, Arkady, with gentle condescension, replaces his father's volume of Pushkin with Büchner's *Matter and Force*. As the radical critic V. A. Zaitsev explained: "Every one of us would have gone to the scaffold and laid down his life for Moleschott or Darwin."[39]

As Herzen understood, these would-be martyrs for science missed its very point. They could not have differed more from the cautious Darwin, who presented *The Origin of Species* not as a final truth, nor even as a final statement of his ideas, but as a mere "abstract" proposing provisional theories subject to revision in light of criticism and evidence. No blinding revelation led Darwin to his conclusions; they evolved (like species) step by step toward an unpredetermined and unstable outcome as he proceeded cautiously "by patiently accumulating and reflecting on all sorts of facts which could have any bearing" on the issues. Errors are doubtless present, he wrote in the book's introduction, "for I am well aware that scarcely a single point is discussed in this volume on which facts cannot be adduced, often apparently leading to conclusions directly opposite to those at which I have arrived. A fair result can be obtained only by fully stating and balancing the facts and arguments on both sides of each question."[40]

For Darwin, science is all about the skeptical weighing of evidence and attending to "both sides of each question." By contrast, "science" attracted Chernyshevsky and his followers precisely because, in their view, it made skepticism unnecessary, indeed impossible. It allowed them to be, as they liked to say, "mathematically certain," and they proceeded by deducing unchallengeable conclusions from *a priori* principles. The appeal of scientific materialism is itself spiritual, Dostoevsky's Grand Inquisitor explains; it banishes uncertainty.

"From science," Semyon Frank observed, "the *intelligent* takes a few propositions—popularized, distorted, or fabricated *ad hoc*—and although he is frequently even proud of how 'scientific' his faith is, he indignantly rejects both scientific criticism and all pure, disinterested scientific thought."[41]

The narrator of *Fathers and Children* remarks that "young Russians studying physics and chemistry" in Heidelberg "who at first astound the naïve German professors by the soundness of their view of things, later astound the same professor no less by their complete inactivity and absolute idleness."[42] They are idle, Turgenev suggests, because for them the whole point of chemistry lies in the materialism with which they began.

Critics of the intelligentsia frequently pointed out that "science" so conceived is really pseudoscience. In real sciences, some propositions are always more firmly established than others. It is more likely that future work will modify a new theory about a limited domain than one tested countless times across many domains. If that were not so, science could not progress at all. But even well-established theories may be revised in what we now call a scientific revolution. Only in a pseudoscience is everything equally unchallengeable, and those who treat science as a single dogmatic block—you can't go against science!—have transformed it into a pseudoscience. What they say may by chance be true, but, as Mill observed, "truth thus held is but one superstition the more."[43]

## Some Scientific Discoveries

For *intelligents*, it was Chernyshevsky who first enunciated the "scientific," and therefore irrefutable, answers to all social, political, and moral questions. In his celebrated essay on "The Anthropological Principle in Philosophy," he explained that "the English word 'science' does not by any means cover all the branches of knowledge" (like German *Wissenschaft* and Russian *nauka*), but only "the branches of knowledge we call the 'exact' sciences" such as "mathematics, astronomy, physics, chemistry, botany, zoology."[44] Only recently, Chernyshevsky asserted, have history, psychology, politics, economics, and ethics also achieved scientific status in this restricted sense.

"Not so long ago," Chernyshevsky wrote, "the moral sciences could not have had the content to justify the title of science ... and the English were quite right then in depriving them of a title they did not deserve. The situation today has changed considerably." Today "all the progressive thinkers ... studying the moral sciences have begun to work out these problems with the aid of precise methods similar to those by which the problems of the natural sciences are being worked out." As a result, they have arrived at "the exact solution of moral problems, too."[45]

To be sure, Chernyshevsky allowed, these moral sciences are still in their infancy, but they are sciences nonetheless. "In their present form the moral sciences differ from the so-called natural sciences only in that they began to be worked out in a truly scientific way later, and therefore have not yet been developed to the same degree of perfection as the latter."[46] Almost all proponents of a putative new science have found this "young science" argument convenient. It licenses them to argue that since chemistry once was just beginning, and it developed into a science, so the new discipline will develop as chemistry did. But many promising disciplines—including, in our own time,

Freudian psychology—whose proponents advanced this argument failed to develop into a science.

And what has Chernyshevsky's new science discovered? In his essays and in his utopian fiction *What Is to Be Done?*, Chernyshevsky, or the characters who speak for him, enunciate a series of "scientific conclusions" that are "definitely known" and "indubitable."[47] These include:

1. Absolute determinism: one and only one thing can happen at any given moment.
2. The law governing all human behavior: people always act according to what they perceive as their greatest advantage.
3. The denial of free will: the sensation of choosing "is only the subjective impression that accompanies the genesis of thoughts or actions" actually produced by causal necessity.[48]
4. The nonexistence of fault: a person "cannot be blamed for one thing or praised for the other" since nothing could be different and "everything depends on circumstances [and] relationships (institutions)."[49]
5. The denial of "human nature": people become whatever conditions make them. (This argument, sometimes called the absolute malleability of human beings, is shared by virtually all utopian thinkers.)
6. The solution to all crime: to eliminate it, one need only change the circumstances that make people regard socially destructive behavior as personally beneficial.
7. Utopianism: the perfect society, where "no one will ever be poor or unhappy again," is not only imaginable but inevitable.[50] Indeed, Chernyshevsky suggests in *What Is to Be Done?* that it will be achieved in a few years.

In short, all the questions baffling earlier thinkers are not only solvable but easily so. "At the very first application of scientific analysis the whole thing turns out to be as clear as can be." No longer do we see as through a glass darkly. Social evil "is solved so easily that it cannot even be called a problem: it contains its own solution."[51] Almost immediately this "science" became all but obligatory; to challenge it was to place oneself outside the intelligentsia.

## Superfluous Advice

The disdain with which Chernyshevsky advanced his shabby reasoning irritated many more sophisticated thinkers. He failed to grasp that no experiment could ever establish determinism (or indeterminism). A determinist might show that this or that outcome is predictable, but determinism is the thesis that *everything* is in principle predictable; one counterexample refutes it. Demonstrating the predictability of one process—or many—does not advance the argument a bit. The same reasoning applies to indeterminism: any apparent chance event may have been produced by undiscovered laws. As Dostoevsky suggested and William James argued, one becomes a determinist or indeterminist by temperament.[52]

It was also obvious to critics that Chernyshevsky contradicted himself. Speaking for the author, the enlightened hero of *What Is to Be Done?* maintains that each person "is governed exclusively by the calculation of his own advantage"—if they were only sometimes governed by this principle, how could human behavior be scientifically predictable?—yet in the very next sentence he claims that unselfish "sublime emotion or ideal aspiration . . . is completely insignificant [*sic*] in comparison with each person's pursuit of his own advantage."[53] But an "insignificant" exception refutes a categorical law as surely as a significant one, just as one tiny miracle overturns iron determinism.

It was easy enough to point to passages in *What Is to Be Done?* that first deny free will and then advocate one choice rather than another. Despite his claim that people "exclusively" and inevitably act to further their advantage, Lopukhov ardently advises Vera Pavlovna to do so![54]

"The intelligentsia asserts that the personality is wholly a product of the environment," wrote Sergei Bulgakov, "and at the same time suggests to it that it improve its surroundings, like Baron Münchausen pulling himself out of the swamp by his own hair."[55]

## Purposeful Science

Critics found it especially odd that leading *intelligents* favored "sciences" attributing purpose to nature. It was, of course, the banishment of "final causes" that underwrote modern science. As Francis Bacon famously declared: "The research into final causes, like a Virgin dedicated to God, is barren and produces nothing."[56] We must not anthropomorphize nature and attribute human purposes to it, he insisted. "For God forbid that we should give out a dream of our own imagination for a pattern of the world."[57]

"It is only necessary for experimental science to introduce the question of a final cause [or purpose] for it to become nonsensical," wrote Tolstoy.[58] To attribute human purposes to nature is to smuggle God into one's theory while claiming to have banished the supernatural.[59] For how else could nature have acquired any purposes, let alone human ones? Modern astronomy had shown that our world is not at the universe's center and is one of countless worlds; geology had proven that the earth existed long before humans inhabited it; and Darwinian evolution had exploded the last remnants of the argument by design: all these conclusions made nonsense of theories supposing that the world had been created to further human goals. Sheep did not evolve to provide us with wool. As Herzen frequently pointed out, no providence, whether divine or not, guides the universe for our benefit. If instead of invoking God one posits a God substitute—a principle that, without God, does what a providential God would do—all one has done is rephrase medieval cosmogony in new language.[60]

Intelligentsia thinkers found such objections repellent, if not immoral. For science, they argued, exists only to serve people; it has no value in itself. It teaches materialism and so refutes religion; it discovered evolution, which replaced the Bible; and it revealed the laws of human behavior that make utopia inevitable. Science for science's sake is no better than art for art's sake.

The anarchist Peter Kropotkin gave up his career as a distinguished geographer because the knowledge he was acquiring did not seem to offer immediate help to the unfortunate. "Science is an excellent thing," Kropotkin observed. "I knew its joys and I valued them. . . . But what right had I to all these joys, when all around me was nothing but misery . . . ?"[61]

If science is morally neutral, this line of reasoning went, it might as well not exist. The only true science leads to socialism. "The mere idea of knowledge becomes in Russia almost wholly blended with that of something subversive," explained the terrorist Lev Tikhomirov, who meant this comment as praise.[62]

To be worthwhile, knowledge had to promote desirable social change. To confine oneself to "questions of cellular reproduction, the transformation of species, spectrum analysis and double stars," populist theoretician Pyotr Lavrov asserted, was to be "a Philistine of learning." Such questions matter "only insofar as they lead to a better understanding" of social problems "and facilitate their resolution."[63]

If so, then accumulating more scientific knowledge is not important. "We already know much!" Kropotkin maintained. The important thing is that already accumulated "knowledge . . . should become the possession of all."[64] The prestige of *zhurnalisty* as popularizers far exceeded that of Russian scientists. "It should always be remembered," wrote Pisarev, whose essay "Progress in the Animal and Vegetable Worlds" popularized Darwin, "that people do not exist for science and art," but science and art for the welfare of people. "If science and art impede life, if they disunite man, if they lay the foundation of caste divisions, then we shall have no truck with them."[65] We preserve them not because knowledge is an end in itself but because, and only because, it is useful in transforming society.

As in economics, what mattered most in science was not creation but distribution. "Science today is accumulating heaps of great truths which remain almost barren," remarked Pisarev, "because the masses can neither understand nor use them. . . . There is in mankind only one evil—ignorance; for this evil there is only one cure—science; but this medicine must be taken not in homeopathic doses but by the bucket and barrelful." Since nothing inaccessible to the masses matters, "it would be good to expel from science everything that can be understood only by the few and can never become common knowledge."[66]

## The Cunning of Matter

But how can one guarantee that knowledge will serve the right purpose? After all, if one seeks objective truth, it may not. In *August 1914* historian Olda Andozerskaya shocks students who demand that what they learn must "contribute to the liberation of the people." "History isn't politics, my dears, with one loudmouth echoing or contradicting what another loudmouth has said," she replies. "Sources, not opinions, are the material of history. And we must accept the conclusions as they come, even if they go against us."[67] The students find such impartiality novel.

The hard sciences, of course, pose an even greater challenge. It is one thing to discover purpose in the history of people—who are themselves purposeful—but it is quite another to ascribe it to inanimate objects. Somehow, one must show that matter is not inert, that it is heading somewhere good. Or as Berdyaev observed, "materialism mythologizes about matter."[68]

Semyon Frank asked rhetorically: "If the universe . . . is determined only by blind material forces, then how is it possible to hope that historical development will inevitably lead to the reign of reason and the building of an earthly paradise?" Why should "blind and mindless elements" act according to "the controlling force of [human] reason"? And by what means could "cosmic forces which have nothing to do with man" have been directed toward the human dream of a "serene paradise of human well-being"?[69]

Requiring "a metaphysical substantiation of [its] moral needs," Frank wrote, the intelligentsia has disguised wish-fulfillment as science. And so "atheistic materialism is calmly combined with the staunchest faith in future world harmony. The 'scientific socialism' professed by the vast majority of the

Russian intelligentsia even assumes that this metaphysical optimism is 'scientifically proven.'"[70]

"Scientific socialism," in short, makes as much sense as cellular capitalism or chemical feudalism. The noun expresses human purposes while the adjective precludes them. The same contradiction may be found in "dialectical materialism." Dialectics, after all, is a form of human rhetoric or thought, so how can matter be dialectical? Electrons repel each other, but do they argue? Yet when such phrases become familiar, the sense of contradiction is lost. As in medieval philosophy, it seems as if nature were cognizant of human desires.

## Lavrov and Mikhailovsky: Scientific Subjectivity

How did thinkers discover human purpose in nature?[71] For Hegel and Marx, History was itself an agent and, as such, had goals. It was a God substitute, and the enormous appeal of these thinkers for Russians lay in the substitution. No longer did atheism suggest that goals are arbitrary human constructs.

In Marx's case, the dynamics of matter itself ultimately lead inevitably to communism. For the Soviets, it followed that doubting "historical materialism" was like disputing the law of gravity. From this perspective, the late Soviet practice of confining dissidents in madhouses made sense.

In the nineteenth century, various non-Marxist approaches also endorsed laws of inevitable progress. Although Darwin himself denied that evolution leads anywhere and insisted on the role of sheer chance, he was easily reinterpreted, in Russia as elsewhere, as proving that human history continued the purposeful laws of natural history. To satirize such thinking, the philosopher Vladimir Soloviev paraphrased what he called the intelligentsia's syllogism: man is descended from the apes; therefore love thy neighbor as thyself.[72]

The populist philosophers Pyotr Lavrov and Nikolai Mikhailovsky chose a different solution. For Lavrov, the "objective" view of natural science, which rules out considering human purposes and goals, omits the very reason we study the world. And since humans are themselves part of nature, the human tendency to view the world in terms of purpose and to evaluate it morally is a natural fact; purpose must therefore be taken into account. Not to do so, Mikhailovsky observed, is like "measuring weight with a yardstick."[73]

Kant had argued that even though space, time, and causality belong to the mind rather than to the world, we are fully justified in employing them; following this logic, Lavrov contended that we not only may but must see purpose in the world. Specifically, we cannot help arranging the facts of history in terms of progress leading to ourselves at the present moment. "We inevitably see *progress* in history," Lavrov contended, and from the standpoint of our present ideals "all phenomena become identified as . . . morally good or evil . . . in the historical perspective set by our moral ideal we stand at the end of the historical process; the entire past is related to our ideal as a series of preparatory steps which lead inevitably to a definite end." It followed that we must "see history as a struggle between a beneficent principle and a harmful principle, where the former . . . has finally reached the point at which it is for us the supreme human good."[74]

Herbert Butterfield described this way of thinking as a fundamental fallacy, which he called "Whiggism" after the Whig historians who viewed history as leading to the triumph of their liberal values. Whiggism, he explained, is not confined to Whigs. It derives from "a trick in organization . . . [that] is the result of abstracting things from their historical context and organizing the story by a system of direct reference to the present," as if the historian's present offered an extrahistorical vantage point. So situated, the historian is enabled "to make judgments of value, and to count them as the verdict of history." Butterfield described such bias as "an unexamined habit of mind," but Lavrov chose it consciously. And while Butterfield cautioned us to avoid such thinking, Lavrov proclaimed this "subjective" approach not only desirable but also unavoidable.[75]

After providing his definition of progress, Lavrov observed: "I regard the concepts contained in this formula as fully definite and not open to different interpretations" because the subjectivity in question pertains not to one individual or cultural perspective among many, but to humanity as such.[76] The judgments this formula authorizes are therefore as certain as those in any "objective" approach. No less than Marxist dialectics, it authorizes the ascription of teleology to history.

For critics, such thinking mistook wish-fulfillment for science. Berdyaev referred to "the almost insane tendency to judge philosophical doctrines and [factual] truths according to political and utilitarian criteria."[77]

## The Vitality of Matter

Official Soviet philosophy, of course, had no use for "subjectivity." To authorize judging facts and theories on political grounds, it adopted Engels's *Dialectic of Nature* as an infallible guide for discovering objective purposefulness in nature and history. Dialectical materialism had supposedly demonstrated that the inevitability of communism derived from teleology inherent in matter itself.

In Soviet parlance, to deny purpose to matter was to engage in "mechanistic" rather than dialectical materialism. Mechanistic materialism, characteristic of Diderot, La Metrrie, and other eighteenth-century thinkers, led directly to the "right deviation" from the true Leninist line, a deviation apparent in Bukharin's partiality to models of "equilibrium" rather than revolutionary upheaval.[78]

Newton referred to the inertia of matter: to make something move, or to change its speed or direction if it is already moving, an external force must be applied ($F = ma$). But for Soviet Marxists, matter already contained the principle of motion, from which the dynamics of human history ultimately derive. Had not Marx observed in *The Holy Family*: "Among the qualities inherent in matter, motion is first and foremost, not only in the form of mechanical and mathematical motion, but chiefly in the form of an impulse, a vital spirit, a tension"?[79]

In Engels's view, the idea that motion required an external force implied that the universe itself required such a force, supplied by God. "Motion," Engels wrote, is "an inherent attribute of matter."[80] Following Engels, Soviet philosophy affirmed matter's "self-movement" (*samodvizhnost'*), which, following the dialectical process of thesis-antithesis-synthesis, generated ever higher configurations.[81] The three laws of the dialectic that Engels described—the transformation of quantity into quality, the interpenetration of opposites, and the negation of the negation—explain how the dialectic operates, from the smallest particle to the most sophisticated social structures.

## Primitive Empiricism

In Vasily Grossman's novel *Life and Fate,* Viktor Shtrum, a physicist, contends with rejection of discoveries satisfying the criteria of physics but violating the principles of dialectical materialism. He encounters the essential theoretist faith: If experimental facts contradict theory, the facts must yield.

Shtrum disagrees. Told that his ideas "contradict the materialist view of the nature of matter and need to be reconsidered," he incautiously replies "that it was no concern to physics whether or not it confirmed philosophy" and that the logic of physics was "more powerful than that of Engels and Lenin; that it was for . . . the Scientific Section of the Central Committee to accommodate Lenin's views to mathematics and physics, not for mathematicians and physicists to accommodate their views to Lenin's."[82] Shtrum challenges not just Marxist-Leninist theoretism but theoretism itself.

In Solzhenitsyn's *In the First Circle*, Sologdin rejects Rubin's orthodox view that the three laws of dialectics explain the world scientifically. He challenges Rubin to use them to make specific predictions. His point is that these "laws" are general and flexible enough to accommodate anything after the fact, whereas a scientific theory predicts one thing rather than another. It can be tested or, as we would say today, is falsifiable: if it doesn't show us "the direction of development [i.e., what will happen] . . . we don't know a damn thing." This reasoning appalls Rubin. "If Marxism isn't science, what is?" he replies. "You base your epistemology on the empirical principle," which, in the Marxist view, is "primitive" thinking.[83] For the theoretist, empiricism is necessarily inferior to theory.

## Crime and Punishment: *"Unhinged by Theories"*

The great Russian fiction writers subjected the theoretist mindset to intense and revealing criticism. Characters in Dostoevsky's novels often ridicule utilitarian reasoning. If people always seek their own advantage, the hero of *Notes from Underground* asks, why do they deliberately hurt themselves? If civilization is guided by a law of progress, why are people "more loathsomely bloodthirsty than before?"—a passage frequently cited in the twentieth century. The only way to maintain the rationality of history, the underground man continues, is to rule out counterexamples. One can say almost anything about history—it is grand, it is variegated, it is monotonous—but, he asserts, "the only thing one cannot say is that it is rational. The very word sticks in one's throat."[84] Utilitarians reply that apparently irrational behavior must be rational according to standards not yet identified, but that is to assume what is to be proven.

In short, such theories amount to "mere logical exercises." What they really demonstrate is that "man is so fond of systems and abstract deductions that he is ready to distort the truth intentionally, he is ready to deny what he can see and hear to justify his logic."[85]

As we have seen, Raskolnikov, the hero of *Crime and Punishment*, embraces several incompatible theories and cannot specify which one led him to kill. That is, it was the theoretical impulse itself, not any particular theory, that led to the murders. Under its influence, he lived a life of "abstraction," in both senses: theoretical ideas and detachment from his surroundings. Recognizing this state of mind, the detective Porfiry Petrovich knows that Raskolnikov must be guilty. All the evidence shows that the crime resulted from what the detective calls a mind obsessed with "bookish dreams, a heart unhinged by theories." The murderer was so abstracted that he forgot to shut the door. Planning to rob and kill a pawnbroker, he did not think that he would have jewels to take away! Clearly, money was beside the point; he "murdered two people for a theory."[86]

We have already quoted Porfiry Petrovich's chilling comment that "if you'd invented another theory you might have done something a thousand times more hideous"—like revolutionary terrorism, which this novel frequently mentions.[87] Nothing limits the violence potentially flowing from the theoretist mindset, which can justify anything.

After hearing Raskolnikov's argument that great men, or even men a little above the ordinary, have the right to kill in order to advance their "idea," Raskolnikov's friend Razumikhin, as we have seen, observes: "what is really *original* in all this . . . to my horror, is that you sanction bloodshed *in the name of conscience*, and, excuse my saying so, with such fanaticism. . . . But that sanction of bloodshed *by conscience* is to my mind [. . .] more terrible than the official, legal sanction of bloodshed."[88]

Dostoevsky leaves it to Razumikhin to rail at all those *intelligents* who "believe that a social system that has come out of some mathematical brain is going to organize all humanity at once. . . . Logic presupposes three possibilities but there are millions! Cut away a million and reduce it all to the question of comfort! That's the easiest solution to the problem! It's seductively clear and you mustn't think about it."[89] Ideologies seduce with clarity; novels teach complexity.

## War and Peace: *There Cannot Be a Social Science*

Two years before Dostoevsky published *Notes from Underground*, Tolstoy dissected the fallacious theory of a "law of progress." In his essay "Progress and the Definition of Education" (1862), he explained that "the superstition of progress" operates by dismissing contrary evidence as "non-historical." "I am struck by one incomprehensible phenomenon," he wrote.

> They declare a general law for all humanity from the comparison of one small part of European humanity in the present and past. Progress is a common law of humanity, they say, except for Asia, Africa, and Australia, except for one thousand millions of people.
>
>   We have noticed the law of progress in the dukedom of Hohenzollern-Sigmaringen, with its three thousand inhabitants. We know China, with its two hundred millions of inhabitants, which overthrows our whole

theory of progress, and we do not doubt for a moment that progress is
the common law of all humanity ... and we, the believers in that progress, go with cannon and guns to impress the idea of progress upon the
Chinese.[90]

*War and Peace* extends this argument to "scientific" social theories generally.
They all discover what they posit and blind themselves to exceptions, however
numerous. The novel's generals accept a "science" of battle guaranteeing victory
since "every contingency has been foreseen."[91] But countless contingencies are
unforeseeable; and one might almost say that contingency is the book's only
unconquerable hero. Tolstoy ridicules not just the generals' "science," but any
conceivable social science supposedly capable of prediction.

General Pfühl, as Tolstoy depicts him, believes wholeheartedly in his science "deduced from the history of Frederick the Great's wars—and everything
he came across in the history of more recent wars seemed to him ... crude
struggles in which so many blunders were committed on both sides that these
conflicts could not be called wars; they did not conform to a theory, and therefore
could not serve as material for a science." One might imagine that defeat
would lead Pfühl to reassess his theories, but the very opposite is the case.
"On the contrary, to his mind it was the departures from his theory that were
the sole cause of the whole disaster." The science works only if the plans it
prescribes are carried out to the letter; and since that is never possible, defeat,
far from disproving the theory, verifies it. Like so many people who place
theory above experience, Pfühl "was one of those theoreticians who so love
their theory ... that he positively rejoiced in failure, for failures resulting
from deviations from the theory only proved the accuracy of the theory."[92]

The novel's hero, Prince Andrei, first believes in a science of battle, but experience teaches him the ineradicability of contingency. In battle, he learns, one
faces "a hundred million diverse chances, which will be decided on the instant,"[93] and each chance may have concatenating effects. No one can predict
whether a bullet will hit a brave man who inspires others or a coward whose
fear induces a general panic. Proponents of a social science typically assume
that "the unique features of millions of small-scale brief events become aver-
aged out," but sometimes the reverse happens.[94] Tolstoy develops the idea that
chaos theorists have recently called the "butterfly effect": sometimes a tiny contingency, unforeseeable and perhaps undetectable, may cascade into ever
greater effects. If so, prediction is impossible even in principle.

"What theory or science is possible," Andrei asks himself after listening to
General Pfühl, "where the conditions and circumstances are unknown and

cannot be determined. . . . What science can there be in a matter in which, as in every practical matter, nothing can be determined and everything depends on innumerable conditions, the significance of which becomes manifest at a particular moment, and no one can tell when that moment will come?"[95] "As in every practical matter": Tolstoy intends his critique of a science of battle to apply to all putative social sciences, existing or to come.

The novel's wisest general, Kutuzov, recognizes that in conditions of radical uncertainty, devotion to supposedly scientific planning can deprive one of the presence of mind needed to perceive unforeseeable opportunities. He at last calls an end to the council of war before the Battle of Austerlitz: "'Gentlemen, the disposition for tomorrow—or rather for today, for it is past midnight—cannot be altered now,' he said. 'You have heard it, and we will all do our duty. And before a battle, there is nothing more important [. . .]' (he fell silent), 'than a good night's sleep.'"[96]

If there really were a science of battle, it would pay to lose a night's sleep to get the plan right. But in a world of radical contingency, even the best plans matter less than alertness. Other generals laugh at Kutuzov's ignorance of the latest theories, but the old man appreciates that practical wisdom may be more important than any theory; and wisdom, by its very nature, cannot be formalized.

## War and Peace: *"The Endless Variety of Men's Minds"*

Andrei's friend Pierre presumes that either one has an indubitable theory or one has nothing. Pierre craves relief from the despair assailing him whenever he cannot be absolutely certain. Time and again, he discovers what he regards as a consoling theory of theories only to recognize its shortcomings and fall again into despair. Then a new theory, more preposterous than the one before, attracts him.

When Pierre adopts the complex, and evidently absurd, mythology of Freemasonry, "not a trace of his former doubts remained. He firmly believed in the possibility of the brotherhood of men united in the aim of supporting one another in the path of virtue, and envisaged Freemasonry as such a brotherhood."[97]

Pierre's most extravagant system, which Tolstoy offers as exemplary of theoretism, prompts him to remain in French-occupied Moscow under the delusion that he has been destined to kill Napoleon. Pierre has heard that if one assigns numbers to French letters, as is done in Hebrew, and bears in mind that, according to the Book of Revelation, the number of the beast "speaking

great things and blasphemies" is six hundred and sixty-six, one discovers that
the numerical value of the words "L'empereur Napoléon . . . equals six hundred and sixty six (including a five for the letter *e* dropped by elision from the
*le* before *empereur*), and therefore Napoleon is the beast prophesied in
the Apocalypse." What's more, if one counts up the letters in the word
*quarante-deux* (forty-two), one again obtains 666, "from which it follows that
the limit fixed for Napoleon's power came in the year 1812 when the French
Emperor had reached his forty-second year. This prophecy made a deep impression on Pierre."[98]

Surely the one destined to end Napoleon's power in 1812 must also bear a
name totaling 666! Theoretism typically enables a new kind of research, and
Pierre counts up his own name, but it does not work. No matter: since there
are many ways to transliterate his surname from the Russian alphabet into
the French, and since he is free to include some status corresponding to "empereur," Pierre at last discovers that "Le russe Besuhof" totals 671. "This was
only five too much, and corresponded to the *e*, the very article elided from the
word *le* before *empereur*. By dropping the *e*, though ungrammatically, Pierre
got the answer he sought," as believers in systems always do. "L'russe Besuhof"
came to exactly six hundred and sixty-six. The discovery excited him. How, by
what means, he was connected with the great event foretold in the Apocalypse he did not know, but he did not for a moment doubt the connection."[99]

One wants to ask: If Pierre's name had totaled 666 without dropping the
"e," would he still have decided that he had to drop it and therefore, since his
name now totaled 661, he was not destined to kill Napoleon? If one assumes
that all names must total somewhere between, let us say, 100 and 4100, and that
in 1812 there were approximately forty million Russians, then on average each
number, including 666, represents the total for some 10,000 people: they
could not all have been destined to kill Napoleon! But the whole point of such
thinking is to banish skepticism. The human need for certainty, Tolstoy suggests, almost guarantees that one such system after another will acquire followers, as, indeed, has happened from his day to our own.

Pierre's doubts arise when he encounters contingency or individuality beyond his theory's grasp. The reactions to his speech before his fellow Masons
convince him that the uniformity that systems require is chimerical. For a
theory to banish doubt, there must be no doubt about what it means; if it is to
banish difference of opinion, people must not hold different opinions about
its content. What most bothers Pierre about the reception of his speech,
therefore, is not disagreement but qualified agreement. "Even those members
who seemed to be on his side understood him in their own way, with stipula-

tions and modifications he could not agree to, since what he chiefly desired was to convey his thought to others exactly as he understood it."[100]

Evidently, individuality is essential to humanness, as it is not to molecules. It cannot be presumed away, as Pierre had imagined. "At this meeting," Tolstoy observes, "Pierre for the first time was struck by the endless variety of men's minds, which prevents a truth from ever appearing [exactly] the same to any two persons.... Pierre again found himself in that state of depression he so dreaded."[101]

When Pierre at last attains wisdom, he abandons the quest for theory. With amused acceptance and good-hearted curiosity, he appreciates each person's uniqueness and earns good will by "his acknowledgement of the possibility of every man thinking, feeling, and seeing things in his own way. This legitimate individuality of every man's views, which formerly troubled or irritated Pierre, now became the basis of the sympathy he felt for other people. The difference . . . between one man and another, pleased him and drew from him a gentle, ironic smile."[102] While theoretism engenders intolerant enthusiasm, wisdom leads to "gentle irony."

## Selfhood and the Novel

In discovering individuality, Pierre appreciates what realist novels presume. As Russian thinkers recognized, and as Bakhtin elucidated, literary genres presume truths and values. Much as saints' lives take for granted the existence of God and the value of holiness, and epics presume the existence of heroism and the value of glory, so realist novels presuppose—even if they do not explicitly assert—the existence of individuality and the value of self-knowledge.[103] That is one reason so many novels are named after a hero or heroine: *Jane Eyre, Effi Briest, David Copperfield, Père Goriot, Eugénie Grandet, Cousin Bette, Madame Bovary, Romola, Phineas Finn, Doctor Thorne, Anna Karenina.*

Novels presume the fascinating uniqueness and absolute unrepeatability of each person, who cannot be reduced to material causes. In addition to all those causes might explain, there always something left over that exceeds their grasp. "In Dostoevsky's artistic thinking," Bakhtin explained, "the genuine life of the personality takes place . . . at his point of departure beyond the limits of all that he is as a material being, a being that can be spied upon, defined, predicted apart from its own will, 'at second hand.'"[104]

No matter how many categories one applies to Anna Karenina—social class, epoch, gender, family characteristics, even personality traits—one has not exhausted her individuality. Plutarch, who imagined personalities as composed of a finite number of qualities, could ask what would happen to a given type born into a different situation; and so he produced "parallel lives" comparing Cicero with Demosthenes and Alexander with Caesar. In realist novels, by contrast, no list of categories could be sufficient to account for self-hood. Something is always left over or, as Bakhtin phrased the point, there remains an ineradicable "surplus" with "unrealized potentials":

> An individual cannot be completely incarnated into the flesh of existing sociohistorical categories. There is no mere form that would be able to incarnate once and forever all of his human possibilities and needs, no form in which he could exhaust himself down to the last word, like the tragic or epic hero; no form that he could fill to the brim, and yet at the same time not splash over the brim. There always remains an unrealized surplus of humanness. . . . All existing clothes are always too tight, and therefore comical, on a man. . . . Reality as we have it in the novel is only one of many possible realities; it is not inevitable, not arbitrary, it bears within itself other possibilities.[105]

If one does not understand people this way, one does not write realist novels, although one might compose works belonging to other genres of long fiction like the extended allegory (*Moby-Dick*), the satire (*Joseph Andrews*), the adventure story (*King Solomon's Mines*), the fantasy (*The Lord of the Rings*), the mystery (*The Moonstone*), or the utopia (*Looking Backward, 2000-1887*). Each of these genres concerns itself with something other than the specificity of individuals.

## What Is to Be Done?: *People Are Identical*

Literary utopias are not just uninterested in individuality, they explicitly deny it. In this respect, the utopia and the novel are anti-genres, which is why each alludes frequently to the other. Novels demonstrate that utopians are foolish, utopias that novels are pernicious. For Edward Bellamy, William Morris, and Chernyshevsky, the novelistic idea that human complexity defies any simple formula is a falsehood; and the novelistic assumption that no single social solution could work for all individuals perpetuates an unjust social order.[106]

Chernyshevsky's utopia *What Is to Be Done?* argues these points explicitly. This utopia responds to Turgenev's novel *Fathers and Children*, which in turn answered Chernyshevsky's review of Turgenev's novel *Asya*. From its first pages, the author of *What Is to Be Done?* repeatedly mocks novels and the readers who enjoy them. If by talent one means the ability to construct a typically novelistic plot, the author (as we have noted) proudly claims not to have any.[107] Instead of novelistic talent, the author offers truth; and "truth is a good thing; it compensates for the inadequacies of talent of any writer who serves its cause."[108]

Chernyshevsky's book pictures utopia in the heroine's four dreams, while characters explicate the utilitarian science ensuring the utopian future. It also conducts an overt war against its readers or, rather, the ones who envisage the world as novelists do. Time and again, the author first employs some "conventional ruse of a novelist" and then exposes the falsity—about personality, love, or morality—that makes such ruses appealing. Don't blame me for these tricks, the author tells the reader. "It's your own simpleminded naïveté that compelled me to stoop to such vulgarity. . . . The author is in no mood for such things, dear public, because he keeps thinking about the confusion in your head, and about the useless, unnecessary suffering . . . that results from the absurd muddle of your thoughts."[109]

That muddle includes the unscientific belief in individuality. Ask yourself, Chernyshevsky remarked in his earlier review of Turgenev's novel *Asya*, "whether a man who at first glance seems different from others really differs in anything important from people in his own class . . . and [you] soon come to the conclusion that every man is like every other and that each is made up precisely like the others." Differences seem important "only because they appear on the surface and strike the eye, but beneath the visible, apparent differences is hidden a total identity." Thinking scientifically, one understands that man could not possibly "prove a contradiction of all nature's laws." Just as all cedars and hyssops bloom, and all mice move in the same way, people closely resemble each other. Indeed, even the differences between species are trivial. After all, "the organism of mammals, birds, and fish is identical . . . even a worm breathes like a mammal."[110]

In short, Chernyshevsky concluded, "you have practically reached the limit of human wisdom when you become convinced of the simple truth that every person is like every other one."[111] In *What Is to Be Done?*, Lopukhov advances the same argument; and the author observes that Lopukhov and his friend Kirsanov so resemble each other that "if you encountered them separately, each one would appear to have the very same character."[112] Precisely because people are identical a single formula can make everyone happy. No rational person, if unbesotted by novels, could doubt this "simple truth."

Lopukhov explains that since natural laws are deterministic, free choice must be an illusion and history must lead inevitably to the utopian outcome.

What's more, the book makes clear, the revolution establishing utopia will happen within a few months. So certain is this outcome that the author ends the story two years after the book's actual completion date, when the utopian future is an accomplished fact and what "was still only a hope" has become reality. That is, the future is so certain it can be narrated as if it had already taken place:

> "Excuse me, excuse me," says the reader. . . . Are you starting to describe events of 1865?"
> "Yes."
> "But for pity's sake is that possible?"
> "Why is it impossible, if I have the knowledge? . . . If you don't want to listen now, then of course I must postpone the sequel . . . I hope we won't have to wait too long for that day."
> 4 April 1863.[113]

## Fathers and Children: *The Irony of Origins and the Irony of Outcomes*

As we have observed, Turgenev's *Fathers and Children* perfected the type of fiction at which Russia's greatest writers excelled, the novel of ideas (also called the philosophical novel). Such novels narrate the story of a person who believes in some exalted theory that proves inadequate. The theory in question—which the novel's hero Bazarov and his young disciple Arkady call "nihilism"—closely resembles Chernyshevsky's putative social science.

"Studying separate individuals is not worth the trouble," Bazarov explains. "All people resemble each other . . . each of us has brain, spleen and lungs made alike; and the moral qualities are the same in all; the slight variations are of no importance. A single human specimen is sufficient to judge all the rest . . . no botanist would think of studying each individual birch tree." Bazarov dissects frogs to show that, as Chernyshevsky argued in his review, even the differences between species are trivial.[114] In short, the hero of Turgenev's novel argues against the presuppositions of the genre in which he appears.

In response, Chernyshevsky, favoring Bazarov's values over those of the realist novel, has the heroes of *What Is to Be Done?* "dissect frogs, cut open hundreds of corpses a year."[115] So influential did these fictional dissections become that countless real frogs lost their lives to young people proving their nihilist credentials. "In the splayed frog [*rasplastannoi liagushke*]" the radical critic Dmitri Pisarev (as we have noted) famously declared, "lies the salvation and renewal of the Russian people."[116]

In novels, love unites unique souls revealed by intense emotional experience. But in utopias, and for Bazarov, there is no unique self to reveal. That whole view of love, Bazarov intones, is just so much "romanticism, nonsense, rot, artiness." "And what of all these mysterious relations between a man and woman?" he sneers. "We physiologists know what these relations are. Study the anatomy of the eye a bit; where does the enigmatical glance [described by novelists] come in there?" No novelist ever surpassed Turgenev in using fine shadings of verdure to suggest the elusive shadings of feeling, but for Bazarov feelings are simple and "nature's not a temple, but a workshop, and man's the workman in it."[117]

Setting the pattern for philosophical novels to come, *Fathers and Children* tests Bazarov's theories not by logic, evidence, or counterargument, as philosophical treatises do, but by examining what it means to live by them. Novels subject theories to two kinds of irony, which I like to call the irony of origins and the irony of outcomes.[118]

As we have seen, Turgenev subjects Arkady's views to a rather gentle irony of origins. Voicing shocking views—art is bunk, everything should be destroyed!—becomes his way of demonstrating adulthood. He remains naively unaware that proving one's adulthood is a childish thing to do. Turgenev subjects Bazarov's views to a less forgiving scrutiny, the irony of outcomes. The philosophical novel's master plot, which this novel exemplifies, narrates the encounter of simplifying theory with complex reality. The unexpected and unwelcome consequences to which the theory leads demonstrate its inadequacy.

In *The Brothers Karamazov*, for instance, Ivan maintains first, that good and evil are mere social conventions, and second, that even if evil does exist, it applies only to actions and not to wishes. Contrary to both beliefs, he winds up feeling intense guilt for a murder he has done no more than desire. In *War and Peace*, Prince Andrei's experience of lying severely wounded on the battlefield and contemplating the "infinite heavens" proves to him the triviality of "glory."

True to the genre, Bazarov falls in the sort of love whose existence he has denied. Precisely because he denies it, indeed, a sophisticated woman captivates him all the more easily, especially when she intoxicates him with the beauties of nature he has also dismissed. In the novel's key passage, Turgenev describes his hero "tortured and maddened" by a feeling "he would at once have denied with scornful laughter and abuse, if anyone had ever so remotely hinted at what was taking place in him." Bazarov used to wonder that "Toggenburg and all the minnesingers and troubadours had not been put into a lunatic asylum," but now he cannot overlook that something "was taking root at him, something . . . at which all his pride revolted." Trying to banish these shameful thoughts, Bazarov would "obstinately . . . try to force himself to sleep, in which of course, he did not always succeed."[119] The narrator's favorite phrase "of course"—no explanation is necessary for those experienced enough to understand life—suggests the superior wisdom that he and his presumably mature reader share. In novels, wisdom born of experience outstrips theory born of ratiocination.

## We *and the Rebirth of Self*

When Chernyshevsky argued with Turgenev, utopia confronted the novel. This duel of genres reflected the differences between the intelligentsia and the great writers.

In the first decade after the Revolution, the utopian perspective predominated, with its denial of individuality and its unlimited faith in supposedly scientific laws. But the situation also created an opportunity for a new kind of novel, which we have come to call the dystopia.

Previously, anti-utopian fiction usually focused on the naïveté of idealists eager to replace present society with a perfect one.[120] But the Bolsheviks claimed to be doing just that, and so novelists could plausibly set their story in the imminent utopian future. Dystopia's founding novel, Eugene Zamyatin's *We*—the inspiration for Huxley's *Brave New World*, Orwell's *1984*, Bradbury's *Fahrenheit 451* and many other works—discredits utopian ideals by imagining a world in which they have at last been realized. Instead of the expected heaven, however, the result more closely resembles hell—not because the utopian ideology has been perverted but, quite the contrary, because it has been faithfully put into practice. The irony of outcomes pertains not to individuals but to idealistic humanity as a whole.

In the world of *We*, people are identical. "We" has replaced "I." The narrator, a scientist building a rocket to carry utopian ideals to other worlds, proposes to record his experience. As he explains, that experience is not personal, as in the "ancient" world, but impersonal because personhood has disappeared into the collective. He aims to convey not "the things I think" but "the things *we* think." "'We' is from 'God,' 'I' from the devil," he explains.[121]

People, who are called "numbers," no longer have individual names, just digits; the narrator is D-503 and the heroine is I-330. People think the same thoughts "because no one is *one*, but *one of*."[122] They live in glass houses not so they can hide nothing but because they have nothing to hide; they are totally transparent.

Contingency has been entirely banished and so D-503 marvels that once people did not know the results of elections in advance. There is no more surprise. Dostoevsky's underground man, to whom *We* frequently alludes, argues that if everything were determined according to known laws, then life would resemble "a table of logarithms up to 108,000." Should such a world ever come to pass, the underground man supposes, "everything will be so clearly calculated and designated that there will be no more incidents or adventures in the world."[123] After all, adventures require suspense, which is impossible when everything is known in advance. D-503 rejoices that in his world such tables actually exist, and so "there is no place for contingencies; nothing unexpected can happen."[124]

But it does. The novel's plot, which set the pattern for subsequent dystopias, concerns the rebirth of individual self and, along with it, unpredictable choice. Surprise is surprisingly reborn; the hero of the suspenseful story is suspense itself. As Bazarov discovers he is capable of love, so D-503 develops, to his horror, "an incurable soul."[125] His attempt to find mathematical analogies for an irrational self lends the novel considerable wit. The soul, he suggests, resembles X in an unsolvable equation—an allusion to *The Brothers Karamazov*—or, perhaps, the square root of minus one (an "imaginary" number).

As D-503's soul develops, he finds himself, to his dismay, in an "ancient" novel (as, of course, he really is). In what was to become the dystopian master plot, the hero tries to escape from the "perfect" world and return to "the antediluvian time of those Shakespeares and Dostoevskys," especially the latter. "My records," D-503 ruefully admits, resemble "an ancient, strange novel."[126]

D-503 wonders: perhaps a person is not essentially a particle of "we" but an unrepeatable "I"? Is humanity most at home in a world allowing for surprise and choice? Could the essence of humanness be not utopian but novelistic? "Man is like a novel," I-330 tells him. "Up to the last page one does not know what the end will be. It would not be worth reading otherwise."[127]

## Returning the Ticket

"A single death is a tragedy, a million is a statistic," Stalin supposedly said.[128] That may be how it often seems, but perhaps a million deaths is, in fact, a million tragedies? People are not generalizable. "Man-in-general does not exist," Bakhtin declared. "I exist and a particular concrete other exists—my intimate, my contemporary . . . the past and future of actual human beings."[129]

"Hegel has reduced life to dead schemes," Belinsky wrote to his friend V. P. Botkin on March 1, 1841. "He has turned the realities of life into ghosts clasping bony hands and dancing in the air above the cemetery."[130] Hegel and theorists like him, Belinsky complained, take cognizance only of impersonal world processes. They do not concern themselves with individuals who suffer. The very appeal of such thinkers, their ability to transcend sordid experience, entails enormous moral cost.

"You will laugh at me, I know," Belinsky continued, "but, never mind, I will stick to my view: the life of a subject, an individual, a personality is more important than the fate of the world."[131] We have already cited Belinsky's famous rejection of "Yegor Fyodorovich" Hegel:[132] "if I did succeed in reaching the top of the evolution ladder, I would demand even there an account from you of all the victims of the conditions of life and history, of all the victims of accident, superstition, the inquisition, Philip II, etc., etc.: otherwise I will throw myself headlong from the top rung. I will not have happiness even if you gave it to me gratis unless I feel assured about every one of my blood brothers."[133] Ivan Karamazov, as we have also noted, develops this argument in his attack on all theodicies, including secular ones, that justify or explain away individual suffering. By asking us to compare abstract arguments with heart-rending pictures of suffering children, Ivan does more than refute particular theories; he discredits the theoretist impulse itself. As Belinsky demanded an account of each of the Inquisition's victims, Ivan argues that human salvation must not be based on the suffering of even a single child; and as Belinsky will not accept happiness that entails harming even a single individual, Ivan imagines that, even if God should admit him to heaven, he would "most respectfully return him the ticket."[134]

Belinsky's polemic and Ivan's diatribe virtually defined the Russian anti-theoretist tradition. In novel after novel, both before and after 1917, characters contrast theories with the individual suffering they justify.

Does paradise in the future warrant killing children today? In Alexander Kuprin's novel *Yama (The Pit)*, the anarchist Likhonin wrestles with the apparent inevitability of prostitution. "I am an anarchist," he explains, "because my reason . . . always leads me logically to the anarchist beginning. And I myself think in theory." The theory to which he clings is the apocalyptic one that because things are darkest before the dawn, the worse things are, the better they are:

> [. . .] let men beat, deceive, and fleece men, like flocks of sheep—let them!—violence will breed rancor sooner or later. Let them violate the child . . . let there be slavery, let there be prostitution . . . Let them! The

worse, the better, the nearer the end. There is a great law, I think, the same for inanimate objects as well as for the tremendous and many-millioned human life: the power of exertion is equal to the power of resistance. The worse the better.[135]

"The power of exertion is equal to the power of resistance": Likhonin imagines a law of society, modeled on Newton's third law of motion (for every action there is an equal and opposite reaction). Knowing that law, Likhonin continues, he welcomes suffering. "Let evil and vindictiveness . . . grow and ripen like a monstrous abscess—an abscess the size of the whole terrestrial sphere. For it will burst some time! And let there be terror and insufferable pain" since, by scientific law, they will lead humanity to "a new, beautiful life."[136] This is theodicy with a vengeance.

That's the theory, but after having endorsed it, Likhonin mocks it in the spirit of Belinsky and Ivan Karamazov. "Just so do I and many others theorize, sitting in our rooms, over tea with white bread and cooked sausage, when the value of each separate life is so-and-so, an infinitesimally small numeral in a mathematical formula," Likhonin explains. "But let me see a child abused, and the red blood will rush to my head from rage. And . . . I am thrown into hysterics for shame at my algebraic calculations . . . there is a something incongruous, altogether illogical, but which is a hundred times stronger than human reason."[137]

"Our misfortune is that we begin thinking at the end," declares the wise Ananyev in Chekhov's story "Lights." "From the first start . . . we mount to the very topmost, final step, and refuse to know anything about the steps below."[138]

## Crime and Punishment: *Life and Theory*

In *Crime and Punishment*, Raskolnikov embraces murderous theories not out of hard-heartedness but, quite the contrary, out of an extreme sensitivity to others' suffering that he is powerless to prevent. The more suffering affects him, and the more powerless he feels, the more attractive he finds any theory purporting to show that his moral horror is pointless.

After the Marmeladovs's heartrending condition overwhelms him, Raskolnikov first leaves them the little money he has and then, unable to do more, escapes into the theory that the concept of "good and evil" is just unscientific "prejudice." If so, then moral qualms like his are "simply, artificial terrors and . . . it's all as it should be" because things are as the laws of nature inevitably make then. You might as well complain about the law of gravity. In much the same way, Raskolnikov first summons a policeman to save an oblivious girl pursued by a sexual predator but then "in an instant a complete revulsion of feeling came over him." Look at it all from the perspective of the latest social science, he tells himself, and you will see that "a certain percentage . . . must every year go [. . .] that way." But this explanation provokes yet another reversal: "A percentage! What splendid words they have; they are so scientific, so consolatory [. . .] Once you've said 'percentage,' there's nothing to worry about. . . . But what if [my sister] Dunya were one of the percentage?"[139]

After his nightmare about peasants torturing a horse to death, Raskolnikov wakes to the horrible realization that he, too, is planning violence—"that I shall . . . split her skull open . . . tread in the sticky warm blood. . . . Good God, can it be?" But instead of allowing that feeling to discredit his theories, and of returning to his impotent sensitivity, he tries to dismiss his emotional reaction as mere weakness. "Granted, granted that there is no flaw in all that reasoning, that all I have concluded in the last month is as clear as day, as true as arithmetic . . . I couldn't do it!"[140]

Even after he confesses to the murders, Raskolnikov still deems his theory correct and faults only his cowardly failure to live up to it. "'In what way,' he asked himself, 'was my theory stupider than others . . . ? One has only to look at the thing quite independently, broadly . . . and my idea will no longer seem so . . . strange. Oh, skeptics and half-penny philosophers, why do you halt half way? . . . My conscience is at rest.'"[141]

Only on the novel's final pages does he grasp, not by theoretical reasoning but by direct feeling, that his compassionate impulses contain more wisdom than any conceivable theory. "He could not have analyzed anything consciously" precisely because instead of analyzing "he was simply feeling. Life had stepped into the place of theory."[142]

Life or theory? For Chernyshevsky and the intelligentsia, theory provided the proper blueprint for life. For Dostoevsky and the realist novel, life must take the place of theory. Raskolnikov's inner dialectic between the two positions exemplifies a central argument of the Russian experience.

# 7 What Is Not to Be Done?

## Ethics and Materialism

> My conscience is at rest.
>
> —RASKOLNIKOV, IN *CRIME AND PUNISHMENT*

"WE ARE ALL SEEKING, thirsting, waiting [...] waiting for someone to tell us what is to be done," wrote N. A. Dobrolyubov in his celebrated article, "When Will the Real Day Come?"[1] *What is to be done?* (chto delat'?): this question, usually followed by its supposedly indubitable answer, became a rhetorical constant in Russian thought. Most famously, Chernyshevsky used the phrase as the title of his influential utopia *What Is to Be Done?*, as Lenin did for one of his most important books. Neither had any doubt that what they demanded would justify any violence. Perhaps it would have been wiser, as many from Dostoevsky to Solzhenitsyn have thought, to begin with a different question: what is *not* to be done?

In his memoirs of Lenin, Nikolay Valentinov recalled expressing shock at hearing Lenin's view "that nothing, however vile, should be condemned if it is committed by a man who is useful to the party. It is easy this way to arrive at Raskolnikov's 'all is permitted.'"[2] He was even more shocked by Lenin's reply: "What Raskolnikov are you talking about?"—which sounded as strange as someone today asking, "What Macbeth?" or "Hamlet Who?"

By this point the phrase "all is permitted"—as spoken by Raskolnikov in *Crime and Punishment* and Ivan Karamazov in *The Brothers Karamazov*—designated a complex of arguments denying that morality has any objective foundation. It also alluded to an anguished reaction to those arguments. But for Lenin the issue had long since been settled and only fools suffered any pangs about it: "'All is permitted!'" he replied with venom. "That's what we've arrived at—the tender and fine words of a spineless intellectual who wants to drown the problems of the Party and the revolution in moralizing vomit!"[3]

Several lines of reasoning led to Raskolnikov's famous phrase. To begin with, science describes the world in terms of cause and effect acting on purely material objects. There is no room in science for moral categories. If I drop a stone, it falls at 9.8 meters per second per second: is this behavior moral or immoral? The question obviously makes no sense; but if people are just complex material objects, it makes no more sense to ask about the morality of their behavior. Everything is as it is, and that is all.

Ivan Karamazov, a student of natural science, is torn apart by his simultaneous belief in this "scientific" amoralism and his overpowering sense of evil when people inflict suffering on children. In the chapter "Rebellion," he relates horrendous examples of child abuse, which he cannot dismiss on scientific, theological, or any other grounds. Moralism may be primitive, but amoralism is loathsome. How can this contradiction be resolved?

When the Karamazovs meet in Father Zosima's cell, the monks discuss one of Ivan's articles. Like almost everything Ivan says, this article is written in a code enabling him to explore issues without committing himself to any answer.

The article ostensibly concerns the jurisdiction of ecclesiastic (as opposed to state) courts, and we are told that while most readers disputed which side the author was on, "some sagacious people" at last opined that "the article was nothing but an impudent satirical burlesque."[4] Only Father Zosima recognizes the argument as an allegory about the reasons people should not commit crimes. By "state courts" Ivan means the purely pragmatic consideration that one might get caught. If that is the only consideration, then, if one is sure one will not get caught (or the benefit is great and the chance of being caught minimal), there is no rational reason not to commit the crime.[5] So far as this approach goes, there is nothing essentially different between murder and littering. By "church courts" Ivan means that one does not commit crimes simply because it is morally wrong to do so. This way of thinking treats right and wrong as no less objective than astronomical laws.

For all his allegorical disguises, Zosima (as we have seen) tells Ivan, the question of morality

> "is still fretting your heart. . . . That question you have not answered, and it is your great grief, for it clamors for an answer."

"But can it be answered by me? Answered in the affirmative?" Ivan went on asking strangely. . . .

"If it can't be decided in the affirmative, it will never be decided in the negative. You know that is the peculiarity of your heart, and all its suffering is due to it. But thank the Creator who has given you a lofty heart."[6]

Zosima means that Ivan will either answer his question in the affirmative—that is, he will cease to doubt that morality is real—or else he will keep on looking; but he will never, like his terrible father, complacently accept amorality. In his tormenting inner argument, Ivan enacts the drama of this "accursed question" of Russian thought.

## Environment

Other arguments, many still with us, also led to amoralism. We have already examined Chernyshevsky's contention that choice is merely the subjective accompaniment of causes acting outside our awareness and without regard to our will. Our will, in fact, is itself the product of these causes, so that even if we could choose what we will, we cannot will what we will. In that case, as Chernyshevsky maintained, it makes no more sense to blame people for their behavior than to blame Mars for traveling in an elliptical orbit.

In one version of this argument, favored by Chernyshevsky, the real cause of crime lies in the "environment," a term that meant the social environment shaping us all. People do what society educates them to do, and "in the final analysis everything depends exclusively on circumstances." It followed for Chernyshevsky that "one ought not to blame people for anything at any cost" since the social circumstances, not the individual made by them, are alone responsible:"Before you accuse someone, perceive first whether circumstances and social customs are responsible," as they always are.[7] Since the same simple motivations govern all human behavior, everyone educated in the same way must automatically make identical "choices." The judge who condemns a malefactor would, in the same circumstances, behave as he did.[8] "What is necessary here is not punishment of a particular person, but a change in the conditions of a whole class."[9]

We can appreciate how rapidly and widely this exculpation for misbehavior spread when, at the beginning of *Anna Karenina*, Anna's brother Stiva, who is anything but an intellectual, comforts himself with it after being caught in infidelity. "It's all my fault, but I'm not to blame," he thinks. That is, the action happened through him but anyone in his situation would have behaved

the same way. It's simply nature. Later in the novel Anna offers the same excuse for infidelity: "But I was not to blame," she tells her sister-in-law Dolly.
"And who is to blame? What's the meaning of being to blame? Could it have
been otherwise? What do you think? Could it have happened that you didn't
become the wife of Stiva?"[10]

This argument especially appalled Dostoevsky, who attacked it repeatedly,
not just because it licensed crime but also because it turned human beings
into objects. Objects do not have "human dignity," a concept that, by Chernyshevsky's logic, derives from the superstition that man was created in God's
image.[11] Since there is no moral reason not to do what one likes with objects,
Chernyshevsky's argument invites unspeakable cruelty.

In his article "Environment," Dostoevsky observed that Russian juries,
misled by the new doctrine of "environment," have recently succumbed to a
"mania for acquittal." Clever lawyers explain "that there are no crimes at all,
and 'the environment is to blame' for everything." Soon enough, people are
bound to take the next step and "consider crime even a duty, a noble protest
against the environment. 'Since society is organized in such a vile fashion, one
can't get along in it without protest and crimes.'"[12]

Dostoevsky's article contrasts the environmental theory with Christianity,
which, while acknowledging that people's circumstances matter and calling
for mercy, "still places a moral duty on the individual to struggle with the environment, and marks the line where the environment ends and duty begins." In
holding the individual responsible, Dostoevsky continues, "Christianity
thereby acknowledges his freedom" and his difference from mere material objects. It affirms the value of human life. "The doctrine of the environment," by
contrast, "reduces him [man] to an absolute nonentity, exempts him totally
from every personal moral duty and from all independence, [and] reduces
him to the lowest form of slavery imaginable."[13]

Dostoevsky asks us to consider the case of a peasant recently acquitted for
brutally beating his wife, with their child watching. "Have you ever seen how a
peasant beats his wife? I have," Dostoevsky begins his description of the crime.
The scene he imagines, as only Dostoevsky could, goes beyond cruelty to positive sadism, and beyond physical abuse to utter humiliation. First the peasant
starves his wife and, to torment her the more, leaves out bread she is forbidden
to touch. He hangs her by the heels like a chicken to beat her upside down. At
last the woman hangs herself. "Mama, why are you choking?" the child asks.[14]

The jury pronounced the peasant guilty "but with a recommendation for
clemency"![15] As for the little girl who testified against her father, she was to be
returned to him.

Dostoevsky next imagines how a defense attorney would excuse the peasant's behavior as the inevitable result of "backwardness, ignorance, the environment." And yet there are millions of peasants "and not all hang their wives by the heels." Besides, if the environment causes everything, the same argument could be made for "an educated person [who] . . . hangs his wife by her heels." "Enough contortions, gentlemen of the bar," the article ends. "Enough of your 'environment.'"[16]

Another possibility is sure to arise. "And what if the criminal, consciously preparing to commit a crime, says to himself: 'There is no crime!'"[17] In *The Idiot* Dostoevsky depicts a scoundrel thinking just this way.[18] Theories about crime are themselves part of the environment that shapes the criminal, and by no means the least important part. Planets do not alter their behavior in response to theories describing them, but people do. In article and novel, Dostoevsky argues in the novelistic way: he examines ideas by showing the consequences of believing them.

## It's All Relative

When Alyosha Karamazov visits his brother Dmitri in prison, he learns that the *intelligent* Rakitin has bombarded the captive with fashionable ideas excusing crime. Rakitin plans to launch his career with an article applying all the right progressive theories to Dmitri's famous case. "He wants to say 'he couldn't help murdering his father, he was corrupted by his environment,' and so on. . . . He is going to put in a tinge of Socialism." Rakitin has explicated his version of physiologist Claude Bernard's deterministic doctrine (which influenced Zola). Disgusted, Dmitri excoriates Rakitin and all other cynical "Bernards": "They are all scoundrels. And Rakitin will make his way. Rakitin will get on anywhere; he is another Bernard. Ugh, these Bernards! They are all over the place."[19]

Rakitin has also explained cultural relativism to Dmitri: "Goodness is one thing for me and another with a Chinese person, so it's a relative thing," Dmitri paraphrases Rakitin. "A treacherous question! You won't laugh if I tell you it's kept me awake two nights. I only wonder how people can live and think nothing about it."[20] Russian *intelligents*, who took historical relativism even more seriously than cultural relativism, concluded that good and evil are just "conventions" or, for Marxists, "false consciousness." "It is self-evident," wrote Marx and Engels in *The German Ideology*, "that . . . 'the higher being,' 'concept,' 'scruple' are merely the idealistic, spiritual expression . . . of very empirical fetters and limitations, within which the mode of production of life and the form of intercourse coupled with it move."[21]

Why stop at historical and cultural relativism? Morality, declared Pisarev, is simply a matter of personal taste. "If one gourmet likes to have sherry for dinner and another prefers port, there will hardly be a critic in the world able to prove conclusively that one of the two is right and the other wrong . . . but heaven forbid if he voices an independent opinion on morality."[22]

## Are You Your Brain?

Dmitri is most shaken by Rakitin's paraphrase of the extraordinarily influential ideas of physiologist Ivan Sechenov (who had studied with Bernard).[23] Sechenov's book *Reflexes of the Brain* (1863), published in the weekly *Medical Herald*, had originally been submitted to the widely read *Contemporary* under the title "An Attempt to Explain the Origin of Psychical [Psychological] Phenomena," but failed to pass the censor. Today we would refer to Sechenov's argument as neurological reductionism, the theory that consciousness and thought can be exhaustively explained by brain activity—or in Sechenov's words, "that the spirit is the product of the functioning of the brain."[24]

The diversity "of external manifestations of cerebral activity can be reduced ultimately to a single phenomenon—muscular movement," Sechenov explained. "Whether it's the child laughing at the sight of a toy, or Garibaldi smiling when persecuted for excessive love for his native land, or a girl trembling at the first thought of love, or Newton creating universal laws and inscribing them on paper—the ultimate fact is muscular movement." Muscular movement, in turn, "can be subjected to mathematical analysis and expressed by formulas." Even artistic expression is "a purely mechanical act . . . the time will come when men will be able to analyze the external manifestations of the functioning of the brain [in artists] as easily as the physicist analyzes now a musical chord or the phenomenon of a freely falling body."[25] And again, we see how widespread these ideas rapidly became when Stiva Oblonsky excuses one of his actions as simply "reflex action of the brain."[26]

In a similar tone, Chernyshevsky proclaimed the identity of "the process which occurred in the nervous system of Newton when he discovered the law of gravity and the process which takes place in the nervous system of a hen picking grains of oat in a heap of rubbish and dust."[27] One way to show how "scientific" one is, is to dismiss what unenlightened people take for granted—genius, selfhood, human dignity, good and evil, moral responsibility, choice—as so much prescientific prejudice.[28] As we have noted, the radical critic

M. A. Antonovich, who described the formulation of abstract ideas as an "involuntary" process happening by "physiological necessity," used the passive voice to describe thought processes, which he compared to the reflex actions of frogs with their brain removed.[29]

The neurological explanation of consciousness brings Dmitri to despair:

> Imagine: inside, in the nerves, in the head—that is, these nerves are there in the brain [...] (damn them!) there are a sort of little tails, the little tails of those nerves, and as soon as they begin quivering [...] that is, you see, I look at something with my eyes and then they begin quivering, those little tails [...] and when they quiver, an image appears ... an object, or an action, damn it! That's why I see and then think, because of those tails, not at all because I've got a soul, and that I am sort of image and likeness.... And yet I am sorry to lose God.[30]

With updated terminology, essentially the same statement could be made—and often is—today.[31] And the same question is begged: how could quivering tails, or neurological discharges, create the subjective experience of consciousness? An image appears—to whom?[32]

In *Anna Karenina*, Levin overhears a conversation between his brother, the thinker Sergey Ivanovich Koznyshev, and a Kiev professor about these very questions. "The point in discussion," Tolstoy explains, "was the question then in vogue: is there a line to be drawn between psychological and physiological phenomena in man, and if so where?"—that is, can all psychological phenomena be reduced to physiological process and if not, which ones are irreducible? Levin had come across the articles they were discussing, but now sees for the first that these "deductions as to the origin of man as an animal, as to reflex action, biology, and sociology" pertain to the questions about ethics and meaning that trouble him. Sergey Ivanovich denies that we derive all our ideas from sensations since the "idea of existence" itself corresponds to no sensation; the professor cites the usual reply that the idea of existence comes from the conjunction of all senses; and Levin, impatient to get beyond the cut and thrust of academic argument, asks if that means we do not have a soul. The professor winces in pain at such a naïve question, coming from a man who looks more like a barge hauler than a philosopher, but Sergey Ivanovich, who understands "the simple and natural point of view from which the question was asked," smiles indulgently.[33] These questions had already been "in vogue" for over a decade.

## Justice without Guilt or Innocence

Absolving individuals from responsibility may seem humane until one recognizes that, by the same logic, preemptive punishment makes as much sense as retributive. If no one is responsible, then punishment exists not to ensure justice but to direct behavior, and the only question is which punishments are most effective in doing so. Guilt is beside the point, and the concept of innocence disappears. What reason could there be not to lock up those who might commit crimes to prevent them from doing so? That is precisely the conclusion drawn in Soviet justice.

The Soviet criminal code therefore specified potential crimes as crimes in themselves. The OSO (Special Council of the State Security Ministry) used the initials PSh for the crime of "Suspicion of Espionage" (actual espionage was covered under a different article). One step further away from actual criminal activity was SVPSh, "Contacts Leading to Suspicion of Espionage."[34]

Even these "actions" were not necessary to qualify for arrest. Simply belonging to the wrong class, or otherwise qualifying as SOE (Socially Dangerous Element) was sufficient. After all, if all crime results from bad social conditions, and if one belongs to a group that might want to preserve those conditions, then one merits elimination simply by virtue of belonging to that group. For that matter, why not preemptively arrest the whole group? As prosecutor general and People's Commissar of Justice Nikolai Krylenko observed, we take cognizance of what people *might* do, or as he expressed the point: "We protect ourselves not only against the past but also against the future."[35] Krylenko was himself executed in 1938.

And why stop at suspicious groups? Might it not have a desirable effect to terrorize society as a whole? As we have noted, one difference between Soviet and Nazi totalitarianism is that in the USSR even the most loyal officials were arrested *en masse*; the Soviet secret police was constantly arresting its own agents. After all, everyone was potentially criminal. General terror prevented anyone from trusting anyone else enough to conspire with him or her.

After his arrest, former Bolshevik leader Nikolay Bukharin wrote to Stalin: "There is something *great and bold about the political idea of a general purge*. . . . This purge encompasses (1) the guilty, (2) persons under suspicion; and (3) persons potentially under suspicion."[36] Anyone who *might* have reason to hold anti-Soviet attitudes, including friends and relatives of arrested people, qualified for arrest. NKVD chief Yezhov's famous Order No. 00486 specified that wives of "traitors of the motherland" were to be sen-

tenced to between five and eight years in a labor camp. Their children of fifteen years or older, since they were "capable of anti-Soviet activity" and might
wish to take revenge, were to be dispatched to labor colonies.[37]

Though the Soviets made wide use of the concepts of potential counterrevolutionary activity and the collective punishment of whole groups, they
did not invent it. They inherited it from non-Marxist intelligentsia circles. In
1907, the "Maximalist" terrorist theoretician Ivan Pavlov—not to be confused
with the famous psychologist—published *The Purification of Mankind* (*Och-
istka chelovechestva*) in which he divided humanity into two ethical (rather
than ethnic) "races." All those associated with government, all capitalists, and
all other exploiters, constituted a race of worthless predators. Since their
children were bound to "exhibit the same malice, cruelty, meanness, rapacity,
and greed," the entire race had to be exterminated.[38] Pavlov therefore called
for a civil war in which one section of the population would annihilate the
other. As historian Anna Geifman observed, it is noteworthy that Pavlov's
doctrine "aroused no negative feelings, indignation, or protests, and even failed
to provoke controversy within the ranks of the Maximalists." Although the
Maximalists did not adopt Pavlov's position as their formal program, "he
continued to be considered the brightest ideologist of Maximalism.'" Another
Maximalist, M. A. Engel'gardt, also argued for a Red Terror to eliminate "no
fewer than twelve million counter-revolutionaries, including land and factory
owners, bankers and priests."[39]

According to this way of thinking, one is a counterrevolutionary not
because of anything one has done, but simply because of one's class background. In 1918, Cheka (secret police) leader M. I. Latsis instructed revolutionary tribunals dispensing summary justice to disregard personal guilt or
innocence: "Do not seek in your accusations proof of whether the prisoner
rebelled against the Soviets with guns or by word. First you must ask him to
what class he belongs, what his social origin is. . . . These answers must determine the fate of the accused. That is the meaning of the Red Terror."[40]

When Stalin conducted his campaign to "liquidate the kulaks as a class"
and waged his war in the countryside to collectivize agriculture, he used just
this logic, which derived not only from Marxism-Leninism but also from
broader intelligentsia tradition. If individuals are not responsible for crime,
then there is no point in judging them as individuals. Instead, one must eliminate whatever groups that, according to one's theory, foster undesired values
or conditions. Since the number of ways to identify groups—by profession,
education, place of residence, ethnic background, and more—is unlimited,
anyone could be a target.

In Grossman's *Life and Fate*, the Chekist Katsenelenbogen explains that "the concept of personal innocence is a hangover from the Middle Ages. Pure superstition! Tolstoy declared that no one in the world is guilty. We Chekists have put forward a more advanced theory: 'No one in the world is innocent.' ... Yes, everyone has the right to a warrant. Even if he has spent his whole life issuing warrants for others."[41]

The logic of preemptive punishment of potentially untrustworthy groups also led to the forcible deportation to remote regions of entire ethnicities—Koreans, Chechens, Crimean Tatars, Volga Germans, and others. Those who survived the journey found themselves in unpopulated barren wastes, where many, if not most, died. Jews, especially after the creation of the state of Israel, became potential agents of a foreign power. Only the death of Stalin prevented their deportation.[42]

For the Soviets, as for Pavlov, class was a heritable trait. One might falsify one's class background, as many tried to do, but one lived in terror of "unmasking"—that is, the possible discovery of one's origins.[43] Victor Shtrum, the hero of Grossman's *Life and Fate*, has accepted the logic of "question 6" on endless questionnaires regarding class origin. "Victor had always felt that this sixth point was a legitimate expression of the mistrust of the poor for the rich. ... He thought to himself: 'To me, a distinction based on social origin [rather than individual responsibility] seems legitimate and moral.'" But when the Soviets turn on the Jews, he asks himself "whether there really was such a gulf between the legitimate Soviet question about social origin and the bloody, fateful question of nationality as posed by the Germans" who, after all, "obviously consider a distinction based on nationality to be equally moral."[44] In both cases, people become targets not on account of their actions but because of their ancestry.

Shtrum protests with his whole being against Nazi murder of people, however gifted, kind, or sensitive, simply because they are Jews: "But then we have the same principle: what matters is whether or not you're the son of an aristocrat, the son of a merchant, the son of a kulak. ... And we're not talking about the merchants, priests, and aristocrats themselves—but about their children and grandchildren. Does noble blood run in one's veins like Jewishness? Is one a priest or a merchant by heredity? Nonsense."[45]

Grossman, a Jew who had been the first to report on the Holocaust as it unfolded on Soviet territory, came to equate Nazis and Soviets. Marxism, in his view, is racism by class.[46] In fact, as he also recognized, Marxism itself could, when convenient, easily become classism by race or ethnicity. And with the Soviet anti-Semitic campaign, it did.

## Ends and Means

If morality is mere prejudice—in Raskolnikov's phrase, "artificial terrors"[47]—is there any limit to what one might do to achieve one's ends? *Intelligents* asked: Does the end justify *any* means? For instance, should terrorists hesitate to kill their target if children are also bound to die? For that matter, is there any reason not to target children themselves as a way to terrorize a population?

If building socialism requires killing thousands, even millions of people, should one do so? In *The Possessed*, the radicals contemplate taking "a hundred million heads and so lightening one's burden, so that one can jump over the ditch [to the new utopian society] more safely."[48] Uniquely for his time, Dostoevsky thought such mass killing entirely possible and, indeed, as the well-known *Black Book of Communism* established, the bare minimum of civilian deaths caused by Communist regimes in the twentieth century is a hundred million.[49]

The novel's leading revolutionary, Pyotr Stepanovich, knows he can get gentler souls to go along with revolutionary violence if he represents opposition as insufficiently liberal or "not advanced enough." We have already quoted the major in *The Possessed*: "I confess I am rather in favor of a more humane policy. But as all are on the other side, I go along with the rest."[50]

Historians have wondered: why was Dostoevsky the only person to foresee that the twentieth century would not be one of increasing human rights and welfare for everyone, but of the unprecedented horror we have come to call totalitarianism? Why were characters in *The Possessed* able to describe it in detail? The answer, I think, is threefold: (1) Dostoevsky took seriously what *intelligents* said they would do in power; (2) he recognized the psychology leading people (like the major) to support ever more extreme positions; and (3) he understood that, in the absence of sufficient resistance, there was no limit to how far things could go. That much was evident to him from the example of the terrorist Sergei Nechaev (on whom Pyotr Stepanovich is loosely based), a revolutionary who horrified Dostoevsky but favorably impressed Lenin.

For the revolutionary, Nechaev wrote, "everything that promotes revolution is moral; everything that hinders it is immoral."[51] In *Landmarks* Semyon Frank outlined how "the non-recognition of absolute, truly binding values" combined with "the cult of the material benefit of the majority, provide justification for the primacy of might over right" and "the idolatrous worship of party interests."[52] Quoting Plekhanov's speech endorsing the most cynical

tactics and falsehoods, Bogdan Kistyakovksy, another *Landmarks* contrib-
utor, observed that "the idea proclaimed in this speech—that force and
usurped power are supreme . . . is simply monstrous." So deeply has this way
of thinking penetrated, he continued, that even liberals, who supposedly believe in the rule of law, advocate suppressing contrary opinions and "even
physical coercion."[53]

Chekhov, too, was appalled. Commenting on the revolutionaries' strategy
of exacerbating, rather than ameliorating, the epidemic of cholera (the worse,
the better), he wrote to his friend Suvorin (on August 1, 1892) that "if our
socialists are really going to exploit the cholera for their own ends, I shall
despise them. Repulsive means for good ends make the ends themselves
repulsive."[54]

The question of whether, in the absence of God or some other objective
foundation for morality, the ends justify any means—whether literally "all is
permitted"—arose constantly.

## The Moral Minimum

Lenin gave new meaning to "the end justifies the means." Until I started examining his thought in detail a few years ago, I thought that a fair statement of
his view is that, if necessary, one could employ whatever violence might be
required to achieve one's ends. This formulation would aptly describe anarchist Peter Kropotkin's view, but not Lenin's.

"The question is, then," Kropotkin explained, "how to attain the greatest
results with the most limited amount of civil war, the smallest number of
victims, and a minimum of mutual embitterment."[55] For Lenin, concern
about "the smallest number of victims," let alone "a minimum of mutual embitterment," was not only ridiculous but counterrevolutionary.

In his memoirs of his time working in the early Bolshevik government
Isaac Steinberg contrasted Lenin with populist theorist Peter Lavrov, who
maintained that "the banner of the revolution must remain spotless and un-
sullied by a single unnecessary drop of blood. The ethical purity of the socialist struggle must never be in jeopardy."[56]

In an article entitled "Ethics and Politics," a review of Savinkov's novel "What
Never Happened," Socialist Revolutionary leader Victor Chernov argued that
revolutionaries could not, of course, accept the moral maximum of Tolstoy's
doctrine of nonresistance to evil, but they could and must maintain a moral
minimum. "Revolutionary despotism is on the same level as counterrevolutionary despotism," he asserted. "Revolutionary ethics rejects the instinct for

revenge both of those who oppress the people and of those fighting for their liberation. It repudiates the persecution of ideas, be they retrograde or progressive."[57] For Lavrov, Kropotkin, and Chernov, the noble end justified violent means only to the extent necessary.

Appalled by Bolshevik violence beginning right after the October 1917 seizure of power, the writer Vladimir Korolenko, long regarded as a national conscience, objected to Bolshevik ethics. Anatoly Lunacharsky, the first head of the People's Commissariat of Education (Narkompros), debated him and, upon Korolenko's death in 1921, wrote a eulogy entitled "A Righteous Man." Since Bolsheviks viewed the whole concept of "righteousness" as a mystification, the title was ironic, if not sarcastic. "Righteous men are appalled by the blood on our hands. Righteous men are in despair over our cruelty," Lunacharsky wrote. "The righteous man will never understand that . . . it is not only a question of self-sacrifice (this he understands) but also of the sacrifice of others."[58]

## Lenin: "Find Tougher People"

Lenin repeatedly expressed utter contempt for the "moral minimum" idea, and his reasoning became the Soviet position on ethics, taught to generations of schoolchildren. To prefer "the smallest number of victims," "a minimum of mutual embitterment," and the avoidance of "a single unnecessary drop of blood"—for Lenin, such thinking presumed the absolute value of human life, a doctrine that ultimately derived either from religion or from Kant's quasi-religious imperative always to treat people as ends, not means.[59] Lenin and Trotsky, who regarded themselves as uncompromising materialists, sneered at the whole idea of "the sanctity of human life."

In their view, people are material objects like any other, with no immortal or infinitely valuable soul. What's more, objective ethics of the Kantian or any other kind does not exist. Each class defines "right and wrong" to suit its own interests. The idea that human life is valuable regardless of class interests is, they held, a bourgeois mystification.

All the same, Lenin argued in his speech "The Tasks of the Youth Leagues" (October 2, 1920), it is slanderous to say that Bolsheviks have no ethics. "Very often the bourgeoisie accuse us Communists of rejecting all morality," he instructed. "This is a method . . . of throwing dust in the eyes of the workers or peasants." What we do reject, Lenin explained, is ethics "in the sense given to it by the bourgeoisie, who based their ethics on God's commandments . . . or . . . on idealist or semi-idealist phrases, which always amounted to something very similar to God's commandments."

All ethical theories except dialectical materialism mistakenly presume that ethics is somehow objective, like the laws of arithmetic, but Bolsheviks know that ethics is a strictly class concept. Bolsheviks repudiate "any morality based on extra-human and extra-class concepts. . . . That is to say that to us there is no such thing as a morality that stands outside human society; that is a fraud."

Lenin's point is *not* that in the extreme situation of revolution one can set aside the principles of morality. That view still acknowledges the reality of the "extra-human and extra-class" morality one has set aside. By the same token, the interests of the Revolution do not outweigh all other moral principles combined; there are no other moral principles. "To a Communist all morality lies in . . . conscious mass struggle against the exploiters. We do not believe in an eternal morality, and we expose the falseness of all the fables about morality."[60]

To appreciate how odd Lenin's notion is, imagine someone protesting that it is slanderous to say he has no moral standards because he has one to which he always adheres: look out for number one! One might reply that "look out for number one" is not morality at all. Morality by definition entails concerns beyond the self; it begins with number two.

Lenin lamented that Bolshevik morality exceeds most people's capability. Having been educated to regard others as ends rather than means, most people regrettably hesitate before killing; they fret about individual guilt; and they find it difficult to execute children. Torture, public hangings, mass hostage-taking, or destruction of whole cities shocks them. Lenin reproached his subordinates for all these vestiges of religion and bourgeois morality. When peasants objected to the seizure of their grain without payment, Lenin wrote to the Bolsheviks in Penza:

> Comrades! The kulak uprising in [your] 5 districts must be crushed without pity . . . An example must be made. 1) Hang (and I mean hang so that the people can see) not less than 100 known kulaks, rich men, bloodsuckers, 2) Publish their names, 3) Take all their grain away from them. 4) Identify hostages . . . Do this so that for hundreds of miles around the people can see, tremble, know and cry: they are killing and will go on killing the bloodsucking kulaks. Cable that you have received this and carried out [your instructions].
>
> Yours, Lenin.
>
> P. S. Find tougher people.[61]

"Find tougher people": Lenin worried about insufficient rather than excessive cruelty. "Any display of weakness, hesitation, or sentimentality . . . would be an immense crime against socialism," he instructed.[62] The Party, as one historian observed, "had to threaten provincial soviets with severe punishment for failing to implement its terroristic directives."[63] "When we are reproached with cruelty," Lenin declared in a sentence cited above, "we wonder how people can forget the most elementary Marxism."[64] From this point on, they remembered.

In his speech at the "Promparty" trial, Krylenko famously observed that in the early days of the regime, when Bolsheviks were surrounded by enemies, they mistakenly, if understandably, showed—not unnecessary violence or cruelty but "unnecessary leniency and unnecessary softheartedness."[65]

Historians have pointed out that, far from responding to oppositional activities, Bolshevik violence, which began before there was any active opposition, fostered them. If anything, it made holding on to power more difficult. But to argue this way, as westerners naturally do, is to presume that cruelty requires justification. On the contrary, for Lenin, Stalin, Trotsky, Bukharin, and their Bolshevik followers, it was "leniency" and "softheartedness" that were questionable. Unless one grasps the point that cruelty was the default position, one cannot understand Soviet decisionmaking.

As atheists and materialists, Bolsheviks extirpated (or, rather, tried to extirpate) all inclination to mercy. To show compassion was to risk the accusation of covert religiosity and so of counterrevolutionary thinking. It therefore paid to be as cruel as possible. Cruelty, in short, became an atheist virtue. When Lenin learned that the Second Congress of Soviets had abolished the death penalty, Trotsky recalled, he became "utterly indignant." "It is a mistake, he [Lenin] repeated, impermissible weakness, pacifist illusion and so on." "And so on," "etc.," and similar phrases appear commonly in Lenin's dictates, as if there must be no limit to Bolshevik relentlessness. We aim at "the *cleansing of Russia's soil of harmful insects, of scoundrels, fleas, bedbugs—the rich*, and so on," he wrote.[66] Lenin also loved italics: nothing was said without emphasis.

Trotsky sneered at those who objected to the policy of "finishing off the dying class." "You are indignant . . . at the petty terror which we direct against our opponents," he taunted in a December 2, 1917, speech. "But be put on notice that in one month at most this terror will assume more frightful forms. . . . Our enemies will face not prison but the guillotine."[67] Within a week the Cheka came into being.

In *The Economics of the Transition Period*, Bukharin—often thought of as a moderate for opposing Stalin's violence against the peasantry—listed groups to be subjected to "concentrated violence." These groups included: "the parasitic strata (former landowners ... bourgeois entrepreneurs not directly involved in production)"; "skilled bureaucrats—civilian, military, and clerical"; "the technical intelligentsia ... (engineers, technicians, agronomists, veterinarians, doctors, professors, lawyers, journalists, most teachers, etc.)"; "the well-off peasantry"; "the middle and, in part, petty urban bourgeoisie"; and "the clergy, even the unskilled kind." Historian Yuri Slezkine explained that "'concentrated violence' included arrests, searches, killings, censorship, forced labor, suppression of strikes, takeover of property, confiscation of produce, and confinement in concentration camps. The targets were identified ... according to a flexible class taxonomy."[68] One needs precision to avoid applying a decree too broadly; flexibility is desirable to prevent its application too narrowly.

As we have seen, when Dmitri Kursky was formulating the new Soviet law code, Lenin cautioned him that "the law should not abolish terror ... it should be substantiated and legalized in principle, clearly without evasion or embellishment."[69] Once again, we recognize what I think of as Lenin's "hollowing out" principle: much as a "morality" that enjoins self-interest is entirely empty of morality, so "law" that mandates extra-legal government action is the definition of lawlessness.

It says a lot about Soviet ethics that the person who founded the Cheka, the Pole "Iron Feliks" Dzerzhinsky, became a revered hero. "The difference between the Jacobin and Bolshevik terrors," observed Richard Pipes, "is perhaps best symbolized by the fact that in Paris no monuments have been raised to Robespierre and no streets named after him, whereas a giant statue of Feliks Dzerzhinsky ... stands in the heart of the city [of Moscow], dominating a square named in his honor."[70] In Warsaw, where the Soviets also set up a Dzerzhinsky statue, I overheard a Pole saying that Dzerzhinsky really should be honored—as the Pole who killed the most Russians.

## Lenin: Zero-Sum Thinking

If morality is identified with the Party's interests, then any reluctance to press an advantage is automatically immoral. Lenin therefore regarded all interactions as zero-sum. To use the phrase with which Lenin is frequently identified, everything is a matter of "Who Whom?"—who dominates whom, who does what to whom, ultimately who annihilates whom. To the extent that we gain, you lose.

Contrast this view with the one taught in basic microeconomics: whenever there is a non-forced transaction, both sides benefit, or they would not make the exchange. For the seller, the money is worth more than the goods he sells, and for the buyer the goods are worth more than the money. Lenin's hatred of the market, and his attempts to abolish it entirely under War Communism, derived from the opposite idea, that all buying and selling is *necessarily* exploitative. When the Bolsheviks used the term "speculation," we recall, they meant all exchanges outside of government control.

If the enemy is weak enough to be destroyed, and one stops simply at one's initial demands, one is objectively helping the enemy, which makes one a traitor. The following statement from Lenin's most famous book, *What Is to Be Done?*, is typical (the italics are Lenin's): "The *only* choice is: either the bourgeois or the socialist ideology. There is no middle course (for humanity has not created a 'third' ideology, and, moreover, in a society torn by class antagonisms there can never be a non-class or above-class ideology). Hence to belittle the socialist ideology *in any way, to turn away from it in the slightest degree*, means to strengthen bourgeois ideology." No middle ground exists. If one does not absolutely agree on all points, one is a traitor. There is no such thing as a loyal opposition. In short, there is either rule by the bourgeoisie or dictatorship of the proletariat: "Every solution that offers a middle path is a deception ... or an expression of the dull-wittedness of the petty-bourgeois democrats."[71]

The more inhumane a policy sounded, the more Bolshevik it was presumed to be. What was called "compulsory labor"—or at times "slavery"—was introduced almost immediately. "We ought to begin introducing compulsory labor immediately," Lenin wrote in 1918. And they did. Workers and specialists were drafted into a labor army, where disobedience was treated as treasonous and quitting as desertion. "Not a single rogue (including those who shirk their work) should be allowed to be at liberty, but kept in prison, or serve his sentence of compulsory labor of the harshest kind."[72]

Since people are lazy, Trotsky maintained, "the only way to attract the labor power necessary for economic tasks is to introduce *compulsory labor service*." Speaking to the Ninth Party Congress (March 1920), he made clear that compulsory labor was no temporary measure. "We are making the first attempt in world history to organize labor in the interests of the laboring majority," he explained. "But this, of course, does not mean liquidating the element of compulsion. . . . No, compulsion plays and will play an important part for a significant period of history."[73]

When sentimental Mensheviks argue that compulsory labor is unproductive, Trotsky continued, "they are captive of bourgeois ideology and reject the very foundations of the socialist economy." Remarkably, Trotsky went on to defend serfdom. In the days of serfdom, he explained, it was not necessary for gendarmes to stand over peasants, who "only rebelled from time to time." In any case, if forced labor is unproductive, "the whole socialist economy is doomed to be scrapped, because there is no other way of attaining socialism except through the command allocation of the entire labor force."[74]

Economists routinely point out that the only alternative to the market is compulsion, so one might assume that the Bolsheviks were forced into this position. I think this argument falls short because the Bolsheviks did not have to be forced into inhumane behavior. They favored it. They needed reasons *not* to choose it.

## Soviet Ethics

Soviet ethics, explains the hero of Grossman's final novel, *Forever Flowing*, bases itself on a reverse categorical imperative, "a categorical imperative counterposed to that of Kant": always use human beings as mere means.[75] One did not have to be immoral to squander human life. On the contrary, one could readily regard oneself as an ethical person and, by official standards, actually be one.

In her memoir *Within the Whirlwind*, Evgeniya Ginzburg described the official Kaldymov, who directed agriculture produced by slave labor in the frozen far north. Once a philosopher by profession, and therefore adept at dialectical materialism, Kaldymov calculated that it makes no sense to preserve the lives of political prisoners arrested during the Great Terror. They did not produce enough to justify their food rations. One could always get fresh contingents and, during the war years, not just intellectuals resembling "walking corpses," but also healthy peasants. Ginzburg once overheard Kaldymov order that bulls be removed from a building unfit for habitation and that female prisoners, much less valuable than bulls, be housed there instead. In his view, he was simply correcting his predecessor's mistake resulting from "extreme thoughtlessness" in the management of resources. Ginzburg stressed that Kaldymov was no sadist and would have been "fearfully surprised if anyone had called him to his face a slave owner." "Wastage"—the term for convict mortality—"was to him no more than a routine malfunction of the production line, akin, let us say, to the wearing out of a silage cutter. . . . He was totally unaware of his own cruelty" because his training in Marxism-Leninism made such thinking "routine."[76]

People were simply material objects, governed by natural laws. Memoirists frequently pointed out that prisoners in camps (as well as nonprisoners in forced labor armies) received treatment far less humane than Russian serfs had endured. Although they could be bought and sold, Russian serfs had still been regarded as human beings with a soul. Their lowly standing and lack of rights notwithstanding, they were people like their owners and attended the same churches. Soviet prisoners, by contrast, were so much raw material. We have already cited Dmitri Panin's observation that they were worse off not only than serfs but even than ancient Egyptian slaves: "the slaves who erected the pyramids were fortunate men by comparison. . . . The Egyptians were quite well fed. . . . Since a slave had market value, he warranted some care."[77]

## Do Unto Others

In addition to a reverse categorical imperative, what might be called a reverse golden rule operated: always treat others—meaning class or other enemies— as you would not want to be treated yourself. It was immoral not to. Westerners find it hard even to comprehend that in Soviet ethics compassion, pity, and kindness were vices, since they might lead one to spare a class enemy. As we teach children to restrain their natural selfishness, Soviets taught them to overcome the impulse to compassion.

Personal integrity and the admonitions of conscience became foreign concepts. As Orlando Figes has observed, "Communist morality left no room for the Western notion of the conscience as a private dialogue with the inner self. The Russian word for 'conscience' in this sense (*sovest'*) almost disappeared from official use after 1917 . . . replaced by the word *soznatel'nost'* [usually translated as consciousness], which carries the idea of consciousness or the capacity to reach a higher moral judgment and understanding of the world." To have attained *soznatel'nost'* was to have internalized "a higher moral-revolutionary logic, that is, Marxist-Leninist ideology."[78]

Ginzburg recounted how her interrogator tried to persuade her to denounce another person by saying that he had already denounced her. When Ginzburg replied, "That's between him and his conscience," the interrogator answered: "What are you, a Gospel Christian or something?" When she answered, "just honest," he "gave me a lecture on the Marxist-Leninist view of ethics. 'Honest' meant useful to the proletariat and the state."[79] As a dedicated communist, Ginzburg knew that the interrogator was right. She had no choice but to recognize that the ideology to which she was devoted equated "conscience" with belief in God and "extra-class values."

When nineteenth-century novelists exposed the hypocrisy of cruel people pretending to be kind, observed Nadezhda Mandelstam, they testified to the

unquestioned acceptance of kindness as a virtue. As La Rochefoucauld observed, hypocrisy is the tribute vice pays to virtue. But "for our generation,
kindness was an old-fashioned, vanished quality, and its exponents were as
extinct as the mammoth. Everything we have seen in our times—the dispos-
session of the kulaks, class warfare, the constant 'unmasking' of people . . . all
this has taught us to be anything you like except kind." To be sure, kindness
survived, but it "had to be sought in remote places that were deaf to the call of
the age. Only the inert kept these qualities as they had come down from their
ancestors. Everyone else had been affected by the inverted 'humanism' of the
times."[80]

"Inverted humanism" turns old virtues into new vices. Classic Soviet fiction often narrates how a hero learns to overcome compassion.[81] Literary
critic Rufus Mathewson observed that this plot predated the establishment
of socialist realism as Party doctrine. In Dmitri Furmanov's *Chapaev* (1923),
the hero observes that "to cut down a human being . . . to shoot him with one's
own hand is a hard job at first for anyone . . . it always makes him feel confused, ashamed, and remorseful," until one has overcome such "incorrect"
impulses.[82]

In Mikhail Sholokhov's *Seeds of Tomorrow* (part of *Virgin Soil Upturned*),
which deals with the collectivization of agriculture, the hero Davidov reproaches Andrei for his reluctance to kill class enemies. "I've not been trained
to fight against children!" Andrei implores. It's not like killing armed enemies
at the front, he continues. "Do you call it right? What am I? An executioner?
Or is my heart made of stone?" When he had to shoot Gayev and his eleven
children, Andrei laments, "it made my hair stand on end . . . I screwed up my
eyes, stopped my ears, and ran out into the yard. . . . And I shall cry! My own
dead little lad maybe."[83]

This speech infuriates Davidov. "You're sorry for them [. . .] You feel pity
for them. And have they had pity on us? Have our enemies ever wept over the
tears of our children?"[84] Davidov narrates how capitalists sent his father to
Siberia after a strike and similar old regime horrors. If one asks, but what had
Gayev's children to do with cruel capitalists?, one comes up against a key
principle not only of Soviet ethics but of all political movements that divide
people into two categories—exploiter and exploited, our race or nation and
theirs, or any other binary. Each person in the bad category is automatically
responsible for—is essentially the same as—all others. Unless one grasps this
principle, one might be tempted to focus on a person's individual innocence
rather than his membership in a previously privileged and powerful group.

Another character, who has been watching this confrontation, unexpectedly leaps to his feet. "Snake!" he denounces Andrei. "How are you serving the revolution? Having pity on them? . . . You could line up thousands of old men, women, and children and tell me they'd got to be crushed into the dust for the sake of the revolution, and I'd shoot them all down with a machine gun!"[85]

Party policy defines the moral. And the "policy of our Party," Davidov explains, is to "destroy the kulak as a class, hand over his property to the collective farm . . . Comrade Stalin has reckoned it all up . . . and said: 'Free the kulak of his life!'"[86]

## Unlimited Violence

As we have seen, prerevolutionary terrorists often found the appeal of violence irresistible; but except in rare cases, they did not find killing morally unproblematic. In Figner's memoirs, in the novels of Savinkov and Stepniak, and in various ideological statements, we find arguments justifying lethal violence *even though* people die and *even if* it often corrupts the terrorist. It took the Bolsheviks to make maximal violence not only acceptable, not only morally unproblematic, but also morally imperative. It is reluctance to kill that became immoral. Violence was not a regrettable necessity, but good in itself.

"The violence of the totalitarian State is no longer a means to an end," Grossman explained in *Life and Fate*. "It becomes an object of mythical worship."[87] Consider Yuri Piatakov, whom Lenin once called one of the six most promising rising Communists. In 1928 Piatakov met his old friend N. V. Volsky (whom we have encountered as Nikolay Valentinov) in Paris, who reproached him for having repudiated his former Trotskyite views. Piatakov attributed his turnabout to his enthusiastic belief that the Party could achieve things that human beings had always regarded as impossible. It could achieve miracles:

> According to Lenin, the Communist Party is based on the principle of coercion which doesn't recognize any limitations or inhibitions. And the central idea of this principle of boundless coercion is not coercion itself but the absence of any limitation whatsoever—moral, political, and even physical, as far as that goes. Such a Party is capable of achieving miracles and doing things which no other collective of men could achieve. . . . A real Communist . . . that is, a man who was raised in the Party and had absorbed its spirit deeply enough to become in a way a miracle man.[88]

To impose any limitation—moral or any other—on unbounded coercion was to renounce the Party's most essential feature. Without it, the Party would become like all other governing bodies that have ever existed, not a worker of miracles. For such a Party, Piatakov told Volsky, "a true Bolshevik will readily cast from his mind ideas in which he had believed for years. A true Bolshevik has submerged his personality in the collectivity, 'the Party,' to such an extent that he can make the necessary effort to break away from his own opinions and can honestly agree with the Party—that is the test of a true Bolshevik."[89]

"Honestly" believe what one does not believe? When Orwell described doublethink he had just this sort of thinking in mind: "To know and not to know, to be conscious of complete truthfulness while telling carefully constructed lies, to hold simultaneously two opinions which cancelled out, knowing them to be contradictory and believing in both of them . . . to repudiate morality while laying claim to it . . . and above all to apply the same process to the process itself—that was the ultimate subtlety. . . . Even to understand 'doublethink' involved the use of doublethink."[90] Piatakov continued that a true Bolshevik "would be ready to believe that black was white and white was black, if the Party required"—not just to affirm it, but actually believe it![91]

In 1936 Piatakov wrote to the Party secretariat to denounce himself for not having revealed his wife's Trotskyite connections. To make up for this lapse, he offered not only to appear as a witness for the prosecution but, after her condemnation, to shoot her. In fact, Piatakov himself soon became the leading defendant in a round of show trials and was shot.[92] He was not allowed to execute himself.

## No Other Foot

Westerners often refute an opponent's defense of his actions by asking: what if the shoe were on the other foot? If the other party had done the same thing and offered the same defense, would you accept it? However natural this question might seem to us, many Russian revolutionaries not only dismissed it, but even, at times, seemed not to grasp it. Without a shade of irony, Vera Figner condemned the government for using violence to suppress revolutionary violence. How dare they defend themselves! She expressed moral outrage that Sophia Perovskaya—who had directed the assassination of Alexander II—"was treacherously seized on the street."[93] Treacherously?

Having described techniques of deception, disguise, disinformation, banditry, infiltration, and "impersonation of pretenders to the throne," Figner was profoundly shaken by the discovery that one of the top revolutionaries with whom she worked, Degayev, had actually been a police agent. She could not get over the fact that he had behaved deceitfully. Degayev's falsehoods, she explained, "had shaken the foundations of life itself, that faith in people without which a revolutionist cannot act.... He had lied, dissimulated, and deceived.... To experience such a betrayal was a blow heavy beyond all words. It took away the moral beauty of mankind, the beauty of the revolution and of life itself."[94] It evidently never dawned on her to reflect on her own life of deception.

One reason Valentinov gave for breaking with Lenin was an inability to "accept the [Leninist] principle that *what is wrong for them is right for us.*"[95] In *August 1914*, Vera responds to her aunts' praise of the terrorist tradition by observing that in pursuit of noble goals the revolutionary may do "some not very pretty things [...] before he ever fires a shot or explodes a bomb," such as forge letters, pretend to be another person, "or abuse someone's simple trust in his fellows in order to murder him.... That way people could lose all trust in one another—lose something that may be more important than the liberation of the people."[96]

These objections shock the aunts not only because, in their view, nothing could be more important than the liberation of the people, and not only because "to a revolutionary everything that contributes to the triumph of the revolution is moral," but also because Vera was applying the same moral standards to revolutionaries that she applied to others. "Now she had gone too far!" they think. "The unfeeling girl was equating the oppressors of the people and its liberators, speaking as though they had the same moral rights!"[97]

One cannot ask "what if the shoe were on the other foot?" because to do so is to suggest "an equality of moral rights," the way one foot resembles the other. Revolutionary morality adopts what might be called "the principle of no other foot."

For the Bolsheviks, that principle derived directly from the idea that there is no standard of morality outside the interest of the Party. When Sologdin, a character in Solzhenitsyn's *In the First Circle*, asks the dedicated Communist Rubin a "shoe-on-other-foot" question, Rubin is genuinely "astonished." "How can you equate the two?" he demands. If one person is "objectively ... for socialism" and the other is objectively an enemy, "can you really say there's any comparison?"[98]

## The Limits of the Human

If there is such a thing as humanness, if we are not just material objects like any other, if we do have something that might be called human dignity, then,

Russian writers have repeatedly asked, what exactly constitutes that human-ness? Or in Dostoevsky's phrase, what is "the man in man"?

One way to examine this question is to see how much can be removed from a person without destroying his or her personhood. Gogol's stories may be seen as a series of such thought experiments by subtraction. In "The Over-coat," for instance, he gives us a minimal human being. The occupation of copying clerk fits Akaky Akakievich so perfectly he seems a copy himself, a mere simulacrum of a human being. The only thing surprising about him is his complete incapacity to surprise. Years pass, department chiefs come and go, and Akaky Akakievich "was always seen in the same place, in the same position, at the very same duty, precisely the same copying clerk, so that they used to declare that he must have been born a copying clerk, uniform, bald patch, and all."[99]

Even after work, Akaky Akakievich amuses himself by copying some-thing, an occupation in which "he found an interesting and pleasant world of his own . . . certain letters were favorites with him, and when he came to them he was delighted." When other people were out seeking diversion—that is, something different—Akaky Akakievich goes to bed "smiling at the thought of the next day and wondering what God would send him to copy."[100]

When necessity forces Akaky Akakievich to save for a new overcoat, this desired object becomes his substitute for normal human love. He has his dream: "the eternal idea of the future overcoat. His whole existence became fuller, as though he had married . . . as though he were no longer alone but an agreeable companion had consented to walk the path of life hand in hand with him, and that companion was the new overcoat with its thick padding and its strong, durable lining."[101]

Gogol's characters typically lack sufficient humanness to be capable of the usual sins. Lust is beyond them; gluttony often replaces it. They are "dead souls," if they are souls at all. Only when the public prosecutor in *Dead Souls* gives up his soul—that is, dies—does it become clear he actually had one. The miser Pliushkin's life, we learn, has been a process of subtracting one human quality after another until one must ask: "And is it to such insignifi-cance, such pettiness, such vileness that a man could sink?"[102] Gogol com-mented on how, as years pass, pettiness can "so encumber and envelop" a person "that no self remains in him, but only a heap of conditionings and re-flexes that belong to the world. And when you try to break through to the soul, it's no longer there."[103]

Gogol's key comic device is to show us a substance that turns out to be an absence. In *Dead Souls*, Chichikov buys peasants who are legally alive but in fact nonexistent. In *The Inspector General*, people mistake a visiting "nonentity" for a government inspector who exposes their emptiness. The narrator of the story of the two Ivans begins with enthusiastic praise of these interesting friends and ends, famously, with dejected contemplation of "the same fields . . . the same monotonous rain, the tearful sky without one gleam of light in it—It's boring in this world, gentlemen."[104] "Everything is a cheat, everything is a dream, everything is other than it seems!" concludes the narrator of "Nevsky Avenue." "And the devil himself lights the street lamps to show everything in false colors."[105] Instead of people, some sort of shadowy zombies—or even mirages of shadowy zombies—populate the world. Everything is a counterfeit with no original and everyone is an imposter impersonating a nonexistent person.

Dostoevsky explored the psychology of people in situations that dehumanize them. His first novel, *Poor Folk*, shows how the worst deprivation poverty inflicts is not the lack of things but the lack of dignity. As Belinsky immediately recognized, no one has ever described humiliation more profoundly than Dostoevsky.[106] His novel about his prison experiences, *The House of the Dead*, examines how prisoners value the ability to make a choice of their own, even a self-destructive choice, more than anything else because without choice they are not human at all. Other important prerevolutionary works explore various extreme situations threatening the most basic human dignity: prostitution in Kuprin's *Yama*, brutality in Chekhov's "In the Ravine" and *Sakhalin Island*, and drunkenness in Tolstoy's *The Power of Darkness*.

## To Get at the Soul

Extreme conditions in real life do what Gogol does in imagination: they strip away one human quality after another to reveal the raw soul. The Soviets created conditions far more extreme than nineteenth-century authors ever anticipated and so the stripping away of human qualities went that much further. Except for Dostoevsky, humane writers who condemned tsarist injustice did not remotely understand what ideologically motivated people might do. Solzhenitsyn observed:

> If the intellectuals in the plays of Chekhov who spent all their time guessing what would happen in twenty, thirty, or forty years had been told that in forty years interrogation by torture would be practiced in Russia; that prisoners would have their skulls squeezed within iron rings; that a human being would be lowered into an acid bath; that they would be trussed up naked to be bitten by ants and bedbugs; that a ramrod

heated over a primus stove would be thrust up their anal canal ("the secret brand"); that a man's genitals would be slowly crushed beneath the
toe of a jackboot; and that, in the luckiest possible circumstances, prisoners would be tortured by being kept from sleeping for a week, by
thirst, and by being beaten to a bloody pulp, not one of Chekhov's plays
would have gotten to its end because all the heroes would have gone off
to insane asylums.[107]

Soviet life performed an experiment and Russian literature recorded its
results. In Isaac Babel's *Red Cavalry* stories, drawn from his experiences in the
Bolshevik invasion of Poland, the narrator examines how extreme suffering,
inflicted or endured, reveals the soul. One of the characters, indeed, tortures
others for that very reason. In "The Life and Adventures of Matthew Pavlichenko," narrated by Pavlichenko himself, a Bolshevik commander takes
revenge on his former master Nikitinsky, but his main motive isn't revenge. All
right, shoot me, Nikitinsky says, "but I wasn't going to shoot him." Instead

> I stamped on my master Nikitinsky, trampled on him for an hour or
> maybe more. And in that time I got to know life through and through.
> With shooting—I'll put it this way—with shooting you only get rid of a
> chap. Shooting's letting him off, and too damn easy for yourself. With
> shooting you'll never get at the soul, to where it is in a fellow and how it
> shows itself. But I don't spare myself, and I've more than once trampled
> an enemy for over an hour. You see, I want to get to know what life really
> is, this life that we live.[108]

"I don't spare *myself*": Pavlichenko forces himself to perform an arduous scientific experiment in the pursuit of the most important knowledge, the nature of the human soul. Apologists for the USSR have often referred to "the
Soviet experiment" as if millions lost their lives to advance social scientific
knowledge.

## The Worst Punishment

"Our present system is unique in world history," observed Solzhenitsyn in his
essay "As Breathing and Consciousness Return," "because over and above its
physical and economic constraints, it demands of us total surrender of our
souls. . . . To this putrefaction of the soul . . . human beings who wish to be
human cannot consent."[109]

According to Leninist ethics, it is criminal not to inflict the maximum harm on an enemy. But what is the worst thing one can inflict? Clearly, it isn't death, which might well constitute an escape. That is why suicide (or attempted suicide) by an accused person was considered yet another crime, a way to elude Party judgment. Suicide enraged Stalin, who called it one of "the most cunning and easiest means by which one can spit at and deceive the Party one last time."[110]

Could the worst be torture? Interrogation by torture became routine halfway through the great purges; before that was the phase that Anna Akhmatova called "vegetarian."[111] But even torture did not really "get to the soul," as Pavlichenko supposed. It was simply a means to something still worse.

What was the justice system—including interrogation with torture and false confessions, forced labor often in frozen wastes, and gradual starvation—designed to accomplish that shooting could not? We have noted that historian Adam Ulam referred to Stalin's terror as "preposterous" because it did not spare those most loyal to the regime. One may also wonder at the extraordinary waste of resources, which makes nonsense of the theory that the prime goal of the camp system was economic. What economic sense did it make to ship people to the Far East in box cars unheated in winter and unventilated in summer while feeding them only salted food without water, so that some (occasionally all) died en route and the rest lost the strength for labor? What economic considerations would dictate converting experienced engineers, technicians, and scientists into manual laborers in "the north pole of cold"?

But the system does make sense in terms of the Leninist imperative: inflict maximum harm, not just to the body but also to the soul; not just to eliminate but to dehumanize enemies. It also makes sense if the creation of a new type of human being (the "new Soviet person") required utterly destroying the old order, not just institutions and people but also everything that used to constitute humanness. Grossman's narrator poses the central question of *Life and Fate*: "Does human nature undergo a true change in the cauldron of totalitarian violence? . . . The fate of both man and the totalitarian State depends on the answer to his question. If human nature does change, then the eternal and world-wide triumph of the dictatorial state is assured; if his yearning for freedom remains constant, then the totalitarian State is doomed."[112]

The best writers of the Soviet period examined Soviet dehumanization. They asked: what did extreme conditions actually reveal about the soul? No one explored this theme more profoundly than former Kolyma prisoner Varlam Shalamov. The narrator of his story "Captain Tolly's Love" refuses packages from his wife because, he explains to a fellow prisoner, "you and I are not only beyond good and evil; we're also beyond anything human."[113] Kolyma prisoners lose all their former interests and concerns. In Shalamov's story "An Epitaph," Glebov, who has even forgotten his wife's name, knows he would not return home if he could because he would no longer be able to share normal human concerns. Neither could he begin to explain what he has witnessed. Only by experience could anyone know what the narrator of "Major Pugachev's Last Battle" calls "hunger that lasts for years and breaks the will."[114] Nor could anyone who has not been arrested grasp "how impossible" it is for prisoners (and former prisoners) "to tear your eyes from the sight of a man eating."[115]

If selfhood resides in the continuity provided by memory, as Locke presumed, then many prisoners lost both together. "I had forgotten everything," explains the narrator of Shalamov's story "Dominoes." "I didn't even remember what it was like to remember."[116] Evgeniya Ginzburg met people whose "past seemed to have been obliterated. . . . These unfeeling puppets, without moral standards or memory, never attempted to recall the days when they were still free and still human beings."[117] To be sure, their bodies retained traces of their former life (authorities could identify their corpses), but their souls apparently did not. Or were biography and selfhood just very deeply hidden?

## Remembering and Forgetting

In *Anna Karenina*, the hedonist Stiva Oblonsky has developed the ability to forget whatever is unpleasant to remember. It's not that he has a poor memory; rather, he has an excellent forgettory.[118] Whole societies can develop the same ability.

Only if one appreciates the possibility—and horror—of losing one's past can one grasp the enormous value Shalamov and other writers placed on memory. In "The Train," a released prisoner feels "as if I had just awakened from a dream that had lasted for years." Suddenly fear grips him. "I was frightened by the terrible strength of man, his desire and ability to forget. I realized that I was ready to forget everything, to cross out twenty years of my life," as many released prisoners do. Recognizing this desire, "I conquered myself. I knew I would not permit my memory to forget everything that I had seen."[119]

Anything can be forgotten. In his story entitled "The Procurator of Judea," Shalamov recalls that Anatole France gave that title to one of his stories. "In it, after seventeen years, Pontius Pilate cannot remember Christ."[120] Pilate has erased the most important event of his life.

Nadezhda Mandelstam described her horror at former camp prisoners whose memories were so garbled that they could not distinguish between their own experiences and those they had heard of. Times, places, and dates "were all jumbled up in the minds of these broken people." "Listening to these accounts, I was horrified by the thought that there might be nobody who could ever properly bear witness to the past. Whether inside or outside the camps, we had all lost our memories."[121]

The heroine of Grossman's *Forever Flowing* describes witnessing the terror famine, when Stalin "intentionally, deliberately killed people by starvation." In excruciating detail, she describes the stages of starvation in adults and children. "Every starving person dies in his own particular way" [*kazhdyi golodnyi po-svoemu umiraet*—an allusion to the opening line of *Anna Karenina*], she reflects. Some went insane. "These were the people who cut up and cooked corpses, who killed their own children and ate them." All wound up beyond the human, too indifferent to move even when they had the strength. Then she asks: "what has become of all that awful torment and torture? . . . Can it really be . . . that it will all be forgotten without even any words to commemorate it?"[122] Reading such passages, one begins to understand the intense moral loathing so many felt for those Western journalists who, like celebrated, Pulitzer Prize–winning *New York Times* reporter Walter Duranty, knowingly denied that starvation, let alone forced starvation, was happening.[123]

As in the Holocaust, horror became that much worse if forgotten. Ginzburg mentioned those whose response to revelations of Stalinist killings amounted to "That was a long time ago and it never happened."[124] Solzhenitsyn, too, described people who told him not to dig up the past. They cited a proverb that begins: "Dwell on the past and you'll lose an eye," but, he observes, they always omitted how that proverb continues: "Forget the past and you'll lose both eyes."[125]

"The preservation of the cultural environment is no less essential than the preservation of the natural environment," observed literary scholar Dmitri Likhachev, himself a former camp inmate. It is necessary for humanity's "spiritual and ethical life," and so we must attend not just to natural ecology but also to "mental ecology."[126] "It later turned out," Nadezhda Mandelstam observed, "that there were people who had made it their aim not only to save themselves, but to survive as witnesses."[127] She herself made her life into an act of memory of her husband's thoughts and verses.[128]

Here again we arrive at the enormous importance of literature for Russians, whether fiction, memoirs, or verse. As an individual loses identity along with memory, so does a people. Literature is for the nation what memory is to the individual person. In the preface to "Requiem," Anna Akhmatova recalls spending "seventeen months in the prison lines of Leningrad" with people hoping for information about arrested relatives. Someone asked her:

> "Can you describe this?"
>     And I answered: "Yes, I can."
>     Then something that looked like a smile passed over what had once been her face.[129]

## Indifference

Some writers agreed that what Dostoevsky calls "the man in man" resides in the will.

In his memoirs, dissident Vladimir Bukovsky describes how, in order "to see to what degree ants were better than people," he caught three ants and put them in a mug. Whenever they tried to climb out, he shook the mug so they wound up on the bottom again. When they tried again, he shook the mug again. After 180 attempts, "they gave up, crawled toward one another, and settled in a circle." They made no more attempts to get away. Bukovsky left the mug for three days, "but they simply stayed there in the mug, twitching their whiskers—probably telling one another jokes."[130] Did they lose even the desire to escape?

Absolute hopelessness erodes the will. The narrator of Shalamov's story "The Used-Book Dealer" compares lengthy interrogation to relentlessly dripping water. These "water clocks didn't count or measure minutes; they measured the human soul, the will, destroying it drop by drop, eroding it just as water erodes a rock." The prisoner Fleming, once an NKVD officer, describes the many "will-suppressants"—"more . . . than you could shake a stick at"—his former employees employed. They called some "chemistry" (pharmacology) and others "physics" (torture). "Chemistry" explained why the accused at show trials could be counted on to behave properly: "the secret of the trials was the secret of pharmacology."[131]

"Physics," however, enjoyed greater prestige. "The physicists . . . viewed beatings as a means of revealing the moral foundations of the world. Once revealed, how base and worthless were the depths of the human essence!" Was Piatakov right that unlimited coercion could work miracles? Apparently, yes: "Beatings could achieve any testimony. Under the threat of a club, inventors made scientific discoveries, wrote verse and novels." NKVD agents commonly boasted that they could get Karl Marx to confess he was a tsarist agent. Combined with perpetual starvation, beatings "worked miracles."[132]

The destruction of will produces a state of complete indifference, descriptions of which shock more, perhaps, than accounts of torture. Grossman attributes extreme indifference to the central character in his story "The Road," a mule. (He could not have published such a story about a prisoner.) "To be or not to be—to Giu this was a matter of indifference. The mule had resolved Hamlet's dilemma." And yet, the mule's indifference is not complete because "this indifference towards himself was his last rebellion" and to rebel one must retain will.[133]

In Shalamov's "Carpenters," the narrator explains that one did not need a thermometer to know the temperature in the labor camp. For example, when it was colder than "sixty degrees below zero, spit froze in mid-air." He adds: "the same frost that transformed a man's spit into ice in mid-air also penetrated the soul. If bones could freeze, then the brain could also be dulled and the soul could freeze over. And the soul shuddered and froze—perhaps to remain frozen forever."[134] The narrator of his story "Dry Rations" explains that "all human emotions . . . had left us with the flesh that had melted from our bodies" from slow starvation. "We understood that death was no worse than life, and we feared neither. We were overwhelmed by indifference."[135] In ordinary life, emotions overwhelm; in camps, indifference.

Shalamov observed that addition, as well as subtraction, reveals the soul. Near death, the hero of "Sententious" is transferred to a prospecting group, where he is no longer starved. He begins in a state of "indifference and fearlessness. I realized I didn't care if I was beaten or not, given dinner and the daily ration, or not." But human feeling returns as he gains weight, and, observing human emotions born anew, he notes which ones—presumably the most basic—come first. Not love. "How little people need love. Love comes only when all other human emotions have already returned. . . . Or does it return?" Fear came first, then envy: "I envied my dead friends who had died in '38." Pity for animals, he notes scientifically, "returned earlier than pity for people."[136] Envy before love, pitying animals before people: what do these facts tell us about human nature? Has any anthropologist been in a position to observe them? Or imagined conducting such fieldwork?

With his language long reduced to a few words, the narrator is frightened "when there appeared in my brain (I distinctly remember that it was in the back of the skull) a word totally inappropriate to the taiga, a word which I didn't myself understand." He shouted it out: "Sententious!" He remembered the word's sound long before he recalled its meaning; and so it was for other words, one after another. "Each appeared on the tongue and only later in the mind."[137] Has any linguist ever observed this fact about human language?

## The Soul and Fear

Even free people found their souls threatened. Dostoevsky stressed that individuality can emerge only in relation to others. Or as Bakhtin argued, self-hood develops in dialogue. One might have supposed that socialism would therefore promote truly social selfhood, but in practice the very opposite was the case. The Party promoted maximal atomization.

As the term implies, totalitarianism includes the aspiration to, if not the achievement of, total control of people, so that no aspect of life would remain outside Party policy, at least in principle. How else could a wholly new type of person develop? As Lunacharsky explained in 1927, "the so-called sphere of private life cannot slip from us, because it is precisely here that the final goal of the Revolution is to be reached."[138] So far as possible, that goal meant eliminating or poisoning horizontal relations (person to person) not specified by vertical ones (Party to person). The model was the economy, where exchanges had to be routed through the central planners.[139] In *1984*, Winston Smith rebels with an unlicensed love; his soul is destroyed when each lover betrays the other. The novel's concluding words—"He loved Big Brother"—horrify because they signify the absolute destruction of self.

In the 1920s, family became suspect because, as historian Orlando Figes has observed, "the family was the biggest obstacle to the socialization of children." While Americans in recent years have presumed that children above all need the sense of being loved, Figes cited the Soviet educational thinker Zlata Ilina: "By loving a child, the family turns him into an egotistical being, encouraging him to see himself as the centre of the universe." *The ABC of Communism*, coauthored by Nikolai Bukharin and Evgenii Preobrazhensky, looked forward to a time when parents would no longer use the word "my" to refer to their children, but would care equally for all children.[140] The celebration of the boy Pavlik Morozov for denouncing his own father to the NKVD (1932) transformed children into spies.[141] It also made it even more difficult to talk freely at home.

Communal apartments, with several families sharing a kitchen and bathroom, began in part as a policy to promote collectivist, instead of family, consciousness. Of course, such living arrangements also made it likely that someone would overhear a questionable remark and file a denunciation. To prevent people from forming horizontal relationships, it was necessary to destroy trust. One reason for the condemnation of doctors (in 1938 and in the postwar doctor's plot) was to ruin trust where it was most needed. "Nobody trusts anybody," wrote Aleksandr Arosev in his diary on August 13, 1936, "and even the very principle of the need for trust has been shaken." "The world of fraternal comradeship," as historian Yuri Slezkine explained, "had turned into a Hobbesian state of nature."[142]

Fear, even panic, prevailed, as memoirists constantly repeat. "It was essential to smile—if you didn't, it meant you were afraid or discontented," Nadezhda Mandelstam remembered. "Everybody . . . had to strut around wearing a cheerful expression."[143] In principle there was nowhere to hide: even thinking the wrong thoughts became criminal. Among the commonly used initials for crimes, KRM meant "Counter-Revolutionary Thought."[144] "There's more than a grain of truth in the old expression that so-and-so was arrested because he 'smiled counter-revolutionarily,'" Andrei Sinyavsky explained. "The merest hint of skepticism, of doubt, of irony, of humor had become a crime." Sinyavsky recounts an incident in which a woman told her neighbor about dreaming she had sex with commissar of defense Kliment Voroshilov and was arrested "for having unethical dreams about the leaders."[145]

In his autobiography, the Sovietologist Wolfgang Leonhard, who grew up in the Soviet Union and became an official in the East German government before escaping to Yugoslavia, recounts the popular "4 a.m. joke" (an allusion to the time when arrests frequently took place). The five families living in a Moscow house wake up at 4 a.m. to the sound of loud knocking and the demand to open the door. Everyone is too fearful to do so. At last, one tenant takes "his courage in both hands" and opens the door. He is heard whispering. At last he returns and, sighing with relief, exclaims: "Comrades, relax! The house is on fire."[146]

Innokenty Volodin, in Solzhenitsyn's *In the First Circle*, asks himself: "If we live in a state of constant fear, can we remain human?"[147] Nadezhda Mandelstam reports her husband Osip saying "that they [the authorities] always knew what they were doing: their aim was not only to destroy the people, but the intellect itself"[148]—and with it, the soul.

## The Test

Extreme conditions tested moral outlooks. In that respect, they continued the work of novels of ideas, which assessed ideas by the consequences of living by them. How did people with a given philosophy behave when arrested, tortured, and starved?

In *The Gulag Archipelago*'s core chapter, "The Ascent," Solzhenitsyn observes that at some point arrestees, prisoners, and camp inmates face a choice: should one "survive *at any price*"? "'At any price' means: at the price of someone else." Does one take away the food of a weaker prisoner, steal his boots, denounce him to gain favor, become a stool pigeon, betray one's comrades, anything to survive and even "get oneself set up comfortably"?[149]

"This is the great fork of camp life," Solzhenitsyn instructs. "From this point the roads go to the right and to the left. One of them will rise and the other will descend. If you go to the right—you lose your life; and if you go to the left—you lose your conscience."[150] Kolyma posed this question in a way tsarist prisons, like Dostoevsky's "house of the dead," never did.

The regime taught that since nothing exists beyond the chain of cause and effect governed by materialist natural laws, the only materialist standard of morality is an action's consequences: "the result is what counts." This idea "has long since been inculcated in our Fatherland—and they kept on inculcating it over and over." So deeply has the "concept that only the material result counts" penetrated Soviet culture, Solzhenitsyn observes, that when prominent Soviet leaders were accused of treason "people only exclaimed in a chorus of astonishment: '*What more could they want?*' Now that's a high moral plane for you!" People evidently assumed that since these leaders "had a belly full of chow, and twenty suits, and two country homes, and an automobile, and an airplane, and fame—what more could they want?!!" Millions of Soviet people could not imagine that a person "might have been motivated by something other than material gain! To such an extent has everyone been indoctrinated with and absorbed the slogan 'the result is what counts.'"[151]

The Bolsheviks took over this ideology from the Russian socialist tradition, Solzhenitsyn explains. "The result is what counts! It is important to forge a fighting Party! And to seize power! And to hold power! And to remove all enemies!" When people who think this way become prisoners, they still reason that the result is what counts, and so "one must survive at any price."[152]

So let us ask: who behaved better under pressure, imprisoned Bolsheviks or religious believers? Materialists or those who acknowledged absolute standards of good and evil? Who acted nobly and who behaved like a scoundrel?

To the astonishment of Leninist materialists like Evgeniya Ginzburg, believers in God passed the test that others failed. They cared about other people. Ginzburg describes how Lydia, a German whom Ginzburg describes as "a fanatical Seventh-Day Adventist," comforted her when she felt intolerable guilt "as though in the grip of some incarnate Evil, almost mystic in its irrationality." Lydia showed "ordinary human kindness," the pity that, according to Soviet morality, was so much counterrevolutionary nonsense. "She stroked my head and repeated several times, in German, the words of Job: 'For the thing which I greatly feared has come upon me, and that which I was afraid of is come upon me.' This broke the spell." Ginzburg then "fell to sobbing in the arms of the strange woman, from a world unknown to me. She stroked my hair and said again and again in German, 'God protects the fatherless. God is on their side.'"[153]

No matter the consequences, believers whom Ginzburg met simply would not do what they regarded as wrong. She tells the story of some "semi-literate 'believers' from Voronezh" whose courage kept up other prisoners' morale. Refusing to work on Easter, they were made to stand barefoot on an ice-bound pool. "I don't remember how long the torture, physical for the 'believers,' moral for us, lasted. Barefoot on the ice they went on praying" while the other prisoners wept or beseeched the guards.[154] The moral torture Ginzburg suffered by watching the voluntary suffering of others testified to her nonmaterialist, anti-Marxist-Leninist belief in something other than either Party success or one's own interests.

Reflecting on the believers' courage, the others asked: "Was this fanaticism, or fortitude in defense of the rights of conscience? Were we to admire them or regard them as mad? And, most troubling of all, should we have had the courage to act as they had?" The very fact that these questions occurred to them made them aware of their respect for absolute values, for goodness irreducible to consequences. The question about personal courage especially disturbed them because it suggested to these well-educated people that there was no connection, or perhaps even a negative connection, between education and nobility of character. Ginzburg began to sense "manifestations of that Supreme Good which, in spite of everything, rules the world."[155]

Ginzburg remained a Marxist, but others like her converted to belief in moral absolutes and, in some cases, in God. In addition to the positive example of believers, they witnessed the negative ones of intellectuals like themselves. Faster than anyone, Shalamov reports, "the intellectual becomes a coward and his own brain provides a 'justification' of his own actions. He can persuade himself of anything, attach himself to either side in a quarrel." When it is to his advantage to do so, he can align himself readily with the violent professional thieves who dominate over other prisoners. With great facility, he rationalizes this behavior by pronouncing these criminals fighters for "people's rights. A blow can transform an intellectual into the obedient servant of a petty crook. Physical force becomes moral force."[156]

Solzhenitsyn adds: when arrested, Bolsheviks behaved the worst, and the higher up they had been, and the more executions they had authorized, the baser they proved. "The victims of the Bolsheviks from 1918 to 1946 never conducted themselves so despicably as the leading Bolsheviks when lightning struck them. If you study in detail the whole history of the arrests and trials of 1936 to 1938, the principal revulsion you feel is not against Stalin and his accomplices, but against the humiliatingly repulsive defendants—nausea at their spiritual baseness after their former pride and implacability."[157]

Nerzhin, the hero of *In the First Circle*, discovers the pusillanimity of the intellectual elite he has so admired. "In circumstances in which only firmness, willpower, and loyalty to friends showed the true worth of a prisoner and determined the fate of his comrades, these refined and highly educated connoisseurs of the exquisite rather often turned out to be cowards, quick to surrender, and, thanks to their education, disgustingly ingenious in justifying their dirty tricks."[158]

*In the First Circle* tells the story of Innokenty Volodin, a well-placed Bolshevik official who accepts the regime's official morality. Believing that only the result counts, he organizes his personal life to maximize his own well-being—or, as he expresses it, he lives as an Epicurean. When he finds himself under arrest, Epicurean philosophy proves ridiculous. "It was all very well philosophizing under shady boughs" or in comfortable university offices, but in the face of Soviet interrogation, "the great materialist's wisdom seemed like the prattle of a child."[159]

Ethical relativism—regarding good and evil as only an expression of class interest, social conditioning, or personal taste—now seems preposterous to Volodin. He had always agreed with Epicurus that "our inner feelings of satisfaction and dissatisfaction are the highest criteria of good and evil," but now he objects: "Stalin . . . had enjoyed killing people"; does that make it "good"?[160] By the highest moral criteria?

"How wise it all seems when you read these philosophers as a free man! But, for Innokenty, good and evil were now distinct entities."[161] He recalls his former reactions to his mother's diaries and letters from before the Revolution. She had written: "Goodness shows itself first in pity," and he had thought: "Pity, a shameful feeling . . . so he had learned at school and in life." Her old-fashioned idea that one should "respect other people's opinions" previously led him to wonder: "If I have a correct worldview, can I really respect those who disagree with me?" And contrary to everything he had been taught, she and her friends believed in absolutes and "in all seriousness, they began certain words with capital letters—Truth, Goodness, Beauty, Good and Evil, the Ethical Imperative. In the language used by Innokenty and those around him, words were more concrete and easier to understand—progressiveness, humanity, dedication, purposefulness."[162]

When Nerzhin asserts that he believes in "a family of one's own" and the "inviolability of the person," Rubin asks how he could believe in such "amorphous, protozoic concepts in the twentieth century? Those are all class-conditioned ideas!" Nerzhin replies that "justice is never relative ... [it] is the cornerstone, the foundation of the universe," but Rubin calls that, too, a class concept. Like Lenin, he allows only two positions—either with the Party or against it: "You'll have to declare someday which side of the barricade you're on."[163]

In his earlier conversation with Kondrashov, Nerzhin discusses the prevailing idea that "there's no need to spell 'good' and 'evil' with capital letters" and that "as everybody knows, being determines consciousness." To the contrary, Kondrashov replies, "every man is born with a sort of inner essence ... the innermost core of the man, his essential self. No 'being' ... can determine him." What's more, "every man carries within himself an image of perfection, which is never dimmed and sometimes stands out with remarkable clarity! And reminds him of his chivalrous duty!" Don't laugh at such a medieval concept: "in the days of chivalry, there were no concentration camps! No gas chambers!"[164]

An artist, Kondrashov has sketched a picture showing "the moment any man may experience, when he first catches sight of the image of perfection," in this case, "the moment when Parsifal first caught sight of the [. . .] castle of the Holy [. . .] Grail!" Heedless of the abyss before his horse, Parsifal stares in rapt amazement at an orange-gold radiance suffusing the sky and emanating "perhaps from the sun, perhaps from a still purer source concealed by the castle. . . . [R]ising to a needle point in mid-heaven at the top of the picture, hazy and indistinct, as if spun from shifting cloud, yet discernible in all the details of its unearthly perfection, ringed in a blue-gray aureole by the invisible supersun, stood the castle of the Holy Grail."[165]

## Incarcerated Poetry

For many prisoners, Russian tradition suggested another holy grail shining from a source purer than the sun: poetry, or more broadly, literature. Countless former prisoners describe how memorized verse consoled them. It preserved their past life and their continuity with it. And it was something the authorities could not take away. Once stories about prisoners reciting poetry circulated, new prisoners understood that reciting verse linked them to earlier ones, and that this whole tradition of incarcerated poetry reciters constituted a chapter in the history of Russian literature.[166] Above all, poetry—like goodness or God—became an absolute value and reciting it a kind of prayer. It affirmed that the universe contained something besides the chain of material cause and effect dictated by natural laws. It contained as well absolute values for which one might meaningfully live or die.

In his story "Cherry Brandy," Shalamov imagines the death of the great poet Osip Mandelstam at a transit camp on the way to a place of forced labor he was not strong enough to reach. "The poet was dying," the story begins. Mandelstam believed in immortality—not of "his human form, as a physical entity," but of his poetry. "He had nevertheless achieved creative immortality ... and for the first time the meaning of the word 'inspiration' was revealed to him in its fulness. Poetry was the life-giving force by which he had lived.... He had not lived for poetry, he had lived through poetry." It is now "so obvious, so palpably clear that inspiration had been life ... that life had been inspiration." Verse could express everything in the world. "All life entered easily into verse and made itself comfortably at home there. And that was the way it should be, for poetry was the Word."[167]

Did it matter that he was composing verse that would never be recorded? Not at all: verse belongs not to this world but to the other world, not to the chain of causes but to the realm of values. "Who cared if it was written down or not? Recording and printing was the vanity of vanities. Only that which is born selflessly can be without equal. The best was that which was not written down, which ... melted without a trace, and only the creative labor he sensed ... proved that the poem had been realized, that beauty had been created."[168] One does not equate beauty, or any absolute value, with its effects.

For other prisoners the absolute value was knowledge. Solzhenitsyn describes a group of intellectuals—real intellectuals, not *intelligents*, professionals, or simply educated people—all on the brink of death within days, who decide to spend their remaining time conducting a "seminar" in which each would lecture on his specialty. "From one session to the next, participants were missing—they were already in the morgue ... the sort of person who can be interested in all this while growing numb with approaching death—now that is an intellectual!"[169] It is not the consequences of knowledge they value.

## Suffering

Suffering brought Solzhenitsyn, and many others, to God. In Russian literary tradition, suffering can either deform or exalt the personality. In *The Brothers*

*Karamazov*, it has made Fyodor Pavlovich totally loathsome. Through it, he has acquired the psychology of a victim for whom it is "pleasant to take offense."[170] Being offended puts one in a position of moral superiority, and so one may seek out insult or detect it where there is none. Dostoevsky's novels explore this aspect of human psychology in a way no philosopher, psychologist, or other writer has come close to matching. All his novels could be given the title of one of them, *The Insulted and the Humiliated*.

But Dostoevsky also described with unparalleled power how suffering can uplift the soul. The epigraph to *Karamazov*—"Verily, verily, I say unto you, except a corn of wheat fall into the ground, it abideth alone; but if it die, it bringeth forth much fruit" (John 12:24)—expresses how "dying" in life can redeem it.

Russian literature might almost be described as the literature of conversion. (We noted some famous instances in Chapter 3.) Time and again, suffering leads to awareness of Truth or apprehension of God. Tolstoy's autobiographical *Confession* recounts his own discovery of God. Prince Andrei in *War and Peace* and Karenin in *Anna Karenina* experience Christian love for an enemy, the only psychologically convincing descriptions of this kind of love in world literature. We also find conversions in "Master and Man," "The Death of Ivan Ilych," "God Sees the Truth," and other Tolstoy stories. Several Chekhov tales—including his favorite, "The Student"—make spiritual transformation plausible. And in Bulgakov's *The Master and Margarita* even Pontius Pilate becomes a believer. The extreme conditions of the Soviet period offered ample opportunity for the corn of wheat to die and, occasionally, bear fruit.

In Svetlana Alexievich's *The Unwomanly Face of War* we hear the voice of a female anti-aircraft gunner reflecting on the people she killed. "I left for the front a materialist," she explains. "An Atheist. I left as a good Soviet schoolgirl who had been well taught. And there [. . .] There I began to pray." She continues praying, she tells Alexievich, because it has come home to her that she has killed people and, whatever Soviet materialist ethics may affirm, their deaths lie on her conscience. "I'm old now," she reflects. "I pray for my soul. I told my daughter that when I die she should take all my medals and decorations, not to a museum, but to a church. Give them to a priest."[171]

Solzhenitsyn invites us to read *The Gulag Archipelago* as his own conversion story. That is why he presents such an unattractive portrait of himself before his arrest and traces the stages by which he came to change his beliefs. What he endures and witnesses tests him and, perhaps vicariously, tests us, if we reflect on it. *Gulag*, subtitled "an experiment in literary investigation," adapts the bildungsroman (novel of education).

Once you reject the morality of "survive at any price," Solzhenitsyn explains, you implicitly acknowledge values that cannot be reduced to expediency. You recognize that what counts most "is not the result—but *the spirit!* Not *what*—but *how.*" This recognition transforms your character "in a direction most unexpected to you.... You are ascending." Your soul, once dry, "now ripens from suffering" and you begin to look at your fellow prisoners differently. "For the first time you have learned to recognize genuine friendship!"[172] Aristotle distinguished instrumental friendship, in which people are primarily concerned with "what is pleasant to themselves," from "perfect friendship," where each friend is concerned with the flourishing of the other: "Now those who wish well to their friends for their own sake are most truly friends," Aristotle concluded.[173] Or in Solzhenitsyn's terms: you learn to appreciate friendship not for the "result" but for the "spirit."

As you ascend, you grasp that "the meaning of earthly existence lies not, as we have been used to thinking, in prospering, but [...] in the development of the soul." If so, then punishment "*holds out hope.*" In his case, Solzhenitsyn recalls, he came "to understand the truth of all the religions of the world: They struggle with the *evil inside a human being* (inside every human being)" instead of attributing evil entirely to external conditions.[174] Having learned to compose and memorize verse, Solzhenitsyn records lines as they occurred to him:

> Not with good judgment nor with desire
> Are its [my life's] twists and turned illumined.
> But with the even glow of the Higher Meaning
> Which became apparent to me only later on.
>
> And now with measuring cup returned to me,
> Scooping up the living water,
> God of the Universe! I believe again!
> Though I renounced you, you were with me![175]

Tolstoy and other classic writers deemed it their duty to curse prison, but Solzhenitsyn, who served time in conditions those writers could not have begun to imagine, can "say without hesitation: '*Bless you, prison, for having been in my life!*'"[176]

# 8  Who Is Not to Blame?

## *The Search for an Alibi*

> The fundamental rule of the times was to ignore the facts of life . . . to see only the positive side of things.
>
> —Nadezhda Mandelstam

At the very time when he considered himself infallible, Solzhenitsyn confessed, he was, for that very reason, cruel.[1] Reflecting on himself, he inquired into the causes of evil.

For Solzhenitsyn, Grossman, and other twentieth-century Russian writers, the traditional question of theodicy—"why does God permit evil in the world?"—changed to "*how* [does] a human being become evil"?[2] Responsibility belongs not to God but to ourselves.

The horrors of the Soviet period, so much greater than under the repressive tsars, led writers to chart new territory in the kingdom of evil. According to Solzhenitsyn, when writers of the past—Shakespeare, Schiller, Dickens—inquired into the nature of evil, what they had in mind seems trivial compared to what the twentieth century has witnessed. In much the same spirit, Bakhtin observed that, however great the plays of Aeschylus, Sophocles, and Euripides may be, these dramatists were still "naïve, quite naïve" because "they didn't come into contact with the abyss, weren't really familiar with actual terror, didn't know it yet. Indeed, they couldn't have known it yet. They were, despite their incredible power and stature, children" compared to those who witnessed the twentieth century.[3]

What made people capable of such unprecedented evil? Or as Solzhenitsyn phrased the question, why was it that Macbeth and Iago destroyed only a few people whereas Lenin, Stalin, and Hitler killed millions? Solzhenitsyn answered that Macbeth and Iago had no "ideology," no all-encompassing system defining good and evil and removing responsibility for an individual's actions. And that makes all the difference, because real evildoers do not resemble literary villains who rejoice in doing evil. No, they imagine they are doing good.

Before a person can do evil, Solzhenitsyn explained, he must discover "a justification for his actions" so that he can tell himself that his stealing, destroying, killing, and torturing serve the good. "Macbeth's self-justifications were feeble—and his conscience devoured him." But ideology strongly justifies anything. "Ideology—that is what gives evil-doing its long-sought justification and gives the evil-doer the necessary steadfastness and determination. That is the social theory which helps to make his acts seem good instead of bad in his own and others' eyes, so that he won't hear reproaches and curses but receive praise and honors." The Spanish Inquisitors invoked Christianity, the Nazis race, and "Jacobins (early and late) . . . equality, brotherhood and the happiness of future generations."[4]

As the age of ideology, the twentieth century licensed evil that the nineteenth century did not contemplate. "Thanks to ideology, the twentieth century was fated to experience evildoing on a scale in the millions." Solzhenitsyn mentioned a widely circulated rumor that since many condemned prisoners were useless, and since shooting them would leave corpses to dispose of, some were fed live to crocodiles in the zoo. After all, in those years of famine, any other source of food would have to be taken from the working class. Solzhenitsyn explained that he had no idea if this rumor is true, but his point is: from the Soviet perspective there would be no reason not to feed prisoners to crocodiles if it was "expedient" to do so. As we saw in the last chapter, the Soviet moral formula was: It's the result (and only the result) that counts. That idea draws a line "that the Shakespearean evildoer could not cross. But the evildoer with ideology does cross it, and his eyes remain dry and clear."[5]

## The Alibi

Ideology provides what Bakhtin, in his early essay on ethics, called an "alibi." The logic of the alibi is: it may look as if I performed this act, but it was not I. Someone or something else is responsible. One thinks: my "I" was, or might as well have been, far away, since the agency was not mine.[6]

When one claims an alibi, one can perform an otherwise heinous action while disclaiming responsibility for it. One performs it, as Bakhtin said, "representatively": not I, but the group or abstraction I merely represent, is doing this. The assertion of such an alibi is "especially frequent in the case of political answerability [*otvetstvennost'*]," Bakhtin observed.[7]

Such thinking is literally irresponsible: invoking the alibi, a person disclaims responsibility that cannot be disclaimed. One is—you are and I am—always responsible for what one does or fails to do in an unrepeatable moment of time. Each moment offers a "once-occurrent" opportunity for which I alone—not humanity in general—must answer. "Man-in-general does not exist; *I* exist and a particular concrete *other* exists." The fundamental fact about responsibility is that it cannot be displaced in any way whatsoever. Bakhtin calls this fact the "non-alibi." We must "sign" our actions and must recognize: "That which can be done by me [now] can never be done by anyone else [ever]."[8]

Nineteenth-century Russian literature offers a catalogue of alibis. We have already seen Stiva Oblonsky and his sister Anna Karenina invoke determinism: "It's all my fault, but I'm not to blame," Stiva excuses himself, and Anna tells Dolly she cannot be blamed because things could not have happened otherwise. In Goncharov's novel *The Precipice*, Raisky tells himself that people do not really have a will for which they can be held responsible since "what people call will, that imaginary power is not at all under man's command . . . it is, quite to the contrary, subordinate to some extraneous laws according to which it operates, not asking man's consent."[9]

The idea that people are entirely products of their environment—of their society, of the age in which they live—offers a wide range of possible alibis. "I am nothing in myself, a mere particle in a necessary social evil," the doctor in Chekhov's *Ward Six* excuses himself. "Consequently, it is not I who am to blame for my dishonesty, but the times [. . .] If I had been born two hundred years later, I should have been different."[10]

Laevsky, the hero of Chekhov's novella *The Duel*, has mastered a litany of eloquent excuses of this sort. As Von Koren, acidly but not unjustly, observes:

> As a friend I remonstrated with him, asked him why he drank so much, why he lived beyond his means and incurred debts, why he did nothing, read nothing . . . and in answer to all my questions he would smile bitterly and say: "I'm a failure, a superfluous man," or: "What do you expect from us, old man, the dregs of the serf-owning class?" . . . Or

he'd start a long rigmarole about Onegin, Pechorin, Byron's Cain, Bazarov, of whom he would say "they are our fathers in spirit and in flesh."
So we are to understand that it is not he who is to blame that government
packets lie unopened for weeks at a time . . . it's Onegin, Pechorin, Turgenev who are to blame . . . The cause . . . you see, lies not in himself, but
somewhere outside in space . . . [it is] "We of the eighties" . . . his licen-
tiousness, ignorance, and slovenliness constitute a historical phenomenon, sanctified by inevitability . . . and . . . we should burn a candle
before Laevsky, since he is the destined victim of the age.[11]

## Who Is Doing These Things?

According to Soviet ideology, right-thinking people were *supposed* to act
"representatively"—ideally always. According to the doctrine of Partyness, as
we have seen, the true Bolshevik did not even have to bring his thoughts in
line with the current Party line since he had so absorbed Party spirit that he
thought the proper way automatically. As Lev Kopelev explained: "The ability
to see everything—theory and practice, the past and present, others and
oneself—precisely as required by the Party at any given moment; the ability to
think and act only in the interests of the Party under any and all circumstances—
that was Bolshevik 'partyness,' as we called it. This 'partyness' was an almost
mystical concept."[12] The true Bolshevik acted as if he were a machine at the
Party's command. As Igor Shafarevich observed, "Once upon a time J. V. Stalin
whimsically referred to us all as 'cogs' and even proposed a toast to the health
of the 'cogs.'"[13]

When Klara (*In the First Circle*) questions Ernst about Bolshevik cruelty,
he replies "gently but firmly. . . . 'Who is doing these things? Who wants to do
them? It is history. History does what it wants. You and I sometimes find it
horrible, Klara, but it's time we were used to the fact that there exists a law of
large numbers. The more material involved in a historical event, the greater the
likelihood of individual incidental errors . . . what matters is the conviction
that the process itself is necessary and inevitable."[14] Klara finds this argument
convincing.[15]

Kopelev recalled that as a young man he was proud of seizing food from
starving peasants. "I took part in this myself, scouring the countryside,
searching for hidden grain . . . stopping my ears to the children's crying and
the women's wails. . . . For I was convinced that . . . their distress and suffering
were a result of their own ignorance or the machinations of the class enemy."[16]
Above all, Kopelev explained, he did it because "the action was moved by 'his-

torical necessity,' in which I believed more ardently than, as a child, I had believed in God." He was ashamed not of starving the peasants but of pitying
them while doing so. "I belonged to the one and only righteous Party! I was a
fighter in a just war for the victory of the historically most progressive
ideas—and hence for the ultimate happiness of all mankind." Kopelev recognized that "the fate of one person—or of a hundred thousand—was mathematically insignificant." Just as in battle one sometimes has to sacrifice a company
to save a regiment, so in the cause of world revolution "it was permissible to
sacrifice whole countries and peoples—Poland, Finland [. . .]"[17]

Kopelev did not exonerate himself by pointing to his indoctrination. Doing
so would just displace his responsibility to a different alibi. When the Bolshevik regime fell, many excused their deeds by blaming "totalitarianism," but
as S. Dovlatov asked: "who wrote four million denunciations?"[18] Those who
refused this excuse maintained: we will have learned our lesson when we stop
complaining about what they did to us and start repenting for what we did.

## What Is Self-Deception?

"I believed because I wanted to believe," Kopelev explained.[19] The Soviet experience gave new meaning to a central theme of realist novels: self-deception.
There was so much more to deceive oneself about and many new ways to
do it.

Understanding selfhood as bafflingly complex, realist novels explore a key
source of this complexity, our myriad methods of deceiving or blinding ourselves. "Self-love," La Rochefoucauld famously remarked, "is cleverer than the
cleverest man in the world."[20] It is always one step ahead of our shrewdest attempts to outwit it. We are never more likely to be deceiving ourselves than
when we imagine we are free from self-deception.

*Intelligents*, and utopians generally, treated self-deception as the product of
exploitative social conditions and therefore bound to disappear with them. In
the future society, Pisarev explained, "the new men arrange their lives so that
their personal interests in no way contradict the real interests of society." "In the
lives of the new men," he continued, "there is no discordance between inclination and moral duty," and so no need to be dishonest with oneself. If such a
person discovered he had been dishonest with himself, Pisarev memorably observed, "he would surely spit in his own face."[21] In the utopias of Bellamy,
Morris, Chernyshevsky, and others, self-deception has vanished along with
capitalism and human nature has been revealed in its pristine, crystalline
wholeness.[22]

Realist novels, by contrast, treat self-deception as essential to the human condition. Like self-love, it comes in countless forms. In Jane Austen's novels, "pride and prejudice" distort our perceptions so that we see what we are inclined to see and miss disconfirming evidence. In *Emma*, Austen shows how this process works by inducing readers to make the same interpretive mistakes as Emma herself. Bulstrode in George Eliot's *Middlemarch* manages to convince himself that his self-interested actions are just "what God's glory required" and, when morality and the accumulation of power seem to conflict, "he went through a great deal of spiritual conflict and inward arguments in order to adjust his motives" so that what he should do coincides with what he wants to do.[23]

Paraphrasing Bulstrode's thoughts from within, Eliot shows us one way this process works. When he wants to do something dishonest, Bulstrode avoids envisioning the contemplated action as a whole so that "for him at that distant time, and even now in burning memory, the fact was broken into little sequences, each justified as it came by reasoning which seemed to prove it righteous."[24]

Eliot portrays Bulstrode's psychology far more subtly than the great satirists depict typical hypocrites. He is no Tartuffe. "There may be coarse hypocrites, who consciously affect beliefs and emotions for the sake of gulling the world," Eliot observes, "but Bulstrode was not one of them. He was simply a man whose desires had been stronger than his theoretic beliefs, and who had gradually explained the gratification of his desires into satisfactory agreement with those beliefs."[25]

As she often does, Eliot then turns on the reader to say that the rest of us are no different. We enlightened folk may have comforted ourselves by attributing Bulstrode's dishonesty to his religious beliefs, which we look down upon, but in doing so we have ourselves engaged in self-deception. We resemble Bulstrode more than we care to admit, and "if this [Bulstrode's thinking] be hypocrisy, it is a process which shows itself occasionally in us all, to whatever confession we may belong, and whether we believe in the future perfection of our race . . . or have a passionate belief in the solidarity of mankind," as right-thinking secular people do. Bulstrode's "implicit reasoning is essentially no more peculiar to evangelical beliefs than the use of wide phrases for narrow motives is peculiar to Englishmen. There is no general doctrine which is not capable of eating out our morality if unchecked by the deep-seated habit of direct fellow feeling with individual fellow-men."[26]

The plot of *The Brothers Karamazov* turns on Ivan's reluctance to admit, even to himself, his desire to see his father Fyodor Pavlovich dead. Indirectly, in code, Smerdyakov lays out a series of steps sure to result in the old man's death if only Ivan will leave town so events can take their course. Smerdyakov sets things up so that action on Ivan's part is needed to prevent, not instigate, the murder. Consent requires no more than Ivan's failure to think things through and object to the plan in which his only role is to absent himself. Smerdyakov addresses Ivan's desires without engaging his conscious will.

Ivan could easily decipher the code. He might ask himself why he is beset by "all sorts of strange and almost surprising desires; for instance, after midnight he suddenly had an intense irresistible longing to go down . . . and beat Smerdyakov. But if he had been asked why, he could not have given any exact reason, except perhaps that he loathed the valet as one who had insulted him more gravely than anyone in the world."[27] If he only inquired into the reason for this feeling, he would have found it immediately and understood what he was agreeing to. Then the murder would not have happened. But that is precisely why he does not inquire.

Instead, "Ivan tried 'not to think'" about this feeling or about why he experiences "a sort of inexplicable humiliating terror."[28] Nor does he ask, as he leaves town, why he calls himself a scoundrel.

Like many of us, Ivan arranges something he desires to happen "against his will." His "action"—Dostoevsky puts the term in quotation marks—is a non-action: he misdirects his attention so that what he is agreeing to is never fully present to his mind. If it were, he would reject it. When we wish to avoid knowing something inconvenient, we arrange for alarm bells to go off when we get too close to realizing it. And our responsibility lies precisely in that arranging.

Ivan has maintained that people bear no responsibility for their wishes— "who has not the right to wish?"[29]—a position that directly contradicts the Sermon on the Mount, which deems not just bad actions but also unworthy desires sinful. Dostoevsky has constructed a plot showing just why the Gospel is psychologically correct. Most evil happens not because supremely evil people actively create it but because ordinary people like ourselves wish it and let it happen. So long as one retains plausible deniability to oneself, self-deception offers an alibi.

## When Is Self-Deception?

Philosophers have had difficulty understanding self-deception. How is it possible to get oneself to believe what one knows is untrue? When one lies to another person, one can conceal some material fact, but when one lies to oneself one knows what one is concealing, so how can it be concealed? How can one believe what one knows one does not believe? The very concept of self-deception seems to involve a philosophical paradox. Does self-deception involve holding two contradictory beliefs without noticing the contradiction, as one philosopher has proposed? But surely, as philosopher Herbert Fingarette has observed, there is a difference "between commonplace inconsistency in beliefs on the one hand, and self-deception on the other."[30] Self-deception is an action; it involves choice.

Encountering the perplexity of philosophers, one wonders why they do not consult the great novelists, who, after all, offer the most detailed description of the dynamics of self-deception. And "dynamics" is the key concept here: self-deception is a process, not a momentary action. In *Anna Karenina*, Tolstoy allows us to witness that process from within Anna's consciousness.

Anna knows that her contemplated infidelity would be wrong (by her own moral standards). She would gravely injure her husband and, potentially, her son. But she deeply desires the affair. She therefore engages in several types of self-deception to excuse her action to herself. Most important is the way she gradually changes how she perceives her husband.

Looking is not passive reception; it is an action that, like other actions, one can perform honestly or dishonestly. That, too, is a key theme of Russian literature.[31] At any given moment there is a range of ways one can see another person that one might acknowledge as honest. Some are more charitable, some less. Over and over again, Anna focuses on the most uncharitable part of this range until it becomes her normal way of seeing her husband and thus the center of a new range with new extremes. Then she repeats this process many times. In this way, she eventually convinces herself that she cannot be hurting her husband because he cannot feel.[32]

Although as the novel begins, Anna knows her husband's feelings intimately, even better than he himself does, she is at last able to say, "he's not a man, not a human being—he's a puppet."[33] When Karenin finally loses his temper at her ignoring his one condition for her carrying on the affair—that she not bring her lover to their house—he is so upset that he stutters: "'The sufferings of a man who was your husband have no interest for you. You don't care that his whole life is ruined, that he is thuff [...] thuff [...]' Aleksey Alexandrovich [Karenin] ... stammered, and was utterly unable to articulate the word suffering. In the end he pronounced it 'thuffering' [he winds up saying *pelestradal* instead of *perestradal*]."

Anna first wants to laugh, next feels ashamed that anything could amuse her at such a moment, and then "for the first time, for an instant, she felt for him, put herself in his place, and was sorry for him." *For the first time:* Anna, we know, is a master at understanding other people's feelings, but over all these months she has not once put herself in her husband's place! If she only dwelled on this first empathetic reaction, she would appreciate the pain she is causing him. Sensing his jealousy and humiliation, she could no longer think of him as a puppet. Her process of self-deception would be revealed to her. That is just what she wants to avoid, and so she tells herself: "No, can a man with those dull eyes, with that self-satisfied complacency, feel?"[34]

Anna's process of self-deception illustrates the mistake of locating all choices at a moment. People mistakenly equate intention with a choice immediately preceding an action, but a person may be responsible without such an immediately prior intention or choice. Instead of a single choice, for instance, there may have been many small ones, none of which were taken with the end result in mind. Choices, in short, may be temporally extensive and never locatable at a precise moment. And yet they are choices, nonetheless. We are responsible for them. And if we have engaged in this process in order to avoid bearing responsibility for the outcome, we are responsible for the falsehood as well.

By teaching ourselves to misperceive, we become responsible for what we miss. It is one thing not to know, it is quite another to avoid knowing. As Bulstrode evaded his own judgment by breaking a dishonest action into separate pieces, each of which could be justified, Anna gradually establishes the habit of misperceiving her husband without ever having the whole sequence present to her consciousness. Of course, she could, at any moment, compare her current perception of Karenin with facts about him in her memory, but she avoids doing so. Each act of avoidance is a choice—not exactly a choice to misperceive him but a choice to avoid any evidence that might reveal her misperception. It is hard to remember what one does not do, so it is easy not to take responsibility for it.

In this way, good people do, or consent to another doing, bad things. They do not persecute individuals or groups they know to be innocent; rather, they make sure not to learn the other side of the case. The readiness to condemn without taking the effort to see things from both sides, the anger at others to whom one makes sure not to listen, the repudiation of those who do listen to both sides: all such acts of willful not-knowing make one morally responsible for what one does not know.[35]

When Anna thinks she is dying after giving birth, she does realize what she has done and makes a point of confessing her falsehood. "There is another woman in me," she hurries to say to Karenin. "I'm afraid of her. I tried to hate you, and could not forget about her that used to be. I'm not that woman.

Now I'm my real self . . . I know it can't be forgiven" although she also knows that he does forgive and that, as she tells him, "you're too good."[36] And she is right, as a feeling of love and forgiveness overwhelms him.

People deceive themselves all the time. Not to understand this fact is not to understand human beings and the nature of human responsibility. Like fatalism of various sorts, self-deception fabricates the alibi we crave.

## *One Way Beliefs Can Change*

People often use a similar process in adopting political convictions. The great novelists show how educated people in particular manage to hold the social and political beliefs most convenient for them to hold.

No one wants to incur the opprobrium of maintaining opinions held to be outmoded or morally questionable. As a good salesman first persuades himself of the value of his shoddy goods, one therefore makes sure to accept sincerely opinions it is advantageous to accept. One does not really choose particular views; rather, one chooses to accept whatever views the people with whom one identifies profess.

Puzzled onlookers sometimes wonder how someone can believe something in the face of all the evidence to the contrary. Such a question presupposes that the person has at some point considered and accepted the belief, but he may never have done so. What he accepted is whatever package of beliefs the right people profess.

Stiva Oblonsky, for instance, "had not chosen his political opinions or his views; these political opinions and views had come to him of themselves, just as he did not choose the shapes of his hat and coat, but simply took those that were in style. And for him, living in a certain social environment . . . to hold [a set of] views was just as indispensable as to have a hat." With his perfect tact and social acumen, Stiva "firmly held those views on all these subjects that were held by the majority and by his paper, and changed them only when the majority changed—or, more strictly speaking, they seemed to change of themselves within him."[37]

What does "firmly held" mean here? It clearly does not mean that, having examined all the relevant evidence and having seriously considered alternative interpretations, Stiva has confidence that each of his beliefs is well-founded. It means simply that these beliefs are not to be shaken so long as they are regarded as the proper ones to hold. Stiva's beliefs change over time, but, again, not because he ever decides they are mistaken. In fact, he exercises no agency at all, which is why, "strictly speaking," his beliefs "seem to change of themselves

within him." Tolstoy has here described a way of believing that can be applied
to almost any set of beliefs and which one can expect to find among educated
people in societies and epochs very different from tsarist Russia.

Later in the novel, Levin becomes curious about how his liberal friend Sviazhsky manages to hold beliefs so at odds with his very conservative way of
living. It would be easy, Levin reflects, just to call his friend a fool, a hypocrite,
or a scoundrel, but Sviazhsky is clearly too well informed to be dismissed as a
fool and too generous and decent to qualify as a scoundrel. When Levin tries to
"sound out Sviazhsky, to try to get at the foundation of his own view of life," he
fails. "Every time Levin tried to penetrate beyond the outer chambers of
Svaizhsky's mind . . . he noticed that Sviazhsky was slightly disconcerted; faint
signs of alarm were visible in his eyes, as though he were afraid Levin would
understand him, and he would give him a kindly, good-natured rebuff."[38]

Sviazhsky, it is clear, is afraid of understanding himself. After all, if he perceived the contradiction between his professed beliefs and his actual way of
life, he would have to think about both seriously and perhaps even change one
or the other. That would be uncomfortable, and for Sviazhsky, warm and generous beliefs not only suit his personality but also foster the hospitable conversations in which he takes such delight.

## Authenticity

In all these cases, we detect an irony of origins: the reason for holding beliefs
is not the reason one gives oneself and others. And this discrepancy raises a
question: if one sincerely believes one thing but one's actions demonstrate belief
in something else, which is one's real belief? Economists speak of "revealed
preferences": if you say you love opera and would attend more performances if
tickets were cheaper, yet when the price goes way down, you still spend your
money on other forms of entertainment, then your "revealed preference"—for
economists, your real preference—is not what you say, however sincerely, but
what your behavior indicates. This is why economists rarely conduct interviews; they look at what people do.[39]

But may not both beliefs, professed and "revealed," be real? And when
would we say that self-deception, if not conscious hypocrisy, is involved?

In *Anna Karenina*, Tolstoy focuses not so much on *what* people believe as on
*how*. Belief is one word but refers to many different states of mind. There are
many ways for people to hold beliefs. And yet, some ways are, in Tolstoy's view,
more authentic than others. When Kitty, understandably dissatisfied with her
life, adopts Madame Stahl's charitable views wholesale, she winds up, as she soon

recognizes, doing more harm than good. It was all "a fake," she decides. When Mademoiselle Varenka helps people, her actions flow from who she really is, but when Kitty imitates Varenka, the apparently identical actions are not really the same because Kitty performs them "to seem better to people, to myself, to God"; they are inauthentic or, as she expresses it, "not from the heart."[40]

At Sviazhsky's, Levin meets "a reactionary landowner" whose views he does not accept but nevertheless recognizes as authentic. "The landowner," Tolstoy explains, "unmistakably spoke his own thought—a thing that rarely happens—and a thought to which he had been brought not by a desire of finding some exercise for an idle brain, but a thought which had grown up out of the conditions of his life, which he had brooded over in the solitude of his village, and had considered in its every aspect."[41] By listening to such views, Levin can access the experiences that have given rise to them. Everyone's experience is partial—based on limited evidence and therefore potentially one-sided—but by taking authentic views seriously, Levin can expand the compass of experiences on which he draws to solve his problems.

## The Magic Spell of Shared Opinion

Dostoevsky's novels satirize those who acquire beliefs in the way he compares with donning a uniform. He speaks as well of "ready-made ideas" and of opinions that echo other people's ideas.[42] In this sort of thinking, one does not first experience the world and then arrive at ideas reflecting that experience; one first adopts a set of ideas and then shapes one's experiences in accordance with it. One lives from the top down.

In Pasternak's *Doctor Zhivago*, Lara discovers the "root cause of all the evil" around her—people's willingness to slaughter and celebrate slaughter—in "the loss of confidence in the value of one's own opinion. People imagined that it was out of date to follow their own moral sense, that they must all sing in chorus, and live by other people's notions, notions that were being crammed down everybody's throat. And then there arose the power of the glittering phrase, first the Tsarist, then the revolutionary."[43] In *The Master and Margarita*, the demonic "choirmaster" Korovyov literally makes people sing in chorus without the ability to stop. As with the beliefs they profess, the agency leading to the words they sing is not their own.

In *November 1916*, the hero, Vorotyntsev, finds himself at a meeting of Kadets (the Russian liberal party). Solzhenitsyn draws on a tradition describing meetings of like-minded people refusing to think for themselves, a tradition including the meeting of revolutionaries in *The Possessed* and the gathering around "the great Gubaryov" in Turgenev's novel *Smoke*. The dynamics of such meetings depend less on the particular ideology shared than on the methods of preventing any independent thought. Social dynamics do not just forestall the expression of skeptical opinion, they preclude the formation of such opinions in the first place.

Vorotyntsev listens as everyone voices the proper views they all already hold and yet regard as "imperative . . . to meet and hear all over again what they collectively knew. They were all overpoweringly certain they were right, yet they needed these exchanges to reinforce their certainty."[44] They hold forth on topics they know nothing about, like how ordinary soldiers think, but about which Vorotyntsev, a colonel intimately acquainted with countless common soldiers, knows a great deal. Not only do they not want to learn what he has experienced, they also stare at him disapprovingly when he says something that doesn't fit their beliefs.

To his surprise, Vorotyntsev soon feels the need to join in expressing what he knows he disbelieves. "What is it," he asks himself, "that always forces us to adapt to the general tone?" It was like a magic spell: "if you tried to say something yourself, however clear your thoughts were, you looked ridiculous." Under this spell, Vorotyntsev finds himself saying what he regards as false. "He had lied, prevaricated, betrayed his beliefs. Why couldn't he manage it? Say this is *my* opinion. . . . Why was he so feeble?" When as a mere colonel he had attacked incompetent generals, he had not been afraid, yet "*here* he was afraid; his behavior was reactionary, and that was the most damning word of all. . . . It was like a contagious disease." Unless one understands how this sort of pressure to conform works, one will not grasp what governs political life or the reason that experience which contradicts people's views fails to persuade them. At last, Vorotyntsev manages to resist: "A jolt. He was free. Free from the unbearable bewitchment. . . . He spoke loudly, challengingly addressing the whole gathering."[45]

## Double Conscience

Memoirists and novelists describe with fascination a particular state of mind, characteristic of the Soviet period, in which one trains oneself to sincerely accept contradictory beliefs. One belief derives from one's actual experience and the other from official ideological assertions one needs to profess. One soon recognizes that the only way to profess prescribed beliefs flawlessly is to "believe" them.

As Kopelev explained, one had to subordinate "subjective truth" to the "objective truth" of the Party. We examined in Chapter 1 how, when Vasily

Grossman had difficulty getting a novel published, he asked Gorky for help. He pleaded that what he had described was "the truth," but Gorky replied that the writer has to ask "which truth. . . . We know that there are two truths and that, in our world, it is the vile and dirty truth of the past that quantitatively predominates. But this truth is being replaced by another truth that has been born and continues to grow." It is this second truth—the truth of the necessary future already discernible in the present—that the writer must describe.[46]

We also saw how, in Grossman's novel *Stalingrad*, Marusya criticizes Zhenya's realistic painting on just these grounds. "How many times do I have to tell you there are two truths? There's the truth of reality forced on us by the accursed past. And there's the truth of the reality that will defeat that past." The surgeon Sofya Osipovna replies for the author: "You're wrong. I can tell you as a surgeon, there's one truth, not two. When I cut someone's leg off, I don't know two truths. If we start pretending there are two truths, we're in trouble."[47]

Wolfgang Leonhard remarked on how, despite the arrest of his mother, friends, and teachers in 1937, he was delighted to be admitted to the Komsomol: "Somehow I dissociated these things, and even my personal impressions and experiences, from my fundamental political conviction. It was almost as if there were two separate levels—one of everyday experiences, which I found myself criticizing; the other of the great Party line which at this time, despite my hesitations, I still regarded as correct, from the standpoint of general principle."[48] How does one maintain belief in an ideology that, with time, becomes ever more obviously at odds with reality and ever more morally hideous? How to keep the "two separate levels" firmly apart? If one doesn't, one loses one's alibi for participating in the destruction of innocent people.

In *Life and Fate*, the dedicated Bolshevik Krymov finds himself asking how it is possible to believe that all the leading Bolsheviks who helped Lenin make the revolution, except Stalin, had turned out to be traitors and foreign spies? "Questions like these were best forgotten. But tonight Krymov was unable to forget them." Why, Krymov asks himself, did I lack the strength to say that I did not believe Bukharin was a saboteur and assassin, but instead raised my hand and signed? "What am I trying to say? That I am a man with two consciences? Or that I am two men, each with his own conscience?"[49]

Czesław Miłosz reflected on how "after long acquaintance with his role, a man grows into it so closely that he can no longer differentiate his true self from the self he simulates, so that even the most intimate of individuals speak to each other in Party slogans. To identify self with the role one is obliged to play [. . .] permits a relaxation of one's vigilance. Proper reflexes at the proper moment become truly automatic [. . .] Acting on such a scale has not occurred often in the history of the human race."[50]

One can forget one is acting, but one can also become aware that one does not believe what one professes. Solzhenitsyn described how he once re-marked to a Jewish fellow-prisoner, Boris Gammerov, that, of course, Presi-dent Roosevelt's public prayer was hypocritical. Gammerov demanded to know why Solzhenitsyn did not admit the possibility that Roosevelt might actually believe in God.

This question shocked Solzhenitsyn. "To hear such words from someone born in 1923? I could have replied to him very firmly, but prison had already undermined my certainty, and the principal thing was that some clean, pure feeling does live within us, existing apart from all our convictions, and right there it dawned on me that I had not spoken out of conviction but because the idea had been implanted in me from outside."[51] The realization that one's convictions are not really what one believes, that they have been "implanted from outside": this self-knowledge proves as important as it is unusual. In this case, it changed Solzhenitsyn's life by leading him to ask whether other beliefs he professed also came from outside. In this way, he began his journey to faith.

## Refusing Alibis

Grossman's Krymov realizes that it was not fear alone that motivated him. "It was the revolutionary cause itself that freed people from morality in the name of morality, that justified today's pharisees, hypocrites, and writers of denunciations in the name of the future, that explained why it was right to elbow the innocent into the ditch."[52] Krymov is right that fear is too simple an explanation. It does not explain why people betray themselves and the truth without fear. "Revolutionary fervor" also matters, but Krymov errs in thinking it explains everything that fear omits.

The key moment in *Life and Fate* occurs when the hero, Victor Shtrum, proves false to himself by signing a document affirming the so-called doctor's plot. Again, it is not fear that motivates him, and it is certainly not revolu-tionary fervor. After Stalin had called Shtrum to encourage the research that had only recently been condemned as "Talmudic," and after Malenkov had personally given him support, Shtrum's fall from status had reversed itself. Ev-eryone is now friendly to him, and "the most extraordinary thing of all was that these people were quite sincere now, they really did wish Victor well."[53]

Something he never anticipated takes place in Shtrum. "Without his real-izing it, everything that had happened to him began to seem quite normal, quite natural. His new life was the rule, he had begun to get used to it. His past life had been the exception, and slowly he began to forget what it had been like." The people who persecuted him turn out to have families and human interests like his own. "Deep down, of course, Victor understood that nothing had really changed," and yet something in him has changed, "both in his understanding and in his actual memory of things. . . . Yes, something was changing in him. He could feel it, but he didn't know what it was."[54]

When Shtrum's colleagues present him with the letter denouncing doctors for having murdered Gorky, he knows it is absurd. All the same, "though he had not forgotten the past," Victor had accepted his colleagues' friendship and "felt paralyzed by their trust and kindness. He had no strength. If only they had shouted at him, kicked him, beaten him," he would have gotten angry and recovered his strength. Just as Vorotyntsev could face cannon fire and stand up to generals but finds it hard to resist the pressure of liberal opinion, so Shtrum, who has risked his life rather than betray his scientific integrity, discovers how hard it can be to resist friendly gestures.

As he considers what to do, he "felt overwhelmed by disgust at his own submissiveness. . . . He was paralyzed not by fear, but by something quite different—a strange, agonizing sense of his own passivity." The doctors had confessed, after all, and there was only one thing that could make innocent people do that, but wouldn't it be insane to imagine they had been tortured? He rehearses a litany of reasons for not signing; he doesn't like the letter's condemnation of Babel, Pilnyak, Meyerhold, and other writers and artists, he might say, but they would be glad to change that part. "For the love of God! Please understand that I have a conscience. I feel ill," he thinks, but conscience, of course, is not a Bolshevik category. Fear plays a role in his decision to sign, of course, but fear alone cannot account for his "sense of impotence, a sense that he had somehow been hypnotized" much as Vorotyntsev experienced "bewitchment." He tries to see who else has signed, as if to hide behind someone else's back; he imagines delaying but then spending an agonizing night to no effect. At last, "he took out his pen. . . . How docile the rebel had now become."[55]

But that is not the end of the story. Shtrum immediately regrets what he has done. He experiences un-Bolshevik emotions: how could he have thrown stones at defenseless people, how could he have imagined himself pure enough to condemn others? He pitied the doctors' suffering and recognized his own baseness. "He realized with sorrow and horror how incapable he was of protecting his own soul. The power that had reduced him to slavery lay within him."[56] It would be easy enough for Shtrum to excuse himself: he could plead the risk of his life and the lives of his family; the importance of his work; and the pointlessness of not signing. But Shtrum refuses all these alibis.

Shtrum also refuses another excuse: evidently, that is who he is, and one cannot help who one is. "A man's character is his fate," as Heraclitus said. He could have told himself, given who he is, given all that has made him as he is, he could have done nothing else. This especially insidious excuse, which few resist, does not appeal to Victor. Neither does the argument that the past is over and so there is nothing to be done.

Victor has signed the document. Now, to use Bakhtin's term for taking responsibility, he "signs" his actions. "Good men and bad men alike are capable of weakness," he at last thinks. "The difference is simply that a bad man will be proud all his life of one good deed—while an honest man is hardly aware of his good acts, but remembers a single sin for years on end."[57] Sinners sleep soundly. The sign of a good person is a troubled conscience. Victor realizes it is not too late to act differently.

Effectiveness is not the point: that is the regime's criterion. As the family matriarch Alexandra Vladimirovna senses in the last chapter, one cannot control one's life and fate, but one can live as a human being.[58]

## Decency

Solzhenitsyn recognized that "some clean, pure feeling does live within us, apart from our convictions."[59] Not ideas but something he calls "conscience" leads Shtrum to accept responsibility. Krymov asks himself what prevented him from helping the families of those arrested, while "old women, lower-middle-class housewives . . . these superstitious domestics and illiterate nannies, would even take in children whose mothers and fathers had been arrested." "Members of the Party, on the other hand avoided these children like the plague. Were these old women braver and more honorable than Old Bolsheviks . . . ?"[60] The heroine of *The Master and Margarita*, given the chance to have any wish granted, begs mercy for a soul being tortured for eternity. In *August 1914*, when the politically radical Ensign Lenartovich, forced by Colonel Vorotyntsev to help carry a corpse, demands whether Vorotyntsev would show the same respect even for an arch reactionary's corpse, Vorotyntsev shocks him by telling him that "political differences are just ripples on a pond." In that case, Lenartovich inquires, "what sort of differences do you consider important?" Vorotyntsev answers: "The difference between decency and indecency."[61]

Ideology readily leads us to commit immoral acts. Even without ideology, we can talk ourselves into them. Basic decency provides the check. And there is no substitute for it.

In *Gulag*, Solzhenitsyn recalls how he and others in the Komsomol were once invited to join the NKVD and almost did so. The appeal to patriotism and the ideology that Solzhenitsyn accepted came close to persuading him, but something he could not identify, something "not founded on rational argument," restrained him. "People can shout at you from all sides: 'You must!' And your own head can be saying also: 'You must!' But inside your breast there is a sense of revulsion, repudiation. I don't want to. *It makes me feel sick.* Do what you want with me; I want no part of it."[62] A moral sense within us, deeper than all convictions, makes us draw back from indecent actions, whatever arguments justify it.

Nadezhda Mandelstam recounted how, when she lived in a town through which prisoner trains constantly passed, one woman defied the prohibition against helping prisoners when she managed to throw a piece of chocolate—a rare commodity—though the bars of an open window. This small act of kindness, this decency despite threats, made all the difference. "Will anybody in a future generation ever understand what that piece of chocolate with a child's picture on the wrapper must have meant in a stifling prison train in 1938 . . . [to] half-dead human beings, forgotten outcasts who had been struck from the rolls of the living . . . who now suddenly received . . . a little piece of chocolate to tell them that they were not forgotten . . . ?"[63]

In Dostoevsky's great novel about ideology, *The Possessed*, one character—Shatov—sets aside his ideology when his unfaithful wife returns. What is remarkable is that the ideology Shatov transcends is the one Dostoevsky himself professed in his journalism. But in this novel, even the best ideology pales before basic decency and spontaneous love—love that lends Shatov's face a "look of new life and spontaneous radiance. This strong, rugged man, all bristles on the surface, was suddenly all softness and shining gladness." "The convictions and the man are two very different things," he reflects. "We are all to blame, we are all to blame [. . .] and if only all were convinced of it!"[64]

"Men have made subdivisions for themselves in this eternally moving, unending, intermingled chaos of good and evil," writes the narrator of Tolstoy's story "Lucerne." "They have traced imaginary lines on the ocean, and expect the ocean to divide itself accordingly." Century after century, they come up with one system after another, all derived from the hubristic sense that one has found the final answer to moral questions. But we have only "one unerring guide, and only one—the Universal spirit which . . . bids us instinctively draw closer together."[65]

The love of mortals costs something, an angel learns in Tolstoy's story "What People Live By." Gratuitous love and kindness that make no sense from a rational point of view: this is what makes human life possible. Though we imagine otherwise, it is "what people live by."

Grossman places his faith in ineradicable decency. A prisoner in a Nazi camp, Ikonnikov has recorded his credo, which the Bolshevik prisoner Mostovskoy regards as the writings of someone "unhinged." People keep imagining they have discovered the true moral system, Ikonnikov has written, but whenever that happens "the very concept of good becomes a scourge, a greater evil than evil itself. . . . Whenever we see the dawn of an eternal good that will never be overcome by evil . . . the blood of old people and children is always shed."[66] Ikonnikov notes that even the Christian idea of love, when made into an ideology, caused immense suffering.

Ideology transforms good into evil. During the collectivization of agriculture and the terror of 1937, Ikonnikov reflects, "I saw people being annihilated in the name of an idea of good . . . I saw whole villages dying of hunger . . . I saw trains bound for Siberia with hundreds and thousands of men and women from Moscow, Leningrad, and every city in Russia." Even the German Fascists, Ikonnikov continues, committed their crimes in the name of what they considered good. Ikonnikov recalls when he thought that goodness is to be found in nature, only to recognize that nature itself is "a struggle of everything against everything."[67] He discerns the nature not of Wordsworth but of Darwin.

"And yet," he still maintains, "ordinary people bear love in their hearts, are naturally full of love and pity. . . . Yes, as well as this terrible Good with a capital 'G,' there is everyday human kindness. The kindness of an old woman carrying a piece of bread to a prisoner, the kindness of a soldier allowing a wounded enemy to drink from his water-flask . . . thoughtless kindness; an unwitnessed kindness . . . senseless kindness. A kindness outside any system of social or religious good."[68]

This "stupid kindness" is "what is most truly human in a human being," Ikonnikov concludes. "This dumb, blind love is man's meaning."[69] The power of this kindness lies in its very powerlessness, its reason in its irrationality, and its wisdom in its apparent foolishness. Even if we do not see it, or even if we reject it, it is always there hidden in plain view.

## The Consolation of Suffering

The Russian experience demonstrates the danger of ideologically based alibis. Over the past century such alibis have often prevailed. Time and again, they have divided humanity into two groups, with good belonging entirely to one and evil to the other. This division absolves people of individual responsibility. It also offers the heady feeling of moral superiority.

Even some who find themselves in the despised group can enjoy this gratifying feeling. They may pride themselves on the readiness to admit—no, proclaim—the sins of their own group. Only the group's lesser people, they may reason, insist on defending it. More enlightened, their betters demonstrate their superiority by acknowledging "our" guilt. By "our" they tacitly mean their groups' more benighted members, and only nominally themselves. One might call this locution "the self-excluding we."

In *The Brothers Karamazov* Father Ferapont, who loves to mortify his sinful flesh, also claims moral superiority for that very reason. Tolstoy's Father Sergius (the hero of his novella by that name) takes pride in his own humility, but, unlike Bulstrode and Ferapont, recognizes the contradiction and seeks to overcome it.

The appeal of moral dualism represents a still greater danger for those who class themselves as belonging to the good group of oppressed people endowed with the right to attack their oppressors. Victim psychology, indeed, constitutes another of the great themes of Russian literature. Herzen warned that "the oligarchic pretensions of the have-nots to possess a monopoly on suffering in society is as unjust as all forms of exclusiveness and monopoly . . . in the ultrademocrats, as Proudhon has observed, it is confined to the feeling of envy and hatred."[70] Envy, of course, is an emotion one attributes to others; one calls the same emotion in oneself a passion for justice.

"The egoism of the unhappy," observes the narrator of Chekhov's "Enemies," often makes them morally worse. "The unhappy are egoistic, spiteful, unjust, cruel, and less capable of understanding each other than fools. Unhappiness does not bring people together but draws them apart, and even where one would fancy people should be united by the similarity of their sorrow, far more injustice and cruelty is generated than in comparatively placid surroundings."[71]

Evgeniya Ginzburg agreed. "Suffering made me callous," she regretted. "The egoism of those who suffer is probably even more all-embracing than the self-regard of those who are happy." "The new barbarians," she explained, consisted of both "butchers and victims . . . this division did not invest the victims with moral superiority, for slavery had corrupted their souls."[72]

Discussing the psychology of those who denounced others to the NKVD, Grossman identifies those who, out of a sense of their own victimhood, felt morally entitled to even the score. Such a person wears "a permanently tense, offended, irritated expression. Someone has always just stepped on his toes, and he is invariably engaged in settling accounts with someone. The passion of the state for exposing enemies of the people was a find for him."[73]

Victimhood offers an alibi for evil because it allows one to regard the harm one inflicts as a form of justice. Evildoers are punished, and oppressors, or those who belong to the group of oppressors, suffer what they have long deserved. It follows that those who wish to inflict suffering will seek to view themselves as victims; and if they are genuine victims, the alibi will feel all the more airtight. In his account of working with the early Bolshevik government, Steinberg was appalled by those who regarded maximal violence as an uncompromising pursuit of justice: "Woe . . . to the new society," he concluded, "in which yesterday's slaves become today's rulers."[74]

No one has ever described victim psychology as profoundly as Dostoevsky. Precisely because of his immense compassion for those who suffer, Dostoevsky keenly discerned how suffering may debase as well as ennoble. Ivan Karamazov observes that people like Smerdyakov—who lives in a constant state of insult and who correctly regards himself as the victim of injustice— will make the Revolution. Readers may shudder at this prediction if they recognize at least two reasons that former victims make the worst tyrants. First, they feel justified in inflicting on others what they have suffered; and second, they know better than anyone else what hurts the most.

The villain of *Crime and Punishment*, the psychologically insightful Svidrigailov, observes that "human beings in general . . . greatly love to be insulted," a fact he uses to license insulting them.[75] Whenever he hits or insults his wife, she immediately orders her carriage so she can make the rounds of the neighbors and tell them all about it. In *Karamazov*, Dmitri's fiancée Katerina Ivanovna positively encourages his infidelity so that she can dramatize her nobility in sticking by him. As both Ivan and Dmitri observe, she loves not him but her own virtue. She even plans a life of ever-increasing victimization enabling her to rise to unprecedented moral heights.

We have seen that Fyodor Pavlovich, who claims it is positively beautiful (*krasivo*) to be insulted, recalls how he was once asked why he hates so-and-so so much, and "he had answered, with his shameless impudence, 'I'll tell you. He had done me no harm. But I played him a nasty trick'" and have never forgiven him for it.[76] The apparently absurd logic of this statement makes psychological sense if one reflects that the person harmed becomes morally superior and the person inflicting harm warrants opprobrium in his own eyes. The injured person occasioned Fyodor Pavlovich's guilt, and has, in this sense, wronged him, which is why Fyodor Pavlovich hates him. One can confirm this analysis by reflecting that, if it should turn out the victim was not so innocent after all, the hatred for him would diminish.

Here then is another reason Dostoevsky, and Dostoevsky alone, foresaw in detail what we have come to call totalitarianism. He detected in intelligentsia ideology a systematization of victimhood psychology, which licenses unlimited harm and provides a perfect alibi for those who inflict it.

## Where the Line between Good and Evil Is

"It is by now only too obvious," wrote Solzhenitsyn, "how dearly mankind has paid for the fact that we have all throughout the ages preferred to censure, doubt, and hate others" while excusing ourselves.[77] He described the key moral error behind the Soviets, Nazis, and similar regimes as the division of humanity into the evil and the good.

That is not how things actually are. Not only are moral questions more complex than such a division allows, and not only does it ignore one's own evil deeds, it also convicts everyone in the wrong group of the evil deeds of everyone else in that group, in the past as well as the present. But responsibility for crimes is not inherited. Babies are not born into guilt for their ancestors' actions, let alone for the actions of the group to which some ideology happens to assign them. Neither can one inherit moral superiority and the right to punish. Even victimhood one has endured oneself does not automatically make one morally superior. Moral superiority consists in what one chooses to do.

This whole way of thinking creates spurious alibis because it removes one's own responsibility. I began this chapter with Solzhenitsyn's comment that prison taught him "*how* a human being becomes evil and *how* a human being becomes good." He recognized that, before his arrest, he had "felt he was infallible, and was therefore cruel. . . . In my most evil moments I was convinced I was doing good, and was well supplied with systematic arguments" that displaced personal responsibility. Only when lying on rotting straw in prison, Solzhenitsyn continues, did he sense the first stirrings of real goodness. He realized the moral truth that precludes spurious alibis: "Gradually it was disclosed to me that the line separating good from evil passes not through states, nor between classes, nor between political parties either—but right through every human heart—and through all human hearts."[78]

# 9 What Time Isn't It?

## *Possibilities and Actualities*

> I had thought, much and often, of my Dora's shadowing out to me what might have happened, in those years that were destined not to try us. I had considered how the things that never happen are often as much realities to us, in their effects, as those that are accomplished.
>
> —CHARLES DICKENS, *DAVID COPPERFIELD*

COULD THINGS HAVE BEEN DIFFERENT? Is it possible that something else might have happened? Is more than one future possible? Can chance, choice, or sheer contingency alter the course of events?[1]

Some of our emotions, like guilt and regret, presuppose that more than one course of events is possible. So does suspense. But emotions may mislead us. Could suspense reflect nothing more than ignorance of a predetermined future? The eighteenth-century astronomer and mathematician Pierre-Simon Laplace, who contributed to the development of probability theory, insisted that probability applies not to events, which are certain, but only to the state of our knowledge. It measures the accuracy of our predictions.

Aristotle defined a contingent event as one that can either be or not be, and, unlike Laplace, he believed that contingency is real. It pertains to events themselves, not just our knowledge of them. In Aristotle's view, it is unacceptable to say that "nothing takes place fortuitously, either in the present or in the future . . . that there are no real alternatives, but that all that is or takes place is the outcome of necessity." Experience confirms

> that both deliberation and action are causative with regard to the future, and that, to speak more generally, in those things which are not continuously actual there is a potentiality in either direction. Such things may either be or not be; events also therefore may either take place or not take place. . . . It is therefore plain that it is not of necessity that everything is or takes place, but in some instances there are real alternatives.[2]

Aristotle's view contradicts the one that Dostoevsky's underground man fears, in which chance and choice are illusions and people resemble piano keys or organ stops on which the laws of nature play.

The key question, William James argued in his essay "The Dilemma of Determinism," is whether there are more possibilities than actualities. For the determinist, nothing else could have happened, and therefore the number of possibilities and actualities are the same. For the indeterminist, possibilities exceed actualities. In addition to events that did happen and those that did not and could not have happened, there is a third type: those that did not but could have happened. If the same circumstances were repeated—if the tape were played over—the outcome might be different. In such cases, one cannot know what will happen until it does.[3]

If possibilities outnumber actualities, the present moment does not derive automatically from preceding ones. Each present contains more than one possibility and so suspense is not illusory. The moment is truly momentous. As Bakhtin expressed the point, some events display "eventness." People make real choices and exhibit "surprisingness," which is what distinguishes people from mere objects.[4]

Russian thinkers addressed these issues as they pertain to nations as well as to individuals. Is Russia's future already determined, or does it depend on what Russians do? Was the path followed by Western Europe one that Russia is bound to imitate? Or could Russians create a wholly different society? Are there iron historical laws, or just soft tendencies? If the future is already given, could we at least speed it up?

Determinism assures us of a desired outcome, while indeterminism creates the sense of urgency motivating people to act. Both have their appeal. Is there a way to combine them?

## Certainty

Certainty about the future feeds complacency. In Bulgakov's *The Master and Margarita*, it is just such complacency that the devil Woland, having assumed the form of a foreign professor, ridicules with his practical jokes. In the opening chapter, Berlioz, instructing the young poet Bezdomny, voices absolute certainty that God does not exist and that "man himself," having learned the laws of history, controls events. "I'm sorry," replies Woland,

> but in order to be in control, you have to have a definite plan for at least a reasonable period of time. So how, may I ask, can man be in control if he can't even draw up a plan for a ridiculously short period of time, say, a thousand years, and is, moreover, unable to ensure his safety even for the next day? And indeed . . . suppose you were to start controlling others and yourself, and just as you developed a taste for it, so to speak, you suddenly . . . got lung cancer . . . and there goes your control![5]

No wonder five-year plans fail.

For example, Woland remarks to Berlioz, you don't even know what will happen to you today. When Berlioz provides his schedule, Woland announces that Berlioz's head will be cut off, which, to Bezdomny's amazement, soon happens, and in just the way Woland foretold. Even if the future is already given, we can never know it.

Believing they had mastered economic laws, the Soviets presumed they could manage an entire economy scientifically. The key distinction between Soviet and market economics pertains to the extent of possible knowledge. If knowledge can be comprehensive, the economy can be managed from the center; if not, local agency responding to unforeseeable contingencies works better. The economic question was therefore an epistemological one.

How certain can one be? Is economic planning possible? In chapter 18, Berlioz's uncle from Kiev, the economic planner Maximillian Andreevich Poplavsky, journeys to Moscow in response to a perplexing telegram: "I have just been cut in half by a streetcar at Patriarch's. Funeral Friday 3 p.m. Come. Berlioz."[6] How is one to explain a posthumous message? Could Berlioz, foreseeing his end, have written the telegram just before dying? But how would he know the funeral would be at exactly 3 o'clock? It is one thing to foresee one's death from a wasting disease, but how could Berlioz know that a streetcar would cut him in half?

As an economic planner, Poplavsky displays great intelligence, and "what are smart people for, if not to untangle tangled things?"[7] The solution, he decides, is "very simple." The message had been garbled; the word "I" had come from some other telegram and placed where "Berlioz" should have been. Woland repeatedly contrives evidently impossible events, and Muscovites respond, as Poplavsky does, by explaining their strangeness away. That is the key principle of Soviet thought: nothing is essentially strange or inexplicable. To think otherwise is anti-Leninist agnosticism. But the world is indeed strange, and the devil delights to demonstrate as much.

When Likhodeyev is transported instantly to Yalta, no one can explain how, even with the fastest airplane, he could suddenly be there. No sooner has an explanation been formulated than he sends another telegram refuting it. At last his associates agree that a drunken Likhodeyev was telegraphing from the new Yalta restaurant, which hardly explains why police in the real Yalta would be requesting verification of his identity.

After Woland and his retinue depart, authorities explain supernatural tricks according to their rationalist ideology. Ordinary people may whisper about "evil powers," but "needless to say, truly mature and cultured people did not tell these stories about an evil power's visit to the capital." Still, "facts are facts . . . and cannot simply be dismissed without explanation."[8]

As always, Soviet investigators proved equal to the task. The strangest events "were all explained, and one can't but concede that the explanations were both reasonable and irrefutable." It turned out that everything "was the work of a gang of hypnotists and ventriloquists magnificently skilled in their art," so skilled that "they could easily convince whoever came into contact with them that certain objects or people were present in places where really they were not, and, conversely, they could remove from sight those objects or people that actually were in sight." As telegrams from the Yalta police demonstrated, "the band of hypnotists was [even] able to practice long-distance hypnosis, and not just on individuals, but on whole groups of people at one time."[9]

The problem with this "explanation" is that it can fit anything. Any counterevidence can be dismissed as the result of hypnosis. These "scientific" explanations fail the first test of a scientific theory, that it must allow for disconfirmation. But don't Marxism-Leninism and other putative social sciences also fail that test?

The devil who visits Ivan Karamazov describes himself as "x in an unsolvable equation." He exists so that surprising events can happen. I would love to praise God, the devil confides, but I am forbidden to do so because, everyone says, "there'd be nothing without you. If everything in the universe were sensible, nothing would happen. There would be no events without you, and there must be [unpredictable] events."[10] In much the same spirit, Bulgakov's demonic agent of surprise upsets a world that has ruled out the possibility of surprise. Wonder confronts certainty.

## Semiotic Totalitarianism

If chance does not exist, and socialist planning is scientifically flawless, then, as we have seen, economic failures must result from sabotage undertaken by "wreckers." The more socialist planning failed and the emptier the store shelves became, the more sabotage was detected. In 1937 a campaign for the "liquidation of the consequences of the destructive work of saboteurs, spies, and wreckers" intensified. As historian Yuri Slezkine observes, "there was no longer such a thing as a mistake, an accident, or a natural disaster ... any deviation from virtue—not only in human thought and deed, but in the world at large—was the result of deliberate sabotage by well-organized agents of evil."[11] There were no misprints, just wrecking disguised as "simple error." After Sergei Kirov's murder in 1934, chief censor Boris Volin informed local censors that "expertly camouflaged work of the class enemy" had been detected "on the arts front." Artists and graphic designers smuggle messages into apparently innocent pictures:

> By means of different combinations of colors, lights, and shadow ... the enemies are smuggling counterrevolutionary content.
> The symbolic painting by the artist N. Mikhailov, *By Kirov's Coffin*, in which a certain combination of light, shadow, and color represent the outline of a skeleton, has been qualified as a disguised counterrevolutionary act.
> The same has been detected on the tin can labels printed by Supply Technology Publishers. . . .
> In light of the above, I order that:
> All censors working with posters, paintings, labels, photo montages, etc. undertake the most thorough scrutiny possible of such material, not limiting themselves to superficial political meaning and overall artistic value, but considering carefully the entire artwork from all angles ... frequently resorting to a magnifying glass.[12]

One might ask: why would saboteurs inscribe messages that only a magnifying glass could reveal? The answer is: since there are no accidents, what other explanation is possible?

## The Law of Progress

In nineteenth-century Russia as elsewhere in Europe, the law of progress, which asserted that History guides the world to inevitable improvement, seemed obviously true—weren't Europeans better off than they had been a century before?—as well as proven by science itself. Providence operated over time and so history acquired a meaningful story. This faith in a law of progress appealed to liberals, Hegelians, and socialists, and, after 1859, imposed a progressive interpretation on Darwin's theory of evolution.

Belinsky expressed the common view. In his essay "The Idea of Art" (written 1841) he enthused that the earth, the creatures inhabiting it, and the human beings who have mastered it, all progress "toward . . . perfection. It is the law of all evolution that every subsequent moment is higher than the preceding one." "Every important event in the life of mankind occurs *in its time,*" Belinsky asserted. "Every great man . . . expresses in his activity the spirit of the times in which he was born and developed." Modern freedom developed along with "that utter subjugation of Nature by the spirit, as expressed in the steam engines which have practically conquered time and space." In short,

> from the first awakening of the timeless forces and elements of life . . . to the crown of creation—man, from the first association of men in a community to the latest historical fact of our time there is a single chain of evolution without a single break. . . . Both in nature and in history it is not blind chance that holds sway, but a rigorous, inexorable inner necessity.[13]

In "A View of the Principal Aspects of Russian Literature in 1843," Belinsky applied this idea to the history of literature. Literature, too, is "moving forward by the inevitable law of steady progress," which proponents of the "*greybeard literature*" of the past will never appreciate. Innovations are superior precisely because they are innovations.[14]

"History is on our side," later is better: such reasoning, as Nadezhda Mandelstam observed, disables thought.[15] Instead of asking whether some new social theory is true or whether its recommendations make sense, one simply places it on a timeline. Those who should have known better therefore acquiesced in brutal practices justified as more up-to-date than old-fashioned humane values. In her view, Bolshevik leader Nikolai Bukharin, later executed by Stalin, realized "that the new world he was actively helping to build was horrifyingly unlike the original concept" but also believed that any questioning of History's agent, the Party, was unscientific. "Determinist theory . . . boldly outlawed any study of real life: Why undermine the system and sow unnecessary doubt if history was in any case speeding us to the appointed destination?"[16]

To grasp nineteenth-century Russian thought and its Soviet inheritor, one must appreciate this use of the word "history" to designate not the passive record of events but an active agent with purposes of its own. Things do not just happen in history; History itself accomplishes things. As the Greeks attributed the behavior of the sea to Poseidon and of streams to naiads, so nineteenth-century thinkers personified History.

## Tolstoy Rejects the Law of Progress

As we have seen, Dostoevsky's underground man argues that the law of progress can be validated only by excluding counterevidence. We have also seen that Tolstoy, in his essay "Progress and the Definition of Education," argued that "proponents of the superstition of progress" advance the "unproved assertion that humanity in former days enjoyed less well-being, and the farther we go back the less, and the farther forward the more." They conclude that "by the law of progress, every historical action will lead to an increase of the general well-being . . . while all attempts to arrest or even oppose the movement of history are fruitless."[17]

Proponents "prove" their theory, Tolstoy continues, by illustrating it, but any cockamamie theory can be illustrated by picking the right example. One tests a theory by looking not for examples but for counterexamples. Yet believers in a law of progress systematically exclude counterexamples, which they deem "non-historical." And so they point to progress in England and the tiny dukedom of Hohenzollern-Sigmaringen, with its three thousand inhabitants, while ignoring the fact that China, with its two hundred million inhabitants, contradicts the theory. "Progress is a common law of humanity," they say, "except for Asia, Africa, America, and Australia, except for one thousand millions of people."

If one considers counterevidence, one discovers that "the well-being of people now increases in one place, in one stratum, and in one sense, and now diminishes." However comforting a law of progress may be, "it is as easy to subordinate history to the idea of progress as to any other idea or to any imaginable historical fancy."[18]

What makes the idea of progress so appealing to learned people? "Those who believe in progress are sincere in their belief," Tolstoy explained, "because that faith is advantageous to them and so they preach their faith with passion and fury."[19] Who but the learned could be the agents of progress? Who but they should govern?

In his *Confession*, Tolstoy describes his own state of mind when he, too, believed in the law of progress. It was easy to do so, he asserts, because other educated people accepted it and because it made life seem meaningful: "It then appeared to me that this word meant something. I did not as yet understand that . . . in my answer 'Live in conformity with progress,' I was like a man in a boat who when carried along by the wind and waves should reply to what for him is the chief and only question, 'whither to steer,' by saying, 'We are being carried somewhere.'"[20] "Ashamed as I am to confess it," Tolstoy continues, "it was only much later that I recognized why the theory of progress seemed so convincing to me." "It was just the time" when "my muscles were growing and strengthening, my memory was being enriched, I was growing and developing; and feeling this growth in myself it was natural for me to think that such was the universal law in which I should find the solution of my life."[21] But the time came when I felt I was "fading, my muscles were weakening, my teeth falling out, and I saw that the law not only did not explain anything to me, but that there never had been or could be such a law, and that I had taken for a law what I had found in myself at a certain period of my life."[22]

By the same token, since progress, defined as educated people do, depends on educated people, we should hardly be surprised that they are the main "believers in progress" while its enemies include "the master mechanics, the factory workmen, the peasants . . . the more a man works the more conservative he is, and the less he works the more he is a progressist."[23]

## *Herzen: No Libretto*

Herzen's *From the Other Shore*, a collection of essays and dialogues responding to the failure of the 1848 European revolutions, offers an especially profound (and influential) critique of optimistic historical theories. In the book's three dialogues, each between an old skeptic and a young idealist, Herzen exposes the shallowness of the conventional views that he himself adopts in the book's five essays.

For all our disappointed hopes, the idealist intones, one thing remains, "faith in the future; sometime, long after our death, the house for which we have cleared the site will be built." The skeptic replies that "there is no reason to believe that the new world will be built according to our plans" because both circumstances and ideals change. The young man evidently assumes that his image of perfection reflects unchanging values, but it actually participates in the historical process. You are taking away my last consolation, the young man answers, "murdering my dreams, like Macbeth."[24]

The real difference between us, the skeptic decides, is that "you are looking for a banner, I am trying to lose one. . . . Where are the necessities in virtue of which the future must act the precise role that we have devised for it?" You justify your hopes with historical theory, but "life has its own embryogenesis which does not coincide with the dialectic of pure reason." You are misled, he continues, "by categories not fit to catch the flow of life." Who guaranteed the end you seek, "who conceived it, who declared it? Is it something inevitable or not? If it is, are we mere puppets?"[25]

The idealist reminds the skeptic that he has "forgotten that throughout all the changes and confusion of history there runs a single red thread binding it into one aim. This thread—is progress. . . . Is it possible that in all this you do not see a goal?"[26]

"The path is not determined," the skeptic replies, and that is a good thing. "If humanity marched straight towards some kind of result, then there would be no history, only logic; humanity would have come to rest, a finished article, in an absolute *status quo*, like animals." Operatic optimism notwithstanding, "there is no libretto. If there were a libretto, history would lose all interest, become . . . ludicrous." Human effort would become so much play acting in a drama with a predetermined denouement. But the very opposite is the case: "In history, all is improvisation, all is will, all is *ex tempore*; there are no frontiers, no itineraries."[27]

What is more, the skeptic continues, a comet or a geological cataclysm could end human life tomorrow. Impossible, the idealist replies; "would it have been worth while to have had a development for three thousand years with the pleasant final prospect of suffocating from sulphuric fumes? How can you not see that this is an absurdity?" This question implies the world operates purposefully, the skeptic retorts, and that is precisely what is at issue. "Who guaranteed the immortality of the planet?" Nature has no desires, it is perfectly "indifferent to the result."[28]

Possibilities team but they cannot all be realized, the skeptic asserts. "In nature, as in the souls of men, there slumber countless forces and possibilities."[29] Each past moment could have been different, and the future can be many things. It is a mistake to treat future moments as specific states of affairs, like past moments. The future does not exist, and any particular future we imagine can "either be or not be."

## Is the Future Historical?

The Soviets treated the future as already given. Events to come are already determined and unchangeable, even if we have to wait to know them. As philosopher Arthur Danto has argued, Marx and Engels, like other "substantive philosophers of history," were inclined, despite their atheism, "to regard history through essentially theological spectacles, as though they could perceive a divine plan, but not a divine being whose plan it was." Their statements about the future are not predictive, but prophetic, Danto explains. A prophecy, in this sense, is a specific type of statement about the future,

> an *historical* statement about the future. The prophet is one who speaks about the future in a manner which is appropriate only to the past, or who speaks of the present in the light of a future treated as a *fait accompli*. A prophet treats the present in a perspective ordinarily available only to future historians, to whom present events are past, and for whom the meaning of present events is discernible.[30]

Soviet Marxist-Leninism assessed the present the way a critic, having completed a novel, assesses the import of events taking place chapters earlier. In Solzhenitsyn's *In the First Circle*, Gerasimovich reproves Nerzhin for wanting to go "back to the past" and change history's direction. "If only I believed that there is any backward and forward in human history!" Nerzhin answers. "For me there's no word so devoid of meaning as 'progress.'" Not only have people not become better over the centuries, but they have become worse—and precisely because they believed in "beautiful ideas" like progress.[31]

"History" in the sense used by Hegel, Marx, and other theoreticians of progress—History as an agent heading in a certain direction—does not exist, argues Ivan Grigorievich in the closing chapter of Grossman's *Forever Flowing*. "Yes, and the word 'history' itself has been dreamed up by men. There is no history—it is like grinding water."[32]

## *The Fallacy of the Irrelevant Future*

What obligation do we owe to future generations? Proponents of two opposing views justified their reasoning as the necessary consequence of unsentimental materialism. To the great writers, both positions, taken to extremes, appeared erroneous. Let us call these twin errors "the fallacy of the irrelevant future" and "the fallacy of the actual future."

If the chain of cause and effect is all there is, if the result is all that matters, and if the ascription of absolute significance to any value is merely superstition contrary to materialism, then, people have reasoned since antiquity, we should live our lives so as to experience as much pleasure as possible. As we have seen, Innokenty Volodin, in Solzhenitsyn's *In the First Circle*, draws this "Epicurean" conclusion.

In *Anna Karenina*, Stiva, who "never could make out what was the object of all the terrible and high-flown language about another world when things might be so very amusing in this world,"[33] squanders his wealth, accumulates debts, and sells off his wife Dolly's forests. As Dolly never forgets, their children will consequently have nothing. At one point Stiva realizes to his horror that he has actually begun to worry about his children's future, but he soon adopts the more sophisticated "Petersburg" view:

> His children? In Petersburg children did not prevent their parents from enjoying life. The children were brought up in boarding schools and there was no trace of the wild notions that prevailed in Moscow . . . that all the luxuries of life were for the children, while the parents were to have nothing but work and anxiety. Here people understood that a man is in duty bound to live for himself, as every man of culture should.[34]

For Levin, Stiva's attitude constitutes a betrayal of his status as an aristocrat. Stiva readily sells one of Dolly's forests to a scheming merchant who will cut down the trees for timber. Levin, by contrast, regards himself not as the owner of his inherited land, free to do with it as he pleases, but as its steward, morally bound to pass it down to his children in the same state as he received it. In Levin's view, aristocracy exists to ensure that those concerned only with present pleasure do not ruin the future for others.

Conversing with the "reactionary landowner," Levin wonders why they both choose to earn so little from their work on the land when they could sell their trees and make much more. Levin attributes this choice to "a sort of duty one feels to the land."[35] But how can one have a duty to an inanimate entity? What he means is that he has a duty to coming generations. In Chekhov's stories and plays, what we would call "environmentalism" also derives from a duty to the future. Doctor Astrov in *Uncle Vanya*, who charts the disappearance of forests and birds, imagines, each time he plants a tree, how people will someday benefit. In *The Cherry Orchard*, which ends with the merchant Lopakhin cutting down the splendid orchard to build profitable summer cottages, the trees represent a beautiful past, exquisitely vulnerable in a materialistic age.

Debt, waste, carelessness, and the destruction of beauty spoil the world for those to come. They are forms of robbery. The "fallacy of the irrelevant future" entails serious moral consequences.

## The Fallacy of the Actual Future

The Bolsheviks adopted a collectivist interpretation of radical materialism. In building Communism, the Party, rather than the individual, operates according to the maxim that only the result counts.

Bolsheviks reasoned: since the number of future generations is indefinitely large, and the total population of the future dwarfs that of the present, it is morally permissible—in fact, obligatory—to sacrifice any number of people today to ensure happiness in the future. Such thinking, though justified by materialism, does not require it. It characterizes utopians generally.[36]

Utopians usually presume that future people are as real as present ones. The historian of Russian philosophy George L. Kline contested this widespread proposition.[37] Bertrand Russell, for instance, maintained that "time is an unimportant and superficial characteristic of reality. Past and future must be acknowledged to be as real as the present" and that "it is a mere accident that we have no memory of the future." "For us . . . physicists," Einstein explained, "the distinction between past, present, and future is only an illusion, if a stubborn one."[38] Or as some philosophers argue, events occur tenselessly.[39]

The fate of characters in a novel is already recorded: it exists on a page to come. In much the same way, these philosophers suppose, the time to come already exists. A time we cannot experience is no less real than a space we cannot reach. This spatialization of time entails a denial of the temporal asymmetry we usually sense, that the past has been determined while the future is open to multiple possibilities.[40] The future is no different from, and no less irrevocable than, the past. It is the past to come, and already has pastness.

In a novel, events are caused not only by prior events, as in life, but also by future ones to which they are destined to lead. They complete a structure, and when a well-crafted work ends, the reader sees why each event and each detail could be no other way. The end is present in the beginning and everywhere along the way. Causation works in both directions, backward as well as forward, as it does in the view, as Peirce concluded from physics, that "the future determines the past in precisely the way the past determines the future."[41]

It follows that future people have the same moral claim on us as distant people. One utopian thinker asks rhetorically, "How is the sacrifice of (part of) one generation for all later ones different in principle from sacrificing parts of one generation for another?" which, he says, happens all the time in "pre-utopian" societies. Kline cited other philosophers who refer to "future persons" or "actual persons of the future" and maintain, as one philosopher expresses it, that "future people are, after all, still people. . . . And future people are *real*. They differ from us by virtue of their location in time, just as others do by their location in space. This doesn't make them any more 'unreal' than the Chinese."[42]

Contemplating the bloodshed to which such reasoning has led, Kline concluded that the claims of future people are "*weaker* than the claims of actual present persons," and that we should decisively reject "the instrumentalizing of living persons."[43] In a country where terrorism flourished and a regime sacrificed millions in the name of building communism, the question of "future persons" seemed anything but abstruse. Writers answered it in several ways.[44]

One answer follows from Tolstoy's idea that responsibility diminishes with what might be called moral distance. Levin, the hero of *Anna Karenina*, refuses to share the martial enthusiasm of the educated for helping Balkan Slavs resist Ottoman atrocities. This argument continues to perplex thinkers today: do we have a moral obligation to rescue people from genocide or should we renounce military interference abroad? Dostoevsky believed strongly in the obligation to intervene and, in *A Writer's Diary*, contested Levin's arguments.

Levin would surely feel the need to prevent torture occurring right before his eyes, Dostoevsky supposes. Then why not feel the same obligation when torture occurs far away? "Is it simply the distance that influences the matter?" Dostoevsky asks. To be sure, people exhibit the "*psychological* peculiarity" of diminished pity for distant people, but the same moral obligation remains. "Imagine that there are people living on the planet Mars and that they are piercing the eyes of some infants there. Do you think we'd feel any pity here on earth, any great amount of pity, at least?" Should we? If not, "if distance really does have such an influence on humaneness of itself, at what point does love of humanity end?"[45]

These questions presume, as most philosophical systems do, that we owe the same obligation to everyone. Tolstoy (and the autobiographical Levin) regarded this presumption as monstrous. In Dickens's *Bleak House*, Mrs. Jellyby utterly neglects her own children as she raises money for people in "Borrioboola-Gha." By contrast, Dolly, the moral compass of *Anna Karenina*, devotes unflagging attention to her growing family. Philosophers notwithstanding, she and Levin acknowledge that some people have a greater moral claim on us than others. As the ancient Stoics maintained, responsibility comes in concentric circles.[46] We owe the greatest obligation to our family, then to relatives, neighbors, and friends, then to people in our community, and only many circles later to people on the other side of the world (or "Martians"). Responsibility never disappears, but it diminishes with moral distance.[47]

The same argument applies to the moral distance separating us from future generations. We can help the people around us. We know their needs reasonably well, which is one reason we have greater responsibility for them. But we know little about people to come, especially those centuries away. We may be harming them by the very sacrifices we make to help them, as Russian experience demonstrates.

Countless people are possible, but only a small percentage of them will come to be. We cannot tell which ones, or what they will need and desire. We contemplate a future not of actual but of possible people, and the status of "possibility" confers moral distance and diminishes responsibility.

## The Harm of Charity

Why should one provide charity? The fallacy of the actual future suggests that we should not. Lenin was not the only revolutionary to argue that charity is positively immoral. The worse, the better: the more people suffer, the closer the revolution eliminating all suffering forever. For revolutionaries, our obligation is to the countless people of the future, not the few alive today. During the famine of 1891–1892, while Tolstoy organized relief, Lenin argued against help. "Psychologically, this talk of feeding the starving," he remarked, "is nothing but an expression of the saccharine sweet sentimentality so characteristic of our intelligentsia."[48] Many radicals shared this view.

Defense of charity, in fact, became a conservative position. In *The Idiot*, Ippolit maintains "that people were wrong in preaching and maintaining, as many do now, that individual benevolence was of no use. . . . Anyone who attacks individual charity . . . attacks human nature and casts contempt on personal dignity."[49] We become fully human in sacrificing ourselves for our neighbors.

Ippolit mentions a retired general who devoted his life to helping prisoners, both materially and with sympathetic listening. Each act of charity may soften a soul who then does the same for someone else, Ippolit explains. "How can you tell . . . what significance such an association of one personality with another may have on the destiny of those associated [. . .] You know, it's a matter of a whole lifetime, an infinite multitude of ramifications hidden from us." One personality interacts with another: that is a part of charity that those focusing only on material benefits miss, and it is possible only when two people are present. "In scattering the seed, scattering your 'charity,' your kind deeds, you are giving away . . . part of your personality, and taking into yourself part of another."[50]

In *Landmarks*, Semyon Frank traced how concern for future people, and for humanity in the abstract, leads to cruelty. "Intoxicated with the ideal of the radical, universal achievement of the people's happiness," *intelligents* regard "simple, person-to-person aid, mere relief of current sorrows and needs," not only as insignificant but even as "a harmful waste of time and . . . a betrayal of all mankind and its eternal salvation for the sake of a few individuals close at hand." So widespread has this attitude become, Frank noted, that charitable people feel compelled to justify their generosity as a way for revolutionaries to gain people's confidence.[51]

Future people are an abstraction, living people actually suffer. And so, Frank continued, "the abstract ideal of absolute happiness in the remote future destroys the concrete moral relationship of one individual to another and the vital sensation of love for one's neighbor, one's contemporaries, and their current needs." He maintains, as we have seen, that the socialist is not an altruist. "He does not love living people, only his *idea*. . . . Since he is sacrificing himself, he does not hesitate to sacrifice others." For him, contemporaries are either victims he cannot help or perpetrators he must destroy. "Thus, great love for future humanity engenders great hatred for people."[52]

Utopians inflict real suffering while the glorious future remains as distant as ever. "I want to live now, not 'in the long run,'" Nerzhin tells the Leninist Rubin in *In the First Circle*. "I know what you are going to say . . . this is a transitional period, a temporary state of affairs—but this transitional period of yours makes my life impossible." After all, *all* states of affairs are "temporary." Nerzhin continues: "We ridicule the Christians . . . living in hopes of paradise and putting up with absolutely everything on this earth! But . . . for whose sake do we suffer? For our mythical descendants. What difference does it make whether it's happiness for posterity or in the next world?"[53]

What is more, unrestrained means create a worse, not a better world. Utopian violence injures not only present people but future ones as well. The argument that future well-being justifies present pain tacitly depends on the strict separation of the present, where violence is committed, from the future, where utopia flourishes. It presumes that today's suffering, once over and done with, will not become routine and lead to more suffering later. But it does.

Sologdin tells Rubin (*In the First Circle*) that "the loftier your aim, the nobler must be your means. Treacherous means destroy the end itself."[54] We do not first employ means, then enjoy ends; the means persist. The worse, the worse.

## The Last Number

What if the society envisaged by utopians should be realized? Anyone familiar with the history of utopian plans will appreciate how, time and again, earlier utopias seem hellish by later standards. Presumably, the same will happen to today's ideas of perfection. Today's dreams may be tomorrow's nightmares, as literary dystopias show.

Utopians presume an end of history, when perfection is reached and the flux of values ceases. They regard their values as extra-historical. But they are not. In Zamyatin's dystopia *We*, I-330 asks the hero, D-503, to "name the last number":

> "What is. . . . I cannot understand, which *last?*"
>
> "The last one, the highest, the largest."
>
> "But I-330, that's absurd! Since the number of numbers is infinite, how can there be a last one?"
>
> "And why do you think there is a *last* revolution?"[55]

Historians passing moral judgments speak as if they were outside history, Tolstoy observes in *War and Peace*. They presume their values are the final standard. But all their praise and blame of a historical figure means only that he "did not have the same conception of the welfare of humanity . . . as a present-day professor," who will, in turn, be treated the same way by professors to come.[56]

The future will never reach finality. Those who sacrifice present lives in the name of a utopian future understand the future even less than the present.

If people may be sacrificed for the perfect future, Herzen objects, what happens if perfection is never reached? In that case, each generation will be sacrificed for a benefit that never arrives. In the most famous passage of *From the Other Shore*, the skeptic asks:

> If progress is the end, for whom are we working? Who is this Moloch who, as the toilers approach him, instead of rewarding them, only recedes, and . . . can give back only the mocking answer that after their death all will be beautiful on earth? Do you truly wish to condemn all human beings alive today to the sad role of . . . wretched galley slaves, up to their knees in mud, dragging a barge . . . with . . . "progress in the future" inscribed on its bows? Those who are exhausted fall in their tracks; others, with fresh forces take up the ropes; but there remains . . . as much ahead as there was at the beginning because progress is infinite. This alone should serve as a warning to people: an end that is infinitely remote is not an end, but, if you like, a trap; an end must be nearer—it ought to be, at the very least, the laborer's wage, or pleasure in the work done.[57]

## Herzen: The Purpose of the Present

To regard the present as merely a bridge to a providential future, Herzen maintains, is to foist purposes on nature. "The aim of each generation—is itself. Nature not only never makes one generation the means for the attainment of some future end, she does not concern herself with the future at all." No moment, no culture, no people, exists merely for the benefit of times to come.

> Life . . . always pours the whole of herself into the present moment . . . each historical moment is complete and self-contained. . . . That is why each period is new, fresh, full of its own hopes, carrying within itself its own joys and sorrows. The present belongs to it. But human beings are not satisfied with this. They want the future to be theirs as well.

The young idealist voices the need to "see . . . in the future the harbor towards which he is moving." If life is to make sense, each moment must have a purpose, an end to which it is directed, he implores. The skeptic replies: "And what, pray, is the end of the song that the singer sings?" If you look beyond the song "for some end," you will suffer "remorse because, instead of listening, you were waiting for something else. You are misled by categories not fitted to catch the flow of life."[58]

If we are mere puppets existing only for the sake of the future, the skeptic continues, then we are no longer "morally free beings . . . I prefer to think of life, and therefore of history, as an end attained rather than as a means to something else."[59]

## Tolstoy: Absorption in the Present Moment

Without entirely disregarding consequences, we need the ability to immerse ourselves in the present. What Tolstoy calls life's "finest moments" require presentness.[60]

In Tolstoy's view, fiction is especially well adapted to capturing presentness. "The historian is concerned with the results of an event, the artist with the very fact of the event," he explained in his essay "Some Words About the Book *War and Peace*."[61] Focusing on where events actually led, historians omit where they might have led. Those unrealized possibilities were essential to the moment when it was experienced, and when historians overlook them, they mispresent it. Novelists try to restore the open presentness of past moments.

As the Russian army retreats, Prince Andrei finds himself back on his own estate. There he experiences great joy as he witnesses girls stealing plums. "A new sensation of solace and relief came over him. . . . Evidently these little girls passionately desired one thing—to carry away and eat those green plums without being caught—and Prince Andrei shared their wish for success in this enterprise."[62] Watching their total absorption in the present, Andrei experiences the same absorption observing them.

But Andrei usually focuses on consequences. This Bolkonsky family characteristic enables prudence but inhibits the total absorption in the moment that comes so readily to the improvident Rostovs. Right after witnessing the girls stealing plums, Prince Andrei watches the soldiers under his command bathe in the river. Heedless of the future, one soldier crosses himself and plunges into the water while another "stood up to his waist in water, twitching his muscular body and snorting with satisfaction as he poured water over his head with his blackened hands." Andrei cannot share their enjoyment of the moment because he cannot help imagining the horrors of imminent battle. "'Flesh, bodies, cannon fodder,' he reflected, looking at his own naked body and shuddering, not so much from cold as from a state of revulsion, incomprehensible even to himself, aroused by the sight of all those naked bodies splashing in the muddy water."[63] What Andrei anticipates happens, but, from Tolstoy's perspective, he showed more wisdom contemplating the girls stealing plums.

Nikolai Rostov displays a keen appreciation of presentness when, on leave from the army, he participates in a wolf hunt. Lying in wait for the wolf, he addresses God "with that passionate compunction with which men pray in moments of intense emotion arising from trivial causes. 'Why, what is it to Thee,' he said to God, 'to do this for me? I know . . . that it is a sin to ask this, but for God's sake make the wolf come my way and let [my dog] Karai get his teeth into his throat.'" And indeed the wolf suddenly appears. "The greatest happiness had come to him—and so simply, unheralded by pomp and fanfare. Rostov could not believe his eyes, and he remained in doubt for over a second."[64] The wolf seems to get away, but a lucky accident enables Karai to overtake it. In a sentence only he could have written, Tolstoy observes: "That instant when Nikolai saw the wolf in the gully struggling with the dogs, saw her gray coat and outstretched hind leg under them, her head with ears laid back in terror and gasping (Karai had her by the throat), was the happiest moment of his life."[65]

Tolstoy knows: this is not just a happy moment, but the happiest moment in Nikolai's life. Why? The answer is ultimately mysterious, but we may remark that the moment lies outside any story Rostov might tell of his life. It has nothing to do with his military career or his love for Sonya and Princess Marya. For that matter, if this whole scene were omitted from the book, the reader would sense nothing missing. The happiest moment of our lives, Tolstoy suggests, lies beyond narrative and is complete in itself. Like Nikolai, we may never remember it.

Nikolai experiences what the psychologist Mihaly Csikszentmihalyi has called "flow," an exhilarating moment experienced by thinkers, athletes, or anyone totally absorbed in a challenging activity to which one's abilities are just barely adequate. One strains one's utmost, develops one's skills in unanticipated ways, and experiences the moment in all its fullness. As Csikszentmihalyi observes, "concentration is so intense that there is nothing left over to think about anything irrelevant, or to worry about problems. Self-consciousness disappears, and the sense of time becomes distorted. An activity that produces such experiences is so gratifying that people are willing to do it for its own sake, with little concern for what they will get out of it, even when it is difficult, or dangerous."[66]

Tolstoy's best-known description of flow occurs in *Anna Karenina* in yet another scene that, so far as the novel's plot is concerned, could have been omitted. We accompany Levin as he learns to mow. Tutored by the peasant Titus in how to wield a scythe, Levin tries to keep up with the peasants in this strenuous labor. After describing the stages preliminary to flow, as Levin learns "to swing less with my arm and more with my whole body" and to "strain every nerve not to drop behind the peasants," Tolstoy dwells on the exhilarating moment when concentration is total.

> Levin lost all sense of time, and could not have told whether it was late or early now. A change began to come over his work, which gave him immense satisfaction. In the midst of his toil there were moments during which he forgot what he was doing, and it came easy to him, and at those same moments his row was almost as smooth and well cut as Titus's. But as soon as he recollected what he was doing . . . he was at once conscious of the difficulty of his task, and the row was badly mown.[67]

Levin falls in and out of perfect flow—a process that is part of flow itself and, taken as a whole, obliterates the sense of passing time and surrounding conditions. When Titus announces a break for lunch, Levin is amazed so much time has elapsed. He has felt rain, but only when he stops mowing does he reflect on its significance, that the drenched hay may be spoiled. Totally absorbed, he had no attention to spare, not even the minute amount needed to draw an obvious conclusion.

## Chekhov's Flow

Chekhov's descriptions of flow are easily overlooked because, like Tolstoy's, they lie outside the main plot line. In "Gooseberries," Ivan Ivanovich and Burkin, who have taken shelter from the rain at Alekhin's estate, join him for a swim in the pond. Exhilarated, Ivan Ivanovich becomes so absorbed that he loses all sense of time.[68] The hero of *A Dreary Story*, an old professor facing imminent death, recalls the intense joy he experienced when lecturing. "To lecture well, that is, with profit to your listeners without boring them," requires skill, practice, and unflagging effort, he observes. Attention must never flag, and "you must keep your wits about you and never lose sight of the point in question for an instant":

> A good conductor ... does twenty things at once: he follows the score, waves his baton, keeps an eye on the singers, makes a sign to the drums, the French horn, and so on. It is the same with me when lecturing. I see a hundred and fifty faces before me, each one different from the others. . . . My aim is to conquer this many-headed Hydra. If, at every moment when I am lecturing, I have a clear conception of the degree of its attention and the measure of its comprehension, it is in my power. . . . At every moment I must have the skill to pluck from this mass of material what is most important and most essential and, keeping pace with my own speech, to present my thoughts in a form that is both accessible to the monster's mind and effective in rousing its interest; at the same time I must see to it that my ideas are presented not as they come to me, but in the order required for a proper composition of the picture I want to paint.

Nothing compares with this experience, the professor remarks. "No scientific debate, no sort of game or entertainment, has ever given me so much pleasure as lecturing. Only then have I been able to abandon myself completely to a passion, to have realized that inspiration is not an invention of poets, but is real."[69]

## Are There Historical Alternatives?

Does history offer genuine alternatives? Specifically, was Russia bound to follow the path marked out by Western European countries? Was their present its future? If not, what role does human initiative play? If so, can initiative at least affect history's tempo?

Russia's historical significance includes its experience as the first country to undergo rapid westernization. It defined the issues that would preoccupy Turkey, Japan, Iran, and other westernizing societies. It was clear that for a country to preserve its independence, let alone to prosper, it needed to adopt Western technology. Did it have to adopt Western culture and values as well? Westernizers maintained that innovations cannot be separated from the culture that produced them; Slavophiles (or their equivalents elsewhere) thought it possible to adapt technology to local mores.

In an article published in 1832, Slavophile thinker Ivan Kireevsky posed the question in these terms: "When will our civilization attain the degree of development of the civilized states of Europe? What should we do to attain this goal? . . . Should we draw our civilization from our inner selves or receive it from Europe?"[70]

When Singapore's leader Lee Kuan Yew, the architect of its rapid economic development, advocated "Asian values," he was, essentially, giving the same answer as the Russian Slavophiles. As Michael D. Barr has observed, "the surprising fact that ideas with such a narrow, remote base of origin [as Singapore] have found widespread resonance throughout East and Southeast Asia suggests that the concept contains elements that reflect widespread Asian cultural concerns and legitimate aspirations of which Western observers should take cognizance."[71]

Slavophiles favored modernization that respects Russian habits of life, thought, and faith. They therefore rejected the example of Peter the Great, who westernized at breakneck speed, radically reconstructed essentially every institution, forced the nobility to dress and behave like Europeans, and made a point of insulting Russian faith and customs.

In *Anna Karenina*, Tolstoy addressed the debate on modernization in his account of Levin's attempt to modernize his estate. He tries to make the land more productive and the peasants more prosperous by introducing Western agricultural machines and techniques, as other progressive landowners were doing. Time and again, Levin discovers that what works in England fails in Russia: imported seeds are ruined, expensive foreign machines break, and new work schedules are not observed. The problem, Levin realizes, is not sabotage or ill will. Rather, there seems to be some "elemental force" that subverts all plans.[72] Eventually he recognizes that English machines were designed to fit English work habits, which Russians do not share, and so delicate machinery is bound to be misused. The same principle applies more broadly:

one cannot just copy a model as if culture did not matter. If one is to introduce innovations that take, one must proceed not from the top down, but from local customs up. That, indeed, is true of all reforms.[73]

Levin at last encounters a prosperous peasant family that has successfully introduced some modern methods. These peasants have not followed a model or simply copied English farmers. Instead, they have chosen whatever new methods fit their particular circumstances. As these methods became familiar, the family acquired new and modified habits, which allowed for still more innovations. With other families and in other conditions, the same strategy would probably produce a different pattern of innovation. The result is a patchwork of the old, the new, and the highly adapted. Levin reflects: Might it not be that all change is best approached this way?

## History's Grandchildren

If moderate westernizers like Turgenev or Botkin favored adopting Western institutions as rapidly as possible, radical westernizers like Herzen sometimes echoed the Slavophile idea that Russia should follow its own path. As economic historian Alexander Gerschenkron astutely observed, "the respective positions [on economic modernization] were succinctly expressed in the two prayers of the antagonists—Herzen: 'God save Russia from the bourgeoisie'; Botkin: 'God give Russia a bourgeoisie.'"[74]

Herzen, like Slavophile A. S. Khomyakov, maintained that Russia could bypass Europe's repellent bourgeois culture. Russia's very backwardness, Herzen and others reasoned, might prove advantageous. Just as Russia could borrow advanced technology without having to invent it step by painful step, so it could leap over the West's long social history. Khomyakov, himself an inventor, explained the "advantages of backwardness": "With regard to railroads, as in many other things, we are particularly fortunate; we did not have to expend energy on experiments and to strain our imagination; we can and shall reap the fruits of others' labor." He continued: "We have been imitating Europe for nearly a century and a half, and we shall continue to do so. . . . Possibly the time may come when we, too, shall serve in many respects as a model for Europe."[75]

For Herzen, this argument also applied to social forms. Addressing the West, Herzen explained that Russia

> need not pass through those swamps which you have crossed. . . . We
> have no reason to repeat the epic story of your emancipation, in the

course of which your road has become so encumbered by the monuments of the past that you hardly are able to take one step ahead. . . . History is very unjust. The latecomers receive instead of gnawed bones the [right of] precedence [at the table] of experience. All development of mankind is nothing else but [an expression of] that chronological ingratitude.[76]

Chernyshevsky agreed: "History is like a grandmother, it loves the younger grandchildren."[77]

Those who supposed Russia could leap over the capitalist stage straight to socialism placed their hopes on the village commune. Russia could use this archaic institution as a model for a specifically Russian socialism. "The Russian peasant has no other morality than that which flows instinctively and naturally from his communal life," Herzen supposed. "The commune has preserved the Russian people from Mongol barbarism, from Imperial civilization, and from the German bureaucracy," he declared in "The Russian People and Socialism." "By good fortune it has survived right into the period that witnesses the rise of socialism in Europe."[78]

## Herzen and Turgenev: One Path or Many?

Turgenev objected to Herzen's historical views. "An enemy of mysticism and absolutes, you mystically abase yourself before the Russian [peasant] sheepskin coat and see in it . . . the new and original social forms of the future," Turgenev wrote to Herzen. "All your idols have been shattered, but one cannot live without an idol, so let's raise an altar to this new, unknown god." When peasant behavior contradicts your description of it, you reply "that this behavior is temporary, chance, forcibly imposed on it by an external power. . . . Your god accepts precisely what you reject in its name," but you "avert your eyes, stop up your ears—and with that ecstasy peculiar to all skeptics who have grown sick of skepticism . . . you keep talking about 'spring freshness, blessed storms,' and so on."[79]

Nothing can shake your beliefs, Turgenev continued, "not even . . . that indubitable fact that we Russians belong linguistically and racially to the European family, 'genus Europaeum,' and consequently, by the invariant laws of physiology, must proceed along the same path. I have yet to hear of a *duck* which, belonging to the genus *duck*, breathed through gills like a fish."[80] To be sure, "Russia is no Venus of Milo . . . but [she is still] a young woman no different from her [European] sisters—except that she is a bit broader in the beam."[81]

Herzen replied with what historian Aileen Kelly called "an attack on the deterministic assumptions common to all forms of Russian liberalism." Addressing Turgenev's argument about "the invariant laws of physiology," Herzen appealed to evolution's forking paths: "The general plan of development allows for an endless number of unforeseen deviations," he observed. "There are any number of variations on the single theme of the dog: wolves, foxes, harriers, borzois, water spaniels and pugs." In human history, think of the number of forms Christianity has taken.[82] Contingencies of time, place, and habits matter.

As Kelly correctly observes, Herzen arrived at a model resembling Darwin's—not as conventionally depicted but as *The Origin of Species* actually outlines.[83] Both thinkers chart a path between sheer chance and deterministic laws. Loose regulatory principles operate in the background and contingency operates in the foreground. The principles limit possibilities but do not determine any single outcome.[84] Whatever happens, something else might have. In Herzen's formulation, "universal laws . . . remain the same, but may lead to opposing results . . . developments in nature and history, far from being unable to deviate, are *bound* to do so, conforming to every influence . . . resulting from the absence of precise aims." As a result, "a multitude of possibilities . . . lies slumbering at every step."[85]

## Lenin's Voluntarism

The idea that Russia must follow the West insulted national pride and dampened revolutionary enthusiasm. Were all our efforts, many asked, to end in making us German burghers?

As Herzen appealed to contingency, others went further and adopted radical voluntarism in their quest for a separate Russian path. They believed passionately that individuals like themselves could affect the course of history. When Russia's "first Marxist," Georgi Plekhanov, argued against the efficacy of individuals (or of groups), he had just such voluntarism in mind. Events are governed by "historical *necessity*," Plekhanov insisted. The individual "*serves as an instrument of this necessity and cannot help doing so*, owing to his social status and to his mentality and temperament, which were created by his status. This, too, is *an aspect of necessity*." This necessity does not compromise "freedom" inasmuch as the individual "passionately desires, and cannot help desiring" what historical laws dictate. "This is *an aspect of freedom*, and, moreover, of freedom that has grown out of necessity."[86]

Voluntarism proved far more attractive, because it not only allotted Russia its own (superior) destiny, but also endowed the intelligentsia with genuine agency. Voluntarism fed the sense of urgency, as determinism could not. Russia was at a crossroads, *intelligents* concluded. At critical moments only they could make a difference and no moment seemed more critical than the present. Every year was exceptional.

As early as 1861, the radical Nikolai Shelgunov asked: "Who can assert that we must travel the same path as Europe, the path of some Saxony, or England, or France? . . . We believe in our own fresh powers; we believe that we are called upon to bring to history some new principle, to say our own word and not to repeat the past errors of Europe."[87] Populists tended to embrace historical voluntarism. So did terrorists, who acted to realize "the people's will." As we have noted, terrorism implicitly affirms the historical efficacy of at least two individuals, victim and assassin.

As a determinist philosophy, Marxism at first seemed to imply quietism. In *Encounters with Lenin*, Valentinov explained that although Marxism's optimism was appealing, its determinism frustrated the intelligentsia's sense of urgency. "Don't you really understand that you are powerless?" he recalled a Marxist lecturer explaining. "In Marx's words . . . no social order perishes before the full development of the new productive forces latent in it. Not a single hair will fall from the head of the serf-owning autocratic system, and this system will not perish, until Russian capitalism develops," which will not happen for many years. Valentinov called such thinking "requiem Marxism."[88]

Understandably, Lenin's radical voluntarism attracted Valentinov. "To the idea that 'not a single hair can fall from the head of the autocracy until capitalism develops' . . . Lenin answered: 'Give us an organization of real revolutionaries and we will turn Russia upside down.'" Like Tkachev, whom he admired, Lenin "put forward the image of the 'professional revolutionary,' of a St. George the Dragon-killer" and "glorified the 'selfless determination,' 'energy,' 'daring,' 'initiative,' 'conspiratorial skill' of the revolutionary, and argued that personality can work 'wonders' in the revolutionary movement." More than other forms of Marxism, Leninism "was shot through with out-and-out voluntarism and . . . we responded heart and soul to its call to 'will.'"[89]

According to Lenin, professional revolutionaries could not just speed up the revolution; the revolution could not happen without them. Class consciousness could only be brought to workers "from without. The history of all countries shows that the working class, exclusively by its own effort, is able to develop only trade union consciousness." Marx and Engels, after all, were bourgeois intellectuals and in Russia, too, social democracy was not "the spontaneous growth of the working-class movement" but the outcome of "ideas among the revolutionary socialist intelligentsia."[90] In Soviet parlance, "spontaneity" must yield to "consciousness" (party dictates).

Lenin polemicized against other Marxists who argued that one could not establish socialism unless the requisite productive forces (or "level of culture") had developed. In his 1923 article "Our Revolution," Lenin denounced all those preening fools who, "proud as a peacock . . . keep repeating this incontrovertible proposition over and over again." Lenin objected: "But what if peculiar circumstances drew Russia, first" to revolution? What if "the complete hopelessness of the situation, by stimulating the efforts of the workers and peasants tenfold, offered us the possibility of creating the fundamental requisites of civilization in a different way from that of the West European countries?"[91] As many have noted, Lenin was adopting an essentially populist position.

If the economic prerequisites of socialism are absent, Lenin asked, "why cannot we begin by first achieving the prerequisites . . . in a revolutionary way, and *then*, with the aid of the workers' and peasants' government and the Soviet system, proceed to overtake the other nations?"[92] This suggestion, commentators have noted ever since, turned Marxist economic determinism upside down. Instead of the economic "base" determining the "superstructure," including politics, Lenin supposed the superstructure could create the base.

How, other Marxists wondered, is that Marxism at all? Marx had famously maintained that "it is not the consciousness of men that determines their existence, but, on the contrary, their social existence determines their consciousness," and Engels had insisted that "the final causes of all social changes and political revolutions, are to be sought not in men's brains . . . but in changes in the mode of production and exchange." Thinkers cannot accelerate history, he continued. "For only when the means of production and distribution have *actually* outgrown" the conditions under which they operate, and only when the next stage has become "*economically* inevitable" can socialism be realized.[93] Non-Bolshevik Marxists could not square Leninism with Marx and Engels.

## The Kingdom of Freedom

Leninist voluntarism does accord with Engels's famous argument in the *Anti-Dühring* and "Socialism: Utopian and Scientific" that once the revolution takes place, humanity will leap "from the kingdom of necessity to the kingdom of freedom." It will remake the world as it wills.

With the coming of socialism, Engels explained, human beings will no longer be dominated by economic laws but will control them. Having abolished the market with its "absence of plan . . . accident . . . [and] anarchy," humanity will control economic activity by central planning. Free from the economic constraints bourgeois economists regard as immutable, they will achieve productivity behind humanity's wildest dreams. Humanity will escape the constraints of natural laws as well. Instead of being subject to "extraneous objective forces" and "the necessity imposed by nature and history," humanity will be subject only to its own will.[94]

> Then for the first time man . . . emerges from mere animal conditions of existence into really human ones. The whole sphere of the conditions of life which . . . have hitherto ruled man, now comes under the dominion and control of man who for the first time becomes the real, conscious lord of nature because he has now become master of his own social organization. . . . Only from that time will man himself, with full consciousness, make his own history—only from that time will the social causes set in movement by him have, in the main and in a constantly growing measure, the results intended by him. It is humanity's leap from the kingdom of necessity to the kingdom of freedom.[95]

Bolsheviks gave Engels's idea an extreme interpretation. What took place in October 1917, they reasoned, was not just a political change, one revolution like others, but a change in the relation of humanity to the universe. Humanity had gone through three qualitatively different epochs. An animal stage once gave way to history, which was now supplanted by a "truly human" existence. This scheme secularized the Christian three-stage process from Eden, to fallen human history, to the final Kingdom of God. The key difference is that Christians placed the heavenly kingdom in the (perhaps remote) future while the Bolsheviks, after 1917, imagined they already inhabited a posthistorical world.

So understood, time is not just a matter of earlier and later. It also changes qualitatively. In Bolshevik thought, the future—that is, the Soviet present—differs profoundly from all earlier periods. Unless one grasps that the change was considered metaphysical, one will not understand the essentially mystical conception of the command economy. In the earlier world, governed by the market, forces dominated people; now people control forces. Permitting any trade or enterprise outside central control represented not merely an economic concession but a metaphysical betrayal of history itself.

As we saw in Chapter 5, after the attempt to create communism by abolishing money and relying on sheer force led to mass famine, the Bolsheviks retreated to a "New Economic Policy" allowing a modicum of market activity. Many regarded this decision as a betrayal of their ideals. Stalin could therefore count on enthusiastic support when he returned to strict control. The violence occasioned by collectivization and industrialization reignited revolutionary enthusiasm celebrating the renewal of post-historical time.

## Trotsky: Controlling Everything Human

Consider Trotsky's famous description in *Literature and Revolution* of what the "kingdom of freedom" would create. Humanity would remake the earth and itself. "The present distribution of mountains and rivers, of fields, of meadows, of steppes, of forests, and of seashores, cannot be considered final. . . . Faith merely promises to move mountains. . . . Man will . . . earnestly and repeatedly make improvements in nature. In the end, he will have rebuilt the earth . . . according to his taste. We have not the slightest fear that this taste will be bad." Soon, "man in Socialist society will command nature in its entirety, with its grouse and sturgeons. He will point out places for mountains and passes. He will change the course of rivers."[96] Even in the Soviet Union's final years, leaders contemplated reversing the course of northern rivers. Such thinking explains the unprecedented environmental damage that Bolshevism entailed.

"Communist life will not be formed blindly, like coral islands," Trotsky continued, "but will be built consciously . . . will be directed and corrected. Life will cease to be elemental." Conscious planning will remake everything human. "Breathing, the circulation of the blood, digestion, reproduction" will all be subordinated "to the control of reason and will. Even purely physiological life will become subject to collective experiments." The psyche will also come under conscious control, so there will be no more subconscious. No longer will blind genetic processes operate without human guidance. We have already quoted the book's striking conclusion: "The average human type will rise to the heights of an Aristotle, a Goethe, or a Marx. And above this ridge new peaks will rise."[97]

## Stalin: "Bound by No Laws"

Under Stalin, Soviet thought became still more voluntaristic as "mechanistic" Marxism yielded to "dialectical" Marxism. The former presumed determinism, constraints on action, and the absence of individual agency. It looked forward to "the withering away of the state."

Stalin condemned his rival Bukharin for holding the mechanistic view. According to Bukharin's "equilibrium" theory, planners can act only within narrow limits. Stalin wanted to exceed those limits. "Our task is not to study economics but to change it," he famously declared. "We are bound by no laws. There are no fortresses which Bolsheviks cannot storm. The question of tempos is subject to decision by human beings."[98]

"We are bound by no laws": When Alexey Stakhanov purportedly mined 102 tons of coal in less than six hours—fourteen times the already ambitious quota—he exemplified the Bolshevik capacity to do the apparently impossible. The Stakhanovite movement encouraged workers to break ever more records. Since the total number of productive units were all that mattered, many of the goods produced were useless. The heady goals of the first Five-Year Plan (begun in 1929) repeatedly increased. The plan's originally specified growth of 18 to 20 percent, as Robert Conquest noted, "had already been achieved in the only way it was ever to be achieved, on paper."[99] Stalin soon doubled this rate, and the slogan "five in four," plastered everywhere, envisaged (and therefore achieved) the plan's goals a year early.

It turned out that mechanistic Marxists had taken the "mystical" view that past conditions determine subsequent developments. Bolsheviks do not yield to such fatalism. The Central Committee's 1936 decree on "Pedagogical Perversions in the System of the People's Commissariat of Education" rejected the "two-factor" theory, which held that people were the product of heredity and environment. This "profoundly reactionary" idea expressed the exploiting class's impulse to limit their victims' potential remedies. In addition to heredity and environment, two other factors—training and self-training—enabled the supposedly impossible.[100]

If by human freedom one means not individual choice but collective power to achieve goals, then, however odd it may seem, the greatest champion of human freedom was Stalin. Since the power of the collective (that is, the Party) depends on government power, the state had to be strengthened as much as possible. How was this strengthening to be reconciled with the Marxist doctrine of the state's "withering away"? Stalin explained: "We are for the withering away of the state. But at the same time we stand for the strengthening of the proletarian dictatorship, which constituted the most powerful, the mightiest of all government powers that have ever existed. . . . Is this 'contradictory'? Yes, it is. But this contradiction . . . reflects completely the Marxian dialectic."[101]

## Chekhov's Nonaction

After the fact, events seem inevitable. After all, we are the product of what did happen, not what could have happened, and to imagine other possibilities is to imagine ourselves away. What's more, only what happens leaves documentary traces. For good reason, might-have-beens seem insubstantial; and insubstantiality suggests impossibility. We see what is, but not "what if." Russian writers, especially those who believed in contingency and choice, therefore explored ways to restore our sense of other possibilities and make the might-have-beens palpable.

Chekhov sensed missed opportunities especially strongly. His characters regret the life they could have lived. Time and again, either some inexplicable obstacle stands in their way or they themselves fail to act when they should. The result is waste, one of Chekhov's key themes.

The special sadness readers experience when reading Chekhov derives, in part, from the shadow cast by the sense of happiness lost and opportunities missed. By intimating possible plots as well as narrating an actual one, apparently simple tales achieve great depth. For one character or many, each story is shadowed by others, and the shadows cast by all these could-have-beens accumulate in a pattern of poignant possibilities. The combination of real and possible stories into a seamless whole defines Chekhov's narrative art.

The heroine of "The Schoolmistress," a teacher in a remote province who lives a poor and empty life, dreams of other possibilities. These dreams, not the petty cares that overwhelm her, form the center of Marya Vasillyevna's life. She encounters Hanov, a handsome, wealthy man who drinks too much, rushes about as if trying to escape from himself, and fails to "understand this coarse life." She imagines how she would take care of him if she were his sister or wife.

> His wife! Life was so ordered that he was living in his great house alone, and she was living in a God-forsaken village alone, and yet for some reason the mere thought that he and she might be close to one another and equals seemed impossible and absurd. In reality, life was so arranged and human relations were complicated so utterly beyond all understanding that when one thought about it one felt uncanny and one's heart sank.
>
> "And it is beyond all understanding," she thought, "why God gives beauty, this graciousness, and sad, sweet eyes to weak, unlucky, and useless people—why they are so charming."[102]

Anyone who knows Chekhov will recognize this passage as one only he could have written. Sad mystery darkens Chekhov's world, and we do not know why happiness tantalizes us. Several Chekhov stories end with an assertion that life is "beyond all understanding" in this way. As *The Duel* concludes, Von Koren expresses this thought once and Laevsky three times in the same words: "Nobody knows the real truth."[103] Chekhov's play *The Three Sisters* ends with the sisters, who have all missed happiness that seemed possible, lamenting that they must live out their lives without understanding them. The regiment, which had provided the interest and romance of their lives, is leaving to the sound of gay music just as gaiety itself is disappearing, apparently forever.

> *Masha:* Oh, listen to that music! They are leaving us . . . forever; we are left alone to begin our life over again. We must live [. . .] We must live [. . .]
>
> *Irina:* A time will come when everyone will know what all this is for, why there is all this suffering, and there will be no mysteries, but meantime we must live. . . .
>
> *Olga:* . . . The music is so gay, so joyous, it seems as if just a little more and we shall know why we live, why we suffer [. . .] If we only knew, if we only knew. [*The music grows softer and softer* . . .] . . . If we only knew, if we only knew![104]

Often enough, unhappiness results from the failure to empathize. We could put ourselves in the position of others, and so enrich our lives and theirs, but remain locked in our own affairs. In Chekhov's early story "Yearning" (*Toska*), a cabman needs to speak to others about the death of his son, but no one listens, neither his fares nor another cabman, and he grows sadder after each failed attempt to share his grief. At last, he tells his story to his horse.

Chekhov's plays and stories feature a distinct kind of communication failure. As *The Cherry Orchard* begins, Dunyasha longs to share her feelings with Anya, who has just returned from abroad.

> *Dunyasha:* . . . My darling! [*Laughs and kisses her.*] I've waited so long for you, my joy, my precious [. . .] I must tell you at once [. . .] I can't wait another minute [. . .]
>
> *Anya [listlessly]:* What now?
>
> *Dunyasha:* The clerk, Yepikhodov, proposed to me just after Easter.

*Anya:* You always talk about the same thing [. . .] [*Straightening her hair*] I've lost all my hairpins . . .

*Dunyasha:* I really don't know what to think. He loves me—he loves me so!

*Anya [looking through the door into her room, tenderly]:* My room, my windows. . . . [105]

Chekhov's plays revolutionized the theatre because, in contrast to earlier dramas packed with action, they were packed with inaction. More accurately, they feature nonaction, things that might have occurred but didn't and choices that might have been made but weren't. What happens is what didn't happen. As one critic is supposed to have observed, "the only thing that happens in *The Three Sisters* is that three sisters do not go to Moscow."

*Uncle Vanya* and *The Cherry Orchard* both feature a nonproposal, perhaps inspired by Koznyshev's nonproposal to Varya in *Anna Karenina*. What we hear is simply trivial conversation, empty words filled with what they are not saying. In the last act of *The Cherry Orchard*, Lyubov Andreevna urges Yermolai Lopakhin to propose to Varya. If he does not, the opportunity will be lost forever. He agrees—"we even have the champagne," he says—and Varya enters with eager anticipation. Then, for a page, they speak of other things. The scene ends:

*Lopakhin:* Last year at this time, it was already snowing, if you remember, but now it's still and sunny. It's cold though [. . .] About three degrees of frost.

*Varya:* I haven't looked. [*Pause*] And besides, our thermometer's broken. [*Pause*]

[*A voice from the yard calls: "Yermolai Alekseich!"*]

*Lopakhin* . . . Coming! [*Goes out quickly.*]

[*Varya sits on the floor, lays her head on a bundle of clothes, and quietly sobs.*][106]

The stage direction "Pause," which Chekhov constantly uses, marked a startling violation of drama's imperative to keep the action going. Nonaction acts and silence speaks: something might be said or done, but isn't. The hypothetical takes on flesh and provides the drama. In this way, Chekhov's stories and plays offer practice in detecting the might-have-beens.

In his story "Enemies," which we have already mentioned, Chekhov comments explicitly on the horror of missed opportunity. The wealthy Abogin comes to the poor doctor Kirillov—the status of doctors was quite low—to summon him to the bed of his dying wife, but Kirillov's only son has just died. Afflicted by grief, described as only Chekhov can, he is reluctant to leave his wife alone. At last he goes. When they arrive, Kirillov surveys Abogin's wealthy home and notices its signs of high culture, far beyond his reach. He detects condescension as well in Abogin's fashionable, progressive opinions, characteristic of the elite.

It turns out that Abogin's wife has faked her illness in order to run off with her lover. The two men, both grieving, could empathize with each other, but Kirillov instead takes offense. He chooses to regard Abogin's dragging him on a needless errand at such a moment as the careless indifference of the elite to their social inferiors. Abogin responds to his insults in kind.

If they had only extended themselves to care for the other's sorrow, they would both have been far better off. "But what happened was quite different," Chekhov observes. As Abogin grieves, Kirillov's face "gave way to an expression of resentment, indignation, anger." He refuses to listen because listening, he feels, would again make him Abogin's servant. "What are you telling me all this for?" he demands. "Do you consider that I have not been insulted enough? That I am a flunkey . . . ?"[107]

Abogin replies in the same tone, and they

> continued flinging undeserved insults at each other. . . . The egoism of the unhappy was conspicuous in both. The unhappy are egoistic, spiteful, unjust, cruel, and less capable of understanding each other than fools. Unhappiness does not bring people together but draws them apart, and even where one would fancy people should be united by the similarity of their sorrow, far more injustice and cruelty is generated than in comparative placid surroundings.[108]

"One would fancy" grief would draw sufferers closer: that is the possibility that does not happen. As the story ends, Chekhov indicates that political (in this case, class) hatred results from the egoism of the unhappy that affects us all. The consequences of failures of empathy extend farther than we might suppose.

## Solzhenitsyn: The Russia That Might Have Been

The novels comprising Solzhenitsyn's *Red Wheel* narrate counter-history as well as history. As Solzhenitsyn made clear in his memoir, *Between Two Mill-*

stones, as well as in the novels themselves, the revolutionaries diverted Russian history from the path it might have taken, one of reforms leading peacefully to a better society.[109] The pathos these novels evoke derives primarily from the sense that things might well have developed differently. Solzhenitsyn regarded the moment when it became possible to publish his novels in Russia as another historical fork—another February 1917—leading to radically different alternatives. He hoped his novels would affect the outcome.[110]

The first novel in the series, *August 1914*, contains two stories, the path taken and the path that might have been taken. Russia had faced such a historical fork before. When terrorists, aided by luck and the government's poor decisions, succeeded in assassinating Tsar Alexander II, they brought an end to his unprecedented great reforms. "Herd instinct, or the urging of the devil, told the terrorists that this was their last chance to use the gun, that only with bullets and bombs could they interrupt reform and go back to revolution." The murder of his father prompted Alexander III, who "with his generous nature was capable of making concessions," to embrace rigid policies even though "with his love for Russia he would [otherwise] not have strayed from her true [reforming] path." "Over and over again," Solzhenitsyn remarks, "the chance was missed."[111]

The firm stand and extensive reforms of Pyotr Stolypin, prime minister from 1906 until 1911, "could have been, and looked like, the beginning of a new period in Russian history. . . . ('Another ten or fifteen years,' Stolypin would tell his close collaborators, 'and the revolutionaries won't have a chance.')"[112] Lenin agreed. Stolypin's assassination, which would not have happened had he only worn a bulletproof vest that day, allowed the revolutionaries to succeed.

"A fatal shot was no new event in Russian history," Solzhenitsyn concludes. "But there was never one so fraught with consequences—for the whole twentieth century." In addition to domestic reforms, Stolypin planned to end Russia's "territorial expansion" and seek international disarmament agreements. This plan and his "program for the reconstruction of Russia by 1927–1932, perhaps even more ambitious than the reforms of Alexander II, would have rendered Russia unrecognizable." But what "would have" been was usurped by Bolshevism. "Ironically, their [Bolsheviks'] first Five-Year Plan coincided exactly with what would have been the last five-year period of Stolypin's project."[113] Readers contemplate the two possibilities together.

Contrasts between the Russia that was and the Russia that might have been recur in *The Red Wheel*. The hypothetical shadows the actual, as Solzhenitsyn repeatedly demonstrates how possible it was that things might have been different. *March 1917*, the multivolume day-by-day account of the first

1917 revolution, narrates moments when possibilities competed. Instead of focusing on the overall story, Solzhenitsyn slows down the action to evoke the suspenseful presentness of countless instants. Describing the past not as a completed event viewed in retrospect but as a sequence of fraught presents, Solzhenitsyn allows us to sense the pulse of history in the making—unplanned, suspenseful, and open at each instant to multiple possibilities.

## Dostoevsky Shows Us the Cloud of Possibilities

Believing in free will, Dostoevsky explored ways to make alternative possibilities visible. With unparalleled skill, he describes what he calls "critical moments" with radically different possible outcomes. Will the character commit murder, be killed, commit suicide, confess, choose sin or faith? Possibilities hover over the moment like a cloud. One of them, not always the most likely, takes place. If the situation were repeated, another outcome might result.

At such moments, presentness intensifies. When Dmitri holds the pestle over his father's head, unsure whether to kill him; when Nastasya Fillipovna throws a hundred thousand rubles into the fire and invites Ganya to humiliate himself by reaching for them; when Raskolnikov considers fighting his way out of the room where he has killed two women—at all these critical moments readers sense the moment's openness. Our suspense testifies to our awareness of multiple possibilities.

Dostoevsky also discovered ways to describe the cloud of possibilities directly. To do so, he often uses a narrator, a busybody with incomplete information. Unable to decide what happened, the narrator sketches various possibilities. Facts are contradictory. Witnesses disagree. "Some assert," "others affirm," "it is absurd to suppose," "unreliable rumors maintain," "at the club people were completely certain": these and similar expressions suggest the many genuinely plausible courses of events. Usually, Dostoevsky never clarifies what did take place and so the cloud of possibilities does not dissipate. The point is that any of these events *could have* happened.

In *The Possessed*, several characters visit the mad "prophet" Semyon Yakovlevich. Just as people are leaving, Stavrogin and Liza Nikolaevna jostle—or may have jostled—against each other in the doorway.

> I fancied both stood still for an instant, and looked, as it were, strangely at one another, but I may not have seen rightly in the crowd. It is asserted, on the contrary, and quite seriously, that Liza, glancing at Nikolay Vsevolodovich [Stavrogin], quickly raised her hand to the level of

his face, and would certainly have struck him if he had not drawn back in time. Perhaps she was displeased with the expression of his face, or the way he smiled, particularly just after such an episode with [her fiancé] Mavriky Nikolaevich. I must admit I saw nothing myself, but all the others declared they had, though they certainly could not all have seen it in such a crush, though perhaps some may have. But I did not believe it at the time. I remember, however, that Nikolay Vsevolodovich looked rather pale all the way home.[114]

"I fancied," "perhaps," "it is asserted quite seriously"; I saw nothing, but others declared they had, but they couldn't all have seen it, though some may have— perhaps. This is the kingdom of maybe. Possibilities suggested and immediately denied, one qualification piled on another, reliability asserted then withdrawn then perhaps reasserted, dubious evidence after the fact—the narrator has no idea what to believe. He did not believe the report "at the time," but doesn't say whether he believes it now, and if he does, how reliable would that judgment be?

Still more puzzling, the "action" that might or might not have happened is a slap that *almost*, but did not, take place. Did the nonaction occur or not? If it did, it may have had different motivations, some stated and many presumably unknown.

Rhetoric like this gives us many possible stories. The point is not which one did happen but that any of them, and many more, could have happened. We discern not the fact but the cloud of possibilities. And that is what time is really like, even at noncritical moments.

## Tolstoy: Development Itself

*War and Peace* dramatizes sheer contingency, which makes "scientific" prediction impossible. Before the battle of Borodino, as we have seen, Prince Andrei asks: "What are we facing tomorrow? A hundred million chances, which will be decided on the instant by whether we run or they run, whether this man or that man is killed."[115] What happens is decided "on the instant," not before: the moment matters. It is not the automatic derivative of prior moments.

Tolstoy discerned in the very form of the novel a challenge to representing contingency. How can there be contingency when events in novels are caused not only by prior events but also by subsequent ones? Occurrences must conform to the structure visible as a whole when the novel is completed. Contemplating that structure, readers appreciate why what happened had to happen. Time reveals what is already determined, what has already happened in the future.

In short, the very fact that novels have structure and closure—a final moment when loose ends are tied up and the plan of the whole becomes visible—makes it almost inevitable that they will convey a sense of closed time, the very doctrine Tolstoy wanted to refute. To do so, he had to find a way to overcome this bias of the artifact.

In his drafts for an introduction to *War and Peace* and his essay "Some Words about the Book *War and Peace*," Tolstoy explained his decision to avoid structure and closure because they falsify the nature of time. Even the most realistic novel mispresents temporality. *War and Peace* cannot be called a novel, he asserted, if by a novel we mean a narrative "with a plot that has growing complexity, intrigue and a happy or unhappy dénouement, at which point interest in the narration ceases" and the work ends.[116] Whatever you call *War and Peace*—Tolstoy called it simply a "book"—it conforms to a different, nonstructural poetics, a poetics of process. It therefore deliberately precludes an ending, a point when the structure is completed. Rather than end, the book would simply break off. In principle, it could always be continued.

Should this new poetics of process work as intended, Tolstoy explained, readers would sense each present moment not as inevitable but as just one possible outcome of preceding moments. They would anticipate many possible futures. Only one would be realized, but others would leave a trace. Moments would display the same presentness as in life.

To achieve such open temporality, Tolstoy proposed to make serialized publication not just the way the work happened to appear, as was the case, for instance, with Dickens's *Great Expectations*. Rather, serialization would be essential to the work's poetics.[117] "In printing the beginning of this work," Tolstoy explained, "I do not promise either to continue or conclude it." No predetermined conclusion would shape character's actions. On the contrary, "I do not foresee the outcome of these characters' relationships in any one of these periods" being described. "Provided I write as I want to . . . interest in my story will not cease when a given section is completed, and I am striving to this end."[118]

In most works, the author's time differs from the time of the characters and readers inasmuch as they do not know the ending while he does. The author of *War and Peace* does not differ from character and reader in this way. He is as ignorant of the future as they are. All exist in the same open temporality. As in life, there is no outside position and no whole to contemplate.

In short, Tolstoy explains, "I strove only so that each part of the work would have an independent interest." And then he wrote and struck out the following remarkable words: "which would consist not in the development of events but in development [itself]."[119] "Development itself" requires unpredetermined futurity and open time.

Dickens died before finishing *The Mystery of Edwin Drood*, which is therefore incomplete. It lacks an ending by accident. *War and Peace* lacks it by design. It remains incomplete in principle and could never have an ending. In place of closure, it relies on what might be called aperture. If aperture governs, causation goes in only one direction. As in life, events are pushed, but not pulled, and no overall structure guarantees significance. By contrast, if structure and closure govern, readers can be confident that events must mean something, or they wouldn't be there. When Pip gives a pie to a convict in the opening chapter of *Great Expectations*, we know it will make a difference.

*War and Peace* does not work that way. Many incidents lead nowhere. Before the battle of Austerlitz, a proud man expects Prince Andrei to move aside for him, but Andrei does not. When Andrei's protégé Boris Drobetskoy asks who that proud man is, Andrei replies portentously that he is "one of the most remarkable but to me most distasteful of men—Prince Adam Czartoryski, the Minister of Foreign Affairs. It is such men as he who decide the fate of nations."[120] Everything points to a future confrontation. The two proud men must meet again, or why are the scene and the portentous comment there? But nothing of the sort happens. In *War and Peace*, as in life, some events that seem to call for development receive it while others do not.

## The Process of The Idiot

Dostoevsky's novel *The Idiot* also exhibits countless loose ends, promises not fulfilled, and other shoes that never drop. In part I, for instance, Ganya tells Myshkin: "I believe you and I shall either be [great] friends or enemies," and three times ominously (and eponymously) calls him an idiot. [121] A confrontation seems inevitable, but it doesn't happen. Ganya for some reason becomes Myshkin's secretary and ceases to be a major character. To take another example, Myshkin confides that his father died awaiting trial but does not know the accusation—and we never learn. Again, we learn that in addition to Myshkin's benefactor Pavlishchev, there is another Pavlishchev, but we never hear anything more about him. In that case, why mention him at all?

Viewed in terms of structure, *The Idiot* is clearly a failure, and some critics have called it one.[122] And yet, as countless readers testify, it is plainly a brilliant success. The reason, I think, is that, as with *War and Peace*, readers respond to a different poetics governing the work, a poetics not of structure but of process.[123]

Tolstoy planned from the outset to write without knowing his characters' destiny. Dostoevsky at first remained ignorant because he was so desperate for money that he had to dispatch installments without a clue as to what would happen next. Having escaped abroad to avoid arrest for debt, Dostoevsky and his bride Anna Grigorievna ran completely out of money. He simply had to produce a novel and earn something, but the one he was working on was not going well and he refused to publish anything mediocre.

At last Dostoevsky abandoned his plan to narrate how an evil man (called "the Idiot") finds God, and decided instead to begin with an entirely good, "perfectly beautiful man"—a Christ figure without supernatural powers—and then see whether such a person would do more good than harm.[124] His hero's goodness might serve as an inspiring example to other characters, but it might also provoke resentment at his moral superiority and so lead to vindictiveness. Dostoevsky had no idea what the balance would turn out to be. Instead of prescribing an ending, he would create scenes to test characters and then record whatever reactions seemed psychologically plausible.

"I turned things over in my mind from December 4 through December 18 [1867]," Dostoevsky explained in a letter to a friend written December 31. "I would say that on average I came up with six plans a day (at least that). My head was in a whirl. . . . At last I sat down to write the novel." He sent the first chapters off with no idea how the story would develop, and, as the notebooks clearly demonstrate, continued to write that way until it was over. "I took a chance, as at roulette: 'Maybe it will develop under my pen as I write it!'"[125] Writing resembled roulette not only because so much was at stake but also because the course of events was radically uncertain.

Dostoevsky soon realized he could make a virtue of necessity by making the openness of time a central theme. What better way could there be to illustrate the multiple possibilities of each moment than to compose without directing characters toward a predetermined ending? Perhaps the fact the novel was appearing alongside *War and Peace* in *The Russian Herald* suggested this idea. Composing in process would dramatize life as a process. By "process" Dostoevsky meant not just a sequence of unfolding events but a particular kind of sequence, one in which each step could lead in multiple directions.

And so, when in part III Ippolit reads his fascinating confession, he explicitly defends the processual understanding of life while saying that he has recorded his thoughts just as they came to him. Ippolit wrote his confession the way Dostoevsky wrote the book in which it appears. It contains the novel's most quoted lines: "Oh, you may be sure that Columbus was happy not when he had discovered America, but while he was discovering it. . . . Columbus died almost without seeing it; and not really knowing what he had discovered. It's life that matters, nothing but life—the process of discovering, the everlasting and perpetual process, not the discovery itself, at all."[126]

## Intention as Process

Dostoevsky and Tolstoy were not the first to hit upon the idea of a poetics of process. They both knew well at least three other processual works: Sterne's *Tristram Shandy*, Byron's *Don Juan*, and Pushkin's *Eugene Onegin*.[127] *The Idiot* and *War and Peace* differ from these predecessors in using the poetics of process to convey a sense of open time. *Tristram Shandy* uses it to satirize neat systems purporting to describe a chaotic world and a mind given to aimless wandering. Byron chose it to dramatize improvisation. As one canto appeared after another, readers watched the author improvising ever new forms of improvisation.

Dostoevsky's later attempt to write a processual work, *A Writer's Diary*, not only appeared periodically but took the form of a periodical. Periodicals eventually stop but they do not end. The *Diary's* essay on the Kairova case outlines exactly how intentionality can be processual. Having discovered that her lover was betraying her by sleeping with his wife (!), and doing so in Kairova's own apartment, Kairova procured a razor, sat outside the apartment for a while, eventually entered, and began to attack the wife. She was stopped by the awakened couple. The jury was asked to decide whether Kairova intended to kill the wife and whether, had no obstacle intervened, she would have done so.

Dostoevsky argued that this question is unanswerable because it relies on a mistaken idea of intention. In his *Essay on Human Understanding*, John Locke traces all actions to a prior complete intention formed at some particular moment. We may, of course, alter our intentions and may "hold our wills undetermined until we have examined" relevant facts, but if we are to act at all, we must at some point arrive at an intention. If nothing intervenes, "what follows after that follows in a chain of consequences, linked one to another, all depending on the last determination of the will."[128]

In Dostoevsky's view, some intentions do not conform to Locke's account. They extend over time and are never complete or locatable at any single moment. Kairova's intention, for instance, evolved step by step, with each action leading to a decision about the next, but not subsequent ones. At every moment, more than one choice was possible. The actions she took followed not from some prior complete intention—some "last determination of the will"—but evolved along with an incomplete process not directed to a predetermined aim.

Dostoevsky did not mean that Kairova did not know what she was doing. On the contrary, at every moment she knew just what she was doing; but she did not know what she would do next. Indeed, Dostoevsky stated, if the identical situation could be repeated, the result might be quite different. He outlines a few possibilities: perhaps Kairova would have passed the razor over the wife's throat, then shuddered and run away. Or she might have made a slash and then turned the razor on herself. Or she might have "flown into a frenzy when she saw the first spurts of hot blood and not only murdered Velikanova [the wife] but even begun to abuse the body."[129] The processually developing intention allowed for all these possibilities and more.

There is no inevitability. Dostoevsky concludes: "all [these outcomes] could have happened and could have been done by this very same woman and sprung from the very same soul, in the very same mood and under the very same circumstances."[130]

Identical situations leading to multiple outcomes: that is the definition of indeterminism. There are more possibilities than actualities. Dostoevsky argued for the openness of time while his poetics of process allows us to sense it.


The poetics of process suggests that no fate predetermines our future. Possibilities ramify. Constraints limit choices but allow for more than one. There will never be a moment when everything fits and stories are all complete. The future, like the past, will be a series of present moments, and each present moment is oriented toward multiple futures. Time's potential is never exhausted. "Nothing conclusive has yet taken place in the world," wrote Mikhail Bakhtin. "The ultimate word of the world and about the world has not yet been spoken, the world is open and free, everything is still in the future and will always be in the future."[131]

# 10 What Don't We Appreciate?

## Prosaics Hidden in Plain View

> God must have loved the common people, because He made so many of them.

—ATTRIBUTED TO ABRAHAM LINCOLN

IS LIFE PRIMARILY A MATTER OF GREAT, dramatic events or small, ordinary ones? Is a person's experience best understood in terms of its most memorable occurrences—which would make a good story—or is its essential quality defined by the countless infinitesimal impressions that elude narrative? Is history made by cataclysms, like wars and revolutions, or do cataclysms themselves result from myriad small incidents that, taken together, are far more consequential? If we wish to improve our lives, individually or collectively, should we focus on grand exploits or daily habits? Is it wiser to empower a central authority to implement a comprehensive plan top down or to promote uncoordinated initiatives from the bottom up? Do we notice life's true heroes? Could it be that most heroes are heroines?

Anyone contemplating intelligentsia ideologies might conclude that Russians all favor the dramatic, the noticeable, and the narratable. The predominant view identified Russianness with extremism: patience and gradual change betray the people, and every moment is especially urgent.

Nothing repels those who think this way more than mediocrity and vulgarity. For Herzen and many others, the petty bourgeois virtues of prudence, caution, and persistence stank of *poshlost'* (tastelessness).[1] Such "German" qualities drain life of meaning.

Precisely because melodrama dominated Russian history and thought, several thinkers explored the opposite view. They formulated a perspective I like to call "prosaics" for three reasons. First, it places the greatest emphasis on the ordinary (the prosaic). Second, it treats great prose literature—especially the realist story and novel—as the best expression of the prosaic viewpoint. Third, as a theory of literature it departs from traditional "poetics," which, as the word implies, sees literature as verse and deems prose literary only insofar as it uses poetic devices, like metaphor. Examining novels, prosaics instead attends to distinctively novelistic qualities and devices. In this third sense, Bakhtin may be considered the inventor of modern prosaics.[2]

According to Bakhtin, each genre conveys its own view of life and values. Realist novels, which Bakhtin regarded as humanity's greatest treasury of wisdom, exhibit a uniquely profound "prosaic intelligence." Their "prosaic wisdom" reflects "the prosaic vision" of "the novelist's eye."[3]

## Prosaic Prose

Realist novels represent Russia's greatest literary achievement, but Russian writers, of course, neither invented this genre nor discovered the efficacy of the ordinary. All realist novels presume that everyday experience, small turnings of consciousness, and prosaic events shape human life. "If we had a keen vision and feeling of all ordinary life," wrote George Eliot in *Middlemarch*, "it would be like hearing the grass grow and the squirrel's heart beat, and we should die of that roar which lies on the other side of silence."[4] Tolstoy seems to echo this passage in *Anna Karenina* when Levin realizes that he can actually detect the grass growing.

Many novelists acknowledge the importance of everyday events without finding life's fundamental values in them. In fiction exhibiting the sensibility of romance or epic—like *A Tale of Two Cities*, *Wuthering Heights*, *Villette*, or most of Turgenev's novels—quotidian events control life but do not constitute its meaning, which lies in the transcendent. In these works, the songs of the troubadours, not the routines of Tolstoy's "family happiness" (the title of his early novella), define love. Heroism lies in rare acts of great sacrifice, like Sidney Carton's at the end of *A Tale of Two Cities*. The fact that transcendence must soon succumb to the pressure of the quotidian creates the distinctive tragic sensibility shaping Turgenev's stories.

The world-weary narrator of *Fathers and Children*, for instance, addresses his tale to readers with sufficient experience to understand the romantic dreams that bewitched Pavel Petrovich (and Turgenev himself) while knowing they inevitably leave a legacy of disappointment. Having lost the sphinxlike woman who enchanted him for many years, Pavel Petrovich "undertook nothing. He aged and his hair turned grey; to spend his evening at the club, in jaded boredom, and to argue in bachelor society became a necessity for him—a bad sign, as we all know. He did not even think of marriage, of course."5 "As we all know," "of course"—these phrases, which Turgenev uses frequently, presume readers who do not need to be told why romance both exalts and devastates.

Some realist novels (and stories) do not just recognize the efficacy of prosaic circumstances but also locate life's meaning in them. This tradition, which I call "the prosaic novel," regards a good life as one lived well moment to moment. The moral choices that matter most are the small ones we make a thousand times a day. We behave well or badly each time we choose where to direct our attention and whether to regard others charitably or resentfully. The plot of "prosaic novels" typically concerns the hero's or heroine's growing ability to appreciate the world immediately around them.

Beginning with Jane Austen, prosaic authors include Anthony Trollope, George Eliot, Tolstoy, Chekhov, and some lesser-known twentieth-century writers, such as Barbara Pym. For reasons we shall explain, many prosaic novelists are women. Even male writers belonging to this tradition often focus on heroines, like Trollope's Alice Vavasor (in *Can You Forgive Her?*) and Lady Glencora (in all six Palliser novels). They call our attention to those "excellent women" (as Pym calls them) whom we underappreciate if we notice them at all.

Some prosaic authors leave their prosaic philosophy implicit, but the three greatest—Eliot, Tolstoy, and Chekhov—propound it explicitly and profoundly. The epilogue to *Middlemarch*, for instance, observes that the heroine, Dorothea, did not accomplish any famous deeds. That is no cause for regret, however, because the best people, on whom we all depend, are those we usually overlook.

> Her finely-touched spirit had still its fine issues, though they were not widely visible. . . . But the effect of her being on those around her was incalculably diffusive; for the growing good of the world is partly dependent on unhistoric acts; and that things are not so ill with you and me as they might have been, is half owing to the number who lived faithfully a hidden life, and rest in unvisited tombs.6

Such views ran counter to the prevailing Russian ethos and to Russian historical experience. Tolstoy, whom contemporaries called a *nyetovshchik*—one who says *nyet* (no) to what others affirm—enunciated a prosaic philosophy in the teeth of prevailing opinion. He could count on no sympathy, so had to develop it with exceptional power.

## How All Happy Families Resemble Each Other

*Anna Karenina* begins with one of world literature's most famous aphorisms: "All happy families resemble each other; each unhappy family is unhappy in its own way." Though widely quoted, it has been poorly understood.

In *War and Peace*, in his diary and letters, and in a variant of *Anna Karenina*, Tolstoy quotes or alludes to a French saying: "*Les peoples hereux n'ont pas d'histoire*" (happy people have no history).[7] The logic of this saying resembles the proverbial curse, "May you live in interesting times!" What makes times interesting and lives dramatic is crisis and catastrophe. "The happiest women, like the happiest nations, have no history," George Eliot observes in *The Mill on the Floss* (book 6, chapter 3). "Happy that Nation—fortunate that age," wrote Benjamin Franklin, whom Tolstoy greatly admired, "whose history is not diverting."[8]

I believe Tolstoy meant that happy families resemble each other because they lack striking events. Their lives are rich in ordinary, daily, small problems and joys. There is no story to tell about them. But unhappy families, like unhappy lives, are dramatic. They each have a story, and every story is different.

Another "bias of the artifact" confronted Tolstoy: Novels require a plot, and interesting plots narrate dramatic events. How is the writer to convey the importance of the ordinary when only the extraordinary makes a good story? In Chapter 9 we examined Tolstoy's efforts to overcome the bias of the (structured) artifact toward closed time. In *Anna Karenina*, he wrestled with narrative's bias for the dramatic.

## Pregnant Women

Contempt for ordinary, bourgeois virtues extended far beyond the revolutionists. For all his criticism of the intelligentsia, Berdyaev could not have agreed more with its distaste for the quotidian. "My greatest sin," he wrote, "has probably been my inability and refusal to bear the burden of the commonplace, that which constitutes the very stuff of 'life,' or to see light through the unspeakable darkness of the commonplace." As this comment suggests, Berdyaev regarded this supposed "sin" as a virtue, especially for an intellectual. "My feeling for life," he explained, "has always been accompanied by non-acceptance of the world as it was given to me . . . a deep-rooted disinclination to the habitual . . . and almost morbid weariness of the commonplace." He was imbued, instead, "with an irresistible eschatological [apocalyptic] impulse, which could not be satisfied by any given world."[9]

Although Berdyaev possessed "a strong and well-formed body," he constantly experienced "a feeling of revulsion against its physiological functions." Talk of sex and everyday quarrels "revolted" him. To Berdyaev, the very fact that mothers bear children constituted a threat to individuality. "Family likenesses have always struck me as a challenge to the dignity of the human person. I held dear only the distinctly individual" and "could never see why people attached such importance to the principle of motherhood." He despised "that well-known abstraction, 'the ordinary man.' Every established way of life was repellent to me, and I longed to break out of the world of workaday existence."[10]

Without reservation, Berdyaev embraced the romantic clichés that Tolstoy, as he well knew, sought to discredit. "True love cannot be a matter of chance or circumstances; it arises in the encounter of two human beings whose destiny is that they should meet." True love is antithetical to marriage and to everyday give-and-take. "Legal love" is not love at all, since "legality is only valid on the level of the commonplace. . . . The so-called institution of marriage is, in fact, a piece of shamelessness." Regarding children as an absurd obstacle to love, Berdyaev was "repelled by the very sight of pregnant women. . . . I could not help seeing in child-bearing something hostile to the personality."[11]

"I may note that despite my great admiration for Tolstoy," Berdyaev explained, "I always repudiated the [anti-romantic] idea underlying *Anna Karenina*. I regarded the marital relations between Anna and Karenin as culpable and immoral, while believing in the excellence and nobility of the love between Anna and Vronsky." Berdyaev preferred Chernyshevsky's ideas on free love and "professed complete agreement with him on social and moral issues" even though he regarded Chernyshevsky's "philosophical ideas" as "pitiful and decrepit" and deemed *What Is to Be Done?* "worthless from the literary point of view."[12]

Nadezhda Mandelstam contrasted her husband Osip's views with Berdyaev's. Given Berdyaev's view that everyday life is "dominated by prose and ugliness," she explained, it makes sense that "Berdyaev's idea of beauty is the direct opposite of what I have always found" in poets like her husband. They "do not look down on ordinary life—on the contrary, it is a source of beauty for them." She cited Osip's observation that "the earth is not an encumbrance or an unfortunate accident, but a God-given palace."[13]

"To think that we could have had an ordinary family life with its bickering, broken hearts and divorce suits!" Nadezhda memorably observed. "There are people in the world so crazy as not to realize that this is normal human existence of the kind everybody should aim at. What wouldn't we have given for such ordinary heartbreaks!"[14]

## Domestic Dirt

For Chernyshevsky, only civic ideas mattered. Better not raise a child at all "than to raise him without the influence of ideas on civic affairs." Outside civic (political) affairs, he affirmed, there is nothing but "the troubled bustling of separate individuals with their personal, narrow worries" and even the best people "fall into empty and filthy vulgarity as soon as their thoughts turn from civic interests."[15]

Recall that the poet Alexander Blok welcomed the revolution because he found "the *boredom*, the *triviality*" of everyday life "nauseating." Offering a lengthy, sarcastic description of bourgeois virtues—"Obey papa and mamma," "Save money for your old age"—he maintained that "the roar is . . . about something *grand*—always. . . . Life is worth living only if we make boundless demands on it."[16]

In fact, boundless demands wound up making life even more trivial. The confrontation of revolutionary enthusiasm with stubborn bourgeois concerns became a persistent theme in the first decades of Soviet literature. Filth, self-ishness, and bribery did not disappear. If anything, they got worse. Bolsheviks spat. "Here's my advice to you: get yourself some curtains," remarks the mechanic in Mayakovsky's play *The Bedbug*. "You can either open them and look out at the street or close them and take your bribes in private."[17] The narrator of Mikhail Zoshchenko's story "Poverty" responds to his house's new electricity—a symbol of socialist modernization—with disgust at the sordid living conditions electric lights reveal. "Now when we turn on the lights," he explains, "we see here someone's old bedroom slipper lying around, there the wallpaper torn in shreds, there a bedbug running away at a trot." His landlady cuts the wires because "with those bright lights of yours . . . I have to keep busy from morning to night with cleaning and washing."[18] As Woland demonstrates in *The Master and Margarita*, if the new Soviet person has been transformed at all, it is only into a still pettier, more grasping vulgarian.

The *Landmarks* contributors foresaw this outcome. The intelligentsia's contempt for the virtues it derided as bourgeois had already created daily squalor. "Any concern with putting one's life in order, fulfilling private and public obligations . . . is declared a bourgeois affair," Izgoev explained. "A man marries, fathers children—what can be done? This is an unavoidable but petty detail that ought not to deflect him from his basic task. The same is true of work."[19] For the past half century, Gershenzon wrote,

> A handful of revolutionaries has been going from house to house and knocking at every door: "Everyone into the street! It's shameful to stay at home!" And every consciousness, the halt, the blind, and the armless poured out into the square: no one stayed home. For half a century they have been milling about, wailing, and quarreling. At home there is dirt, destitution, disorder, but the master doesn't care. He is out in public, saving the people—and that is easier and more entertaining than drudgery at home.[20]

## Tolstoy's Prosaics: The Fallacy of the Notable

People display a natural tendency to assume that the most notable events are the most important. Individuals most readily recall striking occurrences, from which they assemble a coherent story. By the same token, contemporaries typically record striking events, from which historians fabricate a narrative. But to equate the notable with the important is to think fallaciously, Tolstoy insisted. It is "just as incorrect as for a person, seeing nothing but treetops beyond a hill, to conclude that there is nothing but trees in that locality."[21]

Because of this error, Tolstoy explains in *War and Peace*, individuals misperceive their lives and historians misrepresent past epochs.

> We who were not living in those days . . . tend to imagine that all Russians, from the least to the greatest, were engaged solely in sacrificing themselves, in saving the fatherland, or in weeping over its ruin. . . . But in reality it was not like that. It appears so to us because we see only the general historic issues of the period and do not see all the personal, human interests of the day. And yet actually those personal interests of the moment . . . were of the greatest service at the time. . . . In Petersburg . . . ladies and gentlemen in militia uniforms lamented the fate of Russia and the capital and talked of self-sacrifice and all that sort of thing; but in the army . . . no one swore vengeance on the French; they were all

thinking about their pay, their next quarters, Matryoshka the canteen woman, and the like.[22]

Memory plays a trick on us. Since it is impossible to recall countless small events, we remember the ones fitting a recognizable kind of narrative. We have already cited Tolstoy's example of memory's distortions: Talk with soldiers and officers right after a battle, and you will form a complex, vague, confused, and infinitely varied impression of what the battle was like. Then the officers turn in their reports, and to make them comprehensible, organize events into a relatively neat story resembling those they have read. At the next level their superiors assemble a still neater story, a process that continues until the official story is composed, disseminated, and believed. "Everyone is relieved to exchange his own doubts and questions" for this false and clear account and their memory reshapes itself accordingly according to the official report. People who were miles apart will recall witnessing the same striking incidents.[23]

When Nikolay Rostov recounts his battle experience, this truthful young man, "who would on no account have told a deliberate lie ... began with the intention of relating everything exactly as it happened, but imperceptibly, unconsciously, and inevitably he slipped into falsehood.... To tell the truth is very difficult, and young people are rarely capable of it."[24] Only with great experience and a habit of skeptical self-observation can one overcome the false neatness that memory and narrative convention tend to impose. Indeed, Tolstoy demonstrates, sometimes even initial perception regularizes an impression by filtering out whatever escapes the general picture.

*War and Peace* and *Anna Karenina* offer practice in overcoming such regularization and discerning ongoing events and thought processes as they really are.[25] More aware of how our minds work, we will be able to recover experience in all its fullness.

## Tiny Alterations

Tolstoy redirects our attention to the countless ordinary events we miss but which, taken together, shape the quality of experience. What we do at dramatic moments arises primarily from the climate of our minds shaped by countless tiny events. In his essay "Why Do Men Stupefy Themselves?" Tolstoy discredited the common view that, while drunkenness is dangerous, surely the minor fogging of consciousness by a glass of wine cannot cause harm. To argue this way, Tolstoy countered, "is like supposing that it may harm a watch to be struck against a stone, but that a little dirt introduced into it cannot be harmful."[26]

The most terrible actions flow from almost imperceptible movements of consciousness. The painter Bryullov once corrected a student's sketch, Tolstoy observed. "Why you only touched it a tiny bit," the amazed student exclaimed, "but it is quite a different thing." Bryullov replied: "Art begins where that 'tiny bit' begins." Tolstoy draws his prosaic moral:

> That saying is strikingly true not only of art but of all life. One may say that true life begins where the tiny bit begins—where what seem to us minute and infinitely small alterations take place. True life is not lived where great external changes take place—where people move about, clash, fight, and slay one another—it is lived only where these tiny, tiny, infinitesimally small changes occur.[27]

To explain his idea, Tolstoy asked us to imagine the "tiny, tiny" alterations taking place in Raskolnikov's consciousness (in the first part of *Crime and Punishment*) as the process leading him to murder develops. "Raskolnikov did not live his true life when he murdered the old woman and her sister," Tolstoy explained. By that point he was acting "like a machine ... discharging the cartridge with which he had long been loaded." Raskolnikov

> lived his true life ... when he had not yet killed any old woman ... nor held the axe in his hand, nor had the loop in his overcoat by which the axe hung. He lived his true life when he was lying on the sofa in his room, deliberating not at all about the old woman, nor even as to whether it is or is not permissible at the will of one person to wipe off the face of the earth another, unnecessary and harmful, person, but whether he ought to live in Petersburg or not, whether he ought to accept money from his mother or not, and on other questions not at all relating to the old woman. And then ... the question whether he would or would not kill the old woman was decided. That question was decided—not when, having killed one old woman, he stood before another, axe in hand—but when he was doing nothing, when only his consciousness was active; and in that consciousness tiny, tiny alterations were taking place.... Tiny, tiny alterations—but on them depend the most immense and terrible consequences.[28]

No one ever described the tiny alterations of consciousness better than Tolstoy. Matthew Arnold famously declared that *Anna Karenina* is not a piece of art but a piece of life; Isaac Babel remarked that "if the world could write by itself, it would write like Tolstoy"; Virginia Woolf, herself an expert chronicler of stream of consciousness, regarded Tolstoy as far superior to all other novelists.[29] "Nothing glances off him unrecorded," she wrote.[30] Tolstoy's unsurpassed realism derives, I suspect, from his amazing sensitivity to the tiny alterations of consciousness that others miss.

## Hidden in Plain View

Tolstoy's heroes learn to seek meaning not in grand events or impressive philosophical systems but in ordinary incidents. In *War and Peace*, Pierre, who has sought meaning in one philosophy after another, at last finds it where he least expected, immediately before him. "He felt like a man who, after straining his eyes to peer into the remote distance, finds what he was seeking at his very feet. All his life he had been looking over the heads of those around him, while he had only to look before him without straining his eyes."[31]

Pierre had assumed that meaning lies elsewhere, or he would already have found it. But to see, truly to see, what is always present requires great insight. In everything near and commonplace Pierre had discerned only what was insignificant and "limited" because "he had equipped himself with a mental telescope and gazed into the distance" where things "hidden in the mists of distance had seemed to him great and infinite only because they were not clearly visible." Now, however, he appreciates the richness of ordinary events and the people he encounters daily. "He had learned to see the great, the eternal, the infinite in everything, and therefore ... he naturally discarded the telescope through which he had till then been gazing over the heads of men, and joyfully surveyed the ever-changing, eternally great, unfathomable, and infinite life around him."[32]

Cloaked in their ordinariness, the truths we seek are hidden in plain view.

## True Heroes and Saints

Tolstoy's conception of heroism derived from these ideas. In military campaigns, he insists in *War and Peace*, we honor the wrong people. The ones who make the difference are the competent officers with no special abilities, people barely mentioned in the sources. About generals Dokhturov and Konovitsyn, for instance, the historians of 1812 have little to say, Tolstoy observes, but the fate of Russia depended on people like them. Those who do not understand how a machine works may imagine that some useless but noticeable chip that has fallen into the works "is the most important part of the mechanism. Anyone who does not understand the construction of the machine cannot conceive that it is not the chip . . . but that noiselessly revolving little transmission gear which is one of the most essential parts of the machine."[33]

In *Anna Karenina*, Dolly plays the role of the noiselessly revolving transmission gear. Life depends not on dramatic people like Anna and Vronsky, but on hard workers, like Levin, and still more, on good mothers whose efforts are as indispensable as they are unappreciated. If by the hero of a work we mean the person whose values most closely resemble the author's, then Dolly is the true hero of *Anna Karenina*. The book's moral compass is not its eponymous heroine. It is Dolly—whose life after the opening scene contains nothing eventful enough to make a good story—who understands life the best.

Tolstoy solved the problem of making a novel out of prosaic events by letting Anna provide the drama. Riveting our attention, she exemplifies the wrong way to live and think. To find the wiser alternative, readers must examine the heroine of the undramatic background.

Dolly exemplifies the wisdom of the Schcherbatsky family, which Levin must acquire from his bride Kitty, whom he initially underestimates. Against his wishes, she accompanies him to his dying brother's bedside, where only she can ease the invalid's sufferings. While Levin focuses on the big picture and the horror of dying, Kitty watches the tiny alterations of the sick man's bodily movements:

> It never entered his [Levin's] head to analyze the details of the sick man's condition, to consider how that body was lying under the blanket, how those emaciated legs and thighs and spine were lying huddled up and whether they could not be made more comfortable. . . . It made his blood run cold when he began to think of all these details. . . .
>
> But Kitty thought, and felt, and acted quite differently. On seeing the sick man, she pitied him. And pity . . . aroused . . . a desire to act, to find out the details of his condition, and to remedy them. . . . The very details, the mere thought of which reduced her husband to terror, immediately engaged her attention.[34]

Tolstoy uses the word "details" (*podrobnosti*) four times in this passage. Like Dolly, Kitty grasps that it is details that comprise life. That is where God is. Levin acknowledges that his unphilosophic wife has shown more wisdom than all the philosophers.[35]

The hero of Tolstoy's novella "Father Sergius" aspires to sainthood and achieves wide renown for his holiness. He eventually realizes that the true saint is really an old childhood friend, Praskovya Mikhailovna, who neglects going to church, supports her family, and performs small acts of kindness. A characteristically Tolstoyan conclusion follows: we never know who is a saint, but we know that those honored as such are not.

## Gold in Sand

Anna, Vronsky, Stiva, and Karenin all miss life's most important events, which belong to Dolly. Like Rostov's happiest moments during the wolf hunt in *War and Peace*, Dolly's most significant moments could easily be omitted without our noticing anything missing. They occur when, having gone to the country to save money, she finds that her frivolous husband Stiva has not equipped the house as children require. Dolly despairs, but then she and the servant, Matryona Filimonovna, jury-rig solutions. At last

> Darya Aleksandrovna [Dolly] began to realize, if only in part, her expectations, if not of a peaceful, at least of a comfortable life in the country. Peaceful with six children Darya Aleksandrovna could not be . . . hard though it was for the mother to bear the dread of illness, the illnesses themselves, and the grief of seeing signs of evil propensities in her children—the children themselves were even now repaying her in small joys for her suffering. These joys were so small that they passed unnoticed, like gold in sand, and at bad moments she could see nothing but the pain, nothing but sand; but there were good moments too when she saw nothing but the joy, nothing but gold.[36]

Dolly experiences the book's most meaningful moments, which usually "pass unnoticed." *Anna Karenina* gives us practice in noticing them in our own lives and valuing them in the lives of others.

## Prosaic Evil

As Dolly represents prosaic goodness, her charming, irresponsible husband embodies prosaic evil. We usually think of evil as grand, dramatic, and Satanic, but most evil—though not the worst evil—is, like goodness, an everyday affair. It results primarily not from malice—Stiva exhibits no malice at all—but from a sort of criminal negligence.

Having trained himself to overlook anything that might cause distress, Stiva, who wishes his family no harm, causes a great deal of it. Although Stiva intended to be a good husband and father, Tolstoy remarks archly, "he never could keep in his mind that he had a wife and children."[37] His good "forget-tory" directs his attention away from anything that might diminish his enjoy-ment of the moment.

So accomplished is Stiva at creating an atmosphere of pleasure that every-one loves him. We enjoy evil, or why would there be so much of it? Most de-rives from people like us. Thinking of it as superhuman or alien allows us to persist in it. That, too, is an alibi.

Partly under Tolstoy's influence, Dostoevsky, Chekhov, and some others developed what might be considered the Russian idea of evil: evil as negli-gence. It manifests itself as an absence. Russia perpetrated countless sins of commission, of course, so it is especially noteworthy that its greatest writers called our attention to sins of omission as well.

The devil who haunts Ivan Karamazov resembles Stiva. (Dostoevsky had written a review focusing on Stiva.)[38] Dressed like a gentleman, but with linen not too clean, Dostoevsky's petty demon resembles those nobles who, like Stiva, forget about their children. The devil holds conventional opinions, which means, oddly enough, that he is an agnostic and a materialist! It turns out that the other world as a whole keeps up with the times, as cultured people should; it has even adopted the metric system and so one sinner must walk "a quadrillion kilometers" in the dark. Such banality disgusts Ivan. Is there nothing grand even in the world to come? Does Satan, too, resemble all the trivial people Ivan already knows? "I repeat, moderate your expectations, don't demand of me everything grand and noble,'" the devil cautions. "You are really angry with me for not having appeared to you in a red glow, with thunder and lightning, with scorched wings, but have shown myself in such a modest form. You are wounded, in the first place, in your aesthetic feelings, and, secondly, in your pride. How could such a vulgar devil visit such a great man as you!"[39]

Like good, evil is fundamentally prosaic and so its personification looks familiar. He is all the scarier for that.

## An Onion

Father Zosima tries to teach the pious Alyosha Karamazov that goodness consists of small deeds. He bids the monks greet others warmly, because kindness is infectious and each small act ramifies beyond measure. Alyosha adores Zosima, but such thinking runs counter to his nature. Like others in his generation—the narrator means the radical intelligentsia—Alyosha was "honest in nature, desiring the truth, seeking for it and believing in it, and . . . seeking for immediate action." No gradualist, he was ready to sacrifice everything for the sake of "swift achievement." In spirit, Alyosha resembled the radicals, the narrator explains, except that they placed their faith in revolution, while he anticipates miracles.[40]

When Father Zosima dies, Alyosha confidently expects the traditional miracle confirming his mentor's sainthood: that his corpse will not stink but emit a pleasant odor. To Alyosha's horror, not only does that not happen but the corpse, as if to mock his hopes, stinks especially strongly. In despair, Alyosha goes to the infamous Grushenka so he can rebel through sin, but happens to arrive just when she, too, is undergoing a spiritual crisis. The two reach out to each other.

Grushenka recounts a Russian folktale about a wicked woman who dies and is condemned to the burning lake. Pitying her, her guardian angel recalls that the woman did one good deed in her life: she gave an onion to a beggar. You take that onion, says God, and pull her out of hell with it. As the angel lifts the woman from the burning lake, other sinners grab onto her and she kicks them away: "it's my onion, not yours!"[41] At that moment, the onion breaks, and she has been rotting in hell ever since.

The smallest good deed, like giving an onion, can save someone. Other small deeds recur in the novel. When Dmitri was a neglected child, Dr. Herzenstube gave him a pound of nuts, and Dmitri remembered the kindness decades later. Waking from sleep after a grueling interrogation, Dmitri rejoices to find that some good soul has placed a pillow under his head. This small, gratuitous act of kindness greatly moves him. The onion fails to save the wicked old woman, but the story of the onion restores Alyosha's faith.

Returning to the monastery, Alyosha hears Father Paissy reading the story of Cana of Galilee over Zosima's corpse. In *Crime and Punishment*, Dostoevsky chooses the most dramatic of Christ's miracles, the raising of Lazarus, as the epitome of Christian faith, but here he makes the opposite choice. The miracle of Cana, where Jesus turns water into wine at a poor wedding, occurs in only one of the four Gospels; as he says, it has nothing to do with his mission; and most people at the wedding do not even notice it. "Was it to make wine abundant at poor weddings He had come down to earth," Alyosha asks himself, and the answer is that, in a sense it was.[42] It is the small acts of goodness that are truly miraculous.

Alyosha dreams he attends an eternal, heavenly marriage of Cana, where Father Zosima explains that Alyosha is there for the same reason as Zosima himself: "I gave an onion to a beggar, so I am here too. And many here have given only an onion each—only one little onion."[43] At last Alyosha realizes that faith must be based not on "immediate deeds," "swift achievements," and dramatic actions, whether miracles or revolutions. It is not a matter of moving mountains, as the villainous Smerdyakov supposes, but of prosaic kindnesses and gifts as small as an onion. As the devil is ordinary, so is everything truly saintly.[44]

## Chekhov's Bourgeois Virtues

Chekhov made no apologies for upholding values others disparaged. Dirt, poor hygiene, disorder, rudeness, imprudence, financial dishonesty, petty malice, and thoughtlessness: all these apolitical, nonphilosophical vices appalled him. So did the usual excuses proffered by "the wood lice and mollusks we call the intelligentsia" about being concerned with higher things.[45] "In my opinion," Chekhov wrote in a famous letter to his talented but irresponsible brother, people of culture must fulfill the following conditions:

1. They respect the human personality and are therefore forbearing, gentle, courteous, and compliant. They don't rise up in arms over a misplaced hammer or a lost rubber band . . . they do not say, "It is impossible to live with you!"
2. They are sympathetic not only to beggars and cats. . . .
3. They respect the property of others and therefore pay their debts.
4. They are pure of heart and therefore fear lying like fire. They do not lie even in small matters. . . . They don't pose. . . .
5. They do not humble themselves in order to arouse sympathy in others. . . . They don't say: "I'm misunderstood!" . . .
6. They are not vain. . . . Sincere talent always remains in obscurity. . . .
7. If they have talent, they respect it. . . .
8. They develop an aesthetic taste. They cannot bear to fall asleep in their clothes, look with unconcern at a crack in the wall with bedbugs in it, breathe foul air, walk across a floor that has been spat on. . . .

. . . Such are cultured people. It is not enough only to have read *Pickwick Papers* and to have memorized a monologue from *Faust*. . . .

What you need is constant work.[46]

Laevsky, the hero of Chekhov's novella "The Duel," could profit from this advice. Although the army doctor Samoylenko respects Laevsky's education, he "disliked extremely" his vices: "Laevsky drank a great deal and at unsuitable times ... despised his work, lived beyond his means, frequently made use of unseemly expressions in conversation, walked about the streets in his slippers, and quarreled with [his mistress] Nadezhda Fyodorovna before other people."[47] Far from embarrassed at such behavior, Laevsky prides himself on despising everything bourgeois.

Given to role playing, Laevsky endows his most tawdry thoughts and actions with cultural significance by finding literary parallels. Having fallen out of love with Nadezhda Fyodorovna, he finds her neck repulsive and immediately reflects "that when Anna Karenina got tired of her husband what she disliked most of all was his ears." He compares his irresponsibility to Hamlet's indecisiveness. Above all, he deems his shortcomings the inevitable outcome for high-minded Russians of his generation. In Chapter 8, we quoted his self-description as "the destined victim of the age" and his irritating comparison of himself with literature's "superfluous men," Onegin and Pechorin.[48]

Nadezhda Fyodorovna also accumulates debts while professing high ideals. "I don't understand how it is possible for anyone to be seriously occupied with bugs and beetles," she reproves zoologist Von Koren, "when people are suffering."[49]

No one but Chekhov, I imagine, would have created Nadezhda Fyodorovna's conversation with the properly bourgeois Marya Konstaninovna, whom she had assumed looked up to her. Instead, Marya Konstantinovna reproves her. "When we were at the bathhouse," she observes,

> you made me shudder. Your outer clothing is passable, but your petticoat, your chemise [...] my dear, I blush! ... Your house is dreadful, simply dreadful! No one else in the whole town has flies, but ... your plates and saucers are black with them. Just look at the windows and tables—they're covered with dust, dead flies, glasses. ... Why, my dear, at this hour of the day hasn't your table been cleared? And one is embarrassed to go into your bedroom.[50]

"The Duel" develops in an unexpected way. The proximity of death in a duel shocks Laevsky into reexamining his life, while Nadezhda Fyodorovna's shame at her repeated acts of infidelity alters her outlook as well. Their moral change can be discerned, first of all, in their habits. By the novella's end, they have married, embarked on a respectable life, and begun to repay their debts.

Von Koren admits he was wrong about them: "It's amazing . . . how he has buckled down! . . . His marriage, the way he works all day for a crust of bread, a certain new expression in his face . . . it's all so extraordinary I don't know what to call it."[51] Who but Chekhov would have dared lay such stress on daily habits and prosaic virtues?

## Chekhov and Histrionics

Chekhov's dramas dramatize the falsity of living dramatically. In most plays, theatrical behavior reflects nothing but the demands of theatre; but in Chekhov's plays, where the norm is nonaction, it appears histrionic, as it is in life. Believing that "true life" resides in critical moments, desperate actions, and romantic self-assertion, Chekhov's self-dramatizing characters create "scenes." Those who understand life correctly often live lonely lives and usually win no appreciation.

The more dramatically a character acts, the more inauthentic is his life. In *Uncle Vanya*, the old professor Serebryakov constantly appeals to literary examples while demonstrating cruel unconcern for others. He makes even his diseases into literary echoes: "They say that Turgenev developed angina pectoris from gout. I am afraid that I may have it." When he summons the family to propose they sacrifice everything so he can buy a house in Finland, Serebryakov cannot refrain from beginning with hackneyed quotations from Shakespeare ("lend me your ears") and from Gogol's comedy *The Inspector General*: "I invited you here, ladies and gentlemen, to announce that the Inspector General is coming."[52]

Voinitsky (Vanya) responds by behaving like a wronged character in a play, which, of course, he is. Since the professor has really exploited him, Voinitsky's histrionic rage combines poignancy and slapstick humor in a way that has become Chekhov's signature. "My life is over!" he declaims. "I was talented, intelligent, self-confident. . . . If I had lived a normal life, I might have been a Schopenhauer, a Dostoevsky."[53] Dostoevsky?

Both sincere and self-dramatizing, Voinitsky speaks in theatrical clichés: "Wait, I haven't finished! You have ruined my life! I haven't lived! Thanks to you, I have destroyed, annihilated the best years of my life! You are my worst enemy!"[54] Outside of literature, people speak this way only when they are imitating literature. To miss the histrionic element here—to imagine that Chekhov wrote these clichés seriously—is to diminish the subtlety of his psychological insight and the brilliance of his artistic achievement.

"I know myself what I must do! [*To Serebryakov*] You will remember me!" Voinitsky vows, running out of the room. It isn't clear whether he intends suicide or murder, but he evidently foreshadows some portentous action. It is one thing for an author to engage in foreshadowing, quite another for a character to do so.

Few productions of the play's crucial moment get it right:

> Serebryakov [runs in, staggering with fright]: Hold him! He's gone mad!
>
> [Elena Andreevna and Voinitsky struggle in the doorway.]
>
> Elena Andreevna [trying to take the revolver from him]: Give it to me! Give it to me, I say!
>
> Voinitsky: Let me go, Hélène! Let me go! [Freeing himself, runs in and looks around for Serebryakov] Where is he? Ah, there he is! [Shoots at him.] Bang! [Pause] Missed him! Missed again! Oh, damn, damn! [Throws the revolver on the floor and sits down exhausted.][55]

Voinitsky first shoots and then *says* "Bang!" If the scene is performed as written, the audience will first hear the sound of the pistol shot and then hear Voinitsky imitate a stage sound of a pistol shot. Directors almost invariably leave out Voinitsky's "Bang!" and so miss a key point of the scene. Is Voinitsky trying to shoot the professor or dramatize a desperate role? Does he know himself?

Is this attempted murder or attempted attempted murder? Throughout this scene, Voinitsky resembles a child narrating his actions as he performs them. In real life people often act histrionically, as if they were characters in a play, and Chekhov's plays dramatize such self-dramatization. When people work themselves up to a theatrical rage and then take that rage as a sign of how much they have been wronged, they behave as Voinitsky does. How many murders are committed in just this way?

## The Apocalypse of Squabbles

"Ivan Petrovich," Elena Andreevna explains to Voinitsky in act 2, "you are an educated, intelligent man, and I should think you would understand that the world is being destroyed not by crime and fire, but by . . . all these petty squabbles."[56] She is right: life is spoiled more by prosaic enmity than by dramatic disappointments. And yet, even she cannot abstain from apocalyptic rhetoric.

The play's morally best characters behave differently and do not speak that way. The old nurse quietly comforts people. As readers of *Anna Karenina* usually underestimate Dolly, audiences of *Uncle Vanya* underestimate its real hero, Sonya. She plays only a minor role in the main plot, but everything depends on her work on the estate, which provides everyone with income. The estate, in fact, is legally hers, as we learn only by chance.

Solzhenitsyn brilliantly ended his story "Matryona's Home" with praise for the heroine's unappreciated importance:

> She was misunderstood and abandoned even by her husband.... She was a stranger to her sisters, a ridiculous creature who stupidly worked for others without pay. She didn't accumulate property against the day she died....
>
> We had all lived side by side with her and never understood that she was that righteous one without whom, as the proverb says, no village can stand.
>
> Nor any city.
>
> Nor our whole land.[57]

Much the same could be said about Sonya, but Chekhov leaves the praise implicit—perhaps because plays lack a narrator and perhaps because Chekhov appropriately refrains from calling attention to the unnoticed.

The play's moral compass, Sonya remains in the background. Few reflect that she is present—tacitly—in the play's title, since only she could call Voinitsky "Uncle Vanya."

In the play's concluding scene, Sonya comforts Vanya—caring for others is her role—with the hope that after their life of hard work, "you and I, Uncle, dear Uncle, shall behold a life that is bright, beautiful, and fine. We shall rejoice and look back on our present troubles, with tenderness, with a smile—and we shall rest. I have faith, Uncle, I have fervent, passionate faith.... We shall rest!"[58] The audience can look at their lives tenderly now.

Doctor Zhivago praises Pushkin and Chekhov above other Russian writers. The greatness of these two writers for Zhivago lies above all in their "modest reticence ... in high-sounding matters."[59] No one had a better nose for the fake and bombastic than Chekhov.

In Grossman's *Life and Fate*, Madyarov, evidently speaking for the author, praises Chekhov as Russia's greatest writer. "Our Russian humanism has always been cruel, intolerant, sectarian," he explains, "but Chekhov said: let's put God—all these grand progressive ideas—to one side. Let's begin with man: let's be kind and attentive to the individual man.... Let's begin with compassion and respect for the individual." The only reason that the Soviet regime honors Chekhov, Madyarov concludes, is that "it doesn't understand" him.[60]

## Work

People who produced the goods sustaining life earned the intelligentsia's contempt, especially if they engaged in trade or trades. In Chekhov's novella "My Life," Dr. Blagovo tells the hard-working narrator, a nobleman who has scandalously become a tradesman, that "it was unworthy of a free man to plow, reap, and tend livestock, that in time all such crude forms of the struggle for existence would be relegated to animals and machines."[61]

Even Marya Viktorovna, who at first unrealistically idealizes work, eventually rejects it precisely because its effects are so unspectacular. "Let us suppose that you work for a long, long time, all your life, and in the end obtain certain practical results," she argues, "what are they, these results of yours, what can they possibly do against such elemental forces as wholesale ignorance, hunger, cold, degeneration? A drop in the ocean!" Like Alyosha Karamazov, she rejects slow progress. "Other methods of fighting are necessary—strong, bold, quick! If one really wants to be of use, one must get out of the narrow circle of ordinary activity."[62] The alternative to work is terror.

How much more glamorous were utopianism and revolution! Prosaic effort, the slow acquisition of skills, the gradual accumulation of wealth, and strict probity in financial dealings: these "German" virtues, many felt, contradicted the Russian character. For utopians generally, work usually figures as drudgery to be overcome. The narrator of Chekhov's story "The House with a Mezzanine," who describes himself as "condemned by destiny to perpetual idleness," disparages his neighbor Lida's unflagging efforts to aid, educate, and doctor the poor, because such actions change nothing fundamental. Like the anarchist Peter Kropotkin or like many utopians, he supposes that if only everyone worked a few hours a day people could produce enough to devote the rest of their time to higher, spiritual activities. Then "all of us, as a community, could search for truth and the meaning of life, and I am convinced that the truth would be discovered very quickly; man would escape from this continual, agonizing dread of death, and even from death itself."[63]

Why should people labor to learn a particular trade? Isn't such expertise acquired at the cost of becoming one-sided? While Adam Smith viewed specialization and the division of labor as fabulous multipliers of productivity, utopians, perhaps especially in Russia, saw them as dehumanizing. Marx famously observed in *The German Ideology* that in the present world labor is "divided" and so "man's own deed becomes an alien power opposed to him, which enslaves him instead of being controlled by him." Under capitalism, man cannot work as a whole person. "He is a hunter, a fisherman, a shepherd, or a critical critic, and must remain so if he does not wish to lose his means of livelihood." In communist society, by contrast, no one "has any exclusive field of activity . . . society . . . makes it possible for me . . . to hunt in the morning, fish in the afternoon, rear cattle in the evening, criticize after dinner, just as I have a mind, without ever becoming hunter, fisherman, shepherd or critic."[64] The populist Mikhailovsky concurred in condemning the division of labor and looked forward to a society with "the least possible division of labor between men."[65] It is difficult to find prominent thinkers who regarded specialization as an opportunity to achieve excellence.

Work is prosaic, utopianism spectacular: this view seemed obvious to the intelligentsia. We have already cited Izgoev's observation in *Landmarks* that an *intelligent* typically "regards his profession as something incidental, a sideline that does not deserve respect. If he is enthusiastic about his profession and devotes himself to it whole-heartedly, he can expect the cruelest sarcasm from his friends."[66]

One might suppose that the Soviets, with their fixation on rapid economic development, would value the most diligent and talented workers, but the opposite was usually the case. Specialists were suspect, not only because they belonged to the wrong social class, but also because their practical ethos ran counter to the revolutionary frame of mind. In *August 1914*, we recall, Solzhenitsyn describes engineers who shock young revolutionaries by their preference for construction over destruction. "Don't imagine that once the monarchy goes the good times will arrive immediately," Ilya Isakovich points out, but that is just what they imagine. "The more violent the storm, the better, eh?" Ilya Isakovich paraphrases their attitude. "That's simply irresponsible. I've built two hundred mills, steam or electric . . . and if a violent storm breaks out, how many of them will still be grinding?" If they stop, what will people do for food? Extremist thinking precludes real achievement. "On this side you have the Black Hundreds, and on this side the Red Hundreds," he concludes, "and in between . . . a handful of practical people. . . . They will be squashed flat!"[67]

Stalin indeed squashed them flat. And not only the engineers; he did everything possible to destroy successful, hard-working peasants, branded as "kulaks." Proclaiming the "liquidation of the kulaks as a class," Stalin targeted peasants who were (often marginally) more successful and industrious than their neighbors. As Solzhenitsyn observed, the process was one of "counterselection" in that "the most . . . valuable people were extirpated from the population."[68]

Did Stalin devise "dekulakization" to create a docile peasantry incapable of resistance? Probably, but he also shared, or perhaps relied on others to share, a utopian hostility to dedicated hard work as such. As we have seen, for instance, in Sholokhov's *Seeds of Tomorrow* (part of *Virgin Soil Upturned*), the hero Davidov enthusiastically embraces the liquidation of the kulaks. One reason is that they work too hard. "Destroy the kulak as a class, hand over his property to the collective farm," he demands. "We put up with the kulak because . . . they supplied more bread than the collective farms did. But now it is the other way around. Comrade Stalin has reckoned it up to the last figure and said 'Free the kulak of his life!'"[69]

Davidov describes the peasant Titok's transformation from brave Red Army soldier to hardworking, prosperous agriculturalist as a moral decline, indeed, as a betrayal of the Revolution. "Although we warned him again and again," Davidov explains, "he worked day and night . . . went about in a single pair of canvas trousers winter and summer." Still worse, he bought oxen, acquired a windmill, and hired other peasants to help with all the work. "More than once we've tried to make him feel ashamed of himself . . . threatened we would trample him in the earth . . ."[70]

## The Russian Perhaps

Numerous educated characters in nineteenth-century Russian fiction talk incessantly about how people should work instead of talking incessantly. Like Turgenev's Rudin, they speechify about the futility of mere speechifying. They like the idea of work, but not actually working.

Was such an attitude part of the Russian character, many wondered? In *Oblomov*, Goncharov offers a generally admirable portrait of the hardworking and successful Stolz, but, as his name suggests, Stolz's industriousness reflects his ethnic German origins. In his justly celebrated article "Time Horizon in Russian Literature," economic historian Alexander Gerschenkron pointed to the cliché that patient work for long-term results—what Gerschenkron called a high time-horizon—"is something that is downright unRussian and by contrast fits the contemptible way of life of the German *Bürger*." He cited a passage from Gogol's story "Nevsky Avenue" describing the tradesman Shiller:

> Shiller was a perfect German in the full meaning of this word. Even when he was twenty, that is to say, at that happy age, when the Russian lives from hand to mouth, Shiller already had measured in advance all his future life . . . in the course of ten years to accumulate a capital of fifty thousands and from the beginning the program was as fixed and unchangeable as fate itself.

Gerschenkron also quoted the narrator of Dostoevsky's novella *The Gambler:*

> It is uncertain what is more revolting, Russian disreputability or the
> German method of accumulation of riches . . . I do not want such virtues. . . .
> After five or such generations . . . continuous work for a century or two,
> patience, intelligence, character, firmness, calculation . . . ! But I prefer
> to squander riotously *à la Russe* or to get rich through roulette.

Gerschenkron called attention to the Russian reliance on *avos',* "which
Pushkin in the tenth chapter of *Eugene Onegin* justly called 'the national shib-
boleth'"—a word meaning, roughly, sheer luck, windfall, something favorable
that one has no right to expect, a sort of miracle, pure perhapsness. *Avos',* Gerschenkron explained, is "a risk-worshipping and risk-adoring term, and as such
the very denial of time horizon."[71] A society relying on *avos'* doesn't invest and
therefore does not develop economically. *Avos'* epitomizes the anti-prosaic
ethos.

Reliance on *avos'* (or the miraculous) recurs in Russian literature and
thought. In Savinkov's terrorist novel *What Never Happened,* for instance,
Alexander, a naval officer in the Russo-Japanese war, hopes for victory in spite
of everything he knows. "I knew the Japanese were stronger," he explains, and
that a Russian ship had already been sunk. "I knew we . . . did not know how
to man vessels. I knew it all, and yet . . . I had faith in our victory . . . I believed
firmly—I wanted to believe—that victory could be secured . . . by the careful
Russian perhaps [*avos'*]."[72] In *August 1914,* General Martos knows that Russians must overcome this characteristic if they are to defeat the Germans.
Martos "could not tolerate Russian sloppiness, the Russian inclination to 'wait
and see,' to 'sleep on it' and leave God to take the decisions."[73] And in Eugene
Vodolazkin's recent novel *The Aviator* (2016), the dying hero consults a
German doctor, who tells him:

> "Expect no miracles from our clinic. . . . But we will do all we can."
> I felt that I was smiling broadly, showing all my teeth:
> "But it's miracles I came for [. . .]"
> "Miracles, that's in Russia," said [Doctor] Meier, his gaze growing
> sad. "There you live by the laws of the miracle, but we attempt to live in
> conformity with reality. It's unclear, however, which is better."
> "When God wishes, nature's order is overcome," I said, expressing my
> main hope, but the interpreter could not translate that.[74]

## The Real Party of Action

Several Russian writers defied prevailing opinion by celebrating prosaic work. In *Anna Karenina*, Levin learns that a good marriage depends not on romantic love or idyllic expectations but on the patient, daily labor he already practices on his estate.

> Levin had been married three months. He was happy, but not at all in the way he had expected to be. At every step he found his former dreams disappointed, and new, unexpected surprises of happiness. . . . On entering upon family life, he saw at every step that it was utterly different from what he had imagined. At every step he experienced what a man would experience who, after admiring the smooth, happy course of a little boat on a lake, should himself get into that little boat. He saw that it was not all sitting still, floating smoothly; that one had to think too, not for an instant to forget where one was floating; and that there was water under one, and that one must row; and that his unaccustomed hands would be sore; and that it was only to look at it that was easy; but that doing it, though very delightful, was very difficult.[75]

Who but Tolstoy could have written this thoroughly unromantic passage?

In utopian literature, people struggle to achieve social perfection, but when utopia has at last been achieved, they rest: the full title of William Morris's influential utopia is *News from Nowhere, or An Epoch of Rest*. Utopia is an eternal sabbath. In much the same way, romantic stories conclude with a marriage, as if that were the end of difficulties. Nonsense, Tolstoy responded. "I couldn't help thinking that . . . a marriage seemed more like a source of complication than diminution" of it.[76]

The thoroughly anti-utopian Chekhov, who labored not only as a writer but also as a physician, knew that the greatest happiness lies not in rest but in work that affords unmatched joy. "The whole secret of success," remarks gardener Pesotsky in Chekhov's story "The Black Monk," "lies not in its being a big garden or a great number of laborers being employed in it, but in the fact that I love the work . . . I love it perhaps more than myself . . . when anyone helps me, I am jealous and irritable till I am rude."[77] This love of the work enables constant attention and care.

In his novel *The Precipice*, Goncharov offers a rare portrait of an honest, industrious entrepreneur. He "lovingly took care" of the trees on his estate. "His woods comprised several thousand acres and his business was organized and managed with a rare meticulousness. He was the only landowner thereabouts to have a steam-powered sawmill, and Tushin managed everything, watched everything himself." When his expertise fell short, Tushin knew enough to hire a specialist—a German, of course—"but rather than blindly following his advice, he used him as a consultant and managed the forest himself."[78]

Tushin's probity impresses the novel's hero Raisky, who appreciates that Russia's future prosperity depends not on revolutionaries but on Tushins. "The Tushins of the world are our real 'party of action,' that solid 'future of ours," he reflects. That future will emerge, he decides, "when all the mirages, all the laziness and overindulgence disappear, to be replaced by real 'work,' by a great variety of real 'work' for everyone. And when the mirages, the voluntary 'martyrs' [for the people] disappear, they will be replaced by 'workers,' by 'Tushins' on all rungs of the social ladder."[79]

Turgenev arrives at a similar conclusion in *Virgin Soil*. While the novel's populist revolutionaries fail miserably, the capable factory manager Solomin, who shares their devotion but not their faith in sudden change, actually helps people. In the novel's final pages, one character praises Solomin in terms resembling Raisky's eulogy of Tushin: "Solomin!... He's a man that'll stick to what he's about! He'll carry anything through!"—just the qualities that Russia needs:

> And the great thing is: he's not trying to cure all the social diseases all in a minute. For we Russians are a queer lot, you know, we expect everything; some one or something is to come along one day and cure us all at once.... Who or what this panacea is to be—why Darwinism, the village commune ... anything you please!... It's all sluggishness, apathy, shallow thinking! But Solomin's not like that—no, he's not a quack doctor, he's first rate![80]

## *Kuprin and Babel: Why Do Women Bother?*

Work fascinated Alexander Kuprin, who tried his hand at many professions. As one critic has observed, this writer worked in "dozens of occupations: soldier, reporter, stevedore, athlete, circus rider, actor, dental technician, psalm reader, shop assistant, forester, hunter, fisherman, bailiff, pig breeder, tobacco grower, editor and critic. It was even rumored that he once committed a robbery so as to learn the feelings of a thief at work."[81] Indeed, among his stories about different professions, "An Insult" features thieves describing, and upholding the honor of, their line of work. Kuprin also was a "pupil in a choir school, student of art and of Esperanto, novice monk, and lavatory pan salesman," a skilled juggler, and so good an actor that Chekhov "urged him to join the Moscow Art Theatre." Kuprin wanted to experience each of these occupations from within. In his novel about prostitution, *Yama* (*The Pit*), one character says that he would "like to live the inner life of everyone I meet and look at the world through their eyes."[82]

In ordinary occupations Kuprin could always discover something fascinating and "strange" (one of his favorite words). What most concerned him was a profession's ordinary moments. In *Yama*, one character observes that by focusing on especially shocking incidents most commentators fail to convey the real horror of prostitution. "No, horrible are the everyday, accustomed trifles, these business-like, daily, commercial reckonings, this thousand-year old science of amatory practice, this prosaic usage, determined by ages," all of which take place like any other trade. "Do you understand," he asks, "that all the horror is just in this, that there is no horror!"[83]

Prosaic kindness also mattered to Kuprin. A key incident in his novel *The Duel* occurs when the hero, the officer Romashov, has exhausted his money and his orderly gives him a package of cigarettes. "You have no cigarettes. I buy. You smoke please. I give," says the orderly, who, "perhaps embarrassed, rushed out of the room banging the door behind him."[84] These are the moments that matter.

Babel may have been developing this scene in "The Death of Dolgushov," a key story in *Red Cavalry*. The narrator Lyutov cannot find it in himself to fulfill a mortally wounded soldier's request to be shot and so avoid falling into the hands of sadistic enemies. Lyutov despairs that his softheartedness has cost him his best friend, who rightly regards his fastidiousness as a form of cruelty. As the story ends, Lyutov, like Kuprin's Romashov, receives unexpected comfort from an orderly, the driver Grishchuk. "Grishchuk produced a shriveled apple from his driving seat. 'Eat it,' he said to me. 'Do please eat it.'"[85]

Grishchuk voices the key question posed by the violence described in *Red Cavalry*: "'Whatever do women go and give themselves such trouble for?' he asked still more mournfully. 'Whatever do they want engagements and marriages for. . . . Makes me laugh,' said Grishchuk sadly, pointing a whip at [the mortally wounded] man sitting by the roadside. 'Makes me laugh, what women want to go and give themselves such trouble for . . .'"[86] Men make war and revolution, which decimate the life women nurture.

The *Red Cavalry* stories, based on Babel's 1920 diary, contrast masculine violence, justified as "revolution," with the daily life soldiers destroy by killing old men, raping women, and vandalizing churches and estates. In both diary and stories, the author treats wanton destruction of beehives as symbolic of war on everyday life. "Total destruction. . . . The orchard, apiary, destruction of hives, terrible, bees buzzing despairingly, the men blow up hives with gunpowder . . . attack the hives, a wild orgy . . . I feel sick about it all,"[87] he wrote in the diary, and one *Red Cavalry* story begins: "I mourn for the bees. . . . We defiled untold hives. . . . There are no more bees in Volhynia."[88] Is the same fate in store for the Jews? Babel wondered in the diary. "Can it be that ours is the century in which they perish?"[89]

Bees matter to the artist Pan Apolek, who scandalizes churchmen by painting Jesus and Mary with the faces of local sinners, as if to show that the sacred resides right before our eyes. He tells a story about how gnats plaguing Jesus on the cross asked a bee to sting him, but the bee refused since Jesus is a fellow carpenter. Soldiers kill industrious bees, but Jesus is their brother.

Struck by "the ineradicable cruelty of human beings," Babel recognized that wanton savagery must follow when revolution, or any breakdown in order, allows people to act on that cruelty. "I must look deeply into the soul of the fighting man, I am trying to, but it's horrible," he wrote. "Wild beasts with principles." "It is hell," he remarked after a massacre. "Our way of bringing freedom—horrible. They search the farm, drag people out, Apanasenko—don't waste cartridges, stick [stab, bayonet] them. That's what Apanasenko always says—stick the nurse, stick the Poles." All this cruelty "is simply a means to an end, one the Party does not disdain."[90] One asks: how could people trained to gain power by violence not continue to use it against anyone opposing them?

## Prosaics Resists Sudden Transformation

How else can change happen? English history offered one model, gradual, unsystematic evolution. Russian history offered another, long periods of stasis followed by far-reaching change imposed by force from the top, whether by tsar (Peter the Great) or dictator (Lenin). The poet Kantemir eulogized "the wise commands of Peter, / Through which we have already become in a moment's time a new people."[91]

"With us everything had to be started from the top downwards," Belinsky remarked in an article praising Peter. "Peter had no time to waste. . . . He could not sow and wait calmly until the scattered seed would germinate, sprout and ripen."[92] In violation of its own laws, nature allowed him to scatter seed with one hand and gather their fruit with the other. Russia relies on miracles: "The new Joshua, he [Peter] stopped the sun midst the sky, he wrested from the sea its ancient domains, he raised a beautiful city out of the swamp. He understood that half-measures would not avail … [and] that sweeping changes … that [elsewhere] have been the work of centuries" had to be accomplished suddenly. The only way to do this is by sheer force aimed at transforming the most basic daily habits.

As Belinsky well knew, no command can actually remake people according to a model. Peter's directive that nobles should copy their European counterparts created a persistent sense that the new manners were a masquerade. How else could it be when the changes went so far? As Yuri Lotman observed, "the area of subconscious, 'natural' behavior became a sphere in which teaching was needed."[93] As a result, this "emphasis on the artificiality of 'correct' social behavior and the fact that its code had to be learned by members as though it were a foreign language" made "civilization" seem superficial generations later.[94] In *A Writer's Diary*, Dostoevsky, observing the polite behavior at a Christmas party, cannot banish the feeling "that people are only pretending and will suddenly commence a first-rate [Russian] row, just as they might in their own homes."[95]

Why exactly is sudden transformation according to a model impossible? The same question can be asked about individuals: why can't someone just become what she admires? Disgusted with her life, Tolstoy's Kitty, as we have seen, finds models in the philanthropic Madame Stahl and her ward Varenka, and winds up doing more harm than good. The reason, she recognizes, is that what is natural for Varenka is for her "all pretense and not from the heart … it was all a fake! A fake! A fake! (*pritvorstvo*)." At first Kitty petulantly resolves to stop helping others entirely—"I'll be bad, but anyway not a liar, a cheat"—but she eventually comes to a wiser decision.[96] Instead of changing everything at once, she will change one small habit at a time. Instead of becoming Varenka, she will become a better version of herself—not by imposing a model but by beginning where she is.

As Levin learns when trying to modernize his farm, one must proceed from the bottom up. Understanding the prosaic explains why. A person is not a system in which everything fits. Each person acquires habits, practices, ways of thinking and behaving—daily, without plan, layering one haphazardly on another. These habits conglomerate rather than cohere, and often run counter to each other. This is one reason our own behavior often surprises us. One can try to reconcile conflicting habits, or overcome counterproductive ones, as therapy aspires to do, but, as anyone who has tried to diet knows, changing even a single habit takes much attention, which is always a limited resource. Sudden extensive, let alone total, transformation is not to be thought of.

Such transformation would be possible if everything about a person flowed from a single principle or emotional complex, as some have supposed. Caligula allegedly wished that Rome had only one head so he could cut it off with a single blow, but it had a million heads.[97] In the same way, we each have countless habits that we cannot alter in a single act of will. Like Kitty, we must become better versions of ourselves. This logic applies to society. Structuralists notwithstanding, cultures do not form a system but result from countless contingent events and choices layered on each other. Like individuals, cultures are palimpsests of habits. Prey to contingency, neither conforms to a neat narrative.

Prosaics resists utopian transformation. That is why Solzhenitsyn insisted that, when Communism fell, Russia should proceed gradually. It should work from the bottom up, adjusting changes as their results become apparent. People should improve their moral character as these efforts proceed, because character—the sum total of our habits and impulses—ultimately limits what is possible. There is no going faster than our habits and inclinations allow. For these reasons, Solzhenitsyn opposed introducing a market economy at once, by "shock therapy." He also urged Russians to give up "great power" ambitions and instead amend the bad habits acquired during seventy years of Communism.[98]

## People and Culture in Realist Novels

Realist novels take for granted that people cannot suddenly transform themselves, as happens in saints' lives and conversion literature.[99] Neither are people immutable, and so novels differ from works that, like Plutarch's *Lives*, presume that character is fixed. Romances, tales of knight errantry, and picaresque stories also narrate how a stable person meets challenges.

Major characters in realist novels develop bit by tiny bit, altering slightly with each contingency, however minor, and each choice, however inconsequential. Their choices do not just reflect who they are, they also change who they are. That is why incidents in realist novels cannot be rearranged whereas episodes in adventure stories can, and often are. Because Anna Karenina and Dorothea Brooke gradually become different, they would not make the same choices if earlier circumstances were repeated. Dick Tracy and James Bond would.

The contingent events that shape people in realist novels are cultural as well as personal. Cultures alter as individuals do, and characters in realist novels are cultural to the core. Cultures shape people and people shape cultures.

Because societies differ, one cannot set the same story in a different country. *Pride and Prejudice* would make no sense in Russia. Jane Austen's novels depend not only on English values but also on English laws preventing women from inheriting, which did not exist in Russia. By the same token, one could not situate *Middlemarch* a half century later, when different issues concerned people. Turgenev's novels trace cultural change so minutely, year by year and even season by season, that historians have used them as anthropological documents. The last words of *Fathers and Children*—August 1861—situate the action precisely. The point is that the story it tells could not have happened, let us say, in 1858.

The prosaic facts of a culture and of a personality interact in idiosyncratic ways. That is why personalities can never repeat. No formulae can explain the world or tell people how to behave. One requires not some social science, but wisdom. Reacting to the intelligentsia's putatively scientific dogmatism, the great Russian writers defended these novelistic assumptions explicitly and extensively.

## Alexievich's Splintered Truths

Novelistic wisdom can extend beyond novels. For Tolstoy, as we have seen, the conventional structure of novels ran counter to his themes of contingency and open time, and so he created a form that went beyond the novel. Solzhenitsyn subtitled *The Gulag Archipelago* "an experiment in literary investigation" largely because he used novelistic insight to examine real events.

Nobel Prize–winning author Svetlana Alexievich devised a nonfictional form to venture further into the prosaic aspects of life. Her new genre presumes the mystery of the prosaic and the difficulty of investigating it, and her books convey the excitement of discovery.

People have so many ways to hide their knowledge of what goes on before their very eyes—sometimes because they want to forget it and sometimes because it contradicts a broadly accepted, more exalted view. The form Alexievich invented conveys not only the process of discovery but also the dynamics of suppression.

One must learn to listen. "Flaubert called himself a human pen," she explained in her Nobel Prize speech. "I would say I am a human ear. When I walk down the street and catch words, phrases, and exclamations, I always think—how many novels disappear without a trace! Disappear into darkness."[100] How is one to discover all these disappearing novels?

Like a good therapist, Alexievich gained the confidence of the people she interviewed. They told her their stories, often for the first time, revealing events they had kept even from themselves. In true dialogue, as Bakhtin defines it, interlocutors don't just take turns expressing what they already know but also make discoveries in the process of responding to each other. Alexievich referred to this revealing process as "the conversational side of human nature," which she strove to "capture."[101] The powerful impression her books convey derives both from the revelations and the drama of reaching them.

Interviews edited, introduced, and orchestrated; scenes set and rambling recollections recorded in all their shagginess; self-justification alternating with self-condemnation; losses irretrievable except for the traces left in suppressed memory; above all, wonder at all we do not understand about life: all this shapes Alexievich's art. "More than once . . . I was the only hearer of totally new texts."[102]

When Bakhtin called Dostoevsky the most dialogic of writers, he had in mind his novels' "polyphony," by which Bakhtin meant that Dostoevsky treats his characters not as objects of his creation but as subjects capable of surprising him. They are as "unfinalizable" (still in the making) as the author himself. The peculiarly intense sense of drama and "eventness" that rivets the attention of Dostoevsky's readers results from their intuitive sense that the author is learning about the characters much as they are. In Bakhtin's terms, Dostoevsky surrendered the author's "essential surplus" of meaning—knowledge authors usually have that characters cannot, such as their destiny—and retained only enough control to devise situations to test them ("that indispensable minimum of pragmatic, purely *information-bearing* 'surplus' necessary to carry forward the story.")[103]

"One could put it this way," Bakhtin explained. "The artistic will of polyphony is the will to combine many wills, a will to the [eventful] event."[104] Alexievich, who referred to Dostoevsky's profound influence on her, strove for this sort of polyphonic—or to use her word, conversational—truthfulness. Some truth not only emerges in dialogue, but is itself dialogic. "It always troubled me that the truth doesn't fit into one heart, into one mind, that truth is somehow splintered," she explained. "There's a lot of it, it is varied, and it is strewn about the world. Dostoevsky thought that humanity knows much, much more about itself than it has recorded in literature."[105] The form Alexievich designed captures varied, splintered truth that cannot be fit into a single heart. Her dialogues actually contain not two but three interlocutors, she explains. "Three people are present: the one who is talking now, the one she was then, and me."[106]

Splintered truths concern, above all, life's prosaic qualities, so uninteresting to connoisseurs of the dramatic and grand. "So what is it I do?" Alexievich asked. "I collect the everyday life of feelings, thoughts, and words. I collect the life of my time. I'm interested in ... the everyday life of the soul, the things the big picture of history usually omits or disdains." The big picture focuses on big people, but "I'm interested in little people. The little, great people is how I would put it."[107]

## Women's War

In the name of colossal achievements guided by an infallible theory, Alexievich explained, Communism ruined the lives of countless little people. Even now, "twenty years after the fall of the 'Red Empire' of the Soviets," she pointed out, the same ideas often prevail. "Many young people are reading Marx and Lenin again ... there are new museums dedicated to Stalin." The romantic belief in high drama has not lost its appeal for people like Alexievich's father, who never abandoned socialism. Today's "idealists" and "romantics," she asserted, "are sometimes called slavery romantics. Slaves of utopia."[108]

Soviet literature and discourse favored epic stories of great heroes and odes to superhuman leaders, but Alexievich's novelistic nonfiction recounts the "history of 'domestic,' 'indoor' socialism ... the history of how it played out in the human soul. I am drawn to that small space called a human being [...] a single individual. In reality, that is where everything happens."[109]

"I believe that in each of us there is a small piece of history," she explained in the introduction to her counter-history of World War II, *The Unwomanly Face of War.* "Together we write the book of time ... the nightmare of nuances. And it all has to be heard, and one has to dissolve in it all ... and at the same time, not lose oneself. To combine the language of the street and literature."[110]

Men embrace official history and epic consciousness, Alexievich asserted. They focus on great deeds, while women attend much more to the prosaic facts of life, the way war is experienced day by day. But even women usually suppress their impressions in favor of the official story. "They tune into the canon." So Alexievich must use all her dialogic skill to tease out suppressed impressions. It may take a day of listening, but sometimes, "you never know when and why, suddenly comes this long-awaited moment, when the person departs from the canon ... and goes on to herself. Into herself," into war as women experience it.[111]

Most histories are "men writing about men.... Everything we know about war we know 'with a man's voice.' ... Women are silent. No one but me ever questioned my grandmother," she explained. When women talk about war to each other, they do not talk about "how certain people heroically killed other people and won." Their stories are entirely different. "Women's war has its own colors, its own smells, its own lighting, and its own range of feelings. Its own words."[112]

Smells play an outsized role. Alexievich described how, when one woman returned from leave, the others sniffed her—literally sniffed her—to detect the distinctive odor of "home." Only those who grasp prosaic life pay such attention to smells. It is such small things, almost inexpressible in words, that matter. What people dismiss as "'small details' are what is most important for me, the warmth and vividness of life," Alexievich affirmed. "History through the story told by an unnoticed witness and participant. Yes, that interests me, that I would like to make into literature."[113]

"Only the familiar transformed by genius is truly great," observes Doctor Zhivago, whose poems achieve greatness in just that way. To understand life, one must appreciate the profundity of ordinary circumstances. The revolutionary Strelnikov, we are told, will never achieve anything great because he lacks "a heart which knows only of particular, not general cases, and which achieves greatness in little actions." "It has always been assumed that the most important thing in the Gospels are the ethical maxims and commandments," observes Nikolai Nikolaevich. "But for me the important thing is that Christ speaks in parables taken from life, that He explains truth in terms of everyday reality."[114]

My goal, Alexievich explained, is to discern in each, specific human being "the eternally human . . . the tremor of eternity." Only by probing the prosaic mysteries hidden in plain view can one "fathom the mystery of life itself."[115]

# 11 What Doesn't It All Mean?

## The Trouble with Happiness

> Not one of you victims of ambition, filthy lucre, refined
> depravity, and your own idle existence, not one of you,
> I say, knows the true meaning of existence.
>
> —ALEXEI PISEMSKY, *ONE THOUSAND SOULS*

DOES LIFE HAVE A MEANING, or is it just one damn thing after another? If it has a meaning, what is it? Why don't people agree about it? Can the answer be communicated in words or must it be learned from experience? Countless Russian novels and stories pose these questions. Russian literature as we know it would scarcely be conceivable without them.

Literary heroes and heroines dedicate their lives to finding an answer. If they cannot find one, they may succumb to despair or commit suicide. Before shooting himself, Svidrigailov in *Crime and Punishment* imagines that, even if there is another world, it must be as pointless and trivial as this one, if not more so. Perhaps "there are only spiders there," he speculates. "We always imagine eternity as something beyond our conception, something vast, vast! But why must it be vast? Instead of all that, what if it's one little room, like a bathhouse in the country, black and grimy and spiders in every corner, and that's all eternity is?"[1]

Svidrigailov distracts himself from existential horror with debauchery—"my only hope is in anatomy," he says[2]—as does Fyodor Pavlovich Karamazov and the hero of *The Possessed*, Stavrogin. As the novel commences, Stavrogin has already tried and discarded several ideologies promising meaning. He escapes from emptiness through shocking practical jokes. Only the novel's other hero, the murderous Pyotr Stepanovich, recognizes that for all his magnetic charm and cold beauty, Stavrogin is embodied nothingness.

Tolstoy's quest for meaning became exemplary. No one has ever described existential despair and the sense of meaninglessness better than he did in his autobiographical *Confession* and in the last part of *Anna Karenina*, where Levin endures what Tolstoy did. Both author and hero found themselves paralyzed by the thought that death would soon obliterate anything they achieved. Knowing that nothing could make any difference, they ceased to desire anything, except by the weakening force of habit. "It had come to this, that I, a healthy, fortunate man felt I could no longer live," Tolstoy explained. "I cannot say I *wished* to kill myself. The power that drew me away from life was stronger, fuller, and more widespread than any mere wish. It was a force similar to the former striving to live, only in a contrary direction."[3] Like Tolstoy himself, Levin tries to outwit this striving for death. Each hides a cord so as not to be tempted to hang himself and each refrains from going out with a gun "for fear of shooting himself."[4]

Tolstoy and several of his characters search assiduously for meaning and, at times, find it. With his example in mind, subsequent Russian writers describe a similar quest. Sofya Lvovna, the heroine of Chekhov's story "Two Volodyas," admires her adopted sister Olga, a nun, because she seems to have found the meaning of her life. "Olga is saved now, she has settled all questions," the heroine says to herself. "If Olga were to see death before her this minute she would not be afraid [because] . . . she has already solved the problem of life for herself." But is there no other way to solve that problem than to enter a convent? Sofya Lvovna asks herself. And what "if there is no God? Then her life is wasted. But how is it wasted? But why is it wasted?"[5]

We ask ourselves: can one's sense of meaningfulness be mistaken? And can one's life be meaningful without knowing that it is?

## Negative Revelations

In *War and Peace*, Prince Andrei repeatedly discovers what the meaning of life is not. He wants to excel at what is truly significant but changes his mind about what that is. As the novel begins, Andrei has recognized the emptiness of his energetic pursuit of social success. Having married the best woman of his circle, he has come to regard her as frivolous. Her insipid thoughts and laughter at silly gossip irritate him, and Tolstoy allows the reader to hear how unpleasant her chatter sounds to him. When Pierre asks him why he is going to war, Andrei replies: "because this life I am leading here—this life is—not to my taste."[6]

Andrei has found a new ideal, glory, and a new hero, Napoleon. Aspiring to be the Napoleon who defeats Napoleon, he prides himself on possessing the very qualities that enabled the French emperor to succeed: intelligence, will-power, and courage. Believing in a science of warfare, he masters it. Events prove he is brave enough to run forward through a hail of bullets while others flee in panic.

Modeling his life on Napoleon's, Andrei is on the lookout for his "Toulon" (the initial triumph that made Napoleon's reputation). On the eve of the battle of Austerlitz, he fantasizes about how he might save the Russian army. For him, as for the heroes of *The Iliad* (to which *War and Peace* repeatedly alludes), life offers nothing more meaningful than glory. Andrei seems like an epic hero transplanted to a realist novel, a sort of genre refugee.[7] In epics, the transcendent value of glory is a given, but in the novel it is, like other ideals, open to question and tested by experience.

In comparison to glory, death itself does not matter. Andrei tells himself:

> if that is what I want—glory, to be celebrated by men and loved by them—I cannot be blamed for wanting that, for wanting nothing but that, and living for that alone. Yes, for that alone! I shall never tell anyone, but, my God, what can I do if I care for nothing but glory and men's love? Death, wounds, the loss of my family—nothing holds any terror for me. And dear and precious as many people are to me—father, sister, wife, those who are most dear, I would sacrifice them all, dreadful and unnatural as it may seem, for a moment of glory, of triumph over men, for the love of men I do not know and shall never know.... Yes, that's how it is, I love and value nothing but triumph over all of them, value only this mysterious power and glory that is hovering over me in the mist.[8]

Glory hovering in the mist: Andrei does not yet know that it is mist and fog that will ensure Russian defeat.

Running forward with the standard in the heat of battle, Andrei suddenly feels as if he has been bludgeoned on the head. Thrown on his back, he gazes at the sky. Literally and figuratively, he has changed his point of view. "Above him there was nothing but the sky, the lofty heavens." Could all human effort be trivial when viewed from the perspective of eternity?

"How quiet, solemn, and serene, not at all as it was when I was running," thought Prince Andrei . . . "how differently do those clouds float over the lofty, infinite heavens. How is it I did not see this before? How happy I am to have discovered it at last! Yes! All is vanity, all is delusion, except those infinite heavens. There is nothing but that. And even that does not exist. . . . Thank God."[9]

Andrei regains consciousness in the presence of Napoleon, who proudly surveys his victory and struts before captured Russian officers. Andrei remembers that Napoleon was his hero, but now everything that engrosses the emperor seems petty, as does Napoleon himself, "with his paltry vanity and joy in victory." When Napoleon addresses him, Andrei remains silent. "Looking into Napoleon's eyes, Prince Andrei thought of the insignificance of greatness, the unimportance of life, which no one could understand, and of the still greater unimportance of death, the meaning of which no living person could explain."[10]

Time and again, Tolstoy gives Andrei a negative epiphany, the realization that what looks meaningful is actually insignificant. Contemplating the icon of the Savior that his sister hung around his neck as he left for war, Andrei dismisses her naïve belief in "that God who has been sewn into this amulet." He expresses his sense of utter meaninglessness, but then corrects himself: "There is nothing except the nothingness of everything that is comprehensible to me, and the greatness of something incomprehensible, but all-important!"[11] Beyond nothingness, something "all-important" exists, and Andrei, after a period of despair, will again quest for it.

As the novel proceeds, Andrei repeatedly loses hope, finds a new ideal, and despairs again. Each transition widens the compass of his disdain, until it embraces life itself. Many regard Prince Andrei's dying, which extends over two hundred pages, as the greatest death in world literature. His final negative epiphany exposes the vanity of living people's concerns. When Andrei hears that Moscow has burned, he can only say "too bad," as if a teacup had broken. Human affairs no longer concern him, and he has trouble understanding the simplest things. Natasha, whom he has loved, and his sister Princess Marya conclude "that he was indifferent to everything, indifferent because something of far greater importance had been revealed to him."[12]

Andrei experiences "alienation from all things earthly" and regards life differently because he sees it as if from outside.[13] He views life as if he were already dead. From this perspective, what conceals life's true meaning is life itself. That is how he understands Jesus's words, "The fowls of the air sow not, neither do they reap, nor gather into barns, yet your heavenly Father feedeth them" (Matthew 6:25); but he knows that if he tried to explain what these words mean to him, Natasha and Princess Marya would not understand. "But no, they would interpret it in their own way, they don't understand that all these feelings they set such store by—all our feelings, all those ideas that seem so important to us, *do not matter*."[14]

The novel by no means endorses Andrei's final conclusions. Tolstoy makes it clear that Andrei's truth is only partial. Even if it were not, one could not live by it. But the view it expresses haunted Tolstoy and attracted him to the negative wisdom of Ecclesiastes, Schopenhauer, and Buddhism. Life ensnares us in activity bound to prove pointless. We pursue phantoms. Schopenhauer reasons: once we understand "that the world, and therefore man too, is something which really ought not exist," we should be indulgent to our fellow sufferers and recognize that "the most necessary of all things" are "tolerance, patience, forbearance, and charity, which each of us needs and therefore owes."[15]

In Tolstoy's last decades, this line of thinking attracted him to Lao Tzu and the *Tao Te Ching*, with its doctrine of "non-action."[16] Tolstoy explained: "The ills of humanity arise, according to Lao Tzu, not because men neglect to do things that are necessary, but because they do things that are not necessary." Westerners mistakenly celebrate work as a virtue and source of meaning (Tolstoy cited a speech by Zola), but it is merely a necessity. One might as well find life's purpose in nutrition. Rather than reveal meaning, activity and purposeful labor merely serve as "a moral anesthetic, like tobacco, wine, and other means of stupefying and blinding oneself to the disorder and emptiness of our lives."[17]

## Happiness

"Man is born for happiness as a bird is made for flight," Korolenko famously observed.[18] Today, this observation appears unremarkable, almost banal. What else could make a life worthwhile if not happiness? In Russia, however, this view of life often seemed selfish, vulgar, and a betrayal of all that is truly meaningful.

Russian thinkers realized, of course, that the doctrine of individual happiness as life's goal was the gift of the Enlightenment. Historian Ritchie Robertson begins his study *The Enlightenment: The Pursuit of Happiness, 1680–1790*: "The Enlightenment declared the conviction that the goal of life was happiness, and that if this goal could be attained at all, it was to be found in the here and now."[19]

The American Declaration of Independence states that the right to pursue happiness is not only inalienable but self-evident. Then why had this view not always been accepted, and why do other cultures, and many people in Western culture, still not accept it? Earlier and elsewhere, other goals—salvation, the carrying out of divine will, or achievements more significant than any individual life—seemed far more important than one's own contentment. Centuries of Christian thought had represented life as a mere prelude to life eternal, a vale of tears where happiness was unattainable. In a well-known treatise on life's wretchedness, Pope Innocent III had observed: "We are all born yelling and crying, to the end we may expresse our myserie."[20]

By the late seventeenth century, this view of life changed. Leibniz defined wisdom as "the science of happiness" and in *The Essay on Human Understanding*, Locke asserted: "I lay it for a certain ground, that every intelligent being really seeks happiness, which consists in the enjoyment of pleasure, without any considerable mixture of uneasiness."[21] Alexander Pope, whose skill lay in expressing memorably "what oft was thought," begins the fourth epistle of his *Essay on Man*:

> Oh Happiness! our being's end and aim!
> Good, Pleasure, Ease, Content! whate'er the name:
> That something still which prompts th' eternal sigh,
> For which we bear to live, or dare to die . . .
> Plant of celestial seed! if dropped below,
> Say, in what mortal soil thou deignst to grow?[22]

Frances Hutcheson and Jeremy Bentham argued that the standard of morality must be the greatest happiness of the greatest number. Bentham called this mathematics of life "felicific calculus."

Doubters still flourished, of course, as we see from the widely circulated story that Julien Offray de La Mettrie, the materialist who regarded life as the satisfaction of sensual pleasures, died "by keeling over at a Berlin dinner table after gorging himself on truffles."[23] More seriously, Kant pointed out that if the purpose of life were happiness, "nature would have hit on a very bad arrangement by choosing reason in the creature to carry out this purpose" since the way to happiness "would have been mapped out . . . far more accurately by instinct."[24] The claim of duty, Kant maintained, must outweigh the claim of happiness. We should follow the moral law, which constitutes "the idea of another and far worthier purpose of one's existence, to which therefore, and not to happiness, reason is properly destined, and to which . . . the private purpose of the human being must for the most part defer."[25]

For Samuel Johnson, to pursue happiness is to chase a phantom. The plot of his philosophical tale *Rasselas* concerns a prince's quest to find the best "choice of life," a quest that Johnson's mouthpiece, Imlac, knows to be futile. "Human life," Imlac explains, "is everywhere a state in which much is to be endured and little to be enjoyed."[26] Voltaire, whose influence on the Russian novel would be hard to overstate, came to a similar conclusion at the end of *Candide*. Instead of madly seeking resplendent happiness, we should "cultivate our garden."[27]

In his philosophical parable "The Story of a Good Brahmin," Voltaire demonstrates that people are not so sure as they imagine that happiness is the highest goal. If they were, they would not hesitate a moment to choose it over anything else, but, as the tale demonstrates, they do hesitate. It seems that a wealthy, wise, and highly educated Brahmin is miserable, while a poor, ignorant old woman who lives outside his palace gates is happy. The Brahmin tells the narrator that he has asked himself many times whether he would exchange places with her and become happy by becoming stupid. Though he cannot explain why, he knows that he would not. Why not, if the goal is happiness? Isn't intelligence valuable simply as a means to that goal?

The narrator realizes that he would also refuse the bargain. When he poses the questions to other thinkers who believe that life's goal is happiness, he can find "no one willing to . . . become an imbecile in order to be content."[28] Do they not believe what they sincerely assert? Do they actually believe that something else is more important than happiness? The story ends with the paradox unresolved.

## The Mystery of Happiness

Happiness strikes many as a simple concept. For Bentham, "happiness," "benefit," "advantage," "pleasure, and "good" all "come to the same thing," as do their opposites, "mischief, pain, evil, or unhappiness."[29] But isn't it possible that happiness is a word we apply to many different, even contradictory, things? Perhaps meaningfulness demands sacrificing happiness, as Dostoevsky thought? Or, as Kant argued, do duty and moral obligation, by their very nature, demand we choose something other than our own welfare? Could it be, as Voltaire's parable suggests, that happiness itself is fundamentally mysterious?

Chekhov agreed that happiness is mysterious, and devoted several stories to probing its perplexing nature. In "Happiness," an old shepherd and his young helper converse with an estate overseer about a great fortune that, legend has it, is buried somewhere nearby. In Russian, the words for "fortune" and "happiness" are the same, so everything said about one applies to the other.

The old man's family has been seeking this fortune for generations, but, he reasons, it is evidently protected by a charm. Without a special talisman, one could be standing right next to treasure and not see it. "There is fortune," the old shepherd explains, "but what is the good of it if it is buried in the earth? It is just riches wasted with no profit to anyone, like chaff or sheep's dung, and yet there *are* riches there, lad, fortune enough for all the country round and no one sees it." The overseer agrees: "Yes, your elbow is near, but you can't bite it."[30] We wonder: if happiness is so close, perhaps it is hidden not in the earth but in plain view? Perhaps we need to discern what is right before our eyes?

But that is not the conclusion the old man draws: "Yes," he reflects, "so one dies without knowing what happiness is like." At this point, Chekhov pauses to describe the vegetation and wildlife in the desolate surroundings: "The endless steppe had a sullen and death-like look: no soul would ever know why they [the barrows] stood there, and what secret of the steppes was hidden under them.... No meaning was to be seen in the boundless expanse of the steppe."[31] Perhaps nature is not just indifferent, but positively spiteful, leading people to seek a happiness that does not exist.

When the overseer leaves, the young shepherd asks: "What will you do with the treasure when you find it?" Strangely enough, this question has never occurred to the old man. "Judging from the expression on his face, indifferent and uncritical, it did not seem to him important and deserving of consideration." The young peasant puzzles over a mystery: why do old people search for hidden treasure, "and what was the use of earthly happiness to people who might die any day of old age?" We leave the two of them pondering, the old man on the treasure's whereabouts and the youth on yet another mystery: "What interested him was not the fortune itself, which he did not want and could not imagine, but the fantastic, fairy-tale character of human happiness."[32]

## Dystopian Happiness

In Dostoevsky's view, happiness could be a curse. When he submitted early chapters of his novel about his prison camp experiences, *The House of the Dead*, the censor initially objected for a reason he had not expected: the descriptions of prison life in the censor's opinion were not horrible enough and therefore would not be a sufficient deterrent to crime! Dostoevsky offered to publish a supplement (it turned out to be unnecessary) explaining that confinement and lack of freedom could turn heaven itself into hell. "Try an experiment and build a palace," he wrote, fit it out with everything you could possibly want, so that your every desire was immediately granted. You might wish never to leave. But let someone make it impossible to leave, and everything changes. Once it becomes compulsory, "in that instant you will wish to quit your paradise. . . . Even more! All this luxury, all this plenitude will only sharpen your suffering. You will even feel insulted."[33]

Dostoevsky concludes: "Happiness lies not in happiness but in the attempt to achieve it."[34] Apparently, something in human nature presumes that choice and effort are constituent parts of what is most desirable. We want to earn what we want, not to be given it. That is something utopians do not understand. The destination includes the journey. Dostoevsky's underground man compares man to a chess player who "loves only the process of the game . . . he likes the process of attaining, but does not quite like to have attained" because then the process of attaining stops. "And who knows . . . perhaps the only goal on earth to which mankind is striving lies in this incessant process of attaining, or in other words, in life itself and not particularly in the goal."[35] As Pascal observed, "we prefer the hunt to the capture." [36]

Today we might cite Robert Nozick's idea of an "experience machine" that stimulates our brains to make us feel we are having whatever experience we might wish. We would be guaranteed a life of perfect bliss. Would you plug it in? After all, Nozick asks, "what else can matter to us other than how our lives feel from inside"?[37] Well, to begin with, one reason we want to experience doing certain things is that we want actually to do them. As Dostoevsky would say, we want to achieve things, not have them happen to us. For another, we want to become, through our choices, a certain sort of person, but a brain connected to electrodes cannot be said to be any sort of person.[38] As Dostoevsky and Bakhtin would say, to be human we must really be responsible for something.

Nozick suggests that we might also wish to go beyond man-made reality to reach something deeper, which cannot happen in a wholly man-made world. In short, "what we desire is to live (an active verb) ourselves, in contact with reality. (And this machines cannot do *for* us.)"[39] In Bakhtin's words, "there is no alibi for being."

Dostoevsky's underground man concludes that man is such a strange creature that he might find perfect happiness intolerable. "Shower upon him every earthly blessing, drown him in bliss so that nothing but bubbles would dance on the surface of his bliss, as on a sea . . . and even then man, out of sheer ingratitude, sheer libel, would play you some loathsome trick. He would even risk his cakes and deliberately desire the most fatal rubbish . . . simply in order to prove to himself . . . that men are still men and not piano keys." Rather than live in paradise, man would choose suffering, the underground man asserts, since "suffering is the sole origin of consciousness" and without it "there will be nothing left but to bottle up your five senses and plunge into contemplation." Even flogging yourself is better than that, he adds. "It may be reactionary, but corporal punishment is still better than nothing."[40]

This passage inspired the genre we have come to call the dystopia. In the first dystopian novel, Zamyatin's *We*, the ruler explains to the hero D-503 that society has taken humanity's dream of happiness "to the logical end. I ask: what was it that man from his diaper age dreamed of, tormented himself for, prayed for? He longed for that day when someone would tell him what happiness is, and then would chain him to it. What are we doing now? The ancient dream of paradise." To choose anything but happiness would be insane, D-503 has himself asserted, to which the heroine I-330 replies: "Yes, yes, precisely. All must become insane" in that way.[41]

In Aldous Huxley's *Brave New World*, Mustapha Mond advances much the same argument as the ruler in *We*. "I don't want comfort," the Savage tells him. "I want God. I want poetry. I want real danger, I want freedom, I want goodness, I want sin. . . . I'm claiming the right to be unhappy." Mustpaha Mond replies that in so doing you are claiming "'the right to grow old and ugly and impotent; the right to have syphilis and cancer; the right to have too little to eat; the right to be lousy; the right to live in constant apprehension of what may happen tomorrow. . . .' There was a long silence. 'I claim them all,' said the Savage at last. Mustapha Mond shrugged his shoulders. 'You're welcome,' he said."[42]

Is it possible that to achieve real happiness, happiness cannot be the goal? Perhaps, as Sergei Bulgakov observed, it should be "incidental to, not an intended concomitant of moral activity and service to the good"?[43] So understood, real happiness must be a byproduct accompanying the achievement of some higher purpose, for which happiness itself may be sacrificed.

## The Way of Stoicism

Some thinkers regarded happiness not as something positive but as the absence of anything distressing. Chekhov's story "In Exile" features an old ferryman who preaches this stoic truth to a young Tatar, exiled for no fault of his own. "And what do you want your wife and mother for?" the old ferryman demands. "It's the devil confounding you, damn his soul! Don't you listen to him. . . . He is at you about the women, but you spite him and say, 'I don't want them!' He is on at you about freedom, but you stand up to him and say: 'I don't want it!' I want nothing, neither father nor mother, nor wife, nor freedom . . ."

Because the ferryman wants nothing, he asserts, "there is nobody richer and freer than I am."[44] He tells the story of an exiled nobleman, whom he has frequently ferried across the river on some desperate pursuit of happiness. Each pursuit ends in misery. The nobleman's wife came to live with him, but in spite of all his frantic efforts to please her, she left him. He raised his daughter, but she has consumption and, in spite of all his chasing after doctors, will soon die. Like some Siberian Schopenhauer, the ferryman argues that pain always exceeds pleasure and that desires, even if satisfied, only magnify misery.

This philosophy appalls the Tatar. "You say, want nothing," he replies in his broken Russian. "But 'nothing' is bad! His wife lived with him three years—that was a gift from God. 'Nothing' is bad, but three years is good. How not understand?" He exclaims that "if his wife came to him for one day, even for one hour, that for such happiness he would be ready to bear any suffering and to thank God. Better one day of happiness than nothing."[45]

At this point in the discussion, the distraught nobleman arrives to cross the river in pursuit of yet another doctor for his daughter. Chekhov describes the ferryman's malicious enjoyment at his distress. "There was a triumphant expression on Canny's [the ferryman's] face, as though he had proved something and was delighted that things had happened as he had foretold. The unhappy helplessness of the man . . . evidently afforded him great pleasure."[46] Does stoicism, like the puritanism of the old or the bohemian's contempt for riches, arise less from wisdom than from envy?

Witnessing this spiteful pleasure, the Tatar exclaims "with hatred and repulsion" that the gentleman is good, but the ferryman is bad. "The gentleman is alive, but you are a dead carcass . . . God created man to be alive, and to have grief and sorrow, but you want nothing, so you are not alive, you are stone, clay! . . . You are a stone, and God does not love you, but He loves the gentleman!"[47]

## Formic Happiness

If human beings are so constituted that even happiness does not make them happy, perhaps the solution is to abridge their humanness. Why not eliminate whatever in us obstructs our satisfaction with perfect bliss? *We* ends with a lobotomy removing the source of all discontent, the imagination. For Dostoevsky, socialism could only work if people resembled ants in an anthill, and his characters wonder whether it would be wise to surrender essential humanness to ensure earthly formic happiness. Become simple! Dmitri Karamazov finds it unendurable that he can simultaneously love debauchery and holiness, or, in his words, "Sodom and the Madonna." "Yes, man is broad, too broad, indeed," he concludes. "I'd have him narrower."[48]

Narrowing people to make them happier: that is the plan of Ivan Karamazov's Grand Inquisitor. Freedom leads to misery, the Inquisitor explains to Jesus. Where there is choice, mistakes are inevitable and so choice necessarily entails anxiety, guilt, and regret. "I tell Thee man is tormented by no greater anxiety than to find someone quickly to whom he can hand over that gift of freedom with which the ill-fated creature is born."[49] To ensure human happiness, the last thing one should do is magnify freedom, as Jesus did.

To escape from freedom, people adopt ideologies promising certainty, the Inquisitor explains. Certainty precludes mistakes. Since disagreement invites doubt, some nations conquer others with different religions or philosophies, as if the absence of disagreement ensured truth. People worship power, since pain is one thing that cannot be doubted. They willingly befuddle their minds with "mystery" to assure themselves that even if their rulers' behavior is inconsistent and their assertions contradict each other, they possess the indubitable truth.

Happiness and freedom are irreconcilable, and so only some form of absolute authority—what we would today call totalitarianism—can ensure the happiness of mankind. For this reason, the Inquisitor explains, Jesus should have accepted the devil's third temptation, to rule all the kingdoms of the world: "Hadst Thou accepted that last counsel of the mighty spirit, Thou wouldst have accomplished all that man seeks on earth—that is, someone to worship, someone to keep his conscience, and some means of uniting all in one unanimous and harmonious ant-heap."[50]

The Inquisitor's program proved appealing. The Soviet project of remaking human nature included narrowing the range of human emotions and merging individual minds with the mind of the Party. Poet Aleksei Gastev, the head of the Central Institute of Labor, advocated the transformation of the proletariat into a machine ("machinism") ensuring "the mechanization, not only of gestures, not only of production methods, but of everyday thinking ... which permits the quantification of separate proletarian units as A, B, or C, or as 325,075 ... and ... the normalization of psychology."[51] The new man, Gastev enthused, will be "soulless and devoid of personality, emotion, and lyricism—no longer expressing himself through screams of pain or joyful laughter, but rather through a manometer or taxometer. Mass engineering will make man a social automaton."[52] Yuri Olesha's novel *Envy* features one hero, Volodya Makarov, who boasts that "I am a human machine" and another, Ivan Kavalerov, who seeks to preserve human emotions condemned by the new order. Kavalerov organizes "a conspiracy of feelings": "I want to find the representatives of what you call the old world," he explains. "I mean feelings like jealousy, love for a woman, vanity.... To me has fallen the honor of conducting the last parade of the ancient, human passions."[53]

## Anti-Gooseberries

In Russian thought of the nineteenth century, opinions and ways of life often seemed immoral precisely because they contributed to happiness! To be happy is to live for oneself, this line of thinking went, whereas morality demands sacrifice for a higher, usually political, ideal. Even if we do not know what life's meaning is, we can be sure of what it is not, namely, anything designed to promote individual happiness.

In Turgenev's *Nest of Gentlefolk*, Mikhalevich refutes one of his friend Lavretsky's ideas by saying that it contributes to enjoyment. "You're an egoist, that's what it is! . . . you wanted personal happiness, you wanted enjoyment in life, you wanted to live only for yourself."[54] What could be worse than living for personal happiness? At the beginning of Turgenev's *On the Eve*, Shubin and Bersenyev discuss whether life's meaning lies in happiness. "Damn it all," Shubin exclaims enthusiastically, "we are young, and neither fools nor monsters. We will conquer happiness for ourselves!" "Is there nothing higher than happiness?" Bersenyev replies. A person seeks happiness for himself, "but is that word happiness, one that could unite us . . . and make us clasp each other's hands? Isn't that word an egoistic one; I mean, isn't a source of disunion?" By contrast, he continues, art, country, science, freedom, and justice unite people. "That's all very well for Germans," Shubin answers, but "I want to live for myself; I want to be first." "It seems to me," Bersenyev counters, "that to put oneself in the second place is the whole significance of life."[55]

In Chekhov's story "Gooseberries," Ivan Ivanovich recounts to his friends Burkin and Alekhin his brother Nikolai's successful quest for happiness. The brothers grew up on a little country estate that had to be sold to pay their father's debts. From then on, the only thing that mattered to Nikolai was to possess such an estate where he could retire and grow his own gooseberries, for him the symbol of all he desired. Obsessively accumulating money, Nikolai married a wealthy woman, only to mistreat her enough for her to pine away and die. If he was given a present, he saved it. "Once a man is absorbed by an idea there is no doing anything with him," Ivan Ivanovich observes.[56]

At last, Nikolai bought an estate on a polluted river and became a country grandee. In government service, he had been afraid to express any opinions, but "now could say nothing that was not gospel truth, and uttered such truths in the tone of a prime minister." Nothing made him so happy as eating his own gooseberries. Just looking at them made tears come to his eyes; "he could not speak for excitement."[57]

At this point, the story switches focus, as it often does with Chekhov. It turns out to concern not Nikolai's way of life but Ivan Ivanovich's reaction to it. "I saw a happy man whose cherished dream was so obviously fulfilled, who had attained his object in life," a sight that overcomes Ivan Ivanovich "with an oppressive feeling that was close to despair." He reflects sadly about "how many happy people there really are! What a suffocating force it is!"[58] Look around and you see countless people going about their daily routines, "talking their silly nonsense, getting married, growing old," but very few of them see or hear all those who suffer because "what is terrible in life goes on somewhere behind the scenes . . . nothing protests but mute statistics." Happiness, Ivan Ivanovich reflects, depends on the silence of the unhappy, and "without that silence happiness would be impossible."[59]

It follows for Ivan Ivanovich that happiness is positively immoral. "There ought to be behind the door of every happy, contented man someone standing with a hammer continually reminding him with a tap that there are unhappy people." Reflecting on his own life, Ivan Ivanovich realizes that in his own way he, too, "was happy and contented."[60] Rather illogically, this realization leads him to reject gradual reform and embrace revolutionary change. Precisely because reform does not interfere with one's happiness, he reasons, it is contemptible. Indeed, by assuaging one's conscience, it makes one even happier. It does not occur to Ivan Ivanovich to ask whether reform or revolution produces better results.

"What grounds have we for waiting?" Ivan Ivanovich asks his friends. "Wait for the sake of what? Wait till there's no strength to live?" Peace and quiet oppress him, and "there is no spectacle more painful to me now than the sight of a happy family sitting round the table drinking tea."[61] Happiness disturbs him more than misery.

Turning to Alekhin, Ivan Ivanovich pleads: "Pavel Konstantinovich . . . don't be calm and contented, don't let yourself be put to sleep! . . . There is no happiness, and there ought not to be: but if there is a meaning and an object in life, that meaning and object is not in our happiness, but in something greater and more rational. Do Good!"[62]

"Ivan Ivanovich's story had not satisfied Burkin and Alekhin," Chekhov observes, and we see, at least in part, why. What he has said about his brother applies to him: "Once a man is absorbed by an idea there is no doing anything with him."[63]

No less than Nikolai, Ivan Ivanovich recognizes only one question, which seems to him perfectly simple. He favors whatever makes the happy most unhappy. His arguments for revolutionary change derive from his resentment of happiness, that is, from his own emotional needs. Concern with self motivates his plea for selflessness. Had he been motivated primarily by a concern to reduce suffering, he would have asked what change actually produces the desired result.

As strongly as gooseberries and all they symbolize delight Nikolai, they nauseate Ivan Ivanovich. The story's title, we may reflect, applies to both brothers. Ivan Ivanovich has grown as obsessed and narrow as Nikolai, albeit in the opposite direction.

## The Shriveled Plum

Tolstoy's heroes often imagine they know what makes a meaningful life only to discover they have been mistaken. In *Master and Man*, Brekhunov spends his life focusing on his business success; Father Sergius (in *Father Sergius*) endeavors to be a holy man; and Ivan Ilych (in *The Death of Ivan Ilych*) assumes that life is about living pleasantly. Each eventually finds meaning elsewhere.

"Ivan Ilych's life had been the most simple and the most commonplace and therefore the most terrible," Tolstoy asserts. It is so terrible because he has made himself "narrower." Recognizing that everything idiosyncratic conflicts with success in career and society, Ivan Ilych makes himself identical to his roles, with nothing left over. Ironically enough, his one distinguishing characteristic is his remarkable ability to live entirely without distinguishing characteristics. "Even when he was at the School of Law he was just what he remained for the rest of his life: a capable, cheerful, good-natured, and sociable man, though strict in the fulfillment of what he considered to be his duty; and he considered his duty to be what was so considered by those in authority." It is not as if he pretends to be what he is expected to be; no pretense is necessary. He is no hypocrite, or rather, he is not even a hypocrite. As Tolstoy remarks, "neither as a boy nor as a man was he a toady, but from early childhood was by nature attracted to people of high station as a fly is drawn to the light."[64] Beginning with an apparent compliment—he was not a toady—this observation ends by suggesting that it would be better if he were, because a toady's pretense testifies to his difference from his role. For Ivan Ilych, the two "by nature" coincide.

Ivan Ilych is the perfect judge because he automatically "acquired a method of eliminating all considerations irrelevant to the legal aspects of the case . . . completely excluding his personal opinion of the matter."[65]

The house he and his wife select, which suits them perfectly, "was so like the others [belonging to his social class] that it would never have been noticed."[66] Only when Ivan Ilych's illness continues to worsen, and he must confront the fact that he will soon die, does he discover the self apart from his roles. After all, when he dies the roles will continue—another judge will be appointed in his place—but his self, what is unique to him alone, will not. Of course, Ivan Ilych always knew that people are mortal, but there is knowing and knowing. Until he faced death himself, mortality remained an abstract proposition like others with no particular significance for Ivan Ilych personally. The story's most famous passage—one of the most striking in Russian literature—traces the difference made by actually appreciating one's own mortality:

> Ivan Ilych knew that he was dying and was in continual despair.
>
> In the depths of his heart he knew he was dying, but not only was he not accustomed to the thought, he simply did not and could not grasp it.
>
> The syllogism he had learnt from Kiesewetter's Logic: "Caius is a man, men are mortal, therefore Caius is mortal," had always seemed to him correct as applied to Caius, but certainly not as applied to himself. That Caius—man in the abstract—was mortal, was perfectly correct, but he was not Caius, not an abstract man, but a creature quite, quite separate from all others. He had been little Vanya. . . . What did Caius know of the smell of that striped leather ball Vanya had been so fond of? Had Caius kissed his mother's hand like that, and did the silk of her dress rustle so for Caius? . . . "Caius really was mortal, and it was right for him to die, but for me, little Vanya, Ivan Ilych, with all my thoughts and emotions, it's altogether a different matter. It cannot be that I ought to die. That would be too terrible."[67]

The terror that dominates him, described as only Tolstoy could, turns out to reflect "that he has not lived his life as he should have done." A voice seems to ask what he wants, and he replies that he wants to live as he used to do—

"well and pleasantly." But when he surveys his life, Ivan Ilych recognizes to his horror that only in childhood was there anything real. Then his experiences were still particular to him, and he remembers particularities. When he is served stewed prunes, "his mind went back to the raw shriveled French plums of his childhood, their peculiar flavor and the flow of saliva when he sucked their stones, and along with the memory of that taste came a whole series of memories of those days." This is Proust's Tolstoy. It strikes Ivan Ilych that the more he made himself the perfect man of society, and the more pleasantly he has lived, the more rapidly his life became meaningless, "in inverse ratio to the square of the distance from death."[68]

Only when Ivan Ilych fully appreciates that he has lived wrongly does he achieve the possibility of doing something right and so redeeming himself. The sympathy he extends to his family, and especially to his terrified son, relieves the terror he feels. His salvation occurs entirely privately, invisible to others who hear only his cries of physical pain. But that is the whole point: the meaningful experience belongs to him alone.

## What Can Only Be Shown

The greatest Russian writers do not tell us what life's meaning is, but they show us what the discovery of it looks and feels like. That is because meaning is not a proposition we could learn, as we master the binomial theorem. If there were such a proposition, we would all already know it. It would be the first thing we had been taught. In *Karamazov* Madame Khokhlakova implores Father Zossima to prove that something beyond "the menacing phenomena of nature"—something truly meaningful—actually exists. "There's no proving it," Zossima replies, "but you can be convinced of it."[69] The distinction is crucial: some things cannot be adequately addressed from a third-person perspective. Physicalism and materialist philosophy notwithstanding, the world as described "from nowhere" is incomplete.[70]

As it leaves out consciousness, the third-person perspective bypasses meaning. Meaning cannot be learned by scientific demonstration or mathematical proof. Strictly speaking, one does not know it, one senses it; that is why it isn't proved, but rather convinces. And it convinces only if one leads the right sort of life. When Madame Khokhlakova asks exactly what sort of life, Zossima replies: a life of "active love. Strive to love your neighbor actively and indefatigably. In so far as you advance in love, you will grow surer of the reality of God and of the immortality of your soul. If you attain to perfect self-forgetfulness in the love of your neighbor, then you will believe without doubt."[71]

Profoundly influenced by Dostoevsky and Tolstoy, the philosopher Ludwig Wittgenstein read *Karamazov* "so often he knew whole passages of it by heart, particularly the speeches of Father Zossima, who represented for him . . . a holy man who could 'see directly into the souls of other people.'" Tolstoy apparently mattered even more to him, having saved him from suicide ("kept me alive").[72] As Wittgenstein's student, the philosopher Stephen Toulmin, observed, the conclusion of Wittgenstein's *Tractatus Logico-Philosophicus*, which so puzzled analytic philosophers, runs parallel to the eighth part of *Anna Karenina*, where Levin overcomes his existential despair and senses the meaning of things.[73]

So similar are the arguments of these two works that each can be used as a gloss on the other. Overcome by his sense of the futility of all human activity in the face of death, Levin first seeks meaning in natural science, which had taken the place of his former religious faith. "The organism . . . the indestructability of matter, the law of the conservation of energy, evolution were the words that usurped the place of his old belief. These words and the ideas associated with them were very useful for intellectual purposes. But for life they yielded nothing, and Levin felt suddenly like a man who has changed his warm fur cloak for a muslin garment, and, going for the first time into the frost, is immediately convinced, not by reason, but by his whole nature, that he is as good as naked, and he must inevitably perish miserably." He soon recognizes that science, which discerns causes and describes the facts of the world, can never address such unscientific concepts as "goodness" or "meaning." "He was in the position of a man seeking food in a toy shop or at a gunsmith's."[74]

"Thus people today stop at the laws of nature, treating them as something unavoidable, just as God and Fate were treated in past ages," Wittgenstein comments. "The modern system tries to make it look as if *everything* is explained." But that is not so: "We feel that even when all *possible* scientific questions have been answered, the problems of life remain completely untouched."[75] Levin at last realizes that by its very nature goodness cannot be reduced to cause and effect: "If goodness has causes, it is not goodness; if it has effects, a reward, it is not goodness either. So goodness is outside the chain of cause and effect. And yet I know it, and we all know it."[76]

When evolutionary biologists, sociobiologists, and neurophysiologists explain how the concept of goodness has arisen, they imagine they have adequately explained it. Of course, one can explain any human belief, true or preposterous, in these ways; and one can equally well account for any human behavior, whether sadistic or altruistic. What one cannot do is assess the validity of an argument or the rightness of an action. The truth of the Pythagorean theorem cannot be ascertained by any conceivable evolutionary reasoning. Neither can the rightness or wrongness of torturing children be established neurophysiologically. That is what Levin means when he concludes that goodness is not a matter of causes.

Goodness is not a matter of effects or rewards because to perform an action because of the benefits it confers is not to perform it because it is right. As the Grand Inquisitor legend suggests, to behave well in order to be rewarded in the afterlife does not significantly differ from saving for retirement: delaying gratification is a matter of prudence, not goodness.

If so, then, as Wittgenstein maintains, "the sense of the world must lie outside the world. In the world everything is as it is, and everything happens as it does happen. . . . If there is any value that does have value, it must lie outside the whole sphere of what happens and is the case."[77]

Our sense of goodness, Levin concludes, is *given*. "I looked for an answer to my question. And thought could not give me an answer to my question—it is incommensurable with my question. The answer has been given me by life itself, in my knowledge of what is right and wrong. And that knowledge I did not arrive at in any way, it was given to me as to all men, *given* [*dano*], because I could not have gotten it from anywhere."[78]

Levin has hoped for a miracle revealing the meaning of life, but he needed an awareness of what he has known since childhood. The absence of the need for a miracle is itself the miracle: "And I watched for miracles, complained that I did not see a miracle that would convince me. A material miracle would have persuaded me. And here is a miracle, the sole miracle possible, surrounding me on all sides, and I never noticed it. . . . I have discovered nothing. I have found out only what I knew."[79] As so often in Tolstoy, the truth lies not in the distance but in the prosaic facts right before our eyes.

Levin has not exactly found an answer to the question of life's meaning. Rather, he senses the meaning directly and so the question vanishes. As Wittgenstein observes: "The solution of the problem of life is seen in the vanishing of the problem. (Is this not the reason why those who have found after a long period of doubt that the sense of life became clear to them have been unable to say what constituted that sense?)" Levin finds he cannot convey his discovery to others by a chain of argument. Some things cannot be stated; "they *make themselves manifest*."[80]

And yet, something can be done to guide others. One cannot state the meaning, but one can show the process of arriving at it. Realist novels, like

*Anna Karenina*, enable readers to trace a character's moment-to-moment experience from within and so are uniquely adept at such showing. They can do what no philosophical treatise ever could.

Literature, as Russians have usually understood it, does not merely present a digestible version of discoveries made by philosophers. In this respect, as in others, it goes beyond the philosophers. It *shows* what cannot be *stated*.

## Meaning Changes No Facts

In his enthusiasm, Levin expects his life to change completely. "He thought that now his relations with all men would be different."[81] There would be no more aloofness from his brother; he would no longer quarrel with his wife Kitty; friction with Ivan the coachman and his other servants would vanish. Within minutes each of these dreams is shattered.

The sense of meaning changes no fact in the world. It changes one's experience of the world as a whole. "In short the effect must be that it becomes an altogether different world. It must, so to speak, wax and wane as a whole. The world of the happy man is an altogether different one from that of the unhappy man."[82] As the novel ends, Levin understands this truth. "This new feeling has not changed me, has not made me happy and enlightened all of a sudden, as I had dreamed," Levin tells himself. "Faith—or not faith—I don't know what it is—has come . . . through suffering, and has taken firm root in my soul." *Anna Karenina* concludes:

> I shall go on in the same way, losing my temper with Ivan the coachman, falling into angry discussions . . . there will still be the same wall between the holy of holies in my soul and other people, even my wife . . . I shall still be unable to explain with my reason why I pray, and shall still go on praying; but my life now, my whole life apart from anything that can happen to me, every minute of it is no longer meaningless, as it was before, but it has an unquestionable meaning of the goodness which I have the power to put into it.[83]

## Suffering

Levin's reference to learning "through suffering" expresses a key idea in Russian literature: the meaning of life can be revealed only to those who suffer. The happy can doze, the miserable must reflect. "Suffering lays bare the real nature of things," Evgeniya Ginzburg observed. "It is the price to be paid for a deeper, more truthful understanding of life."[84] Suffering sometimes reveals higher meanings and, as Solzhenitsyn insisted, "nothing worthwhile can be built on a neglect of higher meanings."[85]

Svetlana Alexievich observed: The best way to understand human life is to "listen to the pain [...] Pain as the proof of past life ... I think of suffering as the highest form of information, having a direct connection with mystery. With the mystery of life. All of Russian literature is about that. It has written more about suffering than about love."[86] It was a commonplace to identify Russia with the "suffering servant" in Isaiah 53. Alexievich's Nobel Prize speech, we have seen, attributed Russian thinkers' extraordinary insightfulness to the suffering Russians have undergone. "Suffering is our capital, our natural resource," she explained. "Not oil or gas—but suffering. It is the only thing we are able to produce consistently. ... But great books are piled at our feet."[87]

"Your soul, which formerly was dry, ripens with suffering," Solzhenitsyn described his own transformation in "The Ascent," the core chapter of *The Gulag Archipelago*. Instead of focusing on your wrongful imprisonment, you ask about your guilt "before your own conscience ... if you go over your life with a fine-tooth comb and ponder it deeply," you will always find a transgression that actually deserved punishment. Instead of blaming others, you will examine yourself, and that is the only way to become better. What truly matters in life is not anything external but "the development of the soul." You appreciate the truth of all religions that "struggle with the *evil inside a human being* (inside every human being)."[88]

"Lev Tolstoy was right when he *dreamed* of being put in prison," Solzhenitsyn concluded. We have already cited these remarkable words: "All the writers who wrote about prison but who did not themselves serve time considered it their duty to express sympathy for prisoners and to curse prison. I [...] I have served enough time there. I nourished my soul there, and I say without hesitation: '*Bless you, prison,* for having been in my life!'"[89]

Suffering has the capacity to elevate the soul, but it also—and perhaps more often—has the opposite effect. *Karamazov* explores both sorts of suffering. The novel's epigraph declares that suffering can be fruitful: "Verily, verily, I say unto you except a corn of wheat fall into the ground and die, it abideth alone: but if it die, it bringeth forth much fruit" (John 12:24). As the novel ends, the epigraph perhaps promises that the new person Dmitri senses in himself will triumph over the old.

But *Karamazov* also illustrates how suffering can distort the personality. The humiliation that Captain Snegiryov has experienced leads to paroxysms of self-destructive self-assertion. The title of book 4, "Lacerations" (*nadryvy*), refs to the pleasure people take in tearing at their own psychic wounds. Katerina Ivanovna actually arranges to be betrayed by her fiancé Dmitri so that she can play the morally superior role of a martyr. Smerdyakov illustrates how victims can feel justified in inflicting suffering on others. Too often, victims make the worst victimizers, as we have noted, both because they feel entitled to revenge themselves and because they know what hurts the most. Father Zossima tells Fyodor Pavlovich Karamazov that "it can be pleasant to take offense," and he replies that it can also be positively beautiful.[90]

When arrested in 1937, Evgeniya Ginzburg explained, "I used to dream of purging my guilt through suffering. By '49 I already knew that suffering can only cleanse up to a point. When it drags on for decades . . . it simply dulls all sensation." "Suffering made me callous," she recognized. "The egoism of those who suffer is probably even more all-embracing than the self-regard of those who are happy."[91] In *Forever Flowing* Grossman observes that one type of person who denounced others to the NKVD exhibited victim psychology, which could always justify any spiteful action. "In his eyes . . . there is a permanently tense, offended, irritated expression. Someone has always just stepped on his toes, and he is invariably engaged in settling scores with someone. The passion of the state for exposing enemies of the people was a find for him."[92] Ivan Karamazov observes that the revolution will be made by the Smerdyakovs.

## Overcoming False Ideals

The Soviet experience intensified the question of life's meaning as it intensified other ultimate questions. In the torture chambers of the Lyubyanka, the idea that life is about personal happiness seemed absurd. Nadezhda Mandelstam reports her husband Osip asking: "Why do you think you should be happy?"[93]

In *The Gulag Archipelago* Solzhenitsyn remarks that those who behaved bravely under extreme conditions were "those who have a stable nucleus, who do not accept that pitiful ideology, which holds that 'human beings are created for happiness,' an ideology which is done in by the first blow of the work assigner's cudgel."[94]

Solzhenitsyn in exile shocked Westerners. In several speeches, he applied the insights he had gained from Russian literature and Soviet totalitarianism to Western life. "When the modern Western states were being formed," Solzhenitsyn observed in his Harvard address, "it was proclaimed as a principle that . . . man lives in order . . . to pursue happiness. (See, for example, the American Declaration of Independence.)" With technical progress and the welfare state, every citizen has in fact acquired "material goods in such quantity and of such quality as to guarantee in theory the achievement of happiness in the debased sense of the word." What has resulted is not happiness—debased or not—but "a weakening of the personality" that threatens the West's survival. Weapons alone are never sufficient. "To defend oneself, one must also be ready to die; there is little such readiness in a society raised in the cult of material well-being."[95] If there is no ideal above personal happiness, no one will sacrifice life for country, civilization, or anything else.

What Solzhenitsyn calls "the humanistic way of thinking," which fails to recognize "any task higher than the attainment of happiness on earth," led, eventually, to the cult of physical well-being and material accumulation "as if human life did not have any higher meaning." For the American founding fathers, happiness was only one goal, but over the centuries "the meaning of life has ceased to be seen as anything more lofty than the 'pursuit of happiness'. . . . It has [even] become embarrassing to appeal to eternal concepts, embarrassing to state that evil makes its home in the individual human heart before it enters a political system."[96]

The West's spiritual enfeeblement should lead people to ask: "Is it true that man is above everything? Is there no Superior Spirit above him?" Are there no values and "eternal concepts" outside material life? "Let us ask ourselves," he concluded his Templeton lecture, "are not the ideals of our century false?" We must look at existence differently by recognizing that "our life consists not in the pursuit of material success but in the quest for worthy spiritual growth. . . . Material laws alone do not explain life or give it direction." Significant striving, purpose beyond satisfaction, and goals not felt to be arbitrarily chosen, all depend on acknowledging something higher than ourselves. For a life to be meaningful, "it has to be the fulfillment of a permanent, earnest duty so that one's life's journey may become above all an experience of moral growth."[97]

## Ecclesiastes

Characters in Russian literature often oscillate between uncompromising idealism and absolute relativism, with no middle ground. So far as the great realist writers are concerned, neither extreme allows for a truly meaningful life. We live in a world of better or worse, and our knowledge never attains perfection.

Pierre begins *War and Peace* in a state of absolute, pathological nihilism that leaves him incapable of acting. He cannot keep his promises because, he tells himself, "all these words of honor are mere conventions, having no definite meaning, especially if one considers that one may be dead by tomorrow, or something so extraordinary might happen that there would no longer be any question of honor or dishonor."[98] After his wife's infidelity and his duel with Dolokhov, Pierre thinks:

> I am guilty and I must bear [...] what? The disgrace to my name, the unhappiness of my life? Oh, that's all nonsense ... the disgrace to my name and honor, that's all a convention, all apart from myself.
>
> They executed Louis XVI because *they* said he was dishonorable and a criminal ... and they were right from their point of view, just as right as those who died a martyr's death for him.... Then Robespierre was executed for being a despot. Who is right, and who is to blame? No one [...] And is it worth tormenting oneself when one has only a moment to live in comparison with eternity?[99]

When Pierre finds some philosophy satisfying his hunger for meaning, it sooner or later crumbles to dust. Since there is no middle ground for him, the slightest step away from certainty leads him back to "Louis XVI." As we have seen, Pierre's escape from meaninglessness comes only when he "throws away the telescope" with which he gazed over the heads of people and learns to appreciate the ever-changing life surrounding him.

In several Chekhov stories, a character experiences an "Ecclesiastes moment," in which it seems that all activity, and therefore life itself, is pointless, a striving after the wind. Perhaps the most profound of these philosophical tales is "Lights."

Ananyev, the lead engineer building a railway, finds his effort rewarding. Staring at the lights extending to the horizon, he reflects on the progress of work. "You and I are building a railway," he comments to his assistant Baron Von Schtenberg, "and after we are gone, in another century or two, good men will build a factory, a school, a hospital, and things will begin to move!" Von Schtenberg replies that such optimism is misplaced. The lights remind him of the campfires of ancient peoples before a battle. "Once Philistines and Amalekites were living in this world, making wars, playing their part," he explains, "and now no trace of them remains. So it will be with us. Now we are making a railway ... but two thousand years will pass—and of this embankment and of all those men, asleep after their hard work, not one grain of dust will remain. In reality, it's awful!"[100]

To the story's narrator, Von Schtenberg's "slightly ironical, dreamy face" expresses "spiritual stagnation and mental sloth.... And on his intelligent face I read: I don't see any good in definite work.... It's all nonsense. I was in Petersburg, now I am sitting here. . . . What sense there is in all that I don't know and no one knows."[101]

"I hate those ideas with all my heart," Ananyev replies. "Thoughts of the aimlessness of life, of the insignificance and transitoriness of the visible world, Solomon's 'vanity of vanities,' have been, and are to this day, the highest and final stage of human thought" but only if they are reached through long experience.[102] If one begins with them, these ideas, even if they are expressed in the same words, mean something quite different. Moral ideas differ from propositions in geometry because the process by which they are reached, the life experience they express, necessarily forms an intrinsic part of them.

As we have seen, realist fiction tests ideas by their role in life. "Our thoughts make no one hot or cold," Von Schtenberg objects, but Ananyev asserts that is not so. "Our theory of life is not so innocent as you suppose. In practical life, in contact with human beings," some ideas lead to "horrors and follies."[103] Ananyev then describes how the very ideas Von Schtenberg has propounded once led him astray.

On a visit to the town where he grew up, Ananyev indulged in "the line of thought we have been discussing," which was fashionable in those days. "I was no more than twenty-six at the time, but I knew perfectly well that life was aimless and had no meaning, and that everything was a deception and an illusion . . . that no one is righteous or guilty, that everything was stuff and nonsense." Ananyev recalls finding in this philosophy "something alluring, narcotic in its nature, like tobacco or morphia. It becomes a habit, a craving. You take advantage of every moment of solitude to gloat over thoughts of the aimlessness of life and the darkness of the grave."[104]

Why should such bleak thoughts be so alluring? For one thing, they demonstrate one's superiority to those fools who still believe in something. For another, they free one from moral responsibility. The son of honorable parents, Ananyev felt no uneasiness in paying prostitutes or following high school girls with insulting looks. "One who knows that life is aimless and death inevitable is not interested in the struggle against nature or the conception of sin; whether you struggle or don't, you will die and rot just the same." What's more, this philosophy "denies the significance of each individual personality. It's easy to see that if I deny the personality of some Natalya Stepanovna, it's absolutely nothing to me whether she is insulted or not."[105]

Thinking these thoughts, Ananyev encountered Kisochka, a girl he had known from school. Now a thoughtful woman married to a vulgarian, she is looking for something noble and so Ananyev finds it easy to seduce her. Listening to her, another man might have experienced romantic feelings, Ananyev recalls, but he only thought: "All this is very impressive, but the time will come when of that building and of Kisochka and her troubles and of me with my thoughts, not one grain of dust will remain [. . .] all is nonsense and vanity."[106]

For Ananyev, the affair was an ordinary amatory episode, but for Kisochka, he realizes, it was a complete revolution in life. When in spite of all his vows he abandons her the next day, he unexpectedly feels guilty. "I had committed a crime as bad as murder. My conscience tormented me," he recalls. "To stifle this unbearable feeling, I assured myself that everything was nonsense and vanity, that Kisochka and I would die and decay, that her grief was nothing in comparison with death, and so on, and so on [. . .] and that if you come to that, there's no such thing as free will, and therefore I was not to blame."[107] But these reflections no longer had the desired effect.

For the first time, Ananyev was not just professing fashionable ideas, but "was really thinking eagerly and intensely." Experience reveals that he did not really believe what he thought he believed. Now that he is thinking in earnest, he recognizes that his borrowed ideas are worthless. "Now through suffering I realized that I had neither convictions nor a definite moral standard, nor heart, nor reason; my whole intellectual and moral wealth consisted of specialist knowledge . . . other people's ideas, and nothing else."[108] If Ananyev had not murdered anyone, he reflects, that was not due to any convictions but to habit. And he also realized that a great many people of his generation had also mistaken pseudo-thinking for real thought.

An irritated Von Schtenberg replies that he is not convinced. Of course, Ananyev answers, "do you suppose I claim to do that? . . . To convince you is impossible. You can reach conviction only by way of personal experience." Von Schtenberg mocks Ananyev's "queer logic" that the truth of an idea depends on whether the one who accepts it has gray hair. "If these ideas are poison, they are equally poisonous for all," he asserts. Again Ananyev explains that the same words may not reflect the same experience. Older people's pessimism "comes to them not casually from the outside, but from the depths of their own brains, and only after they have studied . . . have suffered, have made no end of mistakes, when they have climbed the whole ladder from the bottom up." Their pessimism neither feeds the ego nor justifies immoral behavior, but "rests . . . on a Christian foundation because it is derived from love of humanity" rather than love of self. "You despise life because its meaning and object are hidden just from you, and you are afraid of your own death," Ananyev explains, "while the real thinker is unhappy because the truth is hidden from all and he is afraid for all men."[109]

After Von Schtenberg retires, Ananyev observes to the narrator: "Those lights remind the Baron of the Amalekites, but it seems to me that they are like the thoughts of men [...] You know the thoughts of each individual man are scattered like that in disorder, stretch in a straight line towards some goal in the midst of the darkness, and without shedding light on anything, ... they vanish somewhere beyond old age."[110] If meaning can only be earned through experience, and life is too short for anyone's experience to be extensive, then wisdom entails recognizing how little we know. Von Schtenberg errs not only in what he believes, and not only in how he has come to believe it, but in the supreme confidence with which he holds his beliefs. Chekhov's wisest characters arrive not at final answers, but at a deeper understanding of questions.

## An Unbroken Chain

Despair and meaningfulness, the two extremes of human experience: in Chekhov's story "The Student," readers trace the hero's movement from one to the other. A masterpiece of concision, the story has justly earned the reputation as one of the greatest in world literature.

While seminary student Ivan Velikopolsky is returning home on Good Friday, the fine weather abruptly changes. "A cold wind blew inappropriately from the east, and everything sank into silence." It seems to the hungry young man that the cold "had destroyed the order and harmony of things, that nature itself felt ill at ease, and that was why the darkness was falling more rapidly than usual."[111]

The universe appears entirely indifferent to human life. Shrinking from the cold, Ivan thinks

> that just such a wind had blown in the time of Riurik [ninth-century founder of the Russian state] and in the time of Ivan the Terrible and Peter, and in their time there had been just the same desperate poverty and hunger, the same thatched roofs with holes in them, ignorance, misery, the same desolation around, the same darkness, the same feeling of oppression—all these had existed, did exist, and would exist, and the lapse of a thousand years would make life no better. And he did not want to go home.[112]

Ivan approaches a garden belonging to two widows, a mother and daughter. Vasilisa, the mother, "a woman of experience, who had been in service with the gentry . . . expressed herself with refinement," while her stupid daughter Lukerya, "who had been crushed by her husband," remains dumb. As it is Good Friday, Ivan recalls that the apostle Peter also warmed himself by a fire, so it must have been cold then, too. Ivan recounts how Jesus tells Peter that before the cock crows, he will deny him thrice; how Judas betrays Jesus to his tormentors; and how, when Jesus is arrested, a frightened Peter asserts three times that he does not know Jesus. Abruptly remembering Jesus's prediction, Peter, who deeply loved Jesus, "went out and wept bitterly," according to the Gospel. "I imagine it," Ivan elucidates. "The still, still, dark, dark garden, and in the stillness faintly audible, smothered sobbing."[113]

Emotion overcomes the two women. Vasilisa cries and screens her face, while Lukerya's "expression became strained and heavy like that of someone enduring intense pain."[114] Evidently the story resonates deeply with their own lives. We ask: have they, too, been betrayed? Or have they, like Peter, been false to someone they love? Chekhov has the tact not to tell us.

Ivan departs into the cold wind. Evidently winter has returned—a betrayal of the promise of spring?—and it did not feel possible that the day after tomorrow would be Easter. He reflects on the widows' reaction to the story. Clearly what had happened nineteen centuries ago "had a relation to the present—to both women, to the desolate village, to himself, to all people." Vasilisa had wept not because of Ivan's skill at storytelling "but because Peter was near to her, because her whole being was interested in what was passing in Peter's soul."[115]

Joy stirs in Ivan's soul and he senses an entirely different world. Instead of hopeless indifference, he experiences a deep connection with people past and present.

> "The past," he thought, "is linked with the present by an unbroken chain of events flowing one out of another." And it seemed to him that he had just seen both ends of that chain; that when he touched one end of that chain, the other quivered . . . he thought that truth and beauty which had guided human life there in the garden and in the yard of the high priest had continued without interruption to this day, and had evidently always been the chief thing in human life, and in all earthly life.[116]

Chekhov has shown us two contrary states of the human soul. The story ends—almost—with a sense of the world's meaningfulness: "The feeling of youth, health, vigor—he was only twenty-two—and the inexpressible sweet expectation of happiness, of unknown mysterious happiness, took possession of him little by little, and life seemed to him enchanting, marvelous, and full of lofty meaning."[117] "He was only twenty-two": the feeling that possesses Ivan may be a lasting appreciation of life's mysteries, but it may also result from youthful health and inexperience. For that matter, so may his initial despair. Once more, Chekhov does not answer ultimate questions but deepens our understanding of them.

## Unpublished Poetry

Bolshevik ethics notwithstanding, meaningfulness cannot be reduced to effectiveness. Interrogation by torture, enforced starvation, labor at seventy degrees below zero, Nazi death camps: these horrors destroy life and embody evil, but they do not negate the possibility of meaning. The greatest Soviet writers—Shalamov and Grossman no less than Solzhenitsyn—locate meaningfulness, as well as goodness, in an objective realm apart from the chain of cause and effect. As Levin discovers, it cannot be studied by physical science or reduced to social causes. It is not something that just happens to one, but something one must choose and work for. It implies, and depends on, human freedom.

The narrator of Shalamov's story "My First Tooth" describes the appalling conditions under which he and other convicts were transported to Siberia. At roll call, a religious sectarian for some reason refuses to stand up and the guard punches him in the face. "All at once," the narrator explains,

> I felt a burning sensation in my chest and I realized that the meaning of my whole life was about to be decided. If I didn't do something—what exactly, I didn't know—it would mean that my arrival with this group of convicts was in vain, that twenty years of my life had been pointless.
>
> The burning flush of shame over my cowardliness fled from my cheeks. I felt them cool down and my body tighten.
>
> I stepped out of line and said in a trembling voice:
>
> "How dare you beat that man!"[118]

The intervention does no good, of course. And late that night the narrator is punished by being made to stand naked in the snow and then kicked in the face so his tooth falls out. But consequences are beside the point; what matters is doing the right thing.

We recall that in Shalamov's story imagining poet Osip Mandelstam's death, the poet realizes that it does not matter that the verse he is creating will never be published.

It exists eternally. "The poet understood that he was composing real po-etry," the narrator paraphrases his thought. "And who cares if it was written down or not? Recording and printing was the vanity of vanities. Only that which was born selflessly can be without equal. The best was that which had not been written down, which . . . melted without a trace."[119]

The remainder of the story describes how, after the poet's death, his fellow prisoners keep raising his hand for bread so that they can get his daily ration a bit longer. The story concludes: "So he died before the recorded date of his death—a not insignificant detail for future biographers."[120] But what is signif-icant to biographers does not touch what is truly significant, the realm where poetry resides with the Word.

## Life beyond Fate

Grossman's *Life and Fate* describes the Jewess Sofya Levinton's last mo-ments in a Nazi gas chamber. She thinks of the memories she can never share. That is always the case, she reasons, you can never wholly reveal "the secret of your soul. However passionately it might long to, your soul could never be-tray this secret . . . the miracle of a particular individual" whose conscious and unconscious experience over a lifetime has "fused into the mysterious se-cret of an individual life."[121]

Never having had a family, Sofya senses something missing, but finds meaning as she is dying. She has been comforting a Jewish boy as they walk to the gas chamber and clasps him in her arms as he is dying. This act of conso-lation defines her life. "'I've become a mother,' she thought. That was her last thought."[122]

Such a moment would not make anyone else's life meaningful, Grossman comments. That is because every soul is unique and experiences the sound of oceans, the smell of flowers, and the sadness of autumn in its own way. "What constitutes the freedom, the soul of an individual life, is its uniqueness." "Freedom and meaning" depend on one's existence "as a whole world that has never been repeated in all eternity."[123] Such meaningfulness cannot be conveyed in words, but a novel, and only a novel, can describe how it is achieved.

Chepyzhin, Victor Shtrum's mentor in *Life and Fate*, describes why he sacri-ficed his career by retiring from an immoral line of research. Shtrum contem-plates a similar decision, which will deprive him of his laboratory and the possibility of doing the work he loves. "It must be very hard for you," Chepyzhin observes, "but I'm very glad: honesty is never just wiped off the slate."[124] Like Mandelstam's poetry, honesty leaves its mark, and makes a life meaningful, even when it has no discernible effect.

As *Life and Fate* ends, Alexandra Vladimirovna, the matriarch of that novel and its prequel *Stalingrad*, reflects on her life. All those close to her have suffered. Now she was an old woman, "living and hoping, keeping faith, full of anxiety for the living and an equal concern for the dead . . . wondering why the future of those she loved was so obscure and the past so full of mistakes."[125] In the depths of her soul she senses the meaning of her life, even though she could not verbalize it. She knows as well what makes the lives of those near to her meaningful.

Aware that "at times like these no man can forge his own happiness and that fate alone has the power to pardon or chastise" or "to reduce a man to concentration camp dust," she recognizes that neither the State nor any other external force can affect what is most human about human beings like her loved ones. "No," she reflects, "whatever life holds in store—hard-won glory, poverty and despair, or death in a labor camp—they will live as human beings and die as human beings, the same as those who have already perished; and in this alone lies man's eternal and bitter victory over all the grandiose and in-human forces that have ever been or will be."[126]

Life is shaped by fate, but meaning depends on what we choose.

# Conclusion

## *Into the World Symposium*

LIFE IS ETERNAL DIALOGUE, a world symposium that never ends. In Bakhtin's notebooks we discover his core belief:

> The dialogic nature of human consciousness. The dialogic nature of human life itself. The single adequate form for *verbally expressing* authentic human life is the *open-ended dialogue*. Life by its very nature is dialogic. To live means to participate in dialogue: to ask questions, to heed, to respond, to agree, and so forth. In this dialogue a person participates wholly and throughout his whole life: with his eyes, lips, hands, soul, spirit, and his whole body and deeds. He invests his entire life in discourse, and this discourse enters into the dialogic fabric of human life, into the world symposium.[1]

Literature, especially realist novels and related genres, allows us to sense the spirit of symposium. Then we experience the world as people engaged in conversation. If only more of it could be preserved! "When I walk down the street and catch words, phrases, and exclamations," Alexievich explained in her Nobel Prize speech, "I always think—how many novels disappear without a trace! . . . We haven't been able to capture the conversational side of human life."[2] If life is essentially dialogic, what capture could be more worthwhile?

One dialogue exceeds all others in importance: the dialogue about dialogue itself. The rules of conversation constrain or inspire what can be said about any topic.

Should conversation resemble a catechism or an open-ended exchange surprising to its participants? Does it simply convey known truth from master to pupil? Or do interlocutors make discoveries in the process of attending to each other? Real dialogue entails more than interlocutors speaking in turn. It manifests what Bakhtin called *eventness*: speakers arrive at new insights as they consider the views of others. Instead of refuting each other, they approach the exchange as an opportunity to expand the compass of their own experience.[3]

In *Anna Karenina*, as we have seen, Levin converses with a "reactionary landowner" with whom he disagrees. Their host Sviazhsky dismisses the landowner's opinions out of hand, but Levin listens carefully. He learns something important by reconstructing the experiences that have prompted them: "The landowner unmistakably spoke his own individual thought—a thing that rarely happens—and a thought to which he had been brought not by a desire of finding some exercise for an idle brain, but a thought which had grown up out of the conditions of his life, which he had brooded over in the solitude of his village, and considered in every aspect."[4] Everyone's experience is limited, and so each person's views are necessarily partial, in both senses of that word. One can vicariously extend one's experience by understanding the circumstances informing another person's views—so long as those views actually arise from experience rather than from the need for mental exercise or the desire to think as others do.

Rightly conducted, exchange engenders change. Interlocutors look at things differently. For that to happen, one must be willing to bracket one's own position and try to see the world as the other person does. What has made his view persuasive to him? To what case does the generality he defends implicitly refer? How would my principle deal with that case, and how would he address the case that my generality presumes? If his view seems naïve to me, how does my view strike him? Real dialogue requires empathy, both intellectual and emotional.[5]

No one understood empathy better than Chekhov, and the power of his stories largely derives from perspectives layered upon each other so subtly that readers find it difficult to recognize when one has shaded into another. Maxim Gorky's reminiscences describe Chekhov's ability to advocate a view passionately and then, without warning, to look at it from an outside perspective that makes it appear faintly ridiculous. At such moments, Gorky reports,

> a fine network of wrinkles showed at the corners [of his eyes], deepening
> his glance. He looked around him and began making fun of himself.
>     "There you are—I've treated you to a full-length leading article from
> a liberal newspaper. Come on, I'll give you some tea as a reward for your
> patience [. . .]"
>     This was often the way with him. One moment he would be talking
> with warmth, gravity, and sincerity, and the next, he would be laughing at
> himself and his own words. And beneath this gentle, sorrowful laughter
> could be felt the subtle skepticism of a man who knew the value of
> words. . . . There was a shade of his attractive modesty, his intuitive deli-
> cacy in this laughter, too.[6]

Dialogue requires the "modesty" of regarding one's opinion not as the center of truth around which other beliefs revolve, as planets revolve around the Ptolemaic earth, but as one of many possible beliefs, like planets in the Copernican or Galilean solar system. From this "Galilean" perspective, as Bakhtin calls it, one appreciates that firm conviction never guarantees truthfulness.[7]

Herzen's dialogues in *From the Other Shore* exhibit this dialogic spirit with special power. Dostoevsky attributed their success to "Herzen's superb capacity for self-reflection. Self-reflection—the ability to make of his own deepest feelings an object which he could set before him, pay it tribute, and, in the next breath, perhaps, ridicule it—was a thing he had developed to the highest degree."[8] Dostoevsky's own articles often turn unexpectedly into imagined dialogues as he intuits the ironic replies of opponents and then tries, not always successfully, to answer them. Dostoevsky recalled how he once expressed to Herzen his admiration for the dialogues in *From the Other Shore:*

> "What I especially like . . . is that your opponent is also very clever. You
> must agree that in many instances he backs you right to the wall."
>     "Why, that's the essence of the whole piece," laughed Herzen. "I'll tell
> you a story. Once . . . Belinsky . . . sat me down to listen to him read his
> article, 'A Conversation Between Mr. A and Mr. B'. . . . Mr. A, who is Be-
> linsky himself . . is made out to be very clever, while his opponent, Mr. B,
> is rather shallow. When Belinsky had finished reading, he asked me with
> feverish anticipation:

"'Well, what do you think?'

"'Oh, it's fine, very fine, and it's obvious you are very clever. But whatever made you waste your time talking to a fool like that?'

"Belinsky threw himself on the sofa, buried his face in a pillow, and shouted, laughing for all he was worth:

"'Oh, you've got me there, you really have!'"[9]

## The Fox Knows Many Truths

"The fox knows many truths, but the hedgehog knows one big thing," wrote the Greek poet Archilochus in a line that inspired Isaiah Berlin. A Russian thinker given to commenting on other Russian thinkers, Berlin remarked on "the chasm between those [hedgehogs], on one side, who relate everything to a single central vision . . . a single universal organizing principle . . . and, on the other side, those [foxes] who pursue many ends . . . and entertain ideas that are centrifugal rather than centripetal."[10] Dante and Hegel exemplify the first type of thinker, Erasmus and Shakespeare the second. Chernyshevsky outdid Hegel (if that is possible) as a hedgehog, while Chekhov displayed perfect foxiness. Berlin especially loved Herzen's foxy dialogues. Whatever vocabulary one uses to describe it, true dialogue invites us into a world of novelty, playfulness, discovery, and self-discovery.

Berlin describes the moment when he recognized the mistake of assuming that "all genuine questions must have one true answer . . . all the rest being necessarily errors" and that "the true answers, when found, must necessarily be compatible with one another, and form a single whole."[11] On the contrary, a genuine plurality of values obtains and so "some among the Great Goods cannot live together. . . . We are doomed to choose, and every choice may entail an irreparable loss."[12] In Problems of Idealism, Semyon Frank made much the same pluralistic point:

The totality of the moral feelings people experience and the moral principles they recognize cannot be reduced to one supreme axiom from which all of them would derive, like conclusions from a logical premise. There exists no single moral postulate from which it would be possible to develop a logical system of ethics encompassing, without exception, all the judgments that bring phenomena under the categories of "good" and "evil." The complex and intricate pattern of the moral world cannot be unraveled by finding the end of one of its threads, for this pattern is formed from many interweaving and mutually intersecting threads . . . a number of basic principles that are independent of each other.[13]

We may recall Pierre's acknowledgment, at the end of *War and Peace*, "of the possibility of every man thinking, feeling, and seeing things in his own way. This legitimate individuality of every man's views, which formerly troubled or irritated Pierre, now became the basis of the sympathy he felt for other people and the interest that he took in them."[14] Given human difference and the plurality of viewpoints, wisdom consists in learning to see the world from the perspectives of others. By intellectual as well as emotional empathy, we can bring discrete positions into open-ended dialogue. When we do, we enrich both ourselves and the world.

## Singing in Chorus

Hedgehogs often triumph over foxes because they promise more. Has anyone ever founded a school or commanded a significant following by limiting his claims to the evidence?[15] Those certain they know the truth once and for all—the certaintists—often regard skeptics as cowards and consider open-ended dialogue pointless. As there can be no "honest disagreement" about Newton's laws, only noxious bourgeois vermin (as Lenin referred to his opponents) could benefit from a free-wheeling conversation about the science of Marxism. For hedgehogs, dialogue can make no further discoveries because there is nothing left to discover.

For certaintists, open-endedness can only lead participants astray. Encountering someone who disagreed with him, Lenin, as we have seen, regarded discourse not as a vehicle for discovery or negotiation but as an opportunity to "pin the convict's badge" on him and his supporters. Vera Figner, as we also saw, presumed that if all means of persuasion fail, then, of course, one had to resort to dynamite.

Sometimes the one "with the truth in his pocket" (as socialist leader Victor Chernov described Lenin) encounters a willing listener.[16] In that case, the exchange consists of the teacher's statements and the student's acknowledgments of their correctness. After the initial conversation with Thrasymachus, Plato's *Republic* consists largely of Socrates's explications of his ideas and Glaucon's expressions of assent: "Unquestionably," "I agree," "Yes," "Quite true," "I think that is perfectly true."[17] Such undialogic dialogues characterize all literary utopias, since they presume that the truth is known and only needs to be implemented. They recur in William Morris's *News from Nowhere*, Edward Bellamy's

*Looking Backward, 2000–1887,* and countless less influential works.[18] In Chernyshevsky's *What Is to Be Done?,* Marya Alekseevna eavesdrops on a conversation between Vera Pavlovna and Lopukhov:

"[...] But must one view life that way?" (These were the first words Marya Alekseevna overheard.)

"Yes, Vera Pavlovna, one must."

"In other words, those cold and practical people are telling the truth when they say that man is governed exclusively by the calculation of his own advantage?"

"Yes, they are telling the truth" ...

"Let us assume that you're right—yes, you are right. All actions, as far as I can see, can be explained by advantage. But isn't that theory rather cold?"

"Theory is supposed to be cold. The mind is supposed to make judgments about things coldly."[19]

Such dialogues might as well be lectures, and Solzhenitsyn's *In the First Circle* features a lecture on dialectical materialism in which the speaker proclaims as an absolute truth that "there are no absolute truths." Listening to the lecturer assert that "matter is indestructible, that is not open to dispute!" a physicist, thinking of Einstein's theory of matter's convertibility into energy, wonders how the lecturer would account for the vanishing of "four million tons of solar substance ... in a single second," but does not dare voice this question.[20] Certainty precludes dialogue.

One might laugh at putative certainty, however, and in Soviet conditions jokes ridiculed what could not be argued against.[21] *The Master and Margarita* begins with Woland's mockery of Berlioz's smug atheism. Woland's assistant and "translator," the "ex-choirmaster" Korovyov, plays practical jokes based on the Soviet project of transforming each "I" into a mere particle of "We." Under his spell, one official literally becomes an empty suit. And as we have seen, a group of office workers, constantly dragooned into clubs, find themselves unable to stop singing in chorus. "And suddenly they started singing the second verse as if of their own accord. . . . They went back to their places, but before they could manage to sit down, they started singing against their will. It was beyond their power to stop."[22]

Singing in chorus feels so much easier than thinking for oneself! "The main misfortune, the root of all the evil to come," Lara explains in *Doctor Zhivago,* "was the loss of confidence in the value of one's own opinion. People imagined that it was out of date to follow their own moral sense, that they must all sing in chorus, and live by other people's notions."[23] As we have seen, Solzhenitsyn described the moment he realized that his atheism was not a real conviction but "a thought planted from outside."[24] Evgeniya Ginzburg, too, recalled the time when she first thought for herself: "For the first time in my life I was faced by the problem of having to think things out for myself—of analyzing the circumstances and deciding my own attitude."[25]

Dostoevsky appealed to readers not to don the "uniform" of "other people's opinions." We recognize Stiva Oblonsky's inauthenticity when Tolstoy explains that his opinions always coincided with those of his circle, and he changed them only when others did—"or, more accurately speaking, they seemed to change of themselves within him."[26]

There can be no true dialogue when participants efface their particularity. Individual perspectives must exist before they can interact. Dostoevsky, Solzhenitsyn, and Grossman offer subtle accounts of the special "hypnosis" (as Grossman calls it) and "bewitchment" (Solzhenitsyn's term) that inclines people to agree with others. "Only people who have never felt such a force can be surprised" by its power, Grossman observes.[27] As we saw, Solzhenitsyn's Vorotyntsev experiences that power and asks himself: "What is it that always forces us to adapt the general tone? . . . He tried not to show even by his expression how much he disagreed." Though he opposes the views shared by all others at the Kadet gathering, Vorotyntsev "gave ground, held his peace. Not because he felt he was wrong, but out of fear of saying something *reactionary*."[28] "Courage in war and courage of thought are two different things," Alexievich observed. "I used to think they were the same."[29]

"What we wanted was for the course of history to be made smooth . . . so . . . everything would flow evenly and according to plan," Nadezhda Mandelstam explained the desire to replace dialogue with monologue. We looked to "Wise Leaders" for "foolproof prescriptions," with no disagreement or doubt allowed. As Dostoevsky's Grand Inquisitor foresaw, certainty about means and goals was a goal in itself. "In our blindness we ourselves struggled to impose unanimity—because in every disagreement, we saw the beginnings of a new anarchy and chaos. And so by silence and consent" we aided the regime's accumulation of ruthless power.[30]

Dostoevsky compared the ideal of perfect agreement to an anthill, and the sociologist Pitirim Sorokin, hiding in a forest from the Bolsheviks, came across "a huge anthill and I sat down to watch their communistic labors. . . . Not from Marx or other ignorant ideologists, but from these ants should the Communists and Socialists have learned their theories. If they could but transform the human race into ants ... what an ideal communistic society they would create. But as long as human beings love freedom and independence [of thought] ... communistic aspirations must forever fail." Bolshevik success, he opined, depended on "mob mind."[31]

## Laughter

"It would be extremely interesting to write the history of laughter," remarked Herzen.[32] Bakhtin quotes this observation in his book on Rabelais, which offers one chapter in that history.

In laughter, and especially in laughter at oneself, Bakhtin discovered the dialogic spirit. The one who laughs stands outside the world and regards himself as no less limited, and therefore no less comic, than anyone else.[33]

Laughter is not just a bodily reflex, Bakhtin explained, it "has a deep philosophical meaning, it is one of the essential forms of truth concerning the world as a whole ... the world is seen anew, no less (and perhaps more) profoundly than seen from the serious standpoint."[34] By contrast, utopian writers are nothing if not dead serious. Possessing the one truth to redeem the world from misery, they detect in frivolity nothing but the frivolous. Humor seems uncalled for, inappropriate, even scandalous, which is why Socrates, in *The Republic*, proposes to rewrite the Homeric poems so that heroes should not "be overmuch given to laughter."[35] To the extent that utopian fiction does allow for humor, it casts irony on the ideal it describes.[36]

Jokes could be fatal in the Soviet Union. "In 1938 M[andelstam] even declared he had invented a device for the suppression of jokes as a dangerous thing," Nadezhda Mandelstam recalled. "He would move his lips silently and point at his throat to indicate the position of the cut-off device. But the 'device' didn't help and M. couldn't stop telling jokes."[37]

Laughter withers ideologies. Claims of infallibility preclude "standing outside" one's beliefs. Since laughter often erupts spontaneously, a humorist can provoke an audience of certaintists to betray unawares the ideology they profess. Before they realize it, they have viewed their beliefs less than seriously. Soon enough, they may sternly deny that what they laughed at is the least bit funny.

Bakhtin cited Herzen's observation that "Voltaire's laughter was more destructive than Rousseau's weeping." For Bakhtin, Rabelais expressed the spirit of laughter better than any other writer. "No dogma, no authoritarianism, no narrow-minded seriousness can coexist with Rabelasian images," he observed. "These images are opposed to all that is finished and polished, to all pomposity to every ready-made solution in the sphere of thought and world outlook."[38] Play dethrones certainty and humor encourages fearless experimentation. Together they bring what had been reverentially distant near to us, where we can detect its flaws and pretensions. "Laughter has the remarkable power of making an object come up close," Bakhtin observed, "of drawing it into a zone of crude contact where one can finger it familiarly on all sides, turn it upside down, inside out, peer at it from above and below, break open its external shell, look into its center, doubt it, take it apart, dismantle it, lay it bare and expose it, examine it freely and experiment with it."[39] When laughter erupts, the indubitable becomes doubtful.

## Novelistic Truth

> When I walk down the street and catch words, phrases, and exclamations,
> I always think—how many novels disappear without a trace! . . .
> We haven't been able to capture the conversational side of human life.
>
> —SVETLANA ALEXIEVICH, NOBEL PRIZE LECTURE

Comic genres promote dialogue, but it is the realist novel that allows dialogue to flourish the most. Beginning with Jane Austen, novelists allowed readers to trace a character's thoughts and feelings from within and, in this way, to identify with people unlike themselves.[40] One lives in the minds and hearts of people from a different nationality, epoch, gender, profession, social class, manners, and set of cultural assumptions. One need not be a Russian, an aristocrat, a woman, or a holder of nineteenth-century values to identify with Anna Karenina and wince at her self-destructive choices. Across all the social categories distinguishing us from her we recognize in her shortcomings our own bad mental habits.

We recognize them in other major characters as well. Readers of *Middlemarch* and *Anna Karenina* inhabit several consciousnesses in turn, so when people with different beliefs argue they sense from within why each reacts to the others in a specific way. In so doing, readers can come to understand even misunderstanding.

Novels also realize the potential conflict of points of view that in life have not yet encountered each other. We attend to dialogues that may someday happen. When they do, the novelist seems prophetic, as Dostoevsky often has.

Switching perspectives from character to character, readers practice empathy and learn to regard their own views from the outside. Gradually, consciousness becomes "foxy" and "Galilean." Stories that depict how others respond to stories may dramatize how this change of consciousness happens.[41]

Unlike utopias and saints' lives, realist novels do not presume they possess the absolute truth. The realist novel speculates in categories of ignorance, makes its home in uncertainty, and dwells in the land of opinion. The author never claims to have understood everything about a person. She presents her own beliefs as challengeable. They derive not from divine revelation, mathematical proof, or scientific demonstration, but from experience. They are not definitive, and what they offer is not perfect knowledge but unformalizable wisdom. Because they are open to challenge, they invite conversation.

Realist novels represent views not as impersonal propositions but as emotionally charged thoughts in the consciousness of particular people. They give us not the objective view from nowhere, but a perspective from somewhere specific. As Ananyev explains in Chekhov's "Lights," the "same" belief means something different when it is the product of a different experience. Novelists and story writers reveal the subjective roots of each claim to objectivity. Each enunciated truth resounds in the voice of a specific person with her own psychology and social experience.

Only the personal voice can enter into dialogue. Abstract positions do not contain the potential for surprise, and when they encounter each other they interact mechanically. As Bakhtin explained, that is the difference between Hegelian or Marxist "dialectics" on the one hand and real dialogue on the other: "Take a dialogue and remove the voices . . . remove the intonations (emotional and individualizing ones), carve out abstract concepts and judgements from living words and responses, cram everything into one abstract consciousness—and that's how you get dialectics." Dialogue cannot be reduced to "a mechanical contact of 'oppositions.'" It presumes "the world as an event (and not as existence in ready-made form)."[42]

It is even possible to conceive of truth itself as dialogic, in the sense that one approaches it most closely not as separable abstract propositions from which a system can be built but as an open-ended conversation. A "monologic" system can in principle be contained in a single consciousness. It can be fixed and "finalized," whereas a dialogic conversation is eventful and "unfinalizable." Both conceptions of truth have their place, and we need each for different aspects of experience. "It is quite possible," Bakhtin explained, "to postulate a unified truth that requires a plurality of consciousnesses, one that cannot in principle be fitted into the bounds of a single consciousness, one that is, so to speak, *full of event potential* and is born at a point of contact among various consciousnesses."[43]

Just as Aristotle maintained we need both theoretical and practical reasoning, the same may be said of "monologic" (systemic) and dialogic conceptions of truth. Ethics and cultural understanding, but not mathematics or astronomy, require empathy. "The monologic way of perceiving cognition and truth is only one possible way. It arises only where consciousness is placed above existence."[44]

For action arising from empathy, for understanding among specific people, and for ethics requiring personal commitment, conversational truth may be most appropriate. There is no alibi for dialogue. Could that be one reason our richest understanding of ethics is to be found in novels?

## The Conversation Continues

If this study has a hero, it is Chekhov. When criticized for not adopting a "tendency," he insisted that the writer's job is to deepen our understanding of the facts of the world. The facts he had in mind include the perception of facts and the perception of other people's perceptions of facts. We live in a world of active consciousnesses. Responding to his friend A. S. Suvorin's criticism that his story "Lights" (which we considered in Chapter 11) does not conclude by endorsing a particular philosophy, Chekhov explained "that the writer's function is only to describe by whom, how, and under what conditions" questions arise, not to answer them.[45] "It is time for writers . . . to admit that you can't figure out anything in this world" once and for all.[46] We recall that Chekhov's novella *The Duel* closes with several utterances of the sentence "Nobody knows the real truth," and that his play *The Three Sisters* ends with Olga repeating: "if we only knew, if we only knew!"[47]

"You are right in demanding that an artist approach his work consciously," Chekhov observed to Suvorin, "but you are confusing two concepts: *the solution of a problem and the correct formulation of a problem.* Only the second is required of the artist. Not a single problem is resolved in *Anna Karenina* or [*Eugene*] *Onegin*, but they satisfy you completely only because all the problems in them are formulated correctly."[48]

The greatest literature advances understanding not by supplying final answers to eternally open questions but by revealing new depths in the questions themselves. Wisdom begins with better questions posed more thoughtfully, and literature, if it accomplishes what it should, leaves its readers wiser.

Near the end of *The Master and Margarita*, Pontius Pilate dreams he

> set out on a shining road and ascended straight to the moon. He even laughed in his sleep with happiness, so splendid and unique was every-

thing on that light-blue, transparent road. He was accompanied by [his faithful dog] Banga and alongside him was the vagrant philosopher [Jesus]. They were arguing about something complex and important, and neither one of them could convince the other. They did not agree about anything, and that made their dispute all the more engaging and endless.[49]

Rightly conducted, the conversation about ultimate questions remains "engaging and endless."

Let us keep the conversation going.

.

# Abbreviations

A1914    Aleksandr Solzhenitsyn, *August 1914: The Red Wheel /
          Knot I*, trans. H. T. Willetts (New York: Farrar, Straus and
          Giroux, 1990).

AK         Leo Tolstoy, *Anna Karenina,* Garnett translation revised by
          Leonard J. Kent and Nina Berberova (New York: Modern Library,
          1965).

AKDoC   Aileen M. Kelly, *The Discovery of Chance: The Life and Thought of
          Alexander Herzen* (Cambridge, MA: Harvard University Press,
          2016).

AWD      Fyodor Dostoevsky, *A Writer's Diary*, ed. and trans. Kenneth
          Lantz (Evanston, IL: Northwestern University Press, 1993 [vol. 1]
          and 1994 [vol.2]).

BK         Fyodor Dostoevsky, *The Brothers Karamazov,* trans. Constance
          Garnett (New York: Modern Library, 1950).

C&P       Fyodor Dostoevsky, *Crime and Punishment,* trans. Constance
          Garnett (New York: Random House, 1950).

Ch13     Anton Chekhov, *The Tales of Chekhov,* trans. Constance Garnett,
          13 vols. (reprinted New York: Ecco Press, 1984–1987). Volume 1 =
          Ch13-1, volume 2 = Ch13-2, etc.

ChSS     A. P. Chekhov, *Sobranie sochinenii,* ed. V. V. Ermilov (Moscow:
          Pravda, 1950).

CRP     Richard Wortman, *The Crisis of Russian Populism* (Cambridge: Cambridge University Press, 1967).

DZ     Boris Pasternak, *Doctor Zhivago*, trans. Max Hayward and Manya Harari (New York: Random House, 1958).

F&S     Ivan Turgenev, *Fathers and Sons*, ed. Ralph E. Matlaw (New York: Norton, 1966).

FTOS     Alexander Herzen, *"From the Other Shore" and "The Russian People and Socialism,"* trans. Moura Budberg and Richard Wollheim (Oxford: Oxford University Press, 1979).

FUTR     Alexander Solzhenitsyn and six others, *From Under the Rubble*, trans. by six translators under the supervision of Michael Scammell (Chicago: Regnery Gateway, 1981).

HAH     Nadezhda Mandelstam, *Hope Against Hope: A Memoir*, trans. Max Hayward (New York: Atheneum, 1976).

IiR     "Intelligentsiia v Rossii," in *"Vekhi," "Intelligentsiia v Rossii": Sborniki statei, 1909–1910* (Moscow: Molodaia gvardiia, 1991).

ITFC     Aleksandr Solzhenitsyn, *In the First Circle*, trans. Harry T. Willetts (New York: Harper, 2009).

L&F     Vasily Grossman, *Life and Fate: A Novel*, trans. Robert Chandler (New York: Harper and Row, 1987).

MWS     Gary Saul Morson and Morton Schapiro, *Minds Wide Shut: How the New Fundamentalisms Divide Us* (Princeton, NJ: Princeton University Press, 2021).

P     Fyodor Dostoevsky, *The Possessed*, trans. Constance Garnett (New York: Modern Library, 1963).

RP2     *Russian Philosophy*, ed. James M. Edie et al., vol. 2 (Chicago: Quadrangle Books, 1969).

S     *Signposts*, trans. and ed. Marshall S. Shatz and Judith E. Zimmerman (Irvine, CA: Charles Schlacks, Jr., 1986).

SR     *The Solzhenitsyn Reader*, ed. Edward E. Ericson, Jr. and Daniel J. Mahoney (Wilmington, DE: ISI Books, 2015).

TSK  Anna Geifman, *Thou Shalt Kill: Revolutionary Terrorism in Russia, 1894-1917* (Princeton, NJ: Princeton University Press, 1993).

UFW  Svetlana Alexievich, *The Unwomanly Face of War: An Oral History of Women in World War II*, trans. Richard Pevear and Larissa Volokhonsky (New York: Random House, 2017).

UR  Stepniak, *Underground Russia: Revolutionary Profiles and Sketches from Life*, 2nd edition (New York: Scribners, 1888).

W&P  Leo Tolstoy, *War and Peace*, trans. Ann Dunnigan (New York: Signet, 1980).

WITBD  Nikolay Chernyshevsky, *What Is to Be Done?*, trans. Michael R. Katz (Ithaca, NY: Cornell University Press, 1989).

# *Notes*

## Introduction

1. For Bakhtin's extensive discussion of the "dialogue of the dead" as a form of Menippean satire with special relevance to Dostoevsky, see Mikhail Bakhtin, *Problems of Dostoevsky's Poetics*, trans. Caryl Emerson (Minneapolis: University of Minnesota Press, 1984), chapter 4.

2. Matthew Stewart, *The Courtier and the Heretic: Leibniz, Spinoza, and the Fate of God in the Modern World* (New York: Norton, 2006); Steven Nadler, *The Best of All Possible Worlds: A Story of Philosophers, God, and Evil* (New York: Farrar, Straus, and Giroux, 2008); David Edmonds and John Eidenow, *Wittgenstein's Poker: The Story of a Ten-Minute Argument Between Two Great Philosophers* (New York: HarperCollins, 2001); Dennis C. Rasmussen, *The Infidel and the Professor: David Hume, Adam Smith, and the Friendship That Shaped Modern Thought* (Princeton, NJ: Princeton University Press, 2019).

3. As cited in Stephen Miller, "The Death of Hume," *Wilson Quarterly* 19, no. 3 (Summer 1995): 32.

4. Voltaire, "Conversation of Lucian, Erasmus, and Rabelais," *Candide and Other Writings*, ed. Haskell M. Block (New York: Modern Library, 1956), 469.

5. Much of the humor in Ivan Karamazov's conversation with the devil derives from the devil's insistence that the other world *is* historical and follows human intellectual fashions. Cosmology completely shifted after Copernicus, and nowadays distances are measured according to the metric system, he explains.

6. BK, 277–278.

7. AWD, 942.

8. BK, 776.

9. P, 249, 253.

10. W&P, 471–472.

11. Alexei Pisemsky, *One Thousand Souls*, trans. Ivy Litvinov (New York: Grove, 1959), 291–293.

12. Ivan Turgenev, *A House of Gentlefolk*, trans. Constance Garnett (London: William Heinemann, 1894; reprinted New York: AMS, 1970), 143–144. *A Nest of Gentlefolk* is the literal translation of the Russian title.

13. DZ, 456.

14. As John Ellis has observed, "literary texts are defined as those that are used by society in such a way that *the text is not taken as specifically relevant to the immediate context of its origin*." John M. Ellis, *The Theory of Literary Criticism: A Logical Analysis* (Berkeley: University of California Press, 1974), 44.

15. Harold Orel, "English Critics and the Russian Novel, 1850–1917," *The Slavonic and East European Review* 33, no. 81 (June 1955): 459.

16. John Cowper Powys, *Visions and Revisions: A Book of Literary Devotions* (New York: G. Arnold Shaw, 1915), 235.

17. Virginia Woolf, "The Russian Point of View" (1925), in *The Essays of Virginia Woolf, 1925–1928*, ed. Andrew McNeillier, vol. 4 (Orlando, FL: Harcourt, 1994), 186.

18. Woolf, "Russian Point," 187–188.

19. Woolf, "Russian Point," 189.

20. Arnold Bennett, "Russian Fiction," *The Savour of Life: Essays in Gusto* (Garden City, New York: Doubleday, Doran, and Company, 1928), 127.

21. Henry James, "Preface to *The Tragic Muse*," *The Art of the Novel* (New York: Scribner's, 1934), 84.

22. "To lie to him is impossible," Gorky said of Tolstoy. Maxim Gorky, *Reminiscences of Tolstoy, Chekhov, and Andreyev* (New York: Viking, 1959), 16.

23. Powys, *Visions and Revisions*, 241.

24. J. Middleton Murry, *Fyodor Dostoevsky: A Critical Study* (New York: Russell and Russell, 1966), 33–34.

25. Murry, *Fyodor Dostoevsky*, 5.

26. See the Marquis de Custine, *Empire of the Czar: A Journey Through Eternal Russia* (New York: Doubleday, 1989) and the essay by André Gide in *The God That Failed*, ed. Richard Crossman (New York: Harper Collins, 1949), 165–195.

27. Robert Conquest, *Harvest of Sorrow: Soviet Collectivization and the Terror-Famine* (New York: Oxford University Press, 1986), 1.

28. Dimitri Panin, *The Notebooks of Sologdin*, trans. John Moore (New York: Harcourt Brace, 1976), 232.

29. Panin, *Notebooks*, 81.

30. George Eliot, *Middlemarch* (New York: Modern Library, 1984), II, 335.

31. David Hume, *A Treatise of Human Nature*, ed. L. A. Selby-Bigge, 2nd edition revised by P. H. Nidditch (Oxford: Clarendon Press, 1992), 214.

32. Hume, *Treatise*, 269.

33. Alexander Herzen, "The Russian People and Socialism: An Open Letter to Jules Michelet," FTOS, 200.

34. AWD, 288.

35. Joseph Frank, *Through the Russian Prism: Essays on Literature and Culture* (Princeton, NJ: Princeton University Press, 1990).

36. S, 10–12.

37. C&P, 445.

38. To clear up frequent misunderstandings of Solzhenitsyn's thought, consult Daniel J. Mahoney, *The Other Solzhenitsyn: Telling the Truth about a Misunderstood Writer and Thinker* (South Bend, IN: St. Augustine's Press, 2014).

39. As Turgenev illustrates in *Fathers and Children*, the thinkers of the 1860s responded to their great predecessors from the 1840s, Herzen, Bakunin, and Belinsky. Turgenev's novel is in fact dedicated to Belinsky.

40. As cited in Irina Paperno, *Chernyshevsky and the Age of Realism: A Study in the Semiotics of Behavior* (Stanford, CA: Stanford University Press, 1988), 28.

41. Pyotr Lavrov, *Historical Letters*, in RP2, 138.

42. V. G. Korolenko, *The History of My Contemporary*, trans. Neil Parsons (London: Oxford University Press, 1972), 178.

43. Korolenko, *History*, 177.

44. AK, 841.

45. An interesting school of criticism, inspired by Lydia Ginzburg, examines literature and models for living. See Lydia Ginzburg, *On Psychological Prose*, ed. and trans. Judson Rosengrant (Princeton, NJ: Princeton University Press, 1991); Paperno, *Chernyshevsky*; Irina Paperno, *Suicide as a Cultural Institution in Dostoevsky's Russia* (Ithaca, NY: Cornell University Press, 1997); Eric Naiman, *Sex in Public: The Incarnation of Early Soviet Ideology* (Princeton, NJ: Princeton University Press, 1997). See also essays in Ju. M. Lotman and B. A. Uspenskii, *The Semiotics of Russian Culture*, ed. Ann Shukman (Ann Arbor: Michigan Slavic Contributions, 1984) and *The Semiotics of Russian Cultural History*, ed. Alexander D. Nakhimovsky and Alice Stone Nakhimovsky (Ithaca, NY: Cornell University Press, 1985), and essays by Joan Delaney Grossman, Irina Gutkin, Alexander Lavrov, Irene Masing-Delic, Olga Matich, Irina Paperno, and Michael Wachtel in *Creating Life: The Aesthetic Utopia of Russian Modernism*, ed. Irina Paperno and Joan Delaney Grossman (Stanford, CA: Stanford University Press, 1994).

46. On Russian terrorism, see TSK.

47. Kropotkin observed of hopes for Alexander III's reign: "all young heirs to thrones are supposed to be liberals." Peter Kropotkin, *Memoirs of a Revolutionist* (New York: Dover, 1971), 315.

48. On Alexander II's several reforms, see Michael T. Florinsky, *Russia: A History and An Interpretation*, vol. 2 (New York: Macmillan, 1970); W. Bruce Lincoln, *In the Vanguard of Reform: Russia's Enlightened Bureaucrats, 1825–1861* (DeKalb: Northern Illinois University Press, 1986); and W. E. Mosse, *Alexander II and the Modernization of Russia*.

49. As cited in Nicholas Riasanovsky, *A History of Russia* (New York: Oxford University Press, 1963), 417.

50. Dostoevsky discusses Spasovich in chapter two of the February 1876 issue of *A Writer's Diary*. On the relation of the trial to Dostoevsky's thinking see Ronald LeBlanc, "The Karamazov Murder Trial: Dostoevsky's Rejoinder to Compassionate Acquittals," *Languages, Literatures, and Cultures Scholarship* (2018), 451. https://scholars.unh.edu/lang_facpub/451.

51. UR, 17.

52. Adam B. Ulam, *In the Name of the People: Prophets and Conspirators in Prerevolutionary Russia* (New York: Viking, 1997), 257.

53. UR, 6.

54. Extract from the proclamation "Young Russia" (*Molodaia Rossiia*) in *A Source Book of Russian History from Early Times to 1917: Volume 3, Alexander II to the Revolution*, ed. George Vernadsky et al., (New Haven, CT: Yale University Press, 1972), 640.

55. "Young Russia," 640, 641.

56. "Young Russia," 641.

57. Alexis de Tocqueville, *L'Ancien Régime*, as cited in *The Oxford Dictionary of Quotations*, ed. Elizabeth Knowles, 6th edition (Oxford: Oxford University Press, 2004), 795.

58. Adam Ulam, *In the Name of the People* (New York: Viking, 1977), 244.

59. Korolenko, *History*, 176.

60. Nikolay Valentinov [N. V. Volsky], *Encounters with Lenin*, trans. Paul Rosta and Brian Pearce (New York: Oxford University Press, 1968), 25–26.

61. Aleksandr I. Solzhenitsyn, *The Gulag Archipelago, 1918–1956: An Experiment in Literary Investigation*, trans. Harry Willetts, vol. 3 (New York: Harper and Row, 1978), 91.

62. *The Yale Book of Quotations*, ed. Fred R. Shapiro (New Haven, CT: Yale University Press, 2006), 814.

63. V. G. Belinsky, *Selected Philosophical Works* (Moscow: Foreign Languages Publishing, 1956), 358.

64. See I. Sechenov, *Reflexes of the Brain*, Russian text ed. K. Koshtoyants, trans. S. Belsky and ed. G. Gibbons (Cambridge, MA: MIT Press, 1965).

65. James H. Billington, *The Icon and the Axe: An Interpretive History of Russian Culture* (New York: Random House, 1970), 407. On the history of Russian and Soviet science, see Alexander Vucinich, *Science in Russian Culture, 1861–1917* (Stanford, CA: Stanford University Press, 1970), *Darwin in Russian Thought* (Berkeley: University of California Press, 1988), and *Einstein and Soviet Ideology* (Stanford, CA: Stanford University Press, 2001); Loren Graham, *Science in Russia and the Soviet Union: A Short History* (Cambridge: Cambridge University Press, 1994); *Science and Philosophy in the Soviet Union* (New York: Random House, 1974); *What Have We Learned About Science and Technology from the Russian Experience?* (Stanford, CA: Stanford University Press, 1998); and *Lonely Ideas: Can Russia Compete?* (Cambridge, MA: MIT Press, 2013); David Joravsky, *Russian Psychology: A Critical History* (Oxford: Basil Blackwood, 1989).

66. See Molly Brunson, *Russian Realisms: Literature and Painting, 1840–1890* (DeKalb, IL: NIU Press, 2016).

67. On Russian music and its relation to Russian literature and thought, see Caryl Emerson, *Boris Godunov: Transpositions of a Russian Theme* (Bloomington, IN: Indiana University Press, 1986), *The Life of Musorgsky* (Cambridge: Cambridge University Press, 1999), and *All the Same the Words Don't Go Away: Essays on Authors, Heroes, Aesthetics, and Stage Adaptations from the Russian Tradition* (Brookline, MA: Academic Studies Press, 2011); Boris Gasparov, *Five Operas and a Symphony: Words and Music in Russian Culture* (New Haven, CT: Yale University Press, 2005); Richard Taruskin, *Musorgsky: Eight Essays and an Epilogue* (Princeton, NJ: Princeton University Press, 1993) and *Defining Russia Musically* (Princeton, NJ: Princeton University Press, 2000).

68. Sechenov, *Reflexes*, 123. Koshtoyants notes in his biographical sketch that when sent to *The Contemporary* the work was entitled "An Attempt Physiologically to Explain the Origin of Psychical Phenomena," but failed to pass the censor. It appeared in *Meditsinskii vestnik* in 1863 (123).

69. On Russian literary journals and their importance, see the superb essays in *Literary Journals in Imperial Russia*, ed. Deborah A. Martinsen (Cambridge: Cambridge University Press, 2010). On Katkov, see Susanne Fusso, *Editing Turgenev, Dostoevsky, and Tolstoy: Mikhail Katkov and the Great Russian Novel* (DeKalb, IL: Northern Illinois University Press, 2017).

70. C&P, 334.

71. W&P, 164.

72. Unmasking, *oblichenie*, could also be translated as "exposure" or "denunciation."

73. L&F, 13.

74. SR, 588, 586.

75. SR, 588.

76. SR, 588.

77. Matthew Arnold, "Count Leo Tolstoi" (1887), in *Leo Tolstoy: A Critical Anthology*, ed. Henry Gifford (Harmondsworth, UK: Penguin, 1971), 63. See also Gregory Carleton, *Russia: The Story of War* (Cambridge, MA: Harvard University Press, 2017).

78. See Andrew Baruch Wachtel, *The Battle for Childhood: Creation of a Russian Myth* (Stanford, CA: Stanford University Press, 1990) and *An Obsession with History: Russian Writers Confront the Past* (Stanford, CA: Stanford University Press, 1994). Wachtel's study belongs to a scholarly genre—the broad overview of the Russian tradition from a particular angle—that have included many interesting works: David M. Bethea, *The Shape of Apocalypse in Modern Russian Fiction* (Princeton, NJ: Princeton University Press, 1989); James H. Billington, *The Face of Russia* (New York: TV Books, 1998); Michael C. Finke, *Metapoesis: The Russian Tradition from Pushkin to Chekhov* (Durham, NC: Duke University Press, 1995); Catriona Kelly, *Russian Literature: A Very Short Introduction* (Oxford: Oxford University Press, 2001); Martin Malia, *Russia Under Western Eyes: From the Bronze Horseman to the Lenin Mausoleum* (Cambridge, MA: Harvard University Press, 1999); Irina Paperno, *Suicide as a Cultural Institution in Dostoevsky's Russia* (Ithaca, NY: Cornell University Press, 1997); Kevin M. F. Platt, *History in a Grotesque Key: Russian Literature and the Idea of Revolution* (Stanford, CA: Stanford University Press, 1997); Andrew Baruch Wachtel and Ilya Vinitsky, *Russian Literature* (Cambridge: Polity, 2009).

79. At least that is what Dostoevsky tried to do. I discuss the peculiar poetics of *A Writer's Diary* in Gary Saul Morson, *The Boundaries of Genre: Dostoevsky's "Diary of a Writer" and the Traditions of Literary Utopia* (Austin: University of Texas Press, 1981); "Introductory Study" of AWD, 1–117.

80. See William Mills Todd, *The Familiar Letter as a Literary Genre in the Age of Pushkin* (Princeton, NJ: Princeton University Press, 1976) and *Fiction and Society in the Age of Pushkin: Ideology, Institutions, and Narrative* (Cambridge, MA: Harvard University Press, 1986).

81. Boris Tomashevskij, "Literature and Biography," in *Readings in Russian Poetics: Formalist and Structuralist Views*, ed. Ladislav Matejka and Krystyna Pomorska (Cambridge, MA: MIT Press, 1971), 51.

82. See Victor Shklovsky, "Sterne's *Tristram Shandy*: Stylistic Commentary," in *Russian Formalist Criticism: Four Essays*, ed. Lee T. Lemon and Marion J. Reis (Lincoln: University of Nebraska Press, 1965), 44. Since the Russian text reads, "Blood in art is not bloody, it rhymes with love" (the words for "blood" and "love" rhyme in Russian), Lemon and Reis give: "Gore in art is not necessarily gory; it rhymes with *amor*." Victor Shklovsky, "Art as Technique," in *Russian Formalist Criticism*, 44.

83. Important works in English on Dostoevsky include: Carol Apollonio, *Dostoevsky's Secrets: Reading Against the Grain* (Evanston, IL: Northwestern University Press, 2009); Robert L. Belknap, *The Structure of "The Brothers Karamazov"* (Evanston, IL: Northwestern University Press, 1989) and *The Genesis of "The Brothers Karamazov"* (Evanston, IL: Northwestern University Press, 1990); Anna Berman, *Siblings in Tolstoy and Dostoevsky* (Evanston, IL: Northwestern University Press, 2015); Ksana Blank, *Dostoevsky's Dialectics and the Problem of Sin* (Evanston, IL: Northwestern University Press, 2010); Julian W. Connolly, *Dostoevsky's "The Brothers Karamazov"* (London: Bloomsbury, 2013); Paul J. Contino, *Dostoevsky's Incarnational Realism: Finding Christ among the Karamazovs* (Eugene, OR: Cascade, 2020); Yuri Corrigan, *Dostoevsky and the Riddle of the Self* (Evanston, IL: Northwestern University Press, 2017); Kate Holland, *The Novel in the Age of*

*Disintegration: Dostoevsky and the Problem of Genre in the 1870s* (Evanston, IL: Northwestern University Press, 2021); Steven Cassedy, *Dostoevsky's Religion* (Stanford, CA: Stanford University Press, 2005); Joseph Frank's five-volume biography (Princeton, NJ: Princeton University Press, 1976–2002); Frank, *Lectures on Dostoevsky*, ed. Marina Brodskaya and Marguerite Frank (Princeton, NJ: Princeton University Press, 2020); Richard Freeborn, *Dostoevsky* (London: Haus, 2003); Susanne Fusso, *Discovering Sexuality in Dostoevsky* (Evanston, IL: Northwestern University Press, 2006); Kate Holland, *The Novel in the Age of Disintegration: Dostoevsky and the Problem of Genre in the 1870s* (Evanston, IL: Northwestern University Press, 2013); Michael Holquist, *Dostoevsky and the Novel* (Princeton, NJ: Princeton University Press, 1977); Robert Louis Jackson, *Close Encounters: Essays on Russian Literature* (Boston: Academic Studies Press, 2013); Malcolm Jones, *Dostoevsky and the Dynamics of Religious Experience* (London: Anthem, 2005); Jackson, *Dialogues with Dostoevsky: The Overwhelming Questions* (Stanford, CA: Stanford University Press, 1993); Liza Knapp, *The Annihilation of Inertia: Dostoevsky and Metaphysics* (Evanston, IL: Northwestern University Press, 1996); Knapp, *Dostoevsky's "The Idiot": A Critical Companion* (Evanston, IL: Northwestern University Press, 1998); Harriet Murav, *Holy Foolishness: Dostoevsky's Novels and the Poetics of Cultural Critique* (Stanford, CA: Stanford University Press, 1993); Deborah A. Martinsen *Surprised by Shame: Dostoevsky's Liars and Narratives of Exposure* (Columbus: Ohio State University Press, 2003); Greta Matzner-Gore, *Dostoevsky and the Ethics of Narrative Form* (Evanston, IL: Northwestern University Press, 2020); Susan McReynolds, *Redemption and the Merchant God: Dostoevsky's Economy of Salvation and Anti-Semitism* (Evanston, IL: Northwestern University Press, 2011); Robin Feuer Miller, *Dostoevsky and "The Idiot": Author, Narrator, and Reader* (Cambridge, MA: Harvard University Press, 1981); Miller, *"The Brothers Karamazov": Worlds of the Novel* (New York: Twayne, 1992); Miller, *Dostoevsky's Unfinished Journey* (New Haven, CT: Yale University Press, 2007); and Vadim Shneyder, *Russia's Capitalist Realism: Tolstoy, Dostoevsky, and Chekhov* (Evanston, IL: Northwestern University Press, 2020).

Interesting anthologies include Svetlana Evdokimova and Vladimir Golstein, eds., *Dostoevsky Beyond Dostoevsky: Science, Religion, Philosophy* (Boston: Academic Studies Press, 2016); and Robert Louis Jackson, ed., *A New Word on "The Brothers Karamazov"* (Evanston, IL: Northwestern University Press, 2004).

Significant recent works on Tolstoy include Berman, *Siblings in Tolstoy and Dostoevsky*; Brett Cooke, *Tolstoy's Family Prototypes in "War and Peace"* (Brookline: Academic Studies Press, 2020). Liza Knapp, *Anna Karenina and Others: Tolstoy's Labyrinth of Plots* (Madison: University of Wisconsin Press, 2016); Knapp, *Tolstoy: A Very Short Introduction* (Oxford: Oxford University Press, 2019); Inessa Medzhibovskaya, *Tolstoy and the Religious Culture of His Time: A Biography of a Long Conversion, 1845–1887* (Lanham, UK: Rowman and Littlefield, 2018); Donna Tussing Orwin, ed., *Tolstoy's Art and Thought, 1847–1880* (Princeton, NJ: Princeton University Press, 1993); and Justin Weir, *Leo Tolstoy and the Alibi of Narrative* (New Haven, CT: Yale University Press, 2011). Anthologies include Orwin, ed., *Anniversary Essays on Tolstoy* (Cambridge: Cambridge University Press, 2010) and *The Cambridge Companion to Tolstoy* (Cambridge: Cambridge University Press, 2003).

Important recent works on Chekhov include Michael C. Finke, *Metapoesis: The Russian Tradition from Pushkin to Chekhov* (Durham, NC: Duke University Press, 1995); Finke, *Seeing Chekhov: Life and Art* (Ithaca, NY: Cornell University Press, 2005); Serge Gregory, *Antosha and Levitasha: The Shared Artistic Lives of Anton Chekhov and Isaac Levitan* (DeKalb: Northern Illinois University Press, 2105); Janet Malcolm, *Reading Chekhov: A Critical Journey* (New York:

Random House, 2002); Shneyder, *Russia's Capitalist Realism*; and the anthologies, Carol Apollonio and Angela Britlinger, eds., *Chekhov for the 21st Century* (Bloomington, IN: Slavica, 2012); Michael C. Finke and Michael Holquist, *Approaches to Teaching the Works of Anton Chekhov* (New York: MLA, 2016); Vera Gottlieb and Paul Allain, eds., *The Cambridge Companion to Chekhov* (Cambridge: Cambridge University Press, 2004); Savely Senderovich and Munir Sendich, eds., *Anton Chekhov Rediscovered: A Collection of New Studies With a Comprehensive Bibliography* (East Lansing, MI: Russian Language Journal, 1987).

84. Mikhail Bakhtin, *The Duvakin Interviews, 1973*, ed. Slav N. Gratchev and Margarita Marinova, trans. Margarita Marinova (Lewisburg, PA: Bucknell University Press, 2019), 41.

85. S, 60.

86. A. P. Chekhov, letter to A. N. Pleshcheev, 7–8 October 1888, ChSS, vol. 12, 95.

87. A. P. Chekhov, letter to A N. Pleshcheev, 27 August 1888, as cited in Ernest J. Simmons, *Chekhov: A Biography* (Boston: Little, Brown and Company, 1962), 165.

88. Leo Tolstoy, *Resurrection*, trans. Mrs. Louise Maude (New York: Dodd, Mead, and Company, 1901), 210.

89. See Robert Chandler, "Translator's Introduction" in L&F, 9.

90. Alexandra Popoff, *Vasily Grossman and the Soviet Century* (New Haven, CT: Yale University Press, 2019), 275.

91. A notable exception was Solzhenitsyn's *One Day in the Life of Ivan Denisovich*.

92. See Kathleen F. Parthé, *Russia's Dangerous Texts: Reading Between the Lines* (New Haven, CT: Yale University Press, 2004).

93. Aleksandr Solzhenitsyn, *Between Two Millstones: Book I, Sketches of Exile, 1974–1978*, trans. Peter Contsantine (Notre Dame, IN: Notre Dame University Press, 2018) and Solzhenitsyn, *Between Two Millstones: Book 2, Exile in America, 1978–1994*, trans. Clare Kitson and Melanie Moore (Notre Dame, IN: Notre Dame University Press, 2020).

94. SR, 539.

95. SR, 596, 573.

## 1. Russian Literature

Epigraph: Cited in Donald Fanger, "Conflicting Imperatives in the Model of the Russian Writer: The Case of Tertz / Sinyavsky" in *Literature and History: Theoretical Problems and Russian Case Studies*, ed. Gary Saul Morson (Stanford, CA: Stanford University Press, 1986), 112.

1. AWD, 1069, 1068.

2. As cited in Peter Finn and Petra Couvée, *The Zhivago Affair: The Kremlin, The CIA, and the Battle Over a Forbidden Book* (New York: Vintage, 2015), 225.

3. Tatyana Tolstaya, *Pushkin's Children: Writings on Russia and Russians*, trans. Jamey Gambrell (Boston: Houghton Mifflin, 2003), 81.

4. Vasily Grossman, *Stalingrad*, trans. Robert Chandler and Elizabeth Chandler (New York: New York Review Books, 2019), 948.

5. As cited in *The Zhivago Affair*, 94.

6. As cited in Donald Fanger, "Conflicting Imperatives in the Model of the Russian Writer: The Case of Tertz / Sinyavsky" in *Literature and History: Theoretical Problems and Russian Case Studies*, ed. Gary Saul Morson (Stanford, CA: Stanford University Press, 1986), 112.

7. https://www.nobelprize.org/uploads/2018/06/alexievich-lecture_en-3.pdf.

8. And Russian Jews, perhaps, are doubly so.

9. HAH, 159.

10. HAH, 222. Mikhail Bulgakov, *The Master and Margarita*, trans. Diana Burgin and Katherine Tiernan O'Connor (New York: Vintage, 1995), 245.

11. Stephen Kotkin, *Stalin: Waiting for Hitler, 1929–1941* (New York: Penguin Press, 2017), 1–2. See also Geoffrey Roberts, *Stalin's Library: A Dictator and His Books* (New Haven, CT: Yale University Press, 2022).

12. Denis Kozlov, *The Readers of "Novyi Mir": Coming to Terms with the Stalinist Past* (Cambridge, MA: Harvard University Press, 2013), 27.

13. See Brian J. Boeck, *Stalin's Scribe, Literature, Ambition, and Survival: The Life of Mikhail Sholokhov* (New York: Pegasus, 2019), 54–55.

14. Kozlov, *Readers*, 26, 2, 3, 88–89.

15. Tolstaya, *Pushkin's Children*, 90.

16. Kathleen F. Parthé, *Russia's Dangerous Texts: Reading Between the Lines* (New Haven, CT: Yale University Press, 2004), 2, 12. David Remnick, *Resurrection: The Struggle for a New Russia* (New York: Random House, 1998), 222, as cited in Parthé, 13. As Parthé calls it, 13, from Joseph Frank, *Dostoevsky: The Stir of Liberation, 1860–1865* (Princeton, NJ: Princeton University Press, 1986), 45.

17. Eugenia Ginzburg, *Within the Whirlwind*, trans. Ian Boland (London: Collins, 1981), 100–101.

18. Olga Adamova-Sliozberg, "My Journey," in *Till My Tale is Told: Women's Memoirs of the Gulag*, ed. Simeon Vilensky (Bloomington, IN: Indiana University Press, 1999), 35.

19. Varlam Shalamov, *Kolyma Tales*, trans. John Glad (London: Penguin, 1994), 393, 266.

20. See Solzhenitsyn, "Playing Upon the Strings of Emptiness," in SR, 585–590.

21. Nikolai Gogol, "On the Lyricism of Our Poets," *Selected Passages from Correspondence with Friends*, trans. Jesse Zeldin (Nashville: Vanderbilt University Press, 1969), 51.

22. Daniil Kharms, "Anecdotes from Pushkin's Life," in *The Man in the Black Coat: Russia's Lost Literature of the Absurd*, ed. George Gibian (Evanston, IL: Northwestern University Press, 1987), 70.

23. *The Collected Tales and Plays of Nikolai Gogol*, Garnett translation revised by Leonard J. Kent (New York: Modern Library, 1964), 49.

24. Pamela Davidson, "The Validation of the Writer's Prophetic Status in the Russian Literary Tradition: From Pushkin and Iazykov through Gogol to Dostoevsky," *The Russian Review* 62, no. 4 (October 2003): 508–536.

25. See Marcus C. Levitt, *Russian Literary Politics and the Pushkin Celebration of 1880* (Ithaca, NY: Cornell University Press, 1989).

26. AWD, 1295.

27. Davidson, "Validation of the Writer's Prophetic Status."

28. Closing words of Percy Bysshe Shelley, "A Defense of Poetry," in *Critical Theory Since Plato*, ed. Hazard Adams (New York: Harcourt, Brace, 1971), 513.

29. As cited in Fanger, "Conflicting Imperatives," 112.

30. On *Petersburg*, see *Andrey Bely's "Petersburg": A Centennial Celebration*, ed. Olga M. Cooke (Boston: Academic Studies Press, 2017); Timothy Langen, *The Stony Dance: Unity and Gesture in Andrey Bely's "Petersburg"* (Evanston, IL: Northwestern University Press, 2005); and David M. Bethea, *The Shape of Apocalypse in Modern Russian Fiction* (Princeton, NJ: Princeton University Press, 1989), 105–144. The novel has been translated several times. See Michael Katz, "'Petersburg'

Only Seems to Exist—Bely in English Translation," *Slavic and East European Journal* 54, no. 1 (Spring 2010): 165–167.

31. D. S. Mirsky, *A History of Russian Literature from Its Beginnings to 1900*, ed. Francis J. Whitfield (New York: Random House, 1958), 177.

32. Max Hayward, "Pushkin, Gogol, and the Devil," *Writers in Russia: 1917–1978*, ed. Patricia Blake (San Diego: Harcourt Brace, 1983), 292–293.

33. To be sure, similar discussions can be found in some Western works—for example, the lengthy discussion of paper production in Balzac's *Lost Illusions*.

34. As cited in Donald Fanger, *The Creation of Nikolai Gogol* (Cambridge, MA: Harvard University Press, 1979), 28.

35. V. G. Belinsky, *Selected Philosophical Works* (Moscow: Foreign Languages Publishing, 1956), 355.

36. As cited in Fanger, "Conflicting Imperatives," 112.

37. In a class on Soviet literature I took with him in 1966–1967.

38. Dmitrii S. Likhachev, *Reflections on Russia*, ed. Nicolai N. Petro, trans. Christina Sever (Boulder, CO: Westview Press, 1991), 150.

39. Likhachev, *Reflections*, 150.

40. Ralph E. Matlaw, ed., *Belinsky, Chernyshevsky, and Dobrolyubov: Selected Criticism* (New York: Dutton, 1962), 102.

41. Peter Kropotkin, *Memoirs of a Revolutionist* (New York: Dover, 1971), 88. The book was written in English; the 1902 Russian edition was a translation from English.

42. https://www.nobelprize.org/uploads/2018/06/alexievich-lecture_en-3.pdf.

43. UFW, xviii, xxv.

44. Brian J. Boeck, *Stalin's Scribe, Literature, Ambition, and Survival: The Life of Mikhail Sholokhov* (New York: Pegasus, 2019), 302.

45. Boeck, *Stalin's Scribe*, 302, 303.

46. Ivan Turgenev, *Rudin: A Novel*, trans. Constance Garnett (London: William Heineman, 1894; reprinted New York: AMS Press, 1970), 33–34.

47. See Andrew Baruch Wachtel, *An Obsession with History: Russian Writers Confront the Past* (Stanford, CA: Stanford University Press, 1994). As Wachtel argues, Russian writers often presumed that the truth was best discovered by an intergeneric dialogue between history and fiction, and so they often wrote both (or combined them in one work).

48. *The Yale Book of Quotations*, ed. Fred R. Shapiro (New Haven, CT: Yale University Press, 2006), 724, which notes "Quoted in *New York Times Book Review*, 28 Sept. 1958."

49. Belinsky, *Selected Philosophical Works*, 310.

50. Matlaw, *Belinsky*, 178.

51. Matlaw, *Belinsky*, 180, 178.

52. See, for instance, D. N. Ovsyaniko-Kulikovskii, "Psikhologiia russkoi intelligentsia," in IiR.

53. AK, 501, 498.

54. On Tolstoy's "negative narration," see Gary Saul Morson, *Hidden in Plain View: Narrative and Creative Potentials in "War and Peace"* (Stanford, CA: Stanford University Press, 1987), 130–189.

55. Leo Tolstoy, Drafts for an Introduction to *War and Peace* and "Some Words about the Book *War and Peace*," in *War and Peace*, ed. George Gibian (New York: Norton, 1966), 1091.

56. Tolstoy, Drafts for an Introduction to *War and Peace*, 1092. Gary Saul Morson, *Narrative and Freedom: The Shadows of Time* (New Haven, CT: Yale University Press, 1994).

57. John Keegan, *The Face of Battle* (Harmondsworth, UK: Penguin, 1978).

58. Tolstoy, Drafts for an Introduction to *War and Peace*, 1092.

59. For a more recent study of how historians project their sense of the shape of events onto the documented facts, see Hayden White, *Metahistory: The Historical Imagination in Nineteenth-Century Europe* (Baltimore: Johns Hopkins University Press, 2014).

60. UFW, xvi.

61. Citations in this paragraph are from Svetlana Alexievich, *In Search of the Free Individual: The History of the Russian-Soviet Soul* (Ithaca, NY: Cornell University Press, 2016).

62. UFW, xvii, xix–xx.

63. UFW, xxi.

64. Vasily Grossman, "The Hell of Treblinka," *The Road: Short Fiction and Articles*, trans. Robert Chandler and Elizabeth Chandler with Olga Mukovnikova (London: Maclehose, 2010), 165.

65. The original Russian title of this volume is *Vekhi*, usually translated as *Landmarks*. The edition I cite here, however, translates the title as *Signposts*.

66. L[ev Aleksandrovich] Tikhomirov, *Russia, Political and Social*, trans. Edward Aveling, vol. 2 (London: Swan, Sonnenschein Lowrey, 1888), 87. Irina Paperno, *Chernyshevsky and the Age of Realism: A Study in the Semiotics of Behavior* (Stanford, CA: Stanford University Press, 1988), 11. Perhaps the only major mid-nineteenth-century writer belonging to this tradition was satirist Mikhail Saltykov-Shchedrin. Alexander Herzen belonged to both camps.

67. Paperno, *Chernyshevsky*, 27.

68. WITBD, 48

69. Valentinov was a follower of Lenin who soon became disillusioned and broke with him. Nikolay Valentinov [N. V. Volsky], *Encounters with Lenin*, trans. Paul Rosta and Brian Pearce (New York: Oxford University Press, 1968), 63–64.

70. Letter to Botkin, January 4, 1858, as cited in Rufus W. Mathewson, Jr., *The Positive Hero in Russian Literature*, (Stanford, CA: Stanford University Press, 1975), 86.

71. *Tolstoy's Letters*, ed. R. F. Christian, vol. 1, 1828–1879 (New York: Scribner's, 1978), 116.

72. *Fathers and Children* is a literal translation of the Russian title, though it became known in English as *Fathers and Sons*. By leaving out daughters, the usual English translation obscures the fact that the original title includes fathers, sons, and daughters—but, significantly, not mothers. I therefore refer to *Fathers and Children* throughout.

73. Ivan Turgenev, "Apropos of *Fathers and Sons*," in *Turgenev's Literary Reminiscences*, trans. David Magarshack (New York: Farrar, Strauss, 1958), 196.

74. Turgenev, "Apropos," 196. For a defense of Chernyshevsky's book, see Andrew M. Drozd, *Chernyshevskii's "What Is to Be Done?": A Reevaluation* (Evanston, IL: Northwestern University Press, 2001).

75. Turgenev, "Apropos," 202.

76. Robert C. Tucker, ed., *The Lenin Anthology* (New York: Norton, 1975), 149.

77. Rufus W. Mathewson, Jr., *The Positive Hero in Russian Literature* (Stanford, CA: Stanford University Press, 1975), 1–2.

78. Mathewson, *Positive Hero*, 21.

79. On types, see Robert Louis Jackson, *Dostoevsky's Quest for Form: A Study of His Philosophy of Art* (New Haven, CT: Yale University Press, 1966), 92–123. Belinsky, *Selected Philosophical Works*, 323.

80. WITBD, 212, 89.

81.  WITBD, 293.

82.  See Mathewson, *Positive Hero*, 211–232. See also Katerina Clark, *The Soviet Novel: History as Ritual*, 3rd edition (Bloomington, IN: Indiana University Press, 2000) and Rolf Hellebust, *Flesh to Metal: Soviet Literature and the Alchemy of Revolution* (Ithaca, NY: Cornell University Press, 2003). For another important study of socialist realism, see Irina Gutkin, *The Cultural Origins of the Socialist Realist Aesthetic* (Evanston, IL: Northwestern University Press, 1999).

83.  Mathewson, *Positive Hero*, 5.

84.  Mathewson, *Positive Hero*, 229.

85.  I cite the exchange between Grossman and Gorky as it appears in Robert Chandler's introduction to Grossman, *Stalingrad*, xxiii–xxiv

86.  Grossman, *Stalingrad*, 96–97.

87.  UFW, xxxv.

88.  Aileen Kelly, *Mikhail Bakunin: A Study in the Psychology and Politics of Utopianism* (New Haven, CT: Yale University Press, 1987), 9.

89.  Kelly, *Mikhail Bakunin*, 9.

90.  Yuri Lotman traces this "theatricality" to the Russian nobility's rapid westernization. Break-neck cultural change engendered a sense that newly adopted behavioral norms were artificial and so "members of the nobility passed their lives as if they were plays." In the early nineteenth century this theatricality shaped the Decembrist revolutionaries' behavior and self-image; and the mythology of the Decembrists, in turn, shaped the consciousness of radicals in subsequent decades. See Ju. M. Lotman, "The Decembrist in Everyday Life," "The Theater and Theatricality as Components of Early Nineteenth-Century Culture," and "The Poetics of Everyday Behavior in Eighteenth-Century Culture," in Ju. M. Lotman and B. A. Uspenskii, *The Semiotics of Russian Culture*, ed. Ann Shukman (Ann Arbor: Michigan Slavic Contributions, 1984).

91.  Boris Gasparov, introduction to *The Semiotics of Russian Cultural History*, ed. Alexander Nakhimovsky and Alice Stone Nakhimovsky (Ithaca, NY: Cornell University Press, 1985), 13.

92.  Matlaw, *Belinsky*, 226.

93.  F&S, 232–233.

94.  Paperno, *Chernyshevsky*, 29.

95.  Paperno, *Chernyshevsky*, 30, and 1–38, is a classic of Russian cultural historical scholarship.

96.  BK, 5–6.

97.  Stepniak, *Underground Russia: Revolutionary Profiles and Sketches from Life* (New York: Scribners, 1888)

98.  Vera Figner, *Memoirs of a Revolutionist*, trans. Camilla Chapin Daniels and G. A. Davidson (DeKalb, IL: Northern Illinois University Press, 1991), 205. Sally A. Boniece, "The Spiridonova Case, 1906: Terror, Myth, and Martyrdom," in Anthony Anemone, ed., *Just Assassins: The Culture of Terrorism in Russia* (Evanston, IL: Northwestern University Press, 2010), 143.

99.  A1914, 452, 441, 455.

100.  Vladimir Alexandrov continues the tradition of treating a terrorist as a sort of secular saint in *To Break Russia's Chains: Boris Savinkov and His Wars Against the Tsar and the Bolsheviks* (New York: Pegasus, 2021).

101.  Lynn Ellen Patyk, "The Byronic Terrorist: Boris Savinkov's Literary Self-Mythologization," in Anemone, *Just Assassins*, 165–166.

102.  Tikhomirov, *Russia*, 103.

103.  Paperno, *Chernyshevsky*, 11.

104. Dmitry Pisarev, "Pushkin and Belinsky: *Eugene Onegin*," in *Russian Views of Pushkin's "Eugene Onegin"*, trans. Sona Stephan Hoisington (Bloomington, IN: Indiana University Press, 1988), 51.

105. Eugene Lampert, *Sons Against Fathers: Studies in Russian Radicalism and Revolution* (Oxford: Clarendon Press, 1965), 335.

106. RP2, 86.

107. Lampert, *Sons*, 329.

108. RP2, 89.

109. Lampert, *Sons*, 333.

110. Kropotkin, *Memoirs*, 298.

111. https://www.marxists.org/subject/art/literature/mayakovsky/1917/slap-in-face-public -taste.htm. Victor Erlich, "The Battle of Manifestoes," *Modernism and Revolution: Russian Literature in Transition* (Cambridge, MA: Harvard University Press, 1994), 80–91.

112. Erlich, *Modernism*, 86.

113. Richard Stites, *Revolutionary Dreams: Utopian Vision and Experimental Life in the Russian Revolution* (New York: Oxford University Press, 1989). For an important study of the interactions of postrevolutionary Russian culture with the genre of biography, see Angela Britlinger, *Writing a Usable Past: Russian Literary Culture, 1917–1937* (Evanston, IL: Northwestern University Press, 2000).

114. Alexander M. Yakovlev, *Striving for Law in a Lawless Land: Memoirs of a Russian Reformer* (New York: M. E. Sharpe, 1996), 55.

115. Kozlov, *Readers*, 64.

116. Yuri Slezkine, *The House of Government: A Saga of the Russian Revolution* (Princeton, NJ: Princeton University Press, 2017), 953–954.

117. On the history and theory of the novel, see Thomas G. Pavel's classic study, *The Lives of the Novel: A History* (Princeton, NJ: Princeton University Press, 2013).

## 2. The Intelligentsia

Epigraph: Richard Pipes, ed., *The Russian Intelligentsia* (New York: Columbia University Press, 1961), 4.

1. Marshall S. Shatz and Judith E. Zimmerman, ed. and trans., *Signposts: A Collection of Articles on the Russian Intelligentsia* (Irvine, CA: Charles Schlacks, Jr., 1986), 60.

2. See, for instance, the essays in "Intelligentsiia v Rossii," in *IiR*.

3. Christopher Read, *Religion, Revolution, and the Russian Intelligentsia, 1900–1912: The "Vekhi" Debate and Its Intellectual Background* (London: Macmillan, 1979), 7.

4. On the term's origin, see Martin Malia, "What Is the Intelligentsia?" in Pipes, *Russian Intelligentsia*, 1–18. As Malia points out, the term's derivation from Latin reflects the importance of seminarians, who studied Latin, in the formation of the group. It may have been first coined by the novelist Boborykin before Turgenev popularized it. See Tibor Szamuely, *The Russian Tradition*, ed. Robert Conquest (New York: McGraw-Hill, 1974), 144. Nicholas Riasanovsky concludes that "the history of the term remains not fully known, as well as disputed" in "Notes on the Emergence and Nature of the Russian Intelligentsia," in *Art and Culture in Nineteenth-Century Russia*, ed. Theofanis George Stavrou (Bloomington, IN: Indiana University Press, 1983), 4.

5. For a skeptical look at definitions of "intelligentsia," see Daniel R. Brower, "The Problem of the Russian Intelligentsia," *Slavic Review*, vol. 26, no. 4 (Dec. 1967), 638–647.

6. Alexander Solzhenitsyn, "The Smatterers," FUTR, 235.

7. Ivan Turgenev, *"A Desperate Character" and Other Stories*, trans. Constance Garnett (London: William Heinemann, 1899; reprinted New York: AMS, 1970), 43.

8. In *Intelligentsia and Revolution: Russian Views of Bolshevism, 1917–1922* (New York: Oxford University Press, 1986), Jane Burbank refers to "the 'broad intelligentsia,' as this group was sometimes called" (8).

9. Adjectives designating the narrower group also included "true," "best," or "young." "As a rule, this 'true' intelligentsia was called in the populist literature by such edifying appellations as 'critically thinking individuals,' 'men of convictions,' 'conscious actors of historical progress,' 'conscious fighters for truth and justice,' 'fighters for social ideals,' 'social fighters,' and 'intellectually and morally developed minority.'" See Vladimir C. Nahirny, *The Russian Intelligentsia: From Torment to Silence* (New Brunswick: Transaction, 1983), 6–7. See also Charles A. Moser, *Esthetics as Nightmare: Russian Literary Theory, 1855–1870* (Princeton, NJ: Princeton University Press, 1989) and Susan K. Morrissey, *Heralds of Revolution: Russian Students and the Mythologies of Radicalism* (New York: Oxford University Press, 1998).

10. So contested is the term, and so complex the history of its usage, that in *Training the Nihilists: Education and Radicalism in Tsarist Russia* (Ithaca, NY: Cornell University Press, 1975), Daniel R. Brower decided to dispense with it: "The solution I have adopted consists of the complete abandonment of the 'intelligentsia' as a tool for scholarly analysis" (35). Since the people Brower studies (the "radicals") did use the term, this solution almost precludes an internal perspective. By contrast, in the collection *Intelligentsia Science: The Russian Century, 1860–1960*, ed. Michael D. Gordin, Karl Hall, and Alexei Kojevnikov, in the journal *Osiris* 23, no. 1, Gordin and Hall draw the opposite conclusion.

11. A1914, 345.

12. Stuart Ramsay Tompkins, *The Russian Intelligentsia: Makers of the Revolutionary State* (Norman, OK: University of Oklahoma Press, 1957), 245.

13. S, 117–118.

14. S, 118.

15. S, 120.

16. Nicholas Riasanovsky concludes: "there was an intelligentsia in Russia by the end of Nicholas I's reign, in fact, if not necessarily in name" (Riasanovsky, "Notes on the Emergence," 19). Riasanovsky refers to an intelligentsia defined as oppositional (4).

17. R. V. Ivanov-Razumnik, *Istoriia russkoi obshchestvennoi mysli*, V trekh tomakh. Tom pervyi (Moscow: Respublika, 1997), 20. In *The Russian Marxists and the Origins of Bolshevism* (Boston: Beacon, 1955), Leopold H. Haimson located the beginnings of the intelligentsia in the 1820s and treated the late 1850s and early 1860s, when the term was coined, as a period when it changed significantly (8–9). In *The Thinking Reed: Intellectuals and the Soviet State 1917 to the Present*, trans. Brian Pearce (London: Verso: 1989), Boris Kagarlitsky located the beginning of the intelligentsia in 1825 (14).

18. Citations in this paragraph are from Ivanov-Razumnik, *Istoriia russkoi obshchestvennoi mysli*, 21–22.

19. Nahirny notes that "the name of 'intelligentsia' has been rarely accorded to creative scholars, scientists, and artists. Rather, it has been closely associated with those educated and half-educated

persons who carried the torch of ideological enlightenment and served various causes" (Nahirny, *Russian Intelligentsia*, 5).

20. FUTR, 234.

21. Kagarlitsky observes: "By their action the contributors to *Vekhi* [*Landmarks*] had put themselves outside the ranks of the Russian intelligentsia." Kagarlitsky, *Thinking Reed*, 33.

22. Paul Miliukov suggested the image of concentric circles. See Boris Elkin, "The Russian Intelligentsia on the Eve of Revolution," in Pipes, *Russian Intelligentsia*, 32. Stuart Ramsay Tompkins explains that if by intellectuals Westerners mean those engaged "in spiritual creativity, especially scientists, artists, high school teachers, pedagogues, and the like," then the apparently equivalent Russian terms *intelligent* and *intelligentsia* "displayed a completely opposite character" because it was "neither a professional or economic group, but an ideological association" (Tompkins, *The Russian Intelligentsia*, 101). See also Abbott Gleason, *Young Russia: The Genesis of Russian Radicalism in the 1860s* (Chicago: University of Chicago Press, 1983).

23. Ivan Turgenev, *Virgin Soil*, trans. Constance Garnett, vol. 1 (London: William Heinemann, 1896; reprinted New York: AMS Press, 1970), 116–117.

24. Ivanov-Razumnik, *Istoriia russkoi obshchestvennoi mysli*, 22.

25. L. Tikhomirov, *Russia, Political and Social*, trans. Edward Aveling, vol. 2 (London: Swan, Sonnenschein Lowrey, 1888), 64. Tikhomirov later repented of his revolutionary activities and switched sides.

26. On Katkov, see Susanne Fusso, *Editing Turgenev, Dostoevsky, and Tolstoy: Mikhail Katkov and the Great Russian Novel* (DeKalb, IL: Northern Illinois University Press, 2021).

27. Tikhomirov, *Russia, Political and Social*, 2:6.

28. N. A. Gredeskul, "Perelom russkoi intelligentsia i ego deistvitel'nyi smysl," in "Intelligentsiia v Rossii," 238; published 1910.

29. Stuart Ramsay Tompkins, *The Russian Intelligentsia: Makes of the Revolutionary State* (Norman: University of Oklahoma Press, 1957), 271.

30. Szamuely, *Russian Tradition*, 143.

31. Boris Elkin, "The Russian Intelligentsia on the Eve of the Revolution," in Pipes, *Russian Intelligentsia*, 32.

32. Szamuely, *Russian Tradition*, 158–159.

33. D. N. Ovsyanniko-Kulikovskii, "Istoriia russkoi intelligentsia," in Ovsyaniko-Kulikovskii, *Sobranie sochinenii*, vol. 7 (St. Petersburg: Obshchestvennaia pol'za, 1911; reprinted The Hague: Mouton, 1969).

34. Tikhomirov, *Russia, Political and Social*, 2:15.

35. Employing the same premise, Malia maintained that the Decembrists did not qualify as *intelligenty* precisely because they did not renounce their place in society; they were, after all, mostly army officers. See Malia, "What Is the Intelligentsia?" in Pipes, *Russian Intelligentsia*, 9.

36. Ivanov-Razumnik, *Istoriia russkoi obshchestvennoi mysli*, 19. Malia argues: "as its members moved away from their estate of origin, they became *déclassé*. One of the primary characteristics of the *intelligenty*, then, was that they could no longer fit into the official estate system." Malia, "What Is the Intelligentsia?," 6.

37. Victor Turner, *The Ritual Process: Structure and Anti-Structure* (Chicago: University of Chicago Press, 1969), 94.

38. A Jew who joined the intelligentsia "had already ceased to feel that he was a Jew and considered himself a Russian *intelligent*." Kagarlitsky, *Thinking Reed*, 35n23.

39. Stepan Trofimovich remarks to the engineer Kirillov: "you want to build our bridge and at the same time you declare that you hold with the principle of universal destruction. They won't let you build our bridge" (P, 94).

40. S, 89.

41. Student life had "its own traditions, customs, morals, rituals, heroes and folk-lore" and the ideal "eternal student ... attending no lectures, passing no examinations, but taking a leading part in every radical activity" clung to that life as long as possible. Szamuely, *Russian Tradition*, 162; Ronald Hingley, *Nihilists: Russian Radicals and Revolutionaries in the Reign of Alexander II (1855–1881)* (New York: Delacorte, 1967), 25. "It is striking," remarked Malia, "how large a number of *intelligenty*, from Belinsky and Herzen to Lenin, Trotsky, and Stalin were expelled or arrested students" (Malia, "What Is the Intelligentsia?" 14).

42. Quotations from *August 1914* in the discussion of Sonya with her father are from A1914, 811–816.

43. As cited in James H. Billington, *Mihailovsky and Russian Populism* (Oxford: Clarendon Press, 1958), 57–58. Even before the coinage of the term intelligentsia, Belinsky wrote: "Peter the Great, blasting his own son with curses, declaring he would rather have a stranger's son but a good son—than his own, but a worthless creature: that is an enviable example." As Belinsky was doubtless aware, Peter did not just curse his son but tortured and executed him. Szamuely, *Russian Tradition*, 165.

44. Tikhomirov, *Russia, Political and Social*, 2:16.

45. As cited in Haimson, *Russian Marxists*, 18.

46. "The Catechism of a Revolutionary," in *Imperial Russia: A Source Book, 1700–1917*, ed. Basil Dmytryshyn (New York: Holt, Rinehart and Winston, 1967), 241.

47. For a superb study of the ethos of *popovichi* (sons of Orthodox parish clergymen) as shapers of the intelligentsia, see Laurie Manchester, *Holy Fathers, Secular Sons: Clergy, Intelligentsia, and the Modern Self in Revolutionary Russia* (DeKalb: Northern Illinois University Press, 2008). "That popovichi brought a secularized religious morality to the revolutionary movement," Manchester writes, "was apparent to their contemporaries from other estates" (191).

48. In *The Possessed*, Stepan Trofimovich tells the narrator and his friends, "I have not observed that narrow-mindedness I found in Petersburg, *chez les séminaristes*." By "*séminaristes*" he means the *intelligents* described in an earlier chapter.

49. Others from a clerical background included radical critics Dobrolyubov, Gregory Eliseev, and Afanasy Shchapov, as well as most members of the Ishutin group. Andrei Sinyavsky cited a definition attributed to the novelist Boborykin: an *intelligent* "is a person who, first, has been expelled from university, and, second, who loves the people." Andrei Sinyavsky, *The Russian Intelligentsia*, trans. Lynn Visson (New York: Columbia University Press, 1997), 2.

50. S, 30.

51. Philip Pomper, *The Russian Revolutionary Tradition* (New York: Thomas Y. Crowell, 1970), 3.

52. S, 30.

53. Aleksandr Solzhenitsyn, *November 1916: The Red Wheel / Knot II*, trans H. T. Willetts (New York: Farrar, Straus and Giroux, 1999), 403.

54. A1914, 442.

55. A1914, 447.

56. A1914, 450.

57.  A1914, 449.

58.  Malia, "What is the Intelligentsia?," 5.

59.  Manchester, *Holy Fathers*, 13.

60.  Theodore Dan, *The Origins of Bolshevism*, ed. and trans. Joel Carmichael (New York: Harper and Row, 1964), 24.

61.  See D. N. Ovsyaniko-Kulikovskii, "Psikhologiia russkoi intelligentsia," in "Intelligentsiia v Rossii," 382–405.

62.  As Alain Besançon has observed, intelligentsia ideology "had created a fossilized image" of reality in which the regime was essentially *defined* as "absolute evil," which is why no reform efforts on the regime's part did or could have made any difference. See Alain Besançon, *The Rise of the Gulag: Intellectual Origins of Leninism*, trans. Sarah Matthews (New York: Continuum, 1981), 100.

63.  Dobrolyubov, "When Will the Real Day Come?" in *Belinsky, Chernyshevsky, and Dobrolyubov: Selected Criticism*, ed. Ralph E. Matlaw (New York: Dutton, 1962), 182.

64.  Tikhomirov, *Russia, Political and Social*, 2:31.

65.  There were important exceptions. Mikhailovsky rejected the prevailing materialism. In her splendid study, *Doubt, Atheism, and the Nineteenth-Century Intelligentsia* (Madison: University of Wisconsin Press, 2011), Victoria Frede argued "not that the intelligentsia was atheistic by definition but that atheism was one particularly provocative answer to the eternal questions that lent meaning to the lives of educated Russians" (7). Religious thought, along with idealism, became important from the 1890s, as the contributors to *Landmarks* show; whether the religious thinkers belong to the intelligentsia is, again, a problem of definition and depends on where one draws lines beyond the classical radicals. *Landmarks* "came to define the intelligentsia in historical memory," Frede observed, and "after the 1917 revolution, [it] seemed prophetic" (14). In the Soviet period, she remarked, "militant atheism" became "the Bolsheviks' state religion" (18).

66.  Richard Pipes, *The Russian Revolution* (New York: Knopf, 1990), 139.

67.  Vera Figner, *Memoirs of a Revolutionist*, trans. Camilla Chapin Daniels and G. A. Davidson (DeKalb: Northern Illinois University Press, 1991), 160.

68.  Aleksandr I. Solzhenitsyn, foreword to Igor Shafarevich, *The Socialist Phenomenon* (New York: Harper and Row, 1980), viii.

69.  Solzhenitsyn, *November 1916*, 455.

70.  I. N. Steinberg, *In the Workshop of the Revolution* (New York: Rinehart, 1953), 9.

71.  See Irene Masing-Delic, *Abolishing Death: A Salvation Myth of Russian Twentieth-Century Literature* (Stanford, CA: Stanford University Press, 1992).

72.  S, 65.

73.  S, xxvii. Gershenzon and Izgoev eloquently invoke the intelligentsia's everyday moral slackness.

74.  See Gary Saul Morson, *The Boundaries of Genre: Dostoevsky's "Diary of a Writer" and the Traditions of Literary Utopia* (Austin: University of Texas Press, 1981), 69–106. On the apocalyptic theme in Russian literature, see David M. Bethea, *The Shape of Apocalypse in Modern Russian Fiction* (Princeton, NJ: Princeton University Press, 2016) and essays in Bethea, *The Superstitious Muse: Thinking Russian Literature Mythopoetically* (Boston: Academic Studies Press, 2009). An excellent study of mythopoetic thinking in life and literature is Gregory Carleton, *Russia: The Story of War* (Cambridge, MA: Harvard University Press, 2017).

75.  Closing lines of Leon Trotsky, *Literature and Revolution*, translator not specified (Ann Arbor: University of Michigan Press, 1971), 256.

76. Citations from Sergei Bulgakov in this paragraph are from S, 32.

77. As cited in Franco Venturi, *Roots of Revolution: A History of the Populist and Socialist Movements in Nineteenth-Century Russia*, trans. Francis Haskell (New York: Grosset and Dunlap, 1966), 296.

78. Irina Paperno, *Chernyshevsky and the Age of Realism: A Study in the Semiotics of Behavior* (Stanford, CA: Stanford University Press, 1988), 7.

79. Alexander Herzen, "To an Old Comrade," in *Selected Philosophical Works*, trans. L. Navrozov (Moscow: Foreign Languages, 1956), 587.

80. RP2, 156.

81. As cited in Michael Karpovich, "Two Types of Russian Liberalism: Maklakov and Miliukov" in *Continuity and Change in Russian and Soviet Thought*, ed. Ernest J. Simmons (New York: Russell and Russell, 1967), 138.

82. From Chekhov's letters to Suvorin, December 27, 1889, and to Pleshcheev, August 27, 1888, in Ernest J. Simmons, *Chekhov: A Biography* (Boston: Little Brown, 1962), 203, 165.

83. To be sure, several thinkers—notably Herzen and Mikhailovsky—took individual freedom seriously, but even they were inconsistent. See Billington, *Mikhailovsky and Russian Populism*.

84. Martha Bohachevsky-Chomiak, *Sergei N. Trubetskoi: An Intellectual Among the Intelligentsia in Prerevolutionary Russia* (Belmont, MA: Nordland, 1976), 12. Haimson also called the use of "intellectual" to translate *intelligent* "deceptive." Haimson, *Russian Marxists*, 8. Kagarlitsky also noted that "originally the concept *intelligentsia* was almost the direct opposite of 'intellectuals'" (Kagarlitsky, *Thinking Reed*, 14).

85. "Princess Ida," *The Complete Plays of Gilbert and Sullivan* (New York: Norton, 1976), 254.

86. Barbara Alpern Engel and Clifford N. Rosenthal, eds. and trans., *Five Sisters: Women Against the Tsar* (DeKalb: Northern Illinois University Press, 2013), 212.

87. Paperno, *Chernyshevsky*, 17.

88. Hingley, *Nihilists*, 16.

89. Paperno, *Chernyshevsky*, 18.

90. Hingley, *Nihilists*, 25.

91. Yuri Slezkine, *The House of Government: A Saga of the Russian Revolution* (Princeton, NJ: Princeton University Press, 2017), 224.

92. Peter Kropotkin, *Memoirs of a Revolutionist* (New York: Dover, 1971), 298.

93. Kropotkin, *Memoirs of a Revolutionist*, 299.

94. WITBD, 285–286.

95. Eugene Lampert, *Sons Against Fathers: Studies in Russian Radicalism and Revolution* (Oxford: Clarendon Press, 1965), 115. The line is also attributed to Turgenev. Evidently the witticism circulated widely.

96. Ropshin [Boris Savinkov], *What Never Happened*, trans. Thomas Seltzer (New York: Knopf, 1917), 146–147.

97. S. Stepniak, *The Career of a Nihilist: A Novel* (New York: Harper, nd), 60.

98. Paperno, *Chernyshevsky*, 32–33.

99. Paperno, *Chernyshevsky*, 32.

100. C&P, 357–358.

101. C&P, 354.

102. C&P, 355.

103. C&P, 357.

104. C&P, 354–361, 411.

105. Alexander Herzen, *My Past and Thoughts: The Memoirs of Alexander Herzen* (New York: Knopf, 1968), 4:1581.

106. F&S, 53.

107. F&S, 52–55.

108. WITBD, 180.

109. C&P, 255.

110. C&P, 254–255.

111. P, 413.

112. C&P, 255.

113. C&P, 258. In *Holy Fathers, Secular Sons,* Laure Manchester observed: "Because popovichi believed their clerical origins christened them the chosen people, they were more than willing to become the nation's self-professed leaders" (9). She concluded that "they viewed themselves as the nation's only leaders, and subsequently they were loath to compromise" (211).

114. C&P, 258.

115. C&P, 258.

116. From his periodical published abroad *Nabat* in 1875, as cited in Haimson, *Russian Marxists*, 16.

117. See Albert L. Weeks, *The First Bolshevik: A Political Biography of Peter Tkachev* (New York: University of London Press, 1968). Weeks cites the recollections of publisher of clandestine literature Vladimir Dmitrievich Bonch-Bruyevich, who supplied Lenin with reading material: "Vladimir Ilych read through . . . most carefully all of this old revolutionary literature, paying particular attention to Tkachev, remarking that the writer was closer to our viewpoint than any of the others. . . . He also recommended that all of us familiarize ourselves with the writings of this original thinker . . . 'Begin,' V. I. would advise, 'by reading and familiarizing yourself with Tkachev's *Nabat*.'" (Weeks, *The First Bolshevik,* 5). See also Deborah Hardy, *Peter Tkachev, the Critic as Jacobin* (Seattle: University of Washington Press, 1977).

118. S, 29.

119. S, 143.

120. See the best study of Russian Terrorism, TSK.

121. Alexander Herzen, "The Cannon Fodder of Liberation" (1862), in *A Herzen Reader,* ed. and trans. Kathleen Parthé (Evanston, IL: Northwestern University Press, 2012), 154.

122. Lenin and Trotsky as cited in Igal Halfin, *From Darkness to Light: Class, Consciousness, and Salvation in Revolutionary Russia* (Pittsburgh: University of Pittsburgh Press, 2000), 156.

123. As quoted by P. B. Akselrod, cited in Weeks, *The First Bolshevik,* xii.

124. "Monopolists of science" and "the revolt of life against science, "as cited in Marshall S. Shatz, *Jan Wacław Machajski: A Radical Critic of the Russian Intelligentsia and Socialism* (Pittsburgh: University of Pittsburgh Press, 1989), 39; "According to Mr. Marx," as cited in Pipes, *Russian Revolution,* 135.

125. See Shatz, *Jan Wacław Machajski,* 50–51. The article's Russian title is "Chto zhe takoe, nakonets, intelligentsia?"

126. HAH, 109.

127. The new state," Jane Burbank observes, "made no place for the intelligentsia of the past, with its functions of political criticism and articulation of alternative ideals." Burbank, *Intelligentsia and Revolution,* 7.

128. See Halfin, "The 'Intelligentsia': Vicissitudes of the Notion," *From Darkness to Light*, 149–204.

129. FUTR, 236.

130. HAH, 332.

131. On the literary culture of the 1920s, see Carol Avins, *Border Crossings: The West and Russian Identity in Soviet Literature, 1917–1934* (Berkeley: University of California Press, 1983).

132. FUTR, 237.

133. FUTR, 238.

134. FUTR, 239.

135. See Igal Halfin, *Terror in My Soul: Communist Autobiographies on Trial* (Cambridge, MA: Harvard University Press, 2003).

136. P, 415.

137. Solzhenitsyn, *November 1916*, 350.

138. FUTR, 239.

139. HAH, 216.

140. HAH, 80–81. In Arthur Koestler's novel *Darkness at Noon*, Rubashov's cultured first interrogator is himself arrested by a much cruder second one.

141. HAH, 164.

142. HAH, 166.

143. HAH, 174.

144. HAH, 167–168.

145. In her review of Richard Stites, *Revolutionary Dreams: Utopian Vision and Experimental Life in the Russian Revolution* (New York: Oxford University Press, 1989), Aileen Kelly pointed out that Stites advocates the very position Nadezhda Mandelstam sought to refute. Kelly wrote: "According to the mythological version of the 1920s [that Stites defends], the system that [eventually] destroyed such people was fundamentally hostile to their ideals. In reality, it derived both its claim to legitimacy and the justification for its violence from a belief that the revolutionary leaders of the twenties, with the willing collaboration of huge numbers of the intelligentsia, had sought unremittingly to inculcate in their society: that the goal of progress was to establish a single, correct . . . system of social existence. . . . It is difficult to separate the elements of pressure from above and voluntary conformism from below." Kelly also noted that the millenarian Proletkul demanded the Party suppress other cultural groups. See Aileen Kelly, "Brave New Worlds," *New York Review of Books*, December 6, 1990, https://www.nybooks.com/articles/1990/12/06/brave-new-worlds/. See also Boris Groys, *The Total Art of Stalinism: Avant-Garde, Aesthetic Dictatorship, and Beyond*, trans. Charles Rougle (Princeton, NJ: Princeton University Press, 1992).

146. For an account of how and why the term intelligentsia went from honorific to insult, see Halfin, *From Darkness to Light*, 153–204. Before the Revolution, it became necessary to distinguish between those *intelligents* who adhered to the Party and the more numerous ones supporting other parties and therefore serving bourgeois class interests and misleading workers. Writing in *Ogonyok* in 1988, Vyacheslav Kostikov described the official image of the (non-Party) *intelligent* as "the sniveling, wavering ninny, terrified of the Revolution and hostile to the working class. This image was closely based on that of the Mensheviks or the Socialist Revolutionary." See Vyacheslav Kostikov, "The 'Lokhankin Phenomenon' and the Russian Intelligentsia," in *The New Soviet Journalism: The Best of the Soviet Weekly "Ogonyok*," ed. Vitaly Korotich, ed, and trans. Cathy Porter (Boston: Beacon, 1990), 193.

147. FUTR, 242; Andrei Amalrik, *Will the Soviet Union Survive Until 1984?* (New York: Harper and Row, 1971), 17.

148. HAH, 332. The editors of the collection of *Intelligentsia Science* observe that "Throughout this volume, one can trace the constant tension between the Stalinist identification of 'intelligentsia' with white-collar workers . . . and a protodissident identification of science as a radical democratic force analogous to the nineteenth-century traditions." Writers who tried to find a place in the Soviet regime without totally surrendering their integrity faced real trials and dilemmas. For a superb study of their moral tests, see Carol Any, *The Soviet Writers' Union and Its Leaders: Identity and Authority under Stalin* (Evanston, IL: Northwestern University Press, 2020). See also Ann Komaromi, *Uncensored: Samzdat Novels and the Quest for Autonomy in Soviet Dissidence* (Evanston, IL: Northwestern University Press, 2015).

149. FUTR, 271. *Glasnost'* and the fall of the USSR provoked many reassessments of the revolutionary intelligentsia that made the revolution. *Landmarks* was printed in the USSR for the first time and widely discussed. For a survey of some of these discussions, see Caryl Emerson, "And the Demons Entered into the Swine: The Russian Intelligentsia and Post-Soviet Religious Thought," *Cross Currents* 43, no. 2 (Summer 1993): 184–20. See also Aleksandr Panchenko, "I Do Not Want to Be an *Intelligent*" ("Ne khochu byt' intelligentom"), *Moskovskie Novosti*, no. 50, (December 15, 1991): 16.

150. FUTR, 268

151. FUTR, 271.

152. FUTR, 273.

153. HAH, 331.

154. HAH, 333.

155. HAH, 333.

156. What is essential for this rebirth, according to Sinyavsky, is that this new intelligentsia remain distant from political power. He cites novelist Andrei Bitov's caution that "I do not see ways for cooperating with power" (Andrei Sinyavsky, *The Russian Intelligentsia*, trans. Lynn Visson [New York: Columbia University Press, 1997], 67).

157. Mikhail Bulgakov, *The Master and Margarita*, trans. Diana Burgin and Katherine Tiernan O'Connor (New York: Vintage, 1995), 111.

## 3. The Wanderer

Epigraph: AWD, 1282.

1. Andrew Louth, ed., *The Way of a Pilgrim: Candid Tales of a Wanderer to his Spiritual Father*, trans. Anna Zaranko (New York: Penguin, 2019), 3. The author's identity and the work's textual history remain the topic of speculation, as Louth explains, ix–xvi.

2. Louth, *Way of a Pilgrim*, 6.

3. See a splendid recent novel, set in the Russian Middle Ages: Eugene Vodolazkin, *Laurus*, trans. Lisa C. Hayden (London: Oneworld, 2015).

4. Nicholas Berdyaev, *The Russian Idea*, trans. R. M. French (Boston: Beacon, 1962), 198–199.

5. Berdyaev, *Russian Idea*, 197.

6. BK, 73–74.

7. AWD, 1289–1290. The word Dostoevsky uses for wanderer is *skitalets*. See F. M. Dostoevskii, *Polnoe sobranie sochinenii v tridtsati tomakh* [Complete Works in 30 volumes] (Leningrad: Nauka, 1972–1990), 26:137.

8. AWD, 1282–1283.

9. Ch13-7, 137.

10. Ch13-7, 139.

11. Ch13-7, 148.

12. Ch13-7, 155.

13. Ch13-7, 150–151.

14. Ch13-8, 201.

15. Ch13-8, 203.

16. Ch13-8, 205–206.

17. Ch13-8, 209.

18. Ch13-8, 210.

19. Ch13-8, 210–211.

20. Ch13-8, 211.

21. Ch13-8, 212.

22. Ch13-8, 212–213.

23. Ch13-8, 213.

24. Ch13-8, 213.

25. Ch13-8, 214.

26. Ch13-8, 214.

27. Ch13-8, 215.

28. TSK, 12.

29. Sergei Stepniak, *Underground Russia: Revolutionary Profiles and Sketches from Life,* 2nd edition (New York: Scribners, 1888), 36.

30. Stepniak, *Underground Russia,* 115.

31. Stepniak, *Underground Russia,* 127.

32. AWD, 501.

33. AWD, 534.

34. AWD, 1287–1288.

35. Ch13-8, 216.

36. Ch12-8, 217.

37. Ch13-8, 221.

38. Ch13-8, 224.

39. Ch13-8, 221.

40. Adam Ulam, *In the Name of the People* (New York: Viking, 1977), 369.

41. Ulam, *In the Name of the People,* 370.

42. Ulam, *In the Name of the People,* 371.

43. Ulam, *In the Name of the People,* 370.

44. Ulam, *In the Name of the People,* 370–371.

45. Ulam, *In the Name of the People,* 371.

46. L. Tikhomirov, *Russia, Political and Social,* trans. Edward Aveling (London: Swan, Sonnenschein Lowrey, 1888), 2:202.

47. Ulam, *In the Name of the People,* 369.

48. Ulam, *In the Name of the People,* 370.

49. Nicolas Berdyaev, *Dream and Reality: An Essay in Autobiography,* trans. Katharine Lampert (New York: Collier, 1950), xiii.

50. Berdyaev, *Dream and Reality*, 32.

51. Berdyaev, *Dream and Reality*, 35–36. See David M. Bethea, *The Shape of Apocalypse in Modern Russian Fiction* (Princeton, NJ: Princeton University Press, 1989).

52. As cited in Isaiah Berlin, "Vissarion Belinsky," in Berlin, *Russian Thinkers*, ed. Henry Hardy and Aileen Kelly (Harmondsworth, UK: Penguin, 1978), 150.

53. E. Lampert, *Studies in Rebellion* (London: Routledge, 1957), 50.

54. P. V. Annenkov, *The Extraordinary Decade: Literary Memoirs*, ed. Arthur P. Mendel, trans. Irwin R. Titunik (Ann Arbor: University of Michigan Press, 1968), 216.

55. On Dostoevsky's interactions with Belinsky, see the material in *Fyodor Dostoevsky—In the Beginning (1821–1845): A Life in Letters, Memoirs, and Criticism*, ed. Thomas Gaiton Marullo (DeKalb, IL: Northern Illinois University Press, 2016) and *Fyodor Dostoevsky: The Gathering Storm (1846–1847); A Life in Letters, Memoirs, and Criticism*, ed. Thomas Gaition Marullo (DeKalb, IL: Northern Illinois University Press, 2020).

56. Berlin, *Russian Thinkers*, 159.

57. Annenkov, *Extraordinary Decade*, 5.

58. Annenkov, *Extraordinary Decade*, 150.

59. AWD, 842.

60. Alexander Herzen, *My Past and Thoughts: The Memoirs of Alexander Herzen* (New York: Knopf, 1968), 2:411.

61. Annenkov, *Extraordinary Decade*, 16.

62. Lampert, *Studies in Rebellion*, 55.

63. Ivan Turgenev, "Reminiscences of Belinsky," in *Turgenev's Literary Reminiscences*, trans. David Magarshack (New York: Farrar, Strauss, 1958), 123.

64. Annenkov, *Extraordinary Decade*, 38.

65. Lampert, *Studies in Rebellion*, 48.

66. AKDoC, 155.

67. Herzen, *Past and Thoughts*, 2:501–502

68. Lampert, *Studies in Rebellion*, 66.

69. Lampert, *Studies in Rebellion*, 56.

70. Lampert, *Studies in Rebellion*, 60.

71. AKDoC, 229.

72. Lampert, *Studies in Rebellion*, 52.

73. Annenkov, *Extraordinary Decade*, 16.

74. Annenkov, *Extraordinary Decade*, 103.

75. V. G. Belinsky, *Selected Philosophical Works* (Moscow: Foreign Languages Publishing, 1956), 160.

76. Herzen, *Past and Thoughts*, 2:402.

77. Lampert, *Studies in Rebellion*, 73.

78. AKDoC, 155, from the letter of September 29–October 8, 1839.

79. Annenkov, *Extraordinary Decade*, 34.

80. Annenkov, *Extraordinary Decade*, 20.

81. Belinsky, *Philosophical Works*, 160.

82. BK, 269. In Kuprin's novel *Yama*, Likhonin echoes these views.

83. BK, 272.

84. BK, 270.

85. Herzen, *Past and Thoughts*, 2:413.

86. Belinsky, *Philosophical Works*, 167.

87. Belinsky, *Philosophical Works*, 168.

88. I allude to Bertrand Russell's essay "The Harm That Good Men Do" (1926).

89. AWD, 284.

90. AWD, 285–286.

91. AWD, 286–287.

## 4. The Idealist

Epigraph: Anton Chekhov, "A Nervous Breakdown," in Ch13-9, 45.

1. Ivan Sergeevich Turgenev, *The Essential Turgenev*, ed. Elizabeth Cheresh Allen (Evanston, IL: Northwestern University Press, 1994), 548.

2. Alexander Herzen, *My Past and Thoughts: The Memoirs of Alexander Herzen* (New York: Knopf, 1968), 2:398–399.

3. P. V. Annenkov, *The Extraordinary Decade: Literary Memoirs*, ed. Arthur P. Mendel, trans. Irwin R. Titunik (Ann Arbor: University of Michigan Press, 1968), 25–26.

4. Herzen, *Past and Thoughts*, 2:503.

5. Annenkov, *Extraordinary Decade*, 81.

6. Herzen, *Past and Thoughts*, 2:504–505.

7. Annenkov, *Extraordinary Decade*, 82.

8. Leonard Schapiro, *Russian Studies*, ed. Ellen Dahrendorf (New York: Penguin, 1988), 346. Schapiro notes the connection with the Turgenev quotation I cite immediately after.

9. Turgenev, *Essential Turgenev*, 564.

10. Turgenev, *Essential Turgenev*, 550.

11. Turgenev, *Essential Turgenev*, 549.

12. Turgenev, *Essential Turgenev*, 555.

13. AWD, 1129–1130.

14. AWD, 1130–1131.

15. Ivan Turgenev, "Yakov Pasinkov," in *"The Diary of a Superfluous Man" and Other Stories*, trans. Constance Garnett (London: William Heineman, 1899; reprinted New York: AMS Press, 1970), 156–157, 159–160.

16. Turgenev, "Yakov Pasinkov," 210.

17. Ivan Turgenev, *Rudin: A Novel*, trans. Constance Garnett (London: William Heineman, 1894; reprinted New York: AMS Press, 1970), 63, 104.

18. Turgenev, *Rudin*, 119–120, 195.

19. Annenkov, *Extraordinary Decade*, 201.

20. Annenkov, *Extraordinary Decade*, 202.

21. On "the irony of origins," see Gary Saul Morson, *The Boundaries of Genre: Dostoevsky's "Diary of a Writer" and the Traditions of Literary Utopia* (Austin: University of Texas Press, 1981), 77; Gary Saul Morson, *Hidden in Plain View: Narrative and Creative Potentials in "War and Peace"* (Stanford, CA: Stanford University Press, 1987), 17; and Gary Saul Morson, *Narrative and Freedom: The Shadows of Time* (New Haven, CT: Yale University Press, 1994), 268; for further references, see Morson, *Narrative and Freedom*, 306.

22. F&S, 12.

23. F&S, 15.

24. F&S, 38.

25. F&S, 39.

26. Fyodor Dostoesvky, *The Notebooks for "The Possessed,"* ed. Edward Wasiolek, trans. Katharine Strelsky (Chicago: University of Chicago Press, 1967), 38.

27. P, 5.

28. P, 6, 31.

29. Dostoevsky, *Notebooks for "The Possessed,"* 90.

30. Dostoevsky, *Notebooks for "The Possessed,"* 79, 83.

31. Dostoevsky, *Notebooks for "The Possessed,"* 90, 142–143.

32. Dostoevsky, *Notebooks for "The Possessed,"* 97–98.

33. Dostoevsky, *Notebooks for "The Possessed,"* 199.

34. Ivan Turgenev, *A House of Gentlefolk*, trans. Constance Garnett (London: William Heinemann, 1894; reprinted New York: AMS, 1970), 295–296.

35. On populism and Russian literature, see CRP and N. Bel'chikov, *Narodnuchestvo v literature i kritike* (Moscow: Sovetskaya literatura, 1934). See also Donald Fanger, "The Peasant in Literature," in *The Peasant in Nineteenth-Century Russia*, ed. Wayne S. Vucinich (Stanford, CA: Stanford University Press, 1968), 231–262.

36. CRP, 68

37. Dostoevsky wrote of "layers of barbarity" and "impenetrable deposits of filth" covering the essence of the peasantry, but hoped one could still find "diamonds in the filth." AWD, 347.

38. James H. Billington, *The Icon and the Axe: An Interpretive History of Russian Culture* (New York: Random House, 1970), 402–433.

39. Cited in Peter Henry, *A Hamlet of His Time: Vsevolod Garshin; The Man, His Works, and His Milieu* (Oxford: Willem A. Meeuws, 1983), 13.

40. Henry, *Hamlet of His Time*, 14, 20.

41. Radical critic Maxim Antonovich went so far as to deny that the brain (let alone the soul or "free will") controls human behavior, much as a frog with a pithed brain can still act by reflex. See Victoria S. Frede, "Materialism and the Radical Intelligentsia: The 1860s," in *A History of Russian Philosophy, 1830–1930*, ed. G. M. Hamburg and Randall A. Poole (Cambridge: Cambridge University Press, 2010), 78.

42. In Pisarev's article "Motivy russkoi dramy," as cited in Irina Paperno, *Chernyshevsky and the Age of Realism: A Study in the Semiotics of Behavior* (Stanford, CA: Stanford University Press, 1988), 272n27. Nicholas Rusanov, having abandoned nihilism for populism, exclaimed: "To the devil with all these frogs and other objects of science, which have made us forget about the people." As cited from N. S. Rusanov's biography of Lavrov in RP2, 113.

43. See Fan Parker, *Vsevolod Garshin: A Study of a Russian Conscience* (Morningside Heights, NY: King's Crown Press, 1946), 11. For a basic introduction to Garshin, see Edmund Yarwood, *Vsevolod Garshin* (Boston: Twayne, 1981).

44. Ch13-9, 45.

45. Ch13-9, 21–22.

46. Ch13-9, 19–20.

47. Ch13-9, 28.

48. Ch13-9, 31.

49. Ch13-9, 37–38.

50. Ch13-9, 33.

51. Ch13-9, 37–38.

52. Ch13-9, 41.

53. Ch13-9, 45–46.

54. Vsevolod Garshin, *The Scarlet Flower*, trans. Bernard Isaacs (Moscow: Foreign Languages, nd), 102.

55. Henry, *Hamlet of His Time*, 37.

56. Vsevolod Garshin, *"From the Reminiscences of Private Ivanov" and Other Stories*, trans. Peter Henry, Liv Tudge, Donald Rayfield and Philip Taylor (London: Angel, 1988), 116–117.

57. Garshin, *"Reminiscences of Private Ivanov,"* 28–29, 32.

58. Garshin, *"Reminiscences of Private Ivanov,"* 33.

59. I explore this theory of disgust in "Laughter and Disgust," in Gary Saul Morson, *Prosaics and Other Provocations: Empathy, Open Time, and the Novel* (Boston: Academic Studies Press, 2013), 161–170.

60. For an enlightening discussion of Dostoevsky's aesthetics of ugliness, see Robert Louis Jackson, *Dostoevsky's Quest for Form: A Study of His Philosophy of Art* (New Haven: Yale University Press, 1966). For the Dostoevskian element in Garshin, see Jackson's *Dostoevsky's Underground Man in Russian Literature* (The Hague: Mouton, 1958; reprinted Westport, CT: Greenwood Press, 1981), 73–81.

61. Garshin, *Scarlet Flower*, 83.

62. "Human anvils" is the translator's invention for the untranslatable *glukhari*, from *glukhoi*, deaf (from the hammering). V. M. Garshin, *Sobranie sochinenii* (Berlin: I. P. Ladishnikova, 1920), 106.

63. Garshin, *Scarlet Flower*, 82–83.

64. Fyodor Dostoevsky, *The Idiot*, trans. Constance Garnett (New York: Modern Library, 1962), 388–389. To Ippolit and Dostoevsky, the Russian word for ugliness, *bezobrazie*, which literally means imagelessness, suggests this possibility. I paraphrase here an argument from Robert Louis Jackson, *Dostoevsky's Quest for Form: A Study of His Philosophy of Art* (New Haven, CT: Yale University Press, 1966), 40–70.

65. Garshin, *Scarlet Flower*, 85.

66. See Gary Saul Morson, "The Reader as Voyeur: Tolstoy and the Poetics of Didactic Fiction," in *Canadian-American Slavic Studies* 12, no. 4 (Winter 1978): 465–480.

67. Cited in Alexandra Popoff, *Vasily Grossman and the Soviet Century* (New Haven, CT: Yale University Press, 2019), 178.

68. Garshin, *Scarlet Flower*, 168.

69. Garshin, *Scarlet Flower*, 169, 174.

70. Garshin, *Scarlet Flower*, 171, 178.

71. Henry, *Hamlet of His Time*, 14.

72. CRP, ix.

73. CRP, 94.

74. AWD, 349.

75. CRP, 4.

76. CRP, 64–65.

77. CRP, 67.

78. CRP, 62.

79. CRP, 20.

80. CRP, 8–9.

81. CRP, 19.

82. CRP, 20.

83. G. I. Uspensky, "Neizlechimyi," in *Sobranie sochinenii v devyati tomakh*, vol. 3 (Moscow: Khodozhestvennaia literatura, 1956), 151.

84. Uspensky, "Neizlechimyi," 153, 155.

85. Uspensky, "Neizlechimyi," 166.

86. Uspensky, "Neizlechimyi," 169.

87. Uspensky, "Neizlechimyi," 181.

88. Uspensky, "Neizlechimyi," 192, 195.

89. Uspensky, "Neizlechimyi," 185, 196, 199.

90. Uspensky, "Neizlechimyi," 199.

91. CRP, 71–72.

92. CRP, 75–76.

93. "Gde-nibud' v glushi, v tishi nastoiashchei derevni." G. I. Uspensky, "Ovtsa bez stada," in *Sobranie sochinenii v devyati tomakh*, vol. 4 (Moscow: Khodozhestvennaia literatura, 1956), 309.

94. Uspensky, "Ovtsa bez stada," 310, 321.

95. Uspensky, "Ovtsa bez stada," 321.

96. Uspensky, "Ovtsa bez stada," 324. The Russian is: "ne sol'esh'sya s vami, a sop'esh'sya!"

97. He may be paraphrasing Mikhailovsky's views about the division of labor.

98. Uspensky, "Ovtsa bez stada," 332–333.

99. Uspensky, "Ovtsa bez stada," 338, 340.

100. Uspensky, "Ovtsa bez stada," 348.

101. Uspensky, "Ovtsa bez stada," 349.

102. CRP, 87.

103. CRP, 94.

104. CRP, 88–89.

105. CRP, 92.

106. CRP, 90.

107. AK, 617.

108. AWD, 735.

109. BK, 99.

110. BK, 291.

111. CRP, 97–98.

112. CRP, 97, 100.

## 5. The Revolutionist

Epigraph: Originally in German as the closing sentence of an article signed Jules Elysard: "Die Lust der Zerstörung ist auch eine schaffende Lust." For a translation of the whole essay, see "The Reaction in Germany," *Bakunin on Anarchy: Selected Works by the Activist-Founder of World Anarchism*, ed. Sam Dolgoff (New York: Random House, 1972), 55–57.

1. As cited in Paul Hollander, *From Benito Mussolini to Hugo Chavez: Intellectuals and a Century of Political Hero Worship* (Cambridge: Cambridge University Press, 2016), 28.

2. As cited in Richard Wolin, *The Wind from the East: French Intellectuals, the Cultural Revolution and the Legacy of the 1960s* (Princeton, NJ: Princeton University Press, 2010), 210.

3. As cited in Marshall S. Shatz, *Jan Wacław Machajski: A Radical Critic of the Russian Intelligentsia and Socialism* (Pittsburgh: University of Pittsburgh Press, 1989), 150.

4. Opening of I. N. Steinberg, *In the Workshop of the Revolution* (New York: Rinehart, 1953), 9.

5. Mikhail Bakhtin, *The Duvakin Interviews, 1973*, ed. Slav N. Gratchev and Margarita Marinova, trans. Margarita Marinova (Lewisburg, PA: Bucknell University Press, 2019), 106.

6. HAH, 126.

7. Leonard Schapiro, *Russian Studies*, ed. Ellen Dahrendorf (New York: Penguin, 1988), 68.

8. TSK, 11.

9. TSK, 20–21.

10. TSK 40–41.

11. TSK, 22, 173.

12. TSK, 12. See also Amy Knight, "Female Terrorists in the Russian Socialist Revolutionary Party," *The Russian Review* 38, no. 2 (April 1979): 139–159; Susan K. Morrissey, "The 'Apparel of Innocence': Toward a Moral Economy of Terrorism in Late Imperial Russia," *The Journal of Modern History* 84, no. 3 (September 2012): 607–642; and Jenny Kaminer, *Women with a Thirst for Destruction: The Bad Mother in Russian Culture* (Evanston, IL: Northwestern University Press, 2014).

13. TSK, 22, 172.

14. Vladimir Lenin, *The Lenin Anthology*, ed. Robert C. Tucker (New York: Norton, 1975), 550, 559–560.

15. As cited in Nathan Leites, *A Study of Bolshevism* (Glencoe, IL: Free Press, 1953), 122.

16. Robert Conquest, *Reflections on a Ravaged Century* (New York: Norton, 2001), 98. Historian Peter Holquist observes: "The Red Terror—modeled on its French revolutionary counterpart, and with the Paris Commune always in mind—was a signal departure in state use of violence." Holquist, "Violent Russia, Deadly Marxism? Russian in the Epoch of Violence, 1905–1921," *Kritika: Explorations in Russian and Eurasian History* 4, no.3 (Summer 2003): 646.

17. Anarchism especially attracted those who valued revolutionary violence for its own sake. A notable exception was Russia's best-known anarchist after Bakunin, Prince Peter Kropotkin. Kropotkin befriended, defended, and sympathized with revolutionary killers, but he favored violence only to the extent needed to make the revolution.

18. On this contradiction in Bakunin's thought, see Aileen Kelly, *Mikhail Bakunin: A Study in the Psychology and Politics of Utopianism* (New Haven: Yale University Press, 1987), 227–256.

19. Kelly, *Mikhail Bakunin*, 126.

20. Kelly, *Mikhail Bakunin*, 210.

21. Michael Bakunin, *God and the State* (New York: Dover, 1970), 6.

22. As Paul Avrich noted in his introduction to the Dover edition of *God and the State*, the pamphlet was probably intended as part of a longer work that Bakunin (of course) never completed, *The Knouto-German Empire*; that is, it is a fragment of a fragment. Bakunin, *God and the State*, x–xi.

23. Alexander Herzen, *My Past and Thoughts: The Memoirs of Alexander Herzen* (New York: Knopf, 1968), 3:1358.

24. Herzen, *Past and Thoughts*, 3:1351.

25. Kelly, *Mikhail Bakunin*, 112.

26. Herzen, *Past and Thoughts*, 3:1353.

27. Kelly, *Mikhail Bakunin*, 169.

28. Ropshin [Boris Savinkov], *What Never Happened*, trans. Thomas Seltzer (New York: Knopf, 1917), 231, 241.

29. Boris Savinkov, *Pale Horse: A Novel of Revolutionary Russia*, trans. Michael R. Katz (Pittsburgh: University of Pittsburgh Press, 2019), 110.

30. I borrow facts from Lynn Ellen Patyk, "The Byronic Terrorist: Boris Savinkov's Self-Mythologization," in *Just Assassins: The Culture of Terrorism in Russia*, ed. Anthony Anemone (Evanston, IL: Northwestern University Press, 2010), 185n12. A year later *Izvestiia* reported that Savinkov had committed suicide by jumping from the fifth-floor window of his luxurious prison cell, but many, including Stalin, believed he had been defenestrated by the secret police. For a recent full-throated defense of Savinkov, see Vladimir Alexandov, *To Break Russia's Chains: Boris Savinkov and His Wars Against the Tsar and the Bolsheviks* (New York: Pegasus, 2021). I discuss Alexandrov's book and some controversies about Savinkov in "Falling in Love with Terror," *The New York Review of Books*, January 13, 2022, 55–57. https://www.nybooks.com/articles/2022/01/13/falling-in-love-with-terror/

31. Barbara Alpern Engel and Clifford N. Rosenthal, eds. and trans., *Five Sisters: Women Against the Tsar* (DeKalb: North Illinois University Press, 2013), 69–70.

32. Boris Savinkov, *Memoirs of a Terrorist*, trans. Joseph Shaplen (New York: Albert & Charles Boni, 1931), 42.

33. Savinkov, *Memoirs of a Terrorist*, 28.

34. Daniel Brower, "Nihilists and Terrorists," in *Times of Trouble: Violence in Russian Literature and Culture*, ed. Marcus C. Levitt and Tatyana Novikov (Madison: University of Wisconsin Press, 2007), 93–94.

35. In the draft of a letter to the People's Will executive committee, Stepniak explained how, when addressing European progressives, the terrorists must present themselves as identical in aspiration to European radicals, while "propaganda in Russian for Russian youth should, of course, have a completely different character." The letter is cited in Peter Scotto, "The Terrorist as Novelist: Sergei Stepniak-Kravchinsky," in Anemone, *Just Assassins*, 106.

36. See Peter Kropotkin, *Memoirs of a Revolutionist* (New York: Dover, 1971). The book was written for *Atlantic Monthly*, where it appeared from September 1898 to September 1899. Kropotkin, *Memoirs of a Revolutionist*, vi.

37. For an account of Zaichnevsky's development and views, see Franco Venturi, *Roots of Revolution: A History of the Populist and Socialist Movements in Nineteenth Century Russia*, trans. Frances Haskell (New York: Grosset and Dunlap, 1966), 285–302.

38. Savinkov, *Pale Horse*, 19.

39. Ivan Turgenev, "A Desperate Character" and Other Stories, trans. Constance Garnett (London: William Heinemann, 1899; reprinted New York: AMS, 1970), 1.

40. Turgenev, "Desperate Character," 10.

41. Turgenev, "Desperate Character," 14.

42. This tradition continues. In Eugene Vodolazkin's novel *The Aviator* (2016), the desperately ill hero consults a German doctor, who tells him to "expect no miracles," but that is just what the narrator wants. The doctor explains that Russians "live by the law of the miracle, but we [Germans] attempt to live in conformity with reality. It's unclear, however, which is better." Eugene Vodolazkin, *The Aviator*, trans. Lisa C. Hayden (London: Oneworld, 2018), 375. This passage is discussed in Chapter 10 of the present study.

43. Turgenev, *"Desperate Character,"* 14.

44. Turgenev, *"Desperate Character,"* 34, 39.

45. Savinkov, *Memoirs of a Terrorist,* 298.

46. On gambling as an index of character in nineteenth-century Russia, see Ian Helfant, *High Stakes of Identity: Gambling in the Life and Literature of Nineteenth-Century Russia* (Evanston, IL: Northwestern University Press, 2002).

47. A1914, 642.

48. S, 125.

49. C&P, 30, 150, 251–252.

50. C&P, 170.

51. Contrast this disregard for specifying what the future society will be with Kropotkin's contrary belief: "No destruction of the existing order is possible, if at the time of the overthrow, or of the struggle leading to the overthrow, the idea of what is to take the place of what is to be destroyed is not always present to the mind." Peter Kropotkin, "Modern Science and Anarchism," in *Kropotkin's Revolutionary Pamphlets: A Collection of Works by Peter Kropotkin,* ed. Roger N. Baldwin (New York: Dover, 1927), 156.

52. Fyodor Dostoevsky, *The Gambler,* in *Great Short Novels of Dostoevsky,* trans. Constance Garnett (New York: Dial, 1945), 100, 118, 120.

53. Dostoevsky, *Gambler,* 119, 126.

54. Dostoevsky, *Gambler,* 120–122.

55. Dostoevsky, *Gambler,* 125.

56. Savinkov, *Pale Horse,* 70–71, 102.

57. TSK, 156.

58. Alexander Blok, "The Intelligentsia and the Revolution," in *Russian Intellectual History: An Anthology,* ed. Marc Raeff (New York: Harcourt, Brace, 1966), 365.

59. Blok, "Intelligentsia and the Revolution," 365–368.

60. Schapiro, *Russian Studies,* 370.

61. Blok, "Intelligentsia and the Revolution," 369, 371.

62. Victor W. Turner, *The Ritual Process: Structure and Anti-Structure* (Chicago: University of Chicago Press, 1969) 95, 116, 139.

63. S. Stepniak, *The Career of a Nihilist: A Novel* (New York: Harper, nd), 310–311, 320. In the anarchist group *Black Banner,* notes historian Paul Avrich, "students, artisans, and factory workers predominated, but there were also . . . self-styled Nietzschean supermen." Avrich, *The Russian Anarchists* (Princeton, NJ: Princeton University Press, 1971), 44.

64. DZ, 195. The phrase could also be rendered "so out of place and out of time." I have modified the translation considerably.

65. DZ, 296–297.

66. F&S, 39, 41.

67. J. Frank Goodwin, "Violence and the Legacy of 'Bakuninism' in the Russian Revolution," in Levitt and Novikov, *Times of Trouble,* 106.

68. Levitt and Novikov, *Times of Trouble,* 106.

69. Richard Stites, *Revolutionary Dreams: Utopian Vision and Experimental Life in the Russian Revolution* (New York: Oxford University Press, 1989), 75–76.

70. "The Catechism of a Revolutionary," in *Imperial Russia: A Source Book, 1700–1917,* ed. Basil Dmytryshyn (New York: Holt, Rinehart, & Winston, 1967), 247.

71. TSK, 138.

72. S, 144.

73. Bernard Yack, *The Longing for Total Revolution: Philosophic Sources of Social Discontent from Rousseau to Marx and Nietzsche* (Berkeley: University of California Press, 1992), 6.

74. S, 145.

75. Stephen Kotkin, *Stalin: Paradoxes of Power, 1878–1928* (New York: Penguin, 2014), 463.

76. Nikolay Valentinov [N. V. Volsky], *Encounters with Lenin*, trans. Paul Rosta and Brian Pearce (New York: Oxford University Press, 1968), 149.

77. Steinberg, *Workshop of the Revolution*, 145, 147.

78. Steinberg, *Workshop of the Revolution*, 149–150.

79. Simon Sebag Montefiore, *Young Stalin* (New York: Random House, 2008), 309.

80. Kotkin, *Stalin: Paradoxes of Power*, 608.

81. Savinkov, *Memoirs of a Terrorist*, 198–199.

82. Savinkov, *Pale Horse*, 23.

83. TSK, 137. Geifman is quoting another scholar, Iuda Grossman.

84. Savinkov, *Memoirs of a Terrorist*, 38.

85. Donna Oliver, "Fool or Saint? Writers Reading the Zasulich Case," in Anemone, *Just Assassins*, 75–76.

86. Engel and Rosenthal, *Five Sisters*, 68–69, 74.

87. Sofya Kovalevskaya, *Nihilist Girl*, trans. Natasha Kolchevska and Mary Zirin (New York: MLA, 2001), 38, 48.

88. Vera Figner, *Memoirs of a Revolutionist*, trans. Camilla Chapin Daniels and G. A. Davidson (DeKalb: Northern Illinois University Press, 1991), 76.

89. Savinkov, *Pale Horse*, 27.

90. Savinkov, *Pale Horse*, 46, citing Revelation 6:8.

91. Savinkov, *Pale Horse*, 108.

92. Savinkov, *Pale Horse*, 112–113.

93. Savinkov, *Pale Horse*, 114.

94. On the Russian Byronic models for Savinkov's novels, see Patyk, "The Byronic Terrorist," in Anemone, *Just Assassins*, 163–189.

95. Savinkov, *Pale Horse*, 29, 69.

96. Ropshin, *What Never Happened*, 186.

97. Kelly, *Mikhail Bakunin*, 97–98, 110–111.

98. Savinkov, *Memoirs of a Terrorist*, 217, 219.

99. Nikolai Erdman, *The Suicide*, trans. George Genereux and Jacob Volkov, in *Russian Literature Triquarterly*, no. 7 (Winter 1974): 25–26.

100. Erdman, *Suicide*, 33–34.

101. Stepniak, *Career of a Nihilist*, 292.

102. Figner, *Memoirs of a Revolutionist*, 116–117.

103. On the Kadets I follow "The Kadets and Terror," TSK, 207–222, and Richard Pipes, *The Russian Revolution* (New York: Knopf, 1990), 169–171.

104. TSK, 214–216.

105. TSK, 224.

106. TSK, 225.

107. Richard Pipes, *The Russian Revolution* (New York: Knopf, 1990), 170.

108.  TSK, 214–215.

109.  Aleksandr Solzhenitsyn, *November 1916: The Red Wheel / Knot II*, trans H. T. Willetts (New York: Farrar, Straus and Giroux, 1999), 78. The quotation also appears in part in Richard Pipes, *Struve: Liberal on the Right, 1905–1944* (Cambridge, MA: Harvard University Press, 1980), 56.

110.  Robert Conquest, *V. I. Lenin* (New York: Viking, 1972), 100.

111.  Anna Geifman, *Death Orders: The Vanguard of Modern Terrorism in Revolutionary Russia* (Santa Barbara, CA: Praeger, 2010), 128.

112.  Conquest, *V. I. Lenin*, 107

113.  Geifman, *Death Orders*, 128.

114.  Peter Holquist noted that Lenin repeatedly called for civil war: "It was not 'circumstances' of war and revolution that forced the Bolsheviks into civil war, thereby derailing an otherwise popular and legitimate revolution. Civil war was what the Bolsheviks *sought*." Holquist, "Violent Russia, Deadly Marxism?" 645.

115.  Philip Pomper, "Russian Revolutionary Terrorism," in *Terrorism in Context*, ed. Martha Crenshaw (University Park: Pennsylvania State University Press, 1995), 81.

116.  TSK, 139.

117.  TSK, 171–172.

118.  Pomper, "Russian Revolutionary Terrorism," 81.

119.  TSK, 173.

120.  Pomper, "Russian Revolutionary Terrorism," 81.

121.  Stepniak, *Career of a Nihilist*, 208.

122.  Arthur Koestler, *Darkness at Noon*, trans, Daphne Hardy (New York: Macmillan, 1958), 46.

123.  Geifman, *Death Orders*, 133.

124.  TSK, 254.

125.  S. P. Mel'gunov, "*Krasnyi terror*" *v Rossii, 1918–1923* (Moscow: PUICO, 1990), 175, as translated in Geifman, *Death Orders*, 142.

126.  TSK, 255.

127.  In this section I draw on Geifman, "When Terrorists Become State Leaders," in *Death Orders*, 122–138.

128.  Geifman, *Death Orders*, 122–123, 126.

129.  Geifman, *Death Orders*, 126.

130.  Geifman, *Death Orders*, 126–127.

131.  TSK, 132 and Mel'gunov, "*Krasnyi terror*," 120–130.

132.  Geifman, *Death Orders*, 124.

133.  Dmitri Volkogonov, *Lenin: A New Biography*, ed. and trans. Harold Shukman (New York: Free Press, 1994), 168. This is the first biography of Lenin to make use of archives opened after the fall of the USSR.

134.  Conquest, *V. I. Lenin*, 100–101.

135.  Conquest, *V. I. Lenin*, 102.

136.  https://www.marxists.org/archive/lenin/works/1920/oct/20.htm.

137.  Volkogonov, *Lenin*, 238.

138.  Volkogonov, *Lenin*, xxxviii.

139.  Schapiro, *Russian Studies*, 372–373.

140. *"Lyubovnaya lodka razbilas' o byt"*: "byt"—everydayness, the daily grind—ultimately triumphs over revolutionary liminality. Vladimir Mayakovsky, "Past One O'clock" (*Uzhe vtoroy*), in *The Bedbug and Selected Poetry*, ed. Patricia Blake (Cleveland: Meridian, 1962), 237.

141. See his speech "Dizzy with Success," www.marxists.org/archive/stalin/works/1930/03/02.htm, originally published in *Pravda*, no. 60, March 2, 1930.

142. Stephen Kotkin, *Stalin: Waiting for Hitler, 1929–1941* (New York: Penguin, 2017), 68.

143. Alexander Herzen, "To an Old Comrade," in *Selected Philosophical Works*, trans. L. Navrozov (Moscow: Foreign Languages, 1956), 577, 579, 582–583.

144. Herzen, "To an Old Comrade," 584, 586.

145. Herzen, "To an Old Comrade," 587.

146. FUTR, 13, 15.

147. Evgenia Semyonovna Ginzburg, *Into the Whirlwind*, trans. Paul Stevenson and Manya Harari (Harmondsworth, UK: Penguin, 1968), 115–117.

148. Ginzburg, *Into the Whirlwhind*, 65.

149. Eugenia Ginzburg, *Within the Whirlwind*, trans. Ian Boland (London: Collins, 1981), 421. These are words she was told Tvardovsky had uttered.

150. Ginzburg, *Into the Whirlwhind*, 179–180.

151. L&F, 214.

152. L&F, 215.

153. "The movement toward socialism," Stalin explained, "must lead to resistance by the exploiting elements against this movement, and the resistance of the exploiters must lead to an inevitable sharpening of the class struggle." Cited in Kotkin, *Stalin: Paradoxes of Power*, 604. As Kotkin noted, this doctrine had already been formulated by Lenin; see the quotations from Lenin on page 954, note 291. Because no such resistance was visible, it must be surreptitious and therefore all the more sinister; hence the need for greater "vigilance," which generated arrests and (forced) confessions implicating others. In this way, "the siege Stalin was imposing," Kotkin observes, "generated evidence of the need for a siege" (601). Terror feeds on itself.

154. Kotkin, *Stalin: Waiting for Hitler*, 307.

155. Kotkin, *Stalin: Waiting for Hitler*, 307.

156. DZ, 381.

157. Stites, *Revolutionary Dreams*, 252.

158. Stites, *Revolutionary Dreams*, 251–253. These are the closing words of the book.

159. DZ, 381–382.

## 6. What Can't Theory Account For?

Epigraph: "Mne milo otvlechennoe: / Im zhizn' ya sozdayu[. . .] / I vse uedinennoe / Neyavnoe lyublyu." Cited in E. Lampert, "Decadents, Liberals, Revolutionaries: Russia 1900–1918," offprint of inaugural lecture at University of Keele, November 18, 1969, 23.

1. Nicolas Berdyaev, *Dream and Reality: An Essay in Autobiography*, trans. Katharine Lampert (New York: Collier, 1950), 34.

2. V. G. Belinsky, *Selected Philosophical Works* (Moscow: Foreign Languages Publishing, 1956), 168.

3. AKDoC, 155.

4. Belinsky, *Selected Philosophical Works*, 416.

5. AKDoC, 208–209.

6. AKDoC, 209. Daniel, of course, read the letters, he did not write them.

7. Isaiah Berlin, "The Hedgehog and the Fox," in *Russian Thinkers*, ed. Henry Hardy and Aileen Kelly (Harmondsworth, UK: Penguin, 1978), 22–81.

8. AKDoC, 225–226.

9. See the introduction to *Rethinking Bakhtin: Extensions and Challenges*, ed. Gary Saul Morson and Caryl Emerson (Evanston, IL: Northwestern University Press, 1989), 7–10, 29–30. See also Caryl Emerson, *The First Hundred Years of Mikhail Bakhtin* (Princeton, NJ: Princeton University Press, 2000).

10. BK, 301

11. Berdyaev, *Dream and Reality*, 74–75.

12. Vera Figner, *Memoirs of a Revolutionist*, trans. Camilla Chapin Daniels and G. A. Davidson (DeKalb, IL: Northern Illinois University Press, 1991), 82.

13. Figner, *Memoirs of a Revolutionist*, 33–34.

14. John Stuart Mill, *On Liberty* (Buffalo, NY: Prometheus, 1986), 43.

15. Figner, *Memoirs of a Revolutionist*, 34–35.

16. Aristotle, *The Basic Works of Aristotle*, ed. Richard McKeon (New York: Random House, 1941), 936.

17. Figner, *Memoirs of a Revolutionist*, 59–60.

18. Eugene Lampert, *Sons Against Fathers: Studies in Russian Radicalism and Revolution* (Oxford: Clarendon Press, 1965), 148–149.

19. Lampert, *Sons Against Fathers*, 149.

20. A more recent Russian thinker, Ayn Rand, shared Chernyshevsky's naïve "objectivism" and failure to understand epistemological issues.

21. V. I. Lenin, *Materialism and Empirio-Criticism* (Peking: Foreign Languages, 1972), 6, 10, 302. Lenin's book concludes with a discussion of Chernyshevsky's epistemological views, pp. 436–439.

22. Lenin, *Materialism and Empirio-Criticism*, 68–69.

23. Lenin, *Materialism and Empirio-Criticism*, 7.

24. See Linus Pauling's comments, http://scarc.library.oregonstate.edu/coll/pauling/bond/notes/1946a.3-ts-01-large.html.

25. Gustav A. Wetter, *Dialectical Materialism: A Historical and Systematic Survey of Philosophy in the Soviet Union*, trans. Peter Heath (New York: Praeger, 1963), 419, 433.

26. Nikolay Valentinov [N. V. Volsky], *Encounters with Lenin*, trans. Paul Rosta and Brian Pearce (New York: Oxford University Press, 1968), 183–184.

27. V. V. Zenkovsky, *A History of Russian Philosophy*, trans. George L. Kline, vol. 2 (New York: Columbia University Press, 1967), 746.

28. Valentinov, *Encounters with Lenin*, 184.

29. Karl Marx and Friedrich Engels, *Basic Writings on Politics and Philosophy*, ed. Lewis S. Feuer (Garden City, New York: Doubleday, 1959), 245.

30. "The Task of the Youth Leagues," October 2, 1920, https://www.marxists.org/archive/lenin/works/1920/oct/02.htm, first published in *Pravda*, nos. 221, 222, and 223, October 5, 6, and 7, 1920.

31. Cited in Raymond A. Bauer, *The New Man in Soviet Psychology* (Cambridge, MA: Harvard University Press, 1959), 108.

32. Bauer, *New Man in Soviet Psychology*, 108–109.

33. See Robert Conquest, *Reflections on a Ravaged Century* (New York: Norton, 2001), 100.

34. Nikolai Erdman, *The Suicide*, trans. George Genereux and Jacob Volkov, in *Russian Literature Triquarterly*, no. 7 (Winter 1974): 29–30.

35. Erasmus-Luther, *Discourse on Free Will*, trans. Ernst F. Winter (New York: Continuum, 1996), 8.

36. Élie Halévy, *The Growth of Philosophic Radicalism*, trans. Mary Morris (Boston: Beacon, 1955), 6.

37. See Jared Diamond, *Guns, Germs, and Steel: The Fates of Human Societies* (New York: Norton, 1999). In the "Epilogue: The Future of Human History as a Science" (403–425), Diamond claims to have established the basis for a science of human history "on a par with acknowledged historical sciences such as astronomy, geology, and evolutionary biology" (408).

38. AKDoC, 483.

39. AKDoC, 483.

40. Charles Darwin, *The Origin of Species: A Facsimile of the First Edition* (Cambridge, MA: Harvard University Press, 1981), 2.

41. S, 137.

42. F&S, 165.

43. Mill, *On Liberty*, 42.

44. RP2, 31.

45. RP2, 33.

46. RP2, 33–34.

47. RP2, 34, 43.

48. RP2, 35.

49. RP2, 39.

50. WITBD, 102.

51. RP2, 38–39.

52. See Dostoevsky's articles on spiritualism in *A Writer's Diary*. The narrator of *Karamazov* strives to offer some medical explanation for Zosima's apparently more than natural insight; one reason this novel uses a narrator, in fact, is to allow us to examine such *ad hoc* assertions. (In the same vein, Dickens has Scrooge try to dismiss Marley's ghost as a fragment of an underdone potato.) In Turgenev's "Strange Story," the skeptical narrator proposes to test a spiritualist's powers by prevailing on him to conjure up his dead tutor, whose appearance, unknown to the spiritualist, "was so original, so unlike any figure of today, that it would be utterly impossible to imitate it." Ivan Turgenev, *"A Desperate Character" and Other Stories*, trans. Constance Garnett (London: William Heinemann, 1899; reprinted New York: AMS, 1970), 53. When the spiritualist actually succeeds, the narrator finds some *ad hoc* "scientific" explanation: "such transferences of sensation are recognized by science" (58). Such unfalsifiability, of course, is the hallmark of pseudoscience.

53. WITBD, 115.

54. WITBD, 116–117.

55. S, 36.

56. For a well-known critique of this aphorism and its interpretation, see D. A. Broad, "The Philosophy of Francis Bacon: An Address at Cambridge on the Occasion of the Bacon Tercentenary," October 5, 1926. http://www.ditext.com/broad/bacon.html.

57. Francis Bacon, *The New Organon* (Indianapolis: Bobbs-Merrill, 1960), 29.

58. Leo Tolstoy, *"A Confession," "The Gospel in Brief," and "What I Believe,"* trans. Aylmer Maude (London: Oxford University Press, 1971).

59. In the celebrated anthology *Problems of Idealism* (1902), Sergei Bulgakov referred to such smuggling as "contraband": The source of this attribution of purpose to nature, he wrote, "is *religious faith*, but a faith that has crept in clandestinely, as contraband … where it was assumed only science was called to rule." In such confused thinking, he observes, "basic problems … are resolved with the help of contraband, that is, by introducing under the flag of positive science elements that are foreign to it." Sergei Bulgakov, "Basic Problems of the Theory of Progress," in *Problems of Idealism: Essays in Russian Social Philosophy*, ed. and trans. Randall A. Poole (New Haven, CT: Yale University Press, 2003), 96, 107.

60. This is a central argument of Aileen Kelly's study of Herzen (AKDoC).

61. Peter Kropotkin, *Memoirs of a Revolutionist* (New York: Dover, 1971), 239–240.

62. L[ev Aleksandrovich] Tikhomirov, *Russia, Political and Social*, trans. Edward Aveling, vol. 2 (London: Swan, Sonnenschein Lowrey, 1888), 14.

63. RP2, 123.

64. Kropotkin, *Memoirs of a Revolutionist*, 240.

65. Pisarev, "Progress in the Animal and Vegetable Worlds," in RP2, 76.

66. RP2, 75, 93–94.

67. A1914, 789.

68. Berdyaev, *Dream and Reality*, 179.

69. S, 142.

70. S, 142.

71. The fallacies involved in discovering purpose in nature, in attributing one's desired goals to a purely causal model, and of somehow finding "what ought to be" contained in "what is" were elucidated by the contributors to the influential and sophisticated anthology *Problems of Idealism* (1902). Randall A. Poole, ed. and trans., *Problems of Idealism: Essays in Russian Social Philosophy*, (New Haven, CT: Yale University Press, 2003). See especially the introductions by Poole and Caryl Emerson and the essays by Struve and P. I. Novogrodtsev.

72. Berdyaev quotes this famous aphorism as: "man is descended from the apes, therefore we ought to love one another." S, 9.

73. RP2, 186.

74. RP2, 131–132.

75. Herbert Butterfield, *The Whig Interpretation of History* (1931; reprint New York: Norton, 1965), 30–31.

76. RP2, 134.

77. S, 5.

78. See Bauer, *New Man in Soviet Psychology*, 21.

79. "The Holy Family," chapter VI 3, "Critical Battle Against French Materialism," https://www.marxists.org/archive/marx/works/1845/holy-family/ch06_3_d.htm. The quote occurs in Marx's paraphrase of Bacon. Also cited in Rufus W. Mathewson, Jr., *The Positive Hero in Russian Literature*, 2nd edition (Stanford, CA: Stanford University Press, 1975), 115.

80. See Friedrich Engels, *Dialectics of Nature* (India: Leopard Books, no date; originally authored 1883), 52, 69.

81. Wetter, *Dialectical Materialism*, 140.

82. L&F, 583.

83. ITFC, 483, 489.

84. Fyodor Dostoevsky, *"Notes from Underground"* and *"The Grand Inquisitor,"* the Garnett translation rev. and ed. by Ralph Matlaw (New York: Dutton, 1960), 21, 27.

85. Dostoevsky, "*Notes from Underground*," 21. The underground man, or his creator, here draws upon a satiric tradition discrediting thinkers who favor abstractions over experience. In Sterne's *Tristram Shandy*, Walter Shandy, "like all systematick reasoners . . . would move both heaven and earth, and twist and torture every thing in nature to support his hypothesis" [Laurence Sterne, *The Life and Opinions of Tristram Shandy, Gentleman*, ed. James Aiken Work (New York: Odyssey, 1940), 53]. Gogol echoes this passage in chapter 9 of *Dead Souls*.

86. C&P, 441–442.

87. C&P, 445.

88. C&P, 258.

89. C&P, 251–252.

90. Lev N. Tolstoy, "Progress and the Definition of Education" in the second, separately page-numbered part, of "*Moscow Acquaintance*," "*Snow-Storm*," "*Domestic Happiness*," "*Polikushka*," *Pedagogical Articles*, "*Linen-Measurer*," trans. Leo Wiener (Boston: L. C. Page, 1904), 162.

91. W&P, 318.

92. W&P, 771

93. W&P, 930.

94. Diamond, *Guns, Germs, and Steel*, 424.

95. W&P, 775.

96. W&P, 323.

97. W&P, 431.

98. W&P, 801–802.

99. W&P, 802.

100. W&P, 528.

101. W&P, 528–529.

102. W&P, 1323–1324.

103. See chapter 7, "Theory of Genres," in Gary Saul Morson and Caryl Emerson, *Mikhail Bakhtin: Creation of a Prosaics* (Stanford, CA: Stanford University Press, 1990), 271–305.

104. Mikhail Bakhtin, *Problems of Dostoevsky's Poetics*, trans. Caryl Emerson (Minneapolis: University of Minnesota Press, 1984), 59.

105. Mikhail Bakhtin, *The Dialogic Imagination: Four Essays*, ed. Michael Holquist, trans. Caryl Emerson and Michael Holquist (Austin: University of Texas Press, 1981), 37.

106. For more on this topic, see Gary Saul Morson, *The Boundaries of Genre: Dostoevsky's "Diary of a Writer" and the Traditions of Literary Utopia* (Austin: University of Texas Press, 1981).

107. WITBD, 48.

108. WITBD, 48.

109. WITBD, 47–48.

110. Ralph E. Matlaw, ed., *Belinsky, Chernyshevsky, and Dobrolyubov: Selected Criticism* (New York: Dutton, 1962), 117.

111. Matlaw, *Belinsky, Chernyshevsky, and Dobrolyubov*, 118.

112. WITBD, 92.

113. WITBD, 444–445.

114. F&S, 14, 66.

115. WITBD, 92.

116. Irina Paperno, *Chernyshevsky and the Age of Realism: A Study in the Semiotics of Behavior* (Stanford, CA: Stanford University Press, 1988), 272n27.

117. F&S, 25, 33.

118. See Morson, *Boundaries of Genre*, 77; and Gary Saul Morson, *Narrative and Freedom: The Shadows of Time* (New Haven, CT: Yale University Press, 1994), 268, 306. These techniques inform European philosophical novels by George Eliot, Henry James, Balzac, and others.

119. F&S, 73.

120. For examples, see Morson, *Boundaries of Genre*, 115–141.

121. Eugene Zamyatin, *We*, trans. Gregory Zilboorg (New York: Dutton, 1952), 4, 121.

122. Zamyatin, *We*, 8.

123. Dostoevsky, "*Notes from Underground*," 22.

124. Zamyatin, *We*, 129.

125. Zamyatin, *We*, 84–85.

126. Zamyatin, *We*, 41, 167.

127. Zamyatin, *We*, 151.

128. Fred R. Shapiro, ed., *The Yale Book of Quotations* (New Haven, CT: Yale University Press, 2006), 724.

129. M. M. Bakhtin, *Toward a Philosophy of the Act*, trans. Vadim Liapunov, ed. Vadim Liapunov and Michael Holquist (Austin: University of Texas Press, 1993), 47.

130. Belinsky, *Selected Philosophical Works*, 159.

131. Belinsky, *Selected Philosophical Works*, 160.

132. The comic name for Hegel in the Stankevich circle, to which Belinsky belonged. Belinsky, *Selected Philosophical Works*, 552n3.

133. Belinsky, *Selected Philosophical Works*, 160.

134. BK, 291.

135. Alexandre Kuprin, *Yama (The Pit)*, trans. Bernard Guilbert Guerney (New York: Modern Library, 1932), 143. The phrase "the worse, the better" is usually attributed to Lenin, but it was often used before. In "Three Crises," published in *Rabotnitsa*, np. 7, July 19, 1917, he quotes Plekhanov using it. https://www.marxists.org/archive/lenin/works/1917/jul/19.htm.

136. Kuprin, *Yama*, 143.

137. Kuprin, *Yama*, 143–144.

138. Ch13-7, 24.

139. C&P, 28, 51–52.

140. C&P, 61.

141. C&P, 526.

142. C&P, 531.

## 7. What Is Not to Be Done?

Epigraph: C&P, 526.

1. Ralph E. Matlaw, ed., *Belinsky, Chernyshevsky, and Dobrolyubov: Selected Criticism* (New York: Dutton, 1962), 204.

2. Nikolay Valentinov [N. V. Volsky], *Encounters with Lenin*, trans. Paul Rosta and Brian Pearce (New York: Oxford University Press, 1968), 241–242.

3. Valentinov, *Encounters with Lenin*, 242.

4. BK, 14.

5. This is Nobel Prize–winning economist Gary Becker's approach to crime. See Gary S. Becker, "Crime and Punishment: An Economic Approach," in *Essays in the Economics of Crime and Punishment*, ed. Gary S. Becker and William M. Landes (National Bureau of Economic Research, 1974), 9, http://www.nber.org/chapters/c3625.pdf; and Gary Saul Morson and Morton Schapiro, *Cents and Sensibility: What Economics Can Learn from the Humanities* (Princeton, NJ: Princeton University Press, 2017), 144–147.

6. BK, 79–80.

7. Matlaw, *Belinsky, Chernyshevsky, and Dobrolyubov*, 115, 119.

8. See Victoria S. Frede, "Materialism and the Radical Intelligentsia: The 1860s," in *A History of Russian Philosophy, 1830–1930: Faith, Reason, and the Defense of Human Dignity*, ed. G. M. Hamburg and Randall A. Poole (Cambridge: Cambridge University Press, 2010), 69–89.

9. Matlaw, *Belinsky, Chernyshevsky, and Dobrolyubov*, 119.

10. AK, 4, 664.

11. Or the concept of human dignity derives from Kant's idea that people recognize moral demands and make laws for themselves to guide their own behavior. "But this lawgiving self, which determines all worth, must for that reason have a dignity, that is an unconditional, incomparable worth. . . . *Autonomy* is therefore the ground of the dignity of human nature and of every rational creature." Cited in Ritchie Robertson, *The Enlightenment: The Pursuit of Happiness, 1680–1790* (New York: HarperCollins, 2021), 767.

12. AWD, 132, 135–137.

13. AWD, 136.

14. AWD, 142–145.

15. AWD, 144.

16. AWD, 145.

17. AWD, 138.

18. See the dispute Myshkin arbitrates between Lebedyev and his nephew. Fyodor Dostoevsky, *The Idiot*, trans. Constance Garnett (New York: Modern Library, 1962), 183–184.

19. BK, 716.

20. BK, 721.

21. Karl Marx and Friedrich Engels, *Basic Writings on Politics and Philosophy*, ed. Lewis S. Feuer (Garden City, NY: Doubleday, 1959), 253.

22. Eugene Lampert, *Sons Against Fathers: Studies in Russian Radicalism and Revolution* (Oxford: Clarendon Press, 1965), 303–304.

23. The heading "Are You Your Brain?" alludes to Jeffrey M. Schwartz, M.D., and Rebecca Gladding, M.D., *You Are Not Your Brain: The 4-Step Solution for Changing Bad Habits, Ending Unhealthy Thinking, and Taking Control of Your Life* (New York: Penguin, 2011).

24. I. Sechenov, *Reflexes of the Brain*, Russian text ed. K. Koshtoyants, trans. S. Belsky and ed. G. Gibbons (Cambridge, MA: MIT Press, 1965), 3, 123.

25. Sechenov, *Reflexes of the Brain*, 3–4. The French materialist Julien Offray de La Mettrie, author of *Man a Machine*, argued, "The human body is a machine, which winds itself up, a living picture of perpetual motion." Quoted in Robertson, *Enlightenment*, 285.

26. AK, 5.

27. Lampert, *Sons against Fathers*, 145.

28. La Mettrie declared that "Man was trained like an animal; he became an author in the same way as he became a porter. A mathematician learns the most difficult proofs and calculations, as a

monkey learns to put on and take off his little hat." In the same spirit, Claude Adrien Helvétius insisted that there is no intrinsic difference between a genius and a dope; the only difference is their education. Robertson, *Enlightenment*, 283–285.

29. Frede, "Materialism and the Russian Intelligentsia," 78.

30. BK, 716–717.

31. See, for instance, Daniel C. Dennett, *Consciousness Explained* (Boston: Little, Brown, 1991).

32. See Raymond Tallis, *Aping Mankind: Neuromania, Darwinitis and the Misrepresentation of Humanity* (London: Routledge, 2014).

33. AK, 27–29.

34. Aleksandr I. Solzhenitsyn, *The Gulag Archipelago, 1918–1956: An Experiment in Literary Investigation*, trans. Thomas P. Whitney, vol. 1 (New York: Harper and Row, 1974), 284.

35. Solzhenitsyn, *Gulag Archipelago*, 1:284, 309.

36. Yuri Slezkine, *The House of Government: A Saga of the Russian Revolution* (Princeton, NJ: Princeton University Press, 2017), 851.

37. Alexandra Popoff, *Vasily Grossman and the Soviet Century* (New Haven, CT: Yale University Press, 2019), 93.

38. TSK, 82.

39. TSK, 82–83.

40. I. N. Steinberg, *In the Workshop of the Revolution* (New York: Rinehart, 1953), 152.

41. L&F, 635.

42. See Jonathan Brent and Vladimir P. Naumov, *Stalin's Last Crime: The Plot Against the Jewish Doctors, 1948–1953* (New York: HarperCollins, 2003).

43. See Sheila Fitzpatrick, *Tear Off the Masks!: Identity and Imposture in Twentieth-Century Russia* (Princeton, NJ: Princeton University Press, 2005).

44. L&F, 578.

45. L&F, 578.

46. See John Garrard and Carol Garrard, *The Bones of Berdichev: The Life and Fate of Vasily Grossman* (New York: Free Press, 1996).

47. C&P, 28.

48. P, 413.

49. Stéphane Courtois, Nicolas Werth, Jean-Louis Panné, Andrzej Paczkowski, Karol Bartošek, and Jean-Louis Margolin, *The Black Book of Communism*, trans. Jonathan Murphy and Mark Kramer (Cambridge, MA: Harvard University Press, 1999).

50. P, 415, 427.

51. "The Catechism of a Revolutionary," in *Imperial Russia: A Source Book, 1700–1917*, ed. Basil Dmytryshyn (New York: Holt, Rinehart and Winston, 1967), 241–247.

52. S, 152.

53. S, 102.

54. ChSS, 12:567.

55. Peter Kropotkin, *Memoirs of a Revolutionist* (New York: Dover, 1971), 291.

56. Steinberg, *Workshop of the Revolution*, 115.

57. Andrei Sinyavsky, *Soviet Civilization: A Cultural History*, trans. Joanne Turnbull with Nikolai Formozov (New York: Little, Brown, 1990), 123.

58. Quoted in Sinyavsky, *Soviet Civilization*, 125.

59. On official Soviet atheism, see Victoria Smolkin, *A Sacred Space is Never Empty: A History of Soviet Atheism* (Princeton, NJ: Princeton University Press, 2018); and Daniel Peris, *Storming the Heavens: The Soviet League of the Militant Godless* (Ithaca, NY: Cornell University Press, 1998).

60. All citations from "The Tasks of the Youth Leagues" are from https://www.marxists.org /archive/lenin/works/1920/oct/02.htm.

61. Dmitri Volkogonov, *Lenin: A New Biography*, ed. and trans. Harold Shukman (New York: Free Press, 1994), 69–70.

62. Robert C. Tucker, ed., *The Lenin Anthology* (New York: Norton, 1975), 429.

63. Richard Pipes, *The Russian Revolution* (New York: Knopf, 1990), 792.

64. Robert Conquest, *V. I. Lenin* (New York: Viking, 1972), 102.

65. Solzhenitsyn, *Gulag Archipelago*, 1:1.

66. Pipes, *Russian Revolution*, 791.

67. Pipes, *Russian Revolution*, 791–792.

68. Slezkine, *House of Government*, 154–155. See Nikolai I. Bukharin, *Economics of the Transition Period, with Lenin's Critical Remarks* (New York: Bergman, 1971).

69. Volkogonov, *Lenin*, 238.

70. Pipes, *Russian Revolution*, 792.

71. Tucker, *Lenin Anthology*, 28–29, 450–451.

72. Tucker, *Lenin Anthology*, 431, 446.

73. Pipes, *Russian Revolution*, 704.

74. Pipes, *Russian Revolution*, 704.

75. Vasily Grossman, *Forever Flowing*, trans. Thomas P. Whitney (New York: Harper and Row, 1986), 76.

76. Evgenia Ginzburg, *Within the Whirlwind*, trans. Ian Boland (London: Collins, 1981), 70–72.

77. Dimitri Panin, *The Notebooks of Sologdin*, trans. John Moore (New York: Harcourt Brace, 1976), 232.

78. Orlando Figes, *The Whisperers: Private Life in Stalin's Russia* (New York: Henry Holt, 2007), 33.

79. Evgenia Semyonovna Ginzburg, *Into the Whirlwind*, trans. Paul Stevenson and Manya Harari (Harmondsworth, UK: Penguin, 1968), 72.

80. HAH, 134.

81. On the Soviet novel, see Katerina Clark, *The Soviet Novel: History as Ritual*, 3rd edition (Bloomington: Indiana University Press, 2000).

82. Rufus W. Mathewson, Jr., *The Positive Hero in Russian Literature*, 2nd edition (Stanford, CA: Stanford University Press, 1975), 185.

83. Mikhail Sholokhov, *Seeds of Tomorrow*, trans. Stephen Garry (New York: Knopf, 1935), 71.

84. Sholokhov, *Seeds of Tomorrow*, 72.

85. Sholokhov, *Seeds of Tomorrow*, 73.

86. Sholokhov, *Seeds of Tomorrow*, 32–33.

87. L&F, 33.

88. Robert Conquest, *Reflections on a Ravaged Century* (New York: Norton, 2001), 77.

89. Conquest, *Reflections on a Ravaged Century*, 78.

90. George Orwell, *1984* (New York: Signet, 1977), 35.

91. Figes, *Whisperers*, 34.

92. Conquest, *Reflections on a Ravaged Century*, 38.

93. Vera Figner, *Memoirs of a Revolutionist*, trans. Camilla Chapin Daniels and G. A. Davidson (DeKalb: Northern Illinois University Press, 1991), 100.

94. Figner, *Memoirs of a Revolutionist*, 46, 150.

95. Valentinov, *Encounters with Lenin*, 9.

96. A1914, 467.

97. A1914, 466–467.

98. ITFC, 515.

99. Nikolai Gogol, *The Collected Tales and Plays of Nikolai Gogol*, Garnett translation revised by Leonard J. Kent (New York: Modern Library, 1964), 564.

100. Gogol, *Collected Tales and Plays*, 564, 567.

101. Gogol, *Collected Tales and Plays*, 574–575.

102. Nikolai Gogol, *Dead Souls*, Guerney translation revised and edited by Susanne Fusso (New Haven, CT: Yale University Press, 1996), 122.

103. Donald Fanger, *The Creation of Nikolai Gogol* (Cambridge, MA.: Harvard University Press, 1979), 189. On Gogol, see also Victor Erlich, *Gogol* (New Haven, CT: Yale University Press, 1969) and Susanne Fusso, *Designing Dead Souls: An Anatomy of Disorder in Gogol* (Stanford, CA: Stanford University Press, 1993). Excellent anthologies include Susanne Fusso and Priscilla Meyer, ed., *Essays on Gogol: Logos and the Russian Word* (Evanston, IL: Northwestern University Press, 1992); and Robert A. Maguire, ed., *Gogol from the Twentieth Century: Eleven Essays* (Princeton, NJ: Princeton University Press, 1974). I am indebted to conversations with Victor Erlich, Michael Holquist, and Robert Louis Jackson.

104. Gogol, *Collected Tales and Plays*, 420; translation amended.

105. Gogol, *Collected Tales and Plays*, 453.

106. AWD, 842.

107. Solzhenitsyn, *Gulag Archipelago*, 1:93.

108. Isaac Babel, *The Collected Stories*, ed. and trans. Walter Morison (New York: Merdian, 1960), 106. I have combined this version with phrases from Val Vinokur's fine translation in *Isaac Babel: The Essential Fictions* (Evanston, IL: Northwestern University Press, 2018).

109. FUTR, 24–25.

110. Brian J. Boeck, *Stalin's Scribe, Literature, Ambition, and Survival: The Life of Mikhail Sholokhov* (New York: Pegasus, 2019), 121.

111. HAH, 211.

112. L&F, 216.

113. Varlam Shalamov, *Kolyma Tales*, trans. John Glad (London: Penguin, 1994), 329.

114. Shalamov, *Kolyma Tales*, 243.

115. "Dominoes," in Shalamov, *Kolyma Tales*, 109.

116. Shalamov, *Kolyma Tales*, 108.

117. Ginzburg, *Into the Whirlwind*, 270–271.

118. On Stiva's "forgettory," see Gary Saul Morson, *"Anna Karenina" in Our Time: Seeing More Wisely* (New Haven, CT: Yale University Press, 2007), 50–54.

119. Shalamov, *Kolyma Tales*, 392–393.

120. Shalamov, *Kolyma Tales*, 176.

121. HAH, 379.

122. Grossman, *Forever Flowing*, 158, 164, 166.

123. See S. J. Taylor, *Stalin's Apologist: The New York Times's Man in Moscow* (Oxford: Oxford University Press, 1990).

124. Ginzburg, *Into the Whirlwind*, 221.

125. Solzhenitsyn, *Gulag Archipelago*, 1:x.

126. Dmitrii S. Likhachev, *Reflections on Russia*, ed. Nicolai N. Petro, trans. Christina Sever (Boulder, CO: Westview, 1991), 78.

127. HAH, 379.

128. On Nadezhda Mandelstam as a writer, see Beth Holmgren, *Women's Work in Stalin's Time: On Lydia Chukovskaia and Nadezhda Mandelstam* (Bloomington: Indiana University Press, 1993).

129. *The Complete Poems of Anna Akhmatova*, ed. Roberta Reeder, trans. Judith Hemschemeyer (Boston; Zephyr, 1997), 384. On the special role of verse in Russia and Poland, see Clare Cavanagh, *Lyric Poetry and Modern Politics: Russia, Poland, and the West* (New Haven, CT: Yale University Press, 2010).

130. Vladimir Bukovsky, *To Build a Castle: My Life as a Dissenter*, trans. Michael Scammel (New York: Viking, 1979), 71.

131. Shalamov, *Kolyma Tales*, 261.

132. Shalamov, *Kolyma Tales*, 263.

133. Vasily Grossman, *The Road: Short Fiction and Articles*, trans. Robert and Elizabeth Chandler with Olga Mukhovnikova (London: Maclehose, 2010), 252.

134. Shalamov, *Kolyma Tales*, 15, 17.

135. Shalamov, *Kolyma Tales*, 32–33.

136. Shalamov, *Kolyma Tales*, 287.

137. Shalamov, *Kolyma Tales*, 290.

138. Orlando Figes, *The Whisperers: Private Life in Stalin's Russia* (New York: Henry Holt, 2007), 8.

139. On Soviet economic planning, see MWS, 167–174; Paul Craig Roberts and Karen LaFolette, *Meltdown: Inside the Soviet Economy* (Washington, D.C.: Cato, 1990); and Nikolai Shmelev and Vladimir Popov, *Revitalizing the Soviet Economy*, trans. Michele A. Berdy (New York: Doubleday, 1989).

140. Figes, *Whisperers*, 8–9.

141. See Yuri Druzhnikov, *Informer 101: The Myth of Pavlik Morozov* (Piscataway, NJ: Transaction, 1997) and Catriona Kelly, *Comrade Pavlik: The Rise and Fall of a Soviet Hero* (London: Grata, 2005).

142. Slezkine, *House of Government*, 792, 794.

143. HAH, 304–305.

144. Solzhenitsyn, *Gulag Archipelago*, 1:284.

145. Sinyavsky, *Soviet Civilization*, 74, 90. Those who have contested the "totalitarian" school point out, correctly, that control was never total and that initiative of various sorts continued. True enough, but when people can be arrested for their thoughts there is an aspiration for total control, and it is that aspiration—not the obviously impossible project of realizing it completely—that distinguishes totalitarianism.

146. I recount the anecdote as I heard it in Leonhard's course on Soviet history when I was a Yale undergraduate. It can be found in his autobiography, *Child of the Revolution*, trans. C. M. Woodhouse (Chicago: Henry Regnery, 1958), 51.

147. ITFC, xix–x.

148. HAH, 363.

149. SR, 256, 261.

150. SR, 256.

151. SR, 260.

152. SR, 260.

153. Ginzburg, *Into the Whirlwind*, 88, 98.

154. Ginzburg, *Into the Whirlwind*, 327–328.

155. Ginzburg, *Into the Whirlwind*, 326, 328.

156. Shalamov, *Kolyma Tales*, 413.

157. Solzhenitsyn, *Gulag Archipelago*, 1:129–130.

158. ITFC, 495.

159. ITFC, 698, 711.

160. ITFC, 710.

161. ITFC, 711.

162. ITFC, 438–439.

163. ITFC, 340.

164. ITFC, 333.

165. ITFC, 334.

166. See Irina Ratushinskaya, *Grey Is the Color of Hope*, trans. Alyona Kojevnikov (New York: Knopf, 1988). My thanks to Frances Padorr Brent for introducing me to this book.

167. Shalamov, *Kolyma Tales*, 69, 71–72.

168. Shalamov, *Kolyma Tales*, 72.

169. SR, 258.

170. BK, 48.

171. UFW, 61–62.

172. SR, 261–262.

173. Book VIII of the *Nichomachean Ethics*, in *The Basic Works of Aristotle*, ed. Richard McKeon (New York: Random House, 1941), 1060–1061.

174. SR, 264, 266.

175. SR, 265.

176. SR, 267.

## 8. Who Is Not to Blame?

Epigraph: HAH, 115.

1. SR, 265.

2. SR, 265.

3. Mikhail Bakhtin, *The Duvakin Interviews, 1973*, ed. Slav N. Gratchev and Margarita Marinova, trans. Margarita Marinova (Lewisburg, PA: Bucknell University Press, 2019), 89.

4. SR, 234.

5. SR, 234.

6. The term alibi in fact comes from the Latin for "elsewhere." For a superb meditation on the "alibi," see Justin Weir, *Leo Tolstoy and the Alibi of Narrative* (New Haven, CT: Yale University Press, 2011). Weir explains: "A narrative alibi works in two ways. In the simplest sense, it can be a story that exculpates, removes blame or transfers responsibility. . . . A narrative alibi can also be a

story that uses the logic of the word *alibi*, which literally means to be 'elsewhere.' An alibi here is a meaningful absence, a place in the text where one is supposed to notice that the author has purposely bypassed or concealed an important aspect of the plot" (Weir, 1–2).

7. M. M. Bakhtin, *Toward a Philosophy of the Act*, trans. Vadim Liapunov, ed. Vadim Liapunov and Michael Holquist (Austin: University of Texas Press, 1993), 53.

8. Bakhtin, *Philosophy of the Act*, 40, 47.

9. Ivan Goncharov, *The Precipice*, trans. and ed. Laury Magnus and Boris Jakim (Ann Arbor, MI: Ardis, 1994), 251.

10. Anton Chekhov, *"Ward Six" and Other Stories*, trans. Ann Dunnigan (New York: Signet, 1965), 27.

11. Chekhov, *"Ward Six" and Other Stories*, 77.

12. Lev Kopelev, *To Be Preserved Forever*, trans. and ed. Anthony Austin (Philadelphia: Lippincott, 1977), 19.

13. FUTR, 284.

14. ITFC, 321.

15. In David Bergelson's Yiddish language novel *Judgment*, about a Jewish community shortly after the Revolution, Doctor Babitsky is summoned to care for Cheka agent Filippov: "It seemed to the doctor that Filipov was sick with a strange illness that nobody had ever heard of. This was an illness that could infect only a man like Filipov. When he ordered someone's death, when he gave the command, 'Shoot!'—there was no wisdom that could dissuade him, because it wasn't Filipov who was giving the orders. It was History. . . .'And who has fallen ill, hmmm? . . . The ambassador of History!'" David Bergelson, *Judgment: A Novel*, trans. Harriet Murav and Sasha Senderovich (Evanston, IL: Northwestern University Press, 2017), 59.

16. Kopelev, *Preserved Forever*, 12.

17. Kopelev, *Preserved Forever*, 259–261.

18. Sergei Dovlatov, "Kto napisal chetyre milliona donosov?," *Izbrannoe*, October 30, 2018, http://www.izbrannoe.com/news/mysli/sergey-dovlatov-kto-napisal-chetyre-milliona-donosov-/

19. Kopelev, *Preserved Forever*, 12.

20. *The Maxims of La Rochefoucauld*, trans. Louis Kronenberger (New York: Random House, 1959), 33.

21. RP2, 97, 99, 102.

22. See Gary Saul Morson, *The Boundaries of Genre: Dostoevsky's "Diary of a Writer" and the Traditions of Literary Utopia* (Austin: University of Texas Press, 1981), 69–104.

23. George Eliot, *Middlemarch* (New York: Modern Library, 1984), 150.

24. Eliot, *Middlemarch*, 589.

25. Eliot, *Middlemarch*, 590–591.

26. Eliot, *Middlemarch*, 591.

27. BK, 326.

28. BK, 326.

29. BK, 170.

30. Herbert Fingarette, *Self-Deception* (Berkeley: University of California Press, 2000), 15. Brian P. McLaughlin and Amélie Oksenberg Rorty, ed., *Perspectives on Self-Deception* (Berkeley: University of California Press, 1988).

31. See Gary Saul Morson, "The Reader as Voyeur: Tolstoy and the Poetics of Didactic Fiction," *Canadian-American Slavic Studies* 12, no. 4 (Winter 1978): 465–480; and Robert Louis Jackson,

"The Ethics of Vision I: Turgenev's 'Execution of Tropman' and Dostoevsky's View of the Matter," in *Dialogues with Dostoevsky: The Overwhelming Questions* (Stanford, CA: Stanford University Press, 1993), 29–54.

32. For more on Anna, self-deception, and the drama of looking, see Gary Saul Morson, *"Anna Karenina" in Our Time: Seeing More Wisely* (New Haven, CT: Yale University Press, 2007), 79–117.

33. AK, 380.

34. AK, 384.

35. These are the themes discussed at length in MWS.

36. AK, 434.

37. AK, 9.

38. AK, 346.

39. My thanks to Morton Schapiro for pointing out the significance of this idea.

40. AK, 248.

41. AK, 350.

42. BK, 4.

43. DZ, 404.

44. Aleksandr Solzhenitsyn, *November 1916: The Red Wheel / Knot II*, trans. H. T. Willetts (New York: Farrar, Straus and Giroux, 1999), 285–286.

45. Solzhenitsyn, *November 1916*, 291, 293–296.

46. Vasily Grossman, *Stalingrad*, trans. Robert and Elizabeth Chandler (New York: New York Review Books, 2019), xxiii–xxiv.

47. Grossman, *Stalingrad*, xxiv.

48. Orlando Figes, *The Whisperers: Private Life in Stalin's Russia* (New York: Henry Holt, 2007), 191.

49. L&F, 526.

50. Figes, *Whisperers*, 472.

51. Aleksandr I. Solzhenitsyn, *The Gulag Archipelago, 1918–1956: An Experiment in Literary Investigation*, trans. Thomas P. Whitney, vol. 1 (New York: Harper and Row, 1974), 612.

52. L&F, 528.

53. L&F, 818.

54. L&F, 820–821, 823.

55. L&F, 835, 837.

56. L&F, 840.

57. L&F, 840.

58. L&F, 862.

59. Solzhenitsyn, *Gulag Archipelago*, 1:612.

60. L&F, 527–528.

61. A1914, 404.

62. SR, 230–231.

63. HAH, 55.

64. P, 578–579, 594.

65. Leo Tolstoy, *Short Stories*, ed. Ernest J. Simmons (New York: Modern Library, 1964), 330.

66. L&F, 406, 410.

67. L&F, 406–407.

68. L&F, 407–408.

69. L&F, 410.

70. AKDoC, 486.

71. Ch13-11, 32.

72. Eugenia Ginzburg, *Within the Whirlwind*, trans. Ian Boland (London: Collins, 1981), 82, 144.

73. Vasily Grossman, *Forever Flowing*, trans. Thomas P. Whitney (New York: Harper and Row, 1986), 76.

74. I. N. Steinberg, *In the Workshop of the Revolution* (New York: Rinehart, 1953), 212.

75. C&P, 277.

76. BK, 48, 99.

77. SR, 530.

78. SR, 265.

## 9. What Time Isn't It?

Epigraph: Charles Dickens, *David Copperfield* (New York: Heritage, 1937), 765.

1. These questions, and their relation to literature, are discussed at length in Gary Saul Morson, *Narrative and Freedom: The Shadows of Time* (New Haven, CT: Yale University Press, 1994).

2. *The Basic Works of Aristotle*, ed. Richard McKeon (New York: Random House, 1941) 47–49.

3. William James, "The Dilemma of Determinism," *"The Will to Believe and Other Essays in Popular Philosophy" and "Human Immortality: Two Supposed Objections to the Doctrine"* (New York: Dover, 1956), 145–183.

4. On eventness and surprisingness, see Gary Saul Morson and Caryl Emerson, *Mikhail Bakhtin: Creation of a Prosaics* (Stanford, CA: Stanford University Press, 1990), 250–259. See also "The Flesh of Time: Mikhail Bakhtin," in Aileen M. Kelly, *Views from the Other Shore: Essays on Herzen, Chekhov, and Bakhtin* (New Haven, CT: Yale University Press, 1999), 192–216.

5. Mikhail Bulgakov, *The Master and Margarita*, trans. Diana Burgin and Katherine Tiernan O'Connor (New York: Vintage, 1995), 8–9.

6. Bulgakov, *Master and Margarita*, 165.

7. Bulgakov, *Master and Margarita*, 165.

8. Bulgakov, *Master and Margarita*, 326.

9. Bulgakov, *Master and Margarita*, 228, 326, 328–329.

10. BK, 780–781.

11. Yuri Slezkine, *The House of Government: A Saga of the Russian Revolution* (Princeton, NJ: Princeton University Press, 2017), 753.

12. Slezkine, *House of Government*, 818.

13. V. G. Belinsky, *Selected Philosophical Works* (Moscow: Foreign Languages Publishing, 1956), 186–188.

14. Belinsky, *Selected Philosophical Works*, 204.

15. On the themes discussed here, see the essays in Aileen M. Kelly, *Toward Another Shore: Russian Thinkers Between Necessity and Chance* (New Haven, CT: Yale University Press, 1998).

16. HAH, 114.

17. "Progress and the Definition of Education," in Count Lev N. Tolstoy, *Moscow Acquaintance, Snow-Storm, Domestic Happiness, Polikushka, Pedagogical Articles, Linen-Measurer*, trans. Leo Weiner (Boston: L. C. Page, 1904), 161–162.

18. Tolstoy, "Progress and the Definition of Education," 162–163.

19. Tolstoy, "Progress and the Definition of Education," 167–168.

20. Leo Tolstoy, *"A Confession," "The Gospel in Brief," and "What I Believe"*, trans. Aylmer Maude (London: Oxford University Press, 1971), 12.

21. Tolstoy, *"A Confession,"* 25.

22. Tolstoy, *"A Confession,"* 25–26.

23. Tolstoy, "Progress and the Definition of Education," 168.

24. FTOS, 27.

25. FTOS, 28, 31, 35.

26. FTOS, 36.

27. FTOS, 38–39.

28. FTOS, 40.

29. FTOS, 40.

30. Arthur C. Danto, *Analytical Philosophy of History* (Cambridge: Cambridge University Press, 1968), 9.

31. ITFC, 670.

32. Vasily Grossman, *Forever Flowing*, trans. Thomas P. Whitney (New York: Harper and Row, 1986), 242.

33. AK, 10.

34. AK, 758.

35. AK, 686.

36. See, for instance, R. R. Palmer's classic study, *Twelve Who Ruled: The Year of the Terror in the French Revolution* (Princeton, NJ: Princeton University Press, 1970; originally published 1941).

37. See George L. Kline, "'Present,' 'Past,' and 'Future' as Categoreal Terms, and the 'Fallacy of the Actual Future,'" *Review of Metaphysics* 40 (December 1986): 215–235.

38. Kline, "'Present,' 'Past,' and 'Future,'" 215.

39. Gary Saul Morson, *Narrative and Freedom: The Shadows of Time* (New Haven, CT: Yale University Press, 1994), which defends open time, maintains the opposite.

40. See chapter 2 of Morson, *Narrative and Freedom*.

41. Kline, "'Present,' 'Past,' and 'Future,'" 216.

42. Kline, "'Present,' 'Past,' and 'Future,'" 231–232.

43. Kline, "'Present,' 'Past,' and 'Future,'" 234–235.

44. Sergei Bulgakov objected to the idea that "the sufferings of some generations form a bridge to the happiness of others; for some reason, some generations must suffer for others to be happy. . . . Our descendants turn out to be vampires, living off our blood." (*Problems of Idealism: Essays in Russian Social Philosophy*, ed. and trans. Randall A. Poole [New Haven, CT: Yale University Press, 2003], 103).

45. AWD, 1095–1096.

46. So Cicero argued in *De Officiis* (On Duties). See Ritchie Robertson, *The Enlightenment: The Pursuit of Happiness, 1680–1790* (New York: HarperCollins, 2021), 601.

47. Gary Saul Morson, *"Anna Karenina" in Our Time: Seeing More Wisely* (New Haven, CT: Yale University Press, 2007), 217.

48. Robert Conquest, *V. I. Lenin* (New York: Viking, 1972), 21–22.

49. Fyodor Dostoevsky, *The Idiot*, trans. Constance Garnett (New York: Modern Library, 1962), 384.

50. Dostoevsky, *The Idiot*, 385.

51. S, 143.

52. S, 143.

53. ITFC, 340–341.

54. ITFC, 515.

55. Eugene Zamyatin, *We*, trans. Gregory Zilboorg (New York: Dutton, 1952), 162.

56. W&P, 1353.

57. FTOS, 37.

58. FTOS, 35, 37.

59. FTOS, 35–36.

60. W&P, 512.

61. L. N. Tolstoy, *Polnoe sobranie sochinenii* [Complete Works], ed. V. G. Chertkov et al. (Moscow: Khudozhestvennaia literatura, 1929–1958), 16:10.

62. W&P, 847.

63. W&P, 848.

64. W&P, 604–605.

65. W&P, 156.

66. Mihaly Csikszentmihalyi, *Flow: The Psychology of Optimal Experience* (New York: Harper, 1991), 71.

67. AK, 265–266.33

68. This scene gives the title to a book with an interesting analysis of this story: George Saunders, *A Swim in a Pond in the Rain: In Which Four Russians Give a Master Class on Writing, Reading, and Life* (New York: Random House, 2021).

69. Anton Chekhov, *"Ward Six" and Other Stories*, trans. Ann Dunnigan (New York: Signet, 1965), 172–173.

70. AKDoC, 98.

71. Michael D. Barr, "Lee Kuan Yew and the 'Asian Values' Debate," *Asian Studies Review* 24, no. 3 (September 2000): 310.

72. AK, 165.

73. See Morson, *"Anna Karenina" in Our Time*, 143–167.

74. Alexander Gerschenkron, "The Problem of Economic Development in Russian Intellectual History of the Nineteenth Century," in *Continuity and Change in Russian and Soviet Thought*, ed. Ernest J. Simmons (New York: Russell and Russell, 1967), 21.

75. Gerschenkron, "Problem of Economic Development," 25.

76. Gerschenkron, "Problem of Economic Development," 23–24.

77. Gerschenkron, "Problem of Economic Development," 27.

78. FTOS, 184–186.

79. AKDoC, 433–434.

80. AKDoC, 434.

81. Leonard Schapiro, *Russian Studies*, ed. Ellen Dahrendorf (New York: Penguin, 1988), 330. Schapiro's discussion of this exchange on pages 321–337 is particularly illuminating, as is Aileen Kelly's in AKDoC, 426–445.

82. AKDoC, 435.

83. See Stephen Jay Gould, *Wonderful Life: The Burgess Shale and the Nature of History* (New York: Norton, 1989), and *The Panda's Thumb: More Reflections in Natural History* (New York: Norton, 1982), discussed in Gary Saul Morson, *Narrative and Freedom: The Shadows of Time* (New Haven, CT: Yale University Press, 1994), 245–251.

84. Two other works adopting this model are William H. McNeil's classic *Plagues and Peoples* (New York: Anchor, 1998) and Joel Mokyr's recent (and future classic?) study, *The Enlightened Economy: An Economic History of Britain, 1700–1850* (New Haven, CT: Yale University Press, 2009).

85. AKDoC, 422, 437.

86. George Plekhanov, *The Role of the Individual in History* (New York: International Publishers, 1940), 17.

87. Schapiro, *Russian Studies*, 139.

88. Nikolay Valentinov [N. V. Volsky], *Encounters with Lenin*, trans. Paul Rosta and Brian Pearce (New York: Oxford University Press, 1968), 24–25.

89. Valentinov, *Encounters with Lenin*, 26.

90. From Lenin's *What Is to Be Done?* in *A Documentary History of Communism*, ed. Robert V. Daniels, vol. 1 (New York: Random House, 1960), 12–13.

91. Daniels, *Documentary History of Communism*, 228–229.

92. Daniels, *Documentary History of Communism*, 226.

93. Karl Marx and Friedrich Engels, *Basic Writings on Politics and Philosophy*, ed. Lewis S. Feuer (Garden City, NY: Doubleday, 1959), 43, 103.

94. Marx and Engels, *Basic Writings*, 97, 109.

95. From part 3 of *Anti-Dühring* by Frederick Engels (1877), https://www.marxists.org/archive /marx/works/1877/anti-duhring/ch24.htm.

96. Leon Trotsky, *Literature and Revolution*, translator not specified (Ann Arbor: University of Michigan Press, 1971), 251–252.

97. Trotsky, *Literature and Revolution*, 254–255.

98. Raymond A. Bauer, *The New Man in Soviet Psychology* (Cambridge, MA: Harvard University Press, 1959), 22.

99. Robert Conquest, *Reflections on a Ravaged Century* (New York: Norton, 2001), 101–102.

100. Bauer, *New Man in Soviet Psychology*, 23, 123–124.

101. Bauer, *New Man in Soviet Psychology*, 36.

102. Ch13-9, 7–9.

103. Chekhov, *"Ward Six" and Other Stories*, 161.

104. Anton Chekhov, *The Major Plays*, trans. Ann Dunnigan (New York: Signet, 1964), 312.

105. Chekhov, *Major Plays*, 319.

106. Chekhov, *Major Plays*, 375–377.

107. Ch13-11, 30.

108. Ch13-11, 32,

109. Aleksandr Solzhenitsyn, *Between Two Millstones, Book 2: Exile in America, 1978–1994*, trans. Claire Kitson and Melanie Moore (Notre Dame, IN: University of Notre Dame Press, 2020).

110. This point is argued repeatedly in Aleksandr Solzhenitsyn, *Between Two Millstones*, 2 vols. (Notre Dame, IN: University of Notre Dame Press, 2018–2020).

111. A1914, 563.

112. A1914, 562.

113. A1914, 600, 605–606.

114. P, 341.

115. W&P, 930.

116. Leo Tolstoy, *War and Peace*, ed. George Gibian, Norton Critical Editions (New York: Norton, 1966), 1363.

117. On serialization of novels I have learned much from the articles of William Mills Todd III. See, for instance, Todd, "*The Brothers Karamazov* and the Poetics of Serial Publication," *Dostoevsky Studies* 7 (1986): 689–696; "'To Be Continued': Dostoevsky's Evolving Poetics of Serialized Publication, *Dostoevsky Studies, New Series* 18 (2014): 23–33; "V. N. Golitsyn Reads *Anna Karenina*: How One of Karenin's Colleagues Responded to the Novel," *Practices of Reading and Literary Communication*, ed. Damiano Rebecchini and Rafaella Vassena, https://books.openedition.org/ledizioni/284?lang=en; "*Crime and Punishment*: The Serial Version" (talk), https://open.library.ubc.ca/cIRcle/collections /77752/items/1.0397245; and "Reading 'Anna' in Parts," *Tolstoy Studies Journal* 8, (Jan. 1, 1995): 125.

118. Tolstoy, *War and Peace* (Norton Critical Edition), 1362, 1364–1365.

119. Tolstoy, *Polnoe sobranie sochinenii*, 13:55.

120. W&P, 310.

121. Dostoevsky, *The Idiot*, 117.

122. See Gary Saul Morson, "Tempics and *The Idiot*," in *Celebrating Creativity: Essays in Honor of Jostein Børtnes*, ed. Knut Andreas Grimstand and Ingunn Lunde (Bergen, Norway: University of Bergen, 1997), 108–134.

123. But see Robin Feuer Miller, *Dostoevsky and "The Idiot": Author, Narrator, and Reader* (Cambridge, MA: Harvard University Press, 1981). Perhaps the best solution is to acknowledge that the novel can be read in terms either of process or (as Miller demonstrates) of structure.

124. Joseph Frank, *Dostoevsky: The Miraculous Years, 1865–1871* (Princeton, NJ: Princeton University Press, 1995), 271.

125. Frank, *Dostoevsky*, 271.

126. Dostoevsky, *The Idiot*, 375.

127. For an extensive discussion of processual poetics, in both narrative and non-narrative literature, see Gary Saul Morson, *Prosaics and Other Provocations: Empathy, Open Time, and the Novel* (Boston: Academic Studies Press, 2013), 33–124.

128. John Locke, *An Essay Concerning Human Understanding*, ed. Alexander Campbell Fraser (New York: Dover, 1959), 1:349.

129. AWD, 477.

130. AWD, 477.

131. Mikhail Bakhtin, *Problems of Dostoevsky's Poetics*, trans. Caryl Emerson (Minneapolis: University of Minnesota Press, 1984), 166.

## 10. What Don't We Appreciate?

Epigraph: Fred R. Shapiro, ed., *The Yale Book of Quotations* (New Haven, CT: Yale University Press, 2006), 464. I have added "because" to accord with the version I have seen most often.

1. The very idea of daily, ordinary morality (or "practical" ethics), regardless of what that ethics might prescribe, offended Berdyaev precisely because it was ordinary. It therefore "usually bears the stamp of banality, offensive to any thinker. . . . We can say that one of the basic tasks of [true] morality is the struggle against philistinism (*meshchanstvo*). . . . Here philosophical ethics declares war

against everyday traditional morals, which philosophy must too often see as the enemy of human individuality and consequently of true morality." N. A. Berdiaev, "The Ethical Problem in the Light of Philosophical Idealism," in *Problems of Idealism: Essays in Russian Social Philosophy*, trans. and ed. Randall A. Poole (New Haven, CT: Yale University Press, 2003), 184.

2. See Gary Saul Morson and Caryl Emerson, *Mikhail Bakhtin: Creation of a Prosaics* (Stanford, CA: Stanford University Press, 1990).

3. Mikhail Bakhtin, *The Dialogic Imagination: Four Essays*, ed. Michael Holquist, trans. Caryl Emerson and Michael Holquist (Austin: University of Texas Press, 1981), 404.

4. George Eliot, *Middlemarch* (New York: Modern Library, 1984), 189.

5. F&S, 23.

6. Eliot, *Middlemarch*, 795.

7. See Gary Saul Morson, *"Anna Karenina" in Our Time: Seeing More Wisely* (New Haven, CT: Yale University Press, 2007), 35.

8. For these and similar quotations, see Morson, *"Anna Karenina" in Our Time*, 235n1–236n1.

9. Nicolas Berdyaev, *Dream and Reality: An Essay in Autobiography*, trans. Katharine Lampert (New York: Collier, 1950), 32, 35–36.

10. Berdyaev, *Dream and Reality*, 16, 35, 46.

11. Berdyaev, *Dream and Reality*, 78–79, 82.

12. Berdyaev, *Dream and Reality*, 79–80.

13. HAH, 263.

14. HAH, 19.

15. Ralph E. Matlaw, ed., *Belinsky, Chernyshevsky, and Dobrolyubov: Selected Criticism* (New York: Dutton, 1962), 123–124.

16. Marc Raeff, ed., *Russian Intellectual History: An Anthology* (New York: Harcourt, Brace, 1966), 365–367.

17. Vladimir Mayakovsky, *The Bedbug and Selected Poetry*, ed. Patricia Blame, trans. May Hayward and George Reavey (Cleveland: Meridian, 1966), 255.

18. Mikhail Zoshchenko, *Scenes from the Bathhouse and Other Stories of Communist Russia*, trans. Sidney Monas (Ann Arbor: University of Michigan Press, 1962), 30–31.

19. S, 86–87.

20. S, 58.

21. L. N. Tolstoy, *Polnoe sobranie sochinenii* [Complete Works], ed. V. G. Chertkov et al. (Moscow: Khudozhestvennaia literatura, 1929–1958), 16:18.

22. W&P, 1126–1127.

23. Tolstoy, *Polnoe sobranie sochinenii*, 16:11.

24. W&P, 298.

25. See Gary Saul Morson, *Hidden in Plain View: Narrative and Creative Potentials in "War and Peace"* (Stanford, CA: Stanford University Press, 1987), 100–129, 161–166.

26. Leo Tolstoy, *Recollections and Essays*, trans. Aylmer Maude (London: Oxford University Press, 1961), 80.

27. Tolstoy, *Recollections and Essays*, 81.

28. Tolstoy, *Recollections and Essays*, 81–82.

29. For these and similar quotations, see Matthew Arnold's review of Anna Karenina in *Tolstoy: The Critical Heritage*, ed. A. V. Knowles (London: Routledge, 1978), 352–361; Christopher Taylor, review of Rosamund Bartlett, *Tolstoy A Russian Life*, November 13, 2010, https://www.theguardian

.com/books/2010/nov/14/tolstoy-russian-life-rosamund-bartlett-review; and Virginia Woolf, "The Russian Point of View," *The Essays of Virginia Woolf: 1926–1928*, ed. Andrew McNeillie, vol. 4 (Orlando: Harcourt, 1994), 181–190.

30. Woolf, "Russian Point of View," 188.

31. W&P, 1320.

32. W&P, 1320.

33. W&P, 1218.

34. AK, 71.

35. "God is in the details" is sometimes attributed to Flaubert. See Shapiro, *Yale Book of Quotations*, 275.

36. AK, 276–277.

37. AK, 274–275.

38. AWD, 872.

39. BK, 786.

40. BK, 25–26.

41. BK, 424.

42. BK, 434.

43. BK, 435.

44. In terms of Dostoevsky's theology, Alyosha has come to appreciate the Holy Spirit. See Morson, "The God of Onions: Dostoevsky and the Mythic Prosaic" in *A New Word on "The Brothers Karamazov,"* ed. Robert Louis Jackson (Evanston, IL: Northwestern University Press: 2004), 107–124.

45. Ernest J. Simmons, *Chekhov: A Biography* (Boston: Little Brown, 1962), 203.

46. March [?] 1886; Simmons, *Chekov*, 111–113.

47. Anton Chekhov, *"Ward Six" and Other Stories*, trans. Ann Dunnigan (New York: Signet, 1965), 66.

48. Chekhov, *"Ward Six" and Other Stories*, 69, 77.

49. Chekhov, *"Ward Six" and Other Stories*, 98.

50. Chekhov, *"Ward Six" and Other Stories*, 110.

51. Chekhov, *"Ward Six" and Other Stories*, 158.

52. Anton Chekhov, *The Major Plays*, trans. Ann Dunnigan (New York: Signet, 1964), 187, 212–213.

53. Chekhov, *Major Plays*, 216.

54. Chekhov, *Major Plays*, 153.

55. Chekhov, *Major Plays*, 217–218.

56. Chekhov, *Major Plays*, 191.

57. SR, 56.

58. Chekhov, *Major Plays*, 230–231.

59. DZ, 285.

60. L&F, 283.

61. Chekhov, *"Ward Six" and Other Stories*, 277.

62. Chekhov, *"Ward Six" and Other Stories*, 284.

63. Ch13-1, 153, 173.

64. Karl Marx and Friedrich Engels, *Basic Writings on Politics and Philosophy*, ed. Lewis S. Feuer (Garden City, NY: Doubleday, 1959), 254.

65. RP2, 115.

66. S, 89.

67. A1914, 814–816.

68. Aleksandr Solzhenitsyn, *"The Russian Question" at the End of the Twentieth Century*, trans. Yermolai Solzhenitsyn (New York: Farrar, Straus, 1995), 81.

69. Mikhail Sholokhov, *Seeds of Tomorrow*, trans. Stephen Garry (New York: Knopf, 1935), 32–33.

70. Sholokhov, *Seeds of Tomorrow*, 35–36.

71. Alexander Gerschenkron, "Time Horizon in Russian Literature," *Slavic Review* 34, no. 4 (December 1975): 696–698.

72. Ropshin [Boris Savinkov], *What Never Happened*, trans. Thomas Seltzer (New York: Knopf, 1917), 403–404.

73. A1914, 505.

74. Eugene Vodolazkin, *The Aviator*, trans. Lisa C. Hayden (London: Oneworld, 2018), 375.

75. AK, 504.

76. Leo Tolstoy, *War and Peace*, ed. George Gibian, Norton Critical Editions (New York: Norton, 1966), 1354.

77. Ch13-3, 117.

78. Ivan Goncharov, *The Precipice*, trans. and ed. Laury Magnus and Boris Jakim (Ann Arbor, MI: Ardis, 1994), 256.

79. Goncharov, *Precipice*, 404.

80. Ivan Turgenev, *Virgin Soil*, trans. Constance Garnett, in 2 volumes (New York: AMS, 1970; reprint of London: William Heinemann, 1896), 2:253–254.

81. Nicholas Luker, *Alexander Kuprin* (Boston: G. K. Hall, 1978), 16.

82. Luker, *Alexander Kuprin*, 16.

83. Alexandre Kuprin, *Yama (The Pit)*, trans. Bernard Guilbert Guerney (New York: Modern Library, 1932), 100.

84. Alexander Kuprin, *"The Duel" and Selected Stories*, trans. Andrew R. MacAndrew (New York: Signet, 1951), 56.

85. Isaac Babel, *The Collected Stories*, ed. and trans. Walter Morison (New York: Merdian, 1960), 90.

86. Babel, *Collected Stories*, 89.

87. Isaac Babel, *1920 Diary*, trans. H. T. Willetts, ed. Carol J. Avins (New Haven, CT: Yale University Press, 1990), 88.

88. Isaac Babel, *The Essential Fictions*, trans. Val Vinokur (Evanston, IL: Northwestern University Press, 2018), 200.

89. Babel, *1920 Diary*, 33.

90. Babel, *1920 Diary*, 46, 69, 74, 77.

91. Alexander D. Nakhimovsky and Alice Stone Nakhimovsky, eds., *The Semiotics of Russian Cultural History* (Ithaca, NY: Cornell University Press, 1985), 53.

92. V. G. Belinsky, *Selected Philosophical Works* (Moscow: Foreign Languages Publishing, 1956), 142–143.

93. Nakhimovsky and Nakhimovsky, *Semiotics of Russian Cultural History*, 68.

94. Nakhimovsky and Nakhimovsky, *Semiotics of Russian Cultural History*, 23.

95. AWD, 305.

96. AK, 248.

97. Elizabeth Knowles, ed., *The Oxford Dictionary of Quotations*, 6th ed., (Oxford: Oxford University Press, 2004), 185.

98. Aleksandr Solzhenitsyn, *Rebuilding Russia: Reflections and Tentative Proposals*, ed. Alexis Klimoff (New York: Farrar, Straus, 1991).

99. I follow Bakhtin, "Forms of Time and of the Chronotope in the Novel," in *Dialogic Imagination*, 84–258.

100. Svetlana Alexievich, Nobel Prize Lecture, https://www.nobelprize.org/uploads/2018/06/alexievich-lecture_en-3.pdf

101. Alexievich, Nobel Prize Lecture.

102. UFW, xvi.

103. Mikhail Bakhtin, *Problems of Dostoevsky's Poetics*, trans. Caryl Emerson (Minneapolis: University of Minnesota Press, 1984), 73.

104. Bakhtin, *Problems of Dostoevsky's Poetics*, 21.

105. Alexievich, Nobel Prize Lecture.

106. UFW, xx.

107. Alexievich, Nobel Prize Lecture.

108. Alexievich, Nobel Prize Lecture.

109. Alexievich, Nobel Prize Lecture.

110. UFW, xxi–xxii.

111. UFW, xvi–xvii.

112. UFW, xvi.

113. UFW, xxi.

114. DZ, 42, 251, 285.

115. UFW, xvi, xviii.

## 11. What Doesn't It All Mean?

Epigraph: Alexei Pisemsky, *One Thousand Souls*, trans. Ivy Litvinov (New York: Grove, 1959), 356.

1. C&P, 283–284.

2. C&P, 279.

3. Leo Tolstoy, "A Confession," "The Gospel in Brief," and "What I Believe", trans. Aylmer Maude (London: Oxford University Press, 1971), 18.

4. AK, 822; see Tolstoy, "A Confession," 18.

5. Ch13-1, 106–107,

6. W&P, 53,

7. In much the same way, Bazarov can be seen as a figure from utopias placed in a realist novel and Anna Karenina is a genre refugee from romance. Realist novels often use genre refugees as a way to examine the assumptions and values of other genres and worldviews. On genre refugees, see Morson, "Genre and Hero / *Fathers and Sons*: Intergeneric Dialogues, Generic Refugees, and the Hidden Prosaic," in *Literature, Culture, and Society in the Modern Age*, ed. Edward J. Brown, Lazar Fleishman, Gregory Freidin, and Richard Schupbach, *Stanford Slavic Studies* 4, no. 1 (1991): 336–381.

8. W&P, 324–325.

9. W&P, 344.

10. W&P, 358–359

11. W&P, 359.

12. W&P, 1170.

13. W&P, 1172.

14. W&P, 1171.

15. Arthur Schopenhauer, *Essays and Aphorisms*, trans. R. J. Hollingdale (London: Penguin, 1970), 50.

16. See Michael Denner, "Tolstoyan Nonaction: The Advantage of Doing Nothing," in *Tolstoy Studies Journal* 13 (2001): 8–22.

17. Leo Tolstoy, *Recollections and Essays*, trans. Aylmer Maude (London: Oxford University Press, 1961), 148, 154.

18. As cited in FUTR, 21.

19. Ritchie Robertson, *The Enlightenment: The Pursuit of Happiness, 1680–1790* (New York: Harper, 2021), 1. See also Paul Hazard, *European Thought in the Eighteenth Century: From Montesquieu to Lessing*, trans. J. Lewis May (Cleveland, OH: Meridian, 1963), 14–25.

20. Robertson, *Enlightenment*, 3.

21. Citations from Leibniz and Locke are from Robertson, *Enlightenment*, 1.

22. Alexander Pope, *Selected Poetry and Prose*, ed. William K. Wimsatt, Jr. (New York: Holt, Rinehart, 1965), 156.

23. Robertson, *Enlightenment*, 5.

24. Immanuel Kant, *Groundwork of the Metaphysics of Morals*, trans. H. J. Paton (New York: Harper, 1956), 63.

25. Robertson, *Enlightenment*, 9. Berdyaev agrees: "Happiness is itself subject to *moral* judgment . . . recognizing it as worthy or unworthy of moral nature" (*Problems of Idealism: Essays in Russian Social Philosophy*, trans. and ed. Randall A. Pool [New Haven, CT: Yale University Press, 2003], 32).

26. Samuel Johnson, *Rasselas, Poems, and Selected Prose*, ed. Bertrand H. Bronson (New York: Holt, Rinehart, 1958), 531.

27. Voltaire, *Candide and Other Writings*, ed. Haskell M. Block (New York: Modern Library, 1956), 183.

28. Voltaire, *Candide*, 109.

29. Jeremy Bentham, *An Introduction to the Principles of Morals and Legislation* (New York: Hafner, 1948), 2.

30. Ch13-6, 258, 260.

31. Ch13-6, 160, 261.

32. Ch13-6, 264–265.

33. Cited in Joseph Frank, *Dostoevsky: The Stir of Liberation, 1860–1865* (Princeton, NJ: Princeton University Press, 1986), 31.

34. AWD, 335. The essay concerns the Russian craze for spiritualism. For a fascinating study of the role of spiritualism in Russian thought, see Ilya Vinitsky, *Ghostly Paradoxes: Modern Spiritualism and Russian Culture in the Age of Realism* (Toronto: University of Toronto Press, 2009).

35. Fyodor Dostoevsky, *"Notes from Underground" and "The Grand Inquisitor,"* the Garnett translation revised and edited by Ralph Matlaw (New York: Dutton, 1960), 30.

36. Blaise Pascal, *Pensées*, trans. A. J. Krailsheimer (Harmondsworth, UK: Penguin, 1987), 68.

37. Robert Nozick, *Anarchy, State, and Utopia* (New York: Basic Books, 2013), 42–45.

38. Not because it is difficult to tell, but because "there's no way he is." Nozick, *Anarchy, State, and Utopia*, 43.

39. Nozick, *Anarchy, State, and Utopia*, 45.

40. Dostoevsky, *"Notes from Underground,"* 27, 31.

41. Eugene Zamyatin, *We*, trans. Gregory Zilboorg (New York: Dutton, 1952), 147, 200.

42. Aldous Huxley, *Brave New World* (New York: Harper, 1946), 163.

43. S. N. Bulgakov, "Basic Problems in the Theory of Progress," *Problems of Idealism*, 100.

44. Ch13-9, 101.

45. Ch13-9, 106.

46. Ch13-9, 110.

47. Ch13-9, 111.

48. BK, 277.

49. BK, 302.

50. BK, 305–306.

51. As cited in Edward Brown, *Russian Literature Since the Revolution* (New York: Collier, 1963), 74.

52. Richard Stites, *Revolutionary Dreams: Utopian Vision and Experimental Life in the Russian Revolution* (New York: Oxford University Press, 1989), 152.

53. As cited in Brown, *Russian Literature since the Revolution*, 89, 91–92.

54. Ivan Turgenev, *A House of Gentlefolk*, trans. Constance Garnett (London: William Heinemann, 1894; reprinted New York: AMS, 1970), 146.

55. Ivan Turgenev, *On the Eve*, trans. Constance Garnett (London: William Heinemann, 1895; reprinted New York: AMS, 1970), 13–14.

56. Ch13-5, 278.

57. Ch13-5, 278, 282.

58. Ch13-5, 282.

59. Ch13-5, 283.

60. Ch13-5, 283.

61. Ch13-5, 284.

62. Ch13-5, 285.

63. Ch13-5, 278, 285.

64. Leo Tolstoy, *Great Short Works*, trans Louise and Aylmer Maude (New York: Harper, 2004), 255–256.

65. Tolstoy, *Great Short Works*, 258.

66. Tolstoy, *Great Short Works*, 266.

67. Tolstoy, *Great Short Works*, 280.

68. Tolstoy, *Great Short Works*, 294, 297, 299.

69. BK, 62–63.

70. See Thomas Nagel, *The View from Nowhere* (New York: Oxford University Press, 1986).

71. BK, 63.

72. Ray Monk, *Ludwig Wittgenstein: The Duty of Genius* (New York: Free Press, 1990), 115, 132, 136.

73. See Allan Janik and Stephen Toulmin, *Wittgenstein's Vienna* (New York: Simon and Schuster, 1973). I twice co-taught a course on Wittgenstein and *Anna Karenina* with Toulmin. I discuss the relation of Levin's meditations and Wittgenstein's ideas more fully in Gary Saul Morson, *"Anna Karenina" in Our Time: Seeing More Wisely* (New Haven, CT: Yale University Press, 2007), 200–202, 210–214.

74. AK, 818–819.

75. Ludwig Wittgenstein, *Tractatus Logico-Philosophicus*, trans. D. F. Pears and B. F. McGuin-ness (London: Routledge, 1977), 6.372, 6.52.

76. AK, 828–829.

77. Wittgenstein, *Tractatus Logico-Philosophicus*, 6.41.

78. AK, 830.

79. AK, 829.

80. Wittgenstein, *Tractatus Logico-Philosophicus*, 6.521–6.522.

81. AK, 834.

82. Wittgenstein, *Tractatus Logico-Philosophicus*, 6.43.

83. AK, 850–851.

84. Eugenia Ginzburg, *Within the Whirlwind,* trans. Ian Boland (London: Collins, 1981), 78.

85. SR, 589.

86. UFW, xxv.

87. Svetlana Alexievich, Nobel Prize Lecture, https://www.nobelprize.org/uploads/2018/06/alexievich-lecture_en-3.pdf.

88. SR, 262, 264, 266.

89. SR, 266–267.

90. BK, 48.

91. Ginzburg, *Within the Whirlwind,* 82, 291.

92. Vasily Grossman, *Forever Flowing,* trans. Thomas P. Whitney (New York: Harper and Row, 1986), 76.

93. HAH, 28.

94. SR, 272.

95. SR, 565, 569, 572.

96. SR, 573, 581.

97. SR, 575, 584.

98. W&P, 59.

99. W&P, 389.

100. Ch13-13, 17–18.

101. Ch13-13, 23.

102. Ch13-13, 23.

103. Ch13-13, 25–26.

104. Ch13-13, 29

105. Ch13-13, 31–32.

106. Ch13-13, 49.

107. Ch13-13, 59.

108. Ch13-13, 60.

109. Ch13-13, 60, 62–63,

110. Ch13-13, 65.

111. Ch13-6, 169.

112. Ch13-6, 170.

113. Ch13-6, 171–172.

114. Ch13-6, 173.

115. Ch13-6, 173.

116. Ch13-6, 174.

117. Ch13-6, 22.

118. Varlam Shalamov, *Kolyma Tales*, trans. John Glad (London: Penguin, 1994), 384.

119. Shalamov, *Kolyma Tales*, 72.

120. Shalamov, *Kolyma Tales*, 75.

121. L&F, 543.

122. L&F, 554.

123. L&F, 555.

124. L&F, 689.

125. L&F, 862.

126. L&F, 862.

## Conclusion

1. Mikhail Bakhtin, *Problems of Dostoevsky's Poetics*, trans. Caryl Emerson (Minneapolis: University of Minnesota Press, 1984).

2. Svetlana Alexievich, Nobel Prize Lecture, https://www.nobelprize.org/uploads/2018/06/alexievich-lecture_en-3.pdf.

3. For a theological perspective on Bakhtin's approach to dialogue, see Alexander Mihailovic, *Corporeal Words: Mikhail Bakhtin's Theology of Discourse* (Evanston, IL: Northwestern University Press, 1997).

4. AK, 350.

5. On empathy, see Alina Wyman, *The Gift of Active Empathy: Scheler, Bakhtin, and Dostoevsky* (Evanston, IL: Northwestern University Press, 2016).

6. Ralph E. Matlaw, ed., *Anton Chekhov's Short Stories*, Norton Critical Editions (New York: Norton, 1979), 277.

7. Mikhail Bakhtin, *The Dialogic Imagination: Four Essays*, ed. Michael Holquist, trans. Caryl Emerson and Michael Holquist (Austin: University of Texas Press, 1981), 366.

8. AWD, 127.

9. AWD, 124–125.

10. Isaiah Berlin, "The Hedgehog and the Fox," in Berlin, *Russian Thinkers*, ed. Henry Hardy and Aileen Kelly (Harmondsworth: Penguin, 1978), 22. See also "Introduction: Two Russian Ideas," in Aileen M. Kelly, *Views from the Other Shore: Essays on Herzen, Chekhov, and Bakhtin* (New Haven, CT: Yale University Press, 1999), 116.

11. Isaiah Berlin, "The Pursuit of the Ideal," *The Crooked Timber of Humanity: Chapters in the History of Ideas* (New York: Knopf, 1991), 5–6.

12. Berlin, "The Pursuit of the Ideal," *Crooked Timber*, 13.

13. S. L. Frank, "Friedrich Nietzsche and the Ethics of 'Love of the Distant,'" *Problems of Idealism*, 198–199.

14. W&P, 1323.

15. I owe this point to Morton Schapiro.

16. Dmitri Volkogonov, *Lenin: A New Biography*, ed. and trans. Harold Shukman (New York: Free Press, 1994), 28.

17. Francis Macdonald Cornford, trans., *The Republic of Plato* (London: Oxford University Press, 1990), 71.

18. See Gary Saul Morson, *The Boundaries of Genre: Dostoevsky's "Diary of a Writer" and the Traditions of Literary Utopia* (Austin: University of Texas Press, 1981), 69–106.

19. WITBD, 114–115.

20. ITFC, 649, 651.

21. See Jonathan Waterlow, *It's Only a Joke, Comrade!: Humor, Trust and Everyday Life under Stalin, 1928–1941* (Oxford: no publisher, 2018). Jokes could therefore be dangerous.

22. Mikhail Bulgakov, *The Master and Margarita*, trans. Diana Burgin and Katherine Tiernan O'Connor (New York: Vintage, 1995), 163.

23. DZ, 404.

24. Aleksandr I. Solzhenitsyn, *The Gulag Archipelago, 1918–1956: An Experiment in Literary Investigation*, trans. Thomas P. Whitney, vol. 1 (New York: Harper and Row, 1974), 613.

25. Evgenia Semyonovna Ginzburg, *Into the Whirlwind*, trans. Paul Stevenson and Manya Harari (Harmondsworth, UK: Penguin, 1968), 64.

26. AK, 9.

27. L&F, 672.

28. Aleksandr Solzhenitsyn, *November 1916: The Red Wheel / Knot II*, trans. H. T. Willetts (New York: Farrar, Straus and Giroux, 1999), 291, 294.

29. UFW, xxvii.

30. HAH, 96.

31. Pitirim Sorokin, *Leaves from a Russian Diary—and Thirty Years After* (Boston: Beacon, 1954), 19, 158–159.

32. Quoted in Mikhail Bakhtin, *Rabelais and His World*, trans. Helene Iswolsky (Cambridge, MA: MIT Press, 1968), 59.

33. See Aileen M. Kelly, "The Flesh of Time," in *Views from the Other Shore*, 192–216.

34. Bakhtin, *Rabelais and His World*, 66.

35. Cornford, *Republic*, 48.

36. As in More's *Utopia*, Diderot's "Supplement to Bougainville's 'Voyage,'" H. G. Wells's *A Modern Utopia*, and other dialogic utopias or, as I have called them, meta-utopias. Morson, *Boundaries of Genre*, 142–185.

37. HAH, 38.

38. Bakhtin, *Rabelais and His World*, 3, 92.

39. Bakhtin, *Dialogic Imagination*, 23.

40. For more on novelistic language, see Gary Saul Morson and Caryl Emerson, *Mikhail Bakhtin: Creation of a Prosaics* (Stanford, CA: Stanford University Press, 1990), 306–365. On dialogue's importance today, see Gary Saul Morson, *Prosaics and Other Provocations: Empathy, Open Time, and the Novel* (Boston: Academic Studies Press, 2013), 183–221; and MWS. While the use of double-voicing (and "free indirect discourse") can easily be found before Jane Austen, she was, so far as I can tell, the first to make it the governing principle of an entire novel. The greatness of her novels does not exhaust her significance in world literature.

41. Robin Feuer Miller's studies of stories and storytelling in Dostoevsky's works remain unsurpassed. See Miller, *Dostoevsky and "The Idiot": Author, Narrator, and Reader* (Cambridge, MA: Harvard University Press, 1981); Miller, *Dostoevsky's Unfinished Journey* (New Haven, CT: Yale University Press, 2007); and Miller, *"The Brothers Karamazov": Worlds of the Novel* (New York: Twayne, 1992). When novels deal with their own creation (a Russian modernist tradition), they

may foreground their novelness: see Justin Weir, *The Author as Hero: Self and Tradition in Bulgakov, Pasternak, and Nabokov* (Evanston, IL: Northwestern University Press, 2002).

42. M. M. Bakhtin *Speech Genres and Other Late Essays*, trans. Vern McGee (Austin: University of Texas Press, 1996), 147, 162.

43. Bakhtin, *Problems of Dostoevsky's Poetics*, 81, 93.

44. Bakhtin, *Problems of Dostoevsky's Poetics*, 81.

45. Aileen M. Kelly observes: "Chekhov is one of the most deeply subversive writers of his own or any other age, a figure whose originality is poorly understood . . . it was precisely his lack of tendentiousness that made his writings so subversive." Kelly, *Views from the Other Shore*, 171.

46. Matlaw, *Chekhov's Short Stories*, 270.

47. Anton Chekhov, *"Ward Six" and Other Stories*, trans. Ann Dunnigan (New York: Signet, 1965), 161; Anton Chekhov, *The Major Plays*, trans. Ann Dunnigan (New York: Signet, 1964), 312.

48. Matlaw, *Chekhov's Short Stories*, 272.

49. Bulgakov, *Master and Margarita*, 271.

*Acknowledgments*

About a decade ago, John Kulka, then at Harvard University Press, suggested this book, which, he said, I was "born to write." On my own I would never have considered such a vast project, which would cover areas outside my immediate specialties. I am by training a student of the nineteenth-century Russian classics but learning the Soviet period has turned out to be a joy and a revelation, which I owe to John.

Covering so much of Russian culture, I became aware that my greatest debt must be to those who created, appreciated, and sustained it, namely, literature-loving Russian people and all those who have valued and studied Russian literature and thought. Russian history is a story of worsts and bests, of horrors and glories, of cruelties and compassion; and it is Russian literature, with its deep wisdom and concern for human suffering, that remains Russia's greatest contribution to the world.

The older I get, the more I am aware of how much I owe to my teachers, especially Victor Erlich, Michael Holquist, Firuz Kazemzadeh, Vadim Liapunov, Charles Moser, Martin Price, Richmond Thomason, Sarah Grey Thomason, and Harry Willetts. It was my dissertation advisor, Robert Louis Jackson, who encouraged me "boldly" to ask the ultimate questions.

Since I began studying Russian literature, many colleagues and friends have sharpened my thinking: Elizabeth Cheresh Allen, Carol Any, Rob Asghar, Carol Avins, David Azerrad, Leonard Babby, Connor Bain, Steve Balch, Leonard Barkan, Dan Ben-Amos, David Bethea, Helen Brenner, Andrew Bingham, Karen Blair, Irene Blumenkranz, J. J. Blumenkranz, Jostein Børtnes, Bracht Branham, Gary Browning, Bud Bynack, Steven Cassedy, Bill Clinton, Ralph Cohen, Peter Dougherty, Freeman Dyson, Nancy Easterlin, John Ellis, Joseph Epstein, Ahmet Evin, Donald Fanger, Leon Forrest, Joseph

Frank, John Garrard, Boris Gasparov, Marcia Gealy, George Gibian, Sanford Goldberg, Nina Gourianova, Gerald Graff, Thomas M. Greene, Robert Gundlach, Jean Gurley, Anne Drury Hall, Robert Harriman, Christine Helmer, Leland Hutchinson, Dell Hymes, Norman Ingham, Stewart Justman, Noreen Kaminski, Thomas Kaminski, Marvin Kantor, Aron Katsenelinboigen, Michael Katz, Andrew Katzenstein, Adam Keiper, Richard Kieckhefer, Roger Kimball, Alan Kors, Neal Kozody, Sherry Kujala, Krisztina Lajosi-Moore, Diane Leonard, Marcus Levitt, Lawrence Lipking, Dan Lowenstein, Phyllis Lyons, Janet Malcolm, Herb Marks, Kathe Marshall, Susan McReynolds, Arthur Milikh, Robin Feuer Miller, Kenneth Mischel, Elliott Mossman, Martin Mueller, Catherine O'Connor, Barbara O'Keefe, Dan O'Keefe, Robert Orsi, Donna Orwin, Julio Ottino, Irina Paperno, Clara Claiborne Park, Kathleen Parthé, Janice Pavel, Roy Pea, Abe Peck, Jean Perkins, Marjorie Perloff, Randall Poole, Sarah Pratt, Gerald Prince, Mark Ratner, Thomas Remington, Milt Rosenberg, Dalya Sachs-Bernstein, David Satter, Roger Schank, Alissa Schapiro, Mimi Schapiro, Peter Scotto, James Seaton, Seth Singleton, Frank Silbajoris, Larry Silver, Jurij Striedter, Strobe Talbott, Helen Tartar, William Mills Todd, Andrew Wachtel, Irwin Weil, Stevan Weine, Justin Weir, Dennis Weiscopf, Robert Whittaker, Meredith Williams, Michael Williams, Ruth Wisse, Robert Wittebort, and Alexander Zholkovsky.

Although I had not been their student, Robert Belknap and Wayne Booth encouraged and mentored me when I needed it. Daniel Mahoney guided my reading of Solzhenitsyn and encouraged me to pursue my ideas. Aileen Kelly's splendid books and articles served as a model for how literary sensitivity and intellectual historical perspicuity can inform each other. Jonathan and Fran Brent encouraged, helped, and inspired over four decades. Robert Alter, Frederick Crews, and Thomas Pavel stood by me and offered sage advice and good humor.

At difficult moments over decades several Northwestern staff and administrators offered needed help: Andrew Baldovsky, David Cohen, Lawrence B. Dumas, Anne Fish, Dan Linzer, Marilyn McCoy, Elizabeth Murray, James Sheridan, and Arnold Weber. I can't begin to say how much I appreciate the care and attention of Judi Remington.

Co-teaching is one of the most fruitful forms of dialogue. Some four decades ago I had the privilege of giving an interdisciplinary course on Russian culture with historian Alfred Rieber, and his critiques of my ideas still resonate in my thinking. Teaching an NEH Summer Seminar with Michael Williams, I discovered fallacies in my favorite formulations and learned needed skepticism of my fuzzier concepts. Every year I miss the multi-part course I gave with Robert Gundlach. Readers of this book will recognize my enormous debt to Stephen Toulmin, with whom I co-taught courses on Bakhtin and Wittgenstein and on his favorite novel, *Anna Karenina*. The class Morton Schapiro and I co-taught, on how different disciplines understand decision-making and on the different ways they ask and answer questions, has been for the past twelve years the experience that enriched my thinking the most.

Morty and I also did three books together, and there is no form of intellectual exchange that is more meaningful. I still think wistfully of the year in which Caryl Emerson and I wrote our book on Bakhtin; no one is more dedicated and more capable of intellectual growth than she.

I have learned more than I can say from my students. Every time I thank them this way, I remember, right after the book has gone to press, some whom I can't believe I missed. But let me try to name a few graduates from whom I learned so much: Ece Agalar, Christina Allen, Carla Arnell, Lindsay Sergeant Berg, Sara Burson, Wendy Cheng, Olyvia Chinchilla, Leah Culligan, Elizabeth Durst, Brandon Enriquez, Mason Fritz, Andrew Gruen, Robert Gurley, Omar Hassan, Jacob Hoeflich, Joshua Hoeflich, Kelle Hutchinson, Belle Kleinberg, Ann Komaromi, Timothy Langen, John Mafi, Lori Singer Meyer, Sarah Kube Mohler, Joanne Mulcahy, Femke Munting, Jacob Roth, Mehek Sehti, Ryan Serrano, Aarohi Shah, Karthik Sivashanker, Trish Suchy, Jonathan Sun, Ruud Teeuwen, Peter Thomas, Andrew Thompson, Barbara Starke Tishuk, Ryan Vogt, Christina Walker, Cindy Wang, Annabel We, Justin Weir, Jennifer Yeung, Joy Zhao, and Pat Zody. Nava Cohen and Nina Wieda were especially helpful in my research for this book. Matthew Morrison continues to inspire me with reports on his reading and thinking. Special thanks to each and every one of the "dead souls."

Reading not just every word, but every letter of this manuscript, Gene Moore lent his incomparable eye for the smallest errors, along with his unfailing warmth and humor.

Alexander Morson and Emily Morson continue to enliven my life and always will. Altaluna Martinez, Josh Fishbein, and Leah Fishbein have enriched it since I have known them.

I was more than fortunate that, when John Kulka left Harvard University Press, Kathleen McDermott assumed responsibility for this book. Her generosity, care, and sage advice—such as I have never received before—made all the difference. Katrina Vassallo did a splendid copyediting job.

Not a day goes by when I do not think, with love and amazement, of my rich conversations with Michael André Bernstein. Those who knew him will detect places in this book when I am tacitly continuing conversations with him. The appreciation of Steven Blumenkranz, whom I have known since I developed the capacity to remember, means more than I can say. I did not let a word escape the judicious eye of Katharine Porter, who has sustained my soul and spirit.

I dedicate this book to my dearest friend alive, Morty Schapiro.

# Index

"Lucerne" (Tolstoy), 274

Lucian, 1

Lunacharsky, Anatoly, 229, 248

Luther, Martin, 192

Luzhenovsky, Gavrila, 167

Macbeth, 258

Machajski, Jan, 91, 147

machinism, 364

magic words: the people, 26, 81, 148; revolution, 81, 148; socialism, 81, 148

"Major Pubachev's Last Battle" (Shalamov), 244

Makhaevists, 91

Maklakov, Vasily, 83

Malebranche, Nicholas, 2

Malia, Martin, 71, 79, 412n4, 414nn35–36, 415n41

*Managerial Revolution, The* (Burnham), 91

Manchester, Laurie, 80, 418n113

Mandelstam, Nadezhda: on alibi, 257; on happiness, 374; hypocrisy of cruel people, 235–236; on intelligentsia, 92, 94, 95–96; on kindness, 274; on law of progress, 184; on living in constant fear, 249; on Osip's device for suppressing jokes, 391; on Osip's state of confusion, 419n145; on poetry, 43; on prisoners' memories, 245, 249; on prosaics, 324, 325; on revolution, 148, 175. See also *Hope Against Hope: A Memoir*

Mandelstam, Osip: death imagined in "Cherry Brandy," 254, 381–382; on happiness, 374; on intelligentsia, 94, 96; on jokes as dangerous, 391; on living in constant fear, 249; on meaningful life, 383; poem mocking Stalin, 43; on prosaics, 324–325; on revolution, 148

*March 1917* (Solzhenitsyn), 312–313

marginal revolution, 190

market vs. planned economy, 281, 348

marriage and family, 21, 64, 86–87, 248, 323–324, 343

martyrdom, 161–163, 193

Marx, Karl, 25, 91, 189, 199, 201, 221–222, 288, 303–304. See also *Das Kapital; German Ideology, The; Theses on Feuerbach*

Marxism and Marxism-Leninism: "agnosticism," 189, 282; "bourgeois objectivism," 36, 61; choice and humanness and dehumanization, 243; and determinist philosophy, 303; and division of labor, 339–340; economic determinism, 304, 305; justice without guilt or innocence, 172, 224–226; on maximum harm to enemy, 243; mechanistic vs. dialectical, 68–69, 306–307; as racism by class, 225–226; "requiem," 22; sabotage, 191; and science, 91, 189, 388; self-movement, 201; *sovest'* vs. *soznatel'nost'*, 235; "two-factor theory," 307; tyrannize in name of liberty, 91; voluntaristic, 302–307; "withering away of state," 307

*Master and Man* (Tolstoy), 255, 367

*Master and Margarita, The* (Mikhail Bulgakov): on certainty, 281; decency in, 273; devil in, 4, 43, 268; on dialogue, 394–395; "for the drawer," 37; freedom of thought, 389; jokes in, 389; on poetry, 96; on prosaics, 325; revealing truth, 52; on suffering, 255; surprise and "surprisingness," 282

master plot, 11–12, 211, 213

*Materialism and Empirio-Criticism* (Lenin), 188, 189

Mathewson, Rufus, 59–60, 61, 236

"Matryona's Home" (Solzhenitsyn), 338

*Matter and Force* (Büchner), 193

matter and materialism: cunning and vitality of, 198–199, 200–201; Einstein's theory of matter, 389; Engels on, 189, 190; and epicureanism, 201–202; and ethics, 250–251; and fallacy of the actual future, 290–292, 447n44; and fallacy of the irrelevant future, 288–289; idealism, 80, 127, 131, 416n65; ideal of, 199–200; Marx on, 189, 190; meaning of life, 358; in *The Possessed*, 127, 227; realism, 68; "self-movement" of, 201; in *The Unwomanly Face of War*, 255; works by radical materialists, 25, 290–292 (*see also specific writers*). See also dialectical materialism

maximalists, 21, 22, 225

Mayakovsky, Vladimir, 68, 86, 174, 325

meaning and meaninglessness. *See* meaning of life

Soloviev, Vladimir, 34, 74; "intelligentsia's syllogism," 199

Solzhenitsyn, Aleksandr: argument with Sakharov, 175; on arrested Bolsheviks, 252; atheism as not real conviction, 390; on beliefs, 271; "bewitchment," 390; "Bless you, prison," 256, 373; on causes of evil, 257; on consequences of Stolypin's assassination, 312; on decency, 273; enumeration of torture and sadism, 241–242; on happiness, 374–375; heroes in, 338; on human dignity, 241–242; on intelligentsia, 72, 73–74, 77, 78–79, 92, 94–95; on Lenin, Stalin, and Hitler killing millions, 258; "line between good and evil . . . every human heart," 278; on meaning of life, 374–375, 381; new people, 60; on postmodernism, 31, 46; on prisoners' memory, 245; on psychology of "self-persuasion," 93; realist purposes, 33; revenge and, 231–232; on Russian experience, 15; on "the Russia that might have been," 311–313; "secret brand," 242; "seminar" conducted by incarcerated intellectuals, 254; on socialism, 81; soul "ripens from suffering," 256, 273; on suffering, 373; "thought planted from outside," 390; untouched by modernism, 30–31, 37; on urgency, 23; writer as second government, 47. *See also* "As Breathing and Consciousness Return"; *August 1914*; *Gulag Archipelago, The*; *In the First Circle*; *March 1917*; "Matryona's Home"; *November 1916*; *Red Wheel, The*

"Some Words About the Book *War and Peace*" (Tolstoy), 54, 295–297

"Song of the Merchant Kalashnikov, The" (Lermontov), 112

Sorokin, Pitirim, 390

*Sorrows of Young Werther* (Goethe), 63

soul: and brain, 424n41; Chekhov on contrary states of, 380–381; destruction of, 249–253; and essential self, 241–242; and extreme cold, 248–249; and fear, 248–249; in Gogol, 241; as hero of Russian literature, 37; iron for, in "Incurable," 140–142; reborn in *We*, 213; and return of emotions, 252–253; revela-

tion of by extreme conditions, 241–242; ripens through suffering, 256, 273, 372–374; total surrender of, 248–249; uniqueness of in *Life and Fate*, 271–273

*sovest'* vs. *soznatel'nost'*, 235

Soviet ethics: compassion, 231, 235–236, 273–275; described, 234–235; Golden Rule, reverse, 235–237; honor, as outmoded idea, 94; innocence as outmoded concept, 224, 225, 236; integrity as foreign to Soviet discourse, 235; materialism, 255; pity, 252; "result is what counts," 250; reverse process, 95–96. *See also* ethics and morality

Soviet experiment, 242

"So What Then *Is* the Intelligentsia?" (Lozinsky), 91

Spasovich, Vladimir, 19

speculation, 233

Spinoza, Baruch, 2

Spiridonova, Mariya, 66, 167

spiritualism, 434n52

spontaneity vs. consciousness, 304

Stakhanov, Alexei, 174, 307

Stakhanovite movement, 307

Stalin, Joseph: arrests by quota, 21; attack on non-Party-minded writers, 60; Bukharin's letter on purge, 224; on "cogs," 260; criminalization of thoughts and actions, 9, 30; on death, 213; execution of Bukharin, 284; ex-seminarian, 78; "free the kulak of his life," 237, 341; "greatest pleasure" of, 161, 252; identification of intelligentsia, 420n148; importance of literature, 43–44; intensification of class struggle after revolution, 177–178; liquidation of the kulaks, 225, 340–341; mass terror, 173; on movement toward socialism, 432n153; official thinking, 36; "preposterous" terror," 177–178, 243; revival of revolutionist and revolution, 170–171, 172, 174; on Savinkov's suicide, 428n30; Soviet thought, 306–307; on suicide, 243; terror famine, 245; "thaw" following death, 44; torture and sadism, 161, 170, 171, 174; on volunteerism, 307; war on hard workers, 340–341

*Stalingrad* (Grossman), 11, 42, 62, 270, 383